Pilgrims
and
Sacred Sites in China

This volume and the conference from which it resulted were sponsored by the Joint Committee on Chinese Studies of the American Council of Learned Societies and the Social Science Research Council, with funds provided by the National Endowment for the Humanities and the Ford Foundation.

Pilgrims
and
Sacred Sites in China

Edited by

Susan Naquin and Chün-fang Yü

University of California Press
Berkeley   Los Angeles   Oxford

University of California Press
Berkeley and Los Angeles, California

University of California Press, Ltd.
Oxford, England

Library of Congress Cataloging-in-Publication Data

Pilgrims and sacred sites in China/edited by Susan Naquin and Chün-
fang Yü.
    p. cm.—(Studies on China; 15)
    Papers originally presented at a conference held at Bodega Bay,
Calif., in Jan. 1989 and sponsored by the Joint Committee on Chinese
Studies of the American Council of Learned Societies and the Social
Science Research Council.
    Includes bibliographical references and index.
    ISBN 0-520-07567-6 (cloth : alk. paper)
    1. Buddhist pilgrims and pilgrimages—China—Congresses.
2. Pilgrims and pilgrimages—China—Congresses. I. Naquin, Susan.
II. Yü, Chün-fang, 1938–   III. Joint Committee on Chinese Studies
(U.S.) IV. Series.
BQ6450.C6P55 1992
291.3'5'0951—dc20   91-20671
                                           CIP

Printed in the United States of America
1 2 3 4 5 6 7 8 9

The paper used in this publication meets the minimum requirements of American National
Standard for Information Sciences—Permanence of Paper for Printed Library Materials, ANSI
Z39.48-1984. ∞

STUDIES ON CHINA

A series of conference volumes sponsored by the Joint Committee on Chinese Studies of the American Council of Learned Societies and the Social Science Research Council.

1. The Origins of Chinese Civilization
   edited by David N. Keightley
   University of California Press, 1982

2. Popular Chinese Literature and Performing Arts in the People's Republic of China, 1949–1979
   edited by Bonnie S. McDougall
   University of California Press, 1984

3. Class and Social Stratification in Post-Revolution China
   edited by James L. Watson
   Cambridge University Press, 1984

4. Popular Culture in Late Imperial China
   edited by David Johnson, Andrew J. Nathan, and Evelyn S. Rawski
   University of California Press, 1985

5. Kinship Organization in Late Imperial China, 1000–1940
   edited by Patricia Buckley Ebrey and James L. Watson
   University of California Press, 1986

6. The Vitality of the Lyric Voice: *Shih* Poetry from the Late Han to the T'ang
   edited by Shuen-fu Lin and Stephen Owen
   Princeton University Press, 1986

7. Policy Implementation in Post-Mao China
   edited by David M. Lampton
   University of California Press, 1987

8. Death Ritual in Late Imperial and Modern China
   edited by James L. Watson and Evelyn S. Rawski
   University of California Press, 1988

9. Neo-Confucian Education: The Formative Stage
   edited by Wm. Theodore de Bary and John W. Chaffee
   University of California Press, 1989

10. Orthodoxy in Late Imperial China
    edited by Kwang-Ching Liu
    University of California Press, 1990

11. Chinese Local Elites and Patterns of Dominance
    edited by Joseph W. Esherick and Mary Backus Rankin
    University of California Press, 1990

12. Marriage and Inequality in Chinese Society
    edited by Rubie S. Watson and Patricia Buckley Ebrey
    University of California Press, 1991

13. Chinese History in Economic Perspective
    edited by Thomas G. Rawski and Lillian M. Li
    University of California Press, 1992

14. Bureaucracy, Politics, and Decision Making in Post-Mao China
    edited by Kenneth G. Lieberthal and David M. Lampton
    University of California Press, 1992

15. Pilgrims and Sacred Sites in China
    edited by Susan Naquin and Chün-fang Yü
    University of California Press, 1992

In memory of
Anna K. Seidel (1938–1991),
who encouraged us in this project
but did not live to see its completion

CONTENTS

ILLUSTRATIONS

FIGURES

MAPS

ACKNOWLEDGMENTS

The genesis of this volume can be dated to conversations between the editors at the Association for Asian Studies meeting in Philadelphia in the spring of 1985. In separate research, Naquin on Peking temples and Yü on the cult of Kuan-yin, we had become increasingly aware of the important place of pilgrimage in the religious lives of the Chinese people. Aware also that this topic, widely studied in other cultures, had scarcely been investigated for China, we decided to plan a conference on the subject. We later received a grant from the Joint Committee on Chinese Studies of the American Council of Learned Societies and the Social Science Research Council, the funds generously provided by the National Endowment for the Humanities and the Ford Foundation, and so embarked on the joint project of which this book is the result. A circular letter to colleagues in the field soliciting paper proposals elicited an enthusiastic response, and from this pool the conference participants were selected.

We received formative advice from Raoul Birnbaum, Willard Peterson, P. Steven Sangren, and Michel Strickmann, who attended a planning committee meeting in February 1986. The conference itself, "Pilgrims and Sacred Sites in China," was held in the pleasant surroundings of Bodega Bay, California, in January 1989. As always, it was a pleasure to work with Jason Parker and the staff of the ACLS, whose assistance has been invaluable.

Many colleagues have helped shape the conference and this volume. Papers by Timothy Brook, William Powell, P. Steven Sangren, and Michel Strickmann, and comments by Raoul Birnbaum, Prasenjit Duara, Patrick Geary, and Alan Morinis contributed breadth, insight, and humor; this volume, and particularly the introduction, has benefited from their influence. Paul Katz was our able rapporteur. Patrick Geary, Valerie Hansen, Laurel Kendall, Philip Kuhn, John Lagerwey, Victor Mair, Barbara Metcalf, Nathan Sivin, Lowell Skar, and Hung Wu all read the introduction in various versions and gave us frank and useful comments, as did Daniel Overmyer, Dorothy Solinger, and Stephen Teiser on the book as a whole. We are also grateful to the staff of the University of California Press, to other students of pilgrimage who have written us about their work, and to friends who gave us needed encouragement. There are many ways that this topic could have been studied; responsibility for roads not taken rests, of course, with us.

Susan Naquin
Chün-fang Yü

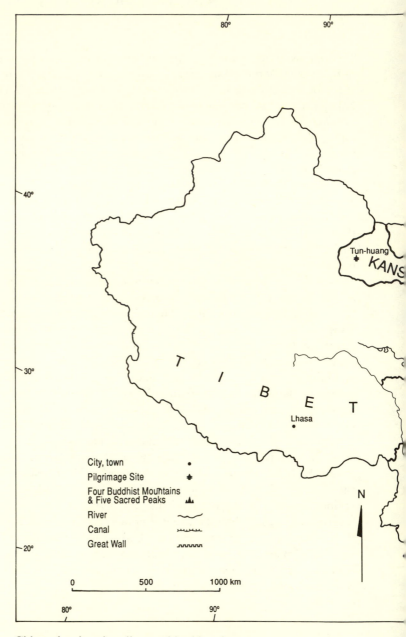

China, showing sites discussed in this volume

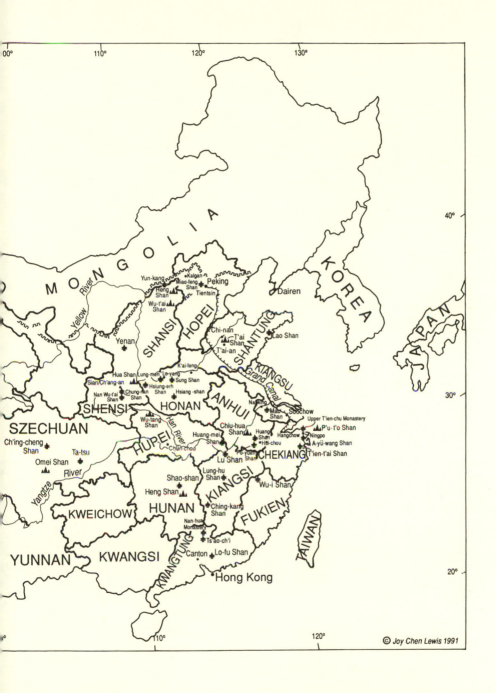

© Joy Chen Lewis 1991

INTRODUCTION:

PILGRIMAGE IN CHINA

Susan Naquin and Chün-fang Yü

PILGRIMAGE IN COMPARATIVE PERSPECTIVE

Throughout history and across cultures, human beings have given shape and pattern to natural space and passing time. Certain intervals acquire special meaning and become demarcated from the everyday; calendars articulate and reinforce such patterns. Similarly, some places are thought to stand out from their surroundings and become associated with special experiences and part of an ordered geography. In any religion, some places and times are viewed as particularly favorable for establishing contact with supernatural powers, and we find people in most cultures making journeys to such places for this purpose. Conceived somewhat differently in each case, these pilgrimages, as we may term them, reflect central ideas about time, space, and sacred power and are a fruitful point of entry into the study of the religious culture of a people.

This volume will concentrate on the pilgrims and sacred places of China, a topic not extensively treated in the popular or scholarly literature. The nine chapters that follow will present various sacred sites in China, typically mountains, and the pilgrims who by their visits affirmed the powers of these sites and helped make them more numinous. For those unfamiliar with Chinese religion or with the comparative literature on pilgrimage, we hope that this introductory chapter will provide useful background. Necessarily superficial and preliminary, it draws on a variety of secondary works, which are listed in the two bibliographies at the end of this introduction.

Pilgrimages are common to all the major world religions. In Judaism, Christianity, and Islam, the paradigmatic pilgrimage is a journey to a holy city. In Judaism, pilgrimage was a central ritual act defining a person as a Jew. The Old Testament specified that every male was required to visit the

Temple in Jerusalem three times a year, on the festivals of Passover, Sha-
vuot, and Sukkot. According to the Mishnah, a second-century legal text,
only minors, women, and the unfit were excepted. Indeed, during the era of
the Second Temple (sixth century B.C. to first century A.D.), this holy place
probably attracted more pilgrims than anywhere in the Mediterranean
world. With the destruction of the Temple in A.D. 70, the desire to make this
journey merged with the determination of Jews to put an end to the exile
from Jerusalem. The joys associated with being in that sacred city were remembered for centuries in grief. For Jews, pilgrimage encapsulated this experience of exile and uncertain return so central to their identity.

In Islam, pilgrimage was (and remains) obligatory for both men and
women. The Koran stipulated that a journey to the holy city of Mecca at
least once in one's lifetime—a journey known as the *hajj*—was one of the five
duties of every capable Muslim. Thus enshrined from the seventh century,
the *hajj* became central to this religion, both an expression of obedience to
God and a link with the holy places in the life of the Prophet. As believers
assembled during the pilgrimage season from increasingly vast distances,
this occasion for ritual purification and forgiveness of sins also became by
modern times a potent and moving symbol of the unity of the Islamic world.
Over the centuries, other Muslim sacred places also developed, particularly
the tombs of saints and holy men; in quite a different category from Mecca,
these were often more accessible and attracted a more eclectic set of pilgrims.

Although never obligatory, pilgrimages have likewise been made by
Christians since the formative period of their religion. Journeys to Jerusalem
began as early as the fourth century. While there, pilgrims visited sites sanctified by the life of Christ, the Virgin, and the Apostles as well as those
commemorated in the Old Testament. Later, with the growing influence of
the Catholic Church, Rome, the capital of Christendom, became the Holy
City and a destination for pilgrims, rivaling even Jerusalem. During the Middle Ages, those pilgrims who made the arduous journeys to Jerusalem or
Rome were given special legal protection, supported by hospices, and rewarded with indulgences. Suffering en route was understood as a penance
that would be rewarded with unmediated contact with divine power.

For most Christians, pilgrimage was more frequently on a smaller scale.
The increasing popularity of the cult of the saints and of the Virgin first in
Eastern and then Western Europe expanded the number of sacred places and
brought them closer to home. Compostela, Canterbury, Vezelay, and Tours
became famous, and more recently Lourdes, Fatima, and a host of others in
Europe and the Americas. Shrines acquired reputations for special efficacy,
collections of miracles at the site were compiled, and the potency of holy
relics and images was advertised. Churches competed for possession of such
objects and incorporated the saints' festivals into the liturgical calendar.

The experience of the pilgrim was sometimes seen as analogous to that of human beings who were exiled from Eden and journeyed through life anticipating heaven; thus, pilgrimage could also become a metaphor for the Christian life. People wrote accounts of this experience that became popular reading and set the precedent for an understanding of pilgrimage as a significant personal quest. Despite criticisms that accompanied the Reformation, miracles, shrines, and pilgrimages have continued to be important in Catholic Europe and Latin America down to the present day.

In each of these three related religions, pilgrimage gave individuals a direct experience of the transcendent and an opportunity to show devotion and seek blessings. More particularly, pilgrimage usually involved long and difficult journeys, defined a community as those to whom a certain place was sacred, and so, in a world of competing faiths, reconfirmed religious identity.

The words used for pilgrimage in these religions nevertheless reveal variety in conceptualizing this process. The root of the English term *pilgrim* emphasizes the idea of a traveler, while *holy* is related to health and wholeness. Both pilgrimage and wayfaring involve traveling, and they bear some resemblance, although the latter lacks a specific destination. There is no special term for a pilgrimage center as distinct from a shrine, sanctuary, or church. German differentiates between short and more frequent pilgrimages (*Wallfahrt*) and longer, rarer ones (*Pilgerfahrt*). The Semitic root of both the Hebrew word *hag* (pilgrimage feasts) and the Arabic word *hajj*, in contrast, refers not simply to a journey but to circular movement. The central sanctuary in Mecca is the Kaaba, understood as the house of God, which pilgrims circumambulate. A quite different term, *ziyara*, describes visits to Muslim saints' tombs.

It is in the context of Judaism, Christianity, and Islam that scholarly writing about pilgrimage has developed in the West. Similarities between journeys to sites important in the history of these religions or to shrines dedicated to prophets, saints, and holy people suggested that pilgrimage was a general human phenomenon, while pilgrims' accounts directed attention toward the experience itself. As the study of religion has been taken up by anthropologists and historians in the last half-century, much attention has been directed toward Christian pilgrimage, specifically the medieval period on the one hand—the "golden age of pilgrimage"—and the contemporary period on the other. Scholarship on this pilgrimage tradition is by far the most developed and has concentrated on the hagiography of saints, the history of sites, cults, and miracles, and the role of pilgrimage in society.

To study pilgrimage cross-culturally, scholars have had to shake off the influence of Western religions—with their clear definitions of religion and believer, identifiable acts of worship, and assumption of hardship as part of the pilgrimage journey. Needing a definition of pilgrimage that would accommodate other religions, most scholars have accepted for comparison—as we do here—any journey to a sacred place to perform some religious act.

When we use the term *sacred*, we are keenly aware of its associated meaning of *transcendent* and its implied opposition to *profane*, terms derived from Western religious traditions. Such implications are natural in the three related religions that affirm the existence of a transcendent god, but they cannot be extended to other cultures, including those of East Asia, where the religious object is not separated from but located within nature. As it is difficult to do without familiar terms, the reader should take note that we use *sacred* without these connotations.

In Catholicism and Islam, practitioners readily differentiated pilgrimage from various related actions; elsewhere, such distinctions were not always obvious, and, as a result, scholars have also had to rethink the perimeters of the phenomenon. They have had to consider, for example, how to make distinctions between pilgrimage and (1) ordinary worship at a sacred place (without a journey), (2) travel to historical or scenic places, and (3) processions of gods, sacred objects, and devotees to a series of holy places. The mixture of the religious with the mundane and secular, so common to pilgrimage, has made it necessary to caution those who expect clear distinctions between these terms.

The academic study of pilgrimages in non-Western traditions, slower to develop, has now become part of an enlarged comparative vision of religion in other times and places. The area of greatest recent scholarly interest has been South Asia, especially the Hindu world of India.

The professed goal of a Hindu is release from the repeated cycle of birth, death, and rebirth, escape from time and space. Progressing toward this ultimate freedom, one seeks, in each lifetime, a better rebirth. Life is likened (as it is in the related Buddhist religion) to crossing a river to reach the other shore. Pilgrimage is expressed as *tīrtha-yātrā*, literally, "journeying to a fording place." To visit a pilgrimage site, a place for "crossing over" both literally and metaphorically, is highly meritorious and helps loosen one's bonds to this life. People still come to Benares, on the sacred river Ganges, for example, to bathe and to pray, even to die and be cremated. Pilgrims also go for the *darshan* (seeing, vision) of the place, its deities, and its holy persons, hoping to be "seen" in return. In the exchange of gazing, blessings are received and wishes are fulfilled. Many pilgrimages follow regular circuits and schedules; for instance, it is considered especially auspicious to go on a pilgrimage once every twelve years to Hardvar, where the Indus and Ganges converge. Thousands of places sacred to a variety of deities dot the landscape of India, and anthropologists have led the way in studying pilgrimages to them. They have seized opportunities to visit these centers, to watch and interview pilgrims, and even to make the pilgrimage themselves. Journeys to sacred places have been readily identified and similarities with European religious behavior easily noted.

Although Buddhism exerted a critically important influence on East Asia, the study of Buddhist pilgrimages has concentrated on South Asia (where the religion began) and Southeast Asia (where it later spread). Buddhism does not have a special term for pilgrimage. At one level, the Mahayana idea of *śūnyatā* (void) implies undifferentiated space and is thus deconstructive of sacred geography. Yet the path (*mārga*) to enlightenment and nirvana, taught by the Buddha in his first sermon and followed down the ages, has served as a significant metaphor for pilgrims.

Buddhist pilgrimages, like many others, were directed toward places sanctified by history and marked by remains of enlightened beings. As in other religions with identifiable founders, later followers of the Sakyamuni Buddha (sixth to fifth century B.C.) wanted to travel to the sites in India commemorated by his life, specifically his birth, enlightenment, first sermon, and death. Of these, the most important has been Bodhgaya, where he attained enlightenment, which continues to attract pilgrims from all over the world.

Early in the development of the religion, sutras (scriptures) recorded the enshrinement and worship of relics of the Buddha and his famous disciples in closed, dome-shaped shrines called stupas. Such relics (Sk. *śarīra*, Ch. *she-li* 舍利), like those of Christian saints, included corporeal remains (bones, hair, teeth) as well as objects associated with the holy person's life. In the third century B.C., according to legend, the Indian King Aśoka recovered, redivided, and dispersed relics of the Buddha by building eighty-four thousand stupas to house them. This story justified a proliferation of stupas throughout the Buddhist world.

As in the other world religions, later cults of holy people (usually monks) created additional foci for clerical and lay pilgrimage. Monks were people who "went forth" or "retired from the world" (*pravrajya, ch'u-chia* 出家), and their life of nonattachment to things and places was a model for pilgrims. Like the Hindu renunciate who entered into the fourth stage of life and the palmers of medieval Europe, Buddhist monks might spend their whole lives traveling from place to place. The paradigmatic pilgrim was the young monk Sudhana, who went on a pilgrimage to visit fifty-three "good friends" who led him to enlightenment, a story told in the widely known *Flower Garland Sutra* (*Avataṃsaka sūtra, Hua-yen ching* 華嚴經).

The Japanese religious tradition is, like the Chinese, a combination of Buddhism and indigenous religion, and an extensive comparison of pilgrimage in the two cultures would be most interesting but more than we can attempt here. The Shinto shrine at Ise, which initially received exclusively imperial patronage and pilgrimages, was later the goal of pilgrim organizations and became increasingly important in the modern period. Simultaneously, a variety of new Buddhist sites (many mountains) were developed by monks and lay people.

The language of pilgrimage shows characteristically Japanese distinctions. *Mairi* 詣い and *mōde* 詣で, related terms commonly used for visits to holy places, did not distinguish local temples from distant sites. Other terms reflected a preference for pilgrimage circuits: *kaikoku* 廻国 (touring the nation), *junrei* 巡礼 (performing rites at a series of temples), and *henro no tabi* 遍路の旅 (pilgrimage journey). In Japan, sets of sacred sites came to form pilgrimage circuits. Famous examples are the thirty-three temples dedicated to Kannon (Avalokiteśvara, Kuan-yin) in the western part of mainland Japan and the eighty-eight stations connected with the holy monk Kūkai (774–835) scattered through Shikoku. Other sites are intended to be visited within a prescribed number of days. For a thousand days extended over a period of seven years, the Tendai monks on Mount Hiei, for example, would walk thirty to eighty kilometers a day, following three routes circling the mountain. They would stop to chant the appropriate *mantra* (spell) and form ritual hand gestures at more than two hundred fifty stations along the way, including temples and shrines to Vedic, Buddhist, Shinto, and Taoist deities; tombs of Tendai patriarchs; and sacred peaks, hills, stones, forests, bamboo groves, cedar and pine trees, waterfalls, ponds, and springs.

The study of pilgrimages outside these major world religions has been scattered and unsystematic, but a number of conferences in the last decade reflect efforts to push into new areas. Some have looked just at pan-European and pan-Christian pilgrimage, while others have been more broadly comparative; a multidisciplinary and multicultural context is now taken for granted. For the modern period, some work is being done on secularization and on the transformation of pilgrims into religious tourists or ordinary travelers, a transition sometimes set within larger theories about the commoditization of culture in industrial societies.

The scholarly pilgrimage literature is empirically rich but theoretically somewhat less so. Some scholars have tried to create typological schemes (unfortunately not always transferable across cultures); others have concentrated on functional analyses (e.g., pilgrimage as a force for social integration, an enactment of the social order, etc.); some have been more interested in individual motivation and psychology.

Victor Turner, an anthropologist with early fieldwork experience in Africa, turned to the study of Marian pilgrimages in Europe and Mexico and emerged in the 1970s as the leading theoretician in the field. Interested in the pilgrim's experience and inspired by the anthropologist Arnold von Gennep's schema of the stages of rites of passage (separation, transition, and incorporation), Turner characterized pilgrimage as a "social process." Pilgrims leave home, he explained, enter a liminal state while traveling to the sacred place, and return, transformed, to be reincorporated into their home communities. For the duration of their travels, pilgrims disengage themselves from the "structure" of ordinary society and contribute to the formation of a different mode of relatedness, the climax of which is the emergence among pilgrims of what Turner called an egalitarian, undifferentiated, and open-

ended "communitas." Structure and communitas are not to be seen as dia-
metrically opposed, however, but as dialectically connected.

This elegant and attractive theoretical model highlights pilgrimage as a
powerful—and universal—transformative experience. In consequence, as a
pioneer of contemporary pilgrimage studies, Turner has had an enormous
and unrivaled influence. Many have sought to test his model, and some have
ended up questioning and modifying his theory. Pruess, Eickelman, and
Morinis—working on Thai Buddhist, Moroccan Islamic, and Bengali Hindu
pilgrimages, respectively—have found, for instance, that while pilgrimage
could be said to create a liminal state, the experience of communitas that is a
crucial part of Turner's theory is sometimes absent. But whether they agree
with his theory or not, most researchers have felt the need to address his
ideas. Turner's other insights and hypotheses on the dialectical relationship
of peripherality and centrality of the pilgrimage centers or the dynamics of
growth and decline of the pilgrimage phenomena have, by contrast, received
less scholarly attention.

Turner has done a great service by distilling a general model from the
confusion of a vast variety of pilgrimages. As a result, much scholarly interest, especially among anthropologists, has been directed toward similarities underlying the pilgrim's experience, away from differences and away
from the site itself. We have found, for reasons explained in more detail below, that it may be time to reconsider the chaos of pilgrimage and to listen
again to the cacophony.

It is in the context of this work on pilgrimage that the 1989 conference that
produced this volume was organized. Our simplest goal was to add to the
general literature several case studies from China, a civilization with a long
history of pilgrimage shaped by its own indigenous traditions as well as by
Buddhism, but scarcely mentioned in comparative works. At the same time,
we have hoped to bring the study of pilgrimage to the China field by introducing here the comparative literature and its concerns. Chinese realities
and Chinese sources, have, furthermore, necessitated different methods and
emphases.

The most fruitful research on pilgrimage has been done in cultures where
ample historical sources (including pilgrims' accounts) have been combined
with contemporary fieldwork. Such a combination is not easily attained in
the Chinese case. Fieldwork is problematic for a variety of reasons, and there
are other constraints on historical studies. Literacy was not widespread, and,
as Pei-yi Wu's chapter in this volume notes, educated people did not usually
provide personal testimonies about their emotional lives. Like accounts of
religious experiences generally, reports of travels to sacred places were written by monks much more rarely in China than in Europe and the Middle
East. At the same time, extensive and varied historical materials on pilgrimage centers themselves do exist. In consequence, we have been encouraged to

shift our focus from anthropology to history, away from the pilgrim's journey and toward the sacred sites themselves. Setting the Turner debate to one side, we have chosen instead to look at pilgrims through the sites that were, in effect, created by their devotions.

The comparative study of the places that are the goals of pilgrims has been influenced—not altogether positively—by another line of intellectual inquiry, one that grew out of the study of myths and comparative religion. Mircea Eliade, the founder of the discipline of the history of religion in the United States, argued in 1959 that all holy places had similar characteristics. Each was a "hierophany," a place where divine or supernatural power was manifested and discovered (not chosen or created) by people. Each was a center, an axis mundi where heaven and earth intersected, a microcosm of a larger whole.

Subsequent work in this vein by Paul Wheatley and others on Asian holy cities has concentrated on symbolic layout, architecture, myths, and legends. Such studies have not integrated the historical or anthropological work on the diversity of popular religion that has contributed much to our understanding of pilgrimage. Moreover, since Chinese cities, unlike Jerusalem or Rome, did not usually attract pilgrims, work on China's capitals has not provided a foundation for further work on this topic.

Descriptions of sacred sites as representations of the unadulterated essence of an entire culture smoothes away contradictions and only reinforces misleadingly sharp distinctions between religions (or denominations). The three Western religions have often emphasized the exclusivity of their sites: Fatima was a shrine to the Virgin and drew Catholic pilgrims, the Wailing Wall holy to orthodox Jews, the Kaaba forbidden to all but Muslims. Scholars have, of course, studied a site's preexisting cults, which were usually incorporated into the later, more dominant religion: the *hajj*, for example, fused older rites in Mecca and on the adjacent plain of Arafat. But the religious establishment—Hindu Brahmans and Buddhist monks as well as Catholic priests, Jewish rabbis, and Muslim mullahs—often controlled pilgrimage sites and presented their histories in a more self-serving fashion. The stories of centers sacred to many different groups, daunting to study in their entirety, are thus often told as separate histories of succeeding eras or as expressions of the tensions between hostile neighbors.

These kinds of compartmentalization are misleading, even in the West, and certainly in East Asia. Jerusalem, for instance, has been made what it is by a complicated overlay of Christian, Jewish, and Muslim pilgrimages that were not only simultaneous but, as with the Dome of the Rock, sometimes even focused on the same spot. A Christian shrine to St. John survives within the Great Mosque of Damascus, while visitors of many faiths visit the Hagia Sophia in Istanbul, a church incompletely converted into a mosque. Within a single tradition, moreover, different sects and religious orders compete for control of certain shrines (the Church of the Holy Sepulcher, for example). This kind of complexity was commonplace in China.

In China, the clerical power of Buddhist and Taoist professionals was rarely undisputed and declined over the centuries. Furthermore, because the state checked and coopted the power of organized religion yet was not itself strong enough to dominate the religious sphere, a diversity of religious systems and interpretations was normal. Pilgrimage and pilgrimage sites thus could, as elsewhere, provide direct access to holy power independent of orthodox intermediaries, but were rarely the exclusive possession of one group. The study of Chinese sites therefore has to proceed on the assumption of considerable heterogeneity and diversity among pilgrims. Like Diana Eck, whose book on Benares is a beautifully successful attempt to describe one city's multiple and changing grounds of attractiveness to pilgrims, we have had to assume that sites are pluralistic and many-faceted.

Pilgrimage, moreover, did not occupy the same central position in Chinese culture that it did in Christianity, Islam, Judaism, Hinduism, or monastic Buddhism. It was not a religious obligation or a metaphor for the place of human beings in the universe (except perhaps for monks), and the boundaries with ordinary worship and travel were more blurred. Nevertheless, to study pilgrimage necessitates identification of what constitutes worship, the sacred, and the sphere of the religious more generally. Through pilgrimage we may still get a glimpse into the heart of Chinese religion.

PILGRIMAGE IN CHINA

While there are undeniable social, economic, and political dimensions to pilgrimage, it is fundamentally a religious activity. To the nonspecialist, Chinese religion presents, alas, a dauntingly fragmented and confusing picture. There is not even a consensus as to whether one should speak of a single Chinese religion reflecting the culture as a whole or many Chinese religions representing different elements of the tradition. Until this century, the Chinese themselves have not had an equivalent of the Western term *religion*. For many centuries Chinese elites have claimed a distinction between what they saw as the sophisticated philosophies of the educated and the vulgar superstitions of ordinary people. Western views (whether liberal, Christian, or Marxist) have reinforced such categories, and Confucianism has generally been understood, in both China and the West, as a philosophy, while Buddhism and Taoism are designated religions. Ordinary people are sometimes said to believe in one or the other, or all three, or none.

This confusion is due in part to the two lines of inquiry along which Western knowledge of Chinese religion developed. The first proceeded from the study of the elite tradition and investigated the ideas and authors of texts of Confucianism, Buddhism, and Taoism. Scholars, especially intellectual historians and those in the humanities, were interested primarily in the history of ideas, major thinkers, formative scriptures, and formal religious institutions. The second type of inquiry started with the "folk religion" and drew on fieldwork to study the beliefs and rituals of uneducated people. These social scientists concentrated on the diffused form of Chinese religion (to use C. K. Yang's term) as manifested in family life and village communities. Texts were of marginal importance, as were religious professionals. The tensions between these two approaches have still not been resolved, and questions about the relationships between written and oral traditions, elite and popular culture, philosophy and religion, one religion or many are still being debated.

In our view, Taoism and Buddhism are relatively clear-cut categories only when one speaks of religious professionals, their rites, and their scriptural materials; similarly, one can identify the Confucian classics that were the basis of elite education and the specialists in Confucian rituals performed for the state and the family. Moreover, each of these religious traditions offered its own paths (*tao* 道) of individual self-transformation and salvation.

At the same time, the guidelines for behavior and methods for dealing with life that these identifiable traditions prescribed actually shared much common ground and experienced considerable mutual influence over the centuries. Community rituals, furthermore, were themselves not exclusive; indeed, they readily accommodated the different private understandings of participants. A Chinese might thus profess to have a Confucian, Buddhist, or Taoist identity, but still join in such rites and subscribe to a broad range of values widely shared in the society. The Chinese preference for blurring, not sharpening, religious identity was expressed in the ideal of "the three religions being one" (*san-chiao ho-i* 三教合一).

Chinese popular religion should be understood, we think, as those religious practices of everyday life shared by members of the entire society, not excluding either religious professionals, educated people of elite status, or any who may have somewhat different understandings of those practices. Although there were many regional variations (probably decreasing over time), popular religion constituted an important part of being Chinese and helped define that culture against those of its neighbors and domestic minorities.

Pilgrimage was one of these shared, popular religious practices, and all kinds of people made these journeys. Pilgrimage centers were built by monks, nuns, laymen and laywomen, rich and poor, learned and ignorant, powerful and powerless. Although some sites have been labeled Buddhist, Taoist, or Confucian, the chapters of this volume will show that such labels usually represented disputed claims.

As the field of Chinese religion developed, it relegated pilgrimage to a marginal position. Pilgrimage was not a central cultural metaphor, after all, or a religious duty, or an action emphasized in the great books. Village studies have usually excluded activities beyond the community, and the capitals studied as "sacred cities" were not actually pilgrimage centers. In the early part of the twentieth century, however, both Chinese travelers and foreign visitors described places that attracted people they readily identified as pilgrims; virtually all of them were mountain temples. But Edouard Chavannes's scholarly study of Mount T'ai concentrated on that North China site, not its pilgrims, as did Michel Soymié's work on Mount Lo-fu near Canton. Ku Chieh-kang's pioneering research on Miao-feng Shan did not spur imitators. Today, Western books and articles on Chinese religion might have a paragraph or a few pages on the subject, while Chinese works (except on Taiwan) ignore it altogether. In general, little sustained research has been done in any language in the last fifty years. It may therefore be helpful to draw together here at the outset our incomplete knowledge about China's pilgrimage tradition. We eagerly encourage other scholars to make corrections and help fill in the blanks.

In China, sacred sites are places where the power of a deity is manifest, places that are *ling* 靈 (numinous, efficacious). The classic form of pilgrimage involves a journey to a temple on a mountain peak, with stops along the way at other spots that are also *ling*. The principal objective is to make contact with the resident deity (*shen* 神), whose image is enshrined in the mountain temple. (The holy ground of ordinary temples echoes the mountain analogy: the entrance to the compound, for example, is called "gate to the mountain" [*shan-men* 山門]).

A mountain (*shan* 山) in the Chinese context can mean a single peak (as at Miao-feng Shan), a cluster of hills (Chiu-hua Shan), or a whole mountain range (Wu-t'ai Shan), not to mention caverns in a mountain (Mao Shan) or an island (P'u-t'o Shan). (These sites were discussed in the conference papers of Naquin, Powell, Gimello, Strickmann, and Yü, respectively. See the map on pp. xii–xiii.) Because Chinese were by preference lowlanders, these mountains, although not always at a great remove, necessitated a journey of some difficulty, and many were indeed very high. China is a land with many mighty summits piercing the clouds, and such peaks seem from very early times to have been viewed as points of access to heaven or places where deities dwelled. Not all pilgrimage sites or sacred places in China were mountains, but they were the prototype and most typical sort.

The Chinese phrase that means going on a pilgrimage—*ch'ao-shan chin-hsiang* 朝山進香—implies neither journey nor circuit. *Ch'ao-shan* means "paying one's respects to a mountain," as one would in an audience with a ruler. *Chin-hsiang*, "to present incense," refers to the acts of bringing and then burning incense so as to make contact with the deity. (In contrast, *shao-hsiang*

燒香, "burning incense," describes everyday worship at a family altar or community temple.) Both terms convey the subordinated relationship of the humble petitioner to a powerful god.

References to incense pervade the language of pilgrimage. An incense burner (*hsiang-lu* 香鑪) set before the god defines the ritual center of a temple; pilgrims are called *hsiang-k'o* 香客 (incense visitors), and their organizations, *hsiang-hui* 香會 (incense associations). A temple or cult's popularity can be expressed as a measure of its "incense fires" (*hsiang-huo* 香火). In contemporary Taiwan, the language of incense links temples to the same deity. In several cults, fragrant cinders from a mother temple are taken to a newly founded branch and used to light the new burner, a process known as "dividing incense" (*fen-hsiang* 分香). To renew this relationship, parishioners from the branch temple make annual pilgrimages to the mother temple, taking cinders to be redeposited there and returning with smoking incense for their own censer (this is called "cutting incense" [*ko-hsiang* 割香]).

Chinese pilgrims, like their counterparts in other parts of the world, have had a great variety of motivations for undertaking pilgrimages. They might go to seek a vision of the deity, perform a penance, ask for heirs or cures, or pray for good health and long life for themselves and their family members. The vague phrase "to obtain blessings and avert calamities" is often used to describe such goals. Many such journeys are undertaken as part of specific personal exchanges with a god, expressed in the contractual language of making promises to a deity (*hsu-yuan* 許願) and fulfilling such vows (*huan-yuan* 還願).

Historically, the language of pilgrimage includes other terms, and, as the chapters in this volume will show, sacred sites also attracted visitors whose purposes and understandings of the power of the place were differently phrased. More work is needed to assemble a full range of changing vocabulary and actions.

Pilgrimage-like behavior has a long history in China. We hypothesize that individual pilgrims, real and imaginary, appeared no later than the fourth century B.C., while large-scale pilgrimages developed during the medieval period (eighth to twelfth centuries) out of the interaction of deeply rooted indigenous ideas with beliefs imported to China through Buddhism. We will, therefore, with apologies for the crudeness of these stages, look first at pilgrimage activities before the arrival of Buddhism, then at Buddhist ideas and practices, and finally at the resultant combination.

For the early history of China, our knowledge is necessarily sketchy. As in other agricultural societies, nature was invested with considerable potency and sometimes imagined in animal form. Such powers then began to take second place to more mighty supernatural forces envisioned as the spirits of deceased men (usually rulers) or as an impersonal "heaven" (*t'ien* 天). These various forces were worshiped, that is, offerings were made to them on a regular basis. The tumuli of kings were one important focus for rites; shamans were also thought to be capable of making spiritual journeys to establish contact with these spirits. As the documentation improves in later eras, we see more clearly how China's rulers continued to monopolize access to these most powerful forces.

By at least the Eastern Chou period (seventh to third century B.C.), mountains and waterways formed one of the symbolic grids that defined the empire, while mountains held an even more special place in the rituals of China's kings. Five mountains had been designated as the northern, eastern, southern, western, and central peaks; according to the "Classic of History," the legendary emperor Shun set the precedent of following an annual cycle of visits presenting offerings to each. Such behavior was described in terms of the subordination of the mountains (which were likened to ministers) to the ruler. (This grand macrocircuit was supposed to have been matched by comparable local ones.)

Other classic texts of the first millennium B.C. contributed to the model for this type of royal progression (*hsun-hsing* 巡幸). In the "Account of the Travels of Emperor Mu" the pattern encapsulated in the phrase *ch'ao-shan* was set for imperial pilgrimage: a ruler toured his realm and visited mountains and rivers to receive the homage of the deities dwelling there, as they yielded up treasures in return for protection. In the late third century, Ch'in-shih-huang, creator of the first empire, set a well-documented precedent (recorded in Ssu-ma Ch'ien's *Shih-chi*) by visiting a host of sacred peaks (and rivers) to legitimize his rule; he also performed the rare *feng-shan* 封禪 rites to heaven and earth at Mount T'ai. An imperial sacred geography that would last for nearly two thousand years was thus gradually constructed.

In the later Chou and subsequent Han period (through the second century A.D.), we can see other strands of belief that also shaped ideas about pilgrimage. It was thought, for example, that immortal beings lived in remote uninhabited regions, forever free of human needs. Some resided on the fabulous mountains of central Asia, far to the west, others on islands in the eastern seas. (Han incense burners shaped like mountains rising from the sea show the early and intimate connection between islands and mountains and gods.)

The "Classic of Mountains and Seas" described the taming of the waters and ordering of the natural world by the mythical emperor Yü. Together with the "Travels of Emperor Mu" and the *Huai-nan tzu*, it also contributed to the idea of the early classic sacred mountain. Such works provide much lore about the Queen Mother of the West and her dwelling place in the distant western reaches of the known world, Mount K'un-lun, describing it as a critical link between human and heavenly realms, a magical place where there was access to immortality.

Any mountain seems to have been potentially sacred, the dwelling place of gods and a passage to another sphere. By the early fourth century the philosopher Ko Hung could write, "No matter whether the mountain is great or small, gods and numinous spirits are found without fail therein." Since mountains were powerful and awesome places, one could not venture there carelessly but had to follow strict protocols as to the proper time and proper behavior for "entering the mountain" (*ju-shan* 入山). Ko Hung provided talismans that could afford protection for those whose purpose was finding the elixir of immortality and other secrets of nature kept by the mountain deities.

The dead were also viewed as powerful spirits requiring ritual attention and regular visits, and tombs were shaped like mounds, similar to mountains. Nevertheless, in China, even in early times, graves never became foci of public worship. Confucius himself was concerned about the funeral rituals performed by children for parents, but his assertion that such responsibilities devolved upon descendants became a standard that kept most graves from becoming objects of pilgrimage.

Documented imperial processions are probably the clearest example of pre-Buddhist pilgrimage-like activity; information about the religious lives of private individuals is harder to come by for the early periods of Chinese history. But in the "History of the Later Han," we do have a simple but clear reference to an individual pilgrim. A certain Hsu Jun fell seriously ill and went to Mount T'ai (the sacred peak of the east, long patronized by rulers) to "pay a visit" (*ye* 謁) and pray for a long life.

With the coming of Buddhism in the first and second centuries A.D., new impulses influenced China's pilgrimage tradition. The pioneers were monks, and the direction of their journeys was, at first, toward India. For a thousand years, monk-pilgrims would brave the dangerous deserts, remote mountains, and treacherous oceans to make the difficult and perilous journey to seek instruction in Buddhist teachings, find scriptures, and visit famous sites sanctified by the life of the Buddha.

By far the most famous of the monk-pilgrims who journeyed west to "seek the dharma" (*ch'iu-fa* 求法) was Hsuan-tsang (ca. 596–664), the Tripitaka Master, who spent sixteen years in India. Later widely popularized in stories, plays, and the novel "Journey to the West," this pilgrim (*hsing-che* 行者) became a perennially powerful symbol. His journey served as an idealized depiction of a real pilgrimage, involving great dedication and self-sacrifice, danger and high adventure, good companionship and spiritual realization.

The *Sutra of Great Decease* (*Ta-pan nieh-p'an ching* 大般涅槃經 *T* 7:374–77), first translated into Chinese about A.D. 300, introduced the basic ideas about stupas (*t'a* 塔), that is, funerary mounds housing relics that, if visited, would promote one's faith and help obtain a better rebirth. This scripture served in

China, as in other Buddhist countries, as a charter for pilgrimage and for a cult of relics.

As Buddhism became domesticated, in a process parallel to that of Christianity in medieval Europe, believers began to create a sacred geography on their native soil, marked here by relics, the miraculously preserved bodies of monks, famous temples, and finally the four great Buddhist mountains (and many lesser ones). A celibate clergy set standards for pious laypeople who could now become pilgrims in their own country. As China achieved a powerful cultural influence on other East Asian countries, Korean and Japanese Buddhist pilgrims went there rather than to India.

Legitimized by the legend of the Aśokan stupas, some monasteries gained great prestige and patronage from their possession of Buddhist relics. The Fa-men Monastery in the suburbs of the T'ang capital, for instance, achieved great fame in the ninth century because it claimed to have a finger bone of the Buddha. (The casket containing the bone together with a treasure of gold and precious gems has recently been excavated.) Such relics were publicly worshiped by the faithful, from the emperor, nobility, and monks down to the common people. These devotions could inspire enormous religious zeal, even frenzy, and worshipers might cut off their fingers and arms as offerings. Many stupas were built, usually near monasteries, to contain ashes and relics of especially holy clerics, outward signs of their invisible spiritual greatness. Such stupas began to attract visitors, initially other monks but eventually laypeople as well. As Bernard Faure's chapter shows, in the eighth century, monks of the school of meditative Buddhism known in China as Ch'an (and in Japan and the West as Zen) began saving the miraculously preserved bodies of enlightened teachers. Other monks started coming to pay respect and make offerings to these *jou-shen* 肉身, "bodies with the flesh still intact."

Although Buddhism provided new reasons for people to go on pilgrimages, paradoxically it also brought challenges to traditional notions. The many legends of Buddhist masters using their universal religion to subjugate and convert local gods, erasing their particularism, encapsulate the confrontation of world views. Furthermore, Buddhist monks in general (and Ch'an monks in particular) asserted that an internal journey might be as conducive to salvation as a physical one, and the latter might even be disruptive and unnecessary. The Pure Land (Western Paradise) was said to be no different from one's own mind, and Amitābha Buddha (faith in whom could lead to rebirth there) was considered identical with one's self-nature. Indeed, like other religions, Chinese Buddhism, Taoism, and Neo-Confucianism all developed mystical traditions that emphasized spiritual growth and access to the divine through introspection or meditation.

Ch'an Buddhism downplayed the notion of pilgrimage but stressed the value for clerics of wandering peregrinations from one major Buddhist center to another (*yu-fang* 遊方, "traveling in all four directions," or *ts'an-fang* 参方,

"traveling to every quarter of the country") on foot (*hsing-chiao* 行脚) to broaden their understanding of the dharma and to inquire after, study with, or meditate under a famous master. The mendicant was called a "monk of clouds and water" (*yun-shui seng* 雲水僧), for he was supposed to be as free and unattached as flowing water and floating clouds. In time, however, important monasteries where famous masters had lived or died evolved into what were essentially pilgrimage centers for monks.

For lay pilgrims, accumulating merit in this world and securing benefits for themselves and their loved ones in the next were common motives for pilgrimages. Images (sculpted or painted) soon became an important focus for devotions. Buddhist associations were formed in pre-T'ang times to fund the creation of monumental images in caves along the road to India and near the capitals of Buddhist rulers, at Tun-huang, Yun-kang, Lung-men, and Ta-tsu. These and other associations created from the Sung on for group invocation of the Buddha's name (*nien-fo hui* 念佛會) or for freeing animals (*fang-sheng hui* 放生會) may have developed into the pilgrimage organizations of later periods.

Buddhist images had a profound influence on Chinese religious art. Explained as aids to believers in focusing their emotions and thoughts on the deity, they became easily copied embodiments of religious ideas. Some images were understood to have been miraculously produced, self-manifested, or created by the deity; others were capable of miracles. Shrines built to house them became temples and, if miracles occurred, pilgrimage sites.

As efficacious sites became better known, Buddhist sutras provided names and imagery that could be used to (in Robert Gimello's words) "transfigure" them. While the Indian idea of the island-mountain Potalaka, Kuan-yin's home, provided scriptural authority for the further blurring of these concepts in China, the *Flower Garland Sutra* served as the basis for mapping and naming important sites. The same scripture also provided one of the central paradigms for Buddhist pilgrimage: the visits of young Sudhana (Shan-ts'ai) to fifty-three teachers in his search for enlightenment. Starting in the tenth century, this theme came to be widely celebrated in art and literature, and Shan-ts'ai became a model for clerical and lay pilgrims. All the important bodhisattvas of Chinese Buddhism, the enlightened ones dedicated to saving all sentient beings—Maitreya (Mi-le), Mañjuśrī (Wen-shu), Samantabhadra (P'u-hsien), and Avalokiteśvara (Kuan-yin)—make their appearances as guides to the young pilgrim.

As Chün-fang Yü's chapter explains, the designated homes of three of these bodhisattvas—Mount Wu-t'ai in Shansi (for Mañjuśrī), Mount Omei in Szechwan (for P'u-hsien), and Mount P'u-t'o, an island off the coast of Chekiang (for Kuan-yin)—together with Mount Chiu-hua in Anhui, the home of Kṣitigarbha (Ti-tsang), came to constitute the four great Buddhist mountains (*ssu ta ming-shan* 四大名山), situated at the four imaginary cardinal points of the Chinese empire and at the same time representing the four constitutive elements of the universe. Founding myths credited the bodhisattvas' hierophanies, visions granted to devotees and miracles dispensed to seekers. By at least Ming times (1368–1644), these four mountains formed a grand Buddhist pilgrimage circuit. The birthdays of these four divinities had, moreover, been incorporated into annual liturgical calendars and marked for special celebration.

Buddhist ideas and institutions thus made dramatic contributions to the development of Chinese pilgrimage, building on, adapting to, and altering the earlier traditions. During the same period (the first millennium A.D.), the emerging schools of Taoism encouraged and affected these trends, and, as Michel Strickmann's paper for the conference illustrated, greatly enriched China's mountain lore.

Taoist scholar-adepts sought lives of ascetic isolation in the mountains, while Taoist scriptures elaborated ideas about peaks and caverns and the transcendent beings who inhabited them. Continuing the ideas of Ko Hung and T'ao Hung-ching (456–536), Taoists created a sacred geography centered on mountains and caves. The classical Five Peaks, for example, were reinterpreted as the five fingers of the cosmic Lao Tzu. By the eighth century, such sacred places were systematized into the ten major and thirty-six minor cavern-heavens (*tung-t'ien* 洞天) and the seventy-two "blessed lands" (*fu-ti* 福地) under the sacred peaks. These sites, supposedly linked by subterranean networks, were to be found the length and breadth of China; they were both secret environments called up by Taoists through meditation and real places visited by pilgrims. (As both the Yü and the Gimello chapters illustrate, Buddhists also favored cave temples, for they were thought suitable to reclusive meditation and likely loci for a vision of the deity.)

Emperors continued, in the meantime, to worship at special shrines to the mountains and rivers of the empire and to make intermittent journeys to specially favored sacred peaks. They generously enfeoffed mountain gods with titles and rewarded deities who brought benefits for the nation as a whole. Since Han times, these designated Five Peaks (*wu-yueh* 五嶽) were Mount T'ai, Mount Heng (in Shansi), Mount Sung (in Honan), Mount Hua (in Shensi), and Mount Heng (in Hunan), Mount T'ai being the most important. Imperial patronage could be crucial to the development of a cult and center, as John Lagerwey shows for Mount Wu-tang.

At the same time, state efforts to strip the wealthy Buddhist and Taoist establishments of significant economic power were rather successful, and after the ninth century, religious institutions did not acquire wealth and property on the scale of their counterparts elsewhere in the world. Neo-Confucianism (the reformulation of Confucian thought that became elite orthodoxy after the twelfth century) similarly challenged the intellectual authority of its rivals, even as it borrowed from them. Nevertheless, toleration and coexistence were generally the norm, and state attempts to register temples and clerics, control unauthorized worship, and discourage pilgrimage became ever more difficult as China grew in size and population.

The growth of regional cults to Buddhist bodhisattvas and many other deities from Sung times on, promoted by local elites and rewarded with imperial patronage, was a strong spur to pilgrimage. Many of the deities who were gradually achieving empirewide recognition—Kuan-yin, Chen-wu, Pi-hsia Yuan-chün (each described in subsequent chapters), Ma-tsu, Wen-ch'ang, and Kuan-ti—developed wide followings in and after the medieval period. Temples where they responded to the prayers of the devotee competed with one another, and each, cult and site, fueled the growth of the other.

Literati education in imperial times did not encourage imitation of the pilgrimage behavior of clerics or pious laypeople. Instead, educated elites created their own models (and by following them, defined themselves as literati). Like Confucius, who spent many years making the rounds (*chou-yu* 週遊) of the various feudal states in search of a ruler who would adopt his counsel, Neo-Confucians such as Chu Hsi (1130–1200) and Wang Yang-ming (1472–1529) traveled about giving lectures. Places associated with the lives of these masters would then draw other literati visitors, who came in remembrance and so recharged the sites with new attractive power. The White Deer Hollow Academy in Kiangsi established by Chu Hsi (who later was buried there) became such a site. In another exception to the privatization of graves, Confucius' tomb in Shantung also received both imperial and scholarly visitors.

Benefiting from improving transportation in an expanding empire, Sung, Yuan, Ming, and Ch'ing literati (between the tenth and nineteenth centuries) set forth to enjoy nature and to "seek teachers and visit friends" (*sheng-shih fang-yu* 省師訪友). Volumes of travel accounts (*yu-chi* 遊記) survive today, describing visits to historical monuments, scenic spots, and religious sites of renown. Such travel, termed *yu* 遊 (leisurely touring), encompassed a large constellation of activities: enjoying natural beauty, investigating history, communing with the past, and immortalizing these moments by composing a poem, painting a picture, or writing a short essay. These writings characteristically shunned discussions of religion and showed disdain for the religious fervor of the common masses. Some literary and artistic genres thus actively constrained their authors. (Such attitudes are illustrated in the Cahill, Wu, and Dudbridge chapters and contrast with earlier material provided by Gimello and Yü.)

Fortunately, Chinese literati were also historians. More than a hundred mountain gazetteers (*shan-chih* 山志) survive, for example, and these histories of mountain sites incorporating a variety of primary sources provide important bases for the studies of Mounts T'ai, Huang, Wu-t'ai, P'u-t'o, and Wu-tang in this volume.

Literati began painting landscapes (*shan-shui* 山水, lit., "mountains and watercourses") in medieval times with mountains as their subjects. But even when artists selected peaks famous as pilgrimage centers, they expressed different values and concerns. Some mountains, such as Mount Lu in Kiang-si province, became famous among painters over the centuries because they had been so well (or so often) rendered; others became the subjects of albums or a series of scrolls that allowed a record from multiple perspectives; most were commemorated in poetry as well. James Cahill's chapter treats one such place. As he shows, crowds, temples, and religious activity at Mount Huang were decidedly secondary to the artist's experience of the natural setting.

At the same time, mountains, miniaturized as rocks, were being trans-ferred from the wild into the garden and home and there played an important role in elite culture. The garden, like the handscroll and album, was also suited to leading a viewer on a winding path through a landscape. The small basin holding a rock and a tree (*p'en-ching* 盆景, related to the Japanese *bonsai* and connected to the earlier incense-burner-as-mountain) encapsulated na-ture on an even smaller scale.

By the beginning of the early modern period (around the sixteenth cen-tury), many tributaries had fed Chinese pilgrimage culture. Differentiated literati, imperial, clerical, and lay traditions existed together with a con-tinuously growing set of shrines to a variety of local, regional, and national deities. With increasing ease of travel within the empire, facilitated by route books and encouraged by economic growth and political integration, pil-grimage flourished. In many parts of China, associations developed that promoted these journeys and cared for the growing numbers of pilgrims. (Some are described in the Lagerwey, Naquin, Wu, and Dudbridge chap-ters.)

Although a few centers steadily accumulated sacred power over the cen-turies, even their development was not always smooth and continuous; more commonly, a site's popularity rose and fell. Mount Wu-t'ai, for example, ex-panded first in the medieval period but underwent a revival and transforma-tion in later times when it also became a Tibetan Buddhist center. As new sites developed, older ones were sometimes forgotten, as the Faure and Yü chapters illustrate. In general, those mountains sacred to a variety of pil-grims outlived those with narrower constituencies.

Pilgrims often wore particular clothing and performed distinctive acts. Holmes Welch provides some modern examples that undoubtedly had earlier antecedents. The Ch'an master Hsu-yun went on a pilgrimage in 1882 from P'u-t'o to Wu-t'ai to ask Mañjuśrī to help his dead parents achieve early rebirth in the Western Paradise. Making prostrations every third step, it took him two years to travel the fifteen hundred kilometers. A more severe form of austerity was undertaken by lay penitents expiating a serious offense or redeeming a great vow: an incense burner would be suspended from a hook that pierced the flesh of the pilgrim's arm or a talisman plaque pinned to the skin of the chest. There were also pilgrims in traditional times who, swept up by the ecstasy of seeing a manifestation of the deity, leapt suicidally off mountain cliffs to join it. Although most pilgrims did not engage in these extreme forms of mortification, they refrained from sexual activity and ate a vegetarian diet for the duration of the journey.

As Timothy Brook's conference paper showed, travel had become a key element in the religious training of monks. The author of the 1827 guidebook *Knowing the Fords on the Way to Knowledge* provided special guidelines for monk-pilgrims, whose goal in visiting famous mountains should be to achieve early enlightenment. En route they were to beg for their food, seek lodging in monasteries, endure the hardships of travel, and always behave in accordance with the monastic rules. He advised his readers to travel with other monks for companionship, assistance, and protection; to make an itinerary and stick firmly to it; but not to set a time limit on the journey. Relinquishing desire for fame and profit and setting their minds resolutely on the Way, they should regard the road as their home and spend their days without worry. Like government officials, however, monastic authorities worried about control. Chu-hung, an influential late Ming Buddhist master, typified this ambivalent attitude: he criticized both extensive seclusion and extended travel and urged a proper sequence tailored to a life-long program of spiritual development. And nuns, he argued, should not travel at all!

China also continued to be part of larger pilgrimage networks. The religious pluralism of medieval times, when Manicheans, Nestorians, Zoroastrians, Christians, Jews, and Muslims could be found in China's capital, had declined in later eras. Imperial patronage of Central Asian Esoteric (so-called Lamaist) Buddhism in the sixteenth to nineteenth centuries helped develop new sites, transformed old ones, and attracted pious Mongol and Tibetan pilgrims to China. As Islam spread to China after the eighth century, it was taken up first by non-Han peoples of Inner Asia and western China and later by the inhabitants of China proper. Chinese Muslims became part of worldwide networks as they journeyed to Mecca, while, by Ch'ing times (1644–1911), the tombs of Sufi saints within the empire had become important Islamic pilgrimage sites. Thus, by the twentieth century, when knowledge of European culture increased and travel beyond China became easier, Chinese Christians could visit Rome or Jerusalem and Chinese Marxists journey to London or Leningrad.

Within China, the remote location of many pilgrimage mountains protected them somewhat from the disorders of the twentieth century, but not from government-sponsored attacks on popular religion as superstitious, wasteful, and reactionary. Since 1949 on Taiwan, governmental ambivalence and prosperity have allowed religious activity to flourish, as P. Steven San-gren's conference paper showed. In the same period, as Rudolf Wagner explains in his chapter here, the People's Republic has attempted to wipe out the past and create a new sacred geography validated by historical connections with the Communist Party and its leaders: the area of the 1930s Soviet in Kiangsi, the wartime headquarters at Yenan, the birthplaces of Mao Tse-tung and of the Party, the mausoleum and other monuments of T'ien-an-men Square in Peking. Recently some of the temples and shrines that attracted pilgrims in the past have been rebuilt and reopened, and religious connections between Taiwan and the mainland have been reestablished. It remains to be seen how pilgrimage will be affected by further modernization.

THE MAKING OF PILGRIMAGE SITES IN CHINA

With these comparative and historical frameworks in mind, let us now turn to the project of this volume. Our approach to the study of pilgrimage in China has been shaped in the first instance by the constraints of our sources. Fieldwork—the mainstay of much pilgrimage research around the world—was feasible on the mainland in the first part of this century but impossible after 1949. The Chinese revolution has introduced a seemingly radical break between contemporary and past religious practice, and only in the mid-1980s did opportunities arise to visit these sites and interview present-day pilgrims. Although field research has been possible in Taiwan and Hong Kong—and has produced interesting results—both areas have had to adapt to abrupt detachment from their larger cultural regions a century ago. Thus, China has not presented the same opportunities for anthropologists as India, Latin America, or Europe.

Other constraints have affected the written accounts historians rely upon. China's most famous pilgrims were those who left the Middle Kingdom to journey to India; moreover, no other identifiable body of domestic pilgrimage accounts is known, and the writings of the proportionally small number of literate travelers rarely discuss "religious" sentiments or activities. The histories of the mountains that drew pilgrims, however, are extensively documented, with much information about buildings, layout, and successive patrons. Biographies of Buddhists and Taoists who visited or resided in these temples, as well as a large travel literature (Chinese and foreign), present further sources of information. Such materials are relatively substantial for the Ming and Ch'ing periods and diminish in quantity as one goes back in time.

We planned our conference with the knowledge that interest in pilgrimage in China was increasing. Although many of the conference participants had visited their sites, only a few had done interviews (Yü and Powell in particular). For the volume we have therefore focused instead on the historical study of pilgrimage. We do so to call attention to the challenge of studying this topic with few personal accounts and without talking to pilgrims. It is in their use of historical sources for pilgrimage sites that these essays are strong and can provide models for other scholars.

We would like to show how one can learn about pilgrimage by studying a site and to argue that this is a needed corrective to the overemphasis on the pilgrims' experience by Turner and others. We hope to illustrate the methodological problems of working without the firsthand accounts of pilgrims and perhaps offer some solutions. A considerable amount of conference time was devoted to the question of whether it was valid to "read" a site and create an "implied pilgrim" (as Rudolf Wagner and William Powell did in their papers). How does one make the connection between the visible (and documented) site and the invisible (and unrecorded) experience? Did these centers provide similar experiences for pilgrims with different motivations? If so, how? What are we to make of the diversity at many of these sites? The chapters that follow provide some answers.

We have taken each person who wrote about or went to a pilgrimage site as someone who helped build it. In this sense the distinction between pilgrims and tourists does not seem useful. Readers who do not appreciate this point may be working with a definition narrower than ours. Moreover, we think that the separate, splintered points of view of such visitors and their partial, partisan descriptions of sights should all be recognized. Assembled to show the range of meanings and polyphony of voices brought to and embedded in a site, their cumulative effect and areas of overlap may reveal much that was inevitably shared. This approach requires a sensitive handling of sources, each of which has not only its own filter (which screened out unwelcome information on aspects of the site and its visitors), but usually a vested interest in defining the meaning of a site in a particular, sometimes exclusive way.

Although pilgrimage in China was traditionally directed toward a temple on the top of a mountain, most sites were much more extensive, complicated, and multifocal. *Mountain* often referred to a range of peaks, but even a simple summit usually involved many paths of ascent and descent and a variety of sights and nodes of interest. The intrinsic numinosity of nature—summits, cliffs, vistas, caves, springs, rocks, trees—was the foundation on which much could be built, physically and imaginatively. Stupas, tombs, inscriptions, ritual arenas, shrines, sculpture, paintings, and pavilions were constructed over a wide area; relics and texts were imported and produced; religious specialists were drawn to set up residence nearby; records of facts and myths were set down and published. Part of the heterogeneity of a site came from this physical diversity. Part came from the variety of pilgrims-cum-patrons,

past and present: emperors, Ch'an and ordinary Buddhist monks, professional Taoists, hermits, tourists, and lay pilgrims. As the chapters in this
volume show, rarely was a single type of pilgrim responsible for a successful
site. These kinds of diversity, which are relatively easy to see, enumerate, and
study, can tell us much about pilgrimage.

Widely different and sometimes opposing ideas of what was sacred were
held by different people at different times in China. Moreover, pilgrims and
visitors each came with their own expectations and experiences. It is possible, although difficult, to try to reconstruct these expectations. Contemporary information about pilgrimage sites was often transmitted in ephemeral
forms: oral accounts by pilgrims, miracle tales, scriptures, woodblock prints,
paintings and albums, maps, sketches, drawings, travel essays, novels, pilgrimage association announcements, guide books, historical and geographical studies. These different media prepared the pilgrim for the journey to
come, but, changing over time, they advertised the site in different ways and
conditioned different audiences. Indeed, like most propaganda, these descriptions asserted one set of meanings at the expense of others.

At the same time, it was possible for a pilgrim to resist the influence not
only of such advertisements but of the very structure of a site. Each pilgrim
came preoccupied with particular concerns. These formed a filter that highlighted certain points of attraction and screened out or devalued others. Each
person surely had his or her own mental map, and even those who traveled
the same route at the same time surely looked at different things or saw the
same things differently.

The chapters in this volume illustrate some of this complexity. Lagerwey
and Yü describe how a site was built up over time by different types of
pilgrims—clerics, emperors, literati, and commoners—one in a generally
Taoist environment, the other Buddhist. Faure shows the bid for domination
of several sites by Ch'an monks. Wagner reveals how political factions tried
to embed different values in the physical structure and decorations at Mao's
mausoleum. The Wu and Dudbridge chapters make clear the sharp differences between literati and "popular" experiences of the same mountain,
while Naquin sees differences in the goals of organized and unorganized pilgrims.

No single pilgrim's view can reveal the diversity of any site, and we have
to be cautious in our assumptions about typicality. A simple list of all the
points of attraction of a site, giving each equal weight, cannot, however,
capture the pilgrimage experience either. A structuralist analysis, furthermore, often ignores the processes of development and decline and glosses
over conflict and interplay. The accretion of meanings laid down over centuries and embedded at the sacred place and in other accounts needs careful
excavation to draw out the changing sets of competing and complementary
perspectives. (Fortunately, even though some pilgrims and patrons came, at

different times, to dominate a given site and its historical record, evidence of multiple readings has usually also been preserved.) Because the site itself must be seen as something built by pilgrims, we can use it as a way of studying the pilgrims themselves.

This diversity of views did not detract from the fame of a site; on the contrary, it reinforced it. Like the retelling of myths (what Prasenjit Duara has called "superscription"), adding new and variant layers of meaning to a pilgrimage site, rewriting its history, or rerouting its pilgrims enhanced a site's powers. An enduringly popular site seems to have been the result of the interaction between the many different pilgrims who built and maintained it. Pilgrims both ignored and competed with one another, it is true, but through a process of what P. Steven Sangren, in his conference paper, called mutual authentication, the entire site derived an increased aura of power from these partial visions of it. Just as rivalry between sites dedicated to a single deity could actually enhance the reputation of the god, so, as pilgrims competed to build a sacred site, they contributed collectively (if inadvertently) to its general fame. The whole became more than the sum of the parts.

The contentious and energizing pluralism within a flexible framework of pilgrimage sites seems to be particularly (but certainly not uniquely) Chinese, an exaggeration of a situation common elsewhere, and a product of both history and culture. The weakness of organized religion in China and the preoccupation of elites with ritual activities in cities meant there was less centralized control and less effective emphasis on exclusivity than in some other cultures.

There were in China, after all, no requirements like daily prayer, baptism, bar mitzvahs, or last rites, no compelling obligations to go to confession or mass, the synagogue on the Sabbath or church on Sunday. The rituals of daily life and rites of passage, not formally enforced, were shared across the culture and served as markers separating Chinese from "barbarian." More closely prescribed imperial rites were imposed on only a few people. Despite rivalry (most explicitly expressed in competition for imperial patronage), no single group of religious professionals triumphed for long, niches were developed, and other systems came to be seen as complementary alternatives. Most would have agreed with (even if they could not fully explain) the inscription on a Ming stele on Mount Wu-tang quoted by Lagerwey: "The three teachings use different paths, but they all come down to the same thing."

This was a culture that allowed for, even insisted upon, multiple understandings. James Watson has argued that there was an emphasis on similar behavior at the expense of shared doctrine. As pilgrimages illustrate, popular religious rituals were simple in China and implied no formal or exclusive creed. Literati painters, sharp-eyed novelists, and officials on duty could burn incense in a temple exactly as did the exhausted penitent or resident monk. Temples accommodated many different images, could serve different communities, and were open to all. Pilgrimage, like worship generally, was a wholly voluntary act; site, route, and timing (except for the "pilgrimage seasons" connected with some cults) were up to the individual. Religion's power to promote community integration in China derived in part from such flexibility.

Understanding this aspect of pilgrimage suggests that it is insufficient to describe Chinese culture in terms of dichotomies and oppositions (elite vs. popular, Buddhist vs. Taoist, orthodox vs. heterodox, etc.) or of eclecticism and syncretism (Confucianism plus Buddhism plus Taoism, the three-religions-are-one, etc.). Scholars must also focus on how the overarching unity of shared ideas and practices developed and survived in the context of competing doctrines, specialists, classes, and institutions.

The chapters that follow will present information on nine multivocal pilgrimage sites during (primarily) the tenth to nineteenth centuries; two present translations as illustrations of (among other things) multiple points of view of a single site; one deals with the construction of a twentieth-century monument.

Glen Dudbridge's translation of two chapters of a mid-seventeenth-century novel vividly conveys the human dimension of pilgrimage, the sights and sounds of "real" people as they made the ascent of Mount T'ai. At the same time, the educated author reveals the ironic distance that literati preferred to maintain between themselves and ordinary (especially female) pilgrims. This chapter should also make us consider the advantages and problems of using fictional sources. Pei-yi Wu, whose material nearly parallels Dudbridge's in time and place, takes us some distance into the mind of an early seventeenth-century literatus who climbed Mount T'ai not once but twice. This lively account helps us understand the ways in which elites did (and did not) share the experiences of other pilgrims and introduces us to the constraints of the *yu-chi* genre of travel writing.

Robert Gimello translates a rare extended firsthand account of a pilgrimage by a member of the elite. The literatus and pious lay Buddhist Chang Shang-ying's description of his trip to Mount Wu-t'ai in 1087 provides an unusually explicit discussion of religious concerns and, like Faure's essay, is a window onto the medieval period. Bernard Faure's chapter explores the development in medieval times of pilgrimage centers by Ch'an Buddhists; by comparing Ts'ao-ch'i (where the Sixth Patriarch's flesh body was preserved) with Mount Sung (which lost its Ch'an constituency), he illustrates not only the rivalries between sites but the fragility of their fame. Chün-fang Yü writes about one of China's four Buddhist "mountains": P'u-t'o, the island sacred to Kuan-yin off the central China coast on which there was a large complex of temples and sights. Using collections of miracle tales and successive editions of the mountain gazetteer in particular, she shows how a Chinese

Potalaka, the sacred site of scriptural fame, was created here, despite many alternatives on the mainland.

Turning to another medium, James Cahill traces the development of literati paintings of Mount Huang, a regional site of considerable natural beauty taken up by the local elites of Hui-chou in southern Anhui in the Ming-Ch'ing period. This essay calls our attention to the role of illustrations of varying levels of artistic quality in spreading a mountain's fame.

John Lagerwey deals with the varied patrons of Mount Wu-tang in Hupei, where shrines to Chen-wu, the Dark Warrior, were located. He uses a broad range of sources, including many Taoist ones. Mount Miao-feng near Peking, discussed by Susan Naquin, had a much smaller, regional clientele and owed its popularity to its status as an offshoot of the temple atop Mount T'ai and to the energetic efforts of urban and rural pilgrimage associations. She and Lagerwey both show how stele inscriptions that survive in situ can be used as sources for more ordinary pilgrims.

Rudolf Wagner's chapter is remote from the others in its subject matter— the construction of the memorial hall for Mao Tse-tung in 1976–77—but its method is of considerable relevance. Contemporary sources expose how patrons of a site built meaning into the physical setting in the hope (not always successful) of conditioning the experience of the visitor. These data reveal clearly how competing symbols can be incorporated into a single structure. Understanding this process encourages us to imagine something similar occurring at more traditional sites and to inspect the buildings and layout more closely. It also reminds us of the many new, modern pilgrimage sites that have been created in China in recent decades.

Although we have not written a full history of Chinese pilgrimage, we hope that this volume will introduce the reader to a range of pilgrims and pilgrimage sites in China and show through specific cases more general processes. At the same time, by arraying before the reader a variety of available source materials and by suggesting methods for unpacking the dense historical record, we hope to stimulate continued research on this subject. There is obviously much that we have not done and could not do. The ever more voluminous comparative literature on pilgrimage shows many aspects of the topic that bear investigation in the case of China and yet are only mentioned in passing in this volume. In the hope of stimulating further work, we therefore close this introduction with a preliminary survey of some of what needs to be done.

We would like to know more about the place of pilgrims in their home communities. Anthropologists who have lived in Indian villages and then joined in pilgrimages provide excellent models. What kinds of people went on pilgrimages? Was a certain age or sex or occupation more common? Can we separate the push from the pull factors? How did people learn about the pilgrimage in advance and prepare for it? How did returned pilgrims then affect the life of their families and communities?

We have all wished for more accounts by pilgrims, especially by men and women of different classes. Have we underestimated the extent of such material among our Chinese sources? Where can these accounts be found? Direct testimony about the goals and meaning and experience itself, while not the whole story, might provide data comparable to that for other religions and allow a serious discussion of some of Turner's issues. Fieldwork data might also help us understand better how pilgrims looked at a site, ignoring some things and noticing others. Even the better-known material on the experience of monks and literati has not been adequately investigated. The ample poetic literature on Chinese mountains, whose richness is suggested by Demiéville, Schafer, and Kroll, might be combined with representations in painting and prints and thus teach us about genres as well as individuals. The massive Ch'ing collection of travel literature in the *Hsiao-fang-hu-chai yü-ti ts'ung-ch'ao*, for example, could bear systematic study. How can we make better use of fictional material? How do we study poorly documented female pilgrims? The pilgrims' songs sung by women and collected by Chün-fang Yü in 1987 (included in her conference paper but not here) suggest some avenues of access.

Can we recover some of the advertising media that publicized sites, fixing expectations and memory—the iconographic representations of places (e.g., Mount Wu-t'ai) and deities (e.g., Kuan-yin), for example, or the miracle literature that also validated the pilgrimage? Scattered references in our conference papers indicate that there were guidebooks to pilgrimage centers. These should be located and systematically studied; Brook (1988) is a good place to start.

Another rich source might be the popular scriptures known as *pao-chüan* 寶卷 (precious volumes). The Ming dynasty *Ling-ying T'ai Shan Niang-niang pao-chüan* (Precious volume spoken by our efficaciously responsive Lady of Mount T'ai), for example, argues for the special efficacy of this site and promises an easy trip for the single-minded pilgrim and a difficult one for the insincere. Written in alternating prose and verse intended for recitation, these scriptures told stories in vivid language that could lodge in the pilgrim's memory and make a deep impression.

What about the distinctive costumes of pilgrims? What were the enduring emblems: staff, rosary, gourd water-container, bag for carrying incense, hats, belts, sandals, and armbands? How much variation was there across time, space, and class? Are these useful markers for distinguishing pilgrimage from ordinary worship at a community temple or for differentiating pilgrims from tourists? Fiction and painting may be useful sources.

A few papers mention pilgrimage organizations, but we know too little about them and their development. How did the groups of pious laypeople who collectively donated money to carve Buddhas at Tun-huang in the medieval period differ from those who handed out tea or porridge to pilgrims in the Ch'ing dynasty or from the societies (*she* 社) organized for the communal sponsorship of funerals and other philanthropic deeds? Did this organizational form evolve, and if so, how?

Accounts by foreign pilgrims to China, arbitrarily excluded from our conference, are quite valuable. The diary of the ninth-century Japanese monk Ennin is the best known in English, but other accounts by Japanese and Koreans exist and could be compared. Indeed, the travel literature of visitors from East Asia who went to China to commune with the roots of their culture, just as Americans made pilgrimages to Europe, might open up a large category of pilgrimage behavior.

Despite several volunteers, we did not include papers at the conference on Hsuan-tsang, China's most famous pilgrim, although much is known about him, his journey, and the many influential transformations of the tale. What can this "Journey to the West" tell us about pilgrimage in China, the idea and the actuality? Exactly how did the story serve as a model for pilgrims?

What about the religious professionals (and others) who were in residence at these centers? At Mecca and in Indian pilgrimage centers, guides are crucial to visitors. How important were such people in shaping the experience of pilgrims in China (viz., Gimello's chapter)? How did the monks at the different temples interact with each other? How did clerics deal with resident or visiting shamans, mediums, diviners, and heads of pilgrimage associations? What were the micropolitics of these sites? What was the place of pilgrims in monastic life? The work of Birnbaum should be followed up; the vision quests and other pilgrimages undertaken by clerics need investigation.

The history of Chinese state policy toward religion does not yet include either a systematic account of official attitudes toward pilgrimage or the personal patronage of pilgrimage sites by emperors. Most of the chapters here show these factors to have been quite important, and documentation is ample. Many emperors (and their wives and mothers) made journeys to pray at the pilgrimage centers popular in their times. What could detailed studies of these journeys reveal about imperial attitudes and pilgrimage more generally?

Chinese minority peoples and religions are not represented here at all. What do we know about Chinese Muslims who made the *hajj* to Mecca? Recent work indicates the importance of Muslim saints' tombs in western China in the early modern and modern period. Were pilgrimages to these tombs influenced most by Islamic or Chinese practices? A great many of the nomadic peoples on China's frontiers have been followers of Tibetan Buddhism since at least the sixteenth century. Some literature exists on the arduous pilgrimages undertaken by penitents to Lhasa, but what of travels to important shrines in China such as Mounts Omei or Wu-t'ai?

Much more needs to be done with the layout and architecture of shrines and sites. Here, the work of art historians can be combined with mountain gazetteers. A great many sites with long histories still survive, in varying states of disrepair. We would like to read more about sculpture and wall paintings and how they were a source of stories told to pilgrims who came to and through a site. Were mountain sites physically different from temples in urban and rural communities? How did geomancy affect the siting and building of temples and stupas? How were places that attracted visitors but had no temples—that is, monuments, historical relics, or sites of famous events—different from the kinds of pilgrimage centers discussed here?

Pilgrimage elsewhere has usually existed side by side with commerce and trade. Surely this was as true in China. How permanent were the services to travelers? Who ran them? What commodities were produced for pilgrims: incense, candles, paper money, religious souvenirs? A local-history approach might help us understand the economic role of each of these sites in their regions. Were the major pilgrimage mountains too remote to serve as the sites of important fairs? Did other sites have fairs that were sources of regional economic or cultural integration (like the T'ien-chu pilgrims' fair mentioned in Yü's conference paper)? Who were local patrons of these sites (like the Tientsin merchants at Mount Miao-feng in Naquin's paper or the Huichou families in Cahill's who helped make Mount Huang famous)? Even nationally famous sites probably had regional constituencies. Will visits to sites provide now rare lists of donors (carved on the back of stelae or elsewhere recorded)? Can these be used to reconstruct the economics of these sites?

The chapters here introduce a few of the cults that formed pilgrimage nodes across the empire and do cover the major regions of China, but a fuller history is needed—not simply of the better-known nationwide figures but of regional gods and shrines, their iconography and history. How were links between shrines to one deity expressed: was the language of dividing incense commonly used? How were rivalries played out? Faure's chapter suggests how fruitful an investigation of Ch'an monks and their stupas would be.

Timothy Brook's paper for the conference introduced an 1827 pilgrim's guidebook that implied the existence of a nationwide network of sites for ecclesiastical pilgrims. Would it be useful to map all of China's pilgrimage centers at a given moment, as Bhardwaj did for India? Were there nested hierarchies? How do they fit into G. W. Skinner's macroregional systems? Most sit on the peripheries of regions, but their catchment areas are often much bigger. What routes were used by pilgrims? What would an annual calendar of those same nationwide sites reveal? Did the progressive integration of China parallel the creation of intermeshed national networks of sites? One might also want to write a history of the famous sets of sites—the four Buddhist centers, five imperial peaks, and so forth.

Our conference discussion turned occasionally from sacred places to the more neglected topic of sacred time and the calendars that shaped lives and thoughts. Were regional cycles of gods' birthdays integrated into a national cycle, and if so, when? Did the Chinese distinguish secular from sacred time? Were pilgrimage sites liminal in Turner's sense? How did time change when one entered a sacred place?

A full understanding of the place of pilgrimage in Chinese culture will include other dimensions we similarly excluded for lack of space. There is much to be learned from the study of visions. China has a rich literature of metaphorical travel, within and beyond the body. Do such voyages use (or shape) the language of pilgrimage? There is, furthermore, a wide range of symbolic links (developed unevenly over the centuries) to be explored— between mountains and caves, grottoes, islands, paradises, palaces, temples, tombs, rocks, bones, lungs, and bodies. The relationships between pilgrimage and death, mountains and tombs, indeed, heaven and hell are particularly interesting. How are these associations, found elsewhere in the world, particularly Chinese? Altars, prayers for the dead, suicide cliffs, and elixirs of immortality tell of different ways in which sacred places served as links with the "other world." Chinese also has a rich vocabulary of mountain topography to investigate.

Steven Sangren has begun to explore the boundary between pilgrimage and ordinary temple worship on the one hand and community processions and celebrations on the other. In Taiwan, one finds a continuum between visits to nearby and far-away shrines; was this more generally true? More detailed historical information on local temples and religious behavior is clearly a prerequisite.

The sketchy history of Chinese pilgrimage provided in this introduction needs considerable amplification. We would like to know more about pre-Buddhist patterns, and we suspect there was a major shift in the Sung period, as in other spheres. Important changes, intellectual and institutional, occurred also in the twentieth century. Can we track the impact on pilgrimage of secularization, Western science (which reinforced Confucian rationalism), Marxist campaigns against religion, the creation of new revolutionary pilgrimage sites and behavior, the adjustment of Taiwan to separation from (and reconnection with) the Fukien coast, increased domestic and foreign tourism and travel? Will mountains lose their transcendence as they become too domesticated, too easy to get to, and insufficiently distinct from ordinary life (there are cable cars on Mounts T'ai and Omei and buses on P'u-t'o)?

In short, there is much to be done. Continuing exposure to the literature on pilgrimage and travel in other times and places should help China specialists by exposing what is commonplace, highlighting what is unusual, calling attention to what is missing, and suggesting new methods and sources. Comparisons between Chinese and Japanese pilgrimage seem particularly called for.

The experience of visiting one of China's pilgrimage mountains is poorly conveyed in words, particularly scholarly analyses. Some of us were lucky enough to make journeys to the sites that we here describe, and during our conference we all benefited enormously from hearing the accounts and seeing the slides from these trips. The natural beauty of the sites, the physical exertion and exhilaration of the climb, the aura of sanctity created by history, and the palpable religious devotion of the pilgrims are not easily forgotten. We hope that our readers can fill in this missing dimension by undertaking such a journey themselves.

BIBLIOGRAPHY

Selected Western-Language Bibliography on
Religion and Pilgrimage in China

We have included here our conference papers that either were not included in this volume or contain significant material cut from the published version. There is a more extensive bibliography on China's mountains, including early accounts by Western visitors, on pp. 121–25 and 246–54 of *Chinese Religion in Western Languages: A Comprehensive and Classified Bibliography of Publications in English, French, and German through 1980*, edited by Laurence G. Thompson (Tucson: Association for Asian Studies, 1985).

Baker, D. W. *T'ai Shan: An Account of the Sacred Eastern Peak of China*. Shanghai: Commercial Press, 1925.

Beal, Samuel. *Si-yu-ki, Buddhist Records of the Western Worlds, Translated from the Chinese of Hiuen Tsiang (A.D. 629)*. 2 vols. London, 1884.

Bell, Catherine. "Religion and Chinese Culture: Toward an Assessment of 'Popular Religion.'" *History of Religion* 29:1 (1989): 35–57.

Birnbaum, Raoul. "Thoughts on T'ang Buddhist Mountain Traditions and Their Contexts." *T'ang Studies* 2 (1984): 5–23.

———. "The Manifestation of a Monastery: Shen-ying's Experiences on Mount Wu-t'ai in T'ang Context." *Journal of the American Oriental Society* 106:1 (1986): 119–37.

———. "Secret Halls of the Mountain Lords: The Caves of Wu-t'ai Shan." *Cahiers d'Extrême-Asie* 5 (1989–90): 115–40.

Boerschmann, Ernst. *Die Baukunst und religiöses Kultur der Chinesen*. Vol. 1, *P'u T'o Shan*. Berlin, 1911.

Bokenkamp, Stephen. "Sources of the Ling-Pao Scriptures." In *Mélanges Chinois et Bouddhiques: Tantric and Taoist Studies in Honour of Rolf Stein*, edited by Michel Strickmann, 3: 434–86. Brussels: Institut Belge des Hautes Etudes Chinois, 1981.

Boltz, Judith. *A Survey of Taoist Literature, Tenth to Seventeenth Centuries*. Berkeley: Institute of East Asian Studies, University of California, 1987.

Brook, Timothy. *Geographical Sources of Ming-Qing History.* Ann Arbor: Center for Chinese Studies, University of Michigan, 1988.

———. "Knowing the Fords on the Way to Knowledge: Ecclesiastical Pilgrimage Routes in Late-Imperial China." Paper prepared for the 1989 Conference on Pilgrims and Sacred Sites in China.

Bush, Susan. "Tsung Ping's Essay on Landscape Painting and the 'Landscape Buddhism' of Mount Lu." In *Theories of the Arts in China,* edited by Susan Bush and Christian Murck, 132–64. Princeton: Princeton University Press, 1983.

Cahill, James. *Shadows of Mount Huang: Chinese Painting and Printing of the Anhui School.* Berkeley: University Art Museum, 1981.

Chavannes, Edouard. *Le T'ai Chan: Essai de monographie d'un culte chinois.* Paris: Leroux, 1910.

Chen-hua. *In Search of the Dharma: Memoirs of a Modern Chinese Buddhist Pilgrim.* Translated by Denis C. Mair. Edited with an introduction by Chün-fang Yü. Albany: SUNY Press, forthcoming.

Ch'en, Kenneth. *Buddhism in China: A Historical Survey.* Princeton: Princeton University Press, 1964.

Demiéville, Paul. "La Montagne dans l'art littéraire chinois." In Demiéville, *Choix d'études sinologiques (1921–1970),* 365–89. Leiden: Brill, 1973.

Duara, Prasenjit. "Superscribing Symbols: The Myth of Guandi, Chinese God of War." *Journal of Asian Studies* 47:4 (1988): 778–95.

Dudbridge, Glen. "A Pilgrimage in Seventeenth-Century Fiction: T'ai-shan and the *Hsing-shih yin-yuan chuan.*" Paper prepared for the 1989 Conference on Pilgrims and Sacred Sites in China.

Ennin's Diary: The Record of a Pilgrimage to China in Search of the Law. Translated by E. O. Reischauer. New York: Ronald Press, 1955.

Faure, Bernard. "Space and Place in Chinese Religious Traditions." *History of Religions* 26:4 (1987): 337–56.

Fontein, Jan. *The Pilgrimage of Sudhana: A Study of Gaṇḍavyūha Illustrations in China, Japan, and Java.* Paris: Mouton, 1968.

Ganza, Kenneth. "A Landscape by Leng Ch'ien and the Emergence of Travel as a Theme in Fourteenth-century Chinese Painting." *National Palace Museum Bulletin* 21:3 (1986): 1–17.

Geil, W. E. *The Sacred Five of China.* London: C. W. Daniel, 1926.

Gladney, Dru C. "Muslim Tombs and Ethnic Folklore: Charters for Hui Identity." *Journal of Asian Studies* 46:3 (1987): 495–532.

Hahn, Thomas. "The Standard Taoist Mountain and Related Features of Religious Geography." *Cahiers d'Extrême-Asie* 4 (1988): 145–66.

Hansen, Valerie L. *Changing Gods in Medieval China, 1127–1276.* Princeton: Princeton University Press, 1990.

Hargett, James M. *On the Road in Twelfth-Century China: The Travel Diaries of Fan Cheng-da (1126–1193).* Stuttgart: Franz Steiner, 1989.

Hart, Virgil C. *Western China: A Journey to the Great Buddhist Center of Mt. Omei.* Boston, 1888.

Hay, John. *Kernels of Energy, Bones of Earth: The Rock in Chinese Art.* New York: China Institute in America, 1986.

Huang Shou-fu and T'an Chung-yo. *Mount Omei Illustrated Guide.* Translated by Dreyden Linsley Phelps. Chengtu, 1936. Reprint. Hong Kong: Hong Kong University Press, 1974.

Joachim, Christian. *Chinese Religions, A Cultural Perspective.* Prentice-Hall Series on World Religions. Englewood Cliffs, N. J.: Prentice-Hall, 1986.

Johnson, Reginald Fleming. *Buddhist China.* London: John Murray, 1913.

Jordan, David. *Gods, Ghosts, and Ancestors: The Folk Religion of a Taiwanese Village.* Berkeley: University of California Press, 1972.

Ko Hung. *Alchemy, Medicine, Religion in China of A.D. 320: The Nei-p'ien of Ko Hung (Pao-p'u-tzu).* Translated by James R. Ware. Cambridge: M.I.T. Press, 1967.

Kroll, Paul W. "Verses from on High: The Ascent of T'ai Shan." *T'oung Pao* 49:4–5 (1983): 223–60.

Kupfer, Carl F. *The Sacred Places of China.* Cincinnati: Western Methodist Book Concern, 1911.

Lagerwey, John. "Le Pèlerinage taoïque en Chine." In Chélini and Branthomme (1987), 311–27.

Ledderhose, Lothar. "The Earthly Paradise: Religious Elements in Landscape Art." In *Theories of the Arts in China,* edited by Susan Bush and Christian Murck, 165–83. Princeton: Princeton University Press, 1983.

Loewe, Michael. *Ways to Paradise: The Chinese Quest for Immortality.* London: George Allen & Unwin, 1979.

Magnin, Paul. "Le Pèlerinage dans la tradition bouddhique chinoise." In Chélini and Branthomme (1987), 279–309.

McDermott, Joseph P. "The Making of a Chinese Mountain, Huangshan: Politics and Wealth in Chinese Art." *Asian Cultural Studies* (Tokyo) 17 (1989): 145–76.

Morrison, Hedda. *Hua Shan: The Taoist Sacred Mountain in West China: Its Scenery, Monasteries, and Monks.* Introduction by Wolfram Eberhard. Hong Kong: Vetch and Lee, 1973.

Mullikin, Mary A., and Anna M. Hotchkis. *The Nine Sacred Mountains of China: An Illustrated Record of Pilgrimages Made in the Years 1935–1936.* Hong Kong: Vetch and Lee, 1973.

Munakata, Kiyohiko. *Sacred Mountains in Chinese Art: An Exhibition Organized by the Krannert Art Museum at the University of Illinois.* Baltimore: University of Illinois Press, 1991.

Overmyer, Daniel L. *Religions of China: The World as a Living System.* San Francisco: Harper & Row, 1986.

Powell, William. "A Pilgrim's Map of Chiu Hua Shan." Paper prepared for the 1989 Conference on Pilgrims and Sacred Sites in China.

Reichelt, Karl Ludvig. *Truth and Tradition in Chinese Buddhism.* Shanghai: Commercial Press, 1934.

Robinet, Isabelle. *Meditation taoïste.* Paris: Dervy, 1979.

———. *La Révélation du Shangqing dans l'histoire du taoïsme.* 2 vols. Paris: Ecole Française d'Extrême-Orient, 1984.

Sangren, P. Steven. *History and Magical Power in a Chinese Community.* Stanford: Stanford University Press, 1987.

———. "History and the Rhetoric of Legitimacy: The Ma Tsu Cult of Taiwan." *Comparative Studies in Society and History* 30:4 (1988): 674–97.

————. "Multilectics of Alienation: Worship and Testimony in the Ma Tsu Pilgrimages of Taiwan." Paper prepared for the 1989 Conference on Pilgrims and Sacred Sites in China.

Schafer, Edward. *Mao Shan in T'ang Times*. 2nd ed., rev. Society for the Study of Chinese Religions Monograph no. 1, Boulder, Colo., 1989.

Schipper, Kristofer. "Les pèlerinages en chine: montagnes et pistes." In *Les Pèlerinages*, 303–42. Paris: Seuil, 1960.

————. *Le Corps taoïste: corps physique, corps social*. Paris: Fayard, 1982.

Schneider, Richard. "Un Moine indien au Wou-t'ai chan—relation d'un pèlerinage." *Cahiers d'Extrême-Asie* 3 (1987): 27–39.

Seaman, Gary. *Temple Organization in a Chinese Village*. Taipei: Chinese Association for Folklore, 1978.

Seidel, Anna. "Chronicle of Taoist Studies in the West, 1950–1990." *Cahiers d'Extrême-Asie* 5 (1989–90): 223–347.

Sivin, Nathan. "On the Word 'Taoist' as a Source of Perplexity." *History of Religion* 17:3–4 (1978): 303–34.

Soymié, Michel. "Le Lo-feou chan, étude de géographie religieuse." *Bulletin de l'École Française d'Extrême-Orient* 48 (1956): 1–139.

Stein, Rolf A. *The World in Miniature: Container Gardens and Dwellings in Far Eastern Religious Thought*. Translated by Phyllis Brooks. Stanford: Stanford University Press, 1990.

Strickmann, Michel. "The Mao Shan Revelations: Taoism and the Aristocracy." *T'oung Pao* 63:1 (1977): 1–64.

————. "Building the Sacred Mountain at Mao Shan." Paper prepared for the 1989 Conference on Pilgrims and Sacred Sites in China.

Teiser, Stephen F. *The Ghost Festival in Medieval China*. Princeton: Princeton University Press, 1988.

Thompson, Lawrence G. *Chinese Religion: An Introduction*. 4th ed. Belmont, Calif.: Wadsworth, 1989.

The Travels of Fah-Hian and Sung Yun, Buddhist Pilgrims from China to India (400 AD to 518 AD). Translated by S. Beal. London, 1869; many reprints.

Tibetan Guide to Places of Pilgrimage. Dharamsala, India, 1985.

Wakeman, Frederic. "Revolutionary Rites: The Remains of Chiang Kai-shek and Mao Tse-tung." *Representations* 10 (1985): 146–93.

Watson, James L. "Standardizing the Gods: The Promotion of T'ien Hou ('Empress of Heaven') along the South China Coast, 960–1960." In *Popular Culture in Late Imperial China*, edited by David Johnson, Evelyn Rawski, and Andrew Nathan, 292–324. Berkeley: University of California Press, 1985.

Weinstein, Stanley. *Buddhism under the T'ang*. Cambridge: Cambridge University Press, 1987.

Weller, Robert P. *Unities and Diversities in Chinese Religion*. Seattle: University of Washington Press, 1987.

Welch, Holmes. *The Practice of Chinese Buddhism, 1900–1950*. Cambridge: Harvard University Press, 1967.

————. *The Buddhist Revival in China*. Cambridge: Harvard University Press, 1968.

Wolf, Arthur P., ed. *Religion and Ritual in Chinese Society*. Stanford: Stanford University Press, 1974.

Wu Ch'eng-en. *The Journey to the West*. Translated and edited by Anthony C. Yu. 4 vols. Chicago: University of Chicago Press, 1977.

Wu Hung. "From Temple to Tomb: Ancient Chinese Art and Religion in Transition." *Early China* 13 (1988): 78–115.

Wu Pei-yi. *The Confucian's Progress: Autobiographical Writings in Traditional China*. Princeton: Princeton University Press, 1990.

Wright, Arthur F. *Buddhism in Chinese History*. Stanford: Stanford University Press, 1959.

Yang, C. K. *Religion in Chinese Society*. Berkeley: University of California Press, 1961.

Yü, Chün-fang. "Miracles, Pilgrimage Sites, and the Cult of Kuan-yin." Paper prepared for the 1989 Conference on Pilgrims and Sacred Sites in China.

Zürcher, Erik. *The Buddhist Conquest of China: The Spread and Adaptation of Buddhism in Early Medieval China*. Rev. ed. Leiden: Brill, 1972.

Selected Western-Language Bibliography on Pilgrimage in Other Cultures

Aziz, Barbara Nimri. "Personal Dimensions of the Sacred Journey: What Pilgrims Say." *Religious Studies* 23 (1987): 247–61.

Babb, Lawrence A. *The Divine Hierarchy: Popular Hinduism in Central India*. New York: Columbia University Press, 1975.

Barbhill, David L. "Basho as Bat: Wayfaring and Antistructure in the Journals of Matsuo Basho." *Journal of Asian Studies* 49:2 (1990): 274–90.

Bharati, Agehananda. "Pilgrimage in the Indian Tradition." *History of Religions* 3:1 (1963): 135–67.

———. "Pilgrimage Sites and Indian Civilization." In *Chapters in Indian Civilisations*, edited by J. W. Elder, 85–126. Dubuque, Iowa: Kendell, Hunt, 1970.

Bhardwaj, Surinder Mohan. *Hindu Places of Pilgrimage in India: A Study in Cultural Geography*. Berkeley: University of California Press, 1973.

Bhardwaj, S. M., and G. Rinschede. *Pilgrimage in World Religions*. Berlin: D. Reimer, 1988.

Bishop, Peter. *The Myth of Shangri-La: Tibet, Travel Writing and the Creation of Sacred Landscape*. Berkeley: University of California Press, 1989.

Blacker, Carmen. *The Catalpa Bow, A Study of Shamanistic Practices in Japan*. London: George Allen & Unwin, 1975.

Bowman, Glenn. "Pilgrimage Conference." *Anthropology Today* 4: 6 (1988): 20–23. A report on the July 1988 Interdisciplinary Conference on Pilgrimage, held at Digby Stuart College, Roehampton Institute (England).

Brown, Peter. *The Cult of the Saints: Its Rise and Function in Latin Christianity*. Chicago: University of Chicago Press, 1981.

Burton, Richard G. *Personal Narrative of a Pilgrimage to Al-Madinah and Meccah*. 1893; reprint, London: Dover, 1964, in two vols.

Chélini, Jean, and Henry Branthomme, eds. *Chemins de Dieux: Histoire des pèlerinages chrétiens des origines à nos jours*. Paris: Hachette, 1982.

———. *Histoire des pèlerinages non chrétiens: Entre magique et sacré, le chemin des dieux*. Paris: Hachette, 1987.

Clothey, Fred. "Pilgrimage Centers in the Tamil Cults of Murukan." *Journal of the American Academy of Religion* 40 (1972): 79–95.

Crumrine, N. Ross, and Alan Morinis, eds. *Pilgrimage in Latin America.* New York: Greenwood Press, 1990.

Daniel, E. Valentine. *Fluid Signs: Being a Person the Tamil Way.* Berkeley: University of California Press, 1984.

Davis, Winston. "Pilgrimage and World Renewal: A Study of Religion and Social Values in Tokugawa Japan." *History of Religion* 23:2 (1983): 97–116, 23:3 (1984): 197–221.

Diehl, Carl Gustav. "Replacement and Substitution in the Meeting of Religions." In *Syncretism*, edited by Svan Hartman, 137–61. Stockholm: Almquist and Wiksell, 1969.

Dupront, Alphonse. *Du sacré: croisades et pèlerinages, images et langages.* Paris: Gallimard, 1987.

Eck, Diana L. *Darsan: Seeing the Divine Image in India.* Chambersburg, Pa.: Anima Books, 1981.

———. *Benares, the City of Light.* New York: Knopf, 1982.

Eickelman, Dale. *Moroccan Islam: Tradition and Society in a Pilgrimage Center.* Austin: University of Texas Press, 1976.

Eickelman, Dale F., and James Piscatori, eds. *Muslim Travellers: Pilgrimage, Migration, and the Religious Imagination.* Comparative Studies on Muslim Societies, no. 9. Berkeley: University of California Press, 1990.

Eliade, Mircea. *The Sacred and the Profane.* New York: Harcourt, Brace, Jovanovich, 1959.

———. "Sacred Places: Temple, Palace, 'Center of the World,'" In *Patterns in Comparative Religion*, 367–85 Cleveland: World Publishing, 1963.

Eliade, M., et al., eds. *Encyclopedia of Religion.* New York: Macmillan, 1987. Entry on Pilgrimage, various authors.

Falk, Nancy. "To Gaze on the Sacred Traces." *History of Religions* 16: 4 (1977): 281–93.

Finucane, Ronald C. *Miracles and Pilgrims: Popular Beliefs in Medieval England.* Totowa, N.J.: Rowman & Littlefield, 1977.

Foard, James H. "The Boundaries of Compassion: Buddhism and the National Tradition in Japanese Pilgrimage." *Journal of Asian Studies* 41:2 (1982): 231–52.

Geary, Patrick J. *Furta Sacra: Thefts of Relics in the Central Middle Ages.* Princeton: Princeton University Press, 1978.

Gold, Ann Grodzins. *Fruitful Journeys: The Ways of Rajasthani Pilgrims.* Berkeley: University of California Press, 1988.

Goldziher, Ignace. "Le culte des saints chez les Musulmans." *Revue de l'histoire des religions* 2 (1880): 257–351.

Gombrich, Richard. *Precept and Practice: Traditional Buddhism in the Rural Highlands of Ceylon.* Oxford: Clarendon, 1971.

———. *Theravada Buddhism: A Social History from Ancient Benares to Modern Colombo.* London: Routledge & Kegan Paul, 1988.

Gross, Daniel. "Ritual and Conformity: A Religious Pilgrimage to Northeastern Brazil." *Ethnology* 10 (1971): 129–48.

Hamsa, Bhagwan. *The Holy Mountain, Mansarovar and the Mount Kailas: Being the Story of a Pilgrimage to Lake Marias and of Initiation on Mount Kailas in Tibet*. London: Faber & Faber, 1934.

Hawley, John. *At Play with Krishna: Pilgrimage Dramas from Brindavan*. Princeton: Princeton University Press, 1981.

Hunt, E. D. *Holy Land Pilgrimage in the Later Roman Empire, AD 312–460*. Oxford: Clarendon, 1984.

Hutchison, John A. *Path of Faith*. New York: McGraw-Hill, 1981.

Iancu, Carol. "Les Pèlerinages dans le Judaïsme après 70 et dans Israël aujourd'hui." In Chélini and Branthomme (1987), 345–64.

Karve, I. "On the Road: A Maharashtrian Pilgrimage." *Journal of Asian Studies* 22 (1962): 13–30.

Keyes, Charles F. "Buddhist Pilgrimage Centers and the Twelve-Year Cycle: Northern Thai Moral Orders in Space and Time." *History of Religions* 15 (1975): 71–89.

Kitagawa, Joseph. "Three Types of Pilgrimage in Japan." In *Studies in Mysticism and Religion Presented to Gershom G. Scholem*, edited by E. E. Urbach, R. J. Werblowsky, and C. Wirszubski. Jerusalem: Magnes Press, 1967.

La Fleur, William. "Points of Departure: Comments on Religious Pilgrimage in Sri Lanka and Japan." *Journal of Asian Studies* 38:2 (1979): 271–81.

Large-Blondeau, Marie. "Les pèlerinages tibétains." In *Les Pèlerinages*, 199–245. Paris: Seuil, 1960.

Leclercq, Jean. "Monachisme et pérégrination du IXe au XIIe siècle." *Studia Monastica* 3 (1961): 33–52.

Les Pèlerinages, Egypte ancienne, Israël, Islam, Perse, Inde, Tibet, Indonésie, Madagascar, Chine, Japon. Paris: Seuil, 1960.

Lewis, Bernard. "Hadjdj." In *Encyclopedia of Islam: New Edition* 3: 31–38. Leiden: E. J. Brill, 1971.

Morinis, E. Alan. *Pilgrimage in the Hindu Tradition, A Case Study of West Bengal*. Delhi: Oxford University Press, 1984.

————, ed. *Sacred Journeys: The Anthropology of Pilgrimage*. Delhi: Oxford University Press, forthcoming.

Nolan, Mary Lee, and Sidney Nolan. *Christian Pilgrimage in Modern Western Europe*. Chapel Hill: University of North Carolina Press, 1989.

Preston, James J. "Sacred Centers and Symbolic Networks in South Asia." *Mankind Quarterly* 20:3–4 (1980): 259–93.

Pruess, James B. "Veneration and Merit-Seeking at Sacred Places: Buddhist Pilgrimage in Contemporary Thailand." Ph.D. diss., University of Washington, 1975.

Rotermund, Hartmut O. *Pèlerinage aux neuf sommets; carnet de route d'un religieux itinérant dans le Japon du XIX siècle*. Paris: Centre Nationale de la Recherche Scientifique, 1985.

Rothkrug, Lionel. "Religious Practices and Collective Perceptions: Hidden Homologies in the Renaissance and Reformation." *Historical Reflections* 7:1 (1980): 243–51.

————. " 'The Odour of Sanctity' and the Hebrew Origins of Christian Relic Veneration." *Historical Reflections* 8:2 (1981): 95–142.

Sallnow, Michael J. *Pilgrims of the Andes: Regional Cults in Cusco*. Washington, D.C.: Smithsonian, 1987.

Sax, William S. *Mountain Goddess: Gender and Politics in a Himalayan Pilgrimage*. New York: Oxford University Press, 1991.

Smith, Bardwell, and Holly B. Reynolds, eds. *The City as a Sacred Center: Essays on Six Asian Contexts*. Leiden: Brill, 1987.

Smith, Wilfrid Cantwell. *Faith and Belief*. Princeton: Princeton University Press, 1979.

Snellgrove, David. *Indo-Tibetan Buddhism: Indian Buddhists and Their Tibetan Successors*. 2 vols. Boston: Shambhala, 1986.

Stevens, John. *The Marathon Monks of Mount Hiei*. Boston: Shambhala, 1988.

Stoddard, Robert. "An Analysis of the Distribution of Major Hindu Holy Sites." *National Geographical Journal of India* 14:2–3 (1968): 148–55.

Stoddard, Robert H., and Alan Morinis, eds. "Sacred Places, Sacred Spaces: The Geography of Pilgrimage." Typescript.

Sumption, Jonathan. *Pilgrimage: An Image of Medieval Religion*. London: Faber & Faber, 1975.

Turner, Victor W. *The Ritual Process: Structure and Anti-structure*. London: Routledge & Kegan Paul, 1969.

———. "The Center Out There: Pilgrim's Goal." *History of Religions* 12 (1973): 191–230.

———. "Pilgrimages as Social Processes." In *Dramas, Fields, and Metaphors*, edited by Victor Turner, 166–230. Ithaca: Cornell University Press, 1974.

———. "Death and the Dead in the Pilgrimage Process." In *Religious Encounters with Death*, edited by Frank E. Reynolds and Earl Waugh, pp. 24–39. University Park: Pennsylvania State University Press, 1977.

Turner, Victor W., and Edith Turner. *Image and Pilgrimage in Christian Culture: Anthropological Perspectives*. New York: Columbia University Press, 1978.

van der Veer, Peter. *Gods on Earth: The Management of Religious Experience and Identity in a North Indian Pilgrimage Center*. London: Athlone, 1988.

Vidyarthi, Lalita Prasad. *The Sacred Complex in Hindu Gaya*. Bombay: Asia Publishing House, 1961.

Wallfahrt kennt keine Grenzen: Themen zu einer Ausstellung des Bayerischen Nationalmuseums und des Adalbert Stifter Vereins, München. Munich: Verlag Schnell & Steiner, 1984.

Wensinck, A. J. "Kaʻba." In *Encyclopedia of Islam: New Edition* 4:317–22. Leiden: E. J. Brill, 1978.

Werblowsky, R. J. Zwi. "The Meaning of Jerusalem to Jews, Christians and Muslims." *Jaarbericht Ex Orient Lux* 23 (1973–74): 1–15.

Wheatley, Paul. *The Pivot of the Four Quarters: A Preliminary Enquiry into the Origins and Character of the Ancient Chinese City*. Chicago: University of Chicago Press, 1971.

Wilson, Stephen, ed. *Saints and Their Cults: Studies in Religious Sociology, Folklore, and History*. Cambridge: Cambridge University Press, 1983. There is an extensive annotated bibliography on pp. 309–417; pp. 359–68 cover pilgrimage.

Zacher, Christian K. *Curiosity and Pilgrimage: The Literature of Discovery in Fourteenth-Century England*. Baltimore: Johns Hopkins University Press, 1976.

ONE

Women Pilgrims to T'ai Shan: Some Pages from a Seventeenth-Century Novel

Glen Dudbridge

The novel Hsing-shih yin-yuan chuan 醒世姻緣傳 *appeared some time between 1628 and 1728. Critics have assigned it variously to the late Ming or the early Ch'ing, and opinion is still divided, both on this matter and on the question of the book's authorship. The author's pseudonym Scholar of Western Chou (*西周生*) does, however, betray an attitude of high-minded nostalgia for a society of archaic Confucian perfection, and his book presents a complex commentary on that lost utopia, making rich use of satire by inversion.*

Within this setting we find a two-chapter episode describing a T'ai Shan pilgrimage made by a group of women from Ming-shui 明水, *a township in rural Shantung. We watch the formation of their group under female religious leadership, the financial preparations and planned coordination with local tour operators, the physical hardships and ritual devotions along the way. Above all we witness the domestic tensions generated by one woman's decision to join the pilgrimage and the subtle colorings of class distinction exposed by its conditions of public fellowship. This interesting material needs careful and critical study, both to compare its abundant descriptive detail with other sources of information on the T'ai Shan mass pilgrimage cult and to identify the author's value judgments, expressed and implied. It challenges the interpreter to recognize and verify several different attitudes toward pilgrimage voiced in the text and to scrutinize its presentation of women's views and activities, which here receive unusually lavish attention. The paper in which these tasks are attempted has not been included in the present volume, since it concerns the pilgrims' social dynamics, not the site of their cult.[1] I give here simply a translation of the episode in two chapters, with a few explanatory notes.[2] Map 1.1 shows the main features of the site.*

The novel's complex and highly episodic action falls into two unevenly balanced divisions. These are linked by a scheme of reincarnations, in which flawed relationships between men and women engender later situations and opportunities for personal revenge. At the heart of it all, and central to the chapters translated here, is the perverse rela-

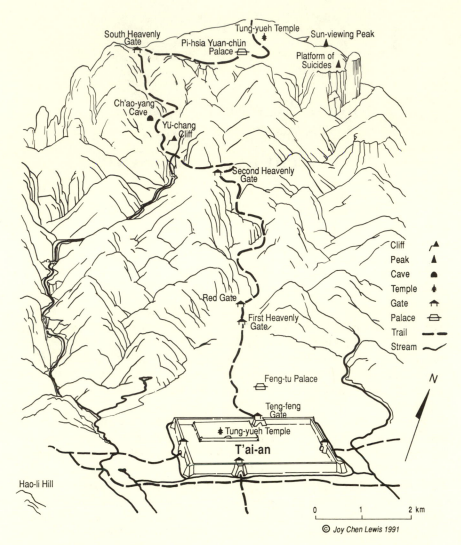

South Heavenly Gate

Tung-yueh Temple

Sun-viewing Peak

Pi-hsia Yuan-chün Palace

Platform of Suicides

Ch'ao-yang Cave

Yü-chang Cliff

Second Heavenly Gate

Cliff

Peak

Cave

Temple

Gate

Palace

Trail

Stream

Red Gate

First Heavenly Gate

Feng-tu Palace

N

Teng-feng Gate

Tung-yueh Temple

T'ai-an

Hao-li Hill

0   1   2 km

© Joy Chen Lewis 1991

Map 1.1. T'ai Shan

tionship between a young provincial academy student, Ti Hsi-ch'en 狄希陳*, and his wife, Hsueh Su-chieh* 薛素姐*, daughter of a provincial professor. In a series of grotesque and often horrifying episodes she sadistically disciplines her weak and submissive husband, shocking the reader with gestures of unashamed social deviance. The pilgrimage suits these purposes well: by joining it Su-chieh can defy the authority of all the senior menfolk in her own and her husband's family while she subjects the wretched Ti Hsi-ch'en to the pain and public humiliation of attending her along the way. She is assisted and directed by two local religious leaders—village women who specialize in organizing grass-roots religious activities among the devout female public. The author begins his narrative of the pilgrimage episode with them, identifying and attacking them with a savage pun on the term* tao-p'o 道婆 *("religious laywomen" or "temple workers") and* 盗婆 *("thieving old women"; here, "temple thieves").*

CHAPTER 68

[969] We return to Hou and Chang, the two religious laywomen from Mingshui. Their sons and husbands plied a single trade: getting a temple built in East Village, a bell cast in West Village, some golden bodhisattva statue made here, some big ceremony for a god's birthday held there—all under the direction of these two temple thieves. Anyone willing to give them alms would earn honor and glory in this life and untold wealth in the next. And the stingy ones who refused would not just be second best in the life to come, they would fall into wretchedness and poverty in this life too. There were wives afraid of their husbands and there were concubines browbeaten by their seniors; if they were prepared freely to give generous alms, then the husbands could be brought back to goodness and made not only to stop bullying their wives, but even to let the wives push them around. And the concubine who gave alms and earned her spiritual reward would make her lord and master treat her like a living Buddha from paradise; even her farts would smell sweet, while the words of the senior wife would smell foul; whatever wild and extravagant things the concubine did would all be under the protection of Buddha's power, as though he had given her a magic herb to make her invisible, so that her lord and master would see nothing. This was more or less the kind of talk they used to lead on simple-minded womenfolk, and they did it so well that simple-minded womenfolk followed them round and round like a [spinning] tortoise.[3]

Women who handled the money in their own households freely and happily gave over sums of silver. Those whose homes were run by their in-laws or whose husbands kept a strict eye on them, so that they could not get their hands on money or sell off provisions, would go behind husbands' and in-laws' backs to sell off their own jewelry or various [970] articles of clothing and donate the proceeds instead. As for concubines, who on top of everything had a senior wife in their way—quite out of the question for *their* alms to be open and above board; they just went slyly and furtively stealing their mistress's things or filching their master's food to fill the needs of those two temple thieves. Women who gave alms openly and for all to see did not mind their in-laws knowing, nor fear their husbands interfering. They would go themselves to where the bells or images were being cast, the temples opened, or the ceremonies held. Their names would be found on the public lists of subscribers. The two temple thieves would still keep back sixty or seventy percent of the funds—though they *would* release the other thirty or forty! And if you were a concubine who went behind your in-laws' or husband's back to give them alms, even shower them with alms, you would not even get a "much obliged" out of them; they would just save up the money to buy land and build houses, cart the sacks of grain and beans off home to be gobbled down and out through their families' rear ends, alter the clothing for their sons and husbands to wear, or put it on themselves. The two temple thieves made a perfect team; each chimed in with the other, and their two families lived very well out of it.

Ever since making Su-chieh's acquaintance in the Temple of the Three Officers that year at the Feast of All Souls,[4] they had seen her as a good prospect—a wife in charge at home, who could easily be taken in. But then they found out that she was Mr. Ti's daughter-in-law. Ti himself was a good, honest sort who would always treat people decently; but his wife Hsiang was such a firebrand that no one in Ming-shui would dare meddle in her affairs. Think as hard as they might, they could find no way in. Then they thought it might be a smart move to wait for Su-chieh to visit her own family and draw her in from there. But, wouldn't you know it, of all people she had to be the daughter of that hidebound Confucian moralist Mr. Hsueh. Would the stuffy old bigot let these two temple thieves into his house? Whichever side they looked, they could find no way to get at her. Later on, when Ti's wife died, the two females bought a tray of paper goods and went off together to pay their condolences.[5] But the Ti family received them on equal terms with other lady guests, and what is more, at the time the senior sister-in-law on the Hsiang side and the third aunt from the Ts'ui family were entertaining them with their company.[6] Besides this, Su-chieh had been beaten by her aunt Hsiang till her face was out of shape, [971] so that there was no chance of a talk even if she wanted one.[7]

Some days later they both went back to the Ti house, and just as they were stepping in through the entrance they came right up face to face with Mr. Ti. They could hardly go straight on in, nor could they go straight out again, so they just wavered there in rather a pathetic way.

Mr. Ti asked them: "To what do we owe the honor, reverend ladies?"

They said: "We'd like to have a word with Mrs. Ti."

"Why talk to a youngster like her? You can say what you have to say to one of us older people," he said. And he would not let them into the family quarters but ushered them firmly into the places reserved for guests, where he sat with them formally and ordered tea to be served. Then he asked: "Please say what you have to say. What do you have to favor us with?"

The two temple thieves said: "The nineteenth of the second month will be the birthday of Our Lady of the White Robe in our White Robe Nunnery.[8] We are celebrating it with a ceremony to last three days and nights, and the Lady from President Yang's residence in our town is the chief sponsor. Our Lady of the White Robe is a most powerful goddess: anyone who has given her alms will get a boy if they pray for a boy or a girl if they pray for a girl, and no one fails to have their prayers answered. We once met Mrs. Ti, and we want to ask her to make a little contribution, so that she will have bonny babies."

Mr. Ti said: "So that's what you wanted to speak about! Very good. Thank you for the guidance." And from his sleeve he took out a small piece of silver. "Here is some silver I just got from selling hemp; it's worth a hundred and twenty cash. Do take it along, ladies, and save me the trouble of sending someone over with it."

The two women accepted the money and left, looking crestfallen and disappointed.

Some time later they both went back to the Ti house. It was a time when the family still enjoyed a prosperous destiny, when the six household gods were all protecting it, so when monsters like this came through the gate they naturally caused a disturbance in the premises, and the shock wave reached the Earth God, who brought out Mr. Ti once again, for no apparent reason, to run right into them.

He asked: "You ladies are back with us once more! It must be some bodhisattva's birthday again, I suppose?"

They said: "The eighteenth of the fourth month is Our Lady of T'ai Shan's birthday; surely you haven't forgotten?"

"Quite true!" said Mr. Ti. "Fancy that—I had forgotten!" And he took out from his sleeve a piece of silver, saying: "This is worth fifty cash. I took it out to spend, but haven't spent it yet. Let's use it to sponsor your ceremony."

They said: "We'll still go through to the back and ask Mrs. Ti to come early on the day and worship the goddess."

Mr. [972] Ti said: "No need to tell her, ladies. Youngsters have no idea of things, and you just might talk her into really wanting to go, which wouldn't be right for a young girl at such a tender age. Any other time you have something to say, just say it to me. Don't speak to the youngsters again; it will do our standing no good."

With this rebuke he dashed the women's hopes altogether, and they made off with wet between their legs.

Two experiences like that in a row had the effect of reining back half their enthusiasm for cheating Su-chieh: there was no plan they could use. Then, by good fortune, old Professor Hsueh died, and there would be a chance they could exploit when Su-chieh went back to her own family. Here, too, they ran into trouble twice: it turned out that Professor Hsueh's wife was even harder to put upon. They stamped twice upon the rock, but stamping a hundred times would not have broken into it. Then, just at that very point, Mme Hsueh died of old age, and they knew that Su-chieh would be with her own family for the funeral—a chance that must on no account be missed.

The temple thieves' designs on Su-chieh had not yet reached a very high pitch. But they had heard that Nun Pai had tricked her out of all that silver,[9] and they reckoned that Su-chieh was a free spender. If she moved fast, they would move fast with her; if slow, they would slow down too—just like the angler fishing for the croaker at Chiu-chiang, who never, eating or sleeping, let it loose for a moment.

So once again they got together to buy a set of underworld paper money, marked it for mourning Mme Hsueh, and went round to the Hsueh residence. Hsueh Ju-pien and his brother were correct young men, but how could they possibly refuse anyone who wanted to burn paper money for their late mother? And when the women came up to the coffin they told the ladies in mourning to return their courtesy and salute in thanks.

When Su-chieh saw these two laywomen she was as warmly welcoming as if she had met her own late mother again. She invited them into a private chamber and offered them tea. But they, seeing Su-chieh so very attentive, deliberately put on an act. "We are particularly busy with arranging for the lady saints in our society to go on a pilgrimage to the top of T'ai Shan. We don't have the time; please don't bother with tea!"

Of course Su-chieh would not let them go. She strenuously ushered them into Lung's bedroom, set out tea and fruit to entertain them, and then wanted to serve cooked food and have them stay for a meal. She told them how grateful she felt to them for taking her to the ceremonies for releasing the lanterns last year in the seventh month.

For their part they pointed out: "We came round twice to your house and both times ran into Mr. Ti, who stopped us outside and wouldn't let us into the family home. On the nineteenth of the second month we held three days and nights of ceremonies for the birthday of Our Lady of the White Robe, and there were masses of people there. [973] What with wives of the gentry from Chi-nan prefecture and ladies of the provincial and county graduates— you couldn't find a gap between all the chairs and horses packed together. Mrs. Ti, you should have gone along! Mr. Ti wouldn't allow us through to the back to tell you about it; he gave us a contribution worth a hundred-odd cash and sent us packing. But the birthday of Our Lady of the Summit on the eighteenth of the fourth month was even finer than Our Lady of the White Robe's birthday. That stirred up the population of all the twenty prefectures.[10] Goods from all over China came to the fair—clothes, ornaments, agates, pearls—absolutely everything was on sale. The ladies all came to the temple and picked out the ones that suited them best."

Before they had finished, Su-chieh was already interrupting: "Shouldn't you have told me about a good thing like this and taken me along?"

"You're telling us! We did actually go round, you know! But we just had to bump into Mr. Ti, who yet again wouldn't let us in, just gave us forty or fifty cash and drove us away. He seemed to feel that we were undesirable types who might cheat you, dear, if we were able to meet you. But building up' merit is something for each of us individually. We hold ceremonies for Our Lady of the White Robe if we are hoping to bear good sons and daughters, we hold them for Our Lady of the Summit if we hope for good fortune and long life. What does Mr. Ti know about it?"

Su-chieh said hotly: "The old scoundrel! He was afraid I would squander the family fortune, so he stood in your way and wouldn't let you see me. And even that rascal husband of mine must be mixed up in it too! They had me completely fooled, kept me from knowing about it! Let them do their worst! I'll get my own back on that fool of mine!"

As she spoke the two laywomen together made to stand up. Su-chieh said: "I so rarely get a chance to meet you—sit with me longer and have a meal. Talk with me some more before you go."

They said: "We wouldn't be willing to leave so soon if we didn't have urgent things to do. The fact is that on the fifteenth the society members will be setting out on their pilgrimage to T'ai Shan, and we two are the society leaders. But the eye shields and blue silk handkerchiefs for all the members have not yet been made! We're negotiating for the animals, but haven't settled the deal. And we've not even worked out the charge. It's only four or five days before we're due to go! Wait until we come back from our pilgrimage. We wouldn't dare go back to your other home, but whenever we hear that you've come across here, my dear, we'll come here to speak with you. Our only worry is that the master here might object to us coming round so much."

Su-chieh said: "Why were you two women made leaders of the society, [974] rather than men?"

The lay women said: "There are no men in this society; it's all women, just about eighty of them!"

Su-chieh asked: "Are there respectable women in the society?"

They said: "Just listen to you, dear! Would they dare come to our society if they weren't in the top bracket? There are five or six ladies from President Yang's residence, the ladies from Mme Meng's in North Street, Mme Hung, Mme Wang and Mme Keng from East Street, Mme Chang in Main Street, Mme Wang in South Street, and Mme Liu in Back Street—all of them ladies from leading families. What room would there be for small fry?"

Su-chieh said: "How far is it from here to T'ai-an chou?"

The laywomen replied: "They say it's two hundred ninety *li*. But the journey is an easy one, less trouble than two hundred *li* on other roads. And along the route there are great temples and monasteries, fine sights to see all the way, the road packed with pilgrims going to and fro, perfumed carriages, jeweled horses, lovely girls, brilliant men—too many good things for the eye to take in, so that you only wish the road were longer."

Su-chieh asked them: "Are there fine things to see on the mountain?"

The laywomen said: "My dear—could there be another T'ai Shan in the world? From the top you get a perfect view of all the lands on earth, the dragons' palaces, ocean treasuries, Buddhas' halls, and immortals' palaces. If such benefits were not to be had, why would men and women come thousands of miles from their homes in Yunnan, Kweichow, Szechuan, Hukuang, Kwangtung, Kwangsi, just to burn incense there? What's more, Our Lady of T'ai Shan controls life and death, luck and prosperity for people through all the world. If people reverently mount the summit and burn incense, then red comes hanging down from heaven and drapes itself about them, while music of reed and pipe comes to the summit to welcome them! If they do not go reverently, then Spirit-officer Wang will bind them up at once, and see if they can move then! The reverent at heart, when they come before Our Lady, see the goddess's true face in the flesh; if not reverent at heart, the face they see is only a gilded face. She is powerful and effective for bringing good luck and forgiving misdeeds. And on the mountain there is no end of wonderful sights, like the South-facing Cave, the Three Heavenly Gates, the Yellow Flower Island, the Platform of Suicides, the Rock for Drying Scriptures, the Stele without Inscription, the Pine of Ch'in, the Cypress of Han, the Golden Slips, the Jade Writings—all these are where the gods and immortals make their dwelling. No one with only average luck could ever get to go there!"

This speech set Su-chieh tingling uncontrollably inside; her thoughts ran wild, and she asked: "The society members who go—will they travel in chairs or ride on [975] horseback? How much will they need for traveling expenses? Will anyone give them hospitality along the way?"

The two laywomen said: "The point of this pilgrimage is partly to build up good fortune, partly to enjoy the sights. It would be far too vulgar to cling to sedan chairs, so everyone will be riding mules. The donkeys we hire for the society come to eight *ch'ien* of silver there and back. If you ride your own animal you get a rebate of eight *ch'ien*. On first joining the society you put in a basic sum of three taels of silver, and when three full years have passed this yields ten taels, including principal and interest. Counting donkey-hire, inn accommodation and [tax] registration, at the most you would still not spend all of five taels. Which leaves another five taels for spending on personal items."

Su-chieh asked: "Can a person not in the society go too?"

The two laywomen said: "That depends on who it is. If it's someone we know well, we would ask her to pay in a sum of silver to match the yield of all the others, then we would report it to them, and then take her along. If it's someone who has nothing to do with us, then we would simply not let her go."

Su-chieh said: "I mean to go with you and see it all, and burn incense to Our Lady, so that I'll be protected in the next life from being second best and bullied by men, as I am in this one. I wonder if you ladies are willing to let me go?"

The two women said: "We'd be only too keen to have you go! Won't it be fun when we all get together for some laughs and chatter! It's just that Mr. Ti is so high and mighty—in your house the high are high and the low are low—and you may not be able to manage things at your own end."

Su-chieh said: "Don't worry! If I mean to go, then I'll go. They will not be able to control what I do. Do those ladies also have proper members of their families going with them?"

"Of course they do. Some have husbands with them, some have sons, some sons-in-law, nephews, or servants—just as it suits them. The only thing is that they each meet their own expenses."

Su-chieh said: "I shall depend on you both to take me. I'll pay in the ten taels of silver and go along too."

They said: "If you want to go we'll have to add on your share of luggage and animals. On the thirteenth we all go to Our Lady's Temple, burn incense, and hold the society procession. Be sure not to miss it! The silver must be sent over at once, too, so that we can add it in for some use or other."

Su-chieh settled with the two women that she would go.

This was on the tenth of the eighth month. Su-chieh's thoughts were entirely engrossed with the pilgrimage; she had no inclination at all to attend to her mother's funeral. On the spot she called Ti Hsi-ch'en [976] before her and said: "I mean to go to T'ai-an chou and burn incense to Our Lady of the Summit. Will you come with me? If you do, I'll have to fit you out with clothes."

Had Ti Hsi-ch'en been a correct and serious man he would have checked her with a stern, moralistic speech; she could hardly grow wings and fly off, after all! But no, Ti Hsi-ch'en was young and fun loving, and he said: "All right, then. Will anyone be going with us?"

Su-chieh said: "Those ladies Hou and Chang who were here just now said that the women in their society will be burning incense and parading the society on the thirteenth of this month, and they set out on the fifteenth. They told me to pay in ten taels of silver: it will be more than enough to cover all the costs, with five taels to spare! And if we don't ride one of the hired donkeys they will even deduct eight *ch'ien* for us."

Ti Hsi-ch'en said: "I'm just afraid that Father won't let us go. What then?"

"You go and speak to Father. If you talk him round I'll be nice to you. If

you don't talk him round to this business, you will never lead a decent existence again, come what may!"

Ti Hsi-ch'en said: "Father is very fond of me. If I go and talk to him, who
knows, he might well agree."

Su-chieh urged Ti Hsi-ch'en back home to say his piece. "I shall expect
you straight back here to report."

Ti Hsi-ch'en dared not delay, but went back home, met his father, and
told him all about his wife's plans to join the society on their pilgrimage.

Mr. Ti said: "I wouldn't mind if we were in an ordinary way of life. But
now you are a member of the academy we count as a cultured family. How
can we send our young womenfolk to join a society on a pilgrimage? Haven't
you seen women who join societies and parade with them? They have dark
blue silk eye shields on their heads and bunches of incense wrapped in blue
silk tied on their shoulders. Men and women walk through the streets all
mixed together. Whatever sort of appearance does that present? Since she
has made up her mind to go, wait until we finish the autumn harvest, when
the animals will be free; then we can get together what you need for expenses
and the two of you can set off in plenty of time. Don't go with that old Hou
woman. Those two are not good types; they came round to our home twice,
and both times I stopped them going inside, gave them a hundred-odd cash,
and sent them away."

Ti Hsi-ch'en at once went to Su-chieh and told her what his father had
said. The effect of this, when she heard it, was to drive her into uncontrol-
lable rage. At once, with face flushed purple, [977] she said: "I go now and
now only! I insist on going! I intend to go along with Hou and Chang! Why
can't I decide for myself on a small thing like this? It would be as well for you
to do as I wish quickly, or you'll be sorry!"

This now put Ti Hsi-ch'en in a real predicament. He was downcast and
miserable, at a loss what to do.

Su-chieh did not even wait for darkness to fall before she was back at
home to collect ten taels of high-grade silver, and the next morning she went
once more to her maternal home to speak to Lung. Behind the backs of
Hsueh Ju-pien and his brother, Lung sent round someone quietly to invite
the two laywomen to their house, where the ten taels of silver were handed
over to them. [Su-chieh] refused out of spite to ride one of the family's mules,
but told them to hire a donkey for her. It was agreed that this would be
picked up at Chang's house first thing on the morning of the thirteenth. Now
that these dispositions were made she did not consult with Mr. Ti or Ti
Hsi-ch'en on the subject any more. On the thirteenth she rose early, combed
her hair, powdered her face white, and decked herself with jewels all over her
head. Ignoring the mourning for her mother, she put on her Ku-embroidered
tunic and skirt. She absolutely insisted that Little Jade go with her; then out
of the gate she flounced, and away.

Mr. Ti and Ti Hsi-ch'en stood at one side simply staring and not daring to utter a word.

We need not go into detail on all the disgusting antics as she joined in with the group of travelers to burn incense with them and take the goddess's sedan in procession. When it was over she went back to her room, stripped off the jewelry and clothes, and sat in her room fuming with anger.

Ti Hsi-ch'en stepped straight into her room before he had time to prepare his defenses. Su-chieh cursed at him: "I thought you had fallen and split your skull open or broken both your legs and couldn't walk, so you didn't go with me, but made me go on my own! Yet lo and behold, here you are still around! Seeing that you didn't go with me, it's a wonder that nobody was bold enough to mistreat me while I was out burning the incense."

Ti Hsi-ch'en said: "If you meant to go, it was for you to go yourself. How could I possibly go with you round the streets in the society's procession with the student's square cap on my head?"

Angrily she said: "Oh, you didn't go with me because you were scared I would disgrace your public standing? But disgrace your public standing is the very thing I am going to do. When I set out on the fifteenth, I shall make you lead along my donkey with your square cap on your head and your student's gown on your back. And when we go up the mountain you will hold my chair for me. If you should stir one step away from me I'll cleave you in two, or not call myself a Hsueh any more! You'll be lucky enough if I let you raise your bloody eyebrows to claim your connection with me! [978] If you go along with me everyone will say: 'Just look what a wife of quality that devil-headed, toad-eyed little runt has got!' I would have said that I was an ornament to your family reputation; how could I possibly make you lose face? I had actually worked out a plan in my mind: if you were going with me we would use the roll of blue silk to make you a lined jacket, and what was left would make you a pair of lined trousers, plus a damask waistcoat, all for you to wear when you climbed the mountain to worship Our Lady. Yet you come out with this high tone! It seems to me that Our Lady of T'ai Shan is still only a woman, and I am perfectly sure that if My Lord of T'ai Shan were an awkward, stubborn customer like you she would not let him off lightly. [. . .][11] One of these days, when I have power in my hands, I shall lay down the law!"

Ti Hsi-ch'en discussed the matter privately with his father. Mr. Ti said: "Her mind is made up—do you think you can win? Even if you made her stay at home she would create so much fuss that you would rather die. And we would have to put up with it in silence! I shall have someone get things ready for you; you'll just have to go along with her."

And Mr. Ti gave orders to prepare the luggage and make ready in advance the rice, noodles, preserved meat, soused fish, pickled cucumbers, black beans, and the like that they would need to take.

To continue. Early on the morning of the fourteenth Lung said to Hsueh Ju-pien's wife: "Your elder sister-in-law is going on a pilgrimage to T'ai-an chou. Shouldn't you wives be giving an 'Off to the Summit' party for her?"

Lien said: "Really? When is she starting? Why haven't we heard anything about it?"

Lung said: "Are you senior wives, then, that must have everything reported to you first? She's been talking about it these past two or three days without you taking any notice, and now you say you know nothing about it!"

Lien hurried straight into her quarters to let her husband know about the matter and told him she wanted to give an "Off to the Summit" party. When Hsueh Ju-pien heard that Su-chieh was going on a pilgrimage he assumed that she would be going along with Ti Hsi-ch'en; but he still frowned severely and said: "I never saw Uncle Ti and Brother Ti behave so irresponsibly before. How can a tender young lady mount the summit? Haven't you seen people riding in those mountain chairs? It's all right on the way up, but on the way down they sit in the chair facing backward, the women face to face with the carrier; if the woman [979] falls backward her feet are more or less right on the carrier's shoulders. Those carriers are lawless dogs and extremely obnoxious: they purposely take advantage of the chair's movements to keep tipping it over. What a dreadful sight! Is that something a scholar's family should go in for? I urge you not to have this 'Off to the Summit' feast. Just let her hold you to blame."

But when he heard that she had entered the woman Hou's society and had already burned incense on the thirteenth, Hsueh Ju-pien said: "How unspeakable!" and gave orders for Su-chieh to be fetched back home and for Ti Hsi-ch'en to be asked round for a talk.

Su-chieh still assumed that they were giving her a summit farewell feast and came back freely and gladly. And Ti Hsi-ch'en dared not refuse to come with her. So, one behind the other, they came in through the gate.

Hsueh Ju-pien asked: "Sister, are you going on a pilgrimage to T'ai-an chou? When are you setting out? Who are you going with?"

Su-chieh told him she had paid silver to join the society and would set out on the fifteenth, with Hou and Chang as society leaders.

Hsueh Ju-pien said: "In my view, sister, you ought not to go. Do women from good families join societies and go on pilgrimages with other folk? Brother Ti is already out of school and into the Imperial Academy; he can afford to ignore people making fun of him. But we brothers, right in the thick of it, still have to attend the county school and meet people there! Someone from a respectable family, running through the streets burning incense, waving flags, and beating drums along the road to T'ai-an chou, showing their face to full view—I don't so much care if people say it's the wife of Ti Hsi-ch'en, but I am afraid they might say this is the sister of Hsueh Ju-pien and Hsueh Ju-chien: 'Her father served a spell as government instructor, and her two brothers are brazening it out in their student's caps, to earn a sister who behaves like this!' "

Su-chieh was already in a rage, but before she burst out with it Lung said in fury: "Just like a dog breaking its stinking wind![12] Why, when your elder sister comes round, does it stop you behaving properly? She is a married woman. If you approve, then you should accept her as elder sister; if you disapprove, then don't accept her as sister and don't invite her into the house. In any case they are perfectly well off in the Ti family and will not be a burden on you for anything!"

Hsueh Ju-pien said: "I gave good advice, and you make trouble out of it! Isn't our brother-in-law right here listening—did I say anything wrong?"

Lung burst into a storm of tears: "Heaven above! Why am I so unlucky? I had a husband, and my husband controlled me. [980] And when my husband died, that senior wife was at me like an ant stinging my leg. I stared at the prison wall, waiting until the senior wife was gone, but now I fall into my sons' hands—and I still don't get my way at all! Sweet heaven!"

Hsueh Ju-pien let her cry and took no notice. He ushered Ti Hsi-ch'en out to go and take the guest's place and said: "My sister wants to go on the pilgrimage, and I imagine you dare not stand in her way, brother. But can't you go with her alone? Why do you have to join those she-villains and their society? What do you mean by it?"

Ti Hsi-ch'en told Hsueh Ju-pien what Mr. Ti had said and the fuss Su-chieh had made about it. But to his surprise Su-chieh was listening just outside the door and burst in through it like a savage tigress. Ti Hsi-ch'en jumped straight out through the door, and she did not get her hands on him. But she did lay hold of Hsueh Ju-pien's lapel and treated him to curses and blows. Hsueh Ju-pien slipped out of his gown and was off like the wind.

Instead of returning to the rear quarters Su-chieh made straight for the Ti residence. Ti Hsi-ch'en knew he had done wrong, so at home he found her some bedding, hunted out a purse for her, had a girdle made for her, bought her bridle and reins, and filled her saucepot, so that everything was complete and waited only for Su-chieh to mount up.

They slept until the fifth watch next morning, when Su-chieh rose and completed her toilet. She put on a short over-jacket in white silk, a lined jacket in pale pink damask, a silk blouse worked with sky-blue damask, a plain skirt of thin twill silk in white, leggings in the same material with white embroidery, cotton-lined shoes in satin with scarlet uppers. On her back she carried incense wrapped in a blue silk handkerchief, and on her head she wore Buddha images printed on paper. She insisted on riding a large donkey hired by the society. When the farmhand detailed by Ti Hsi-ch'en came up and attempted to lead it along she drove him off some distance away with a lash of the whip round his neck and made Ti Hsi-ch'en walk along leading the beast for her. This brought men- and womenfolk down both sides of the street straining for a glimpse of Su-chieh's dashing appearance and Ti Hsi-ch'en's humiliation. Ti Hsi-ch'en was extremely bashful, but that tigress Su-chieh had him terrified: unable to complain of his sufferings, he had no choice but to lead her donkey as he moved along sandwiched among the crowd.

As ill luck would have it, before they covered as much as a mile they ran right into Hsiang Yü-t'ing,[13] who was on his way back from the rear estate. Ti Hsi-ch'en assumed he had not yet seen them and hastily covered his face with a sleeve. But, wouldn't you know it, Hsiang Yü-t'ing had already had a clear sight of them and had deliberately parked himself at the roadside. As Ti Hsi-ch'en came up in front of him [981] Hsiang Yü-t'ing said: "Brother Ti, better move your sleeve away and look at the road, so you can lead your donkey along. You'll get your face bruised if you look with a sleeve over it!" When Su-chieh saw it was Hsiang Yü-t'ing making remarks at their expense she picked up her whip again and brandished it at him a few times.

But then, like a pack of wolves and dogs, the whole herd of women stampeded their donkeys, overtaking one another turn by turn. As they rode on donkey-back, some of them had babies in their arms, some had their hairnets jolted off; some fell off when their saddle slipped sideways, some squealed and shrieked when the animal ran off; some, before they had gone more than a mile or two, said their bowels were unsettled and wanted to get down and find a lonely spot to relieve themselves; some said they had their period and wanted to pull cloths out of their bed sack to go between their legs; some wanted to suckle their children and asked the man with the whip to lead them along by the reins; some said their leg-bones were getting numb and asked people to pull their feet out of the stirrups; some dropped their perfume sachet and asked people to look for it on the ground; some had forgotten their toilet box and told people to go home and fetch it for them. All this stamping about sent the dust rising up to heaven and the rank smell of bodies spreading far and wide.

Such was the scene at the outset, already a most unseemly spectacle. Who knows how many further antics were in store by the time they actually burned their incense? We shall need another chapter to continue with the outcome of this pilgrimage.

CHAPTER 69

[982] In the midst of all those women Ti Hsi-ch'en, wearing his cap and his long gown, marched along leading the donkey. How could a daintily-brought-up young man from a well-to-do family take to walking? Before they had covered six or seven miles he had to take off his scholar's gown, roll it into a bundle, and hold it clasped under one arm. And then blisters gradually came up on both his feet. The pain was unbearable, and though he stretched

out his neck to move forward his legs kept lagging behind. Su-chieh whipped the donkey on to an even faster pace. The farmhand Ch'ang Kung was driv-ing a mule along beside Ti Hsi-ch'en to no purpose: it was meant to be in readiness for Ti Hsi-ch'en to ride, and when Ch'ang Kung saw the plight he was in with walking—short of breath and legs failing—he stepped forward to lay hold of the bridle on Su-chieh's mount, saying: "The master can't walk any more, missus! Why don't I lead your donkey for you and let him get on the mule?"

Su-chieh laid two lashes of the whip on Ch'ang Kung's shoulders and cursed at him: "What difference does it make to your legs whether he can walk or not? I don't care about him—why should you make a fuss? Get yourself right out of my way!" So Ti Hsi-ch'en had no choice but to go on leading the donkey and struggle desperately forward.

In the group was a woman in her forties, wearing a refashioned lined jacket in dark green silk and a purple-patterned linen shawl. She was moving along just behind Su-chieh. Raising her eye shield she asked Ch'ang Kung: "Which family does the lady in front come from?"

Ch'ang Kung replied: "She's the wife of Mr. Ti in Main Street."

The [983] woman said: "Who is that leading her donkey?"

And Ch'ang Kung replied: "Mr. Ti himself."

The woman said: "Just look at that gentleman—why ever is he tiring himself out leading a donkey like that? Doesn't she care?"

Ch'ang Kung said: "They probably had a quarrel at home, and so this will be his punishment!"

She said: "I've never seen punishment like that before" and whipped on her own donkey to catch up with Su-chieh and call out to her: "Is that Mrs. Ti, in front?"

Su-chieh turned her head: "Yes."

The woman asked her: "Who is the young man in the cap leading along your donkey?"

Su-chieh said: "He's my lord and master."

The woman asked again: "And this man leading a mule alongside—is he with you too?"

Su-chieh said: "He's a farmhand of ours."

The woman said: "You leave the farmhand idle, you don't make him lead your donkey for you, but make your husband do it! I can see he is all lame and can't walk any more. He must be a gentleman, for he's wearing a schol-ar's cap. This won't do—stop making him lead the donkey! We have come on this pilgrimage to seek blessings from Our Lady; aren't you falling into sin instead?"

Su-chieh said: "When I was planning to come on the pilgrimage with the society he got together with his father to find all sorts of ways to stop me coming. When I went to burn incense at the procession he wouldn't even come with me, but joined with my spineless brothers, my sister's husband, and my mother's brother, all blaming me behind my back for hurting their reputation. So now I'm making him go on foot and lead my donkey. The mule is free, so I shall make the farmhand ride it."

The woman said: "Listen to me, Mrs. Ti. That won't do. Husbands stand for heaven. A foolish man fears his wife, a worthy wife respects her man. Can a good woman treat her husband badly? For my sake please ask the gentle- man to mount on his mule and have this farmhand lead your donkey."

Su-chieh said: "All right, then—If this lady hadn't spoken up for you I would have made you lead my donkey all the way there and back!—I haven't yet ventured to ask you, Madam—what is your name?"

The woman said: "My name is Liu. My son is Liu Shang-jen, the Ceremo- nial Orderly in the county office. I live at the east end of town; we are in the same street as you. But although I come from a humble family I don't go out unless I have to. And that is why I didn't even know Mr. Ti."

The two became good friends and chatted together all the way. But no more of that.

[984] Ti Hsi-ch'en had walked a good nine miles in one stint, and now his muscles were weak and his bones felt like breaking. When Mrs. Liu spoke up for him and he was able to ride the mule it was more delicious than riding in an eight-man sedan, and he felt more grateful to her than he did to his very parents. That day, with their best efforts, they traveled more than thirty miles and spent the night in Chou Shao-kang's inn at the east gate of Chi-nan prefecture.

Although Su-chieh was traveling in company with many others, they were of course mostly people unknown to her. Hou and Chang, as the two society heads, could not give much special attention to looking after her. So she stuck close to Mrs. Liu, and since Ti Hsi-ch'en also felt deep gratitude to her they all put their baggage together. Hou and Chang had the Holy Mother's great sedan placed on the side facing south, and the whole crowd of women knelt upon the ground. While one of them recited Buddhist chants the congrega- tion cried out with one voice: "Homage to the Bodhisattva Kuan-shih- yin, who saves from suffering and hardship! Amitābha Buddha!" The great unison cry was heard for miles around. When they had finished calling to the Buddhas the host supplied water to wash their faces and served up deep-fried coiled-noodle cakes, "hairy ear" pastries, cooked red dates, and soft dates, as well as four dishes of fruit and nuts to go with their tea. The price of supper was agreed at two *fen* each for as much pancake, bean-curd soup, and rice porridge as they wanted. When all had supped they washed out their mouths, emptied their bladders, and made up their beds and went to sleep.

Since Su-chieh was a good customer newly recruited to the society, Hou and Chang sought her out and joined her. The four women, including Mrs. Liu, spent the night together. Ti Hsi-ch'en slept elsewhere with men from other families. Hou and Chang lay on a k'ang with Su-chieh's group, telling them the whole night through how they should abstain from meat and invoke the Buddhas, how they should worship the Pole Star and read holy books, and how someone who practiced these devotions could commit any sins and wickedness in the world without the ox-head and horse-face demons daring to take or question her, nor would King Yama give her any hard looks, but let her choose whatever rich and noble situation she wished to be reborn in.

Su-chieh asked: "They say that in the underworld there are swift-footed spirit hawks, and no soul, however strong or bad, can escape their clutches."[14]

The woman Hou said: "Rubbish! What swift-footed spirit hawks? If you join our church[15] even the spirit tigers and spirit dragons won't dare show their face, let alone spirit hawks. If you want to go on living you can extend your life for ages long; if you don't like being kept alive you can make your own way to King Yama [985] and get yourself reborn into a fresh life!"

Su-chieh said: "What is it like in your church?"

The woman Hou said: "In our church all new members first put in twenty taels of silver. These twenty taels are invested to create interest for repair of roads and bridges, old-age welfare, and poor relief. And when the birthdays of the Thirty Deities, Eight Vajras and Four Bodhisattvas,[16] and the gods' patrol days come round, we hold ceremonies and recite holy books, meeting at night and breaking up at dawn. That's all—there's no other service to perform. Nor do we put a ban on meat and alcohol or a bar on your sex life. You live like ordinary people."

Su-chieh asked: "Who is the Superior in this church?"

The woman Hou said: "Myself and Master Chang. I am full Superior and she is deputy."

Su-chieh asked: "If I wanted to join this church, would I be allowed to?"

Hou said: "You're so young it's just the right time for you to start religious practices. Elderly people have so short a time left that religious practice is not much use: it merely lets them off some sinful karma, but it doesn't win them any spiritual reward. The only thing is that your father-in-law is difficult to deal with, and your brother Master Hsueh goes even further—abusing Buddhists. Our Lady of the Summit sent me a dream to tell me that this brother of yours has been complaining loudly because you have come on this pilgrimage."

Su-chieh said: "He can't control what I do, though. Even my husband can't control me—let alone a brother from my own family! Just because he tried to stand in my way I punished him by making him lead my donkey a good ten miles. If Mrs. Liu hadn't put so much pressure on me I would have made him walk the whole way there and back, even if it meant him walking his legs into nothing."

Hou and Chang said: "And why not? A husband needs to be dealt a bit of rough treatment to make him afraid of us, or else he'll go and get in the way and stop us doing even the tiniest little thing. Otherwise why didn't we speak up for him when we saw him in such a pathetic state with his walking? Later on we saw him mount up on the mule—so it was Mrs. Liu who pleaded for him!"

Su-chieh said: "I shall get up at the dawn watch and comb my hair; then I shall ask Mrs. Liu to be my witness and formally submit to you both as masters. As soon as I get home I shall offer up the twenty taels of silver, in full."

Hou and Chang readily agreed.

Su-chieh slept until the dawn watch, then rose earlier than everyone else. Ti Hsi-ch'en was already in attendance on her. By the time she had finished her toilet the women Hou and Chang were [986] tidied up and ready. They were ushered up to the top position, where they sat on two chairs while below them Su-chieh performed four double bows and kowtowed heartily sixteen times. Hou and Chang sat there solemnly, accepting it. Then they determined who in the congregation of disciples was her senior and who her junior; they all compared ages and greeted one another with due ceremony. Ti Hsi-ch'en looked on from one side in a daze, not understanding why this was happening.

Su-chieh said: "Now I have submitted myself as a disciple to these two masters. My masters are your masters, so you ought to come over here and pay them a few kowtows."

Hou and Chang said: "But we couldn't accept homage from someone not a member of our church."

Ti Hsi-ch'en had not intended to come over and kowtow, but because he dared not defy Su-chieh he had no choice but to come down below them and perform four kowtows. The two rogues were content to accept and protest in equal measure. From this time on when Su-chieh was with Hou or Chang she called them "Master Hou" and "Master Chang." In Su-chieh's presence the two temple workers called her "disciple," and to other people they referred to her as "the disciple from the Ti family." In Ti Hsi-ch'en's presence they called him "Mr. Ti," but to other people they called him "disciple Ti's husband."

Now that Su-chieh was an acknowledged member of the congregation and had traveled with them a good way, she gradually came to know them well. There were no "ladies from President Yang's residence"—they were all tenant farmers' [wives] and hired staff from President Yang's house. Nor were there any "Mme Mengs" or "Mme Kengs"—they were either former wet nurses from the Meng household or married-off maids from the Keng household. Actually, only Su-chieh was a proper lady from a family. But she was quite happy to be of their company and felt not the slightest disdain for them.

At the end of another day's travel they had covered some thirty miles and spent the night at Wan-te. Of course they put up at an inn, set up the goddess's sedan, recited chants, and called to the Buddhas. No need to go into detail.

Let us go on. Traveling several more miles they passed through Huo-lu. Side by side all down the street in Huo-lu were shops selling fried snacks. Whenever pilgrims came by the waiters in each shop would run out in a noisy rabble into the middle of the road and strenuously pull the pilgrims' donkeys to a halt, then invite them inside for a snack. They hoped in this way to attract business. This disgusting state of affairs was very like the Shensi peddlers of coarse rugs in Peking's East River Rice Lane or like the street-walkers below the walls of the western tile-yard there, [987] who go out into the street and pull at people willy-nilly. Just as Su-chieh and her group were passing through, the whole pack of waiters came charging out like tigers, and without any ceremony a crowd of them pulled to a halt the donkeys ridden by Hou and Chang and struggled to take them off into their premises, saying: "Piping hot snacks, fresh from the pan, done in pure sesame oil! Fragrant and crisp! Come in and have one! The inn is a whole day on from here— make sure you don't go hungry!"

Hou and Chang said: "Thank you, but we only just came from eating in Wan-te. We have to make haste to get to the inn, register our names, and hire chairs."

After repeatedly failing to get the party to stop, the waiters just had to let them go.

This was Su-chieh's first pilgrimage, and she did not know that all travelers passing through suffered the same rough soliciting, pressing you to eat and pay accordingly. When she saw all the shop people mobbing Hou and Chang with their solicitations she thought they all knew them personally, and asked: "Are all these shopkeepers acquaintances of yours, Masters? Why are they pressing you so hard to go in?"

Glibly Hou and Chang replied: "These people are all disciples of ours, but with all of them struggling so hard to invite us in, how can we go to everyone? We're just forced not to go in anywhere!"

When the pilgrims came to the military parade ground in T'ai-an prefecture they were expected there by men who had been sent from Sung K'uei-wu's establishment—an inn well known to them from previous visits. Seeing Hou and Chang arriving at the head of all those society members, the men recognized them a good way off and dashed joyfully up to them. They pulled their two animals to a halt and said: "The master sent us out some days ago to wait here, but we saw no sign of you arriving. Perhaps you started out on the fifteenth? Did you get caught in the rain on the way? Have you been keeping well all this time?" And they led along their donkeys, with the whole company following suit, all the way to the inn.

When Sung K'uei-wu saw them he put on all the true innkeeper's fawning manner to come out and welcome them, mouthing some empty courtesies. They washed their faces and drank tea. They registered their names and hired donkey-chairs. They called to the Buddha, recited sutras. And then they all went first to the T'ien-ch'i Temple[17] to see the sights and worship there. Back at the inn they ate their supper and slept until the midnight watch, when everyone rose. They did their toilet, burned incense, and called to the Buddhas. This done, they all had a meal together.

[988] Hou and Chang saw every single member of the company on to their mountain chairs before they mounted their own to bring up the rear. All the wayside beggars, [fortunetellers], and providers of traveling lamps had lanterns burning, so that all along the way it was as bright as day.

Su-chieh had been born in the deep seclusion of Professor Hsueh's ladies' quarters; she had married into the prosperous Ti family. She rose late and was early to bed; she went abroad in curtained chairs and seated carriages. Now, all of a sudden, she was with this troop of women, only fit for menial housework, who could never sit at a banquet. She had got up in the middle of the night, eyes still fuzzy with sleep; she had eaten a good bellyfull of hard, undercooked rice, salty wheat buns only half cooked, lukewarm vegetables not as clean as they should be; she was riding in a willow-frame mountain chair with half the footrest missing, which was shaking her into a helpless condition. Before they had carried her as far as the Red Gate [Temple] she was already so dizzy that her sight was blurred and so queasy that she had to vomit. What came up first was that assortment of goodies she had risen to eat at midnight; later she brought up brown bile which gave off a powerful stench. She trembled so much that the hair on her bare head flopped down untidily all round; she retched until her fair white face looked as green and yellow as a cabbage leaf.

Hou said to the whole company: "Here is a young person whose heart is not pure enough: Our Lady has got her!" And Mrs. Liu said: "I said she was no good when I saw her put down her husband and make him walk along leading her donkey. And that's how it has turned out—she's driven Our Lady to deal with her. She's the only one of our whole party who has put Our Lady out of humor, but it reflects badly on everybody."

Hou and Chang said: "She may be foolish and may have upset Our Lady, but surely we can't just look on! We'll all just have to beg forgiveness for her."

Thousands of pilgrims from other societies crowded around them so tightly that there was not room enough for a slip of paper between them. There was all sorts of talk about Our Lady binding someone up, and all kinds of questions like: "Where does that pilgrim come from?" "Whatever did she do, to make Our Lady deal with her so harshly?" Some said: "This pilgrim looks quite young, and seeing how well dressed she is she must be with an important master." The people in Su-chieh's society confirmed it: "She's a lady from the Ti family in Ming-shui—the wife of Tribute Student Ti. There's Mr. Ti beside her, isn't he?" The onlookers chattered wildly away among themselves.

[989] Su-chieh sat on the ground with jaundiced face and drooping hair. Now, for one thing she could hear everyone chattering about her; for another, since she had got down from the chair and sat resting on the ground for a while her dizziness and nausea had slowly passed away. She couldn't stand listening to so much drivel, and with a snort she cried out: "Somebody gets dizzy in their chair, feels sick and has a vomit, then sits down for a little rest—and out comes all this flood of crap! What's this about Our Lady binding me up? Have I carried off babies of yours to throw down a well? You're ganging up to curse at me! Why don't you all clear off now? Serve you right if I picked up some dirt and threw it all over your bloody faces!" And standing up she added: "I'm not going to ride in a chair, I'm going to walk by myself for a spell." And she strode off up the slope.

When they all saw how vigorously she walked the society members at last remounted their chairs and moved on. Since Su-chieh was walking on foot Ti Hsi-ch'en could hardly dare sit in a chair, so he followed her closely to give support at her side. Now, Su-chieh had once been a fox before this incarnation, and Mount T'ai had been familiar ground to her.[18] So she climbed that high mountain as easily as treading on level ground, she moved along the winding tracks as if she were walking along well-known paths, making no hardship of it. But this left Ti Hsi-ch'en perspiring with fatigue and panting like an ox driven to exhaustion: gradually one foot could not keep up with another, and his legs went limp. Once again it was lucky that Mrs. Liu said: "Won't it hurt you to walk at such a mad rate, Mrs. Ti? Ride in chairs for a while, you and Mr. Ti—you can always get down and walk again when you feel dizzy." And indeed the two chairs were put down, and only then did Su-chieh and Ti Hsi-ch'en sit in them. But they had not been carried a dozen paces, and Ti Hsi-ch'en had only just settled himself comfortably, when Su-chieh cried out: "Oh no!" Her face looked jaundiced again, she was queasy and dizzy as before. They were forced to make the men put down the chairs again and let her walk by herself. And Ti Hsi-ch'en was again obliged to walk along supporting her.

They made their way by stages to the summit. The man in charge of the pilgrims' tax was the deputy magistrate of Li-ch'eng county; he checked each pilgrim in against their name on the list. When they came up to the front of the Holy Mother's Hall the doors were locked, because inside there were votive offerings of silver currency, robes, figurines in gold and silver, and suchlike, so people were not allowed to go in. Anyone wanting to see Our Lady's golden face had to stand on some support, then gaze in through openings in the door lattice. Su-chieh planted her feet on Ti Hsi-ch'en's shoulders while he grasped [990] her two legs with his hands, so she did after all have a good view. And they did go to make some offerings of silver in the hall.

Once the pilgrims had burned their incense, each of them went round looking at the sights for a while before they all mounted their chairs to go down the mountain. Once again Su-chieh dared not get in a chair, but made Ti Hsi-ch'en support her walking down the mountain as far as the Red [Gate] Temple. Sung K'uei-wu, who had prepared boxed meals with wine, was already there waiting to entertain the company to a "Back from the Summit" party. The women all climbed down together from their chairs, mixing indiscriminately with the men as they promptly put paid to the jumble of food in the partitioned boxes and the weak, vinegary wine of the season. Then they climbed back into their chairs and returned to the inn, Su-chieh riding her own mule along with them and Ti Hsi-ch'en only now permitted to join the rest riding in a chair.

When they reached the inn all the pilgrims of the house who had come down from the summit that same day were seated, men separately from women, in a large marquee, where a banquet was served and theatricals performed in a general farewell party. The man in the seat of honor picked the play *Hairpin of Thorn* and added the scenes "Moonlight Execution of Tiao-ch'an" and "Traveling Alone a Thousand *li*" before the party broke up and all went back to their rooms.

Su-chieh asked: "Master Hou, what story was that they acted just now? Why did Ch'ien Yü-lien get killed by Our Lord Kuan when she had only just been fished out of the river? And even if he did kill her, why did he lead out the two wives to flee away? Was he perhaps afraid they would have to pay with their lives?" And all the others said: "Quite true! She was such a good person—why didn't Our Lord Kuan protect her, instead of killing her? It just shows how unfair things are."[19]

They chatted away, had a night's sleep, and next day, after eating, made ready to set out. Sung K'uei-wu presented Hou and Chang with an umbrella, a woven cane fan, a piece of salt pork, and a copper basin weighing twelve ounces. When all was packed and ready they mounted their animals for the journey back.

On the way they were also going to Hao-li Hill to burn paper money. This hill was a couple of miles distant from T'ai-an prefecture, not particularly high but still possessing a major temple. Along the two side passageways were statues of the Kings of the Ten Courts of Hell and of all the sufferings in the eighteen tiers of Hell. Tradition has it that everyone in the world without exception goes there when they die. Therefore all pilgrims make a point of visiting the place, some to hold services of purification and deliverance for the dead, some to burn paper objects and money. The monks and priests in charge of the temple are also skilled in making profit from others' money by supplying tubes of divination slips, each inscribed with [991] the name of some King in some court of Hell. People burning paper first draw a slip to find out where [their dead ones] have gone. If they then see that the court is a nice place, with no suffering or punishment, the sons and grandsons [of the dead] are pleased. But if it is some bad destination like the mountain of knives, the sea of suffering, the hell of pounding, or the hell of grinding, then they behave just like the dead themselves suffering there, making the earth tremble with their lamentation. Most distressing! "Heaven's signs arise from the hearts of men." How could the sky possibly be clear, the air bright, the sun radiant, or the breeze mild in a place of such unearthly, demonic wailing? Naturally, the sky is dim, the earth dark, the sun and moon lack luster, dark wind makes moan, cold air whistles through. People then read even more farfetched ideas into it and make this Hao-li Hill into the true site of Feng-tu, the Underworld.

We turn now to Ti Hsi-ch'en's mother, the old lady Ti. During her life she had never given her parents-in-law a blow or a hard word, had never railed against heaven and earth, had never ill-treated her maidservants, never spilt rice or wheat flour, nor ever engaged in tittle-tattle or pilfering. The inner and the outer woman were the same: her mouth was the voice of her heart. Such a person, when she dies, represents the moral best of womankind upon this earth. Supposing there were no Kings of Hell, so long as her moral substance remained intact, she would most certainly be reborn in some quarter where justice and enlightenment prevailed. Supposing Kings of Hell really did exist, they would surely feel reverence and respect when they met a person so good: they would instruct the Golden Boy and Jade Girl to guide her over the Bridge of Gold toward her rebirth. How could she possibly still be at Hao-li Hill three or four years after her death? But her son found it safer to believe someone there rather than not there, so he still, in the deity's presence, asked for a slip. On it was clearly written that she was actually in the court of the Fifth King of Hell, renowned among all the ten as a harsh master.

Ti Hsi-ch'en already felt quite upset when he drew this slip, but when he had bought his paper ingots [of imitation silver] and taken his wine round to the Fifth Court, there modeled in clay was a woman tied to a stake, while someone used an iron hook to claw out her tongue and cut it off with a knife. Seeing this, Ti Hsi-ch'en burst out in loud weeping, just as though they really were cutting out his own mother's tongue. He flung his arms around the suffering statue and [992] broke off the hook and the knife in the demon's hands. He wept to make a man of stone dissolve in tears, and everyone felt distressed. The society members tried to talk him out of it: "This is nothing more than a statue of clay. It's meant as a warning to people—why do you treat it like a real thing? We have heard that your mother was a model of virtue when she was alive: how could she be suffering such heavy punishment?"

Su-chieh interrupted: "But that's not necessarily true! When my mother-in-law was alive her talk was really wide of the mark: she would always find fault with people in most outrageous terms. Never mind anyone else—I myself had her picking fault with me more times than I can say. Each time she opened her mouth she attacked me as undutiful. She accused me of hitting and abusing my in-laws and bullying my husband. Slandering good people—surely that alone deserves having your tongue cut off?"

Mrs. Liu said: "You shouldn't talk! If tongues were cut out for clashing with a daughter-in-law, whatever should be cut out for clashing with a mother-in-law?"

While everyone was talking Ti Hsi-ch'en continued to weep. Su-chieh said to him: "Bawling on and on!—how much longer are you going to keep it up? The King is hardly going to let her off having her tongue cut out just because you're crying! Let's be on our way. Wait for your father to die—that will be time enough for you to start crying again!"

Everyone was annoyed with Su-chieh's misbehavior, but Ti Hsi-ch'en duly dared cry no more. He came out of the temple with Su-chieh, and they mounted their beasts.

After seven days' travel, on the twenty-first of the eighth month as the sun was setting, they reached home. Without a word about asking to meet her parents-in-law, Su-chieh pushed straight through to her own room. But T'iao-keng and Ti Chou's wife did go to see her there, and Lung prepared a one-table feast and told Ch'iao-chieh to entertain her sister-in-law to a "Back from the Summit" party.

The next day she dressed up once more in colored clothes, put jewel ornaments in her hair, and made Ti Hsi-ch'en and little Yü-lan go with her to join the company at Our Lady's temple to "return the incense." She brought from home twenty taels of silver which she quietly gave to her two masters, Hou and Chang, as her church entry fee.

Hou and Chang said: "This is a good deed done from a pious heart. Is your silver free of sham and low-grade material? Is it the full amount? Now that you have joined the church you must come at once whenever we summon you to any church functions in future. If you miss out one occasion all your previous merit will unfortunately be thrown away. But your father-in-law will not let us in, so how can we get the summons to you?"

Su-chieh replied: "You can go and tell my family about any activities that I ought to do in future. There will always be someone to let me know."

Hou and Chang both saw what she meant.

[993] In any business the hardest thing is getting started. Now that she had been on one trip to T'ai-an prefecture Su-chieh ever after gave her inclinations free rein. And there were the two temple thieves leading her astray as well. So when any pilgrimage or temple visit came up Su-chieh was always the "licorice in the medicine"—the one essential ingredient they could never

be without. We shall see many a case of this in later chapters, as you can learn by reading on.

NOTES

1. It appears separately, under the title "A Pilgrimage in Seventeenth-century Fiction: T'ai-shan and the *Hsing-shih yin-yüan chuan*," in *T'oung Pao* 77 (1991). Readers of the chapter by Pei-yi Wu in this volume (chap. 2) will find there a description of the same pilgrimage site from a slightly earlier period. And Susan Naquin's chapter (chap. 8) deals with another site dedicated to the same deity.

2. The edition used was published by Shanghai ku-chi ch'u-pan she in 1981. References here are by chapter and page, the latter inserted in brackets throughout the text of the translation.

3. The meaning of the phrase *po kuei* 撥龜, literally "teasing a tortoise," is not clear to me. It reappears in the next chapter to describe the activity of certain people using lanterns on the T'ai Shan mountrainside: cf. 69:988, where I have offered "fortunetellers" as a conjecture.

4. In chapter 56 the two women hold a three-day sequence of ceremonies at a local temple dedicated to San-kuan ta-ti 三官大帝—the Three Agents, gods associated with Heaven, Earth, and Water and with the three Principals of the Chinese ritual calendar. The Middle Principal (*chung-yuan* 中元) corresponds to the Yü-lan season, reaching its climax on the fifteenth of the seventh month. Rituals and offerings are dedicated to rootless and untended souls, perceived as particularly dangerous during this month, but also to ancestral souls nominated by the worshipers. Su-chieh goes alone to watch the spectacle of ritual release of lamps on the waters, attracting huge attention among the simple countrywomen present, and seeks out Hou and Chang to offer them a donation (56:806–10).

5. Old Mrs. Ti died in chapter 59, after a seizure provoked by seeing Su-chieh bullying Ti Hsi-ch'en (59:855). The family mourning follows in the next chapter (60:858 ff.).

6. Old Mrs. Ti was from the Hsiang family. Her elder brother and his wife attend for the funeral preparations, with their son Hsiang Yü-t'ing and his wife (60:858). Third Aunt from the Ts'ui family is a married younger sister of Mrs. Ti (52:758), also present for the mourning observances (60:869).

7. This savage beating administered by Hsiang Yü-t'ing's mother took place when the lady arrived to mourn her sister-in-law, learned of Su-chieh's role in the death, and saw Su-chieh still decked out in flowers and bright clothes. It is one of the moments in the novel when Su-chieh's antisocial behavior provokes a cathartic explosion of discipline from the family hierarchy (60:860–62).

8. The goddess is Kuan-yin 觀音, whose birthday in the ritual calendar indeed falls on this date. The chapter in this volume by Chün-fang Yü (chap. 5) discusses the iconography of the White Robe.

9. Reference to an episode in chapter 64: Su-chieh was tricked into engaging teams of nuns to exorcize the threat of divine punishment from spirit hawks. See below, n. 14.

10. The prefectures of Shantung province.

11. I cannot give a certain translation of the expression "Wang p'i hao lai" (王皮好來).

12. Lung 龍氏 was the concubine of Su-chieh's father, Professor Hsueh (45:659), and is the mother of Hsueh Ju-pien. Hence her claim to address him like this here and in her next speech.

13. See n. 6, above.

14. Early in the novel, when Su-chieh was preincarnate as a fox, the skin of her dead carcass was seized by a sparrow hawk (3:31). She now has a lifelong dread of such birds. Knowing this, her brother later lets one into her room to frighten her into releasing her husband from punitive confinement. He then pretends that the bird brings warning of divine punishment for unwifely conduct (63:904–6). Local nuns confirm the significance of this omen and arrange an elaborate and expensive ritual atonement for her (64:913 ff.).

15. Chinese *chiao* 教, literally, "teaching." I avoid the conventional rendering "sect," which belongs on the lips of outsiders, and prefer "church," which (despite its tendency to suggest the idea of a building) covers both the notion of a minority denomination and that of an integrated religious community seen from the inside.

16. The Thirty Deities, short for the Thirty-three Devas of the Buddhist Trayastrimśās heaven, and Eight Vajras, armed guardians of the Buddhist law, were familiar to Chinese popular culture, as reflected for instance in *Hsi-yu chi* 西遊記 (Peking: Tso-chia, 1954), 8:78, 51:586, 52:602, 58:671, 98:1112, 99:1122. So too were the Four Bodhisattvas—Avalokiteśvara (Kuan-yin), Kṣitigarbha (Ti-tsang), Samantabhadra (P'u-hsien), and Mañjuśrī (Wen-shu)—associated with the Four Great Mountain-sanctuaries (四大名山) of Chinese Buddhism.

17. Temples with this title in the towns of North China were dedicated to Mount T'ai. Here in T'ai-an the pilgrims are evidently visiting the main Temple of the Mount (Tai Miao 岱廟, also called the Tung-yueh Temple), within the north wall of the town, to worship there before their night ascent. See Édouard Chavannes, *Le T'ai chan: essai de monographie d'un culte chinois* (Paris: Leroux, 1910), pp. 27–8, 126–48.

18. The reference is to the opening scene of the novel, in which Ch'ao Yuan meets the fox during his hunt at Yung-shan (1:12).

19. The women ludicrously treat scenes from three different plays as part of the same action. In practice, of course, the female lead in all the scenes might well have been played by the same actress. The loyal wife Ch'ien Yü-lien is saved from suicide by drowning in *Ching-ch'ai chi* 荊釵記 (Hairpin of thorn). The *San-kuo* hero Kuan Yü kills Tiao-ch'an, the woman used by Ts'ao Ts'ao in an attempt to seduce the hero into joining his side, in "Moonlight Execution of Tiao-ch'an." And in "Traveling Alone a Thousand *li*" the same hero, pretending to surrender to Ts'ao Ts'ao, is given charge of the two captured wives of Liu Pei; he then finds a way to take them securely back to Liu, successfully fighting off attempts to prevent him.

TWO

An Ambivalent Pilgrim to T'ai Shan in the Seventeenth Century

Pei-yi Wu

The location of pilgrimage sites sets China apart from most other civilizations. While holy mountains are known in religions outside China, they seldom attract crowds of pilgrims to their lofty peaks. In the Old World, especially, all great centers of religious pilgrimage—notably, Canterbury, Compostella, Jerusalem, and Mecca—are more or less on level ground. In contrast, Chinese sacred geography seems to slight lowlands and cities, which are rarely built on hilltops. A close examination of the two glaring exceptions only confirms the rule. P'u-t'o, which Chün-fang Yü discusses in chapter 5, is an island off the Chekiang coast; Ts'ao-ch'i, which Faure discusses in chapter 4, literally means "Ts'ao Creek." In height they are dwarfed by other great Buddhist centers. But each site consists of a cluster of small hills and other natural features that have been developed and organized to seem, especially to a credulous visitor, not much different from sacred mountains. Altitude and scale were indeed ignored by the believers and writers who suffixed the character *shan* 山 to the two place names, thus elevating an island and a creek to the rank of mountains.[1] Another indication that mountains have been inextricably linked to the idea of pilgrimage is found in one of the two terms that represent the idea better than others (there being no Chinese equivalent to the English word). One is *chin-hsiang* 進香, "to present incense"; the other is *ch'ao-shan* 朝山, "to pay obeisances to a mountain."

Why this is so is perhaps ultimately unanswerable. One may note, however, that in China the idea of sacred mountains goes back to the dawn of history, long before the introduction of Buddhism and the emergence of religious Taoism, perhaps even antedating the beginning of pilgrimage. The most important of the sacred mountains are the Five Marchmounts (*wu yueh* 五嶽). They are East Marchmount (T'ai Shan 泰山, 1,545 meters), West Marchmount (Hua Shan 華山, 2,154 meters), South Marchmount (Heng

Shan 衡山, 1,290 meters), North Marchmount (Heng Shan 恆山, 2,016 meters), and Central Marchmount (Sung Shan 嵩山, 1,512 meters).[2] They, "among the most powerful of the deified natural forces of ancient China, had been regarded as important protectors of the state" (Kroll 225).

The first among the Five Marchmounts, Mount T'ai has always had a special aura not shared by other sacred sites (see map 1.1). Visitors of every type, motivated by various reasons, climbed its lofty peaks. Rulers from the legendary kings of high antiquity down to later tyrants and emperors went to the mountaintop to perform the rites of *feng* 封 and *shan* 禪. Sages like Confucius and philosophers like Wang Shou-jen (Yang-ming) all found it irresistible. Poets and religious adepts sought peaceful and numinous seclusion in its hills; the pious flocked to its various temples and shrines to make offerings and beg for blessings. Almost every literate visitor added his memorable words to the ever-growing literature of T'ai Shan. There have been, however, hardly any accounts of a pilgrimage by the participants themselves, if we define such an account as a prose narrative in which the author describes *unambiguously* his participation in a sequence of events that he himself *explicitly* recognizes as a pilgrimage. This definition, redundant and broad as it may seem, is satisfied by only one work: the *Tai chih* 岱志 by Chang Tai 張岱 (1597–1684?). There are many reasons for the paucity of pilgrim narratives in China; an exploration of them may add to our understanding of pilgrimage in China.

The most plausible explanation is the supposition that few pilgrims were sufficiently literate to write about their activities. Yet we can assume that at least some members of the literati took part in pilgrimages; the question remains why they so seldom wrote about their experiences. A larger question is why so little has been written on the subjective experience of religion. One explanation may lie in the nature of Chinese first-person prose narratives.

Given the limitless variety of styles, the freedom of expression, and the readiness for experimentation taken for granted in modern writing, it is not easy for us to appreciate the constraints under which almost every writer in the premodern world, East or West, had to labor. Only a narrow range of experience—varying of course with the time and place—could be reported, and the manner of reporting was severely circumscribed by narrative conventions that were just as pervasive and demanding as the writer's mother tongue. One might even argue that the very perception of reality was largely shaped by the narrative models available to any particular writer.

In traditional China the emergence of the genre of what I shall call eyewitness account came about rather late, for reasons too complex to go into here.[3] In other words, there may have been first-person narratives, but there were severe restrictions as to what they could do. Such restrictions may not seem reasonable to a modern reader, but until the sixteenth century even an autobiographer could not tell the story of the inner person: an author could only record those facts ostensibly documentable from archival materials or secondhand sources, facts that were public and exemplary. Even an avowedly fanciful genre like fiction could be told only in the third person. The sustained narrative stance of a Sinbad or a Gulliver was not possible. The only exception, the T'ang tale *Yu-hsien k'u* 游仙窟, whose author and narrator are identical, did not survive in China; we know its existence because a copy was preserved in Japan. Consequently, even if a pilgrim had wanted to write about his experience, he would have had no adequate medium of expression. Neither autobiography nor fiction would have been of much use to him. The closest model he would have had was travel literature, which in its early stages would still have denied him much freedom.

The problem is best illustrated by the travel account of the monk Hsuantsang 玄奘 (596–664), the pilgrim par excellence, who roamed India and Central Asia for sixteen years in search of truth and sutras. The *Ta-T'ang hsi-yü chi* 大唐西域記, dictated by the master to a disciple and running to nearly a hundred thousand characters, gives the barest outline of the traveler's own activities but dwells on the description of the some one hundred thirty states that Hsuan-tsang visited. The description is based on secondary sources—local lore and legends—and almost never on his own observations. From his account we can hardly imagine the faith that inspired his great undertaking, the courage that sustained him during perilous trials, or his sense of triumph when he was proclaimed victor in a doctrinal debate presided over by Harsha, emperor of India, and attended by more than sixty thousand. Although Hsuan-tsang's was not the earliest account of a pilgrimage to India—the monk Fa-hsien 法顯 had written his more than two centuries earlier—it could not but set an example for all subsequent Buddhist travelers, given his great fame and accomplishments. For our purpose, Hsuan-tsang demonstrates more than any one else the near impossibility of pilgrimage narratives, for the greatest pilgrim of China, when he dictated his travel account, included almost everything except his pilgrimage.[4]

In defense of the Buddhist master one could argue that in reporting on foreign lands, most of them never visited before by Chinese travelers, Hsuantsang's main concern was credibility—the report was ostensibly meant for the emperor's attention—not entertainment or self-expression. In this connection he was the diametrical opposite of modern travel writers, whose egomania often exceeds their wanderlust. In general, Chinese travel accounts of foreign lands tend to model themselves on the treatises on barbarians in dynastic histories; they often resemble the writings of nineteenth-century European ethnologists or folklorists. In fact, Chou Ta-kuan's 周達觀 *Chen-la feng-t'u chi* 真臘風土記, an account of his visit to Cambodia as a member of an official mission beginning in 1295, stands comparison with the best European ethnology written before the last century.

The works of Hsuan-tsang and other long-distance travelers represent only one of the two genres of Chinese travel writing. The other genre, which I shall call the *yu-chi* 遊記, probably took its cue mainly from landscape and pastoral poetry of the Six Dynasties, hence its relative freedom from ethnology and its amenability to first-person narration. The style of the *yu-chi*, gradually established by T'ang and Sung prose masters such as Liu Tsung-yuan 柳宗元 and Su Shih 蘇軾, remained pretty much the same after 1100. Each work usually begins with the circumstances under which the trip was taken. If the destination or site is one of the *ming-shan sheng-ti* 名山勝地 (famous mountains or unexcelled places) or, to use the usual abbreviation, *ming-sheng* 名勝, the writer is often obliged to touch all bases and compare his impressions with the reports of previous writers. Responses to sites and scenes are more often didactic than introspective, and the companions and their pronouncements are duly noted. (Solitary travelers rarely left records, and even the indefatigable explorer Hsu Hsia-k'o 徐霞客, 1586–1641, was usually accompanied by a monk-guide or servant in his adventures into high mountains and remote gorges.) In shorter pieces of travel literature convivial camaraderie often overshadows the enjoyment of natural scenery.[5]

Although almost all pilgrimage sites are also *ming-sheng*, travel literature does not afford us much information on the explicitly religious aspects of Chinese pilgrimage. If the literary traveler noticed ordinary pilgrims at all, they were usually dismissed with one or two comments. Even on the rare occasions when the writer himself went to the site for a particular purpose that should render his trip a pilgrimage, the fact was invariably given the barest mention, and the travel account does not otherwise depart from the usual format of the *yu-chi*.[6] To illustrate this point and the general characteristics of the genre as well as to have several accounts of T'ai Shan, we could do no better than to take a good look at a representative piece written by one of the most prominent Ming literati.

WANG SHIH-CHEN'S THREE VISITS

For twenty years the proud arbiter of the literary world, Wang Shih-chen 王世貞 (1526–90), poet and critic, distinguished himself also as a prolific historian. His official career was far less happy, but he eventually rose to minister of justice. He received his first appointment in the central government when he was barely twenty-one, and during 1557–59 he served as surveillance vice-commissioner (rank 4a) at Ch'ing-chou, Shantung. Like many visitors to T'ai Shan before and after him, Wang took full advantage of the proximity of his post to the sacred mountain—the Ch'ing-chou circuit was east of T'ai Shan—and the privileges to which his office entitled him.[7] Thus he made three ascents during 1558 and 1559. The account of these trips, written in 1576, follows the *yu-chi* format in every way, including the customary title: *Yu T'ai-shan chi* 遊泰山記. The first trip was begun on the last day of the first lunar month in 1558, right after he had paid an official visit to his superiors in a neighboring city.

> That night I bathed myself in the government hostel together with Mr. Sung Ta-wu. At the third drum I got up. As I opened the northern window of the hall I saw something like a bolt of white silk stretching from the foot of the mountain all the way to the summit. Then it looked like a large collection of fireflies flickering light from hundreds of boxes. When I asked about it, I was told that what I saw was the train of men and women on their way to pay homage to Yuan-chün. I could vaguely hear their prayers and psalms. At dawn when we started our journey the sky was overcast, and clouds flowed so closely by our faces that we could not see anything clearly beyond ten steps. I only noticed that as the sedan chair carriers raised their heels I leaned forward. Even after we arrived at the summit I still could not see a thing. It was so cold that Mr. Sung insisted that we immediately start our descent. We made a short stop at Feng-tu 酆都 Palace, where I had several cups of wine and only then did I stop shivering. The trip was ended in great regret. (*TSC* 5:13a)

Its brevity notwithstanding, the account of Wang's first ascent affords us much information of the genre in general and the T'ai Shan pilgrimage in particular. Wang's great regret for being denied a panoramic view at the summit was shared by some Chinese literati travelers who were, like many a modern day-tripper to the Jungfraujoch, effortlessly brought to the top only to be defeated by bad weather, seeing nothing beyond mist and clouds and enjoying no spiritual uplift. But Wang would never have put up with the rough-and-tumble of mass tourism. In fact, the contrast between the scholar-officials and the mob of common visitors could not have been greater. The former, lodged for the night in clean comfort—bathing, though ritualistic in origin, was routine by the sixteenth century—went up the next morning literally on the backs of others, while the great throng had to spend the night trudging up the mountain. Piety may have caused some to choose the arduous means, but the sheer number of pilgrims and the poverty of the majority of them must have militated against a sufficiency of either convenient lodging or sedan chairs. The differences between the two groups are underscored by the great distance from which Wang saw or heard the pilgrims. During his own ascent he must have either caught up with the tail end of them or run into the first wave of the returnees, but he did not record a close view of the great unwashed. Not even passing mention is made in his accounts of two subsequent visits.

The second occasion for an ascent presented itself a few months later.

> On the last day of the sixth month I went along with Mr. Tuan the censor to inspect T'ai-an. Mr. Tuan invited me for a three-day mountain trip. I knew that quite a few from other government agencies were to join us, and there

would be a shortage of means of transportation. So Mr. Hsu Wen-t'ung, assistant administrative commissioner, and I requested that we be allowed to precede the group by two days. Mr. Tuan gave his consent. (*TSC* 5:13a)

The duties and functions of the censors (*yü-shih* 御史) during the Ming were varied, and their powers were almost limitless. When on inspection tours out of the capital, they enjoyed the precedence and privileges due a provincial governor. There was no need for Wang Shih-chen to spell out what was obvious to himself and his readers, but we can infer from the travel account that the subprefecture of T'ai-an, of which the city by the same name was the capital, provided the logistic support for Tuan and his guests. What Wang chose to narrate does not depart from the usual content of a *yu-chi*: making the rounds of the historical sites and scenic spots, all catalogued and celebrated in earlier writings. He confirmed, challenged, or expanded on the observations of his predecessors; he and his companions jested, drank, and composed poetry. Rainy weather plagued them during almost the entire trip, and the only morning when they could have seen the sunrise—the ultimate treat craved by overnight visitors to any high mountain—they overslept after a night of reveling into the small hours. We are given very few details about the practical aspects of the trip, except that Censor Tuan was lodged at some distance from his guests and that, after four days of rain, "the supplies provided by the subprefecture were exhausted" (*TSC* 5:15a). The group began their descent the following morning in a cold and heavy rain.

The trip, however, had a happy ending. When they reached Yü-chang Cliff 御帳巖 it was very warm and sunny. (See Map 1.1.) The celebrated waterfalls there, which dropped from a height of some two hundred feet, were more torrential than usual.

> I was so inspired by the sight that I became uninhibited. Standing barefoot in the rapid stream next to boulders, I ordered wine and emptied large cups of it in quick succession. My loud singing shook the leaves of the trees overhead. All my companions cheered me on: some harmonized with me while others came down and drank the wine that was being brought to me. After a while it was announced that Mr. Tuan had arrived. Before we took leave of each other we went to Feng-tu Palace for a simple repast. (*TSC* 5:15a)

The account of the third trip, not much longer than half a page, is largely devoted to his rising before the fifth drum and reaching Sun-viewing Peak (Jih-kuan feng 日觀峯) in time to watch the sunrise. Not satisfied with a report of the success that eluded him on previous trips, he goes on to enumerate with regret twenty-four well-known points of interest that he could only view at a distance but not explore. Such inventories are the staple of *yu-chi* literature, but for our purposes the really interesting element in this brief account is the deceptively simple and innocuous beginning.

On the first day of the fourth month in the following year [1559], I passed through Lai-wu on an inspection tour. It happened just then that my father's involvement with border affairs had been temporarily stabilized, and it was decided that an appeal for divine help be made to the god of T'ai Shan. For that reason I made one more ascent. (*TSC* 5:15a)

The brevity of the passage belies its significance, for it indicates unmistakably the nature of Wang's third trip to T'ai Shan, however he chooses to represent the visit in the rest of the essay. Nothing further is said about what we would see as a pilgrimage, but the biography of Wang's father in the *Ming shih* clearly shows why divine intervention was sorely needed in the spring of 1559. Facile and energetic, Wang Yü 王忬 (1507–60), whose own father was once a vice-minister of war, won the favor of the emperor through several brilliant military exploits. Rapid promotions ensued, but his subsequent career was repeatedly marred by mishaps. The emperor found excuses for him and eventually appointed him supreme commander of Chi-Liao. In March of 1559 the Mongols outwitted him and breached the Great Wall through the undefended P'an-chia Pass. After five days of unimpeded and extensive looting, the invaders retreated. The alarmed and angered emperor punished all the military leaders under Wang, but the commander was allowed to stay in service without pay. The temporary stabilization of the father's involvement mentioned in the travel account apparently refers to the state of affairs right after the departure of the invaders. With victorious Mongols still poised at the border and powerful enemies—some of the enmity was incurred by the sharp-tongued son—at the ear of the emperor, Wang Yü needed help from all quarters. The appeal for divine succor, alas, came to naught. Wang Yü's critics reopened the case and brought new charges against him. The emperor, now implacable, overruled the lenient judges and imposed capital punishment on Wang as well as on all the generals under his command. The desperate appeals for clemency made by Wang Shih-chen and his younger brother brought only a short stay, and the father was executed late in 1560.

In light of the facts as recorded in the *Ming shih*, Wang Shih-chen's reluctance to dwell on either his father's misfortune or the fruitless pilgrimage may be understandable. In fact, as he mentions without explaining near the end of the essay, he did not write it until seventeen years after the last visit. By then time must have healed his wounds and softened his grief: he had obtained in 1567 a posthumous rehabilitation of his father. Otherwise it would have been heartless for him to flank the mention of his father with the two joyful highlights of the entire travel account, the exuberant frolic under the waterfalls and the timely and rewarding scaling of Sun-viewing Peak. His sense of triumph was quite in keeping with his station in 1576, when he was indisputably the foremost man of letters in the realm. Or perhaps we may just as easily attribute the way Wang Shih-chen structured his essay to his adherence to the usual format of *yu-chi*, which cannot accommodate an airing of either the father's grievance or the agonies of the filial son. The genre could indeed lend itself to an expression of nostalgia, but nothing more poignant than a mild elegiac mood.

The account of Chang Tai, to be sure, never departs very much from the usual format of the genre. Unlike Wang, he does not even hint at why he ostensibly participated in what was unmistakably a pilgrimage. But the circumstances of his participation and the nature of his pilgrimage gave him an opportunity, rarely made use of by other *yu-chi* writers, to observe at first hand what may be called pilgrimage-tourism. His ability to add his keen observations to the usual T'ai Shan itinerary resulted from a combination of factors. Before we proceed, an exploration of these circumstances and factors seems to be in order.

THE AUTHOR

Chang Tai, a native of Shan-yin (Shao-hsing), Chekiang, came from a long line of prominent scholars and officials. But by the time of his father's generation decadence and extravagance had set in, and Chang himself during the first half of his life indulged in all pleasures as a connoisseur with inexhaustible means. He was reduced to utter poverty after the fall of the Ming. Turning to writing in his later years, he produced several volumes of reminiscences. In some ways he represented the culmination of the trends of what may be called the late Ming dissident style: a disdain of conventions sometimes bordering on iconoclasm, an emphasis on individuality and originality, a readiness to reveal the self to a greater extent than ever before. Writing at a time when the vernacular novel had reached full maturity, Chang shared with the fictionists a keen eye for observation and a willingness to represent the life of the populace in great detail.

Having sustained a great fall from grace without any hope of regaining his former station, Chang wrote with very few illusions. The dissolution of the old order released him from whatever constraints he may previously have felt. He was probably the first Chinese author uninhibited enough to portray his uncles and cousins in a realistic and unflattering light. Chang was even more candid than his peers because he reminisced and wrote almost like a penitent, a self-conscious sinner trying to make amends for his past transgressions through the act of writing.[8] In the autobiographical preface to the collection of essays entitled *T'ao-an meng-i* he lists the contrasts between his former extravagances and present destitution. He goes on to say: "My crimes are seen in the retributions that have been visited on me. . . . How do I bear the thought? I decide to write down things of the past whenever I recall them, and then I bring them before the Buddha and repent them one by one"

(*TAMI* 1). The combination of this confessional mood and an illusionless view of the social realities of late Ming permitted him to write unabashedly about his participation in activities seldom reported by other writers.

Chang's travel account bears no date of composition. It is included in a collection of essays entitled *Lang-hsuan wen-chi*, which contains some pieces written during his old age. Nor is anything said about the year of his ascent. But he provides us with a clue near the end when he states that after the trip he returned to Yen (*LHWC* 43). We know from his biography (*ECC* 1:53) that when his father served as secretary to the eleventh Prince of Lu 魯 in Yen-chou, Shantung, during the years 1627–31, Chang Tai visited him there several times. Therefore it is likely that the ascent of T'ai Shan was made during one of his visits to his father. A highly inquisitive and imaginative man, carefree and idle in his youth but given to all sensual and literary pleasures, he would not have passed up an opportunity—T'ai Shan was only a short detour from the route between his home town and Yen-chou—that few literati would have allowed to slip through their fingers. Furthermore, there is reason to assume that his pilgrimage was made no later than 1629, because in that year, according to the report written by another visitor in the middle 1640s, pilgrimage to T'ai Shan began a precipitous decline (*HYL* 25); Chang noted no such decline.

Let us, then, assume that he took the trip in 1628. That means he went when he was thirty-one, a man without an official position or degree and not yet widely known for his literary talents. His situation set him apart from nearly all other visitors who wrote about their trips. They all seem to have availed themselves of the facilities and services provided by local officials: there is no record that any of them made private travel arrangements. Wang Shih-chen was only one year older than Chang when he made his first ascent, but he had already established his fame both as a man of letters and as a government official. Furthermore, his position gave him jurisdiction over neighboring counties, and he went to the mountain as the guest of the inspecting censor. Chang could not make a similar claim in his own right, nor was his father, unlike the commander-in-chief Wang Yü before the calamity of 1549, sufficiently prominent to ensure that local officials would defer to an obscure person junior in age. Under the circumstances he probably had no alternative to taking what must have been, as we shall see, the equivalent of a twentieth-century package tour.

PILGRIMAGE AND TOURISM

Chang Tai, in common with most literati visitors to T'ai Shan, began the trip from T'ai-an, the capital city of the subprefecture (*chou*) in which Mount T'ai lies. But his account differs from those of others in that it states clearly that, shortly after he left the city, he turned himself over to the agents of what can only be called an organized pilgrimage-tourism business, which saw to all his needs. Occasionally he tried to have his own way, but his account unmistakably reveals that his trip was essentially no different from a package tour. Other men of letters hardly recognized in writing the existence of this mercenary aspect of pilgrimage, let alone admitted their own participation in it, if it ever occurred.[9]

But we are looking at the condition and procedure of his trip from a modern point of view, which would not have made sense to a seventeenth-century member of the Chinese literati. He of course had his own terminology, and his presentation of the facts leaves the modern reader with large areas of opacity and numerous lacunae. The first term that is both revealing and puzzling is *ya-chia* 牙家. A *ya-chia* is at once a guide, a tour director, and a representative of what must have been a tour company. Yet there is no mention of anything equivalent to what we would call a company, a corporation, or a partnership. The only other entity with which Chang and other participants had business dealings was the *tien* 店 or *k'e-tien* 客店, which I shall translate variously as "inn" or "guide company." The two things are of course different, but Chang did not seem to care. Nor did he provide any clue to the question a modern reader is most likely to ask: Are the guides owners or employees of the inn? But let Chang speak in his own words.

> Guides approach the travelers when they are only a few *li* away from the subprefectural city. They lead the horses to the gate of the inn (*tien*). In front of the gate are a dozen stables. There are also a dozen apartments to house the prostitutes and an equal number of accommodations for the actors. I used to think that these matters were run by various people in the subprefecture; I did not know that they are managed by a guide company (*tien*). The company sets a fixed rate for renting rooms, hiring sedan chairs, and paying mountain fees (*shan-shui* 山稅). Visitors (*k'e* 客) are charged on the basis of three classes: upper, middle, and lower (*shang, chung, hsia* 上中下).[10] All the visitors are met upon their arrival, entertained when they descend from the summit, and escorted when they leave. Each day there are several thousand visitors, who will occupy hundreds of rooms and consume hundreds of vegetarian and ordinary banquets; they are entertained by hundreds of actors, singers, and musicians, and there are hundreds of attendants at their beck and call. The guides are from about a dozen families. On an average day eight thousand to nine thousand visitors come, while the number can reach twenty thousand on the first day of spring. The entrance fee is collected at twelve *fen* 分 per person, so the annual collection amounts to two hundred thousand to three hundred thousand taels. The magnitude of Mount T'ai, alas, can be measured by the number of the guides or the amount of the fees! (*LHWC* 37)

A short entry on T'ai-an inns in *T'ao-an meng-i* also describes the package tour; it repeats some of the information contained in the travel account.

When it comes to T'ai-an subprefecture, nobody dares to treat the inns there as ordinary inns. On my pilgrimage to Mount T'ai (*yü chin-hsiang T'ai-shan* 余進香泰山) I stopped at an inn. When I was still more than a *li* from the inn I saw twenty-odd stables for horses and donkeys. A little closer to the inn, I saw twenty-odd houses for the actors. Still closer, there were buildings with tightly closed doors and secluded apartments, where dwelt courtesans with bewitching charms. I had thought that such matters were taken care of by various groups in the subprefecture. Little did I know that one inn could handle them all.

Inn guests first went to an office to register. The standard charge was thirty-eight *fen* per person, plus eighteen *fen* for the mountain tax. There were three classes of pensions. The cheapest would provide only vegetarian meals for the first night and the next morning. On the day of the ascent everyone would be rewarded with a vegetarian lunch—simple wine, fruits, nuts, and seeds—and it was called "postsummit reception" (*chieh-ting* 接頂). There were formal banquets that night at the inn, during which the guides congratulated the inn guests.

The word "congratulate" (*ho* 賀) was used because now that they had burned the incense (*shao-hsiang* 燒香), the customers were going to get what they had come for: an office, a son, or wealth. There were also three classes of congratulations. For the first class, the customer had a table to himself. There would be candies, cakes, five kinds of fruits, ten kinds of meat, nuts and seeds, and theatrical entertainment. The second class would provide the same, except that the table would be shared by two. The third class meant that three or four would have to share a table, and the entertainment would be singing to the accompaniment of a lute rather than theatricals.

In all the inn had to maintain, every day without exception, twenty-odd theatrical troupes, countless numbers of singers, twenty-odd kitchens, and somewhere between one hundred and two hundred waiters and bellhops, so that as soon as the inn guests came down from the summit they could eat meat, drink wine, and frolic with prostitutes as they pleased. They came and went every day, but new arrivals never found their rooms unready; vegetarian and nonvegetarian meals never got mixed up, nor did the employees ever fail to anticipate every need or respond to every wish of the guests. It is simply unfathomable how the inn managed to do everything right. It is even more surprising that in the T'ai-an subprefecture there should have been five or six establishments comparable to our inn. (*TAMI* 59–60)

That Chang Tai went to T'ai Shan as a pilgrim (*hsiang-k'e*) was obvious: he went through all the motions that were included in what we might call a pilgrimage-tour package. It was so obvious that in the travel account he never feels the need to refer to himself as such. But in the piece quoted above he states explicitly his purpose—*chin-hsiang*—for going to T'ai Shan. Why he went on a pilgrimage and why he did so under what must have been a rather unusual arrangement for a member of the scholar-official class he never explains. What emerges from the two passages is his astonishment at and faint distaste for the whole enterprise. Although he merely notes without comment his fellow travelers' easy transition from the nominally sacred to the blatantly profane, the irony in the juxtaposition may have been intentional.

THE TEMPLE OF EAST MARCHMOUNT

The Tung-yueh Temple 東嶽廟 (also known as the T'ien-ch'i Temple), situated at the foot of the mountains, was a large rectangular compound surrounded by walls. The God of East Marchmount, whose image sat in the main hall, was always worshiped by sovereigns, and ceremonies conducted before the god were a part of asserting the legitimacy of a new dynasty or consolidating imperial power. This god had been identified in ancient times with the Lord of T'ai Shan (*T'ai-shan fu-chün* 泰山府君) and later with the King of T'ai Shan (*T'ai-shan wang* 泰山王), who in popular belief determined the life span of every mortal and ruled over the netherworld. The walls in the temple were illustrated with scenes of torture inflicted on the souls of sinners. During the course of the Ming the god of death was gradually eclipsed by the goddess of life.[11] Government officials still appealed to the King of T'ai Shan, as Wang Shih-chen, whose travel account we have quoted before, did in 1559 on behalf of his hapless father; the masses, as we shall see, flocked to Yuan-chün, the goddess who could cure all diseases as well as infertility. In 1324 the Tung-yueh Temple's receipts from the offerings of the worshipers were large enough to cause the emperor to intervene personally in the disposition of the income (Sawada 303). But after that date there is no more record of donations in Sawada's detailed account of financial aspects of T'ai Shan pilgrimage. At one time there had been two other temples dedicated to Tung-yueh, one half way to the top of the mountain and the other near the summit. Wang Shih-chen noted the main one at the bottom without elaboration. As for the middle temple, nothing remained except the foundation. He found the top one in such a poor condition that "the burning of incense and candles was not possible" (*TSC* 5:13B). By the late seventeenth century even the main temple seems to have completely lost its religious significance with ordinary pilgrims. On the occasion of a renovation of the temple the man of letters Chu I-tsun 朱彝尊 (1629–1709) wrote that the temple was seldom used. The imperial court would send an emissary to present a message when there was an important state event. "Besides those occasions, the temple was cleaned and swept only twice a year when the local officials came for spring and autumn sacrifices. This was why, alas, the temple had long been in a state of disrepair" (*TSC* 10:6).[12]

Chang Tai's account says nothing at all about the awesome aspects of Tung-yueh Temple, its functions as a divine judicature, or its location, at least in imaginative literature, as the gate of Hell. Chang is interested only in the dimensions of the compound and that its spacious ground had been yielded to a far from pious crowd.

There was a motley collection of stalls and stands, selling their wares mainly to women and children. The rest of the ground was largely taken up by cock-fighters, football players, equestrians, and storytellers. There were also some ten wrestling platforms and theatrical stages, each attracting hundreds of spectators who clustered like bees or ants. As these performing groups were far apart, they did not interfere with each other no matter how loud was the racket each produced by singing as well as by the beating of drums and gongs. (*LHWC* 37)

TRAVELOGUE

Since Chang Tai's is the only detailed premodern account of a pilgrimage to T'ai Shan I have seen, I shall quote generously from it.

At the fifth drum, water was still dripping from the eaves. I wanted to tarry a bit, but the guide urged me to rise and prepare myself for the ascent. I found the mountain sedan chair waiting at the door. The carrying poles were curved, and the compartment differed from that of an ordinary sedan chair in that it had a square, rather than rectangular, shape. The carriers tied the poles to their shoulders with leather strips. When they climbed up the steps the sedan chair moved sideways like a crab.

We left the lodging before dawn, yet huge crowds of pilgrims (*chin-hsiang jen* 進香人) were already going up or down. One of them would chant "A-mi-t'o-fo" [Amitābha], and he would be echoed by a hundred voices. The shouts were punctuated by the din of copper gongs. Flares from torches and lamps made an unbroken line for forty *li*, as if the Milky Way had come down in a winding flow. One was reminded of Emperor Yang-ti of the Sui, who released bushels of fireflies in the mountains and valleys. For a long time my eyes were dazzled by the burning mountains and shining valleys.

As soon as I mounted the sedan chair my guide took out strings of tin pennies and hung them on the carrying poles of the sedan chair. These pennies, thin as elm leaves and each of them inscribed with the characters *A-mi-t'o-fo*, were to be given to the beggars. Real pennies were worth seven *fen* per thousand, but the tin ones were worth only half as much. Going up the mountain, the pilgrims were handed the pennies by the guides; going down the mountain, the beggars returned the coins to the guides. Although this type of coin circulated only among the local beggars, their total value was no less than several hundred taels of silver. From beyond the Teng-feng Gate there were beggars everywhere along the route. Thrusting out their bamboo baskets to beg money, they did not care if they bumped into people. The higher I went the more beggars I saw, but their number decreased somewhat when I reached the Ch'ao-yang Cave. The variety of ways they begged, chanted, and made themselves up reminded me of the Hell painted by Wu Tao-tzu;[13] their grotesqueness was otherwise really inconceivable.

But the beggars were only one of two abominations; the other was the visitors' disgusting practice of inscribing on rocks as well as on the tablets they erected such trite phrases as "Venerated by ten thousand generations" or "The

redolence continuing for an eternity." The beggars exploited Mount T'ai for
money while the visitors exploited Mount T'ai for fame. The land of Mount
T'ai, once pure, was now everywhere desecrated by these two groups. (*LHWC*
38)

PI-HSIA YUAN-CHÜN

By the time of late Ming, perhaps even earlier, the palace of Pi-hsia Yuan-
chün 碧霞元君 (Goddess of Green Clouds) had become the center, and for
the vast majority of people the only goal, of pilgrimage to T'ai Shan.[14] The
receipts at the palace in terms of taxes and offerings, greater than those collected at any other religious site in the empire, were a chief source of revenue
for Shantung province.[15] An annual sum of a little more than twenty
thousand taels of silver was set aside and delivered to the national treasury in
Peking (*Ming shih* 7:2006). Before we go any further let us return to Chang
Tai's story.

> At the top of the cliff was a mud house owned by the guides. We were invited
> into the house to warm ourselves by an open fire. My hands were so frozen that
> at first I could not even stretch them. We did not leave the house for the sum-
> mit until we were thoroughly warmed. When we got out of the door we were
> surrounded by white clouds as thick as loose cotton. I could hear people from
> my group, but I often could not see them. As we groped our way, our hands
> were always ahead of our toes. After we walked in this fashion for a *li* or so we
> arrived at something like a settlement. Turning left, we climbed up to the gate
> of the Pi-hsia Palace. The right path was for the departing pilgrims. As soon as
> I entered the gate a dozen men lifted me onto their shoulders and, pushing their
> way through the crowd, brought me forward to the iron fence, from which I
> peered in and caught a glimpse of the golden visage of Yuan-chün. The fence
> was made of iron posts as large as beams, and the statue of the goddess, seen
> through the narrow spaces between the posts, did not appear to be very large.
> But this was the case with all divine images in the notable mountains such as
> P'u-t'o, Wu-tang, Ch'i-yun 齊雲, Ch'ien-men 前門, and T'ien-chu 天竺. The
> statue of Yuan-chün was not quite three feet tall, yet she attracted more wor-
> shipers than any other deity in all four great continents.
>   Ying Shao 應劭 in his *Feng shan chi* 封禪記 mentions that when Emperor Wu
> of the Han arrived at the foot of T'ai Shan all the officials greeted him on their
> knees. They placed cash by the side of the road in lieu of fruit offerings as a way
> of imploring blessings on the emperor. This shows that the practice of making
> offerings had a long history, but it was never as flourishing as it is now. Several
> hundred times a day the iron fence in the palace is opened, and baskets of
> money collected from the pilgrims are brought in and emptied on the floor.
> There are statues of three Yuan-chün, and the one on the left is responsible for
> the bestowing of male heirs. Those whose wishes have been granted repay the
> favors with silver figures of boys, the size depending on the circumstances of the
> family. The statue on the right heals ailments of the eye. Those who have

appealed to the goddess and thus regained their sight repay the favors with eyes made of silver. A gigantic gold coin is hung in front of the middle statue. Aiming at it, pilgrims throw coins or small ingots of silver over the fence. They believe that they will receive blessings if they hit the mark. Others give as offerings satin, silk, gold, pearls, precious stones, leg warmers, pearl-strewn shoes, and embroidered handkerchiefs. Consequently, gifts pile up several feet high. To guard the offerings behind the fence soldiers are stationed in the palace every night, and for this purpose a military camp has been established at the foot of the mountain. Four times a year the gifts are swept off and collected under the supervision of an officer. Even allowing for unavoidable encroachments, the annual proceeds amount to several tens of thousands of taels. Every official in Shantung, from the governor down to the petty clerks in the subprefecture, receives a share of the income. (*LHWC* 40–41)

The cult of the Yuan-chün formally began early in the eleventh century when the emperor Chen-tsung had a shrine built near the top of the mountain for a divinity by the name of T'ien-hsien yü-nü pi-hsia yuan-chün 天仙玉女碧霞元君 (Goddess of Green Clouds, the Heavenly Immortal, Jade Maiden). Ming writers traced her origins to one of several female figures in earlier lore of T'ai Shan. She was variously identified with one of several daughters of the god Tung-yüeh, one of the jade maidens (*yü-nü* 玉女) who displayed their kindness to Li Po (Kroll 248–51). The long list of stone and metal inscriptions included in the T'ai-an county gazetteer indicates that the goddess's shrine was noted by a few visitors before the Ming. But nothing was said about the purpose or frequency of the visitors. In 1190 a Jürchen princess, accompanied by her husband, made a pilgrimage to the Temple of East Marchmount. In a short inscription she stated that "next day we went to the summit and made obeisances before the Jade Immortal Shrine (*Yü-hsien tz'u* 玉仙祠)" (*TAHC* 11:35b). The noblewoman and her consort may have gone in the hope of having a son born to them, for there was a Taoist shrine dedicated to the Jade Immortal just outside the Sung capital K'ai-feng, where infertile Sung sovereigns went to pray.

The year 1497 probably marks the beginning of the rise in the Yuan-chün cult. It was the year her palace (*kung* 宮) was renovated (*TAHC* 11:41a). From then until the end of Ming her name appeared with increasing frequency. Her cult must have reached considerable proportions no later than 1516, for in that year the central government, following the advice of the eunuch overseeing the tax revenues of Shantung, began to exact its share of the receipts from the offerings at her shrine (*tz'u* 祠) (*Ming shih* 5:1977). By 1532 her efficacy as a fertility goddess was so well known that the empress dowager sent her the following petition:

Our emperor has already reigned for twelve years, yet there is still no imperial heir to ensure the substantiality of the state. All the hundred spirits and millions of subjects are eager in their wish for a change. We are dispatching a special envoy to perform the most solemn sacrifices at the foot of your altar. We respectfully pray that you, the great Goddess, may silently direct the transformations so that a crown prince shall soon be bestowed on us and our line shall prosper. This greatest possible blessing to the imperial house we entreat with utmost sincerity. (*TAHC* 10:17a.)

The prominent Confucian scholar Han Hsi-tso 韓錫胙 (1716–76) wrote an essay on the goddess. In a sweeping beginning statement he affirms the supreme position of Yuan-chün. "The highest among the divinities (*shen-chih* 神祇) in the world, from ancient times to the present, are those of the Tung-yueh. Among the divinities of the Tung-yueh none is worshiped as greatly as Pi-hsia Yuan-chün" (*TSC* 10:19a). He accepted some of the theories regarding her origins and rejected others. To me the most interesting is one of the rejected.

In recent times those who indulged in Buddhism asserted that Kuan-shih-yin 觀世音 had myriad avatars: in the south she was the Sea Goddess Heavenly Empress 海神天后 with the title Pi-hsia Yuan-chün, and in the north she was the Jade Maiden of T'ai Shan with the same title Pi-hsia Yuan-chün. The two were the same person. (*TSC* 10:19b)

The Buddhists certainly had a good point. Although Pi-hsia Yuan-chün was always worshiped in a Taoist temple and attended by Taoist priests, she shared almost all the traits of the bodhisattva Kuan-yin.[16] Indeed, the two, whatever their beginnings, underwent almost the same transformations in the imaginations of believers. One might say that popular clamor during the centuries that saw the rise of the Marian cult in Europe turned both an Indian divinity of male gender and a coquettish jade maiden of folklore into fertility goddesses. Anticipating modern mythologists, Han Hsi-tso recognized Yuan-chün as an earth-mother, although his intention was to rescue her, in an elaborate and somewhat tortuous fashion, from what he considered as superstitious mobs and restore her to a place sanctioned by Confucian rituals and justified on Confucian principles:

Yuan-chün is the Earth Goddess (*Ti-chih* 地祇). The father is stern and the mother is loving. The mother bears and suckles children, but those she has borne and suckled do not of their own accord know this. Heaven is august and Earth is intimate. Earth produces all the elements and things, but those it has produced do not of their own accord know this. . . .

Now thousands of men and women who wish for a good harvest, health, heirs, or longevity ascend lofty mountains, climbing like monkeys and following each other like ants. They prostrate themselves before Yuan-chün, but wish for things that good luck in the human world could bring. That the Goddess should grant them their wish is not a case of granting immortality through the rite of the golden seal and jade tally (*chin-ni yü-chien* 金泥玉簡), something that should not occur in the human world and that the Goddess cannot grant without defying Heaven.

If her temple is but an elaborate version of the altar to Earth and her idol is but the jeweled representation of the Earth Goddess, she is nothing other than spirituality concentrated and a source of the hundred blessings. Can we not say that she is a true divinity under Heaven (*t'ien-hsia chih cheng-shen* 天下之正神)? I respectfully present this essay to the gentle readers of future generations so that they will have a basis for choosing what to accept or believe. (*TSC* 10:20a)

THE REBELLIOUS PILGRIM

Day-trippers to Zermatt who wish to catch an unobstructed glimpse of the Matterhorn are often defeated by bad weather. So were tourists to T'ai Shan. If Chang Tai showed little credulity in his matter-of-fact tone in describing the adoration of Yuan-chün, his response to the clouds betrayed his basic orientation—not a believer hoping for a miracle but a man of letters eager for great sights:

> When we came out of the Pi-hsia Palace the clouds were so thick that we could not walk. I became very distressed when I thought that I had traveled three thousand *li* only to be denied a real look at Mount T'ai. What had I come for? I wanted to spend the night on the top, but could not find anyone to help me or even a path. People in my group, cold and hungry, absolutely refused to go any further. Reluctantly I let the carriers guide me to the sedan chair and began the descent. (*LHWC* 41)

Chang Tai's disappointment is reminiscent of Wang Shih-chen's on his first trip. But it was much easier for Wang to get over his regret because with all his advantages he could easily, as he did five months later, return for another attempt. Chang had to make the most of what for him must have been a rare opportunity. Whether it was out of desperation or simply to assert his independence, his ensuing behavior set him apart from his fellow pilgrims:

> When I came out of the Red Gate the guide poured wine on my feet and offered me nuts and seeds. This was the so-called postsummit reception 接頂. At night theatricals were provided to entertain us at dinner, and wine was poured to congratulate all the pilgrims who had gone up to the summit during the day. The guide said to us: "Let me offer my congratulations to you in advance, because when you return home those of you who seek fame will gain fame, those who seek wealth will gain wealth, and those who seek heirs will gain heirs." Cheerlessly I went through the motions. Retiring early, I planned to make another ascent next morning. In the middle of the night I got up. I was secretly pleased when I found the sky clear, the air still, and stars as large as wine cups hanging just beyond the eaves.
>
> At the crack of dawn I ordered the old servant to seek a sedan chair. The guide, murmuring his astonishment, said to me: "One is not supposed to make another pilgrimage to the top right after the first one. Bad things will happen to the offender." While feigning compliance I walked out. I hurried to the I-t'ien (First Heavenly) Gate by a side path and only there did I succeed in finding a

mountain sedan chair. Native children and women who remembered having
seen my face the day before pointed at me and broke out in laughter. They
chased after my chair carriers and never stopped asking: "This is the man who
made it to the top yesterday. Why is it that he is here again?" They were
puzzled because while there were pilgrims who spent a night at the top, none
had ever gone up two days in a row. It was a convention that had persisted for a
thousand years, but I finally broke it. (*LHWC* 41)

His boldness in violating a time-honored taboo was rewarded with a clear
view of all the peaks and the surrounding land below. Now apparently free
from his guides and unencumbered by his group, he alternated between
catching distant sights and scrutinizing inscriptions on stone tablets and
cliffs, the sort of pursuits dear to literati in all ages but least attractive to
pilgrims on package tours. Since most of the sites had been shrouded by
dense mist and cloud the day before, he wanted to revisit them, but he was
soon satiated with sightseeing. One remark of his is worth noting: "As I did
not have my mountain ticket (*shan-fu* 山符), I did not make another visit to
Yuan-chün" (*LHWC* 42). Presumably the temple of Yuan-chün was the only
place where ticket collectors were stationed, and Chang's ticket either had
been collected on his first visit or was always in the possession of his guide.

Chang did not linger at any particular site. The last thing he says about
his trip itself is revealing: "When I got down to the [Tung-] Yueh Palace I
sought the stelae there so I could read the inscriptions. My eyes were not
swift nor the day long enough" (*LHWC* 43).[17] If he had begun the ascent as a
member of a pilgrimage, he came down the mountain very much his old self.

THE CULTURAL GAP

There is no indication that on his trip Chang ever struck up a conversation or
made acquaintance with any of his fellow pilgrims. Presumably he could not
escape their company as the group was ushered from one point of interest to
another, nor could he avoid sharing their revelries at the banquet even if
he had a table to himself. Yet in his account he does not mention any individuals or describe the group. His reticence in this regard contrasts sharply
with his usual gregarious behavior revealed in the two collections of essays.
They contain a wealth of miniatures of individuals from all walks of life;
even the humbler souls and total strangers—prostitutes, actors, servants,
acrobats—redeem themselves with an uncommon trait or a rare charm. Can
we conclude, then, that other participants in Chang's package tour had nothing in his eye to recommend them? Or were they summarily dismissed, by
Chang as well as by other literati travelers, because they belonged to a class
socially and culturally, if not always financially, beneath Chang's peers?

These questions cannot be answered with any certainty. We can detect,
however, from Chang Tai's other writings a distaste for other groups of pil-

grims that may throw some light on his attitude toward his fellow travelers to
T'ai Shan. In 1638 he took a pilgrimage to P'u-t'o and wrote an account of it
(*LHWC* 44–53). Again he does not mention any exchange between himself
and other pilgrims. In fact, he criticizes some of them for their excessive
fervor, which resulted in self-mutilations (see Yü, chapter 5 of this volume,
for further discussion). Since P'u-t'o was on an island at some distance from
the nearest shore, pilgrims had to travel by boat. Chang describes in vivid
language the discomfort he suffered from living in close quarters and sharing
unsanitary facilities with hundreds of pious men and women (*LHWC* 51–52;
Yü, chapter 5 of this volume). He wonders how the monks, who as managers
and attendants on the pilgrimage boats (*hsiang-ch'uan* 香船) had to endure
one crossing after another, "put up with all kinds of ugly scenes and all sorts
of vile odors" (*LHWC* 52). To forewarn the gentle readers so they would not
have to repeat his hellish experience, Chang insists that they hitch a ride in
naval ships, locally known as "tiger frigates" (*hsiao-ch'uan* 唬船), which, in an
arrangement probably not unlike what is found in modern freighters, provided accommodations for a small number of passengers in a compartment
designated as "cabin for officials" (*kuan-ts'ang* 官艙). The gap between the
"unwashed, halitotic, defecating, urinating" (ibid.) crowd of pilgrims and
our genteel man of letters could hardly be greater.[18]

It could be argued that pilgrimage to P'u-t'o was a special case. An out-of-
the-way place and very difficult to reach, P'u-t'o was only for true believers,
its great popularity notwithstanding. That it did not attract many visitors
from among the literati is repeatedly asserted in Chang Tai's account. Unlike T'ai Shan, there were no inscribed stelae to gratify our antiquarian-
bibliophile, nor was the local gazetteer adorned with poetry and prose by
celebrated hands (*LHWC* 51). Chang confesses that when he traveled he
always pressed his friends to join him, but few responded when P'u-t'o was
mentioned (52). His distaste for the pilgrims could perhaps be attributed to
the difficult circumstances under which he took his trip.

Harder to explain is another unsympathetic depiction of pilgrims, unsympathetic in a different way. It is contained in an essay on pilgrims' markets
(*hsiang-shih* 香市) that sprang up in Hangchow around the West Lake every
year during the middle of the second month. Two huge waves of pilgrims,
going to and coming back from P'u-t'o and T'ien-chu respectively, intersected each other at Hangchow, which consequently became a vast trading post until the last invader left on the fifth day of the fifth month, the
Tuan-wu festival.[19] What tried Chang Tai's patience was the rude and massive invasion of the idyllic lake when spring was at its best. He was especially
unhappy about the transformation of the permanent market along the two
verandas extending from the Chao-ch'ing 昭慶 Temple, apparently during
happier times a preserve for the elite of Hangchow, to whom Chang owed
allegiance by geography, class, and taste:

The scene was completely altered with the arrival of the motley crowds of pilgrims. The quiet elegance of the gentle people was no match for the gaudy showiness of the rustic folk; the subtle scent of orchids was no match for their pungent herbs; the string and wind instruments were no match for their loud drums and pipes; antique bronzes and fine porcelain were no match for their mud statues and bamboo toys; Sung and Yuan masterworks were no match for their pictures of the Buddha and lake scenes. Millions of men and women, old and young, for four months swarmed the temple daily from all directions. Skittish and furtive, they darted to and fro; you could not push your way through them, nor could you hold back their mad rush. (*TAMI* 91–92)

Chang goes on to report that the Chao-ch'ing Temple was destroyed by fire in 1640 and that two years later the flow of pilgrims was cut off by the Manchu raids into Shantung. The markets then disappeared. From this detail we know that the essay was written after he had taken his two pilgrimages. Can we then say that the compiling of the detailed catalogue of differences between the Hangchow elite and the pilgrims—most participants of the P'u-t'o group originated in Shantung—was somewhat colored by his memories of the two trips?

The list of contrasts clearly shows, at least in Chang's eyes, that there was an unbridgeable chasm between the two groups. The Hangchow elite in general and Chang in particular may have been more precious than most members of Ming literati, and the pilgrims who poured into Hangchow may have been more obstreperous than others. Nevertheless, all evidence points to a real gap between literati travelers and ordinary pilgrims. In fact, additional support for this suggestion may be found in the vernacular novel discussed by Dudbridge in the preceding chapter. The T'ai Shan pilgrims in the *Hsing-shih yin-yuan chuan* are admittedly fictional characters, and the author may have exaggerated their negative traits for comical effect. But nothing about them would have made them acceptable to the literati, even if we discount their sordidness and gaucheries as caricatures.

Although Chang Tai's account and the T'ai Shan episode in the novel were written in different media and meant for different readers, each confirms the essential realism of the other as far as the externals of the pilgrimage are concerned. The two groups of pilgrims were separated in time by some half a century, but they seem to have taken the same type of package tour. There is a great deal of continuity and similarity in the tightly scheduled itinerary of two nights and one day, the type of accommodations, the means of transportation, and other details such as the post-summit reception and the theatricals at the inn.[20] It is an uncanny coincidence that Chang Tai and the heroine of the novel each succeeded in catching a glimpse of the statue of the goddess—a highlight of the pilgrimage coveted by all but gained by so few—from the same vantage point—the shoulders of others. Otherwise the wellborn bibliophile and the illiterate shrew had almost nothing else in common.

We have speculated earlier why Chang Tai took the package tour, rubbing shoulders with people he could not have found congenial. There was, perhaps, another reason for him to travel anonymously. A share of the receipts of the temple offerings that Chang described with such loving detail went annually to the administrative offices of the three imperial princes who enjoyed hereditary fiefs in Shantung (*TS* 13:5a). The princes, although nominally enfeoffed, apparently had few other large sources of revenue. Could it be that Chang Tai was combining tourism with business, a mission on behalf of his father to make a firsthand inspection of the procedure on which the welfare of the Prince of Lu as well as the members of the fief bureaucracy so heavily depended? The need for more revenue might have been especially pressing in view of the prince's extravagances Chang so graphically described (*TAMI* 18–19). Even if he did not undertake such a mission, the consciousness of the link between the pilgrims' generous credulity and his father's emolument—an irony that would not escape a man like Chang even though, or especially because, the Changs were far from impecunious—must have made him a keen observer of things unnoticed by other literati travelers.

NOTES

1. See Yü, chapter 5 of this volume, for the history of P'u-t'o's being included as one of the three or four great Buddhist "mountains." Throughout the *Platform Sutra* the place made sacred by its association with the Sixth Patriarch is referred to as Mount Ts'ao-ch'i (Ts'ao-ch'i Shan; see Faure, chapter 4 of this volume).

2. The figures, culled from *Information China*, represent the elevations of the main peaks. For "marchmount" see Kroll 224, n. 8. I prefer this term to "sacred mountain" or "peak." There are many sacred mountains in China but only five *yueh*. "Peak" won't do either, because each *yueh* is identified with a *shan*, which in turn consists of a cluster of peaks. The situation is complicated enough to justify a neologism.

3. See Wu 3–14 for a history of first-person narratives in China.

4. In light of this severe constraint Chang Shang-ying's record of his miraculous visions during a mountain pilgrimage, discussed and translated by Gimello in chapter 3 of this volume, is unprecedented. Another of Chang's innovations is the use of a narrative style strongly reminiscent of typical Chinese translations of Buddhist texts rather than the standard prose that by his time had been fully established by the T'ang and Sung masters. Given Chang's membership in the literati and his successful official career, his innovations are most unusual. He has had, however, no imitators, not even in late Ming when departure from conventions was relatively common. It is also remarkable that his essay survived in a Buddhist collection and not in any secular anthologies and that his miraculous visions do not seem to have provoked any comments or reactions among Confucian literati.

5. Chinese travel literature did not receive sustained critical attention until re-

cently. Two new studies on this important and vast topic, which I read too late to
make use of in the present chapter, are James M. Hargett, *On the Road in Twelfth-
Century China: The Travel Diaries of Fan Chenda (1126–1193)* (Stuttgart: Franz Steiner
Verlag, 1989) and Richard E. Strassberg, *Inscribed Landscapes: Travel Writing from Imperial China* (Berkeley: University of California Press, forthcoming). It must be added
that Chinese autobiography after 1560 occasionally benefited from having travel literature as a narrative model: thus autobiography could break away from the rigid
format of biography. Teng Huo-ch'ü 鄧豁渠 (1498–1570?) and Kao P'an-lung
高攀龍 (1562–1626) were the most notable among the autobiographers who tell their
life stories more or less as travel accounts (Wu 95–116 and 131–41). They visited
many sites associated with sages and worthies. Each reports his quest for the absolute
truth as a double journey: strenuous upward locomotion accompanying spiritual
progress. The hazardous ascent brought each to a salient point, where a sudden
illumination struck the seeker. Their journeys would have been perfect pilgrimages if
only they had admitted an intent or indicated a specific site. Another autobiographer,
Mao Ch'i-ling 毛奇齡 (1623–1716), made two attempts at scaling the heights of Sung
Shan, the Central Marchmount. During his second, and successful, ascent, he met a
mysterious stranger from whom he received the secret message of true Confucianism,
which transformed his life (Wu 173–86). All three lives as well as a few others discussed in my book can be read figuratively as pilgrimages, but they do not have a proper
place in a volume where pilgrimage is studied primarily as *institution*, not as *metaphor*.

6. Cf. Cahill, chapter 6 of this volume. It seems that the Huang Shan paintings he
discusses share with Chinese travel literature a reluctance in expressing religious
sentiments.

7. The Yü and Lagerwey chapters in this volume (5 and 7) also show many examples of officials stationed near famous sites using the opportunity to make a visit.

8. For a history of what I call *penitential literature*, see Wu 207–34. The genre cul-
minated about the time that Chang put together his reminiscences.

9. Organized pilgrimage groups are discussed in the Lagerwey and Naquin chapters (7 and 8). The fictionalized package tour to T'ai Shan in Dudbridge (chap. 1) is
remarkably similar to Chang Tai's.

10. Here I translate the term *k'e* as "visitor" because the emphasis seems to be on
mundane matters. Later, when the full term *hsiang-k'e* 香客 appears, I shall translate it
as "pilgrim."

11. See Naquin (chap. 8 of this volume) for a contrast between Tung-yueh and
Yuan-chün.

12. The essay is undated. As it is known that Chu served as secretary to the
governor of Shantung from 1668 to 1670, the renovation probably took place in that
period.

13. An eighth-century painter.

14. For details of the cult of Yuan-chün see Naquin, chapter 8 of this volume.
Temples for Yuan-chün and for the God of Tung-yueh, who was believed to be her
father, were established in many places. For the proliferation of the cult of the latter
see Eberhard 55–59.

15. See Sawada 1982 for a detailed history. As Lagerwey notes in chapter 7 of this
volume, mountain taxes were also collected at Wu-tang Shan.

16. See Yü and Naquin chapters (5 and 8) of this volume for further details of the cult.

17. Earlier Chang has expressed his annoyance at the inscriptions that lined the way to the summit, because to him they served no purpose other than advertising the inscribers. Conversely, the literati often valued the inscriptions on temple stelae, usually written by members of the official-scholar class, for their historical and literary worth. To a modern social historian, however, the former writings might be more interesting. See Lagerwey, chapter 7 of this volume, for an astute use of the sort of things Chang would have scorned.

18. Chang Tai's display of olfactory sensitivity could be read as a deliberate device to show the contrast between the name of the boat (*hsiang-ch'uan*, literally, "fragrant boat") and the reality of the conditions on it. Similarly, given the near omnipresence of the character *hsiang* (meaning both fragrant and incense) in the denotations of various aspects of a pilgrimage, we cannot overlook the possibly intentional irony on the part of the anonymous novelist of *Hsing-shih yin-yuan chuan* (discussed by Dudbridge in chapter 1 of this volume) in introducing seemingly gratuitous scatological episodes into the T'ai Shan pilgrimage.

19. Both sites were dedicated to Kuan-yin. Chang's description of the markets, especially their variety of trinkets and wares, hints that some pilgrims brought along goods from their native places and sold them in Hangchow. Markets and fairs associated with specific temples, known as *miao-hui* 廟會, existed in other parts of China. This aspect of Chinese pilgrim economy is worth further investigation. Cf. Turner 36–37.

20. I suspect that those who took the package tours represented only a portion of the mass of pilgrims, many of whom were probably too poor to pay for the inns or sedan chairs. This division, however, is not mentioned in any of the premodern accounts of the T'ai Shan pilgrimage I have seen. Naquin in chapter 8 of this volume speculates that the organized pilgrims were about 20 percent of the total.

BIBLIOGRAPHY

Sources Cited by Abbreviation

ECC   *Eminent Chinese of the Ch'ing Period*, edited by Arthur W. Hummel. 2 vols. Washington, D.C.: U.S. Government Printing Office, 1943–44.

HYL   Ch'en Hung-hsu 陳宏緒. *Han-yeh lu* 寒夜錄. Ts'ung-shu Chi-ch'eng ed.

LHWC   Chang Tai 張岱. *Lang-hsuan wen-chi* 瑯嬛文集. Shanghai: Shanghai tsa-chih kung-ssu, 1935.

TAHC   *T'ai-an hsien-chih* 泰安縣志.1828.

TAMI   Chang Tai. *T'ao-an meng-i* 陶庵夢憶. Taipei: K'ai-ming shu-chü, 1972.

TS   Cha Chih-lung 查志隆. *Tai-shih* 岱史. In *Tao-tsang* 道藏, vols. 1092–96.

TSC   *T'ai-shan chih* 泰山志. 1802.

Other Sources

Eberhard, Wolfram. 1967. *Guilt and Sin in Traditional China*. Berkeley: University of California Press.

Information China. 1989. Oxford: Pergamon.

Kroll, Paul W. 1983. "Verses from on High: The Ascent of T'ai Shan." *T'oung Pao* 69, 4–5:223–60.

Ming shih 明史. Peking: Chung-hua shu-chü, 1974.

Sawada Mizuho 澤田瑞穗. 1982. "Taizan kōzei kō" 泰山香稅考. In Sawada, *Chūgoku no minkan shinkō* 中國民間信仰. Tokyo: Kōsakusha.

Turner, Victor, and Edith Turner. 1978. *Image and Pilgrimage in Christian Culture: Anthropological Perspectives*. New York: Columbia University Press.

Wu, Pei-yi. 1990. *The Confucian's Progress: Autobiographical Writings in Traditional China*. Princeton: Princeton University Press.

THREE

Chang Shang-ying on Wu-t'ai Shan

Robert M. Gimello

The effects these visions produce in the soul are: quietude, illumination, gladness resembling that of glory, delight, purity, love, humility, and an elevation and inclination toward God.
SAINT JOHN OF THE CROSS, *THE ASCENT OF MOUNT CARMEL*, 2:24,6

Pilgrimages and their sacred destinations would seem to belong to the religion of Everyman. Among the many manifestations of the numinous, they seem most characteristic of an anonymous and largely collective sort of religious experience, as distinct from the particularistic religiosity of the self-conscious individual. As Alphonse Dupront has noted, contrasting pilgrimage with the often more private and personal encounter with a sacred image, "Le dialogue avec l'image peut-être le plus souvent individuel et furtif. L'acte pèlerin n'en pas moins, qu'il soit de personne isolée ou de group, fait collectif. La société créatrice du pèlerinage est en effet masse" (Dupront 1974, 201). Thus, scholars who study such things nowadays tend to employ methods and theories best suited to study of collectivities and suprapersonal patterns of meaning—societies, polities, classes, strata, symbols, structures, *mentalités*, *textes* (outside of which, some say, there is naught), and so forth. Nor is it an unhappy coincidence for those scholars that such theories and methods are now available in abundant, not to mention privileged, supply.

Occasionally, however, history allows us to see these religious collectivities and objectivities in refraction—to view them, if not subjectively then at least concretely and prismatically in, say, the particular writings of particular persons living in particular circumstances. To be sure, it is no longer likely that a modern scholar will think of such writings as providing direct or unmediated access to the minds, the subjective consciousnesses, of their authors. Nor do many these days expect either to gain through them some direct purchase on the ages and cultures in which those authors lived or to build upon them general theories of human religious behavior. Nevertheless, such personal writings do allow the stimulation of contemplating large-scale religious phenomena *sub specie temporis*, in which mode they appear to have a magnified vividness. Such idiographic study, in turn, can be a useful check

upon the excessive theoretical ambition that sometimes bedevils the social-
scientific study of religion. In any case, students of pilgrimage and sacred
places who choose China as their field of labor—who choose, that is, a place
where such things as pilgrimage abound but where they have been little
studied—might do well to postpone the nomothetic enterprise, the task of
spinning general theories, so that we may linger a while among the *realia*
of certain religious phenomena as they have been thoughtfully related and
self-consciously interpreted by certain individuals who actually experienced
them. Autobiography and memoir, even though they too are particular
genres with their own rhetoric and their own distinctive tropes and so are
never perfect mirrors of historical reality, can nevertheless be useful supplements to other kinds of scholarly sources.

Upon this hypothesis I would draw attention to a text the core of which
was written in 1088 by the Sung statesman, literatus, Taoist scholar, and lay
Buddhist Chang Shang-ying (1043–1122). This man, a leading intellectual
of his day by any reasonable definition of the term and a consequential
political figure as well, was also a famous and devout pilgrim. In this latter
capacity he is especially noted as a visitor to one of China's premier pilgrimage sites, Wu-t'ai Shan 五台山, otherwise known as Ch'ing-liang Shan
清凉山, in northern Shansi. Now, such a combination of interests and
achievements may seem curious. The modern mind is often puzzled to find
persons and times in which the conspicuous worldly accomplishment and
privilege of the elite, together with the sophisticated critical reflection of the
"reflective few," are combined with dramatic forms of piety of the sort we
more often associate with "the masses" and the "unreflective many."[1] Chang
Shang-ying, however, would appear to have felt no conflict at all among such
diverse values and undertakings. He found it possible to be both pilgrim and
scholar, both visionary and bureaucrat, both Ch'an Buddhist and man of
letters. Thus may he be made to join the literati pilgrims whom Chün-fang
Yü discusses in her contribution to this volume (chapter 5) to remind us—
and we still seem to need reminding—that the modern habit of assuming
"popular religion" and "elite religion" to be mutually antithetical may not
always serve us well in the study of traditional societies. Pilgrimage and the
pursuits of the intellectual's and the statesman's life were all of a piece for
Chang, as they seem to have been for many others of his day. That this
should have been so is especially interesting given that he lived—and was
acutely aware that he lived—at a time in Chinese history when the Chinese
cultural world was "shrinking," an age well described by one modern
scholar as "turning away from pluralism in all its forms," as "suppressing
religious ideals," and as tending toward a "rigid" humanism (Bauer 1976,
205–39).

Chang's record of his miraculous pilgrimage to Wu-t'ai Shan thus offers
the opportunity to reflect on several intriguing questions, for example: Why

might a Chinese intellectual and man of letters become a Buddhist pilgrim? Why in particular might he do so in a time and a place said to be decreasingly hospitable to religious enthusiasms of traditional Buddhist kinds? How might he find meaning in the ardors and adventures of pilgrimage? Why might he then go on to write about such journeys for an audience consisting—at least in part, one must assume—of other members of the intellectual elite? What kind of appeal might pilgrimage have had for a layman whose strongest religious affinities lay with Ch'an, and how might he overcome the seeming conflicts between the apparently credulous Buddhism of pilgrimage and the seemingly skeptical, *entzauberte* Buddhism of Ch'an? These questions are interesting in themselves, but they may also serve as species of an even more interesting generic question, a question with which this whole volume is concerned, namely, how and why did religion flourish in the "China molded by Confucius," the China that a Voltaire could admire for the presumed rationalism and irreligion of its mandarin-*philosophes*? Chang's *Hsu Ch'ing-liang chuan* 續清凉傳 (A further record of Ch'ing-liang) may, therefore, well merit retrieval from the relative obscurity in which it has languished for centuries. Nor is such retrieval a dull or odious task, for the work turns out, despite its difficulties, to be quite a "good read"!

CONCERNING CHANG SHANG-YING

Chang Shang-ying 張商英 (*tzu:* T'ien-chueh 天覺) is not well known to modern scholarship, but not because of his lack of significance or our lack of biographical sources. He was a major personage in the religious, cultural, and political history of the Northern Sung, and both the secular and the Buddhist historiographical traditions preserve ample information about his private life and his official career.[2] He was born in 1043 into a prominent literati family that claimed descent from a high-ranking official who, seven generations earlier, had served the T'ang emperor Hsi-tsung (r. 873–88) and had established his family in Szechwan after accompanying the emperor there on his flight in 880 from Huang Ch'ao's rebellious forces.[3] Chang gained early access to capital and court by earning his *chin-shih* degree in 1065, when he was twenty-two years old. During the reign of Emperor Shen-tsung (1067–85), while serving in a minor post in his home province of Szechwan and there distinguishing himself in military expeditions against certain barbarian tribes, he attracted the notice and the patronage of Chang Tun (1035–1105), one of Wang An-shih's (1021–86) more prominent protégés who was then overseeing the Szechwan pacification campaigns.[4] Chang Tun introduced Chang Shang-ying to Wang An-shih who, in respect of such sponsorship, gave the young scholar his first metropolitan post, that of honorary assistant in the Rites Section of the Secretariat (*Chien-cheng chung-shu li-fang kung-shih* 檢正中書禮房公事). Thus did Chang appear, well placed on the political stage, during the early and heady days of the great reforms, the so-called new policies (*hsin-fa*). He quickly identified himself with Wang An-shih's causes, and, rising quickly through successively higher ranks of service, he came soon to be recognized as one of the inner circle of reformers. His commitment to reform, moreover, seems not to have been uncritical, fleeting, or merely opportunistic. It did not, for example, prevent him from speaking out forcefully against other members of reform administrations whenever he found their conduct in implementing the reforms to be reprehensible. Neither did Chang abandon his advocacy of reform after Wang's fall from power. Thus he would prove to be an outspoken critic of the retreat from reform that began immediately upon Emperor Che-tsung's succession to the throne in 1085. This we see especially clearly in one of the most famous of his bold pronouncements, featured prominently in his *Sung-shih* biography. Ignoring the fact that the retreat was really the work of the empress dowager Hsuan-jen and her conservative advisers, Chang went so far as to insinuate that in so precipitously reversing his father's policies the new emperor was guilty of unfilial behavior.[5] Such brave candor, demonstrated repeatedly in his conflicted career, earned Chang a lasting reputation as the very exemplar of ministerial probity, and it is for this more than for any other trait that he would later be remembered and admired. Throughout the Yuan-yu period (1086–93), during which those opposed to reform held sway, Chang continued openly to criticize such respected and powerful conservatives as Ssuma Kuang, although his criticisms were always conscientious and specific, rather than opportunistic or doctrinaire. Thus did he succeed in preserving his reputation, even in the eyes of his opponents, as a principled and trustworthy reformer. It was perhaps for this reason that he was able to retain an official status during the Yuan-yu era, albeit at a much reduced rank, thereby to survive the period of the most extreme opposition to reform.

After the death of the empress dowager in 1093, when Che-tsung assumed direct control of government and recalled many members of the reform party to high office, Chang's career resumed its rise. With the accession of Hui-tsung in 1100, Chang initially aligned himself with that ruler's favorite adviser, Ts'ai Ching (1046–1126), brother of Wang An-shih's son-in-law. This association further accelerated a career that would reach its apex over the next decade. From June 1110 through September 1111 Chang served as prime minister or grand councilor (*tsai-hsiang*), that is, in the highest of all official capacities.[6] However, during these very same years, Chang found himself increasingly ill disposed to tolerate the autocratic and corrupt leadership of Ts'ai Ching, who proved to be a self-seeking and tyrannical official merely masquerading as a reformer. Nor could he abide the lavish self-indulgence of Hui-tsung's court, which he repeatedly excoriated. His relationship with Hui-tsung was further damaged when he fell afoul of some influential Taoists who had risen to power under imperial patronage and who were encouraging the sovereign in anti-Buddhist policies that Chang strenuously opposed. In consequence of all these pressures Chang was removed from high office only thirteen months after he had reached the pinnacle of the Sung bureaucracy.

This abrupt but entirely honorable reversal of fortunes seems to have marked the culmination of a gradual but fundamental change in Chang's political affiliations and loyalties. He was led finally to profess common cause with the then relatively moderate remnants of the conservative party, whom he found far more reputable and worthy of respect than those who were still pretending to support reform. In retaliation, Ts'ai Ching had Chang's name added to the infamous lapidary lists of condemned and banned "Yuan-yu traitors." Thus did Chang effectively remove himself from the political arena, remaining true to his consistent reputation for incorruptibility and choosing in effect to spend the remaining years of his life (1111–22) in virtual retirement. His last decade was spent largely in scholarly and contemplative, especially Buddhist, pursuits. He died on January 1, 1122.[7]

Even before those last years of relative repose, however, Chang had managed to combine an active political life with a course of committed study and practice of Buddhism. Adopting the Buddhist sobriquet Wu-chin Chü-shih 無盡居士 (Layman of the Infinite), he took the part of friend, lay disciple, and patron to some of the most renowned Ch'an masters of the day—most notably Yuan-wu K'o-ch'in 圓悟克勤 (1063–1135) of the Yang-ch'i 楊岐 branch of the house of Lin-chi 臨濟[8] and such luminaries of the Huang-lung 黃龍 branch as Tou-shuai Ts'ung-yueh 兜率從悅 (1044–1091) and Chan-t'ang Wen-chun 湛堂文準 (1061–1115).[9] Another, younger Huang-lung monk named Chueh-fan Hui-hung 覺範慧洪 (1070–1128) enjoyed an especially close relationship with Chang. Indeed, their lives were so closely intertwined that Hui-hung's career rose and fell in lockstep with Chang's; he was even imprisoned and exiled because of his association with the controversial layman. Hui-hung was a famous poet and literatus, as well as an eminent monk. He left a large corpus of writings in which Chang frequently appears and on which we depend for much of what we know about Chang Shang-ying the man, as distinct from Chang the official. The two men even collaborated in writing influential commentaries on two Buddhist scriptures and in composing other occasional Buddhist pieces.[10] Chang would also come to know Ta-hui Tsung-kao 大慧宗杲 (1089–1163), probably the foremost Ch'an master of the Southern Sung, and in fact it was upon Chang's urging that Ta-hui went on to study with Yuan-wu K'o-ch'in, whose leading disciple he would eventually become.[11]

The "discourse records" (*yü-lu* 語錄) and other genres of Northern Sung Ch'an literature preserve numerous conversations, both delightful and deep, between Chang and these several monks. Many of them were on subjects related to Hua-yen thought, which seems to have been one of Chang's special interests. This interest, in turn, took him on journeys to major sites associated with Hua-yen, like Wu-t'ai Shan. In the course of one of these sojourns Chang rendered a service to the Hua-yen tradition for which he is particularly renowned. While stationed in Shansi in 1088, the very year of his major tour of Wu-t'ai Shan, he visited the nearby mountain on which the mysterious T'ang layman and hermit Li T'ung-hsuan 李通玄 (635–730) was known to have lived.[12] There he came upon several previously obscure works by Li that affected him deeply, all of them explanations of the *Hua-yen ching* 華 ⌐ (Flower garland sutra). He resolved then to disseminate Li's corpus, which thereafter became extremely influential throughout East Asia. It appears, in fact, that Chang had a crucial role to play in fostering the popularity of Hua-yen thought, particularly that of Li T'ung-hsuan, in certain influential Ch'an circles of the late Northern Sung and the Southern Sung periods. His visit to Wu-t'ai, the most sacred of all Hua-yen precincts, probably had helped lead him in this direction.

Among Chang's explicitly Buddhist writings three major works proved sufficiently influential to be included in standard modern editions of the Tripiṭaka. The most important of these, no doubt, is the *Hu-fa lun* 護法論 (Essay in defense of the dharma, *T* 52:648c–67c), an eloquent rebuttal of Tao-hsueh criticisms of Buddhism.[13] Another is a subcommentary on Hui-hung's treatise on the *Lotus Sutra* (*HTC* 47:699–835). The third is the text we are now to consider, the *Hsu Ch'ing-liang chuan*. It is worth noting that not many laymen in Chinese Buddhist history have been honored by the inclusion of three of their works in the canon. There are also a number of shorter Buddhist pieces (prefaces, inscriptions, colophons, etc.) to be found elsewhere in the Tripiṭaka or in other collectanea.[14]

Buddhism, however, was not the only subject on which Chang wrote, and this fact leads us to yet another aspect of his diverse religious and intellectual background. No fewer than four writings credited to Chang may be found in the Taoist Canon (*Tao-tsang* 道藏). Two of these are shorter revisions of ritual libretti that Chang compiled at the command of Hui-tsung as part of that Taoist emperor's project to distribute a collection of standard Taoist ritual texts to temples throughout the realm (van der Loon 1984, 39; Boltz 1987, 50); they are the *Chin-lu chai san-tung tsan-yung i* 金籙齋三洞讚詠儀 (Liturgy of encomia from the three caverns for the golden register rite, *TT* 310) and the *Chin-lu chai t'ou-chien i* 金籙齋投簡儀 (Abbreviated liturgy of the golden register rite, *TT* 498). Yet another work, the *San-ts'ai ting-wei t'u* 三才定位圖 (Diagrams of the cosmic triarchy, *TT* 155) is an illustrated summary of exoteric Taoist cosmology and mystical anthropology. The fourth—and certainly, by the criterion of number of editions, the best known—is the *Su-shu* 素書 (The book of simplicity, *TT* 1178–79). This short treatment of the fundamentals of ethical self-cultivation and polity is said to have been revealed during the Han to the semilegendary Taoist patriarch Chang Liang 張梁 by the entirely legendary immortal Huang Shih-kung 黃石公; Chang Shang-ying claims only to have discovered and annotated it. Modern scholars, however, beginning with the *Ssu k'u* editors (*SKCS* 99:837b–c), have held the work to be from Chang's own brush. It has been said that these four works—all substantively and intentionally Taoist in nature and all adopted as canonical by the Taoist tradition—may actually not have been written or edited by Chang but may only have been ascribed to him later by others intent on borrowing the luster of his name. This allegation, however, has not been proven; and if they are his, then they show that Chang's acquaintance with traditions other than Buddhism was far from superficial. Moreover, even if he had compiled some of them at imperial command rather than on his own initiative, they may well hearken back to a youthful enthusiasm for Taoism that his biographies all record and that seems to have been something of a family tradition. As a young man, for example, Chang made a habit of wearing only Taoist clothes and thereby won himself a reputation as something of an eccentric. In any case, Chang's name is mentioned with respect by later authors of other canonical Taoist texts. The sympathy with things magical and mysterious that a deep acquaintance with Taoism could have fostered may have helped dispose Chang favorably toward analogous aspects of Buddhism, like visionary pilgrimage.

As to Chang's secular learning and his knowledge of the Confucian tradition, we have the evidence of his *chin-shih* degree as well as the displays of classical erudition that may be found even in some of his Buddhist writings. Moreover, the great Sung bibliophile Ch'ao Kung-wu 晁公武 (d. 1171) in his *Chün-chai tu-shu chih* 郡齋讀書志, describes a now lost collection of Chang's writings in thirty-two fascicles (entitled simply *Chang Wu-chin chi* 張無盡集).[15] This *wen-chi* likely included pieces in which Chang took up explicitly secular matters—political questions, for example—and in these he would no doubt have joined in the largely Confucian political discourse of his day. Also extant, but scattered among many sources, is an array of poems, songs, letters, and other occasional pieces that testify to Chang's considerable literary skill.

In short, it is clear that we have in Chang Shang-ying a man of many parts—a wide-ranging, classically educated scholar and man of letters, a high-level bureaucrat who led a consequential career during a period of rapid and controversial political change; a one-time enthusiast and continuing *cognoscente* of Taoism, expert in the arcana of its practice and theory; and—most important for our present purposes—a devoted and deeply informed Buddhist layman.

We know too that the world in which this man lived and on which he left an appreciable mark was undergoing profound changes beneath the surface of politics and public affairs. The revival of the Confucian tradition, now enriched and tempered by its centuries-long encounter with Buddhism; the early growth of the metaphysical and ethical tradition of Tao-hsueh or Neo-Confucianism, later to become China's dominant orthodoxy; the slow and, to those involved, almost imperceptible transformation of Chinese society from an aristocratic to a bureaucratic order; the proportionate increase in social mobility; the growth of literacy and of institutions of education; the growing "inwardness" of Chinese culture as it discarded the more cosmopolitan ethos of preceding centuries and cultivated its renewed autonomy and its recovered sense of self-sufficiency; the renascent utopianism and pervasive confidence in the possibility of far-reaching political reform that so inspired the intelligentsia of the day—all these things and more were signs of a sea change in the character of Chinese civilization.

Curiously intertwined with many of these symptoms of epochal transformation was a deep-seated, often unreasoned, animosity toward Buddhism on the part of many of the era's foremost intellectuals, particularly those of Tao-hsueh persuasion. This animosity may be seen as the resonance, in the realm of Chinese religion and thought, of the deep and systemic changes altering the general tenor of Chinese culture as a whole. The standard charges against Buddhism are well known; they came to be such common stock in the arsenal of Confucian rhetoric that it is difficult to avoid finding them wherever one looks in the early corpus of that tradition. Han Yü's diatribe concerning the "bone of the Buddha" and Ou-yang Hsiu's *Pen-lun* (Essay on fundamentals) are only the most commonly cited examples of an incessant refrain of anti-Buddhist polemic.

Not so well known, however, is the Buddhist response to this polemic. And this ignorance is odd, because Buddhist authors were prolific and eloquent in their replies to their Sung critics. Chang Shang-ying's *Hu-fa lun* is an especially interesting riposte, not least because it was written by a layman rather than by a monk, and by a layman who figured prominently in the very same political and literary culture that produced the most vociferous critics of Buddhism. Thus, the *Hu-fa lun* was not a broadside issued from the still somewhat alien intellectual redoubt of the monastic establishment. Chang met his opponents in the public arena—on their own ground, so to speak—and he was able to speak their idiom. Many of them he no doubt knew personally. His replies to their criticisms, therefore, are apposite in a way in which those of his clerical congeners—for example, Tsung-mi 宗密 (780–841), Ch'i-sung 契嵩 (1007–72), and so forth—were not.

In this connection, we should not forget that among the features of Buddhism most likely to arouse Confucian animosity was its predilection for numinous or otherworldly experience. Think of pilgrimage in this light. To the Confucian, of course, an undertaking like pilgrimage could easily appear to threaten the social and political order simply because it allowed people, large numbers of them, to extricate themselves from their fixed positions in society and to venture, if only for a short time, outside the boundaries of familial, social, and political duty in which they normally led their lives. It was, virtually by definition, a potentially antinomic or anarchic activity. How much more threatening must it have seemed when one considered that it was also often the occasion for powerful and uncanny experiences. As we shall see, pilgrimage was certainly such an occasion for Chang Shang-ying, and his decision to publicize the strange things that befell him at Wu-t'ai Shan was surely made in the sober awareness that many would not believe what he had to say and would strongly disapprove of his saying it. Chang's pilgrimage, then, may have been closely related, either as cause or as effect, to his staunch defense of Buddhism against a kind of Confucian criticism that was growing gradually more influential in the dominant intellectual circles of his day.

CONCERNING WU-T'AI SHAN

Chang Shang-ying's destination as a pilgrim, the sacred purlieu of Wu-t'ai Shan, is in northern Shansi province about one hundred fifty miles southwest of Peking, one hundred miles northeast of T'ai-yuan, and eighty miles southeast of Ta-t'ung. It is commonly spoken of as "a mountain" or as "one of China's sacred mountains," but this terminology can be misleading. It is not a single mountain at all but, as the Chinese name suggests, a cluster of five more or less gently domed or flat peaks dominating a small range of mountains—actually a northern spur of the larger T'ai-hang massif—that extends for several scores of miles in a southwest to northeast direction, running parallel to and southeast of the Heng-shan range. As map 3.1 shows, the five rounded peaks that comprise the pilgrimage site proper encompass an irregularly shaped area of more than a hundred square miles. One can grasp something of the dimensions of the place when one realizes that the northernmost and southernmost of its five individual mountains, that is, the Northern Terrace and the Southern Terrace, are about twelve miles apart, and the Eastern Terrace and the Central Terrace about eight miles apart. Despite their names, these peaks are not arranged precisely according to the points of the compass. Rather, the Western, Central, and Northern terraces lie in fairly close proximity to each other along a diagonal axis extending southwest to northeast. The Eastern Terrace is almost due east of the Central Terrace, but at a significant distance therefrom; and the Southern Terrace, although due south of the Northern Terrace, is so far removed from all the others as to stand in virtual isolation. Altogether, the vicinity of the Five Terraces extends, approximately, from 113°15′ to 113°45′ east longitude and from 38°45′ to 39°45′ north latitude.

A single mountain Wu-t'ai Shan certainly is not, but mountainous it just as surely is. The highest of the five peaks, the Northern Terrace, rises 10,033 feet above sea level; the lowest, the Southern Terrace, is no less than 8,153

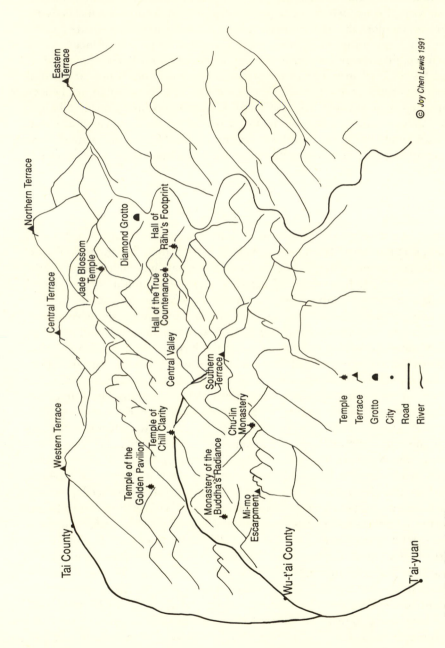

© Joy Chen Lewis 1991

Eastern Terrace

Northern Terrace

Central Terrace

Western Terrace

Jade Blossom Temple

Diamond Grotto

Hall of Rāhu's Footprint

Hall of the True Countenance

Central Valley

Southern Terrace

Tai County

Temple of the Golden Pavilion

Temple of Chill Clarity

Monastery of the Buddha's Radiance

Chu-lin Monastery

Mi-mo Escarpment

Wu-t'ai County

T'ai-yuan

Temple

Terrace

Grotto

City

Road

River

Map 3.1. Wu-t'ai Shan

feet high. Although they may have been somewhat more thickly wooded in Sung times, nowadays the slopes and summits of the mountains have only relatively sparse natural vegetation, largely alpine and evergreen flora scattered amid large sweeps of barren soil and rock. The valleys between the mountains, however, are and were moderately arable, traversed as they are by several small rivers, streams, and creeks. Distinguished by unstable weather throughout the year, the region is especially notorious for its forbiddingly rigorous winters. The permanent or year-round resident population has therefore always been relatively small, and most pilgrimage has been confined to the relatively clement summer months.

As important for an adequate sense of the place as its physical description is an appreciation that it was, and is still, something of a frontier or liminal region. Situated not far south of a stretch of the Great Wall, it marked the boundary between the civilized world of China proper and China's ultima Thule, the vacant expanse now known as Mongolia. Wu-t'ai, therefore, must be seen as a kind of spiritual rampart of the empire. To travel to Wu-t'ai—particularly in earlier times—was to go to the very edge of China's cultural world, there to risk awesome encounters with things genuinely, if not totally, "other." The severe, wind-swept terrain of the place, together with its dramatic weather, no doubt often served to heighten the sense of adventure and holy dread so commonly felt by pious visitors from the more secure and domesticated regions of the Middle Kingdom. For clergy who made of Wu-t'ai their permanent home, these same features must have made the place seem an especially appropriate venue for ascetic effort and a likely location for transcendental visions or powerful personal transformations.

History does not clearly reveal the origins of Wu-t'ai as a sacred place. We do know that it had some kind and measure of religious significance even before it became a Buddhist site. It was once known as Tzu-fu Shan 紫府山 (Purple Palace Mount). Such a name, alluding as it does to the celestial domains of immortals, suggests originally Taoist associations, but this fact is more tantalizing than informative, and we really know nothing specific about Wu-t'ai's role in pre-Buddhist Chinese religion. It was only with the advent of Mahayana Buddhism that the Five Terraces came fully into their own. Various traditions relate that there were Buddhist monasteries at Wu-t'ai as early as the Northern Wei dynasty (424–532), and many of the Buddhist institutions at Wu-t'ai that came to be most famous in later ages are said to have been founded in the fifth and sixth centuries.

During this same period, and by a process we still do not fully understand, Wu-t'ai came to be identified as the residence of the great celestial bodhisattva, Mañjuśrī. Following especially the work of Étienne Lamotte (1960), we may note that the *Hua-yen ching*, a scripture in which Mañjuśrī is one of the major protagonists, contains a list of eight mythic mountains situated in the eight cardinal directions, on each of which dwells a particular bodhisattva.

The Chinese translations of this text, done in 418–20 and 695–99, tell us, in what may be an interpolated apocryphal passage, that Mañjuśrī—the embodiment of, among other things, perfect wisdom or insight (*prajñā*)—is said to dwell on yet another such mountain, the fifth in an expanded series of nine. This is named in Chinese Ch'ing-liang Shan (Mountain of Chill Clarity), and it is said to be somewhere to the east or northeast of India. The *Hua-yen ching* itself makes no mention of this mountain's comprising five peaks, nor does it actually identify it with the five peaks in northern Shansi later called Wu-t'ai. However, other texts—written in or translated into Chinese in increasing numbers during the seventh and eighth centuries—do further specify the precise location and configuration of Mañjuśrī's mountain, situating it specifically in China, noting that it has five peaks, and even identifying it exactly with the former Tzu-fu Shan.

Thus did our Wu-t'ai Shan come to be identified with the mighty Mañjuśrī and with the mythical Ch'ing-liang Shan, by which latter name it has continued commonly to be known. Initially, it would appear, the Mañjuśrī of this mountain cult was presented as a savior whose aid was particularly to be invoked in the time of Buddhism's advanced decline, an age widely thought to have begun by the late sixth century. His cult continued to develop throughout the T'ang, its growth accelerated and amplified by the eighth-century arrival in China of esoteric forms of Buddhism (*mi-chiao* 密教) in which Mañjuśrī played major and complex roles.

Just as Wu-t'ai consists of more than a single mountain, so too does it consist in more—many more—than one man-made edifice. As early as the Northern Ch'i dynasty (550–77) there were said to have been as many as two hundred temples and monasteries at Wu-t'ai. That number grew even larger during the course of the T'ang (618–906), as did the size and population of the institutions themselves; and particularly during the eighth and ninth centuries Wu-t'ai, now widely held to be Mañjuśrī's principal residence, became both a major monastic center and a major destination of both lay and clerical pilgrimage. Inhabited by thousands of monks living in hundreds of monasteries and temples, many of them quite grand, it was also visited, in vast numbers, not only by Chinese Buddhists but also by Buddhists from South and Central Asia as well as from Korea and Japan. Of course, this abundance of piety and devotion was attended, and to considerable extent made possible, by generous imperial support.

Nor did Wu-t'ai decline appreciably after the T'ang. Despite various "barbarian" threats and incursions, it continued to flourish through the Five Dynasties, Sung, and Chin periods (tenth through twelfth centuries). Thus, when Chang Shang-ying arrived there in the late eleventh century it was still a very vital, though by then also a venerable, religious center. When the Mongols took control of the area in the early thirteenth century they established conditions for a new development at Wu-t'ai, the growth of a significant Tibetan presence. This influence, which increased during the Yuan, Ming, and Ch'ing periods (thirteenth through nineteenth century), explains why later visitors to the Five Terraces, including those of modern times, have not failed to note the degree to which "Lamaism," so called, has prevailed there. Even today Wu-t'ai is nearly as much a center of Tibetan Buddhism as of Chinese Buddhism, this being evident not least in the great white Tibetan pagoda (*chorten*) that dominates the central valley and that has become the chief visual symbol of the entire complex. The contemporary visitor to Wu-t'ai who might also read Chang Shang-ying's account would have to count the presence of the Tibetans as a major difference between Wu-t'ai now and Wu-t'ai then.

CHANG'S RECORD OF HIS PILGRIMAGE TO MOUNT WU-T'AI

The very title of the *Hsu Ch'ing-liang chuan* (*HCLC*) would seem to suggest that it was composed as a sequel to two earlier texts of similar title, the *Ku Ch'ing-liang chuan* 古清凉傳 (Old accounts of Wu-t'ai) written about 667 by Hui-hsiang (*T* 51:1092–1100) and the *Kuang Ch'ing-liang chuan* 廣清凉傳 (Expanded accounts of Wu-t'ai) compiled about 1060 by Yen-i 延一 (*T* 51:1101–27). Toward the end of his narrative Chang himself says that he "appended it to the *Ch'ing-liang chuan*." And indeed, at least since the late twelfth century, it has usually been published and reprinted together with those other two works, as the final component of a kind of Wu-t'ai trilogy. Chang Shang-ying's memoir, however, is very different from the other two works. They are miscellaneous collections of lore about the five sacred peaks, part genuine history and meticulous description, part recollected legend and secondhand retelling of myth. Chang's work, by contrast, is the continuous narrative of a single man's visit to the Wu-t'ai mountains, a veritable eyewitness report of a single sequence of events recounted more or less from a single authorial or editorial perspective. Moreover, although many of the experiences that befall its protagonist are wondrous indeed, they are recounted in a rather straightforward narrative style largely unburdened of the sort of solemn rhetoric usually employed in China to recount momentous past events. Indeed, much of the work is given over largely to careful, detailed description of lived experience. It would be quite off the mark, therefore, to think of this work only as a sequel to the earlier Wu-ta'i texts or even to assume that Chang had composed it chiefly with them in mind.[16]

As to the question of the work's authenticity, I see no compelling reason to doubt that it is attributable, at least in some sense of the word, to Chang himself. This I maintain despite the apparent improbability of the events related in it and despite our longstanding sinological tendency to attribute even to literati of eleventh-century China many of our own modern assumptions about which kinds of experiences are to be judged veridical and which illusory or fictive. No strong evidence against the traditional attribution has yet been presented. Moreover, we know beyond doubt that Chang did travel to Mount Wu-t'ai at the time the account purports to describe,[17] and we have available to us reputable testimony written within decades of those events that credits Chang with the authorship of our text. Some have expressed the view that the account is written in a suspiciously crude, inelegant style, falling short of the standards of literary excellence one might expect of an eminent man of letters like Chang Shang-ying,[18] but that judgment seems to apply only to some parts of the text and not to others. It is noteworthy, for example, that those passages that appear to quote from Chang's poems, letters, or memorials are written in a far more polished and erudite style than the rest. The hypothesis I am therefore most inclined now to entertain is that the narrative as we now have it may actually have been compiled or edited by someone other than Chang, although this anonymous editor or scribe may have made use of, at times may even have quoted from, documents that Chang himself had penned. Let us, then, accept the story as Chang Shang-ying's own, in spirit and substance if not always in letter, and let us hear it told before we assess it.[19]

A Further Record of Ch'ing-liang[20]

Narrated
by
Chang Shang-ying

Gentleman in Court Service, Provisionally
Appointed as Judicial Commissioner of the Ho-tung Circuit[21]

PRELIMINARY VISIT

In the Yuan-yu era, during the second month of the *ting-mao* year [1087],[22] Shang-ying[23] journeyed by dream to the Diamond Grotto (Chin-kang k'u 金剛窟)[24] on the Mountain of Five Terraces. When he awoke he thought it strange, for this was not a place he had ever seen or heard of before, nor one he had ever even thought to visit.[25] At the time this dream occurred Shang-ying was serving as a judge in the superior prefecture of K'ai-feng. He related the dream to his clerk, Shao Tsun-chung. Tsun-chung responded in jest, saying, "Perhaps T'ien-chueh will be heading off to Ping-chou."[26] Five months later, when Shang-ying was appointed provisional judicial commissioner of Ho-tung, Tsun-chung observed, "Your earlier dream has now been confirmed. We must go there forthwith. The affairs of a man's life are preordained; how could they possibly be evaded?"

Shang-ying reached his post in the eighth month. In the eleventh month, he visited the Diamond Grotto and confirmed that what was actually to be seen there corresponded entirely to his dream. However, as he had encountered cold weather and feared that sleet and snow would block his journey, he left the mountain after only one night's stay.[27] During the summer of the following *mou-chen* year, the district of Wu-t'ai was beset by packs of bandits who had been allowed to prey at will. Shang-ying undertook a campaign to apprehend them and set off for Wu-t'ai while observing a regimen of complete fasting and abstinence.[28]

FIRST DAY

On the *jen-yin* day, the twenty-seventh day of the sixth month [July 18, 1088], he reached the Temple of Chill Clarity.[29] The chief monk of the temple said, "Three *li* from here is the Temple of the Golden Pavilion (Chin-ko Ssu 金閣寺). Once, some time ago, a certain Supervisor Ts'ui had a vision from there of a 'golden bridge' on

103

the South Terrace, engulfed by a brilliant light."[30] Shang-ying thought to himself, "What sort of person was this Ts'ui, and what kind of person am I?"[31]

When he reached the Temple of the Golden Pavilion,[32] day was giving way to night. The mountain forests were stark and still, without even a wisp of cloud in the sky. The rector Hsing-ch'i came out to greet him, meeting him at the temple's main southern gate. Before they had finished seating themselves there appeared to the side of the South Terrace a white cloud of extremely fine texture, like blossoming white cotton fluff.[33] Hsing-ch'i remarked that this was an auspicious cloud, of a kind rarely seen. Monks assembled to conduct rituals and to chant, hoping soon to see "the mark of radiance."[34] Shang-ying donned pilgrim's garments, burned incense, and bowed repeatedly.[35] Before he had risen from even the first prostration, however, he saw the "golden bridge" and an aureole, gold-edged and deep violet-blue within. But he harbored doubts about these visions, thinking they might be just the effects of the sort of color that is produced when clouds catch the rays of the setting sun. Later, however, when it had grown quite dark, three columns of rosy light arose directly in front of the mountain, and his doubts abruptly vanished.

SECOND DAY

On the morrow, the *kuei-mao* day [July 19], he reached the Hall of the True Countenance (Chen-jung yuan 眞容院)[36] and stopped at the Pavilion of Clear Brilliance (Ch'ing-hui ko 清輝閣). The Northern Terrace was off to the left and the Eastern Terrace in front. Just opposite was Dragon Hill (Lung shan 龍山), below which flowed Gold Precinct Stream (Chin-chieh hsi 金界溪). To the north, behind a balneary, was the Lodge of Mañjuśrī's Transformation (Wen-shu suo-hua chai 文殊所化宅),[37] and above Gold Precinct Stream was the Hall of Rāhu's Footprint (Lo-hou tsu-chi t'ang 羅睺足跡堂).[38] Guide Pien[39] said, "This place too has had numinous lights. Long ago a monk from the Che region prayed for such a manifestation and one appeared, hovering above the balustrade." Shang-ying then made obeisances and reverent prayers. Sometime early in the evening, after the interval of *yu* [5:00–7:00 P.M.], a golden stairway appeared above Dragon Hill. Early in the next hour, the interval of *hsu* [7:00–9:00 P.M.], a great flare appeared above the mountains to the north. Pien said that this was a numinous light of the sort he had earlier mentioned. He then bowed respectfully and another flare appeared, this one lasting for quite some time. Flashes of light shot up on all sides—one playing about the Eastern Terrace, another about the Dragon Hill, and another above Rāhu's Footprint—while behind the balneary appeared two great blazes of light, one following quickly upon the other like successive bolts of lightning. Two more flares appeared to the south, above the Gold Precinct Stream.

Just before midnight, toward the end of the interval of *hai* [9:00–11:00 P.M.], Shang-ying gazed down upon the stream and saw something in the shape of a man holding a large lamp. He thought to himself, "Surely I am suffering a trick of vision; this must be just a monk of the temple or a servant setting out a torch." By that time Pien had already retired for the night, but Shang-ying sent Wang Pan, Chieh Chih, and Ch'in Yuan to rouse Pien and inquire as to what Shang-ying had seen.[40] Pien responded, "There are monstrous tigers in these mountains; where they reside no men venture, nor do any men live there." Shang-ying was doubtful and could not decide what to believe. He looked again at the light of the lamp. First it was large, then small. Its color was pink then white, yellow then green. At one moment it comprised all these colors separately, at the next they had all fused. It lit up the whole grove. Quietly he thought to himself, "This must be a *samādhi* flame. To call it a lamp is to speak merely in conventional terms." He then knelt and announced, "Utterly transcendent is the realm of the sage, well beyond my ken. The range of an ordinary person's consciousness is restricted. If this be no human lamp, then let it appear directly before me."

After he had recited this entreaty ten times, the light above the stream grew red like the sun setting in the sea and then soared aloft, emitting dazzling rays.[41] As it gradually approached the front of the pavilion, its brilliance condensed and intensified until it resembled the sort of garnet sphere the giant basilisk holds in its maw.[42] Shang-ying's whole body shivered violently as though he had been drenched in ice and snow. He then exclaimed, "My doubting mind has been resolved." As soon as he had spoken, the light returned to its original place and shone over the creek. To Ch'in Yuan and the others, who observed it from off to the side, it resembled a golden body arising from a crouch. What the women and servants in the party saw was yet again different.[43] To them it looked like a person seated in the lotus posture with hair done up in a swirl, clad in a purple robe with white collar, brandishing a sword and bearing a horn upon its head. An old monk said, "This is the gold-feathered griffin, the eighth ranked of the heavenly dragons." Sometime later clouds formed above the northern peak. Inside a white cloud there appeared a jewellike light, and after the clouds had clustered there arose a large white orb like the bright disk of the moon.

THIRD DAY

On the following day, *chia-ch'en* [July 20], he reached the Eastern Terrace. An auspicious five-hued cloud appeared, and an orb of white light leapt from the ground, revolving hundreds of times like a chariot wheel. Shang-ying responded by intoning the following verse:

> Clouds cleave to the western peak, the sun rises east,
> A disk of brightness appears amid the clouds.
> Practice is always a matter of groping.[44]
> Fear only that practice may collapse into nothingness.[45]

There then arose a strong wind. Clouds and mists roiled up suddenly as if to topple crags and rend gorges.

FOURTH DAY

The superintendent monk addressed Shang-ying, saying, "As the troops under the command of the military inspector cannot observe the prohibition against cooking meat, I would ask that tomorrow they be sent away." Thus, on the *i-ssu* day of the seventh month [July 21], Shang-ying dismissed his military escort and went to make offerings[46] on the Northern Terrace. That evening they rested on the Central Terrace. As gales blew relentlessly and the four peaks were shrouded in gloom, Pien and the others grew faint. On the slope of the terrace was an old Buddha hall. Shang-ying ordered it swept out and had his attendants perform devotions. The party consisted of the guide Pien, the superintendent, two old wardens, a wine steward, and a tea steward. They then proceeded several paces further north. On the summit of the Central Terrace an auspicious cloud had appeared, resplendent in five hues. Suddenly, the sky to the northwest was opened to reveal a world of blue crystal teeming with legions of bodhisattvas, sumptuous towers and halls, jewellike mountains and forests, ornate pennants and canopies, jeweled terraces and thrones, heavenly kings and arhats, lions and musk elephants, all arrayed in ineffable magnificence. Above the Hall of the True Countenance, under a sumptuous and vast curved-handled canopy woven in the purple mushroom pattern, was the Bodhisattva Mañjuśrī astride a lion. Also, disporting themselves above and below him, gazing upon him from right and left, were seven octads[47] of noble attendants.[48]

At this point the superintendent observed ironically, "I have practiced on these terraces for nineteen years without having seen so much as a single radiance or a single miraculous sign. Hoping that I could rely on the power of merit, I have prayed to see it. But after all my praying, I end up catching a glimpse of such things while hidden in the company of soldiers!"

As the sun gradually darkened, a red flare appeared along the ridge of the Northern Terrace. Shang-ying asked Ch'in Yuan, "Who would light fires hereabouts?" Yuan put the question to Pien, and Pien in turn asked the superintendent. The superintendent said, "That crag is just one large, barren rock, and it is being buffeted by strong winds. What fire could possibly last up there? It must be a numinous light." As they were worshiping this, two other golden lights appeared, and in the intervening valley there was seen a single white light of a hue like burnished silver. Just then the frontier military commissioner, Kuo Tsung-yen, happened by. He immediately sent a messenger to deliver his card. Shang-ying pointed out the light and said to the messenger, "Do you see that or not?" He replied, "I see it." Shang-ying said, "Please give my greetings to the military commissioner." He then gazed worshipfully at the unearthly light. The strong winds having made it impossible to hold a candle, he was not able to write out a reply card. At that point, bowing again and again, he reverently implored, "May the light appear immediately in front of me." He made these supplications repeatedly, first to the west, then to the east. Thereupon, the flare came down from the west, its brilliance coruscating within a violet-blue disk, and two other flares, one from the east and one from the west, converged with it at the same time. From the Northern Terrace to the Central Terrace was a distance of ten *li*, but in the blink of an eye the flare came to within a hundred paces of where he stood. Although it had been vivid and bright far off, close up it softened. Like a globe of red glass kept in a precious chalice of cut white jade, it glowed with a uniform luster. When he arose from his prostrations, it returned to its original place. Then the people on the terrace realized that they had seen something exceedingly rare. They resumed their prayers all the more zealously, and a succession of these jewellike lights returned.

When the night was drawing to a close, and the icy cold had pierced them to the bone, they took their leave bowing and descended the mountain while the flare in the east faded and the other two flares gradually dimmed. Shang-ying then said, "Our task completed, we take our leave. But this feeling of awe with which we are left, how could that soon be dispelled?" As he made this remark, the three flares arrayed themselves together within the purple disk, like the lunar mansion *hsin* in the eastern quadrant.[49] Outside the disk was a red glow that filled the mountains.

FIFTH DAY

That night a storm blew in, and the next day, *ping-wu* [July 22], it remained overcast and foggy. Shang-ying said to himself, in hushed tones, "What I saw last night on the Central Terrace was so splendid! Surely the Bodhisattva will not oppose my now going on to the Western Terrace." When he had gone as far as Fragrant Hill (Hsiang shan 香山), an auspicious cloud covered the top of the terrace. After he had made his offerings, he had a vision just like the first one, except that this time there was no crystalline world. He then proceeded on to the Jade Blossom (Yü-hua 玉華) and Everlasting Repose (Shou-ning 壽寧) temples before returning to the Hall of the True Countenance. There he found Kuo Tsung-yen, the frontier military commissioner; Wu Chün-ch'eng, the controller-general of Tai-chou;[50] Chang Chih-ts'ai, magistrate of Wu-t'ai; Liu Chin, chief military inspector; and Ch'en Yü, leader of the local militia—all gathered in the performance of their duties. Shang-ying told them of what he had seen. Although they all marveled ceaselessly, each reckoning that he had heard of something similar, Shang-ying said, "What you gentlemen relate is [only] what you have heard [and not what you have seen]."[51] That night the sky cleared, and a golden flare was again seen in front of the hall. An adjutant brought word of this to Kuo, Wu, and the others, and when they all gazed above the pines behind the balneary there suddenly appeared an array of lights resembling a string of pearls. Each of the worthy gentlemen kowtowed and bowed repeatedly. After but a moment, the radiance diminished in intensity and the party dispersed. By the side of the Rāhu Hall a great white radiance appeared, like a shooting star, and the area above the pines behind the balneary was shrouded in a white vapor that lasted through the night and then dissipated.

SIXTH DAY

On the morrow, the *ting-wei* day [July 23], Kuo and Wu went to inspect the garrisons to the east, and Chang Chih-ts'ai returned to the north. The sky was heavily overcast. Shang-ying and Ch'en Yü went to see Ts'ao Hsu, mayor of Hsing-shan 興善. That evening they climbed Brahman Sylph Hill (Fan-hsien shan 梵仙山) together. Ts'ao Hsu said, "Last night, I hear, a golden flare appeared to you. I saw it too, later on when I was outside." Yü asked him, "What you saw, sir, where was it?" Hsu replied, "In the sky." Yü kowtowed exclaiming, "Wondrous, wondrous indeed! When I saw it from above, it seemed to be over the stream. When you saw it from below it seemed to be in the sky." Shang-ying, whose every entreaty over the preceding several days had met with a response, took this occasion to exclaim, "For the sake of these two gentlemen I beseech the appearance of an auspicious five-hued cloud." Rising then and changing their clothes, they bowed repeatedly and uttered silent prayers. Suddenly the sky to the southwest cleared. Propitious clouds swirled up and purple mists unfurled. Shang-ying said, "Under these purple mists there must be sages and worthies. I ask that you two gentlemen assume a solemn and grave demeanor, that you may see the holy manifestations." After some considerable time, a magical apparition—castles and towers, halls and pavilions, all teeming with bodhisattvas—magically appeared and disappeared. Shang-ying further proclaimed, "Let the [heavenly] ranks appear that these two men may once see them." As soon as he had spoken, the visions ranged themselves in order. The two men could only sigh. The sun had nearly set when they caught their glimpse of the apparition. Forgetting where they were, the two men said, "Wondrous, wondrous indeed! It is as if they had appeared out of clouds and vapors, then mysteriously vanished. How could they leave not the slightest trace?"

That night they stopped again at the Pavilion of Clear Brilliance. They thought to themselves, "Tomorrow we shall leave the mountain; may the precious lights appear to us yet again." Just as they were removing the bolt to open the doors there appeared above the southern bank of Gold Precinct Stream a great flare, and behind the balneary two beams of light linked east to west arose from the pine boughs and joined together to become a single ray, shining brilliantly, moving from the eastern slope of the hill and proceeding south. Coming to rest above the rocky stream bed at the edge of the copse, it shone clearly and brightly, neither like a cloud nor like mist. After a time two precious lights appeared in the radiance, one of which flew south to join with four other lights above Gold Precinct Stream. And from the Hall of Rāhu's Footprint to the side of Dragon Hill two lights appeared together at one time.

Shang-ying then made this supplication, "If in some previous age I belonged to the family of Mañjuśrī, then may I be blessed to see some miraculous sign." As soon as he had spoken, the two lights vibrated and danced together repeatedly. As Shang-ying looked upon this he pronounced a solemn vow, "When this manifestation is over I will study the limitless teachings of the Buddha. All licentiousness, killing, mendacity, perverse views, and all evil thoughts I will forever exterminate and never allow to arise. Lest I falter for even an instant, I implore the Bodhisattva to watch over me everywhere and always." Thereupon, there appeared two lights, one to the south and one to the north. One shone yellow, the other glowed white. Rising aloft in front, extending down behind, they soared up to the heavens ahead. This occurred at midnight. By the time the lights had returned to their points of origin, it was daylight. Shang-ying went first to the Hall of Rāhu's Footprint. Noticing its dilapidated condition, he resolved soon to repair it. So exceptional was the radiance of the lights[52] seen that night at the Footprint Hall that he donated three hundred thousand cash and charged Rector Ch'i with the task of reconstructing it.

SEVENTH DAY

The following day, *wu-shen* [July 24], he reached the Monastery of the Buddha's Radiance (Fo-kuang Ssu 佛光寺).[53] The abbot, Shao-t'ung, said to him, "This is the sanctuary of Ch'an Master Chieh-t'uo 解脱禪師.[54] His stele and grotto are still here." Chang took the occasion to inspect the stele inscription, which contained the words, "Chieh-t'uo himself is Chieh-t'uo; Mañjuśrī himself is Mañjuśrī." With a deep sigh he said, "What a True Worthy." He then composed a eulogy that said,

> Sage or mere mortal, in the course of life neither leaves the slightest trace.
> Chieh-t'uo or Mañjuśrī, each one has distinguished himself.
> China or India, neither is a place in which to linger.
> Near Fo-kuang Shan, a single niche remains.

As day turned to night auspicious clouds appeared before the monastery, lucent purple and luxuriant. He asked T'ung, "This temple, is it a place of miraculous occurrences? Tell me the circumstances of any propitious forces that have manifested themselves here." T'ung said, "I have heard of a sacred light that appeared once during the Huang-yu era [1049–54]." Shang-ying said, "If this be true it must have been like the light I had prayed to see." "Where was it?" he asked. The monk replied, "In the range of mountains to the south." At dusk and into the night he prayed reverently and, eventually, there did appear in those mountains one silver and two golden lights.[55] They differed only slightly from what he had seen at the Hall of the True Countenance.

EIGHTH DAY

The next day, *chi-yu* [July 25], he went to tour the Mi-mo Escarpment (Mi-mo yen 祕麿巖).[56] When he was ten *li* away, a path of white vapor extended itself from the Five Terraces directly to the top of the escarpment, and in front of the cliff Mañjuśrī appeared astride a lion. When he reached the escarpment itself, the sky had darkened and the apparition had completely vanished. Now there was a certain monk named Chi-che 繼哲 from the Perfect Fruition Cloister (Yuan-kuo yuan 圓果院) in Tai-chou who had built a hut for himself on the southern flank of this mountain and had remained there for three years engrossed in the Tripiṭaka. Shang-ying visited his hut and asked him, "As you have been so long in the mountains, surely you must have had visions?" Che said, "Three years ago, the gate above the cave opened to reveal three monks—one dressed in brown robes, another in yellow, and the third in purple. They stood by the gate for a long time before it closed again, and all the while the interior of the grotto was lit by a numinous light." Che had heard about this but had not seen it himself. Then Che said, "The sky being as dark as it is, it would seem that this poor monk, an uncouth hermit, has allowed you, sir, to come and go in vain![57] Nevertheless, I would ask that you please brighten my den with a verse." Thereupon Shang-ying brushed off the wall and wrote on it the following:

> Perusing all five hundred cases of scripture in the Nāga palace,[58]
> For three years you have not come down from Mi-mo Escarpment.
> But you must understand, you cannot have any place of refuge.
> Strip off the Tathāgata's foul-smelling barbarian's robe.[59]

When he had finished writing, they came out of the hut and gazed at the mouth of the defile. There was an auspicious cloud of golden hue, its radiant coloration dazzling to the eyes. The Bodhisattva then appeared mounted on a green lion and entered into the cloud. Shang-ying said, "Great things have occurred this evening; by no means have I come in vain." The palisade rose to a height of some eight hundred feet, sheer-faced and crag-ridged. As the women and servants in the party gazed eastward at the precipice, bowing repeatedly, praying, and shrinking in awe, two golden lights appeared amid the red cliffs. Shang-ying called Abbot Yung to come see them. Night had just begun to fall. The accompanying troops had not yet settled down for the night when they heard the whole entourage calling out. Each man raised his head to see, and a clamorous noise filled the courtyard.[60] All told, the lights manifested themselves seven times and then disappeared. The reverent prayers continued for many minutes thereafter, but the face of the cliff had become as black as lacquer. Abbot Yung said, "These numinous phenomena appear only for you, sir. How could they occur in the presence of mere servants and underlings? It is a matter of good fortune and has little to do with human determination."

NINTH DAY

The next morning[61] Yung said, "The others have all fallen asleep. We can again pray for a vision." Shang-ying then changed his clothing and prostrated himself. Just as he began reverently to pray, the Bodhisattva—radiant white and life-sized—suddenly appeared to the left of the cliff and stood in the shining light. There were three such appearances. Knowing that he had been vouchsafed something quite rare, Shang-ying made a vow like the one he had made before and intoned, "If in the past I was truly of the family of the Bodhisattva, then again I appeal for the appearance of a marvelous sign." When he had finished speaking, two large golden lights illumined the rocks of the cliff. Shang-ying further intoned, "If in this age of the mere simulation of the dharma[62] the Bodhisattva would wish to charge Shang-ying with its protection, then I beg for a further sign." When he had finished speaking, two rays of light shone forth like flashes of lightning, and a large golden light irradiated the front of the cliff, pouring through the pine branches.

At that point more than ten abbots, together with crowds of followers, made an earnest petition. They said, "We humbly bring to your attention a passage in the *Hua-yen ching* that says, 'In the land to the northeast there is a place named the Mountain of Chill Clarity. From time immemorial many bodhisattvas have resided there. The bodhisattva there at present is named Mañjuśrī. Together with his retinue of a myriad other bodhisattvas, he preaches the dharma continuously.' For thousands of eons past, we know not how many, sages have roamed and dwelt in our mountain. From the time of Emperor Ming of Han, through the Wei, Northern Ch'i, Sui, and T'ang dynasties, up until the beginning of the Five Dynasties period, the successive regnancies have been generous but not excessive in contributing to the upkeep of establishments on Mount Wu-t'ai. When our Emperor T'ai-tsung pacified Mr. Liu[63] he sent functionaries to remit the taxes that had been levied on the monasteries and temples of Wu-t'ai, and none of the subsequent four regnancies has failed to anticipate our needs. Recently, however, there has been instituted a policy of appropriating vacant lands for the support of border garrisons. Thus the mountains and forests of this sacred precinct have been put at the disposal of local militia.[64] The clearing of fields and cutting of forests have exposed the dens of our dragon spirits, and eight or nine of every ten of our monastery buildings have been ruined, their communities of monks left destitute or scattered to the four directions. Thus have the teachings of our master Mañjuśrī come to the verge of extinction. It is for some great purpose that our master has granted Your Honor visions of such rare and wonderful signs. If Your Honor would compose a written record of his experiences that could be used to foster faith throughout the world and among men of these later times,[65] thereby would he fulfill the purpose the Bodhisattva has enjoined upon him."

Shang-ying responded, "My most respectful thanks to this great assembly. How earnestly you have spoken! However, what makes men human is that they see shapes and colors with their eyes, hear sounds with their ears, smell scents with their noses, taste flavors with their tongues, touch material things with their bodies, and perceive mental objects with their minds. They go no further than these six.[66] Yet your master's writing[67] speaks of color and shape that is not color and shape, sound that is not sound, scent that is not scent, taste that is not taste, touch that is not touch, mental objects that are not mental objects. This is utterly divorced from what the world considers as empirical knowledge. Thus, those who live their whole lives never transcending the human realm will not take it as super-natural and so will consider it mere fantastical nonsense. I am concerned only that I myself should believe. How could I arouse the whole world to faith, including even the heterodox of this latter generation?"[68]

When he had finished, a letter arrived from Kuo Tsung-yen and Wu Chün-cheng. It said, "As beneficiaries of Your Honor's influence, we have chanced to witness momentous events. Things which have been reported from of old, but which we have never seen, have now all been verified. It is fitting that there should be a record of this, whereby to arouse faith in men of these latter days."

Chang considered this carefully and then said, "In speaking of holiness to the common person, of silence to the clamorous, of marvels to the mundane, of wisdom to the foolish, of truth to the mendacious, of penetration to the obstructed, of immensity to the small-minded—the differences are so great as to be incommensurable. They are like the difference between the Aśura King who can shake Mount Sumeru with his hands and the ant who cannot lift a mustard seed, or like the difference between Garuḍa, who can traverse the four worlds in seven days, and the tiny mite, which cannot fly even so far as a span. It is not that Shang-ying does not wish to speak; it is only that he fears his words will be of no avail."

Someone said, "Have you ever heard of Shih Fa-chao 釋法照 of the T'ang? During the Ta-li era (766–79) he had visionary experiences of entering the Chu-lin Monastery 竹林寺.[69] Anxious lest he arouse doubt and slander, he did not dare to tell so improbable a story. But he was suddenly visited by a holy monk who said, 'What you have seen are the precincts of Mount Wu-t'ai. Why do you not faithfully record it and publish it widely among all beings for the sake of their greater benefit? Which would you rather do, avoid scandal or effect blessings? If you transmit your message to a hundred persons and just one comes to believe, then transmitting it to a thousand will produce ten believers, and transmitting it to ten thousand will generate a hundred believers. Among a hundred persons who believe it, perhaps only one will practice it, but even this is enough to destroy heretical doctrines and sustain the true dharma. How much more could one expect if a hundred persons were to practice?'"

Shang-ying said, "How excellent a parable! I humbly resolve to write an account of my experiences, to be appended to the *Records of Ch'ing-liang*, and if I should relate even a single falsehood, may I be condemned to billions of eons of evil rebirth."

CHANG'S LATER VISITS TO WU-T'AI

According to the record itself, Chang's audience with the delegation of senior monks occurred on July 26, 1088—nine days after his visit had begun. It marked the end of what we may consider his principal and transformative pilgrimage, but it did not conclude his association with the sacred mountain, nor did it serve as his farewell to the place. The second *chüan* of the *HCLC* opens with a summary account of further visits to Wu-t'ai that Chang made over the course of the next two years. This summary (1130b10–31b25) relates that in less than two months, he had completed his narrative and had sent it back to the Hall of the True Countenance. It was read to an assembly of more than eighty monks, at which time an array of more than forty numinous lights suddenly appeared before them in the Bodhisattva Hall. As a further expression of his gratitude, Chang had also commissioned the sculpting of a clay statue of Mañjuśrī. This he brought back to the hall in late November of the same year. For that occasion he composed an eloquent profession of faith, partly quoted in our text, the recitation of which precipitated still more visions of wondrous lights and auspicious clouds. The following summer (1089) he returned to the mountain for further visions, but he says little about them

A year later, however, in the summer of 1090, the northern Shansi region suffered a drought, and Chang returned to Wu-t'ai once again, this time to pray for rain. On this occasion, the text says, he brought with him a statue of "the Bodhisattva Rāhu." This visit—the last he ever made, so far as we know—lasted for eight days, from July 11 through July 18. Of course, he was again the beneficiary of visions, witnessed this time, we are told, not by himself alone or with only a few companions but also by thousands of other clergy and laity. What is especially interesting about these later visions is that they are described in terms strongly reminiscent of the teachings on the Buddha's radiance (*fo-kuang*) found in the Hua-yen writings of the T'ang layman Li T'ung-hsuan. As we have already remarked, Chang had discovered Li's writings shortly after his 1088 pilgrimage, while returning to T'ai-yuan. He had apparently read them carefully by this time, for we find that the descriptions he gives of the 1090 visions rely heavily on some of the very phrasing we associate with Li. Thus, the miraculous lights Chang and others saw on this occasion prompted him to address Mañjuśrī in prayers that make explicit reference to the *Flower Garland Scripture*, and implicit references to Li's commentaries thereon. He notes, for example, that the scripture speaks of a sublime radiance that emanates from the person of the Buddha and illumines each of the eight cosmic scenes in which the sutra is set. The light he sees on Wu-t'ai he then compares to this supernal Buddha radiance, calling it "the radiance of the dharma nature's fundamental transcendence" (*fa-hsing pen-yu wu-hsiang chih kuang* 法性本有無相之光) and "the radiance that arises from the repletion of all the qualities of the fruition of Buddhahood" (*chu-fo kuo-te yuan-man chih kuang* 諸佛果德圓滿之光).[70] He also sees again (on July 14) the array of lights resembling the constellation Scorpio that he had seen two years earlier, and he takes that vision as an occasion to refer back to his original narrative, which he now labels the *Hsu-chuan* (Further account) and which he is quoted as saying he had "written in a previous year." Retracing his steps of two years earlier, he leaves Wu-t'ai via Fo-kuang Monastery and Mi-mo Escarpment, arriving back at his office in Tai-chou on July 19. Evidently his prayers were answered, for he says that the drought ended and that it rained heavily.

Back in his official quarters, we are told, he set himself immediately to the task of writing an official report (*tsou-wen* 奏聞) on his experiences to be sent back to the emperor. He first summarizes his wonderful experiences and does so in an especially polished style designed, apparently, to impress those in the court who might read it. Then, finally acting on the request the monks of Wu-t'ai had first made of him two years earlier, he proceeds from the description of Wu-t'ai's marvels to a plea on Wu-t'ai's behalf. Specifically, he recommends that the lands on Wu-t'ai that had been requisitioned for the support of border garrisons be forthwith returned to the monasteries. Thereby, he says, the welfare of the monasteries on Wu-t'ai, which had been severely harmed in recent years, would be restored. Thereby too could the present ruler reaffirm the imperial respect and support for this holiest of places that earlier emperors had expressed when they exempted the Wu-t'ai monasteries from all taxation. The memorial reads:

Recently, because of a drought in your minister's territory, he made a personal visit to Wu-t'ai Shan. Before the image of Mañjuśrī and the pool of the five dragons, he prayed for the blessing of rain. The numinous radiances and precious blazes that followed day and night were so uncanny in form and strange in aspect, so gloriously bright and luminously shimmering, that none could put a name to their appearance. On that occasion a crowd of more than a thousand monks and laity from all about gathered together to worship and stare. Their cries of wonder shook the mountains and the valleys. Afterward, the rains poured down, inundating several districts. When your minister had first set out, the plants and trees were withered and exhausted, the farmers disconsolate. But when he returned, the trees, hemp, buckwheat, and pulse were all green and flourishing, and the villages and towns sang and danced in anticipation of an abundant harvest.

It is because our sovereign is possessed of the Tao that all the sages deign to send down their protection. Thus, when officials carry out his edicts, when they spread them even to famous mountains and distant regions, the response is immediate and inevitable, like an echo. Now I have learned in my investigations that there are ten monasteries on Wu-t'ai Shan that once administered forty-two estates. After Emperor T'ai-tsung had conquered Chin,[71] all these holdings were declared tax free, thereby to indicate the imperial esteem in which they were held. But it would appear that the frontier officers have misled the court to believe that these estates are mountain wilderness. Thus, more than four thousand acres (300 *ch'ing*) of good arable land have been confiscated for the support of more than a hundred households of bowmen. The temples have thus been dispossessed, and the resulting litigation has been incessant. Monks and acolytes have dispersed, the temple buildings have fallen into disrepair, and your minister has been embarrassed to see such a state of affairs. He implores that these lands be restored to their original owners and that the matter be thoroughly investigated so that nothing will be left uncovered.

In your minister's humble view "what is outside of this world" is not susceptible to investigation. As for that "man of transformation" [i.e., the emperor], how could he reckon the gain or loss of earthen fields to be a matter of "perfection" or "deficiency?"[72] Men of old bestowed these lands as "fields of blessing" (*fu-t'ien* 福田), but men of later times have taken them to feed militia! If there be any doubts still unsettled, I would request that a commission of inquiry be sent to my post. If anything I have seen or I set forth should prove to be at all untrue, then I request a trial. Forgive me if I ask for the favor of an early disposition of this matter. (*HCLC* 1131b4–22)

To this official document, cast in the typically formal rhetoric of the bureaucrat, the author of our narrative adds a final, and appropriately Buddhist, observation: "Be this as it may," he says, as though to take the reader's attention away from worldly matters of land tenure, "that great being (*ta-shih* 大士, *mahāsattva*, i.e., Mañjuśrī) has taken the entire universe to be the embodiment of Vairocana Buddha. Shang-ying humbly asked for but a few hundred acres. Paltry though his aspiration may have been by comparison, was it not also compassionate?"

The remainder of the *HCLC*, in the expanded Taishō edition we have been using, is something of a miscellany. It consists largely of accounts of later visits to Wu-t'ai, most of which were inspired by Chang's account or served as occasions for recalling his pilgrimage as a point of comparison.[73] Some of these accounts concern persons who were originally skeptical of Chang's reports but who were transformed into believers when their own visits bore out Chang's claims. These later stories and memoirs may have been appended to the basic narrative, presumably by the redactors of the Chin and Ming editions, to provide ample and explicit evidence of the influence his work had for centuries after the events he described, and indeed it does seem as though he had begun a tradition of literati visits to the sacred Buddhist mountain.

INTERPRETATIONS

Like most documents of any appreciable interest to the history of religions, Chang's account of his extraordinary visits to Wu-t'ai Shan may be read on several different levels. At one of those levels, perhaps the one nearest the surface of the text's meaning, it is simply a miracle tale, a story of wonders and mysteries designed to excite religious imagination and arouse piety. To locate the text within this genre is not to dismiss it. Rather it is to treat it primarily as a valuable, and relatively rare, glimpse into currents of popular Chinese religious belief and enthusiasm during an age best known for certain events and doctrines produced by members of only the most elite strata of Chinese society. For these purposes the text's meaning is generic, and questions of authorship and authenticity diminish in significance.

The general history of the Sung has most often, until recently, been told as *histoire événementielle*, and its intellectual history has been written chiefly as "history of ideas." But Chang Shang-ying's text and a few others like it—for example, Hung Mai's *I-chien chih* written about a hundred years later—may be used to go beneath the level of political event to the substratum of social and cultural structure and may assist in excavating the foundational *mentalités* that lie beneath the architecture of deliberately constructed systems of thought. The prospect of using the work in this way is itself enough to confirm its value. In reading it we may be reminded that Sung China was not an entity existing only in the mind of a Chu Hsi or only in the corridors of political power surrounding the emperor's court. After all, as we have already seen, Chu Hsi's own uncle read Chang's book and was so moved by it that he took his own pilgrimage to Wu-t'ai Shan when his soon-to-be-famous nephew was an eleven-year-old boy.[74] We have also seen that Chang himself moved freely between the precincts of politics and the "higher" locales of mountains and mysteries. A truly comprehensive view of Sung China, and of Chinese history generally, must recognize not only that some Chinese lived their lives within settled patterns of bureaucratic hierarchy reflecting a symmetrical cosmos wholly transparent to reason but also that some Chinese, at times the very same men and women, lived lives open to ecstatic experience, quickened by belief in a natural world charged by supernatural forces, invigorated by a sense of the heterogeneity of space and time, and occasionally riven by strong contrasts between order and liminality. The tale of Chang's miracles can help, therefore, at least in a small way, to establish such a more comprehensive sinology.

At the same level of interpretation but apropos of a more specific issue, Chang's text can show that the Chinese religious world was not always so domestic and comfortable a realm as often portrayed. Even the best contemporary work on Sung religion has focused almost exclusively on those popular religious practices and beliefs in which the gods are rather "familiar" to their worshipers. Such gods, for example, were themselves only recently risen (and not too high) from the status of human being; they often behaved in "highly anthropomorphic" ways, sometimes as though they were only a particularly dangerous and irascible sort of corrupt local official or greedy merchant; they were regularly in need of "human recognition," and they were commonly depicted in terms that "exude human warmth" (Hansen 1990, 29–78). Transactions with such gods can barely be counted as "religious experiences" in the most common sense of that term; they fall rather into the same general category as transactions with the mandarinate or in the marketplace. Now, to be sure, such familiarity with the divine, and such divine familiars, were an important part of Chinese religion and should alter our sense of what counts as "religious" for the Chinese, but they were not the whole of Chinese religion. There were also higher deities, supremely powerful spiritual beings who dwelt far beyond the human realm and before whom one could only stand in "fear and trembling." Relations with these truly transcendent beings were possible only in liminal places and conditions, at the tops of forbidding peaks or on the very frontiers of civilization, and such relations were occasions not for reinforcement of established social forms and cultural values but for profound wonder and for the kind of awe in which conventional habits of thought and life were called into question and perhaps transformed. In other words, Chang's pilgrimage story, even when taken simply as a miracle tale, can be a reminder of the persistent dimension of strangeness and otherness in Chinese religion.

But, of course, it is not only as a miracle tale that the work can be read. In addition to being a story of wondrous visions it is also a brief chapter in Chinese institutional and economic history. It is, in fact, a story of church-state relations. To appreciate it as such it is not even necessary that we adopt a "hermeneutic of suspicion," reading political motives between lines of only apparently religious import. The text itself tells us explicitly that the prelates of Wu-t'ai Shan had asked Chang to write an account of what he had seen so that the fame of the mountain as a numinous place would be enhanced. Such an account, they expressly hoped, would lead the political authorities to reconsider their policy of depriving Wu-t'ai monasteries of their land holdings. It follows, then, that our text is, among other things, a kind of pious donation to the sangha and, given the prestige of the donor, an important addition to Wu-t'ai's already impressive panoply of official patronage.

I have not been able to locate independent sources relating to the economic conditions on Mount Wu-t'ai in the late eleventh century or to contemporary government policy toward its monasteries. The conditions Chang describes are certainly plausible, however, particularly because in the period in question "barbarian" forces were pressing hard on China's borders, including the border that lay very near the sacred mountains. It is quite likely, in fact, that soldiers were garrisoned in the area, and their presence could well have had painful consequences for the Wu-t'ai monasteries quite like those alleged. We do not know if Chang's narrative, or the memorial it quotes, had any practical effect on court policy (and the question was soon to become academic, for the Chin forces would conquer the Wu-t'ai region within but a few decades). Nevertheless, we need not draw from the political ramifications of the text any reductionistic conclusions. We need not, for example, assume that political advocacy, special pleading for the economic privilege of certain prominent religious institutions, is somehow the "real" but "covert" meaning of the text. Such advocacy was obviously a significant, and an acknowledged, purpose in the writing and circulation of the work, but it was also a purpose entirely compatible with other motivations operating outside the spheres of economics and politics. One might even suggest that political motivations and religious motivations were mutually entailed, in the sense that an intent to defend Wu-t'ai from governmental depredation would have followed necessarily from a sincere conviction that the mountain was a special venue for the manifestation of supernatural, transcendent forces.

It is also possible that Chang's decision to turn his brush to the defense of Mount Wu-t'ai against economic depredation was part of, or prelude to, his more far-reaching decision to defend all of Buddhism against the analogous but more ideational sort of depredation he found implicit in the nascent rationalism of Tao-hsueh and explicit in Tao-hsueh's public assaults on the dharma. It is a recurrent theme of Chang's later work, for example, the *Essay in Defense of the Dharma*, that contemporary representatives of Confucianism were men of parochial and narrow vision, numb to the transcendent, oblivious of the hieratic, and lacking any capacity for wonder. In Chang's estimation, the world such men would make was barren and constricted, its usages "weary, stale, flat and unprofitable." The numinosity of a place like Wu-t'ai Shan was therefore a resource to be exploited in demonstrating to such men that "there [were] more things in heaven and earth . . . than [were] dreamt of in [their] philosophy." Something like this must have been what he had in mind when, in his memorial to the court, he quoted Chuang Tzu to urge acceptance of "things outside of this world." This kind of apologetic on Buddhism's behalf, based on a conviction that Buddhism preserves a worldview less parochial and more commodious than any other available in China, may well have been another purpose meant to be served by Chang's record.

However, apart from its use as documentation of certain larger currents in popular Chinese religiosity, as an index of economic relations between church and state, or as an antidote to pallid humanism, the *Hsu Ch'ing-liang chuan* has a subtext cutting across the grain of its basic narrative and providing access to a fascinating issue in the study of relations between personal and public spirituality, between elite and popular religion, during a period in history when China was in transition from a "medieval" to an "early modern" stage of cultural development. In fact, our text may be said to exemplify an especially important aspect of that transition.

Let us frame the issue in the form of a pair of questions suggested at the outset of this essay. How is it that, during a period marked for many Chinese intellectuals by the growth of rationalism and humanism,[75] a prominent intellectual, an accomplished man of letters, a distinguished official, and a student of Ch'an Buddhism might undertake a pilgrimage to a place famed for the ecstatic experiences of supernatural and transcendent realities said to befall its visitors? And how is it that, during an age that saw the increasing privatization or interiorization of religiosity among the elite, a leader of the elite should participate in so overt and public a form of religious activity? These questions are not only ours; they do not reflect only a modern puzzlement. They were also of a kind posed frequently in Chang Shang-ying's own age, even by the man himself. In fact, the appearance of conflict between such things was noted widely during the Sung—for example, between the sober rationalism of literati culture or the disenchanting and demythologizing tendencies of Ch'an Buddhism, on the one hand, and the "otherworldly," visionary bent of those forms of Chinese Buddhism more characteristic of earlier times, on the other, or, just as often, between interior religious cultivation and exterior religious display.

Such conflicts were felt with a special urgency in Ch'an, and we must recall that Ch'an, especially, comprised Chang Shang-ying's own Buddhism while also dominating the whole Buddhist intellectual world of the Sung. Consider, then, the following famous passage from a classical Ch'an text especially famous in the Sung, the *Lin-chi lu* 臨濟錄 (Record of Lin-chi):

> There is a kind of student who seeks Mañjuśrī on Wu-t'ai Shan. Wrong from the start! There's no Mañjuśrī on Wu-t'ai Shan. Do you want to know Mañjuśrī? What you do right before your own eyes, which is never uncanny and in no respect dubitable—*this* is the living Mañjuśrī. The nondiscriminating light of your mind in each single instant of thought—in every sense *this* is the true Samantabhadra. That your mind in each single instant of thought can loosen its own bonds and liberate itself in all conditions—*this* is Avalokiteśvara's method of *samādhi*. Since each of these three is alternately either "master" or "attendant," whenever any one of them appears all three appear simultaneously. Each one is all three; all three are each one. Only when you can understand them in this way can you read the sutras properly.[76]

Surely no Sung pilgrim to Mount Wu-t'ai who was also a student of Ch'an could have been ignorant, if not of this very passage, then at least of the standard Ch'an suspicion of such things as pilgrimage that it so forcefully conveys. Moreover, the Sung was an age in which Ch'an Buddhism developed in tandem with the humanism of renascent Confucianism, another tradition that, for its own reasons, also tended to shun the supernatural and the uncanny. Recall, as many Confucians of the day regularly did, the *Analects'* famous remark that "the Master does not speak of strange things" (*tzu pu-yü kuai* 子不語怪, *Lun-yü* 7.20). Such sobriety was not characteristic exclusively of Confucianism; as Lin-chi's and so many other Ch'an remarks indicate, a similar "this-worldliness" also characterized important strains of Sung dynasty Ch'an.

Nevertheless, as well known as Lin-chi's remark and its message may have been, it was equally well known that for centuries past, and continuing even then, numerous Ch'an clergy and laity had been eager visitors to Wu-t'ai or famous residents there. Chang Shang-ying explicitly acknowledges this himself in a rhapsody (*fu*) on Wu-t'ai Shan appended to the body of his narrative (*HCLC* 1129c19–20): "The ordinary person who makes this pious journey loses himself in liberation; when the Ch'an practitioner makes the ascent, the devilish vexations (*māra*) of Ch'an practice all suddenly vanish." Thus we are faced with an apparent contradiction: pilgrimage to distant places in hope of encounters with transcendent beings is said to violate the Ch'an imperative to find enlightenment in the immediacy of one's everyday experience, and yet just such journeys are also celebrated as antidotes to kinds of spiritual tribulation said to be especially endemic to Ch'an practice. As Lin-chi's final comment indicates, the seeming paradox of "Ch'an pilgrimage"—a theme that Bernard Faure also discusses in his contribution to this volume—mirrors the better-known conundrum in which Ch'an Buddhists, proclaiming their tradition's independence from "words and letters," nevertheless devote themselves to deep study of scripture and to prodigious composition of volumes of literature both sacred and secular.

The author of the preface to the two doxologies (*sung* 頌) appended to Chang's narrative tells an anecdote pertinent to this issue.[77]

> Shang-ying once went to Fen-chou[78] to visit Li Chieh 李傑, the state councilor for Hsi-ho.[79] Together they went to pay homage at the memorial pagoda of Ch'an Master Wu-yeh 無業禪師,[80] but they were dismayed to find it in disrepair and made donations so that it might be restored to its original splendor. Chang then had a dream in which Wu-yeh seemed leisurely to beckon him. When he awoke he looked into Wu-yeh's recorded sayings and came across a dialogue between him and Ma Tsu 馬祖 in which Wu-yeh asked Ma Tsu about the meaning of "the mind-seal come from the West." Ma Tsu said, "You're just bothering me. Get out!" As Wu-yeh was leaving Ma-tsu called to him, "Reverend sir." When Wu-yeh turned his head to look back, Ma Tsu said, "What is it?" Upon reading this, Shang-ying clearly understood the visions he had had on Wu-t'ai Shan. He then wrote two stanzas:

> > Four times I entered the Terraced Mountain beseeching wondrous visions.
> > Five times did the clouds shimmer in the fastness.
> > Until now I have not been "playing the drum and flute."[81]
> > One does not repay a Ch'an master by refurbishing his pagoda.
> > "What is it?" "What is it?"

> > Before Rāhu's Hall, a light like flame.
> > I did not wait for Ma Tsu's call to turn.
> > When seen with the vision of Sudhana,[82]
> > The wind at the world's end blows amain, the ninth heaven looms high.[83]
> > When the egret is blind, the fish swim by.

This passage has some of the nearly invincible obscurity that one often finds in Ch'an literature, and I am not confident I have understood or translated all of it correctly. Yet one cannot but note, amid the farrago of elusive and allusive Ch'an tropes, one rather forthright and plain-spoken statement, namely, that Chang had somehow found in the terse and typically Ch'an dialogue between Ma Tsu and Wu-yeh the key to an understanding of the visions he had had on Wu-t'ai.

What could that key have been? What kind of ligature did Chang find to connect the disenchanting, demystifying spirituality of Ch'an with the enchantment and wonder of Wu-t'ai? Wu-yeh, who beckoned Chang in his dream just as Ma Tsu had called to Wu-yeh in the anecdote, was a scholar, a Wu-t'ai pilgrim, and a Ch'an monk; and Chang too is a scholar, a Wu-t'ai pilgrim, and a Ch'an layman. In the original Wu-yeh vignette, Ma Tsu gruffly dismissed Wu-yeh and then, just as Wu-yeh was about to leave (no doubt in some distress at having been dismissed), Ma Tsu called to him, causing him to turn his head and catching him in this moment of vulnerability with a sharp question. Ma Tsu thereby taught his student that Ch'an does not consist of grand and soaring profundities, like the mystery of "the mind-seal come from the West." Indeed, fixation on such exalted abstractions figures prominently among the "afflictions" thought often to bedevil Ch'an practitioners. Rather, Ma Tsu showed that Ch'an consists in immediate experiences of clarity, experiences of the sort that can occur when one is caught off guard and off balance by an arresting insight. Perhaps Chang's numinous visions, and his quest for them, were his equivalent to Wu-yeh's lofty "mind-seal" question. If so, then his initial difficulty in understanding their significance may be in turn the equivalent of Wu-yeh's distress at Ma Tsu's rebuke. Chang too was put off balance and rendered vulnerable. His pilgrimage had left him in a condition of instability and doubt, but also of wonderment and openness. The cumulative effect of such a volatile combination of religious attitudes may have been to make him, like Wu-yeh, susceptible to breakthrough, to the sudden release or relaxation of spiritual tension possible only after tension has reached a peak. The imagery of the poems that follow the anecdote is even more obscure than that of the anecdote itself, but we can still sense a suggestion that the visions Chang had before the Hall of Rāhu had "turned his head" to the same purpose as that to which Ma Tsu's call had turned Wu-yeh's, but perhaps in a more compelling way. Thus, like the primal pilgrim Sudhana, Chang was brought to the very extremities of reality, the outer limit of things where the kalpa-ending wind blows. Those blind to such possibilities, he seems further to suggest, are like sightless egrets, unable to nourish themselves.

We have already noted other anomalous passages, scattered throughout the narrative and punctuating it, that suggest Chang saw a paradoxically complementary relationship between pilgrimage visions and Ch'an. His verse composed on the third day of his visit, after a vision of five-hued clouds and an orb of white light, hints that powerful visionary experience can help sustain one through the struggle of Ch'an practice and can serve as proof against the threat of nihilism. That is to say, it can ward off the danger of mistaking the insubstantiality of worldly things revealed in Ch'an for utter nothingness, which mistake is especially dire because it can too easily lead to quietism, antinomianism, or complete abandonment of religious and moral effort. Likewise, during his visit to Fo-kuang Monastery as he was leaving Wu-t'ai, he recited another verse comparing the Ch'an monk Chieh-t'uo to Mañjuśrī and asserting that both had transcended the mundane order. Nowhere in this world, he says, is there any place to abide, and at Fo-kuang Monastery all that remains of the saint of old is an empty niche. This too is an intimation of the Ch'an tendency to disenchant and demythologize. Cosmic bodhisattva and mortal monk are equated, thereby to bring the former "down to earth" while exalting the latter, and both are said to have left behind an insubstantial and empty world.

But again, as though in compensation for Ch'an's demystification of the world, Chang proceeds immediately from sober Ch'an reflection to further visions of holy lights. Later still, while visiting the Mi-mo Escarpment south of Wu-t'ai and talking with a scholarly hermit-monk, he invokes again Ch'an's capacity to break spells and ruthlessly burst pious illusions. In the disingenuously blasphemous idiom of Ch'an, he goes so far as to compare Buddhism, whenever it is taken as a refuge from immediate experience, to the foul-smelling garment worn by a barbarian and urges that it be cast off. Just then the "barbarian" Mañjuśrī again appears to him, dressed not in putrid robes but in luminous golden raiment and mounted on a green lion!

There is a repeated pattern of significant alternation in all of this, a continuing movement back and forth between the profane and the hieratic, the ordinary and the stupendous, plain daylight and preternatural radiance. In this alternation, I would suggest, we can see a special perception of pilgrimage and its ecstasies, a perception peculiar to the Ch'an intellectual. The intellectual's characteristic suspicion of traditional religious enthusiasm conspires with the pilgrim's heady celebration of the same, and together they provoke, sustain, reciprocate, and cancel each other. Elsewhere in this volume, for example in Pei-yi Wu's and Glen Dudbridge's chapters, we see intellectuals looking upon pilgrimage from the distance of skepticism and irony. They are incredulous of its claims and either unable or reluctant to commit themselves to its euphorias and its unruly energies. By contrast, Chang's view seems much more complex. On the one hand, he seems eager, after some minimal and preliminary doubt, to accept his eventful visit to Wu-t'ai as a genuine encounter with the transcendent. He is openly amazed and deeply inspired. But he is also a Ch'an Buddhist and a Sung intellectual. His Buddhism is not quite the same as the overtly hieratic Buddhism that prevailed in earlier Chinese history. It is not, for example, the esoteric, mystery-intoxicated Buddhism that pervaded Wu-t'ai when Ennin visited there more than two centuries earlier. Ch'an had brought Chinese Buddhism to a condition of spiritual sobriety in which the truly miraculous revealed itself more in quotidian activities like "carrying water and gathering fire-wood" than in visions and transports achieved by leaving the profane realm and entering the heterogeneous space and time of the sacred. It is clear from his explicit references to Ch'an that Chang understood and accepted these aspects of Ch'an. But Ch'an had achieved such down-to-earth sobriety at a cost. It had become a kind of Buddhism that made very heavy demands on those who practiced it, requiring them to be utterly ruthless in their abandonment of all illusions (māras) and denying them the sorts of consolation and support that other forms of Buddhism amply provided through sacramental ritual, mystical transport, vision quests, and the like. This austerity so distinctive of Ch'an could be threatening, and occasionally dispiriting. Not all Ch'an Buddhists could obey Lin-chi's injunction to refrain from "searching for Mañjuśrī" in strange and marvelous places. They needed the strange and the marvelous as spiritual nourishment. And yet, lest such nourishment become addictive, it was necessary somehow to partake of the miraculous liminality of pilgrimage and vision while also undercutting them with sharp Ch'an reminders that, however nourishing they may be, they are still ultimately illusory, whereas true transcendence, of which pilgrimage and visions are but hints, is finally beyond the distinction between the mundane (*lokiya, shih-chien* 世間) and the supramundane (*lokottara, ch'u-shih-chien* 出世間).

Thus can we add another dimension to our interpretation of Chang's memoir. Reading it as an exercise in personal piety, we can reasonably suppose that Chang's pilgrimage to Wu-t'ai Shan and his account thereof may have been deliberate efforts both to confirm and to invigorate his faith. At least it seems to have had that effect, whether or not the effect was intended. Like most Buddhist palmers who traveled to the Five Terraces, Chang hoped to be blessed there with supernal visions, specifically visions of Mañjuśrī and of certain rare phenomena of light and color traditionally thought to signify that celestial Bodhisattva's earthly presence. We have seen that there was good warrant for this. Pilgrimage visions, like the transports and ecstasies of meditation with which they were often associated, had long been held to quicken the doctrines and symbols of Buddhism, to bring them to life so that they might be apprehended not only by the intellect but also by the body, the senses, and the emotions, all now operating in charged and liminal contexts far removed from mundane routine. Pilgrimage and its visions could thus serve both as proof against doubt and as protection against the danger, especially strong in Ch'an, of faith's becoming colorless and anemic. But they could not be allowed to obscure the fact that in the final analysis any pilgrimage taken by a Ch'an Buddhist must be a *via negativa*, a journey into ultimate transcendence beyond even the splendors of sacred places and sacred encounters.

This I take to be the deeper, inherently self-critical message of the *Further Account of Ch'ing-liang*. Chang Shang-ying's work was a miracle tale, to be sure, and by that alone has it merited our close attention. However, as a text of multidimensional meaning, it can also be said, without disparagement of the genre, to be something rather more, or other, than a miracle tale. Much the same may be said of the subject of the text, Chang's visions themselves; they too may have been more or other than that term is usually taken to denote. But then it may be just this abundance of possible meanings that serves best to render both Chang's experiences and his narrative truly worthy to be called miraculous and visionary.

NOTES

1. These terms, of course, are Robert Redfield's, coined in the formulation of his classic distinction between "great" and "little" traditions (Redfield 1956). This distinction, I would suggest, is still useful and rather more applicable to Chinese culture and religion than has recently been averred (Rawski 1985, 404). It is true, however, that in China as elsewhere it should be used as a tool for tracing connections, not only differences, between the two orders of culture.

2. To list only a few of the most important biographical sources: *YYCC* 3:34a–35b; *SS* 116:11095–98; *SSHP* 121:182; *TTSL* 102:1567–71; *CTPT* 23:319–21; *CSFT* 2:898–901; *CSC* 28:897–900; *WTHY* 18:1199–1201; *CYL* 29:632–33; *CWPC* 9:241–43; and *FFCT* 13:951–52. Modern scholarship on Chang is sparse, but the following studies should be noted: Tokiwa 1982, 244–63; Kubota 1931, 522–27; Kubota 1943, 256–64; Andō 1961; Andō 1963; Levering 1978, 214–17; Abe 1986, 393–448; Hsu 1986, 97–100; Abe 1988; and Schmidt-Glintzer 1989.

3. Chang's father, Chang Wen-wei 文蔚 (*tzu:* Yin-chih 隱之, 998–1067), had seven sons, all with names ending in "Ying" 英. Shang-ying was the second of them. His older brother, T'ang-ying 唐英 (1029–71, *tzu:* Tz'u-kung 次功, *chin-shih* in 1043; see *SS* 351), who served as Shang-ying's boyhood teacher, was famous in his own right and until his early death wielded political influence comparable to that his brother would enjoy through most of his career. Chang Wen-wei's tomb inscription, which has been preserved in *YYCC* 2, provides a detailed genealogy of the family. T'ang-ying's tomb inscription, composed by Chang Shang-ying himself, also survives, in the same source; it mentions that the elder brother, like many of his and Chang Shang-ying's forebears, was a devotee of Taoism. In this too he may have been an early influence on his younger brother.

4. Chang Tun (*tzu:* Tzu-hou 子厚; see *SS* 471) was entrusted especially with control of frontier affairs and seems to have had much to do with implementing Wang An-shih's policies in Szechwan. Through this position, apparently, he came to know and sponsor Chang Shang-ying. It is likely, however, that brother T'ang-ying also had something to do with the early advancement of Shang-ying's career. For more on

Chang Tun and the Szechwan frontier during the Northern Sung, see von Glahn 1987, 210 et passim.

5. *SS* 351:11095; quoted also in *TTSL* 102:1569 and in other sources. Citing the classical maxim "To refrain for three years from altering one's father's way—this may be called filial piety," Chang goes on to observe, trenchantly, that "now, before the earth of the previous emperor's tumulus has even dried, the policies are changed; how can this be deemed filial piety!" At about the same time he is also said to have written a letter to Su Shih, inviting him to return to service in the capital; in that missive he reiterated this charge in the form of a euphemistic and sylleptic pun (*sou-tz'u* 瘦辭), an erudite double entendre that turns in part on the political use of a conventional Ch'an phrase—to wit: "An old monk, wishing to abide in crow temple, berates the Buddha and scolds the patriarchs." "Crow temple" (*wu-ssu* 烏寺) is a homonym of *wu-ssu* 烏私 (filial piety). (This locution is an ellipsis of the phrase *wu-niao ssu-ch'ing* 烏鳥私情 [the young crow's solicitude], which is taken from the well-known *Ch'en-ch'ing piao* 陳情表 [Memorial expressing my feelings]. In that famous memorial, preserved in the *Chin-shu* [*chüan* 88] and the *Wen-hsuan* [*chüan* 37], the courtier Li Mi [224–87] declines imperial appointment by pleading that he must care for his aged grandmother, thereby imitating the young crow who, according to popular Chinese belief, cares for its dying mother by disgorging its own food into the parent's mouth.) This remark, the *SS* tells us, got Chang expelled from the capital. Oft-told anecdotes like this, celebrating Chang's outspoken honesty and sharp wit, would endear him to posterity as a man of singular courage and integrity. No wonder that in later Chinese popular fiction and drama he would become a kind of stock character, the very model of the "upright official."

6. The most detailed documentary account of this phase of Chang's career is to be found in *CSPM* 131:3965–81.

7. The commonly given death date of 1121 is off by one day.

8. Best known as the teacher of Ta-hui and the compiler of the Ch'an tradition's single most influential *kung-an* 公案 (Jpn.: *kōan*) anthology, the *Pi-yen lu* 碧巖錄 (Blue grotto record), Yuan-wu (a.k.a. Fo-kuo Ch'an-shih 佛果禪師) was one of the two or three foremost Ch'an masters of his day. For a standard account of his life and representative examples of his style of teaching see the entry on him in *WTHY* 19:1253–57. See also *ZD*, 161–63. Chang Shang-ying appears several times as an interlocutor in Yuan-wu's recorded sayings (*Yuan-wu Fo-kuo Ch'an-shih yü-lu*, 20 *chüan*, *T* 47:713–810—e.g., 735b–c). Another disciple of Yuan-wu, Hu-ch'iu Shao-lung 虎丘紹隆 (1077–1136), was a progenitor of several important lines of Japanese Zen, and it is in part for this reason that Chang Shang-ying came to be known and respected in that country.

9. See *WTHY* 17:1147–49 and 1150–54. The Ch'an tradition's "official" judgment as to Chang's Ch'an lineage is that he was a disciple or descendant of Tou-shuai Ts'ung-yueh. Thus, it is under Tou-shuai's name that Chang's usually appears in most Ch'an lineage charts.

10. *WTHY* 17:1159–60. See also Hui-hung's autobiography in his *wen-chi* (*SMWT* 24:17a–18b). For modern treatments of Hui-hung, see Abe 1986, 449–88, and Yanagida 1988, 30–57 et passim.

11. Chang is mentioned in Ta-hui's writings too. See Levering 1978.

12. Li T'ung-hsuan was a major inspiration for Chang, as he was for many of

Chang's Ch'an contemporaries, perhaps in part because he too was a layman but also because he exemplified a desirable combination of deep Buddhist learning, especially in the Hua-yen tradition, with the practice of meditation and the promise of visionary experience. See Gimello 1983.

13. This frequently reprinted work vies both with Ch'i-sung's earlier *Fu-chiao pien* 輔教編 (*T* 52:637a–46c), which Chang knew and to which he wrote the standard preface, and with Li P'ing-shan's 李屏山 later *Ming-tao-chi shuo* 鳴道集說 for the distinction of being judged the most eloquent and sustained Buddhist response to the Neo-Confucian or Tao-hsueh critique of Buddhism that began in the Northern Sung and achieved orthodox status thereafter. For more on Li P'ing-shan's work see Jan 1979. Literature on Ch'i-sung is more plentiful; see especially Huang 1986. Note too that Chang wrote the standard preface to Ch'i-sung's work.

14. Note especially his postface (*hou-chi* 後記) to Li T'ung-hsuan's *Lueh-shih hsin Hua-yen ching hsiu-hsing tz'u-ti chueh-i lun* 略釋新華嚴經修行次第決疑論 (A brief explanation of the newly translated version of the *Hua-yen ching*, being a treatise which settles doubts concerning the sequence of cultivation; *T* 36:1048c27–49c14). In the opening lines of this postface Chang mentions that he had come upon Li T'ung-hsuan's work in October of 1088 on Fang Shan 方山, a mountain about twenty miles east of the town of Shou-yang 壽陽, itself only about twenty miles east of T'ai-yuan. He had visited Li T'ung-hsuan's shrine on that mountain, the Chao-hua yuan 昭化院, while on his way back from Wu-t'ai Shan to T'ai-yuan. He even mentions specifically the vision he had had at the Mi-mo Escarpment, the one described at the end of the pilgrimage narrative, and says that, having just had visions of Mañjuśrī, he was in a state of exaltation in which he had vowed to undertake the study of Buddhism. This testimony must be borne in mind as one considers the question of the authenticity of the *HCLC*; it would seem corroborative.

15. *CCTS* 4c:21a–b. Other sources mention collections in 53 *chüan* or 100 *chüan* (*SS* 208, 5357), and one source lists a *pieh-chi* in 17 *chüan*; see Hsu 1986, 99. All that actually survives of this large collection is the selection of 58 pieces, culled from various sources, preserved in *STSW* 13–14:195–218.

16. The most readily available and, apart from considerations of punctuation, perhaps also the most complete and reliable version of the *HCLC* is *T* 51:1127a–29c, no. 2100—i.e., the version found in the *Taishō shinshū daizōkyō*, the standard modern citation edition of the Sino-Japanese Buddhist canon published between 1925 and 1932. This version of the text is based, in turn, on that in the *Dainihon zokuzōkyō* edition of the canon published in Kyoto between 1905 and 1912. In the recent Taiwan and Hong Kong reprints of the *Zokuzōkyō*, entitled *Wan-tzu* 卍字 *hsu-tsang ching*, it appears in vol. 150, pp. 492–508. Both these Japanese editions of the *HCLC* are based on a Ch'ing edition privately published in 1884. The Ch'ing edition was based on, but seems not to be exactly the same as, a Ming edition of 1462 that had come into the possession of the great bibliophile Juan Yuan (1764–1849). Because the work had not been included in the *Ssu-k'u ch'üan-shu*, Juan decided to include it in his *Wan-wei pieh-tsang*, where it can still be found (*WWPT* 150). The source of the 1462 edition appears to have been an earlier Ming edition (1396) based on a printed Chin dynasty edition. The preface to this Chin edition, by Yao Hsiao-hsi 姚孝錫 (see *CSCS* 5.3b), is dated 1164. This combined publication also included Hui-hsiang's *CLC* and Yen-i's *KCLC*. We can trace the textual history of the work back no further than this, except to note,

on the basis of internal evidence, that Chang finished composing the main portion of the work in 1088, immediately after his eight-day visit to Wu-t'ai and at the request of the Wu-t'ai monastic community. It was on September 17, 1088, we are precisely told, that the basic narrative, perhaps together with the several Wu-t'ai poems still found appended to it, was bound, wrapped, and given to the Wu-t'ai monks as a gift. That narrative and those poems comprise the first *chüan* of the present expanded edition. Since the monks had expressly asked Chang to write the text to use in defending the interests of their institutions against governmental depredations, we can safely assume that they began circulating it right away. Over the course of the next several years, in connection with later visits to the mountain, several supplements were added, taking the story of Chang's association with Wu-t'ai down to 1090. A number of related pieces—postfaces, accounts of other visits to Wu-t'ai by later pilgrims who compared their experiences to Chang's, and the like—were also added later. All these supplements were eventually incorporated, as a second *chüan*, into the expanded version of the text we now have in the redactions listed above. Note also that the two extant gazetteers of Wu-t'ai Shan—the *Ch'ing-liang shan chih* 清凉山志 of 1596 (*CLSC* 241–54) and the *Ch'ing-liang shan hsin-chih* 新志 of 1701 (*CLSH* 242–60)— include in their entries on Chang Shang-ying the core of our text, but without most of the later supplements. The Ming gazetteer version is, for the most part, simply a condensation of the original text, with some minor rewordings. The Ch'ing gazetteer version, however, is rather more than that. It tells the same story but in language often very different from that of the other versions. Since it seems unlikely (although not impossible) that the compilers of the Ch'ing gazetteer had at their disposal an otherwise unknown alternative version of the text, we are led to assume that they decided simply to paraphrase, or to rewrite from imagination, the more opaque or prolix passages in the original. Indeed, the wording of many passages in this paraphrase is often easier to follow than are the sometimes difficult locutions in the original version. I have sometimes relied on these later gazetteer versions when I have not been able to decipher the original version, but seldom have I done this in the confident belief that the reedited versions are necessarily correct, and in several instances I have found that the gazetteer editors had simply gotten things wrong. Both of these abridged and paraphrastic versions are now conveniently available in the recently published collection of Buddhist monastic gazetteers (*CKFSC* II.29 and III.30). In 1725 the editors of *Ku-chin t'u-shu chi-ch'eng* also included the story of Chang's pilgrimage in their entry on Wu-t'ai Shan in the section on mountains and rivers (*KCTS* 186:1a2–2a2), but their version is only a nearly verbatim repetition of the Ch'ing gazetteer version. The Kyoto University Library and the Kiangsu Provincial Library hold manuscript versions of the text, but I have not had access to them and so know nothing of their provenances or their relations to other redactions. Finally, well after I had finished most of this essay, I learned that in May 1989 the Shansi People's Publishing Company of T'ai-yuan had published a critical and punctuated edition of the whole Wu-t'ai trilogy, including Chang's work, in simplified characters, annotated and punctuated by Ch'en Yang-chiung 陳揚炯 and Feng Ch'iao-ying 馮巧英. I have had the chance barely to glance at this edition. My cursory examination revealed nothing that would require major revision of this article, but this new edition clearly warrants more careful study.

17. Whether or not we can ever positively prove that Chang wrote the *HCLC*, we

can have no doubt that he did visit Wu-t'ai in 1088. Several reliable sources, including other pieces by Chang himself and even two farewell poems by Su Shih (*SSSC* 1566–67) the second of which mentions Wu-t'ai specifically, attest to this visit. That Chang made the visit lends at least some plausibility to the claim that he was also somehow responsible for the account of the visit.

18. Professor Pei-yi Wu raised such doubts during the conference from which this volume derives. He suggested that the work is so clumsily written that it may have been composed by some ill-educated and anonymous author, perhaps a monk, who merely ascribed it to Chang Shang-ying to lend it the luster of an eminent name. Although I confess that I find much of the prose of the *HCLC* awkward and some of it obscure, there are also passages of eloquence and many striking turns of phrase. In any case, I am reluctant to assess authenticity on the basis of stylistic characteristics, and I would require more and different evidence before rejecting the traditional attribution. The admittedly inelegant style in which certain portions of the text are written could perhaps be taken as evidence of its reportorial authenticity. In my estimation, a text originally written by Chang Shang-ying was most likely rewritten, summarized, or enlarged by someone less articulate than he, perhaps one or more of the monks to whom he had made a gift of his holograph (see above). In support of this hypothesis I can note a consistent difference in diction between the narrative portions of the text and those portions that purport actually to quote from documents Chang is said to have composed. The latter are usually more fluent, elegant, and recondite. It is true that the authenticity of another work attributed to Chang has been questioned. The great modern bibliographer of Chinese Buddhism, Ch'en Yuan (Ch'en 1962, 18–19), has cited a thirteenth-century source (*CCL* 4:2202b; see *SB* 313) that says the *Hu-fa lun* was actually composed by Chang's clerical friend and protégé Chueh-fan Hui-hung, who is said merely to have "borrowed Chang Wu-chin's name" for the purpose. However, Andō Tomonobu (Andō 1963) has thoroughly examined this claim, which is made in no other source, and found it to be unlikely. It may derive from a residual prejudice expressed in a refusal to believe that an otherwise respected literatus could have been also a devout Buddhist layman. In any case, doubts about this other work have little bearing on the question of literary style, because Hui-hung was himself a superior stylist, and the *Hu-fa lun* has always been judged a stylistically exemplary work.

19. The section of the expanded *HCLC* translated below comprises 7 registers of the Taishō canon (1127b12–29c13). A word on method and problems of translation is in order at this point. This is a particularly knotty text, preserved in redactions that are frequently faulty and written in a dense style that is sometimes concise to a fault. It does not lend itself well to literal rendering, at least not without the risk of making the text seem less fluent and more awkward than it is in the original. I have therefore chosen to adopt a relatively free style of translation, sometimes verging on paraphrase, and I have taken pains to identify those passages I am not sure I have understood. I should also note that the author of the work seems to have spent much effort in trying to describe precisely the visual or visionary phenomena or both that comprise the core of his work. Several features of the text (e.g., attention to details of distance, direction, time of day, color, names, etc.) suggest that he sought to avoid vague impressionism and strove, perhaps with memory still fresh, for precise description and imagery. This authorial virtue, however, has made the translator's task all

the more difficult. Even where I think I have caught the author's meaning, I continue to suspect that I have missed the detail, the nuance, and thus perhaps much of the intended emotional effect. What I have translated, for example, as "azure" or "purple" may actually be slightly different colors, and much may hang on such differences. Nor can I be sure that I have perceived the real differences among various kinds of "fog," "mist," and so forth—not to mention the much more important differences among varieties of light (e.g., I am not always sure whether a light is a "glow," "blaze," "radiance," etc.). Finally, I should note that I have not been to Wu-t'ai Shan nor even seen a good collection of photographs, and these disadvantages hamper my sense of the geography and atmosphere of the place.

20. The abbreviated and edited version of the text found in the Ch'ing gazetteer of Wu-t'ai (mentioned above) refers to this work by another title, namely, *Shen-teng chi* 神燈記 (The record of the mystic lights); see *CLSH* 5:260. I have not found any other occurrence of this alternate title; it may simply be a designation chosen by the gazetteer editors, but it is descriptive of the actual content of the text in which phenomena of light predominate.

21. The Ho-tung circuit was one of twenty-four large, supraprefectural regions into which the Northern Sung had divided its territory. It encompassed all of what is today Shansi (including Wu-t'ai Shan) as well as parts of the adjacent modern provinces. That Chang was a "gentleman in court service" (*ch'ao-feng lang* 朝奉郎, a prestige title available usually to those of ranks 6a1 to 7a) and that he was "provisionally assigned" (*ch'üan fa-ch'ien* 權發遣) to the office of judicial comissioner would seem to indicate that he was at the time an official of moderately distinguished rank assigned to a lower-order position.

22. The second lunar month of 1087 corresponds to the period from March 8 to April 5. Apropos of this, the Western reader may recall "Whan that Aprille with his shoures soote / The droghte of March hath perced to the roote /. . . Than longen folk to goon pilgrimages." The timing of Chang Shang-ying's dream was fortuitous indeed. In 1087 Chang was forty-four years old (45 *sui*). His official career had begun more than twenty years earlier and had flourished under the patronage of the great reformer Wang An-shih. But Wang's reform regime had been ousted in 1085, and the man himself had died in 1086. In the early years of the subsequent conservative reaction, Chang's fortunes waned somewhat. His appointment as judge (*t'ui-kuan* 推官) in K'ai-feng began at the outset of Che-tsung's reign (actually the dowager Hsuan-jen's regency) in 1085. That position was a demotion from the higher ones he had held at the court of Shen-tsung (e.g., investigating censor and examiner for the rites section of the Secretariat [*chien-cheng chung-shu li-fang chien-ch'a yü-shih* 檢正中書禮房檢察御史]). His posting to the provinces less than two years later can be seen as a further reduction in status. It is no wonder, then, that he should have been inclined to seek the succor of pilgrimage—the liberation it provides from settled structures of unsatisfying worldly experience, affording both distance and entrance into transfigured landscapes. Thus could he transform a moderate kind of exile into a spiritual adventure or quest. In this connection, see Dupront 1974 and note especially his characterization of pilgrimage as "une thérape par l'espace" (190). (The whole of Dupront's essay, even though it draws its examples almost always from the history of Christianity, is recommended as a very rich treatment of pilgrimage from a general and phenomenological point of view.)

23. Throughout this narrative Chang is referred to in the third person, and his personal name, rather than his cognomen or sobriquet, is used. To what extent this was simply a polite convention by which an author might refer to himself or to what extent it might suggest that Chang may not actually have written the piece, I cannot say, but I have chosen to follow the same convention in English.

24. The Diamond Grotto is the invisible cave in Lou-kuan 樓觀 Valley west of the Eastern Terrace in which the Kashmiri missionary and translator Buddhapāla (or Buddhapāli or Buddhapālita; Chinese: Fo-t'o po-li 佛陀波利) was believed to have been secreted. In 676 Buddhapāla had come to Wu-t'ai on pilgrimage, hoping to have a vision of Mañjuśrī. He was met on his arrival by an old man who told him he could not see the Bodhisattva unless he had brought with him a copy of the *Sarvadurgati-pariśodhana-uṣṇīṣavijayā-dhāraṇī (Fo-ting tsun-sheng t'o-lo-ni ching 佛頂尊勝陀羅尼經; T 19, no. 967). This is a tantric text believed to provide remission of karmicly deserved rebirth in one of the three lesser or evil destinies (durgati). Apparently it was deemed necessary to the task of shriving the Chinese Buddhist community, laity and clergy alike, of its endemic sinfulness. As it happened, Buddhapāla had not brought this text with him and so went back to India to retrieve it. When he returned to China several years later (in 683) he went straightaway to Ch'ang-an. At first Emperor Kao-tsung assigned the task of translating the work to others and insisted that he would keep the Sanskrit manuscript in the palace. Eventually, however, he released the manuscript to Buddhapāla, who, with the aid of a Chinese assistant, translated it himself for general distribution (this even though it had already been rendered into Chinese twice before, while Buddhapāla was back in India collecting the text). He then returned to Wu-t'ai with the original Sanskrit text in hand and was met again by the old man, who this time revealed himself as Mañjuśrī. The Boddhisattva led the pilgrim into the Diamond Grotto, which then closed itself up and has not reopened since. Buddhapāla and Mañjuśrī in the guise of an old man are portrayed together in the famous tenth-century panorama of Wu-t'ai Shan found in cave sixty-one at Mo-kao-k'u 莫高窟, Tun-huang.

The Japanese pilgrim Ennin (793–863) visited this grotto in 840 and reported that the place on the face of the cliff where the grotto's entrance had once been was concealed by a tower containing a revolving hexagonal scripture repository. In addition to recounting the Buddhapāla story, Ennin also noted the belief, recorded as early as 667 in Hui-hsiang's CLC, that Mañjuśrī had long ago filled the sealed grotto with many miraculous things—a variety of supernal musical instruments bequeathed by Buddhas of prior aeons, a thirteen-thousand-story pagoda containing "the whole body" of the Buddha Kāśyapa (the second of the seven "previous Buddhas"), Chinese writings in gold ink on silver paper, and billions of scripts from the other lands of the Four Continents. Some 144 years later (i.e., in 984) another Japanese visitor to Wu-t'ai, the monk Chōnen 奝然 (938–1016), who founded Kyoto's Seiryōji 清凉寺, also visited the Diamond Grotto, although he provided no further description of the place. His successor among Japanese pilgrims, the elderly Tendai prelate Jōjin 成尋 (1011–81), may also have seen the grotto during his short stay on Wu-t'ai in the winter of 1073, but he made no explicit reference to it in his travel diary. However, Jōjin did meet Yen-i, the author of the 1060 KCLC, and received from him a copy of that work, to which this record by Chang Shang-ying, penned only twenty-eight years later, has been seen as a kind of sequel.

Concerning Buddhapāla, the Diamond Grotto, and the *Uṣṇīṣa-dhāraṇī*, see the preface to Buddhapāla's translation of the scripture (*T* 19:349b–c); *ENGJ* 124; *CLC* 1095a; *SKSC* 717c–18b; *KCLC* 1111a–b; *CLSC* 55–56 and 186–87; Bagchi 1938, 2:512–14; Ono and Hibino 1942, 26–29 et passim; Waley 1952, 137–38; Reischauer 1955a, 246–48; Reischauer 1955b, 195–96; Lamotte 1960, 86–88; Lessing and Wayman 1968, 115; Tokiwa and Sekino 1975a, 1:94; Tokiwa and Sekino 1975b, 1:84–85; Marchand 1976, 161; Kobayashi 1979, 132. On Jōjin and Chōnen, see Gimello 1987.

Concerning the fact that the cave was sealed, that is, that it was a virtual rather than an actual grotto, see Brown 1981, 87: "For the art of the shrine in late antiquity is an art of closed surfaces. Behind the surfaces, the holy lay, either totally hidden or glimpsed through narrow apertures. The opacity of the surfaces heightened the awareness of the unattainability in this life of the person they had travelled over such wide spaces to touch." Perhaps this characteristic of late antique Christian shrines also marks shrines elsewhere. Note too the association here of a sacred place with sacred texts. In this connection, see Schopen 1975 and note particularly his discussion of the Mahayana Buddhist "cult of the book," which seems originally to have competed with the "cult of the relic." Part of the former cult was a tradition according to which certain places are made sacred just by the presence in them of sacred texts. It is as though the ultimate relic (*śarīra*) were, as normative Buddhist tradition had long held, the "body of the dharma" (*dharmakāya*), rather than any fleshly body or body part. That such beliefs should have flourished in China—a "culture of the book" par excellence—should not be surprising. For more on relics and pilgrimage, see Bernard Faure, chapter 4 of this volume.

25. One wonders, of course—if, in fact, the Diamond Grotto was unknown to him—how Chang was able to identify the place he had visited in his dream. Perhaps, his disclaimer notwithstanding, he had already read earlier accounts of Wu-t'ai. In any case, without denying that Chang's interest in traveling to Wu-t'ai may have been inspired by a dream, we may nevertheless suggest that what we see here, and should not be surprised to see, is an example of a literatus's availing himself of a venerable Chinese literary convention, namely, the motif of the prescient dream journey. Neither should we be surprised that this dream focused on a cave or grotto, for such have always been among the most common Chinese venues for oneiric revelations, particularly in those literary traditions influenced by Taoism, with which, as we have seen, Chang was familiar.

26. The passage mentioning Chang's clerk and quoting his initial comment is a bit garbled in certain versions of the text. I read "Ping-chou" 幷州 rather than the "Ping-lü" 幷閭 of certain corrupt editions. Ping-chou is the ancient name of the region—one of the nine primordial provinces of China—in which Wu-t'ai is situated. It corresponds to the modern areas of northern Shansi and a part of western Hopei.

27. As to the location of Chang's headquarters, one might assume it was T'ai-yuan, for this was the largest city in his jurisdiction and was only about a hundred miles southwest of Wu-t'ai. Another possibility is Hsin-chou 忻州, the seat of Hsin prefecture, situated midway between T'ai-yuan and Wu-t'ai (about sixty-five miles southwest of the mountains) along the main route to the mountains. Still another possibility is Tai-chou 代州, a frontier town about thirty-five miles west of the central Wu-t'ai complex and corresponding to the modern Tai-hsien. In fact, Chang himself tells us that his offices were there a few years later, in 1090. Of course, during

the several years of his tenure in this post he may have conducted his ministerial affairs at various times in all these locations. In any case, he first arrived at his post in the fall of 1087 (between August 31 and September 29), and his initial visit to Wu-t'ai, for the purpose especially of seeing the Diamond Grotto, occurred sometime between November 28 and December 27. That it should have lasted only a day or two is not surprising if one bears in mind that winter weather on Wu-t'ai is often forbidding.

28. That Chang's return to Wu-t'ai the following summer (1088) was occasioned in part by his duty to suppress bandits in the area or to defend against possible invasion must stand as a qualification upon our definition of that visit as a pilgrimage. In contrast, that the visit was marked by a regimen of fasting and abstinence does support such a characterization, for such austerities commonly attend pilgrimages as they do other *rites de passage*.

29. Although "Ch'ing-liang Shan" (Clear and Cold Mountain) is used as an alternative name for the whole of Wu-t'ai Shan, here it refers to a particular monastery (major monasteries were commonly referred to, figuratively, as "mountains"). This Temple of Chill Clarity was given the mountain's name as its own chiefly because, according to tradition, it was the first monastery to have been built in Wu-t'ai's sacred precinct, having been established by Emperor Hsiao-wen of the Northern Wei (r. 471–99). The buildings that now comprise it are said to date back to a Chin dynasty reconstruction of the twelfth century. Ch'ing-liang Monastery is in the Ch'ing-liang Valley near the main route into the Wu-t'ai complex, between the Western Terrace and the Southern Terrace. See *KCLC* 1114b; Kobayashi 1979, 133; Tokiwa and Sekino 1975a, 1:99; Tokiwa and Sekino 1975b, 1:95–96.

30. This "golden bridge" is something of a mystery. I cannot tell if it was an actual bridge of human construction, a natural formation like a ridge, some atmospheric phenomenon like an arc of golden light, or something entirely visionary. One or the other of the latter two possibilities would seem most likely. The Tun-huang panorama of Wu-t'ai includes a cartouche noting a "place where a magical golden bridge appeared"; in the painting this is just east of the Ch'ing-liang Monastery. Perhaps the most famous tale of a golden bridge is that told apropos of Tao-i, the founder of the Chin-ko Monastery (see note 32, below). Also, Yen-i tells us (*KCLC, T* 51:1114b) that another famous eighth-century resident of Wu-t'ai, the Pure Land devotee Fa-chao, saw a "large golden bridge" as part of the vision that led to his establishing the Monastery of the Bamboo Grove (Chu-lin ssu).

31. The identity of Supervisor Ts'ui 崔提舉 is unknown. The *KCTS* entry on Wu-t'ai (186:8bc) tells of a certain "Administrator Ts'ui" who heard miraculous bells during an undated visit to the Central Terrace, but no visions are ascribed to him in this brief account. Chang's observation implying that he and Supervisor Ts'ui had much in common I take to be a reference to his confidence in the possibility of visions even for laymen and worldlings like himself. Such experiences are not reserved, he seems to suggest, exclusively for monks or the saintly. This suggestion, in turn, would seem to support a general claim made for pilgrimage and sacred places in all cultures, namely, that they foster a condition of solidarity and equality (*communitas*) in which social and other sorts of profane status distinctions are dissolved. Ennin had observed the same phenomenon centuries earlier (see, e.g., *ENGJ* 128; Reischauer 1955a, 257–58: "Those who enter these mountains naturally develop a spirit of equality [*p'ing-*

teng chih hsin 平等之心]. When maigre feasts are arranged in these mountains, whether one be a cleric or a layman, man or woman, great or small, food is offered to all equally. Regardless of rank or position, here all persons make one think of [or, 'give rise to thoughts of'—RMG] Mañjuśrī.")

32. The Temple of the Golden Pavilion—original namesake of Kyoto's famous Kinkakuji—is northwest of Ch'ing-liang Monastery. Its history began in 736 when Mañjuśrī vouchsafed to the Ch'an monk and Wu-t'ai pilgrim Tao-i 道義 visions of himself (again as an old man) and of an array of marvelous golden mansions approached by a golden bridge. Some years later Tao-i either returned to Ch'ang-an to apprise the court of his experiences or sent back to the court a painting of his envisioned temple in the hope of eliciting imperial support for the construction of an actual temple built according to the model of his vision. In 766, at the urging of the great Chen-yen 眞言 prelate Amoghavajra (Pu-k'ung 不空, 705–74), the chief sponsor of the Mañjuśrī cult in eighth-century China, and with the support of the devout lay Buddhist minister Wang Chin, brother to the poet Wang Wei, Emperor Tai-tsung made a grant for that purpose. A year later, a truly impressive earthly replica of Tao-i's visionary palace-temple was completed, and Amoghavajra was appointed its first abbot (apparently in absentia, for it seems he did not actually visit Wu-t'ai until 770). The Golden Pavilion, during the T'ang a truly magnificent edifice, became a major center of esoteric Buddhism for the remainder of the dynasty. One of the first of the many Japanese pilgrims to Wu-t'ai, the unfortunate monk Reisen 靈仙 (variant pronunciation: Ryōsen; arrived in China 804; d. on Wu-t'ai of poisoning 825–28) stayed there for a time, leaving behind a piece of his skin on which he had incised an image of the Buddha. Ennin, who described the Golden Pavilion in great detail in his diary, noted that the curious relic was still there in 840. The buildings now comprising the temple seem all to date from no earlier than the Ch'ing, although a thousand-armed Kuan-yin housed in the main hall was constructed during the Ming. For general accounts of the Golden Pavilion, Tao-i, Amoghavajra, and Reisen, see *KCLC* 1113a–c; *ENGJ* 126; *SKSC* 843c–44a; *SPC* 834a; Wang Chin's biography in *CTS* 118:3418; Reischauer 1955a, 252; Reischauer 1955b, 158; Tokiwa and Sekino 1975a, 1:100; Tokiwa and Sekino 1975b, 97–102; Ono and Hibino, 45–56; Birnbaum 1983, 14–16 and 25–38; von Verschuer 1985, 484–85; and Weinstein 1987, 77–89.

33. The atmosphere around Mount Wu-t'ai seems commonly to abound in unusual cloud formations and to be emblazed by strange lights. In fact, these are among the most characteristic objects of visionary experience on the mountain, and they are still reported by modern visitors. See, for example, John Blofeld's account of an experience that befell him during a visit to Wu-t'ai sometime in the late 1930s: "There in the great open space beyond the window [of a tower on the South Terrace], apparently not more than one or two hundred yards away, innumerable balls of fire floated majestically past. We could not judge their size, for nobody knew how far away they were, but they appeared like the fluffy woolen balls that babies play with seen close up. They seemed to be moving at the stately pace of a large, well-fed fish aimlessly cleaving its way through the water; but, of course, their actual pace could not be determined without a knowledge of the intervening distance. Where they came from, and where they went after fading from sight in the West, nobody could tell. Fluffy balls of orange-coloured fire—truly a fitting manifestation of divinity!" (Blofeld 1972, 149–50). Many modern observers of such strange sights might wish to explain

them as meteorological phenomena. Perhaps they can be so explained, perhaps not, but in either case we should not fail to note that radiance also plays an important part in the textual visions of buddhas, bodhisattvas, and their paradises that informed the piety of Wu-t'ai visitors. The *Hua-yen ching*, a crucial text for the formation of Wu-t'ai spirituality, is particularly rich in imagery of incandescence, translucence, reflection, and the like. What we have here may be an example of sacred tradition conspiring with nature to transfigure unusual natural phenomena by investing them with spiritual significance.

34. The phrase "mark of radiance" (*kuang-hsiang* 光相) probably refers specifically to the *vyāmaprabhā* (the span of radiance), one of the thirty-two major marks of a superior person (*dvātriṃśad mahāpuruṣa lakṣaṇa*) thought to grace the bodies of all buddhas and buddhas-to-be. It is classically described (e.g., in the *TCTL* 90c; Lamotte 1966, 277) as a luminous aura extending to a distance of one span on all sides of the body. In Mahayana, of course, this aura grows well beyond a single span in size and is often described as a radiance consisting of myriad shafts of light shining from every pore of the Buddha's or bodhisattva's body and traveling infinitely far in all directions to illumine the entire trichilicosm. In this case, the radiance sought is surely Mañjuśrī's; in the art associated with that Bodhisattva in his role as resident of Wu-t'ai, a nimbus of multicolored rays of light emanating from all sides of his body is a common iconographical feature (see Birnbaum 1983, 19–24).

35. I have translated *kung-shang* 公裳 (literally, "public garments") as "pilgrim's garb" on the assumption that it refers to the special sort of uniform and plain clothing, usually bereft of all indications of secular social status and identity, that pilgrims wear at, and on the way to, their sacred destinations. It is another emblem of peregrine "communitas" and of the askesis so universally characteristic of pilgrimage.

36. The Cloister of the True Countenance, sometimes called a Hall (*tien* 殿) and at certain later times known as the Great Temple of Mañjuśrī (Ta Wen-shu ssu 大文殊寺), was founded in the early eighth century by the monk Fa-yun 法雲, an ardent devotee of Mañjuśrī. It was the site of a series of miraculous appearances of Mañjuśrī (seventy-two "sittings," as it were) before the artist An Sheng 安生, who had undertaken to sculpt a clay image of the sage on Fa-yun's behalf. Mañjuśrī's repeated visits were said to have ensured the accuracy of the clay portrait. The temple was rebuilt in 977 at the order of Sung T'ai-tsung and was shortly thereafter made a repository of one of five copies of the entire Tripitaka, which T'ai-tsung had ordered inscribed in gold characters. Later reconstructions were undertaken during the Yung-lo (1403–24) and K'ang-hsi (1662–1722) eras. The temple is on a hill near the center of the Wu-t'ai complex known from early times as Ling-chiu feng 靈鷲峯 (Gṛdhra-kūṭa, i.e., Vulture's Peak), so named after the original Indian site outside Rājagṛha where Sakyamuni delivered so many of his discourses. The Ming and Ch'ing temples now found on this hill came, during the Ch'ing, under the control of Tibetan monks; even today they comprise the largest of the several Tibetan establishments at Wu-t'ai. Nowadays this monastery (and perhaps also the hill it tops) is most commonly known as Bodhisattva's Crown (P'u-sa ting 菩薩頂), and climbing the 108 stone steps leading up to it is still one of the highlights of any visit to Wu-t'ai. It is only a few hundred yards north of the great white Tibetan Pagoda (*rchod-rten* or *chorten*) which, like the nearby Hsien-t'ung Monastery 顯通寺, is one of the dominant edifices in Wu-t'ai's

central valley. See *KCLC* 1110a–b; *CLSC* 71–72; Tokiwa and Sekino 1975a, 80–81; and Tokiwa and Sekino 1975b, 1:92. Note too that this temple acquired special fame in Chinese popular fiction as the site of a memorable episode in the *Shui-hu chuan* 水滸傳 (chap. 4) in which a boisterous Lu Chih-shen 魯智深, masquerading as a monk, violates the rules against meat and drink and nearly tears the place apart in a drunken rage.

37. I have not been able precisely to identify Dragon Mountain, Gold Precinct Stream, the Pavilion of Clear Brilliance, or the Lodge of Mañjuśrī's Transformation. I suspect, however, that the latter two are subsidiary buildings within or near the larger Chen-jung tien (Hall of the True Countenance). Such must be the case also with the balneary or bathhouse (*yü-shih* 浴室).

38. Mañjuśrī was clearly not the only sacred personage whom pilgrims journeyed to Wu-t'ai to visit. The Rāhu after whose footprint the hall here mentioned was named may have been Gautama's son, Rāhula (in which case the final syllable of his name is simply missing), but possibly he was the Demon (*āsura*) King, Rāhu, who was once subdued by the Buddha after attempting to swallow (eclipse) the moon god. The latter tale was often told and would have been readily available to the Chinese in, for example, the encyclopedic *Great Treatise on the Perfection of Insight* (*TCTL* 135b; Lamotte 1966, 610–12). However, a recent article on a Tun-huang manuscript account of an Indian monk's visit to Wu-t'ai (Schneider 1987, 34, note 28) mentions that Rāhula was one of the many saints whom that pilgrim venerated at Wu-t'ai and also notes that a certain *Tsan jou-shen Lo-hou* 讚肉身羅睺 (Encomium on the flesh-body of Rāhu) connecting him with Wu-t'ai appears on verso pages of two different Tun-huang MSS (p. 4617 and p. 4641). Moreover, Chang himself later (1129c24) refers to "the infant Rāhu," and this reference too would seem to point to Gautama's son. The evidence would seem therefore to suggest that the Rāhu referred to is probably Rāhula. I imagine the footprint itself may have been an unusual rock formation near which a temple or monument of some kind was built and so named. A temple of this name, said first to have been named Lo-Fo Ssu 落佛寺, is still to be found at Wu-t'ai, very near the P'u-sa *ting*, the former Hall of the True Countenance. It is said to have been founded during the T'ang, but what may be seen there now are buildings of fifteenth-century construction. See Tokiwa and Sekino 1975a, 1:92; Tokiwa and Sekino 1975b, 1:81–82. That the name Lo-hou (Rāhu) has been a persistent cause of puzzlement may be seen in the claim, apparently invented out of whole cloth but repeated in all modern guidebooks, that the place is named after two Tibetans of the Ch'ing period who are said to have rebuilt it—namely, Mr. Lo and Mr. Hou!

39. I am not sure who Pien 聱 is or whether my rendering of his title (*chih-k'o* 知客) as "guide" is correct, but I assume he was some kind of attendant or host, possibly but not necessarily a clerical official, in the employ of one of the monasteries. I am informed by Chün-fang Yü and others that the term is still in use today at major Buddhist pilgrimage centers in China where it labels monks whose chief duty is to guide pilgrims on their rounds of sacred sites.

40. I take Wang Pan, Chieh Chih, and Ch'in Yuan to be minor officials or servants—in any case members of Chang's retinue—but I can find no other information about any of them.

41. Chang's reference to a "*samādhi* flame" (*san-mei huo* 三昧火) and his use of the phrase *chih wo ch'ien* 至我前 or *hsien ch'ien* 顯前 (appear directly in front of me), a

locution with strong meditative connotations in Buddhism, indicates that he was familiar with Buddhist traditions concerning the relationship between visionary experience and the kinds of ecstatic transport generated in meditation. Of course, in such traditions, which I assume he took seriously, the distinction between veridical and hallucinatory experience is not so easily drawn. This is worth noting, if only as a reminder that the epistemic assumptions underlying a Sung Buddhist's experiences are probably quite different from our own. Thus, the kinds of question that Chang's descriptions might raise for us—for example, "Is he talking about something like the aurora borealis, St. Elmo's fire, or ball lightning and merely interpreting that as a vision of Mañjuśrī, or has he had a hallucination he has so interpreted?"—would not have arisen in his own mind, at least not in the same terms. This is not to say, however, that Chang did not have his own doubts and suspicions, for we note that at several points in the narrative he confesses that he does not know what to make of what he sees. Note too that the Taishō canon's punctuation at this point is erroneous.

42. "Giant basilisk" is my rendering of the Chinese *ta-ch'ing* 大青 (great green), which I take to be a contraction of *ta-ch'ing-she* 蛇, a mythical, green-blue, enormous reptile first mentioned in chapter 17 of the *Shan-hai ching* (*SHCC* 422) and said, appropriately enough, to inhabit the northern wilds.

43. The "women and servants" or "women and children" (*ch'i-na* 妻孥) to whom Chang here refers may be members of his own party, or they may be other pilgrims who happened to be visiting the Chen-jung yuan while he was there. If the latter, we can assume that despite his high rank he and his small party were not traveling alone, that they may have mingled with appreciable numbers of other, perhaps less exalted, pilgrims. In any case, the reference to these other witnesses reminds us of an ideal feature of pilgrimages, their leveling effect, by which persons normally segregated in secular or profane society are, at least symbolically, integrated into a fluid, ecstatic community of common religious purpose.

44. This line is obscure and seems to have given later editors trouble as well. The Ch'ing gazetteer version of the text reads *p'ing-chü* 憑據 (proof, guarantee) rather than *lao-mo* 捞摸 (groping, searching about). Following that gazetteer version, one might translate: "In practice, there is no way but to put it to the test."

45. Chang's verse is especially intriguing. It reminds us, first, that his Buddhist piety, which seems quite ardent, is also informed by an erudite and sophisticated knowledge of Buddhist doctrine. The phrase translated as "nothingness" (*tuan-k'ung* 斷空) I take to be an allusion to one of the most common, but also one of the most dire, misinterpretations of the cardinal Buddhist doctrine of emptiness (*śūnyatā*, *k'ung*). All Buddhist texts that treat of emptiness also teach that emptiness is not to be confused with annihilation (*uccheda*, *tuan*) or mere nothingness. Chang seems to suggest here that visionary experience—in all its vividness, strangeness, mystery, and powerful immediacy—or at least openness to such experience, may serve as proof against or antidote to the affliction of nihilism that, like the associated maladies of quietism and antinomianism, seem always to threaten the Buddhist religious life. Indeed, the theme of a need to distinguish genuine insight into emptiness from the error of nihilism (the effort at which distinction is what he may mean here by "groping") is prominent in Chang's other Buddhist writings, especially those related to Hua-yen. The implicit suggestion of the verse is that visionary experience, of the sort one might seek out at places like Mount Wu-t'ai, might protect against such error and

such spiritual debilitation. This suggestion may offer new avenues for speculation on the relationship between the forbidding rarefactions of Buddhist doctrine and the vitality of practical Buddhist piety.

46. The term *ch'en-pi* 沈幣 is obscure. My rendering it as "make offerings" is only a guess. It appears later in the text as well (1128b14), in connection with Chang's visit to the Western Terrace. Note too that although Chang's visit may have begun in part as a police action, it is clear that at this point it becomes, above all else, a pilgrimage.

47. The phrase *ch'i-pa* 七八 I have rendered as "seven eights," rather than "seven or eight," in view of the importance of groupings of eight figures in certain of the iconographical traditions associated with Mañjuśrī and Wu-t'ai Shan. See Birnbaum 1983, 87–91.

48. Chang seems here to be relating the veritable theophany that will prove to have been the single most compelling of the many visions he had on Wu-t'ai. It is worth noting—indeed, it is impossible to ignore—that this particular mystic vision, in which Mañjuśrī himself appears, differs significantly from the other visions Chang has related. It is described with particular precision and detail; it is not obviously related to any conceivable meteorological phenomena; it was apparently not in need of labored interpretation or identification on the viewer's part; and it consisted not of lights, clouds, and the like, but of divine figures. Nor does Chang express any doubts about it as he does about some of his earlier visions of phenomena of light. It has occurred to me in this regard that the forms and figures he describes here may have had some special connection with, may even have been somehow inspired by, actual works of art. In 1983 the Shansi Institute for the Preservation of Ancient Monuments published a booklet (*YSS*) of color photographs of remarkable murals from another Wu-t'ai temple, the Yen-shan ssu 岩山寺. These murals were done by a Chin artist about eighty years after Chang's visit, yet, despite their somewhat later date, they may give some impression of the sort of artwork Chang might have found on Wu-t'ai. These paintings could be described in much the same sort of language Chang uses to describe his visions. Also, we should recall that it was a convention of Sung literati culture—and a common conceit of Chinese art criticism generally—to remark on the lifelike, even divine, qualities of fine works of art, that is, to conceive of works of art as themselves visions of a kind. In any case, to suggest that such visions may have been informed by art is not necessarily to call their authenticity into question nor to suggest that Chang was somehow making them up. For more on the Yen-shan ssu and its murals see *YSS*, Karetzky 1980, and Laing 1988–89.

49. Hsin-su 心宿, one of the twenty-eight lunar mansions of traditional Chinese astronomy, is the asterism corresponding in part to the Western zodiacal constellation Scorpio. It is in what the Chinese call the "Eastern Palace," one of the five segments of the Chinese firmament. The middle and brightest of Hsin's three major stars is known to the West as Antares. See Yoke 1985, 131–49.

50. A district corresponding to the modern Tai county in northern Shansi, just northwest of Wu-t'ai.

51. This brief exchange is obscurely worded. The corresponding passage in the gazetteer synopses says simply that when Shang-ying told them what he had seen, although they all marveled ceaselessly, none had ever personally seen such things himself (*wei-chi ch'in-chien yeh* 未及親見也). Possibly Chang is here working a varia-

tion on the Buddhist significance of the terms "seeing" (*chien* 見) and "hearing" (*wen* 聞). Usually the two are used as a pair signifying direct or empirical knowledge, as distinct from merely inferential knowledge, whereas Chang seems to use *chien* to label direct experiential knowledge and *wen* to label mere secondhand or hearsay knowledge.

52. Reading *kuang* 光 (radiance) for *wu* 无 (not), as do the gazetteer versions of the record.

53. The Fo-kuang Ssu lies several miles south of Wu-t'ai Shan proper. Chang's arrival there means that he had left the mountain and was heading south to his headquarters. For more on this monastery see Rhie 1977.

54. Chieh-t'uo (d. 642, var. 650–656) is one of the most famous of the many monks associated with Wu-t'ai and Mañjuśrī. His life and experiences are recounted in detail in Hui-hsiang's 667 *CLC* (*T* 51:1095c14–1096b15) and Fa-tsang's 689 *HYCC* (*T* 51:169a12–c10). The *HKSC* also includes a biography of him (*T* 50:603b11–c16). He had had his famous visions of and conversations with Mañjuśrī before coming to Fo-kuang Ssu, but he is said to have lived the last forty years of his life there, during which time he had many visitors. The Fo-kuang Ssu, it seems, was rebuilt under his direction especially to accommodate the crowds of people who visited him on their way to or from Wu-t'ai proper.

55. The wording of the full text is at this point obscure; unable to decipher it, I have been guided by the simpler reading in the gazetteer version.

56. The Mi-mo yen (or, perhaps, Pi-mo yen) would appear to be a palisade or sheer cliff somewhere near Fo-kuang Ssu, in all likelihood the site of caves or grottos in which lived hermit monks like the one mentioned here. Or it may be a particular grotto in the face of such a cliff; the text is not clear on the point. As to the meaning of the name, I can only guess that the syllable "Mo" may be the first syllable in the Chinese transliteration of "Māra," the name of the great tempter of Buddhist mythology, in which case this would be the Hidden Māra Grotto or Hidden Māra Escarpment. In any case, by Chang's time it had already earned fame in Ch'an Buddhist lore as the home for seventeen years of Ch'ang-yü 常遇 (817–88), also known as Mi-mo Ho-shang 秘魔和尚. This disciple of Ma Tsu, like Chang himself, had had visions of Mañjuśrī on Mount Wu-t'ai before moving to Mi-mo Escarpment. He is especially famous in the Ch'an tradition for his technique of responding to all questions put to him by just hitting the ground with a stick and, when the stick was taken away from him, by just holding his mouth agape. See case no. 19 of the *Pi-yen lu* (*T* 48:159a–60a) and Ch'ang-yü's biography in *SKSC* 21 (*T* 50:845b–c). Note that this place was still on the Wu-t'ai pilgrimage route as late as 1885, when the great modern Chinese Ch'an monk, Hsu-yun 虛雲 (1840?–1959), stopped there. He too went on to have visions of Mañjuśrī (*EC* 21).

57. The editor of the Ch'ing gazetteer's version of Chang's record has altered the wording of this conversation considerably, perhaps because, like parts of the poem that follows, it did not seem to make ready sense. This later version has Chang ask the monk, "Why has this monk not been led to seek the higher Way?" To which the monk laughingly replies, "What higher way is there to seek?"

58. In Mahayana lore the full corpus of Buddhist scriptures is said to be kept in the palace of the Nāga King, the Nāgas being a species of serpentlike mythical beings, protectors of Buddhism, who dwell at the bottom of the sea. "Nāga archives"—or, as

Chinese probably understood it, "dragon archives"—is a poetic label for the vast corpus of sacred Buddhist literature. The use of such a phrase suggests that this hermit monk was the practitioner of a particularly scholarly, textually oriented, kind of Buddhism. Such scholarly proclivities, in turn, would help explain the force of the Ch'an metaphors that follow.

59. This line employs a typically Ch'an rhetorical device reminiscent of the better-known injunction "If you meet a Buddha, kill him." Feigning blasphemy, he compares the Buddha himself to a stinking barbarian ("Ku" 鶻 is part of the name of a particular barbarian people—the Hui-ku 回鶻—thought to live beyond China's western borders). The rank body odor of such barbarians is said to imbue their robes. To urge that one strip off the fetid robes worn by the "barbarian" Sakyamuni—and this is just what Chang advises the monk to do—is to urge that one avoid the danger, the outlandish "stench," of dependent attachment to Buddhism, for such attachment is itself a form of craving deemed by advocates of Ch'an to be even more insidious than worldly attachments. For a more famous example of the Ch'an use of this metaphor see Yuan-wu K'o-ch'in's lecture (*p'ing-ch'ang* 評唱) on the twelfth case in the famous *kung-an* anthology, *The Blue Grotto Record* (*T* 48:153b11–12). The editors of the later gazetteer versions of Chang's memoir apparently missed the meaning of the imagery entirely and were so mystified by it that each arbitrarily reworded it in his own way.

60. One must imagine a temple complex at the base of the cliff, of which the cave itself was one part.

61. Reading *jih* 日 (day) for *pai* 白 (white).

62. The reference here is to the second of the three long stages in the gradual decline of the Buddha's teachings, namely, the age of the simulated, sham, or counterfeit dharma (*pratirūpaka-dharma, hsiang-fa* 像法), which was thought to have begun either five hundred or a thousand years after Sakyamuni's demise and to have lasted itself either five hundred or a thousand years. This age is not quite as dire as the far longer "final days of the law" (*paścimadharma, mo-fa* 末法), but bad enough to require special effort in behalf of Buddhism's protection. See Lamotte 1988, 191–202.

63. I take the "Liu" 劉 referred to here to be a member of the family, originally of Turkish origin and protected by the Liao, who established the short-lived Latter Han dynasty in northern China just before the instauration of the Sung. This dynasty was overthrown in 950, three years after its founding; but a cousin of its last ruler continued to rule the northern Shansi region, including the Wu-t'ai area, and he established a derivative regime, called the Northern or Eastern Han, which was not finally subjugated by the Sung until the late 970s (see Wang 1967, 193–97). However, this passage in Chang's account has been the source of some confusion. Kenneth Ch'en came upon it in his research on the economic history of Chinese Buddhism and took it to refer to T'ang T'ai-tsung (r. 626–49); see Ch'en 1964, 218 and 271, and Ch'en 1973, 139. This might seem likely because the T'ang emperor, too, is known to have defeated a "Liu," in his case the rebel Liu Wu-chou 武周, who, with the support of the Turks, had occupied northern Shansi from 617 to 622. Nevertheless, Ch'en is in error; the T'ai-tsung here mentioned must be Sung T'ai-tsung. There are references in T'ang sources to T'ang T'ai-tsung's support for Wu-t'ai, but I have found none that specify a remission of taxation. Moreover, in the passage in question, the petitioning monks refer specifically to "*our* Emperor T'ai-tsung" (*wo* 我 *T'ai-tsung Huang-*

ti), which must mean Sung T'ai-tsung (r. 976–98). Also, the reference to the "four subsequent courts" fits the Sung far better than the T'ang insofar as there were in fact four emperors who reigned over the Sung during the period between T'ai-tsung and the then reigning Che-tsung, whereas there is no set of "four courts" or even of "four dynasties" following T'ang T'ai-tsung that seems relevant to the question of imperial policy toward Wu-t'ai. Finally, and most convincingly, the Ch'ing gazetteer of Mount Wu-t'ai (*CLSC* 210) specifically credits Sung T'ai-tsung with a 976 edict exempting Wu-t'ai establishments from taxation. Further research in Sung documentary archives might reveal the original edict upon which the gazetteer report is based.

64. Reading *ping* 兵 (soldiers) for *ch'iu* 丘 (hill). Note too that the Taishō canon's punctuation here is incorrect. The full stop should follow rather than precede the phrase *suo-yu* 所有. In light of the monks' complaints, it is no wonder that Chang should so often have encountered military men on his journey.

65. I take the phrase *hou shih* 後世 (later generations) to refer not to posterity but to Chang's contemporaries who, it was thought, lived in times of lamentable spiritual decline. Recall Chang's use above of the more conventional Buddhist expression for this, namely, "age of the simulated law."

66. This reference to the six senses, six sense organs, and six sense objects—to what Buddhists call the eighteen *dhātu*—is an invocation of basic Buddhist epistemological principles according to which the world as revealed to ordinary perception is not the real world because ordinary perception in any of its six modes is a very imperfect instrument of knowledge, tainted as it is by craving and attachment. In Chang Shang-ying's day the contrary opinion—confidence in empirical experience of the concrete world—was enjoying a vigorous revival under Tao-hsueh sponsorship, but such opinion would have been, and indeed was, judged on Buddhist criteria to be a very naive sort of realism.

67. I take this to be a reference to the *Flower Garland Sutra*, which the assembly of abbots had quoted in their petition.

68. This passage, so obviously crucial to an understanding of the author's motivations in writing the work, is somewhat obscure, and I am not entirely confident of my rendering of it.

69. Fa-chao was a visionary T'ang monk (d. ca. 820) associated with what would come to be regarded as the Pure Land tradition of devotional Buddhism. He seems to have hailed originally from Szechwan but moved to Mount Lu in Kiangsi, the home centuries earlier of his admired Hui-yuan 慧遠 (334–416); there he practiced the kind of visualization meditation Hui-yuan himself had practiced. In the course of such contemplations he had visions of the Buddha Amitābha and in one such saw an old man attending upon Amitābha. That old man turned out to be another teacher of Pure Land devotion, a monk named Ch'eng-yuan 承遠 (712–802), who was then living in Hunan. Fa-chao went to Hunan (Nan-yueh Shan or Heng Shan) to study with Ch'eng-yuan and while there had other visions of Amitābha in which he learned a special kind of melodic intonation of that Buddha's name, this being the practice for which he would later best be known. He also had visions of a grand monastery on Wu-t'ai. At the time of the visions the monastery he saw did not exist, but Fa-chao took the visions to mean that he was charged to build it. He therefore moved to Wu-t'ai around 770 and between 777 and 796 oversaw the building of this temple of his dreams, which he named the Monastery of the Bamboo Grove (Chu-lin ssu). This

is one of the temples Ennin would visit and describe only about fifty years later, in 840. It was southwest of the Southern Terrace and seems not to have been on Chang's own pilgrimage route. The story of Fa-chao's hesitation to tell of his visions and of the magical monk who persuaded him to do so is told in Yen-i's *KCLC* (*T* 51.1115b–c). The parable here told to Chang seems to be simply a paraphrase of Yen-i's account, and we are thereby given further good reason to believe that Chang knew of Yen-i's work. For more on Fa-chao and the Chu-lin ssu, see *SKSC* (*T* 50:844a–45b); *KCLC* (*T* 51:1114a–15c); *ENGJ* 105; Tsukamoto 1933, 171–81; Reischauer 1955a, 216–17 and 228; Fujiwara 1974, 134–40; and Weinstein 1987, 73–74.

70. Literally, the term *wu-hsiang* 無相 means "without distinguishing characteristic." It is roughly synonymous with the better-known term "empty" (*k'ung*) and in this case suggests the sense in which ultimate truth is so transcendent to ordinary ways of knowing and experiencing that it is basically uncharacterizable, that is, devoid of any of those "features" or "marks" by which we identify the worldly experiences that ordinarily occur to us as reflexes of our ignorance and craving. The "repletion of all the qualities of the fruition of Buddhahood" or "the fullness of the fruition qualities of all the Buddhas" is a more affirmative rendition of the same claim, stressing that truth, although "empty of delimiting marks," is nevertheless "full" of salvific potential and salvific effect and that Buddhahood is not simply an "emptiness" but also a pleroma. This sort of discourse on Hua-yen themes abounds in the works of Li T'ung-hsuan (see Gimello 1983).

71. "Chin" here is an ancient name for the area of northern Shansi governed from T'ai-yuan, where Wu-t'ai is.

72. Chang here alludes to the "Ch'i-wu lun" 齊物論 chapter of the *Chuang Tzu* 莊子, specifically to the passage concerning the lute player Chao. "What is outside the six realms" (六合之外), that is, beyond the bounds of the cosmos, "the sage acknowledges to exist but does not discuss" (聖人存而不論). This I take to be Chang's way of saying he will not discuss or interpret but only report the supernatural phenomena he has seen. Likewise the emperor, a living sage, should accept Chang's report (admit of the existence of such supernatural phenomena), even if they come unexplained. Earlier in the same passage Chuang Tzu also suggests that considerations of "perfection" (*ch'eng* 成) or "deficiency" (*k'uei* 虧) arise only for those of less than sagely insight. Sages take no notice of mere gain or loss; neither should the emperor. See *CTCS* 1967, 11–13, and Graham 1981, 54–57.

73. In view of the general importance of the entire *HCLC*, of which I have translated only the opening sections, it seems worthwhile briefly to describe the remainder of the full text. The sequence of the appendices is as follows: First is a series of brief appended accounts (*fu-chuan* 附傳) of experiences that befell other scholars and officials who visited Wu-t'ai over the several decades that followed Chang's own visits, having been inspired to do so by reading Chang's account. Here we find further reminders of the relevance of pilgrimage to literati culture and piety and of the fact that pilgrimage was not the exclusive province of monks and imperial patrons. These are followed by two other compositions (commendations or doxologies), preceded by a brief preface and written by two of Chang's associates; one is dated 1101; both sing the praises of both Chang and Wu-t'ai. Then comes a series of three separate pieces by other eminent literati—written in 1101, 1104, and 1141—that recount later visits to Wu-t'ai, particularly to the Chen-jung yuan. Finally, there are three postfaces, one

written in 1396 by the editor of the first Ming edition, another in 1462 by the editor of the second Ming edition, and the third in 1884 by the editor of the Ch'ing edition. The Ch'ing postface ends by quoting the *SKCS* entry on the combined edition of all three Ch'ing-liang accounts and adding further bibliographical comments. A number of these appendices, and particularly the question of how they came to be included in the Chin and Ming editions of the *HCLC*, deserve separate and detailed study. They are interesting in themselves. One, for example (see the following note), was written by an uncle of Chu Hsi! But also important for our immediate purposes is the light they may shed on the later resonances of Chang's narrative and on its still obscure and very complex textual history. Such light, in turn, may help clarify the question of the *HCLC*'s authenticity.

74. This is the *T'ai-shan jui-ying chi* 台山瑞應記 (A record of marvelous responses on the terraced mountain), by Chu Pien 朱弁 (*tzu:* Shao-chang 少章, d. 1144), dated July 27, 1141. It is included as one of the supplementary pieces in *chüan* 2 of the *HCLC* (1133b4–c23). Chu Pien, Chu Hsi's uncle, was a Southern Sung ambassador to the Chin who was held captive in the north for several years (1127–43) and who visited Wu-t'ai during his detention.

75. I have in mind here the characteristics of the Sung Confucian revival outlined in de Bary's classic 1959 article and in other of his writings. De Bary focuses on a distinct school of thought—Neo-Confucianism or Tao-hsueh—but, as he had argued in an earlier study (de Bary 1953), early Neo-Confucianism was intricately bound up with more general patterns of social and cultural change, and in this sense the features he ascribed to Neo-Confucianism per se must also be seen as characteristics of Sung generally. This would seem to be true even though it must also be appreciated that these particular features of Northern Sung history were often in tension with others de Bary did not discuss.

76. This is the conclusion of the fifteenth of the twenty-two discourses or Ch'an homilies that make up the first half of the *Lin-chi lu*. I am indebted to, but have departed from, the translation done by Sasaki et al. (*LC* 16, Chinese text, 9). Lin-chi (810?–66), of course, was the progenitor of all the Ch'an lineages bearing his name, and these in turn were the dominant Ch'an traditions of the late Northern Sung. All the Ch'an monks with whom Chang Shang-ying associated were descendants of Lin-chi, for example; and although Chang never quotes this particular passage, we can assume he had come at some point to know it.

77. *HCLC* 1132a10–19. Note that this preface is curiously missing from all but the *T* and *HTC* editions of the text—yet another problem to be dealt with in researching the work's textual history.

78. Fen-chou corresponds to the modern Fen-yang, in central Shansi, about forty-five miles southwest of T'ai-yuan.

79. Li Chieh (*tzu:* Ying-po 穎伯) earned his *chin-shih* degree in the Hsi-ning period (1068–77) and would later, like Chang, be numbered among the forbidden authors of the Yuan-yu "clique." For biographical sources on him, see *SJCS* 884. Hsi-ho is another name for the Fen-chou area.

80. Also known as Ta-ta Kuo-shih 大達國師, Wu-yeh (760–811) was originally a scholar-monk and an expert in monastic discipline (*vinaya, lü* 律) who received Ch'an transmission from Ma-tsu Tao-i. He then resolved to complete a long Ch'an pilgrim-

age to several sacred sites throughout China (e.g., T'ien-t'ai Shan, Ts'ao-ch'i, etc.). His final destination, however, was Mount Wu-t'ai, where he lived for some time at the Golden Pavilion Temple absorbed in study of the whole canon of scriptures. After a series of eight meteorite sightings, which he took as confirmation that he had fulfilled his vow, he left the mountain and moved to the K'ai-yuan Monastery 開元寺 in Fen-chou, where he lived the remaining twenty years of his life in seclusion. See, among other sources on his life and teaching, *SKSC* 2:772b–73a.

81. A mysterious image. But we can at least note that the phrase "beating the drum" (*ta-ku* 打鼓) is sometimes a Ch'an metaphor for "true transcendence" or "true going beyond" (*chen kuo* 眞過), that is, for a kind of insight in which one has overcome the usual dichotomies of knowledge—especially the dichotomy between "learning" (*hsi-hsueh* 習學, *wen* 聞) or mediated access to the truth and "intimacy" (*lin* 臨) or unmediated access to the truth. See case number 44 of the *Pi-yen lu* (*T* 48:180c–188c).

82. Sudhana (*Shan-ts'ai* 善財) is the mythic pilgrim of the final chapter of the *Flower Garland Sutra* and thus the great archetype of all who search for Mañjuśrī. He is discussed also in Chün-fang Yü's chapter in this volume, apropos his connection with Kuan-yin.

83. *P'i-lan feng* 毘嵐風 (the Varambhaka wind) is the strong cosmic gale that Buddhists believe will blow at the end of the kalpa or cosmic eon. *Chiu-t'ien* 九天 may be the highest heaven in the Taoist firmament, or a set of nine heavenly bodies recognized in Buddhism, or the nine segments into which the sky is divided in ancient Chinese cosmology.

BIBLIOGRAPHY

Sources Cited by Abbreviation

CCLW   *Ch'ui-chien lu wai-chi* 吹劍錄外集. Compiled by Yü Wen-pao 俞文豹.
         1 *chüan. PCHS, hsu-pien* 4.

CCTS   *Chün-chai tu-shu chih* 郡齋讀書志. Compiled by Ch'ao Kung-wu 晁公武
         and Chao Hsi-pien 趙希弁. 17 *chüan* in 2 vols. 1250. *SPTK* #419, *san-
         pien, shih.*

CKFSC   *Chung-kuo Fo-ssu chih hui-k'an* 中國佛寺志彙刊. Compiled by Tu Chieh-
         hsiang 杜潔祥. 90 vols. in 3 series. Taipei: Tan-ch'ing t'u-shu, 1980–85.

CLC   *(Ku) Ch'ing-liang chuan* 古清涼傳. Compiled by Hui-hsiang 慧祥.
         T 51:1091c–1100c.

CLSC   *Ch'ing-liang shan chih* 清涼山志. 8 *chüan* combined in one volume. 1596
         (often reprinted). Reprint. *CKFSC*, 2d series, vol. 29. See also the
         simplified-character edition of this text—based on an 1887 reprint of a
         1755 reprint of the original 1596 edition—edited and punctuated by Li
         Yü-min 李裕民 and published in 1989, in T'ai-yuan, by the Shansi
         Jen-min ch'u-pan she.

CLSH   *Ch'ing-liang shan hsin-chih* 清涼山新志. 10 *chüan* in 1 vol. 1701 (often
         reprinted). Reprint. *CKFSC*, 3d series, vol. 30.

CSC   *Chü-shih chuan* 居士傳. Compiled by P'eng Chi-ch'ing 彭際清. 56 *chüan.*
         1770–75. Reprint. *HTC* 149:791–833.

CSCS   *Chin-shih chi-shih* 金史紀事. Compiled by Ch'en Yen 陳巖. Shanghai: Commercial Press, 1936.

CSFT   *Chü-shih fen-teng lu* 居士分燈錄. Compiled by Chu Shih-ssu 朱時思. 2 *chüan*. 1631. Reprint. *HTC* 147:857–934.

CSPM   *T'ung-chien ch'ang-pien chi-shih pen-mo* 通鑑長編紀事本末. Compiled by Yang Chung-liang 楊仲良. 150 *chüan* in 6 vols. 1253. Reprint. Taipei: Wen-hai, 1973.

CTCS   *Chuang Tzu chi-shih* 莊子集釋. Compiled by Wang Hsien-ch'ien 王先謙. 8 *chüan* in 1 vol. Reprint. Taipei: Shih-chieh, 1967.

CTPT   *Chia-t'ai p'u-teng-lu* 嘉泰普燈錄. Compiled by Lei-an Cheng-shou 雷庵正受. 30 *chüan*. 1202. Reprint. *HTC* 137:40–438.

CTS   *Chiu T'ang-shu* 舊唐書. Compiled by Liu Hsu 劉昫 et al. 200 *chüan*. Peking: Chung-hua, 1974.

CWPC   *Chiao-wai pieh-chuan* 教外別傳. Compiled by Li-mei 黎眉 et al. 16 *chüan*. 1633. Reprint. *HTC* 144:1–402.

CYL   *Chih-yueh lu* 指月錄. Compiled by Ch'ü Ju-chi 瞿汝稷. 32 *chüan*. 1595. Reprint. *HTC* 143:1–743.

EC   *Empty Cloud: The Autobiography of the Chinese Zen Master Xu Yun*. Translated by Charles Luk. Revised and edited by Richard Hunn. Longmead, Shaftesbury, Dorset: Element Books, 1988.

ENGJ   Ennin 圓仁. *Nittō guhō junrei kōki* 入唐求法巡禮行記. Punctuated and collated by Ku Ch'eng-fu 顧承甫 and Ho Ch'üan-ta 何泉達. Shanghai: Shanghai Ku-chi, 1986.

FFCT   *Fo-fa chin-t'ang pien* 佛法金湯編. Compiled by Hsin-t'ai 心泰. 16 *chüan*. 1327. Reprint. *HTC* 148:833–991.

GDZT   *Bukkyō seichi: Godaizan no tabi* 佛教聖地五台山の旅. Tokyo: Chung-kuo jen-min mei-shu ch'u-pan-she and Minomi, 1984.

HCLC   *Hsu Ch'ing-liang chuan* 續清涼傳. By Chang Shang-ying. *T* 51:1127a–35a.

HKSC   *Hsu kao-seng chuan* 續高僧傳. Compiled by Tao-hsuan 道宣. 30 *chüan*. *T* 50:425–707.

HTC   *Hsu tsang-ching* 續藏經. 150 vols. Taipei: Hsin-wen-feng, 1977. Originally published as *Dainihon zokuzōkyō* 大日本續藏經. 750 vols. Kyoto: Zōkyō Shoin, 1905–12. (Note: Citations of works in this series will include the original *chüan* number of the work cited but will give the *HTC* volume and page numbers rather than those of the original Japanese edition.)

HYCC   *Hua-yen ching ch'uan-chi* 華嚴經傳記. By Fa-tsang 法藏. 5 *chüan*. *T* 51:153a–73a.

JAOS   *Journal of the American Oriental Society*.

KCLC   *Kuang Ch'ing-liang chuan* 廣清涼傳. Compiled by Yen-i 延一. *T* 51:1101a–27a.

KCTS   *Ku-chin t'u-shu chi-ch'eng* 古今圖書集成. Edited by Ch'en Meng-lei 陳夢雷 et al. 10,044 *chüan* in 800 *ts'e*. 1725. Reprint. Peking: Chung-hua, 1934.

LC   *The Recorded Sayings of Ch'an Master Lin-chi Hui-chao of Chen Prefecture*. Translated by Ruth Fuller Sasaki et al. Kyoto: The Institute for Zen Studies, 1975.

PCHS   *Pi-chi hsiao-shuo ta-kuan* 筆記小說大觀. Several hundreds of volumes, in more than thirty series. Taipei: 1973–.

SB   *A Sung Bibliography*. Edited by Étienne Balazs and Yves Hervouet. Hong Kong: Chinese University Press, 1978.

SHCC   *Shan-hai ching chiao-chu* 山海經校注. Edited by Yuan K'o 袁珂. 21 *chüan* in 1 vol. Shanghai: Shanghai Ku-chi, 1980.

SJCS   *Sung-jen chuan-chi tzu-liao so-yin* 宋人傳記資料索引. 6 vols. Revised and expanded edition. Edited by Wang Te-i 王德毅 et al. Taipei: Ting-wen, 1977.

SKCS   *Ssu-k'u ch'üan-shu tsung-mu* 四庫全書總目. Edited by Chi Yun 紀昀 et al. 200 *chüan* in 2 vols. 1782. Reprint. Peking: Chung-hua, 1965.

SKSC   *Sung Kao-seng chuan* 宋高僧傳. Compiled by Tsan-ning 贊寧. 30 *chüan*. *T* 50:709–900.

SMWT   *Shih-men Wen-tzu Ch'an* 石門文字禪. Compiled by disciples of Chueh-fan Hui-hung 覺範慧洪. 30 *chüan* in 2 vols. 1597. Reprint. Changchow: T'ien-ning ssu, 1921. Reprint. Taipei: Hsin-wen-feng, 1973.

SPTK   *Ssu-pu ts'ung-k'an* 四部叢刊. 3 series (*pien*), each divided into 4 categories (*pu*), in 3,122 *ts'e*. Shanghai: Commercial Press, 1919–37. (Note: Works in this collection will be cited by series and category and by serial number as given in Karl Lo, *A Guide to the "Ssu-pu ts'ung-k'an"* [Lawrence: University of Kansas Libraries, 1965].)

SS   *Sung shih* 宋史. Compiled by T'o T'o 脫脫 et al. 496 *chüan* in 20 vols. 1343–45. Reprint. Peking: Chung-hua, 1975.

SSHP   *Sung-shih hsin-pien* 宋史新編. Compiled by K'o Wei-chi 柯維祺. 200 *chüan* in 1 vol. Ca. 1557. Reprint. Taipei: Hsin-hai, 1974.

SSSC   *Su Shih shih-chi* 蘇軾詩集. Compiled by K'ung Fan-li 孔凡禮. 8 vols. Peking: Chung-hua, 1982.

STSW   *Sung-tai Shu-wen chi-tsun* 宋代蜀文輯存. Compiled by Fu Tseng-hsiang 傅增湘. 101 *chüan* in 2 vols. 1943. Reprint. Taipei: Hsin-wen-feng, 1974.

T   *Taishō shinshū daizōkyō* 大正新修大藏經. 100 vols. Edited by Takakusu Jun-jirō 高楠順次郎 et al. Tokyo: Daizō, 1924–32. (Note: Citations of works in this collection will provide the original *chüan* number of the work cited followed by the *T* volume, page, and register numbers, sometimes with line numbers as well.)

TCTL   *Ta-chih-tu lun* 大智度論. Attributed to Nāgārjuna. *T* 25:57–714.

TT   *Tao-tsang* 道藏. 1120 *ts'e* in 128 cases. Peking: Pai-yun Kuan, 1445, 1607, 1845. Reprint. Shanghai: Commercial Press, 1924–26. Reprint. Taipei: I-wen, 1962. (Note: Works in this series will be cited by the Harvard-Yenching Index serial number as revised by Kristopher Schipper; see Boltz 1987, 247–50.)

TTSL   *Tung-tu shih-lueh* 東都事略. Compiled by Wang Ch'eng 王偁. 130 *chüan* in 4 vols. 1186. Reprint. Taipei: Wen-hai, 1975.

WTHY   *Wu-teng hui-yuan* 五燈會元. Compiled by P'u-chi 普濟. 20 *chüan* in 3 vols. 1252. New critical edition, punctuated and annotated by Su Yuan-lei 蘇淵雷. Peking: Chung-hua, 1984.

WTS   *Wu-t'ai shan* 五台山. Compiled by the Staffs of the Shansi Department of Commerce and the Tourist Supply Company. Peking: Wen-wu, 1984.

WWPT   *Hsuan-yin Wan-wei pieh-tsang* 選印宛委別藏. Compiled by Juan Yuan 阮元. 150 *ts'e* in 14 cases. Shanghai: Commercial Press, 1937.

YSS   *Yen-shan ssu Chin-tai pi-hua* 岩山寺金代壁畫. Compiled by the Staff of the

Shansi Research Institute for the Preservation of Ancient Monuments.
Peking: Wen-wu, 1983.

YYCC   *Ming-ch'en pei-chuan yuan-yen chih-chi* 名臣碑傳琬琰之集. Compiled by Tu
Ta-kuei 杜大珪. 107 *chüan* in 3 vols. 1194. Reprint. Taipei: Chinese
Materials and Research Aids Service Center, 1986.

ZD   Miura Isshu and Ruth Fuller Sasaki. *Zen Dust: The History of the Kōan and
Kōan Study in Rinzai (Lin-chi) Zen.* New York: Harcourt, Brace, & World,
1966.

Other Sources

Abe Chōichi 阿部肇一. 1986. *Chūgoku Zenshūshi no kenkyū* 中國禪宗史の研究. Revised
and enlarged edition. Tokyo: Kyūbun.

———. 1988. "Chūgoku Zenshū to minshū—shomin shinko tenkai no ikkōsatsu"
中國禪宗と民衆民信仰展開への一考察. *Bukkyō shigaku kenkyū* 佛教史學研究
31.1:1–24.

Andō Tomonobu 安藤智信. 1961. "Sō no Chō Shōei ni tsuite: Bukkyō kankei no jiseki
o chūshin to shite" 宋の張商英について－佛教關係の事蹟を中心として. *Tōhō-
gaku* 東方學 22:57–63.

———. 1963. "Chō Shōei no *Gohōron* to sono haikei" 張商英の護法論とその背景.
Ōtani gakuhō 大谷學報 42.3:29–40.

Bagchi, Prabodh Chandra. 1927–38. *Le Canon Bouddhique en Chine: Les traducteurs et les
traductions.* 2 vols. Paris: Geuthner.

Bauer, Wolfgang. 1976. *China and the Search for Happiness.* Translated by Michael
Shaw. New York: Seabury Press.

Birnbaum, Raoul. 1983. *Studies on the Mysteries of Mañjuśrī.* Boulder, Colo.: Society for
the Study of Chinese Religions.

———. 1984. "Thoughts on T'ang Buddhist Mountain Traditions and Their Contexts." *T'ang Studies* 2 (Winter 1984):5–23.

———. 1986. "The Manifestation of a Monastery: Shen-ying's Experiences on
Mount Wu-t'ai in T'ang Context." *JAOS* 106.1:119–37.

Blofeld, John. 1972. *The Wheel of Life: The Autobiography of a Western Buddhist.* 1959.
Reprint. London: Century Hutchinson.

Boltz, Judith M. 1987. *A Survey of Taoist Literature, Tenth to Seventeenth Centuries.* Berkeley: Institute of East Asian Studies, University of California.

Brown, Peter. 1981. *The Cult of the Saints: Its Rise and Function in Latin Christianity.*
Chicago: University of Chicago Press.

Ch'en, Kenneth K. S. 1964. *Buddhism in China: A Historical Survey.* Princeton, Princeton University Press.

———. 1973. *The Chinese Transformation of Buddhism.* Princeton, Princeton University
Press.

Ch'en Yuan 陳垣. 1962. *Chung-kuo Fo-chiao shih-chi kai-lun* 中國佛教史籍概論. Peking.
Chung-hua.

Cheng Shih-p'ing 鄭石平. 1985. *Chung-kuo ssu ta fo-shan* 中國四大佛山. Shanghai:
Shanghai Wen-hua.

de Bary, Wm. Theodore. 1953. "A Reappraisal of Neo-Confucianism." In *Studies in
Chinese Thought,* edited by Arthur F. Wright, 81–111. Chicago: University of Chicago Press.

————. 1959. "Some Common Tendencies in Neo-Confucianism." In *Confucianism in Action*, edited by David Nivison and Arthur F. Wright, 25–49. Stanford: Stanford University Press.

Dupront, Alphonse. 1974. "Pèlerinage et lieux sacrés." In *Mélanges en l'honneur de Fernand Braudel*. Vol. 2: *Méthodologie de l'histoire et des sciences humaines*, 189–206. Toulouse: Privat.

Fischer, Emil S. 1925. *The Sacred Wu Tai Shan: In Connection with Modern Travel from Tai Yuan Fu via Mount Wu Tai to the Mongolian Border*. Shanghai: Kelly & Walsh.

Fujiwara Ryōsetsu. 1974. *The Way to Nirvāṇa: The Concept of the Nembutsu in Shan-tao's Pure Land Buddhism*. Tokyo: Kyoiku.

Gimello, Robert M. 1983. "Li T'ung-hsüan and the Practical Dimensions of Huayen." In *Studies in Ch'an and Hua-yen*, edited by Robert M. Gimello and Peter N. Gregory, 321–89. Honolulu: University of Hawaii Press.

————. 1987. "Imperial Patronage of Buddhism during the Northern Sung." In *Proceedings of the First International Symposium on Church and State in China*, edited by John E. Geddes, 73–85. Taipei: Tamkang University.

Graham, Angus C. 1981. "*Chuang Tzu*": *The Seven Inner Chapters and Other Writings from the Book "Chuang Tzu."* London: Allen & Unwin.

Hansen, Valerie Lynn. 1990. *Changing Gods in Medieval China, 1127–1276*. Princeton, Princeton University Press.

Hibino Takeo 日比野丈夫. 1958. "Tonkō no Godaizanzu ni tsuite" 敦煌の五台山圖について. *Bukkyō geijutsu* 佛教藝術 34:75–86.

————. 1982. "Tonkō no *Godaizan junreiki*" 敦煌の『五台山巡禮記』. In *Ono Katsutoshi hakushi shōju ki'nen Tōhōgaku ronshū* 小野勝年博頌壽記念東方學論集, 287–300. Kyoto: Hōyū shoten.

Hsu Chao-ting 許肇鼎. 1986. *Sung-tai Shu-jen chu-tso tsun-i lu* 宋代蜀人著作存佚錄. Cheng-tu: Pa-shu Shu-she.

Huang Chi-chiang. 1986. "Experiment in Syncretism: Ch'i-sung (1007–1072) and Eleventh-Century Chinese Buddhism." Ph.D. diss., University of Arizona.

Jan Yün-hua. 1979. "Li P'ing-shan and His Refutation of Neo-Confucian Criticism of Buddhism." In *Developments in Buddhist Thought: Canadian Contributions to Buddhist Studies*, edited by Roy C. Amore, 162–93. Ontario: Canadian Corporation for Studies in Religion, 1979.

Kamata Shigeo 鎌田茂雄 and Hirose Tetsuo 廣瀬哲雄. 1986. *Bukkyō seichi: Godaizan, nihonjin Sanzō Hōshi no monogatari* 佛教聖地—五台山日本人三藏法師の物語. Tokyo: Nihon Hōsō.

Karetzky, Patricia Eichenbaum. 1980. "The Recently Discovered Chin Dynasty Murals Illustrating the Life of The Buddha at Yen-shang ssu, Shansi." *Artibus Asiae* 42:245–61.

Kobayashi Tadashi 小林格史. 1979. *Tonkō no bijutsu* 敦煌の美術. Tokyo: Taiyō.

Kubota Ryoon 久保田量遠. 1931. *Shina Ju Dō Butsu sankyō shiron* 支那儒道佛三教史論. Tokyo: Tōhō.

————. 1943. *Shina Ju Dō Butsu kōshō shi* 支那儒道佛交渉史. Tokyo: Daitō.

Laing, Ellen Johnston. 1988–89. "Chin 'Tartar' Dynasty (1115–1234) Material Culture." *Artibus Asiae* 49:73–126.

Lamotte, Étienne. 1959. "Prophéties relatives à la disparition de la Bonne Loi." *Présence du Bouddhisme*, edited by René de Berval, 657–68. Saigon: France-Asie.

————. 1960. "Mañjuśrī." *T'oung Pao* 48:1–96.

————. 1966. *Le traité de la grande vertu de sagesse de Nagarjuna (Mahāprajñāpāramitāśāstra)*. Vol. 1, chaps. 1–15. Bibliothèque du *Muséon*, vol 18. Louvain: Institut Orientaliste.

————. 1988. *History of Indian Buddhism: From the Origins to the Saka Era*. Translated by Sara Webb-Boin and Jean Dantinne. Louvain: Institut Orientaliste.

Lessing, Ferdinand D., and Alex Wayman. 1968. *Mkhas Grub Rje's Fundamentals of Buddhist Tantras*. The Hague & Paris: Mouton.

Levering, Miriam Lindsey. 1978. "Ch'an Enlightenment for Laymen: Ta-hui and the New Religious Culture of the Sung." Ph.D. diss., Harvard University.

Magnin, Paul. 1987. "Le pèlerinage dans la tradition bouddhique chinoise." In *Histoire des pèlerinages non chrétiens: Entre magique et sacré, le chemin des dieux*, edited by Jean Chélini and Henry Branthomme. Paris: Hachette.

Marchand, Ernesta. 1976. "The Panorama of Wu-t'ai shan as an Example of Tenth-Century Cartography." *Oriental Art*. New Series 22.2:158–73.

Nihashi Susumu 二橋進. 1986. *Godaizan no teradera* 五台山の寺々. Tokyo: Nakayama.

Ogawa Kan'ichi 小川貫弌. 1942. "Nittōsō Reisen Sanzō to Godaizan" 入唐僧 靈仙三藏と五台山. *Shina Bukkyō shigaku* 支那佛教史學 5.3–4:137–44.

Ono Katsutoshi 小野勝年 and Hibino Takeo. 1942. *Godaizan* 五台山. Tokyo: Zayūhō.

Po Huan-ts'ai 白換采. 1958. *Wu-t'ai shan wen-wu* 五台山文物. T'ai-yuan: Shansi jenmin.

Rawski, Evelyn S. 1985. "Problems and Prospects." In *Popular Culture in Late Imperial China*, edited by David Johnson, Andrew Nathan, and Evelyn S. Rawski, 399–417. Berkeley: University of California Press.

Redfield, Robert. 1956. *Peasant Society and Culture: An Anthropological Approach to Civilization*. Chicago: University of Chicago Press.

Reischauer, Edwin O. 1955a. *Ennin's Diary: The Record of a Pilgrimage to China in Search of the Law*. New York: Ronald Press.

————. 1955b. *Ennin's Travels in T'ang China*. New York: Ronald Press.

Rhie, Marylin M. 1977. *The Fo-kuang ssu: Literary Evidences and Buddhist Images*. New York: Garland.

Schmidt-Glintzer, Helwig. 1989. "Zhang Shangying (1043–1122)—An Embarrassing Policy Adviser under the Northern Sung." In *Studies in Sung History: A Festschrift for Dr. James T. C. Liu*, edited by Kinugawa Tsuyoshi, 521–30. Kyoto: Dōbōsha.

Schneider, Richard. 1987. "Un moine indien au Wou-t'ai chan: Relation d'un pèlerinage." *Cahiers d'Extrême-Asie* 3:27–40.

Schopen, Gregory. 1975. "The Phrase 'sa pṛthivīpradeśaś caityabhūto bhavet' in the *Vajracchedikā*: Notes on the Cult of the Book in Mahāyāna." *Indo-Iranian Journal* 17.3:147–81.

Tokiwa Daijō 常盤大定. 1982. *Shina ni okeru Bukkyō to Jukyō Dōkyō* 支那に於ける佛教と儒教道教. 1930. Reprint. Tokyo: Genshobō.

Tokiwa Daijō and Sekino Tei 關野貞. 1975a. *Chūgoku bunka shiseki: kaisetsu* 中國文化史蹟—解説. 2 vols. 1940. Reprint. Tokyo: Hōzōkan.

————. 1975b. *Chūgoku bunka shiseki*. 12 vols. 1939–40. Reprint. Tokyo: Hōzōkan.

Tsukamoto Zenryū 塚本善隆. 1933. *Tō chūki no Jōdokyō* 唐中其の淨土教. Kyoto: Tōhō Bunka Gakuin Kyoto Kenkyūjo.

van der Loon, Piet. 1984. *Taoist Books in the Libraries of the Sung Period: A Critical Study and Index*. London: Ithaca Press.

von Glahn, Richard. 1987. *The Country of Streams and Grottoes*. Cambridge: Harvard University Press.

von Verscheur, Charlotte. 1985. *Les relations officielles du Japon avec la Chine aux VIIIᵉ et IXᵉ siècles*. Geneva and Paris: Librairie Droz.

Waley, Arthur. 1952. *The Real Tripiṭaka and Other Pieces*. London: Allen & Unwin.

Wang Gungwu. 1967. *The Structure of Power in North China during the Five Dynasties*. 1963. Reprint. Stanford, Stanford University Press.

Weinstein, Stanley. 1987. *Buddhism Under the T'ang*. Cambridge: Cambridge University Press.

Yanagida Seizan 柳田聖山 et al. 1988. *Zenrin sōbōden: yakuchū* 禪林僧寶傳—譯注. Kyoto: Kyoto Daigaku Jimbun Kagaku Kenkyūjo.

Yoke, Ho Peng. 1985. *Li, Qi and Shu: An Introduction to Science and Civilization in China*. Hong Kong: Hong Kong University Press.

FOUR

Relics and Flesh Bodies:
The Creation of Ch'an Pilgrimage Sites

Bernard Faure

Unlike the preceding chapters in this book, this one is not concerned primarily with the pilgrim's point of view. It emphasizes one admittedly more narrow, but perhaps as crucial, condition of pilgrimages—the clerical transformation of a given site into a cultic center. Besides functioning as an ideal refuge and a concrete goal for pilgrims of all kinds, sacred sites often constituted an important sectarian stake. The sectarian context, weakened or reinforced by pilgrimages, has been relatively neglected perhaps as a result of the "communitas" model (Turner 1974) that still governs much current scholarship on pilgrimage. Here I examine this sectarian dimension, describing some of the strategies with which space, place, and cultic objects were invested with power and claimed by a specific tradition, in this case Ch'an Buddhism.

The sacred site was never entirely a given but was in constant flux, incessantly modified by the actions and perceptions of residents and visitors. Two of the questions that come to mind are, What happens when a new socioreligious group like Ch'an monks attempts to impose a reading of the site that denies the old types of sacrality yet intends to capitalize on the site's numinous power (*ling*)? and How can the new reading replace the old myths that empowered the site and still attract pilgrims and donations? One of the ways, I believe, was the promotion of a cult of relics, and more precisely, of rituals centered on the "flesh bodies" (mummified corpses) of Buddhist masters. To examine these questions, I will attempt to describe the foundation and evolution of two Ch'an cultic sites, focusing on the T'ang period and providing illustrations from later centuries.

The emergence of the Ch'an school in the early T'ang can be seen as an attempt to redraw the map of Chinese sacred space. This may seem paradoxical in the light of Ch'an's denial of mediations or "skillful means" (*upāya*). Just as "sudden" Ch'an rejected the soteriological notion of a path (*mārga*) toward liberation—a notion that itself served as a metaphor for pilgrimage (see the Introduction)—it tended to downplay the notion of pilgrimage. It still, however, recognized the value of vagrancy, that is, the wandering from monastery to monastery in search of a master.

In theory, true liminality denies any spatial fixation. Whereas traditional Buddhist pilgrimages, to the extent that they imply a specific circuit or goal, provide a relatively artificial and temporary communitas and are still structured (in the Turnerian sense), Ch'an peregrinations (known as *hsing-chiao* 行脚, *yu-fang* 遊方, or *yu-hsing* 遊行) constituted (ideally) a process of "destructuration." This ideal is well expressed, for example, in a poem by the Ch'an master Kuang-jen (837–909):

> My way goes beyond the blue sky,
> Like a white cloud that has no resting place.
> There is in this world a tree without roots,
> Whose yellow leaves return in the wind.
>
> (*T* 51:340a)

Thus, the *hsing-chiao* emphasized the process, the transformative aspect of the "quest" itself. In contrast with the pilgrimage, the goal—the sacred sites—was deemed secondary. In actual practice, however, the wanderings of the "clouds and water" (*yun-shui* 雲水), as Ch'an monks were called, soon became as structured as any pilgrimage, and both notions overlapped. Like other Buddhist sacred sites, Ch'an cultic centers often developed around the cult of relics and of stupas. T'ang imperial edicts tried repeatedly to check itinerant monks and to force them to remain secluded within their monasteries (see Gernet 1956). During the Sung, if not earlier, the establishment of a Ch'an monastic rule undercut the primitive ideal of wandering asceticism (Sk. *dhūta-guṇa*).

Like traditional pilgrimages, Ch'an peregrinations had both integrative and potentially subversive effects. In the long run, they replaced one network of sacred places with another; their goal was no longer worship of the traces or symbols of the Buddha, but meeting with real, living (and sometimes dead) buddhas, the master patriarchs (*tsu-shih* 祖師) of Ch'an. Charismatic Ch'an masters drew large numbers of disciples. Monks and laymen gathered around them "like the clouds following the dragon or the wind following the tiger," as the epitaph for Shen-hsiu 神秀 (606–706), the founder of the so-called Northern school, puts it (see Yanagida 1967, 498). According to his biography in the *Chiu T'ang shu*: "At the time, all, from the princes to the common folk of the capital, vied with one another to see him. Every day, more than ten thousand people came to bow down before him" (*CTS*, *chüan* 191, vol. 16:5110). We also know that the movement of monks between the

Ch'an communities in Hung-chou 洪州 and Chiang-hsi 江西 at the time of Ma-tsu Tao-i 馬祖道一 (709–88) and Shi-t'ou Hsi-ch'ien 石頭希遷 (700–90) was extremely important.

Unfortunately, we do not have any diary like that of the Japanese pilgrim Ennin (794–864) concerning these peregrinations. The *hsing-lu* 行錄 (records of pilgrimages) included in the *yü-lu* 語錄 (recorded sayings) of famous Ch'an masters such as Lin-chi I-hsuan (臨濟義玄, d. 867) are merely a literary device to frame the "dialogues" between eminent monks and do not provide any historical material (see, for example, Sasaki 1975, 50–63). For much later periods, guidebooks for pilgrims, such as the *Ts'an-hsueh chih-chin* 參學知津 (Knowing the fords on the way to knowledge, 1827) by Hsien-ch'eng Ju-hai 顯承如海,[1] provide a general description of pilgrimage routes and details on particular sites, but they lack information concerning wandering monks. The best sources remain local gazetteers and the epigraphical and hagiographical collections. Additional information can be gleaned from travelogues such as Hsu Hsia-k'o's *Travel Diaries* (ca. 1640) (Li Chi 1974) or Ch'i Chou-hua's *Ming-shan tsang fu-pen* 名山藏副本 (ca. 1761). In the case of Sung Shan, for example, the local and epigraphical records are particularly rich,[2] and some of the inscriptions have been well studied by institutional historians.[3] But there is hardly any information on pilgrimage as such, and the scholarship is usually carried out from an exclusive point of view that overlooks the multifunctional nature of these inscriptions. In the case of the well-known Shao-lin stele (728), for example, Buddhist scholars have usually focused on one part of the stele, institutional historians on another (see Yanagida 1981, 317; Twitchett 1956, 131; Tonami 1986).

The consecration of early Ch'an was due primarily to the imperial patronage of a few eminent masters and to the development of "metropolitan" cultic centers on Sung Shan and in the capitals. However, its political success failed to translate right away into institutional autonomy, as Japanese scholars usually assume. Perhaps one should not even speak of a single Ch'an school at this stage, since there were actually a number of competing groups. Nevertheless, from the eighth century onward, they shared an awareness of a specific Ch'an lineage that could be traced back—with some pious lies—to the Indian patriarch Bodhidharma. While Ch'an was emerging as the dominant Buddhist teaching in the T'ang capitals during the first half of the eighth century, with the so-called Northern and Southern schools, its subsequent development was marked by a geographical dissemination, a shift from "metropolitan" to "provincial" Ch'an. The prestige of Ch'an came to depend increasingly on the capacity of local communities to attract believers and donations. After the death of their founders and the subsequent "routinization of charisma," these communities were desperately in need of new strategies to attract believers. To reveal some of these strategies, I will con-

trast two cultic centers that were the strongholds of the Northern and Southern schools, Sung Shan 嵩山 and Ts'ao-ch'i 曹溪.

The mountain range of Sung Shan, near the capital Lo-yang (in Honan),
is the site of the Shao-lin 少林 Monastery where, according to legend, the
first Ch'an patriarch Bodhidharma sat in meditation for nine years. The
Nan-hua Monastery (formerly Pao-lin Monastery), where the Sixth Patriarch, Hui-neng (d. 713), taught and where his flesh body (jou-shen 肉身)
was preserved after his death, is at Ts'ao-ch'i. The evolution of Ch'an communities in both places might tell us something of the role of monks and
pilgrims and monks as pilgrims in the making and unmaking of a sacred site.
I will in this chapter be concerned primarily with the first phase of this process, that is, with the establishment of these two centers during the T'ang
and the various legends concerning the Buddhist attempt to take over these
places. I will—in part heuristically, but also because of the nature of my
sources—emphasize the Ch'an view of the process but will put it in the context of other attempts, imperial and Taoist, to use these sites.

THE "CONQUEST" OF SUNG SHAN

As is well known, in the scheme of the five sacred mountains that developed
as part of the official cosmological system during the Han, Sung Shan was
considered the Central Peak—the place where the primordial energies of the
five phases (wu-hsing) concentrated. The four other mountains—T'ai Shan
泰山, Heng Shan 恆山, Hua Shan 華山, and Heng Shan 衡山—corresponded to the Eastern, Northern, Western, and Southern peaks. This system
played a major role in the official religion and in Taoism at least as early as
the second century B.C.E.[4] According to the Han Wu-ti nei-chuan, for example,
the "true form" of the Five Peaks had been revealed by the mythical Hsi-
wang Mu, the "Queen Mother of the West," to Emperor Wu of the Han in
109 B.C.E. (Chavannes 1910, 421; Schipper 1965). Throughout the Six
Dynasties these Five Peaks, and more particularly T'ai Shan and Sung Shan,
were at the center of imperial ceremonies of dynastic legitimation such as the
feng 封 and shan 禪 rituals of consecration through which the emperor
announced to Heaven and Earth the success of his rule (see Kiang 1975, 64).

Composed of a range of peaks, of which the two major ones are Mount
T'ai-shih 太室 (1,140 meters above sea level) and Mount Shao-shih 少室
(1,512 meters), Sung Shan is some fifty miles from Cheng-chou (Honan),
near the subprefecture of Teng-feng 登封 (a name alluding to the feng sacrifice). According to the Han classificatory system, the god of the Sung
Shan presided over the ground, mountains, rivers, and valleys, as well as
oxen, sheep, and all rice-eating beings (Chavannes 1910, 419). It is famous in
imperial history for its endorsement in 110 B.C.E. of Han Wu-ti's reign; on

that occasion, the mountain resounded with the cry of "Ten Thousand Years," memory of which is preserved in the name of one of its peaks (Wan-sui feng 萬歲峯).

In 676, an imperial edict said to have been inspired by Empress Wu announced that the *feng* and *shan* rituals would be performed by Emperor Kao-tsung on Sung Shan. Adverse circumstances caused postponement of the rituals that year and again in 679. Kao-tsung resumed the preparation in 683 but died before the rites could be carried out (see Chavannes 1910, 195–200; Wechsler 1985, 189). Empress Wu eventually performed them in 696 in the name of her new Chou dynasty. Already in 688, she had conferred on Sung Shan the title "Divine Peak" (*Shen-yueh* 神岳) and on the mountain god "King of the Center of Heaven" (*T'ien-chung wang* 天中王). After completing the rituals successfully, she promoted the mountain god to "Emperor of the Center of Heaven" (Chavannes 1910, 200–201; Forte 1976, 234). After the return to the T'ang mandate in 705, Emperor Hsuan-tsung performed the *feng* and *shan* rituals on T'ai Shan in 725. Too closely associated with the reign of Empress Wu, Sung Shan had temporarily lost its privilege in imperial rituals.

The mountain had been a stronghold of religious Taoism since the Han. Toponymy reveals a wealth of mythical associations with Taoist alchemy: Cave of the Precious Jade Girl, Red Cooking Basin, Jade Mirror Peak, White Crane Peak, Three Storks Peak, Jade Man Peak, and so forth. By T'ang times, the space of the mountain was saturated with mythical references, overpopulated with spirits. According to the *Shen-hsien chuan* 神仙傳, a man named Su Lin 蘇林 (d. ca. 250 C.E.), said to be the "Immortal of the Central Peak" (*chung-yueh chen-jen* 中岳眞人), became the master of another legendary Taoist, Chou Tzu-yang 周紫陽 (Porkert 1979). Lord Lao himself bestowed the title "Celestial Master" on K'ou Ch'ien-chih 寇謙之 (d. 448) on Sung Shan; K'ou was believed to have written prophecies on stone and hidden them on the mountain (Seidel 1983, 353; Forte 1976, 248). One of his prophecies, concerning the rise to power of Empress Wu, was found toward 674 by the subprefect of Teng-feng (Forte 1976, 229, 247–251).

In the Taoist tradition, as it developed in the Six Dynasties, the Five Peaks were sometimes seen as the five fingers of the cosmic Lao-tzu. All were interconnected by an array of caves believed to be the gateways to the Taoist heavenly underworld, the so-called grotto heavens (*tung-t'ien* 洞天; translated by Chavannes as "deep celestial place"). Sung Shan's grotto heaven, believed to be three thousand *li* deep (see Stein 1987a, 293, for a description), figures as the sixth among a list of thirty-six *tung-t'ien*, although it does not appear on an earlier list of ten, used in the Mao Shan 茅山 school in the fifth century (Chavannes 1919, 145). Sung Shan was not included in the reduced list of twenty *tung-t'ien* ordered by Emperor Jen-tsung during the early eleventh century, probably because the Five Peaks were *tung-t'ien* by definition (see Strickmann 1989); the exclusion does not seem to reflect a Taoist decline on Sung Shan. During and after the T'ang, Taoists apparently continued to perform rituals on each of the five sacred peaks on behalf of the ruling dynasty.

Sung Shan became toward the mid-T'ang a retreat for eminent Taoist masters of the so-called Mao Shan (or Shang-ch'ing 上清, i.e., "Supreme Purity") school, which had risen to prominence in the fifth and sixth centuries. The tenth patriarch of the school, Wang Yuan-chih 王遠知 (d. 635), had already performed rituals on Sung Shan when the Sui dynasty established its capital in Lo-yang in 605. The eleventh patriarch, P'an Shih-cheng 潘師正 (d. 682 or 694), and his disciple Ssu-ma Ch'eng-chen 司馬承禎 (647–735) also resided on the mountain. P'an Shih-cheng, who was intimate with Kao-tsung, was a Buddhist-Taoist syncretist who founded various Shang-ch'ing institutions on Sung Shan (see Schafer 1980, 46). After studying on Sung Shan with P'an Shi-cheng, Ssu-ma Ch'eng-chen took residence on T'ien-t'ai Shan and convinced Hsuan-tsung that the true masters of the sacred mountains were not the local gods (a fortiori the Ch'an masters), but the masters of the Mao Shan school. In 727 an imperial edict ordered that temples dedicated to the "pure gods" of the Shang-ch'ing school be founded on the Five Peaks.[5]

Other recluses on Sung Shan in T'ang times included the literati. The most well known is Lu Hung 盧鴻, a contemporary of the Ch'an monk P'u-chi 普寂 (see *CTS, chüan* 192, vol. 16:5119; *HTS, chüan* 196, vol. 18:5603). Distinguished by his erudition and his talent at calligraphy, Lu Hung refused an official position and retired on Sung Shan. The number of his disciples reached, we are told, five hundred. During the K'ai-yuan era (713–41), he was often invited to the court by Hsuan-tsung, who offered him in 718 the position of imperial adviser, which Lu Hung declined. When Lu Hung died, Hsuan-tsung contributed ten thousand cash of silver for the funeral, and Lu Yen monastery was built on the spot of Lu Hung's hermitage (Ch'i 1987, 2). The *Sung Kao-seng chuan* (988), mentioning Lu Hung's relationships with the Ch'an master P'u-chi, hints at the rivalry between the two men. When Lu Hung discovered the mnemonic talents of P'u-chi's young disciple I-hsing, he told P'u-chi that P'u-chi was not qualified to teach such a promising young monk and that he should let the young man go visit other places (*T* 50:732c). I-hsing eventually traveled widely and became a master of the Tantric tradition.

The relationships between Buddhists and other groups were at times strained. Under the Northern Wei, Wei Yuan-sung 衛元嵩, a Buddhist monk who turned to Taoism and wrote an anti-Buddhist memorial in 567, went to Sung Shan to study with the Taoist master Chao Ching-t'ung 趙靜通. After Wei received the sacred scriptures, Chao told him to leave because Sung Shan had become defiled by the presence of Buddhists (Lagerwey 1981, 19).

The political rivalry between Taoists and Buddhists at the court was reflected in the competition over beliefs and sacred places. During the T'ang, however, there are few traces of such rivalry, which seems to have resurfaced under the Sung. Its echoes may still be heard in stories told today by Chinese people. We are told, for example, that during a drought at the time of Emperor Hsien-tsung (r. 1465–87) all the Buddhist monks and Taoist priests of Sung Shan gathered in front of the Dragon King to pray for rain. They began to joke, but the joke turned into a real argument, and they eventually went to ask the arbitrage of the emperor (Wang 1988, 143). On another occasion a Ch'an monk, having learned from the Taoist priests the tricks they used to delude the gullible peasants into asking oracles from the Sung Shan god, had nothing more urgent than to reveal the tricks to the believers (147). Even at the time of their strongest dominance over Sung Shan, however, Buddhists were never able to impose their reading of the mountain; they had to find a modus vivendi with its other inhabitants. The Sung Shan god, who had supposedly converted to Ch'an, retained his status in local, imperial, and Taoist cults.

Conversely, despite their potential rivalries for political power and legitimacy, literati, Taoists, and Ch'an masters were natural allies against what they saw as local folk beliefs, for which they shared a common contempt (see Lévi 1989). Like Confucian officials, and in contrast with the Taoists, Buddhists usually attempted to subdue local deities. Whereas Taoist mythology tended to be localized and to see the mountain as a text to be deciphered, as a succession of spaces encapsulating mythological time, Mahayana Buddhists tried to erase local memory, to desacralize spaces, to debunk or re-encode legends. This attempt, however, did not usually succeed; and we have not only a sedimentation of legends, but a tension between various lores that could be reactivated. This "superscription" of the place, like that of the myths, transformed them into "interpretive arenas" (Duara 1988).

Before the newly arisen Ch'an school established itself on Sung Shan, a number of eminent Buddhist monks had resided on the Central Peak. The most famous perhaps was the Western monk Pa-t'o 跋陀 (also known as Fo-t'o 佛陀), for whom the Shao-lin Monastery was founded by Emperor Hsiao-wen Ti (r. 471–99) of the Northern Wei. Pa-t'o's disciples Hui-kuang 慧光 (468–537) and Seng-ch'ou 僧稠 (480–560) also played a major role in the Buddhist circles of the time. Seng-ch'ou was contrasted with Bodhidharma in Tao-hsuan's 道宣 *Hsu Kao-seng chuan* 續高僧傳 (667) (*T* 50, 2060:596c), while the later Ch'an tradition claimed that Hui-kuang and another Buddhist priest had attempted to poison the Indian patriarch of Ch'an, Bodhidharma (see *Ch'uan fa-pao chi*, in Yanagida 1971, 360).

The legend connecting Bodhidharma to Shao-lin took shape after the first Ch'an monks, Fa-ju 法如 (638–89) and Hui-an 慧安 (d. 709), moved from the East Mountain (Tung Shan 東山) community of Tao-hsin 道信 (580–

651) and Hung-jen 弘忍 (601–74) to Sung Shan (see Yanagida 1967; Faure 1986). Thus, it is during the last decades of the seventh century that the legends of Bodhidharma's nine years of "wall contemplation" (*pi-kuan* 壁觀) in a cave near Shao-lin and of his disciple Hui-k'o's 慧可 (487–593) standing all night in the snow and eventually cutting off his arm to show his religious zeal seem to have taken shape.[6]

Before becoming a Ch'an monastery, Shao-lin had been a flourishing translation and Vinaya center where such monks as Guṇamati and Hui-kuang lived and worked. When the monastery was devastated by rebels toward the end of the Sui, its monks organized themselves militarily and contributed in 621 to the victory of the new T'ang dynasty. Li Shih-min (Kao-tsu, r. 618–26) rewarded them in 624–25 with tax-exempt domains. The Shao-lin school of martial arts created about that time was soon traced back to Bodhidharma himself. Under the reign of Kao-tsung (649–83), the monastery often received the favors of the emperor and of Empress Wu. In 704 an ordination platform was erected, supplementing that of the Hui-shan Monastery 會山寺. Later, the monastery declined; it was restored only in 1245. By that time, it had become a Ts'ao-tung institution, although not all its abbots belonged to that school. It was restored again during the Ch'ing, in 1735.

With the rise to prominence of Northern Ch'an, Sung Shan became a pole of attraction for monks coming from all parts of China. As an inscription written by Liu Yü-hsi 劉禹錫 for the Vinaya master Chih-yen (d. 818) puts it: "Those who speak of Ch'an quietness take Sung Shan as ancestor (*tsung* 宗), those who speak of supranormal powers (*shen-t'ung* 神通, Sk. *abhijñā*) take Ch'ing-liang Shan 清凉山 [i.e., Wu-t'ai Shan] as ancestor, those who speak of the *Vinaya-piṭaka* take Heng Shan 衡山 (i.e., Nan-yueh, the Southern Peak) as ancestor" (*Wen-yuan ying-hua, chüan* 867:4; quoted in Tsukamoto 1976, 546). This statement, of course, simply reflects the tendency of various monasteries to specialize in certain aspects of Buddhism and should not be read as an expression of the type of sectarianism that developed after Shen-hui's attack on Northern Ch'an.

The most famous of these Ch'an monks were Hui-an 慧安 (d. 709), Yuan-kuei 元珪 (644–716), P'o-tsao To 破竈墮 (d.u.), and P'u-chi 普寂 (658–739) and his disciples—for example, I-hsing 一行 (683–727) and Fa-wan 法玩 (715–90). Tradition has it that Nan-yueh Huai-jang 南嶽懷讓 (677–744), one of the two heirs of the Sixth Patriarch, also came to study on Sung Shan with Hui-an. Although this tradition is dubious, we know for sure that another disciple of Hui-neng, Ching-tsang 淨藏 (675–746), lived and died on Sung Shan; his stupa, built in 746, is renowned as the most ancient brick stupa extant in China. Shen-hui (684–758) himself, the man responsible for the schism between Northern and Southern Ch'an, seems to have studied there (see *T* 50, 2061:763c).

The fame of Sung Shan during the T'ang is attested by the large number of stupas and stelae. While the Shao-lin Monastery is well known for its "forest of stupas" (*t'a-lin* 塔林), many of these stelae were later moved to the "forest of stelae" (*pei-lin* 碑林) in Sian. The existence on the precincts of Shao-lin of such a large number of stupas (more than 240) raises some questions. Their existence is probably due in part to the importance of commemorating the master-disciple relationship in a school that claims not to rely on scriptures and tends to consider the master as the *lex incarnata*. However, these stupas and stelae were multifunctional; the funerary stupas, "animated" as they supposedly were by the relics they contained, constituted what Paul Mus (1935) has called "substitute bodies." Like the master himself, his relics and stupas were an embodiment of the dharma. To a certain extent, this is true of the stelae as well; although their commemorative function was clearly important, they served simultaneously to channel the power of the dead and to empower, claim, or promote a site. They also served to legitimize Buddhism, by creating a hybrid discourse in which Ch'an dogma and historical claims were intermingled with the prose of the literati.[7]

For the T'ang, of particular interest are the imperial inscriptions concerning the Shao-lin Monastery, the inscription of the ordination platform (composed by Li Yung in 715), and the epitaphs of Ch'an monks such as Ling-yun 靈雲 (750) and T'ung-kuang 同光 (771); for the Yuan, the epitaph of the Ch'an master Hsi-an 息庵 (1341). These inscriptions show that, by the mid-T'ang, the monasteries on Sung Shan had become largely Ch'an (see McRae 1986; Faure 1988).

The most prestigious of these monasteries is of course the Shao-lin Monastery. Although situated somewhat apart at the northern foot of Mount Shao-shih, it clearly belongs to Sung Shan in collective representations. Almost as important, however, were the Fa-wang Monastery 法王寺—allegedly one of the oldest Chinese monasteries where, at the turn of the seventh century, a fifteen-story stupa containing relics of the Buddha was erected by order of Sui Wen-ti (r. 581–604); the Hui Shan Monastery with its ordination platform; and the Sung-yueh Monastery with Shen-hsiu's thirteen-story stupa (see Mochizuki 1977, 3:2880–81; Faure 1988, 45). Ch'an adepts came from all over the country to study with P'u-chi.[8] Yet despite this overwhelming presence of Ch'an on Sung Shan, the mountain remained a Taoist stronghold. As noted earlier, the Mao Shan Taoists obtained in 727 the foundation of a temple dedicated to Shang-ch'ing gods. It is perhaps significant that this Taoist victory occurred the same year that the Tantric master (and former Ch'an adept) I-hsing died. This polymath, who had been intimate with Emperor Hsuan-tsung, had been instrumental in the imperial recognition of Northern Ch'an and the granting of a tax exemption to the Shao-lin Monastery in 728.

Ironically, I-hsing and his Northern Ch'an masters have acquired in their

legend some of the usual characteristics of their Taoist rivals. Their extraordinary popular appeal had apparently less to do with their teaching than
with their alleged supranormal powers. Taming wild animals such as snakes
and tigers, which were regarded in popular beliefs as the representatives or
emanations of the local deities, is a recurring example of *shen-t'ung* in the
hagiographies of these early Ch'an monks. In one story, P'u-chi confronts the
vengeful spirit of a deceased disciple reincarnated under the form of a huge
snake and pacifies him with a sermon on karmic retribution—predicting his
rebirth as a girl in a neighboring village.[9] Several structurally similar stories
also show a Northern Ch'an master conferring the bodhisattva precepts on
the god of Sung Shan. (These stories illustrating the transmission of local
jurisdiction from a local god to the Buddhist order represent, of course, a
purely Buddhist version of events.)

The motif appears in Hui-an's biography (see *T* 50, 2061:823b) and is
further developed in Yuan-kuei's biography (828c). The latter is particularly
significant for the manner in which the conversion of the Sung Shan god
takes place. According to this story, when the god threatened to kill Yuan-
kuei for his lack of respect, the monk replied: "Since I am unborn, how could
you kill me? My body is empty and I see myself as no different from you; how
could you destroy emptiness or destroy yourself?" Eventually, after conferring the bodhisattva precepts on the god, Yuan-kuei explained to him that
the true *shen-t'ung* is emptiness: "The fact that there is neither dharma nor
master is what is called no-mind. For those who understand in my way, even
the Buddha has no powers; he can only, through no-mind, penetrate all
dharmas" (*T* 50:828c).

Another case in point is that of a disciple of Hui-an nicknamed P'o-tsao
To (Stove-breaker To) because of the following anecdote:

> There was [on Sung Shan] a shamaness (*wu* 巫) who could sacrifice to the
> stove-god and perform exorcisms. . . . One day To visited her. He spoke at first
> to her, then struck the stove, saying: "Whence comes the deity? Where are the
> miraculous spirits?" And he completely demolished it. Everybody was startled
> and terrified. Then a layman in a plain blue robe appeared and bowed respect-
> fully to To, saying: "I have suffered many afflictions here. Now by virtue of
> your sermon on the doctrine of nonbirth, I have been reborn into the heavens. I
> cannot repay your kindness." Having said this, he departed.[10]

The claim of Ch'an takes its full significance when one realizes that the
god of Sung Shan was not understood merely as a local god, but occupied a
very high rank in the cosmological system and in the imperial hierarchy. Its
(repeated) conversion by Northern Ch'an monks took place toward the time
when Empress Wu was conferring on it the title "Emperor of the Center of
Heaven" (see Chavannes 1910, 418). One must keep in mind that charismatic Ch'an masters such as Yuan-kuei were the heirs of Hui-yuan (334–416)

and other Buddhists who had fought to establish that monks were above
mundane rules and refused to respect the traditional (human and spiritual)
hierarchy, at least in principle (and in their hagiography). Northern Ch'an
masters recognized only the emperor as interlocutor and tried to establish
that their lineage was the spiritual equivalent of (and counterpart to) the
imperial lineage—a claim that brought them in direct concurrence with
Shang-ch'ing Taoists.

In all the cases mentioned above, the disruptive power of a *local* spirit is
supposedly pacified by the Buddhist teaching, that is, by the revelation of a
higher understanding of reality, one that implies an overall *unlocalized* vision.
There is a dialectical movement from place to space and from space to
place—the new place being redefined in Ch'an terms. The reterritorializa-
tion of Ch'an was accompanied by a remythologization. As already noted,
Sung Shan was an essential part of the imperial cosmological system inherited from the Han. This system was later reinterpreted, adapted, subverted,
by local traditions and by religious Taoism. However, the fundamental
presupposition—namely, that space is complex and unstable, that it is not
always nor everywhere the same—was never questioned (see Granet 1968).
Even after the collapse of the ideological and cosmological structure of the
Han, the perception of a qualitative, heterogeneous space remained prevalent. However, the construction of monasteries created a new domain, a new
space that may be called a *u-topia* or rather a *heterotopia* (see Foucault 1986),
that decentered or displaced the old spatial frame. Although depending on
society for its subsistence, the monastery was presumed "to represent the
entire cosmos, society included" (Boon 1982, 202); negating the dense and
pluralistic space that characterized popular religion and Taoism, it claimed
to belong to another order of reality.

This epistemological shift was expressed not only in hagiographical discourse, but also more directly in doctrinal terms. Yuan-kuei converted the
mountain god, and P'o-tsao To the stove-god, by preaching to him the truth
of the "unborn," the "sudden teaching" superior to all gradual *upāya* or
"skillful means," the ultimate truth that subsumes and cancels all relative
truths. The nature of this "sudden teaching" is revealed by the physical
violence of To's smashing the stove. "Nonbirth" (*wu-sheng* 無生, Sk. *anut-
panna, anutpāda*) is the equivalent for the Mahayana notion of Emptiness
(*śūnyatā*); because everything is empty, it is called "unborn." Space is
emptied of everything and thereby unified, while all phenomena are deprived
of any ontological status. What seems ultimately to govern the Ch'an attitude is the visual/spatial metaphor; even "sudden awakening"—usually
understood in reference to time—was actually defined as a "simultaneous"
visual perception of space (see Stein 1987b). In Ch'an ideology, space was
perceived as ultimately empty, and all phenomena were compared to illusions, "flowers in the sky." The tabula rasa aimed at by the Ch'an motto of

"nonthinking" (*wu-nien* 無念) was the spiritual equivalent of P'o-tsao To's iconoclasm. Ch'an discourse created a clean, abstract space that could ideally be embraced at one glance. The old boundaries were erased, and boundless space meant boundless sovereignty.

A seeming paradox is that while Ch'an monks were intent on desacralizing mountains and imposing the abstract space of their monasteries, they became engrossed in enshrining relics and erecting stupas, thereby creating new centers, new sacred spaces or places that were protected by local gods and in due time tended to be identified with them. This phenomenon, however, had its source in highly literate monastic circles and should not be read as (merely) the subversion of a larger tradition by local cults. The erection of stupas reflected paradoxically both the humanization of the cosmic sacred places and the sacralization of Ch'an. However, it is important to note that within the Ch'an tradition itself mythology (in the usual sense of stories about gods) came to be replaced by hagiography, and Ch'an faith was anchored in the "lives" of eminent anchorites. A superficial resemblance, namely that these new places of worship were often the same as those of the autochthonous cults, might obscure their opposite meaning and the fundamental change that had taken place in the minds of Ch'an monks; despite superficial similarities, the cult of a stupa is not the same thing as that of a chthonian power.

Sung Shan's mirabilia came to include by the Sung the cave where Bodhidharma practiced "wall contemplation," the stone with his shadow, the place where the second Ch'an patriarch Hui-k'o cut off his arm, the Hermitage of the First Patriarch (Ch'u-tsu An 初祖庵, erected in 1125), the Hermitage of the Second Patriarch,[11] and the stupas of Shen-hsiu and P'u-chi. After the decline of Northern Ch'an, there was also a Cedar of the Sixth Patriarch, Hui-neng. This is how the traveler Hsu Hsia-k'o 徐霞客 describes his visit to the Shao-lin Monastery in 1623:

> Heading northwest from the monastery, I walked past the Terrace of Sweet Dew (Kan-lu T'ai 甘露台) and then past the monastery of the First Patriarch. Making a northern tour for four *li*, I mounted the Five Breast Hill (Wu-ju Feng 五乳峯) and explored the First Patriarch's Cave (Ch'u-tsu Tung 初祖洞); twenty feet deep and somewhat less in breadth, it was there that the first patriarch Ta-mo 達摩 faced the wall for a nine-year meditation. The entrance to the cave faced the temple below, but, on its own level, faced Shao-shih. As there was no water source nearby, no one was living there. Descending to the First Patriarch's monastery, I saw the shadow stone of Ta-mo; less than three feet in height, it was white with the black traces of a vivid standing picture of the foreign patriarch.
>
> In the middle court was a cedar planted by the Sixth Patriarch, an inscription on the stone revealing that it was brought from Kwangtung in a pot by that patriarch. It was already so large it would take three men with outstretched arms to girdle it. (Li Chi 1974, 140)

As this text suggests, famous places on Sung Shan had apparently become part of a kind of pilgrimage or sight-seeing circuit. Ironically, the "wall contemplation" attributed to Bodhidharma and defined as "theoretical entrance" or contemplation of the Absolute came to be misinterpreted as a concrete technique of "facing the wall" (*mien-pi* 面壁), and the wall itself ultimately became a sacred place.

Eventually, however, these Ch'an attempts to create new sacred spaces that would pull the crowds to Sung Shan turned out to be a relative failure.[12] They did not prevent the decline of Sung Shan as a Ch'an stronghold, perhaps in part because the Shao-lin Monastery, despite its popularity, was relatively distant from the other monasteries on Sung Shan (map 4.1). The decline of Buddhism on Sung Shan accompanied that of the Northern school in the eighth and ninth centuries, after the diatribes of Shen-hui against what he called a "gradual" and "collateral" branch of Ch'an. Although the Northern school was later replaced locally by the Ts'ao-tung school—one of the "five houses" of Ch'an that emerged during the late T'ang—the latter never rose to the same prominence, and Sung Shan seems to have lost its appeal for Ch'an pilgrims.

The only exception was perhaps the Shao-lin Monastery, whose fame remained great—probably because of its connection with martial arts. After their military prowess at the beginning of the T'ang at the side of Li Shih-min (see Wang 1988, 33), the monks of Shao-lin continued to appear in the political and military arenas. In 815 a monk of Sung Shan named Yuan-ching participated in a coup on the imperial palace in Lo-yang. Although he was eventually executed after the failure of the rebellion, he impressed his executors by his bravery (see Demiéville 1957, 364). But it was particularly during the Ming, in the fifteenth and sixteenth centuries, that the Shao-lin monks won fame by fighting against the Japanese pirates who scoured the Chinese coasts (367). Their exploits have remained engraved on the collective psyche, inspiring numerous stories (see Wang 1988) and plays (and, more recently, movies), while their martial techniques have been represented on mural paintings in the Shao-lin Monastery (see reproductions in Chavannes 1913, figs. 981–82). The Shao-lin school of martial arts (Shao-lin ch'üan 少林拳) became known as the "exoteric school" by opposition to the "esoteric school" of Wu-tang Shan 武當山, which taught a more interiorized method called T'ai-chi ch'üan, supposedly founded by the Taoist master Chang San-feng 張三丰, who died at the beginning of the Ming (see Seidel 1970 and Lagerwey, chapter 7 of this volume). During the Ch'ing, the monastery's prestige was also enhanced by the coming of august visitors such as the K'ang-hsi Emperor (r. 1662–1723) and the Ch'ien-lung Emperor (r. 1736–95) (see Wang 1988, 227–37).

Judging from the number of stelae, the Shao-lin Monastery seems to have experienced a kind of revival between the Yuan and the Ch'ing. It was re-

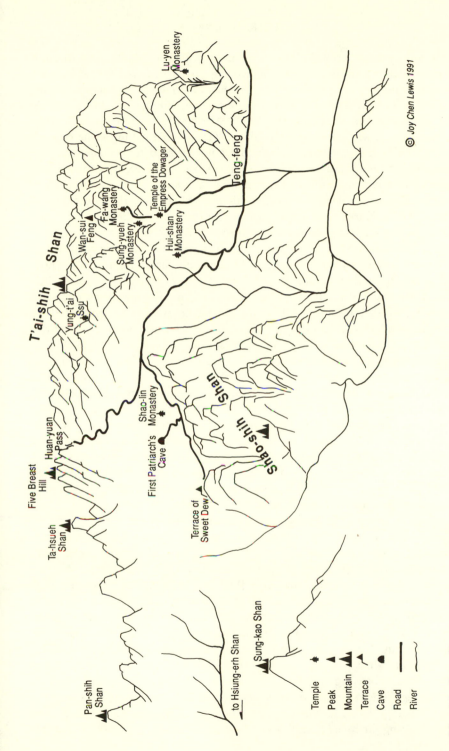

Lu-yen Monastery

T'ai-shih Shan

Wan-sui Feng

Fa-wang Monastery

Sung-yueh Monastery

Temple of the Empress Dowager

Yung-t'ai Ssu

Hui-shan Monastery

Teng-feng

Five Breast Hill

Huan-yuan Pass

Ta-hsueh Shan

Shao-lin Monastery

First Patriarch's Cave

Shao-shih Shan

Terrace of Sweet Dew

Pan-shih Shan

Sung-kao Shan

to Hsiung-erh Shan

Temple
Peak
Mountain
Terrace
Cave
Road
River

© Joy Chen Lewis 1991

Map 4.1. Sung Shan

stored during the Yuan by Hsueh-t'ing Fu-yü 雪庭福裕 (1203–75), a disciple
of the famous Ts'ao-tung master Wan-sung Hsing-hsiu 萬松行秀. Fu-yü's
work was pursued by abbots such as Hsi-an 息庵 (T'ien-ch'ing I-jang
天慶義讓, 1284–1340) and Wu-fang K'o-ts'ung 無方可從 (1420–83). A
Japanese monk named Kogen Shōgen 古源邵元 (1295–1364) came to study
at Shao-lin and wrote a stele inscription ("Hsi-an ch'an-shih tao-hsing chih
pei" 息庵禪師道行之碑) for Hsi-an that still exists on the precincts of the
monastery.[13] Ch'an had been introduced as early as the eighth century into
neighboring countries, and the catchment area of famous cultic centers such
as Wu-t'ai Shan, T'ien-t'ai Shan, A-yü-wang Shan, and the like came to
include Tibet, Korea, and Japan. In the latter country, the Lin-chi (Jpn.
Rinzai) and Ts'ao-tung (Sōtō) sects flourished after the thirteenth century,
and Sung Shan apparently remained a pole of attraction for Zen monks.

The story of the friendship between Shōgen and Hsi-an became legendary
and is still told today.[14] Shōgen settled at Sung Shan for twenty years after
visiting the major Buddhist sites of China, and the itinerary of this eclectic
Zen monk—who, because of his cultural background, was interested as
much in wonders as in Ch'an practice—may be characteristic of that of the
Japanese pilgrims during the Yuan. He first visited Hsueh-feng Shan 雪峯山
(in Fukien), then T'ien-t'ai Shan 天台山 (in Chekiang), where, emulating his
predecessors,[15] he crossed the famous rock bridge to make a tea offering to
the five hundred Arhats (*Lo-han*) and was granted an auspicious vision; he
then went to T'ien-mu Shan 天目山 (near Hangchow in Chekiang) to pay
homage to the stupa of the Ch'an master Chung-feng Ming-pen 中峯明本
(1263–1323), who appeared and preached to him in a dream; he continued
toward Wu-t'ai Shan, where he had a vision of the Bodhisattva Mañjuśrī.
From there, he went to the Yü-ch'üan Monastery in Ching-chou 荆州
(Hupei) and finally to Shao-lin, where he took residence in the Hermitage of
the Second Patriarch (*Honchō Kōsōden* k. 30; Tokiwa 1928, 90).

While the fame of Sung Shan seems to have endured in Japan, it faded
away in China. Sung Shan's loss of prestige was not only a Ch'an phenomenon; it affected the literati too. Most of the extant poems about Sung
Shan were written by T'ang poets such as Sung Chih-wen, Wang Wei, Li
Po, Po Chü-i, and Li Hua. Once described by Wang Wei as "towering aloft
in the skies and piercing half-way into the heaven," Sung Shan came to be
dismissed by later literati travelers as "flat, and lacking in wonders" (Hsu
Hsia-k'o, in Li Chi 1974, 137). Its name, Sung-kao 嵩高, occasioned the
following pun: "Among the Five Peaks, only Sung-kao is not high (*kao* 高)."
As Ch'i Chou-hua puts it, "While Hua Shan seems to be standing, Sung
Shan seems to be lying" (1987, 6–7).

Although the causality at work behind this loss of prestige is complex,
Sung Shan probably declined largely because Lo-yang ceased to be the
capital during the Five Dynasties and thus lost its political and cultural pres-

tige. Yet according to Timothy Brook, during the Ch'ing, Sung Shan and Hua Shan were second only to T'ai Shan in popularity; that the Shao-lin Monastery "operated a hall called Shih-fang (Ten Directions) Cloister opposite its main gate as a combined postal station, itinerant monk's residence, and inn to meet the need of the pilgrims" (*Shao-lin ssu-chih ying-chien*, 8b, quoted in Brook 1988a, 16) seems to bear witness to this popularity. This discrepancy between earlier and later views of the mountain reminds us that our sources, reflecting a limited segment of reality, cannot be entirely trusted. It also suggests that the decline of Sung Shan as a Ch'an site might have coincided with the rise of its popularity in other groups. It seems unlikely, however, that the daily number of pilgrims to Sung Shan could have come anywhere close to the eight or nine thousand people recorded for T'ai Shan. At any rate, the mountain had definitely (if not definitively) lost its popularity by the end of the Ch'ing. As William Geil, a Christian missionary who visited Sung Shan in 1926, two years before the fire that devastated the Shao-lin Monastery, put it: "Verily, the place is all but empty, though by no means swept and garnished. As the old faiths give way, what is to come? Devils worse than before, or the good news of a Heavenly Father?" (1926, 181). An essay by Joseph Hers published ten years later (1936) is subtitled "Sung-shan the Deserted."

THE EMERGENCE OF TS'AO-CH'I AS CULTIC CENTER

What the Buddhist monasteries on Sung Shan had to offer to pilgrims were primarily their "memorials" (stupas, inscriptions). Actually, these were more than memorials, since stupas were frequently reliquaries, and relics are not merely the representation or commemoration of an absent buddha or saint, they imply his numinous presence. However, despite (or because of) its multifocality (and multivocality), Sung Shan could not compete with the Ch'an site of Ts'ao-ch'i on that ground.

Unlike many sacred sites in China, Ts'ao-ch'i (the Stream of Ts'ao) was not strictly speaking a mountain or a mountain range, although it gave its name to the surrounding hills, Ts'ao-ch'i Shan. It was at first a rather obscure place in the countryside, south of Ch'ü-chiang and Shao-chou in northern Kwangtung. It was the site of only one monastery, the Nan-hua Monastery, whose name—Monastery of Southern China—betrayed high ambitions. These ambitions were fulfilled, for it eventually became a national temple or *bodhimanda* (*t'ien-hsia tao-ch'ang* 天下道場), a place to which, according to the Jesuit missionary Matteo Ricci (1522–1610), people flocked in pilgrimage from all parts of China (Gallagher 1953, 222). One reason for its popularity is that the Ts'ao-ch'i community, conveniently situated between Canton and Lu Shan, possessed a wealth of relics of the Sixth Patriarch—"contact relics" such as the robe and the bowl, but also the relic par excellence, Hui-neng himself, "in the flesh." The flesh body of [the sixth patriarch] has been the main object of worship in the Nan-hua Monastery since the eighth century.

Sung Shan's Bodhidharma had unfortunately achieved a kind of Taoist "deliverance from the corpse" (*shih-chieh* 尸解), leaving an (almost) empty grave behind him; the single sandal allegedly found in his coffin never counted among the precious relics of the Shao-lin monastery—if only because the legend had located his grave not on Sung Shan, but on another mountain not too far away, the Hsiung-erh Shan 熊耳山 (Bear's Ear Mountain) in Honan. Nevertheless, the Ts'ao-ch'i community claimed to have the sandal among their relics. The creation ex nihilo at Shao-lin of sacred vestiges such as Bodhidharma's cave, his "shadow stone," or the place where Hui-k'o stood in the snow and cut off his arm might be seen as makeshift epiphanies that could not replace "true" relics. The legend of the "Cypress of the Sixth Patriarch" in Shao-lin Monastery, a tree supposedly grown from a seed brought from Ts'ao-ch'i by Hui-neng himself, can be seen as an attempt by Sung Shan monks to connect their place with Hui-neng. Unlike the latter, Bodhidharma had failed to find a spring (i.e., tame a dragon) near his cave, and the lack of this cosmic and ecological element in his site was another negative factor. As Hsu Hsia-k'o pointed out: "As there was no water source nearby, no one was living there" (Li Chi 1974, 140).

Relics (Sk. *śarīra, dhātu*, Ch. *she-li*) have played a crucial role in the development of Buddhism and more particularly in its acculturation in East Asian countries. Relics in the large sense refer to anything left behind by the Buddha or an eminent monk: ashes, bones, "flesh body," but also a bowl, a robe, or even a text. In the strict sense, the term *śarīra* usually refers to those crystalline fragments left after the cremation of a saintly body. After the extinction (*parinirvāṇa*) of the Buddha in the sixth century B.C.E., his śarīra were supposedly divided and enshrined in eight stupas. Tradition has it that in the third century B.C.E. the Indian king Aśoka collected these relics and magically erected 84,000 stupas all over the southern continent (Jambudvīpa) to enshrine them. According to most sources (see, for example, *Kuang hung-ming chi*, in *T* 52, 2103:201b; also Zürcher 1959, 277–80), nineteen such stupas were "found" in China before the T'ang, the most well known being those of the Ch'ang-kan Monastery 長干寺 (in Chien-k'ang), of A-yü-wang Shan 阿育王山 (Mount Aśoka in Ningpo prefecture, Chekiang), and of Wu-t'ai Shan. Relics were also reported to have appeared in response to meritorious acts. For example, in 744 the monk Ch'u-chin obtained 3,070 grains of śarīra after performing the Lotus samādhi (*fa-hua san-mei* 法華三昧) ceremony (*FTTC, T* 49, 2035:375b; Jan 1966, 61). Additionally, śarīra of saints multiplied after the T'ang with the development of the cremation ritual.

Major relics such as the tooth or the finger bone of the Buddha became the object of a fervent cult in China. In 819 the Confucian Han Yü wrote his famous memorial to protest against the periodic transfer of the finger bone from the Fa-men Monastery 法門寺 in Feng-hsiang to the capital and the collective frenzy it occasioned. As we know from Han Yü's account and various other sources, an important aspect of the cult of relics was self-immolation or self-mutilation (see Gernet 1959; Jan 1965). However, except for one instance—that of the monk Ta-chih, who died on Sung Shan in the early seventh century after burning his arm (*T* 50, 2060:682b)—there is no evidence that Ts'ao-ch'i's flesh body or Sung Shan's reliquaries were the objects of devotional sacrifices like those performed in front of the relics of the Fa-men or the A-yü-wang monasteries (the latter had become a Ch'an monastery by the Sung), where Ch'an monks like Hsu-yun would often mutilate themselves.

The relation between relics and mummies was discussed by Tsan-ning (919–1001) in his *Sung Kao-seng chuan* (988), in relation to the biography of a lay believer of Northern Ch'an named Ting 丁居士, whose true bodhisattva nature was revealed by his "golden bones" (*SKSC, T* 50:830a). In his appended comment, Tsan-ning notes that, although Buddhist saints are said to leave a "linked skeleton" (in the manner of Taoist immortals), in the case of a Buddha, "his whole body is a śarīra."

Beginning with the Sixth Patriarch Hui-neng, many Ch'an masters turned themselves or were turned into mummies or flesh bodies after their deaths. Although this phenomenon is in no way restricted to Ch'an, the majority of known examples are found in this school. Not surprisingly, wonder workers such as Pao-chih 寶誌 (418–514), Wan-hui 萬廻 (d. 711), and Seng-ch'ieh 僧伽 (d. 708) were all said to be self-mummified, although with varying success.

The first recorded case for Ch'an is that of the fourth patriarch Tao-hsin 道信 (d. 651), who might be considered the actual founder of the Ch'an school. After his death, his body was put in a stupa on Huang-mei Shan 黃梅山 (Hupei). The next year, according to the *Ch'uan fa-pao chi* 傳法寶紀 (ca. 720), "the stone doors opened of themselves and his countenance was as majestic as the days when he was alive. His disciples subsequently added lacquered cloth [to the body] and did not dare to reclose the doors. They cut stone and engraved a tablet. Tu Cheng-lun 杜正倫 (587–658), president of the Department of the Imperial Grand Secretariat, composed the text praising his virtue" (Yanagida 1971, 380).

We know that Tao-hsin's successor, Hung-jen, took great pains over the erection of his own stupa, perhaps intending to follow his master's example. However, there is no description of his mummy in the early hagiography. The *Sung Kao-seng chuan* simply mentions that his disciples placed his "whole body" in a stupa (*T* 50:755b). Not surprisingly, a much later work such as the *THCC* is more specific; it speaks of the "true bodies" of Hung-jen and Tao-hsin (2:43b–44a). At any rate, none of Hui-neng's mummified predecessors attracted as many pilgrims as he did, and the existence of these "true bodies" on the mounts of the fourth and fifth patriarchs did not prevent these cultic centers from eventual decline.

The preservation of Hui-neng's mummy, however, probably contributed a great deal to the victory of the Southern school and its rise to the status of Buddhist orthodoxy. It may be that Hui-neng's wide fame as Sixth Patriarch and Ts'ao-ch'i's popularity as cultic center can be attributed to the prodigious success of Hui-neng's mummy. Other Ch'an communities, deprived of this asset, may have attempted, only too late, to emulate Ts'ao-ch'i by producing relics—including perhaps the flesh bodies of Tao-hsin and Hung-jen. At any rate, even if the presence of a mummy was a major condition of prosperity for a Buddhist cultic center, various other geographical, historical, and cultural factors may have played significant roles.

Hui-neng's mummy—together with those of two later Ch'an masters, Han-shan Te-ch'ing 憨山德清 (1546–1623) and Tan-t'ien 丹田 (d.u.)—can still be seen in the Nan-hua Monastery in Ts'ao-ch'i.[16] It has been often described, and the Ts'ao-ch'i local gazetteer contains many poems about it (see, for example, *CTTC, chüan* 5:516; 6:621; 7:638, 653, 669, 708; 8:781). An interesting description is given by Ricci, who was a contemporary of Han-shan. Ricci visited the monastery in 1589, soon after his arrival in China. According to his diary, revised and translated by Trigault:

> The temple itself, magnificent in its grandeur, is built upon the most beautiful of all the hills and is copiously supplied with fresh water from a large mountain, graciously designed and wonderfully built. On the plateau and contiguous to the temple is the cloister, the dwelling, as they say, of a thousand priests of the idols. They are the lords of this demesne, inherited as a benefice from the impious piety of their ancestors. This institution had its origin with a man named Lusu [i.e., *Lu tsu* 盧祖, the "Patriarch Lu," i.e., Hui-neng], some eight hundred years ago. They say that he lived on this very spot and that he acquired a great reputation for sanctity because of his unusually austere manner of living. . . . His body is enshrined in this magnificent temple, which was built in his honor, and the people, who venerate his memory and whatever belonged to him, come here on pilgrimage from all corners of the realm. (Gallagher 1953, 222)

Ricci was particularly impressed by the opulence of the monastery and by the vision of the "idols"—the five hundred Arhats—that filled its main hall. Finally, he was shown Hui-neng's "flesh body": "The temple ministers also showed them the body of Lusu, enveloped in that peculiar shiny bituminous substance known only to the Chinese.[17] Many say it is not his body, but the people believe that it is and they hold it in great veneration" (Gallagher 1953, 223). But Ricci refused to pay homage to the mummy and, putting forward his hosts' "idolatry" as a reason, refused to stay any longer at Ts'ao-ch'i.

A few years later, Ricci's successors recorded how Hui-neng's flesh body was brought from Nan-hua Monastery to the neighboring town of Shao-chou to end a long drought. "So they gave up hope in the city gods, and for the occasion they brought in a celebrated monster from the country. Its name was *Locu* [*sic*]. They paraded it about, bowed before it and made offerings to it, but like its counterparts it remained deaf to their pleading. It was this occasion that gave rise to the saying, 'Locu is growing old'" (Gallagher 1953, 462). The use of Hui-neng's mummy by local religion is attested by a much earlier source, the *SKSC* (988). We are told that during the Five Dynasties, under the rule of the Southern Han (917–71), at the time of the *shang-yuan* 上元 festival (i.e., on the fifteenth of the first month), the mummy of the Sixth Patriarch was always carried to the town (probably Shao-chou) to bring happiness for the people (*Enō kenkyū* 1978, 236; Ui 1966, 246).

Clearly, Hui-neng's flesh body had become a powerful cult object, not only for Ch'an monks, but for the people as well. The process of Hui-neng's apotheosis, however, is not as well documented as that of his contemporary Seng-ch'ieh (d. 710), whose flesh body was also lacquered about the same time (see *FTTC*, *T* 49, 2035:372c) and whom the Sung worshiped in Ssu-chou as a god of navigation (see Makita 1954). Unlike Mao Tse-tung's case, described by Wagner in chapter 9 of this volume, the exact circumstances of Hui-neng's mummification have not been recorded. The earliest document, his epitaph by Wang Wei (see Yanagida 1967, 539) simply tells us that "at an unknown date he told his disciples that he was about to die, and at once a mysterious fragrance permeated the room and a bright rainbow appeared. When he had finished eating, he spread his sitting-cloth and passed away. . . . Again, on an unknown date, his sacred coffin[18] was moved to Ts'ao-ch'i, and his body was placed, seated, in an unidentified place" (Yampolsky 1967, 67). We only know that, like Seng-ch'ieh's body, Hui-neng's was eventually lacquered.

Much of the material of Hui-neng's legend appears in the *Sōkei daishi betsuden* 曹溪大師別傳 (ZZ 2B, 19, 5:483a), a work, lost in China, that was taken to Japan by Ennin. This text, dated 782, was compiled by the disciples of Hsing-t'ao 行韜 (var., Ling-t'ao 令韜), the guardian of Hui-neng's stupa in Ts'ao-ch'i, primarily to establish the legitimacy of the community centered on Hui-neng's relics, a community apparently different from that in which the *Platform Sutra* was compiled. This strategy proved successful: Ts'ao-ch'i soon became a thriving pilgrimage center for monks. After the proscription of Buddhism in 845, Ts'ao-ch'i came to replace, at least for Ch'an adepts, the pilgrimage to the Bodhisattva Mañjuśrī on Wu-t'ai Shan. According to Suzuki (1985, 54), monks would come to pay homage to the stupa of the Sixth Patriarch at Ts'ao-ch'i rather than go to worship Mañjuśrī.[19]

Most of the cases of self-mummification recorded by the Ch'an tradition date from the T'ang or early Sung, but the custom persisted. One of the last

Fig. 4.1. The Nan-hua Monastery at Ts'ao-ch'i. From *CTTC*, 51.

洗心亭 卓錫泉 石坐

伏

Meditation Stone

Hall of the Sixth Patriarch **Fountain of the Planted Staff**

六祖舊殿 Abbot's Rooms

方丈 Stelae

禪

本來堂

Dharma Hall

禪

說法堂

Ch'an Hall

禪

禪堂

禪

平南王生祠

禪

Stupa

陳亞仙祠

Ancestral Temple of Ch'en Ya-hsien

Lo-han Shan

香爐山 羅漢山

Fig. 4.2. Nan-hua Monastery: monastic buildings. From *CTTC*, 52.

well recorded cases is that of the above-mentioned Han-shan Te-ch'ing. Soon after Han-shan's death in 1623, his body, seated in lotus position, was placed in a casket (*k'an* 龕) and enshrined in a memorial hall in Ts'ao-ch'i. In 1625, however, he was transferred to Lu Shan and placed in a stupa. He was eventually returned to Ts'ao-ch'i in 1643. On this occasion, the casket was opened. Han-shan's hair and nails had grown long and he looked "as if alive." He was subsequently painted with sandalwood powder. His flesh body, enshrined in a hall near that of Hui-neng, became an object of intense worship by monks and laymen. The cult of Han-shan grew to the point that, despite his somewhat unorthodox career, he has sometimes been called the "seventh patriarch."

Another Ch'an master of the Ming dynasty, Tan-t'ien (Cinnabar Field), whose name suggests a Taoist influence, was also mummified at the Nan-hua Monastery. According to the monk P'en-kan's preface to the "Eulogy of the Flesh body of the Ch'an Master Tan-t'ien," Tan-t'ien, after his ordination at age thirty-two, spent most of his time reciting the *Vajracchedikā prajñāpāramitā sutra* and died while meditating in 1614 (*CTTC chüan* 6:626). There is unfortunately no other source of biographical information concerning Tan-t'ien. That he died and was mummified nine years before Han-shan seems, however, significant, since his mummification probably influenced Han-shan's determination to leave a flesh body.

The fame of Han-shan's flesh body was supplemented by his restoration of the Nan-hua Monastery. Despite a partial rebuilding in 976, the monastery had fallen into ruins by the time Han-shan arrived in 1600. Its restoration was achieved in 1613. It was again devastated by the end of the Ch'ing, and the second major restoration was carried out by Hsu-yun just before World War II.

As the structure of this sacred site has been modified in the course of its long history (sometimes reluctantly, because any disruption entails danger), it might be useful to locate briefly its main sacred foci. The most important is, of course, Hui-neng's flesh body itself, enshrined in what is now the Later Hall of the Sixth Patriarch (fig. 4.1). The patriarchal robe and bowl had been kept in this two-story building, and Hui-neng's mummy was transferred there from its stupa during the Ch'eng-hua era (1465–88) of the Ming. The hall was renovated in 1980, and the flesh bodies of Han-shan and Tan-t'ien were disposed on each side of Hui-neng, like two bodhisattvas attending a buddha.

In front of the Hall of the Sixth Patriarch is the Precious Stupa (*pao-t'a* 寶塔), a seven-story edifice in which the mummies of Hui-neng and Han-shan were at different times lodged. The year following Hui-neng's death, his body was brought into the stupa. In 812 (Yuan-ho 元和 7), when Hui-neng received his posthumous title (*Ta-chien Ch'an-shih* 大鑒禪師), the stupa was baptized "Yuan-ho Ling-chao" 元和靈照. According to the *CTCL*, it was destroyed by fire during a war at the beginning of K'ai-pao period (968–75), but Hui-neng's body "was protected by the monk in charge and suffered no injury whatsoever" (Yampolsky 1967, 87). The stupa was rebuilt by Emperor T'ai-tsung (r. 976–97) and rebaptized T'ai-p'ing hsing-kuo 太平興國 (Great Peace and Prosperity of the State). Originally made of wood, this stupa was reconstructed in stone in 1477 and subsequently restored in 1516, 1548, and 1568. At the time of its reconstruction, Hui-neng's mummy was transferred into the Hall of the Sixth Patriarch for better preservation, and Han-shan's mummy was placed in the stupa. According to Han-shan's *Ts'ao-ch'i ch'ung-hsing lu* 曹溪重興錄 (see Tokiwa 1928, 79), this transfer resulted from a dream in which Hui-neng appeared to the governor of the commandery and asked to be moved. Hui-neng continued to watch over the destiny of his "mausoleum" until recent times. The "live hagiography" of Hsu-yun records that he saw Hui-neng, first in a vision during meditation, then in several dreams. The meaning of these apparitions, in which the Sixth Patriarch repeatedly told him that it was "time to go back," became evident when, shortly after, the provincial authorities of Kwangtung invited Hsu-yun to renovate the Nan-hua Monastery (Xu Yun 1988, 115).

Hui-neng's and Han-shan's relics were not only the objects of monastic and popular devotion, but also the subjects of many poetic compositions by literati. Although the flesh bodies of the two monks—and to a lesser extent that of Tan-t'ien—had become the central attraction for pilgrims in Ts'ao-ch'i, almost equally important were Hui-neng's robe and bowl, regarded as the equivalent of "dynastic talismans." It seems that some kind of ritual sequence was involved in the seeing of these relics, which were kept in the Hall of the Sixth Patriarch, behind Hui-neng's mummy. The *CTTC* contains several series of poems, apparently forming a literary *topos*: "Entering Ts'ao-ch'i," "The Flesh Body" (var., "flesh patriarch" 肉祖), "Seeing the Robe," "Seeing the Bowl," "The Resounding Shoes" (*hsiang-hsieh* 響鞋), and "The Waist-hanging Stone" (*chui-yao shih* 墜腰石),[20] inter alia, written by literati such as Chao Lin-chi 趙霖吉 (*CTTC, chüan* 8:755) and Wang Ling 王令 (ibid., 775).[21] Another important relic usually on display was a pilgrim's staff (*hsi-chang*), probably the one with which Hui-neng was said to have summoned forth spring waters (see Soymié 1961). At any rate, the existence of poems concerning these relics shows that Ts'ao-ch'i was not merely a pilgrimage site for Ch'an monks, but an attraction for literati as well.[22]

The most famous of these literati is probably Su Shih (1036–1101), who visited the place during his exile and has left many poetical pieces concerning Hui-neng and the Nan-hua Monastery (see *CTTC, chüan* 3:310; 5:474, 481–83, 516; 6:531, 637–38), in particular a poem entitled "On Seeing the True Appearance (*chen-hsiang* 眞相) of the Sixth Patriarch" (ibid., *chüan* 1:638). There is even at Ts'ao-ch'i a hermitage called Su Ch'eng An 蘇程庵, where

Su Shih used to discuss the Way with his friend Ch'eng Te-ju 程德儒 (ibid., 113).

Two other numinous places are the iron stupa called Stupa of the Taming of the Dragon (hsiang-lung t'a 降龍塔), on the left side of the main hall, and the Fountain of the Planted Staff (cho-hsi ch'üan 卓錫泉) at a short distance behind it. The first name refers to the legend of Hui-neng taming a dragon by catching it in his begging bowl after challenging it to reduce its size—a Buddhist variant of a widespread folklorical theme.[23] The stupa allegedly contained the bones left behind by the dragon, but those bones disappeared during the turmoil of the Yuan. The second name refers to another related motif, the saint as source finder. The legend has it that Hui-neng, wanting to wash the robe and the bowl he had inherited from the Fifth Patriarch, caused a spring to well up by driving his staff into the ground. Since that time, whenever the spring appeared to dry up, it was reactivated by the mere presentation of the patriarchal robe—such being the supposed efficacy (*ling* 靈) of this talismanic cloth. Hui-neng is credited with the creation of several other springs in northern Kwangtung, southern Kiangsi, and Hunan (see Soymié 1956, 33–35).

These stories reveal that the conquest of the place by Ch'an, as in the case of Sung Shan, involved some kind of symbolical violence or deception.[24] But their relative scarcity in the case of Ts'ao-ch'i suggests that the place offered much less resistance, for it was not as deeply rooted as Sung Shan in the local, official, and Taoist symbolical systems. Apparently, the only monuments there were the grave and ancestral temple of the donor of the land, Ch'en Ya-hsien 陳亞仙 (*CTTC, chüan* 1:88). To some extent, the "conquest" of Ts'ao-ch'i shares similar features with that of Miao-feng Shan, studied in this volume by Susan Naquin.

Once conquered, the site needed to be promoted. This promotion of the new "local spirit" often prevailed over doctrinal concerns. Beyond the legitimate attachment of the disciples to the relics of their master, we can discern intense sectarian stakes. It is no mere coincidence that all the Ch'an mummies are those of the "founders" of a new school or branch of Ch'an: Tao-hsin for the Tung-shan school, Hui-neng for the Southern school, Wu-hsiang 無相 (684–762) for the Ching-chung 淨衆 school in Szechwan, Fa-ch'in 法欽 (714–92) for the Niu-t'ou 牛頭 school, Wen-yen 文偃 (864–949) for the Yun-men school. The relics of these masters were not only duly venerated, they were also manipulated by their successors to demonstrate the master's power and attract the devotion of believers to the particular temple and school. Ironically, the self-mummified Ch'an master, however independent and undisputed he may have been in his lifetime, became a much disputed collective property after his death.

The possession of relics was at all times an object of intense rivalry. The division of the śarīra of the Buddha, of course, nearly provoked a "war of relics." The case of Hui-neng, however, is a paradigmatic one. Like the translations and *furta sacra* of relics of Christian saints (see Geary 1978 and 1986), Hui-neng's relics were the object of several transfers and perhaps of "sacred thefts." While the *Platform Sutra* simply says that Hui-neng died in the eighth month of 713 and that the "seat of his spirit" (*shen-tso* 神座) was interred on Mount Ts'ao-ch'i in the eleventh month, the *CTCL*, written almost three centuries after the event (1004), alludes to what seems to have been a controversy over Hui-neng's body:

> At this time at both Shao-chou (where he had lived) and Hsin-chou (where he died) sacred pagodas were erected, and none of the monks or laymen could decide [where the body was to be enshrined]. The officials of each county burned incense together and offered an invocation: "Wherever the smoke from the incense leads will be the place to which the Master wishes to return." The smoke from the incense burner rose and moved straight in the direction of Ts'ao-ch'i. On the thirteenth day of the eleventh month, the Master's body was enshrined in its pagoda. He was seventy-six years old. Wei Ch'ü 韋璩, the prefect of Ts'ao-ch'i, wrote the text for his monument. (Yampolsky 1967, 86)

The role of the prefects in this affair suggests that the government was intent on controlling the emerging cult of Hui-neng's flesh body.[25]

According to the Southern Ch'an tradition, Hui-neng's mummy was threatened several times with "sacred thefts." There is first the well-known story, spread by Hui-neng's successor Shen-hui, that the Northern Ch'an master P'u-chi had paid someone to sever the head of the Sixth Patriarch. This attempt is said to have failed (Yampolsky 1967, 28; Hu Shih 1970, 176; Gernet 1949, 94). Even if Shen-hui invented the story to discredit the Northern school, its point is not so much a moral condemnation of Northern Ch'an masters; it is that Hui-neng refused to leave Ts'ao-ch'i for Sung Shan, just as he had allegedly refused to leave it while alive when summoned to the court at the demand of Hui-an and Shen-hsiu. For local believers, the mummy clearly manifested its power by foiling the theft.

Another "sacred theft" (or perhaps a variant of the same) was reportedly attempted in 722 by a Korean. The *CTCL* records what seems to be an ex post facto "prediction" of this event by Hui-neng himself (assuming that the attempts at stealing Hui-neng's head were ever "facts") (see Yampolsky 1967, 86). Chinese sources offer different versions of the event (see *Enō kenkyū* 1978, 214) but agree that the attempt failed. According to the Korean tradition, however, it was successful, and Hui-neng's head was brought back to Korea. Hui-neng himself subsequently appeared in a dream to the thief and told him that he wanted to be enshrined at Sanggye-sa, a monastery on Chiri-san (see Yi Nŭng-hwa 1955, 1:32). This mausoleum still exists, and the relic, compared by the Koreans to that of the sinciput of the Buddha at Wu-t'ai Shan, attracted in 1980 a group of Taiwanese pilgrims. The story proves that

Ts'ao-ch'i's catchment area extended to Korea. We know, for instance, that a famous Korean monk, Toŭi 道義 (d. 825), perhaps unaware or skeptical of this story, came in 784 to pay homage to Hui-neng's flesh body at Nan-hua Monastery (Yanagida 1978, 29). That Ts'ao-ch'i's fame endured is indicated by the unification of Korean Ch'an (Sŏn) in the twelfth century by Chinul (1158–1210) under the label of the Chogye (Ts'ao-ch'i) school. Of course, the toponym "Ts'ao-ch'i" also refers metonymically to Hui-neng himself and might be read as an allusion to the presence of his relic at Sanggye-sa.

However this may be, it is clear that the attempts to steal Hui-neng's head were intended not to harm the mummy, but merely to transfer its power to other Buddhist communities. Relics constituted an apparently inexhaustible source of symbolic and material gain, and recognition of this fact created a "lust for relics." Another Korean allegedly tried to steal the Buddha relic at A-yü-wang Shan in 849 (*FTTC, T* 49, 2035:387a). Whether Koreans were merely the villains of Chinese stories or actual traders in relics remains to be shown.

A similar rivalry over the possession of the remains of Han-shan Te-ch'ing opposed the Ch'an communities of Ts'ao-ch'i and Lu Shan. The scenario is the same. Upon the death of Han-shan, his contending disciples resorted to divination. The monks of Nan-hua Monastery felt entitled by the oracle to build a mausoleum to house Han-shan's mortuary casket. However, one of his disciples had a stupa built for him at Lu Shan and, helped by the supreme commander of Kwangtung, succeeded in 1625 in having the body removed there. It took almost twenty years for the monks of Nan-hua Monastery to convince the local government to return the body to Ts'ao-ch'i. It is on this occasion that the mummy was taken out of its casket and lacquered (Hsu 1979, 100). Another allusion to this episode is found in an inscription related to the Fountain of the Planted Staff inscription according to which, although the fountain had dried up when Han-shan's casket was taken by "someone powerful" to Lu Shan, it flowed again when the mummified body was eventually returned to Ts'ao-ch'i (*CTTC, chüan*4:369).

The Han-shan Hall, where the mummy was enshrined, became afterward a flourishing pilgrimage center. Thus, Han-shan's mummification promoted him to the status of Ch'an patriarch, a status his unorthodox filiation would have otherwise prevented him from acquiring. Without the appeal and power provided by his flesh body, even his restoration of Nan-hua Monastery could probably not have revived Ts'ao-ch'i.

Although a flesh body was the most conspicuous and most valuable relic, it was by no means the only one. We have noted earlier the role played by the local government in the attribution of Hui-neng's and Han-shan's flesh bodies to the Ts'ao-ch'i community. The contest for other patriarchal relics and their role in dynastic legitimization are also reflected in the imperial interest in Hui-neng. In 760, Emperor Su-tsung (r. 756–62) sent an envoy to

Ts'ao-ch'i asking for Hui-neng's robe and bowl in order to enshrine them in the imperial palace. Subsequently, in 765, Hui-neng himself appeared in a dream to Emperor Tai-tsung (r. 762–79), asking for their return. In response to this dream, the emperor ordered the grand general of defense, Liu Ch'ung-ching, to return the robe to Ts'ao-ch'i, saying: "I regard it as a dynastic treasure. Let it be installed properly at the head temple, and be strictly guarded by special priests, who have been recipients of the main tenets of the teachings. Great care must be taken so that it is not lost" (Yampolsky 1967, 87). This famous story concludes the *Sōkei daishi betsuden* (782). According to this work, its author Hsing-t'ao, when asked to come to the court with Hui-neng's robe, declined the invitation and sent his disciple instead. One year after Hsing-t'ao's death in 759, Emperor Su-tsung sent an imperial commissioner to offer incense before the grave of Hui-neng, "whereupon from within the grave a white light leap[t] forth, soaring straight up to a remarkable height" (Yampolsky 1967, 76). This story can be read as a Ch'an claim to provide dynastic legitimization through the intercession of its relics.

The claims of Ts'ao-ch'i were disputed by other communities. The Pao T'ang 保唐 school in Szechwan claimed that Hui-neng's robe had been handed down by Empress Wu to another disciple of the fifth patriarch, Chih-shen 智詵 (603–702).[26] According to the *Li-tai fa-pao chi*, the robe had subsequently been handed down to Wu-chu 無住 (d. 774), the founder of the Pao T'ang school. Despite its political ambition, well reflected in its name (Protector of the T'ang), this school failed to supplant Ts'ao-ch'i in the pilgrims' minds.

Given these threats to their legitimacy, the monks of Ts'ao-ch'i were even more reluctant to deprive themselves of Hui-neng's relics, and they eventually succeeded in convincing the emperor of their right to keep them. Yet they also benefited from the imperial interest in the relics, and the dialectic of legitimization went on for a long time. In 1032, Emperor Jen-tsung (r. 1022–63) required that not only the robe and the bowl, but the flesh body itself be brought to the palace to be worshiped (*CTTC*, 257). However, these "translations" of relics seem to have come to an end with the Ch'ing.

Another important relic was Hui-neng's *dharma-śarīra*, the *Platform Sutra* itself. The claim made by the compilers of the *Platform Sutra*—that the possession of the text was proof of the legitimacy of the transmission—seems to reflect an attempt at loosening the connection between Hui-neng and Ts'ao-ch'i. As Yampolsky points out, "The *Platform Sutra*...is quite specific in its insistence that a copy of the work itself be required as a proof of the transmission of the teaching. Thus the abandonment of the robe as a symbol is compensated for, as far as this work is concerned, by the establishment of the *Platform Sutra* itself as a proof of the transmission" (1967, 113; see also ibid., 162). When the Ts'ao-ch'i community attempted to prevent the dissemination of Hui-neng's charisma by invoking his alleged decision to interrupt the transmission of the robe, other communities tried to overcome this obstacle by turning to other symbols of transmission.[27]

In a similar way, the authors of the *Lotus Sutra* had asserted the priority of the "relics of the Dharmakāya," that is, the teachings of the Buddha as his *Dharmakāya* or cosmic body over the relics of the Buddha's mortal body. Perhaps the main difference is that the *Platform Sutra* was to be the object of an esoteric transmission. Its postcript indicates that after the death of the compiler Fa-hai 法海 (d.u.), it was transmitted to an abbot of the Fa-hsing Monastery 法性寺 (i.e., the Kuang-hsiao Monastery) in Canton.[28] Yet, even as the *Platform Sutra* was being circulated in a way seemingly antithetical to the worship of Hui-neng's relics, its allegedly original text was preserved by the monks of Ts'ao-ch'i as an additional relic, and the Nan-hua Monastery possessed several stele inscriptions (one in particular by Su Shih) eulogizing the *Platform Sutra*. This situation suggests that, although various kinds of relics could be played off against each other in a specific context, they ultimately enhanced each other's symbolic value. They obeyed the same logic of "transcendent immanence" and, while the power (*ling*) circulating through them could not—despite sectarian claims—find its exclusive source in any one of them, each of them was to varying degrees empowered by this circulation.

This logic or ideology of immanence suggests that, beyond narrow sectarian or political concerns characterized by an attempt to bring the accessibility of the sacred in one place and for one group (Brown 1981, 86), a larger change may have taken place at the level of monastic representations. As noted earlier, the process is again a dialectical one. On the one hand, the cult of relics and mummies, while allowing the popularization of Ch'an, implied a humanization of the sacred, a kind of demythologization that often went against local beliefs in cosmic or divine mediators. Mediators became idealized men, Ch'an masters whose power was manifest in and through the relics. This evolution, characterized by the replacement of mythical adhesions by human dominations, set up a new "sacred topography," a new network of pilgrimage anchored in sacred sites such as stupas.

On the other hand, the manipulation of sacred relics triggered what we may call a process of sacralization, which transformed the mummified patriarch into a saintly intercessor and ultimately into a god with a wider audience than monks. Thus, Hui-neng was no longer seen as a man, but as a buddha, that is, a god that was superior to pre-Buddhistic deities yet shared a number of features with them. Centuries after Hui-neng's death, he remained a powerful presence at Ts'ao-ch'i, a protector that could, from his permanent samādhi, influence the course of events. When, in 1276, under the Mongol rule, soldiers opened Hui-neng's flesh body with a sword and saw that his heart and liver were well preserved, they dared no longer profane his remains (see Doré 1916, 7:257). To give a more recent example, reported by the editor of Hsu-yun's "autobiography," when the Japanese air force threatened Ts'ao-ch'i in 1943, two planes collided near the monastery. This accident was apparently interpreted by both Chinese and Japanese as a result of the profanation of the monastery's sacred space, and Japanese bombers subsequently avoided the area (Xu Yun 1988, 128). The possession of relics was, then, not only a means for a monastic community to attract donations from monks or laymen or both in time of prosperity; it was also a way to defend itself against spiritual or physical aggressions. (Unfortunately, the numinous character of Ts'ao-ch'i did not prevent the Communists from arresting and maltreating Hsu-yun in 1951 [ibid., 138].) At any rate, because of the presence of Hui-neng's mummy, the Nan-hua Monastery became widely known as a "prayer temple," one of the "first *bodhimandala* under Heaven," a place where—as on Wu-t'ai Shan and P'u-t'o Shan—miracles could happen (see Yü, chapter 5 of this volume). Even before coming to Ts'ao-ch'i, Hsu-yun himself had a strong interest in relics and traveled widely to the Buddhist sacred sites on the Indian subcontinent and in China, including Wu-t'ai and P'u-t'o. He had, for example, visited the A-yü-wang Monastery near Ningpo several times to pay homage to the relic of the Buddha and even burned one of his fingers in front of it (Xu Yun 1988, 41).

Relics were not only powerful objects of attraction for pilgrims (or repulsion for invaders). As Brown (1981) and Geary (1978) have shown for Christianity, they were themselves mobile. Even mummies could at times travel, as we know from the Jesuit accounts concerning the "celebrated monster" Locu (Hui-neng). One of the latest "translations" of Ch'an mummies occurred in 1944 when Hsu-yun secretly removed the flesh bodies of Hui-neng and Han-shan from Ts'ao-ch'i to hide them from the Japanese (Xu Yun 1988, 131). Paradoxically, the śarīra of Hui-neng and of his five predecessors had also been transmitted in Kamakura Japan within the so-called Bodhidharma school and the Sōtō sect. This geographical and social mobility permitted a "transfer of the sacred" not only from one place to another, but also from one group to others. Like the "dividing of incense" in modern Chinese religion (Sangren 1987), the "dividing of the śarīra" ensured—willy-nilly perhaps—the multiplication of new cultic centers. Another dialectic was at work: the cult that had been at the origin of pilgrimages could also undercut the raison d'être of pilgrimages by bringing the relic to the believer instead of the believer to the relic and disseminating its power instead of concentrating it in one place in the hands of one group.

Although the dialectic of humanization and sacralization was found operating in both sites, one may perhaps heuristically describe their evolution by contrasting the "humanization" of Sung Shan with the "sacralization" of Ts'ao-ch'i. Sung Shan and Ts'ao-ch'i represent what we may perhaps call the "historical" site and the "numinous" site. The growth of Ts'ao-ch'i was due primarily to the symbolic preeminence of its relics and possibly also to the growing importance of the regional capital, Canton, while the eclipse of Sung Shan as a Buddhist site was probably related to its relative lack of relics and to the decline of Lo-yang. However, the wealth of historical associations in the case of Sung Shan made it less vulnerable than Ts'ao-ch'i, whose credibility was tied, not unlike that of the Communist regime after Mao's death (see Wagner, chapter 9 of this volume), to the preservation of a flesh body and to the constant reactualization of its numinous power. Both sites have been restored in the recent past and received some degree of governmental recognition. Chinese President Lin Sen and General Chiang Kai-shek visited Ts'ao-ch'i after its restoration (Xu Yun 1988, 128), perhaps in an attempt to draw on its symbolic capital. It is therefore not surprising that the monastery, for the same reasons, attracted the wrath of the Communists, while the Shao-lin Monastery, perhaps because it was more thoroughly "historicized," was in recent years promoted by the Communist regime as a major tourist site. This dialectic of legitimization between monks and rulers is, in its cumulative effects, the most unilateral of the various dialectical processes that we have seen at work, through the cult of relics, in the construction of the sacred site by monks; the other dialectics—of place and space, sacralization and humanization, fixity and mobility (concentration and dissemination of power)—contributed to the alternations of prosperity and decline that characterized the historical fate of Sung Shan and Ts'ao-ch'i.

NOTES

1. I am indebted to Timothy Brook for lending me his copy of this text. See also Brook 1988a.

2. See, for example, *Sung shu* 嵩書 (1621; rev. ed. in *Sung-shan Shao-lin ssu chi-chih*), *Shuo Sung* 說嵩 (1721), and *Shao-lin ssu chi* (1748), to which one may add the works of Japanese scholars such as Washio Junkei 1932 and Tokiwa Daijō 1972 (1938).

3. These inscriptions, mostly from the T'ang, fall broadly into the following categories: (1) history of a specific monastery (stelae of Shao-lin Monastery by P'ei Ts'ui 裴漼, of Hui-shan Monastery 會山寺 by Wang Chu 王著, of Sung-yueh Monastery 嵩岳寺 by Li Yung 李邕, etc.), a land donation, or some other privileges (inscriptions concerning the ordination platform of the Hui-shan monastery); (2) renovation of monastic buildings (Hall of the First Patriarch); and (3) funerary inscriptions for Ch'an monks that aim primarily at establishing lineage and legitimacy claims.

4. The Buddhist model of the "four mountains"—Omei Shan (Szechwan), Wu-t'ai Shan (Shansi), P'u-t'o Shan (Chekiang), Chiu-hua Shan (Anhwei), which correspond to the four Buddhist elements (*mahābhūta*), the four cardinal directions (west, north, east, south), and the four bodhisattvas (Samantabhadra [P'u-hsien 普賢], Mañjuśrī [Wen-shu 文殊], Avalokiteśvara [Kuan-yin 觀音], and Kṣitigarbha [Ti-tsang 地藏])—corresponds with and reinforces this model. See Chün-fang Yü, chapter 5 of this volume.

5. On this question, see Strickmann 1981, 35.

6. Only much later, with the growing fame of the Shao-lin "fighting monks," was Bodhidharma turned into a martial expert to whom were attributed Taoist treatises of hygiene such as the *I-chin ching* 易筋經 (Classic of the cultivation of the muscles) and the *Hsi-sui ching* 洗髓經 (Classic of the purification of the marrow). See Sekiguchi 1957:391 and 488. The stories of how Bodhidharma created his martial techniques to relieve the fatigue of his "wall contemplation" or how Hui-k'o showed Bodhidharma his fighting skills and became his disciple are still popular (see Wang 1988, 10–20).

7. For a description of the stupas and stelae on Sung Shan, see Sawamura 1925 and Soper 1962.

8. Besides I-hsing, who, as noted earlier, was to become the court astronomer and the patriarch of esoteric Buddhism, and Fa-wan (715–90), already mentioned, other famous Northern Ch'an monks include T'ung-kuang 同光 (700–770), Ch'ung-kuei 崇珪 (756–841), Fa-jung 法融 (d. 853), and Jih-chao 日照 (755–862) (see Faure 1988, 135–37).

9. See *Shen-seng chuan* 7 (*T* 50, 2064:991a). Another popular story, recorded by Wang (1988, 161), tells how one monk of the Sung-yueh Monastery, who believed he was on the way to immortality because he could levitate, was saved in extremis by his friend, a monk of the Shao-lin Monastery, who discovered that his friend's alleged power of levitation was due to a huge snake that was slowly sucking him up. This tale is reminiscent of that of the "immortals" of Lu Shan who were believed to have ascended to heaven until a Buddhist monk discovered they had actually been devoured by a python (see Miyakawa 1979). That the latter legend reveals a rivalry between Buddhists and Taoists on Lu Shan suggests that, behind the present tale of friendship, some rivalry may have existed between the monks of Shao-lin and those of the Sung-yueh Monastery.

10. I have summarized several variants of the story. See, for example, *SKSC*, in *T* 50, 2061:828b.

11. For a description of the two hermitages, see Mochizuki (1977, 3:2807). See also *THCC* 13a–b, which adds a Hermitage of the Third Patriarch.

12. Significantly, the "eight wonders of Sung Shan" visited in the fourteenth century by the Japanese monk Te-shih are no longer Buddhist *mirabilia*, but reflect literati tastes: "The moon in the Sung Shan gate," "The early stroller at Huan-yuan," "Tilled fields in spring by the Ying river," "The shade of the winnowing fan," "Drinking wine by the mountain spring," "Fishing in the jade stream," "Clear snow on the Shao-shih mountain," and the "Lu-ya waterfall." And we are told that "to see all of these one must cover a distance of at least one hundred *li*" (Wang 1988, 169).

13. Shōgen, a monk from Echizen, went to China in 1327. After returning to Japan in 1347, he studied at Tenryūji 天龍寺 with Musō Soseki 夢窓疎石 (1275–1351), then at Tōfukuji 東福寺 (two Rinzai Zen monasteries in Kyoto). His Chinese masters were all in the line of Wu-chun Shih-fan 無準師範 (1174–1249). The lineage of the Ts'ao-tung school is obscure after the Yuan, and Shao-lin was apparently the only place to preserve it. Hsi-an, although abbot of Shao-lin, was not in the Ts'ao-tung lineage. See Tokiwa 1928, 92.

14. See Wang 1988, 132–37. We are told that Hsi-an died from the aftermath of a wound he suffered while trying to protect Shōgen from a falling rock. The storyteller

concludes that the two monks' inscriptions "bear witness to the deep and longlasting friendship between the Buddhist monks of China and Japan" (137). Another story recorded by Wang concerns the visit of a second Japanese monk, Te-shih (alias Sada Mokuzan), whose grandfather had practiced martial arts at Shao-lin from 1312 to 1320 (166–72).

15. This narrow bridge, which only "pure" monks were allowed to cross, had apparently become a test of ritual authentification for Japanese pilgrims. We have accounts of its crossing by late Heian and early Kamakura monks such as Jōjin, Chōgen, Shunjō, Yōsai, and (allegedly) Dōgen. On its legend, see Wen Fong 1958.

16. For photographic reproductions, see Demiéville 1965; Xu Yun 1988, 61 and 76.

17. In his *THCC*, written more than two centuries later (1827), Ju-hai also describes Han-shan's body as having a lustrousness that made him look "as if alive" (*THCC* 1:53b).

18. *Shen-tso* 神座, which Yampolsky translates as "sacred coffin," had a technical meaning in Chinese religion and implies the presence of an enduring principle in the corpse or an effigy of the dead.

19. The first recorded case, predating the Hui-ch'ang era, is that of a disciple of Shih-t'ou Hsi-ch'ien 石頭希遷 (700–790) named Ch'ang Tzu-kuang 長髭曠. Other cases include Tung-shan Ch'ing-ping 洞山清稟 (d.u.) and Ts'ao-shan Pen-chi 曹山本寂 (840–901)—whose toponymic name, Ts'ao-shan, is said to derive from Ts'ao-ch'i. Yun-men Wen-yen 雲門文偃 (864–949) also came to pay homage to the stupa in 911 (Suzuki 1985, ibid.).

20. According to an inscription on it, the "waist-hanging stone" was originally at Huang-mei Shan (Hupei) in the community of the fifth patriarch Hung-jen and was brought to Ts'ao-ch'i during the Chia-ching era (1522–66). Tokiwa (1972) has pointed out various anachronisms and concluded that the inscription was a forgery.

21. Han-shan himself had written a series of such poems (see *CTTC, chüan* 5:478 6:621–23). The autobiography of Hsu-yun also contains a series of poems describing his arrival at Ts'ao-ch'i and his progression from the gates to the Dharma Hall in a kind of ritual taking-over: "At the Ts'ao-ch'i gate"; "At the gate of the Pao-lin Monastery"; "In the Maitreya Hall"; "In front of the shrine of Wei-t'o"; "In the Hall of the Fifth Patriarch"; "In the Hall of the Sixth Patriarch"; "In front of the shrine of Master Han-shan"; "In the Main Hall"; "In the Abbot's rooms"; "In the Dharma Hall." See Xu Yun 1988, 116–19, and Fig. 4.2.

22. According to the Ch'an tradition, Hui-neng, although supposedly illiterate, had contacts with several major literati of the time such as Chang Yueh 張悅 (d. 730) and Sung Chih-wen 宋之文 (d. 712) (see *SKSC, T* 50, 2061:755b). We are told, for example, that Chang Yueh sent another famous man of letters, Wu P'ing-i (d.u.), to Ts'ao-ch'i to offer one of his poems on Hui-neng's stupa. However, the fact that all these men were strong supporters of Northern Ch'an renders these stories dubious. Wu P'ing-i did go to Sung Shan, on Chang Yueh's request, to offer a poem on Shen-hsiu's stupa, and the story of his visit to Ts'ao-ch'i is probably based on this event. Concerning this question, see Fukushima 1938. Other famous T'ang poets who wrote inscriptions for Hui-neng were Wang Wei 王維, Liu Yü-hsi 劉禹錫, and Liu Tsung-yuan 柳宗元, but probably none of them ever went to Ts'ao-ch'i. See *CTTC, chüan* 3:330, 307; 5:454, 473.

23. Interestingly, similar legends were used in Hsu-yun's hagiography. We are told that after his arrival at Ts'ao-ch'i in 1934, he conferred the Buddhist precepts on a tiger (Xu Yun 1988, 116) and on a tree spirit (127) and that three cedar trees from the Sung bloomed again to manifest this renaissance of Hui-neng's dharma (124).

24. Another interesting motif is the story describing the donation of the land of Ts'ao-ch'i, in Fa-hai's "Brief Preface" to the *Platform Sutra* (Yampolsky 1967, 61): Hui-neng convinces a local landowner, Ch'en Ya-hsien 陳亞仙, to give him enough land to spread his sitting-cloth, but when Ch'en does so, the cloth grows to cover the whole area of Ts'ao-ch'i—and Ch'en has to keep his word.

25. On the promotion and cooptation of local cults by the Chinese government, see Watson 1985; Duara 1988; Lévi 1989.

26. The importance of the robe and bowl as both sectarian and "dynastic" talismans can be seen from the first attempt at stealing them from Hui-neng himself, just after he received the dharma transmission from Hung-jen. When Hui-neng offered his bowl to the would-be thief, one of his co-disciples, the latter was unable to move it. As is well known, the weight of a dynastic talisman is proof of its owner's virtue. On this question, see Seidel 1981.

27. The loss of charisma resulting from the transmission was perceived as a very real threat to a community. Thus, the formerly invincible Bodhidharma succumbed to his enemies after transmitting the talismanic *Lankavatara-sutra* to Hui-k'o, and, according to the *Sōkei daishi betsuden* (Yampolsky 1967, 73), Hung-jen died three days after Hui-neng left Huang-mei with the robe and the dharma. Huang-mei disappeared from the Ch'an chronicles and later became a Taoist center.

28. This monastery could boast, however, of another important relic of Hui-neng—his hair, enshrined after his ordination into a seven-story stupa. This event is recorded in an inscription, dated 676, that also mentions the prediction made in 502 by the Tripitaka Master Chih-yao 智藥 concerning the future ordination in that monastery of a flesh body bodhisattva. The authenticity of this inscription has been questioned (see Yampolsky 1967, 65). According to an informant, a *bodhi*-tree is also said to have grown over the place where Hui-neng was buried. At any rate, although this relic could certainly not match those of Ts'ao-ch'i, the rivalry between the two monasteries may have originated the legends.

BIBLIOGRAPHY

Sources Cited by Abbreviation

CTCL *Ching-te Chuan-teng lu* 景德傳燈錄. 1004. Compiled by Tao-yuan 道原 (d.u.). *T* 51, 2076.

CTS   *Chiu T'ang shu* 舊唐書. 954. Reprint. Taipei: Chung-hua shu-chü, 1975.

CTTC *Ch'ung-hsiu Ts'ao-ch'i t'ung-chih* 重修曹溪通志. 1823. In *Chung-kuo fo-ssu shih chih hui k'an* 中國佛寺史志彙刊, vols. 4–5. Reprint. Taipei: Ming-wen shu-chü, 1980.

CTW   *Ch'üan T'ang wen* 全唐文. By Tung Kao 董誥 (1740–1818) et al. Taipei: Hua-wen shu-chü, 1965.

DNBZ *Dai Nihon bukkyō zensho* 大日本佛教全書. 1913–22. Edited by Takakusu Junjirō et al. Tokyo: Yūseidō.

FTTC   *Fo-tsu t'ung-chi* 佛祖統紀. Ca. 1260. By Chih-p'an 志磐. *T* 49, 2035.
HTS   *Hsin T'ang shu* 新唐書. 1043–60. Peking: Chung-hua shu-chü, 1975.
          (Citations are to pages in this edition.)
SKSC   *Sung Kao-seng chuan* 宋高僧傳. 988. By Tsan-ning 贊寧. *T* 50, 2061.
T   *Taishō shinshū daizōkyō* 大正新修大藏經 [Taishō edition of the Buddhist
          canon]. 1924–32. Edited by Takakusu Junjirō. Tokyo.
THCC   *Ts'an-hsueh chih-chin* 參學知津 [Knowing the fords on the way to
          knowledge]. 1827. By Hsien-ch'eng Ju-hai 顯承如海. Edited by I-jun
          Yuan-hung 儀潤原洪 of Chen-chi Monastery 眞寂寺, Hangchow. Reprint.
          Harvard, 1876.
ZZ   *Dai Nihon Zokuzōkyō* 大日本續藏經. 1905–12. Kyoto: Zōkyō Shoin. Reprint.
          Taipei: Hsin-wen feng, 1968–70.

Other Sources

Boon, James A. 1982. *Other Tribes, Other Scribes.* Cambridge: Cambridge University
   Press.
Brook, Timothy. 1988a. "Knowing the Fords on the Way to Knowledge: Ecclesiastic
   Pilgrimage Routes in Late-Imperial China." Paper prepared for the Conference on
   Pilgrims and Sacred Sites in China, Bodega Bay, California, January 1989.
———.1988b. *Geographical Sources of Ming-Qing History.* Ann Arbor: Center for
   Chinese Studies, University of Michigan.
Brown, Peter. 1981. *The Cult of the Saints: Its Rise and Function in Latin Christianity.*
   Chicago: University of Chicago Press.
Chavannes, Edouard. 1909. *Mission archéologique dans la Chine septentrionale.* Publica-
   tions de l'Ecole d'Extrême-Orient, vol. 13. Paris: Ernest Leroux.
———. 1910. *Le T'ai chan: Essai de monographie d'un culte chinois.* Paris: Ernest Leroux.
———. 1919. "Le Jet des dragons." In *Mémoires concernant l'Asie orientale,* 3:53–220.
   Paris: Academie des Inscriptions et Belles-lettres.
Ch'en, Tsu-lung 陳祚龍. 1978. "Sung-yueh ch'an-hsueh yen-chiu tzu-liao hsiao-chi"
   嵩嶽禪學研究資料小集. In his *Chung-hua fo-chiao wen-hua shih san-ts'e ch'u-chi*
   中華佛教文化史散策初集. Taipei: Hsin wen-feng.
Ch'i Chou-hua 齊周華. 1761. *Ming-shan tsang fu-pen* 名山藏副本. Reprint. Shanghai: Ku-chi, 1987.
Ch'uan fa-pao chi 傳法寶紀. Ca. 712. By Tu Fei 杜朏 (d.u.). Edited in Yanagida
   1971.
Ch'üan T'ang shih 全唐詩. 1705–6. Compiled by Sheng Tsu 聖祖. Reprint. Taipei:
   Hung-yeh shu-chü, 1977.
Demiéville, Paul. 1957. *Le bouddhisme et la guerre: Post-scriptum à l'"Histoire des moines-
   guerriers au Japon" de G. Renondeau.* Reprinted in *Choix d'études bouddhiques (1929–
   1970),* 216–99. Leiden: E. J. Brill, 1973.
———. 1965. "Momies d'Extrême-Orient." Reprinted in *Choix d'études sinologiques
   (1929–1970),* 407–32. Leiden: E. J. Brill, 1973.
———. 1973a. *Choix d'études bouddhiques (1929–1970).* Leiden: E. J. Brill.
———. 1973b. *Choix d'études sinologiques (1929–1970).* Leiden: E. J. Brill.
Doré, Henri, S. J. 1911–38. *Recherches sur les superstitions en Chine.* Shanghai. English
   translation: *Researches into Chinese Superstitions,* translated by M. Kennely. Reprinted Taipei: 1966–67.

Duara, Prasenjit. 1988. "Superscribing Symbols: The Myth of Guandi, Chinese God of War." *Journal of Asian Studies* 47, 4:778–95.

Enō kenkyū 慧能研究. 1978. Edited by Komazawa Daigaku Zenshūshi Kenkyūkai. Tokyo: Taishūkan shoten.

Faure, Bernard. 1986. "Bodhidharma as Textual and Religious Paradigm." *History of Religions* 25, 3:187–98.

———. 1987. "Space and Place in Chinese Religious Traditions." *History of Religions* 26, 4:337–56.

———. 1988. *La volonté d'orthodoxie dans le bouddhisme chinois.* Paris: Centre Nationale de la Recherche Scientifique.

———. 1989. *Le bouddhisme Ch'an en mal d'histoire.* Paris: Ecole Française d'Extrême-Orient.

Forte, Antonino. 1976. *Political Propaganda in China at the End of the Seventh Century.* Napoli: Istituto Universitario Orientale.

Foucault, Michel. 1986. "Of Other Spaces." *Diacritics* 16, 1:22–27.

Fukushima Shun'ō 福島俊翁. 1938. "Rokuso Enō zenji to bunjin to no kankei ni oite" 六祖慧能禪師と文人との関係において [The Sixth Patriarch Hui-neng and his relationships with literati]. *Zengaku kenkyū* 29:1–16.

Gallagher, Louis J., trans. 1953. *China in the 16th Century: The Journals of Matthew Ricci, 1583–1610.* New York: Random House.

Geary, Patrick. 1978. *Furta Sacra: Thefts of Relics in the Central Middle Ages.* Princeton, Princeton University Press.

———. 1986. "Sacred Commodities: The Circulation of Medieval Relics." In *The Social Life of Things: Commodities in Cultural Perspective,* edited by Arjun Appadurai, 169–91. Cambridge: Cambridge University Press.

Geil, William E. 1926. *The Sacred Five of China.* Boston: Houghton Mifflin.

Gernet, Jacques. 1949. *Entretiens du Maître de Dhyana Chen-houei du Ho-tsö.* Paris: Ecole Française d'Extrême-Orient.

———. 1956. *Les aspects économiques du bouddhisme dans la société chinoise du Ve au Xe siècle.* Paris: Ecole Française d'Extrême-Orient.

———. 1959. "Les suicides par le feu chez les bouddhistes chinois du Ve au Xe siècle." In *Mélanges publiés par l'Institut des Hautes Etudes Chinoises,* 2:528–58. Paris: Presses Universitaires de France.

Granet, Marcel. 1968. *La pensée chinoise.* Paris: Albin Michel.

Hers, Joseph. 1936. "The Sacred Mountains of China: Sung-shan the Deserted." *China Journal* 24, 2:76–82.

Honchō kōsoden 本朝高僧傳. By Shiban 師蠻 (1626–1710). *DNBZ* 63. Tokyo: Kōdansha, 1970–73.

Hsu Hsia-k'o yu-chi 徐霞客遊記. By Hsu Hung-tsu 徐宏祖. Reprinted Shanghai: Ku-chi, 1980.

Hsu Kao-seng chuan 續高僧傳. By Tao-hsuan 道宣. *T* 50, 2060.

Hsü Sung-pen. 1979. *A Buddhist Leader in Ming China: The Life and Thought of Han-shan Te-ch'ing, 1546–1623.* University Park: Pennsylvania State University Press.

Hu Shih. 1930. *Shen-hui ho-shang i-chi* 神會和尚遺集. Reprint. Taipei: Hu Shih chi-nien kuan, 1970.

Jan Yün-hua. 1965. "Buddhist Self-Immolation in Medieval China." *History of Religions* 4, 2:243–68.

———. 1966. *A Chronicle of Buddhism in China (580–960 A.D.): Translations from Monk Chih-p'an's "Fo-tsu t'ung-chi."* Santiniketan: Visva-Bharati.

Kiang, Chao Yuan. 1975. *Le voyage dans la Chine ancienne, considéré principalement sous son aspect magique et religieux.* Translated by Fan Jen. Vientiane: Editions Vithagna.

Kuang-tung hsin-yü 廣東新語. 1968. By Ch'ü Ta-chün 屈大均. Taipei: T'ai-wan hsueh-sheng shu-chü.

Lagerwey, John. 1981. *Wu-shang pi-yao: Somme taoïste du VIᵉ siècle.* Paris: Ecole Française d'Extrême-Orient.

Lévi, Jean. 1989. *Les fonctionnaires divins: Politique, despotisme et mystique.* Paris: Seuil.

Li Chi. 1974. *The Travel Diaries of Hsü Hsia-k'o.* Hong Kong: Chinese University of Hong Kong.

Li-tai fa-pao chi 歷代法寶記. Ca. 774. *T* 51, 2075.

McRae, John R. 1986. *The Northern School and the Formation of Early Ch'an Buddhism.* Honolulu: University of Hawaii Press.

Makita Tairyō 牧田諦亮. 1954. "Chūgoku ni okeru minzoku bukkyō seiritsu no ichi katei" 中國における民俗佛教成立の一過程 [One process of establishment of folk-Buddhism in China]. In *Silver Jubilee Volume of the Zinbun-kagaku-kenkyusho, Kyoto University,* edited by Kyoto Daigaku Jinbun Kagaku Kenkyūjo, 264–86. Kyoto: Kyoto University.

Miyakawa, Hisayuki. 1979. "Local Cults around Mount Lu at the Time of Sun En's Rebellion." In Welch and Seidel, 83–101.

Mochizuki Shinkō 望月信亨. 1932–36. *Bukkyō daijiten* 佛教大辞典 [Great dictionary of Buddhism]. 10 vols. Reprint. Taipei: Ti-p'ing Hsien, 1977.

Mus, Paul. 1935. *Barabuḍur: Esquisse d'une histoire du bouddhisme fondée sur la critique archéologique des textes.* 2 vols. Hanoi: Imprimerie d'Extrême-Orient. Reprint. New York: Arno Press, 1978.

Nagai Masashi 永井政之. 1976. "Sōtō zensha to Sūzan Shōrinji" 曹洞禪者と嵩山少林寺 [Sōtō Zen practitioners and the Shao-lin Monastery on Sung Shan]. *Shūgaku kenkyū* 18:151–56.

Porkert, Manfred. 1979. *Biographie d'un taoïste légendaire: Tcheou Tseu-yang.* Paris: Collège de France.

Powell, William. 1989. "A Pilgrim's Landscape Text of Chiu Hua Shan." Paper prepared for the Conference on Pilgrims and Sacred Sites in China. Bodega Bay, Calif. January 1989.

Prip-Møller, Johannes. 1937. *Chinese Buddhist Monasteries.* Copenhagen: Gads Forlag.

Reischauer, Edwin O. 1955. *Ennin's Diary: The Record of a Pilgrimage to China in Search of the Law.* New York: Ronald Press.

Sangren, P. Steven. 1987. *History and Magical Power in a Chinese Community.* Stanford, Stanford University Press.

Sasaki, Ruth Fuller, transl. 1975. *The Recorded Sayings of Ch'an Master Lin-chi Hui-chao of Chen Prefecture.* Kyoto: Institute for Zen Studies.

Sawamura, Sentarō. 1925. "Die Stupa im Bezirk des Shao-lin-ssu." *Ostasiatische Zeitschrift* 12:265–72.

Schafer, Edward H. 1980. *Mao Shan in T'ang Times.* Boulder, Colo.: Society for the Study of Chinese Religions.

Schipper, Kristofer. 1965. *L'empereur Wou des Han dans la légende taoïste.* Paris: Ecole Française d'Extrême-Orient.

Seidel, Anna. 1970. "A Taoist Immortal of the Ming Dynasty, Chang San-feng." In *Self and Society in Ming Thought*, edited by Wm. T. de Bary, 483–531. New York: Columbia University Press.

———. 1981. "*Kokuhō*: Note à propos du terme 'tresor national' en Chine et au Japon." *Bulletin de l'Ecole Française d'Extrême-Orient* 69:229–61.

———. 1983. "Imperial Treasures and Taoist Sacraments: Taoist Roots in the Apocrypha." In *Tantric and Taoist Studies in Honour of R. A Stein*, edited by Michel Strickmann, 2:291–371. Brussels: Institut Belge des Hautes Etudes Chinoises.

Sekiguchi Shindai 関口眞大. 1957. *Daruma daishi no kenkyū* 達摩大師の研究 [Research on the great master Bodhidharma]. Reprint. Tokyo: Shunjūsha, 1969.

Shen-seng chuan 神仙傳. *T* 50, 2064.

Shiina Kōyū 椎名宏雄. 1968. "Sūzan ni okeru Hokushū-zen no tenkai" 嵩山にお ける北宗禪の展開 [The development of Northern Ch'an on Sung Shan]. *Shūgaku kenkyū* 10:173–85.

Shuo Sung 説嵩 [On the Sung Mountains]. 1721. By Ching Jih-chen 景日昣. Reprinted in *Chung-kuo ming-shan sheng-chi chih ts'ung-k'an*, 中國名山勝蹟志叢刊, edited by Shen Yun-lung 沈雲龍, no. 21 (n.d.). 4 vols. Taipei, 1971.

Sōkei daishi betsuden 曹溪大師別傳 [A separate biography of the great master of Ts'aoch'i]. ZZ 2B, 19, 5.

Soper, Alexander C. 1962. "Two Stelae and a Pagoda on the Central Peak, Mt. Sung." *Archives of the Chinese Art Society of America* 16:41–48.

Soymié, Michel. 1956. "Le Lo-feou shan: Etude de géographie religieuse." *Bulletin de l'Ecole Française d'Extrême-Orient* 48:1–132.

———. 1961. "Sources et sourciers en Chine." *Bulletin de la Maison Franco-Japonaise* 7, 1:1–56.

Stein, Rolf A. 1987a. *Le monde en petit: Jardins en miniature et habitations dans la pensée religieuse d'Extrême-Orient*. Paris: Flammarion.

———. 1987b. "Sudden Illumination and Simultaneous Comprehension: Remarks on Chinese and Tibetan Terminology." In *Sudden and Gradual: Approaches to Enlightenment in Chinese Thought*, edited by Peter N. Gregory, 41–65. Honolulu: University of Hawaii Press.

Strickmann, Michel. 1977. "The Mao Shan Revelations: Taoism and the Aristocracy." *T'oung Pao* 63, 1:1–64.

———. 1981. *Le taoïsme du Mao chan: Chronique d'une révélation*. Paris: Presses Universitaires de France.

———. 1989. "Building the Sacred Mountain at Mao-shan." Paper prepared for the Conference on Pilgrims and Sacred Sites in China. Bodega Bay, Calif. January 1989.

Sung-shan Shao-lin ssu chi-chih 嵩山少林寺輯志. 1980. 2 vols. In *Chung-kuo fo-ssu shih-chih hui-k'an* 中國佛寺史志彙刊, edited by Tu Chieh-hsiang 杜潔祥, vols. 23, 24. Taipei: Ming-wen shu-chü.

Suzuki Tetsuo 鈴木哲雄. 1984. *Tō Godai no Zenshū: Konan Kōsei hen* 唐五代の 禪宗:湖南江西篇 [The Ch'an school during the T'ang and the Five Dynasties: Hunan and Kiangsi]. Tokyo: Daitō shuppansha.

———. 1985. *Tō Godai Zenshūshi* 唐五代禪宗史 [A history of the Ch'an school during the T'ang and the Five Dynasties]. Tokyo: Sankibō Busshorin.

T'ang hui-yao 唐會要. 961. Taipei: Shih-chieh shu-chü, 1974.

Tokiwa Daijō 常盤大定. 1928. "Nihon sō Shōgen no senbunseru Sūzan Shōrinji no hei" 日本僧邵元の撰文せる嵩山少林寺の碑 [The stele of Shao-lin Monastery on Sung Shan, composed by the Japanese monk Shōgen]. *Tōyō gakuhō* 17, 2:86–110.

———. 1938. *Shina bukkyō shiseki tōsaki* 支那佛教史蹟踏査記 [Record of an investigation of historical remains of Chinese Buddhism]. Reprint. Tokyo: Kokusho Kankōkai, 1972.

Tonami Mamoru 礪波護. 1986. "Sūgaku Shōrinji hei kō" 嵩嶽少林寺碑考 [Reflections on the stelae of Shao-lin Monastery on Sung-yueh]. In *Chūgoku kizokusei shakai no kenkyū* 中国貴族制社会の研究 [A study of Chinese aristocratic society], edited by Kawakatsu Yoshio and Tonami Mamoru, 717–55. Kyoto: Kyoto Daigaku Jinbun Kagaku Kenkyūjo.

Tsukamoto Zenryū 塚本善隆. 1976. *Chūgoku Jōdo Kyōshi Kenkyū* 中國淨土教史研究 [A study of the Chinese pure land doctrine]. Tokyo: Daitō Shuppansha.

Turner, Victor. 1974. *Dramas, Fields, and Metaphors: Symbolic Action in Human Society.* Ithaca, Cornell University Press.

Twitchett, Denis C. 1956. "Monastic Estates in T'ang China." *Asia Major* (n.s.) 5, 2:125–45.

Ui Hakuju 宇井伯壽. 1941. *Daini Zenshūshi kenkyū* 第二禪宗史研究 [Research on the history of the Ch'an school, volume two]. Reprint. Tokyo: Iwanami shoten, 1966.

Wang Hongjun. 1988. *Tales of the Shaolin Monastery.* Translated by C. J. Lonsdale. Hong Kong: Joint Publishing Company.

Washio Junkei 鷲尾順敬. 1932. *Bodaidaruma Sūzan shiseki taikan* 菩提達摩嵩山史蹟大観 [A survey of historical vestiges of Bodhidharma on Sung Shan]. Tokyo.

Watson, James L. 1985. "Standardizing the Gods: The Promotion of T'ien Hou (Empress of Heaven) along the South China Coast." In *Popular Culture in Late Imperial China*, edited by David Johnson, Andrew Nathan, and Evelyn Rawski, 292–324. Berkeley: University of California Press.

Wechsler, Howard J. 1985. *Offerings of Jade and Silk: Ritual and Symbol in the Legitimation of the T'ang Dynasty.* New Haven, Yale University Press.

Welch, Holmes, and Anna Seidel, eds. 1979. *Facets of Taoism: Essays in Chinese Religion.* New Haven, Yale University Press.

Wen Fong. 1958. *The Lohans and a Bridge to Heaven.* Washington, D.C.: Smithsonian Institution.

Xu Yun (Hsu-yun). 1988. *Empty Cloud: The Autobiography of the Chinese Zen Master Xu Yun.* Translated by Charles Luk. Longmead, Shaftesbury, Dorset: Element Books.

Yampolsky, Philip B. 1967. *The Platform Sutra of the Sixth Patriarch.* New York: Columbia University Press.

Yanagida Seizan 柳田聖山. 1967. *Shoki Zenshū shisho no kenkyū* 初期禪宗史書の研究 [Researches on the historical works of the early Ch'an school]. Kyoto: Hōzōkan.

———. 1971. *Shoki no Zenshi, I: "Ryōgashijiki"; "Den hōbōki"* 初期の禪史 I：楞伽師資記、傳法寶紀 [History of early Ch'an I: *"Leng-chieh shih-tzu chi"; "Chuan fa-pao chi"*]. Tokyo: Chikuma shobō.

———. 1978. "Shinzoku tōshi no keifu: Jo (1)" 新續燈史の系譜：叙の一 [The lineage of the "Histories of the Lamp"]. *Zengaku kenkyū* 59:1–39.

———. 1981. *Daruma* 達摩 [Bodhidharma]. Tokyo: Kōdansha.

Yi Nŭng-hwa 李能和. 1918. *Chosŏn pulgyo t'ongsa* 朝鮮佛教通史 [A general history of Korean Buddhism]. 2 vols. Reprint. Tokyo: Kokusho kankōkai, 1955.

Yuan-chueh ching ta-shu ch'ao 圓覺經大疏鈔. By Tsung-mi 宗密 (780–841). ZZ 1, 14, 3–5; 1, 15, 1.

Yun-men shan chih 雲門山志. 1980. In *Chung-kuo fo-ssu shih chih hui k'an*, edited by Tu Chieh-hsiang 杜潔祥, vol. 6. Taipei: Ming-wen shu-chü.

Zürcher, Erik. 1959. *The Buddhist Conquest of China: The Spread and Adaptation of Buddhism in Early Medieval China*. 2 vols. Leiden: E. J. Brill.

FIVE

P'u-t'o Shan:
Pilgrimage and the Creation of the
Chinese Potalaka

Chün-fang Yü

The sacred geography of Buddhist China was marked by sites where great bodhisattvas manifested themselves in human forms. By making a journey to these holy mountains, pious pilgrims hoped to receive blessings and, if they were lucky, obtain a divine vision of the deity. The most famous of these mountains were called the *san-ta tao-ch'ang* 三大道場 (the three great seats of enlightenment) or the *ssu-ta ming-shan* 四大名山 (the four famous mountains). The former term refers to Mount Wu-t'ai 五台 in Shansi, the home of Wen-shu (Mañjuśri); Mount Omei 峨嵋 in Szechuan, the home of P'u-hsien 普賢 (Samantabhadra); and Mount P'u-t'o 普陀 in Chekiang, the home of Kuan-yin 觀音 (Avalokiteśvara). These three bodhisattvas, traditionally called San Ta-shih 三大士 (Three Great Beings), were celestial bodhisattvas who had enjoyed veneration throughout Buddhist Asia. *Ssu-ta ming-shan* includes the same three places as well as a fourth one: Mount Chiu-hua 九華 in Anhui, the home of Ti-tsang 地藏 (Kṣitigarbha). Both expressions came into use quite late. As far as I can ascertain, they were used only after the Sung (960–1279). An early fourteenth-century gazetteer of Ningpo used the first expression. But by the late Ming (1368–1644), both phrases became widely used by the writers of *P'u-t'o shan-chih* (Gazetteer of P'u-t'o; *PTSC*). Ch'iu Lien, the compiler of the 1698 edition of the gazetteer, offered an explanation for the number four. "The four sites symbolized the four great elements. Just as the world was constituted by the four great elements, these elements were in turn represented by the four great mountains, with Wu-t'ai representing wind, Omei fire, Chiu-hua earth, and P'u-t'o water." He went on to comment:

> Chiu-hua is situated right by the [Yangtze] river. Although Wu-t'ai and Omei are quite far, they are nevertheless in the interior of the country and can be reached within reasonable time. P'u-t'o alone is totally isolated, hanging by itself in the middle of the ocean. It is truly both far away and difficult to reach.

Yet during the past several dynasties, faithful men and women of both high status and low birth, Buddhist monks and Taoist priests have been coming here from far away and nearby. Carrying incense and holding scriptures, they walked until their feet became callused, and they knocked their foreheads on the ground until they became bloody. Scaling the mountains and braving the ocean waves, like the gathering of clouds and the roaring of thunders, they came to worship the Great Being [Kuan-yin]. Compared with Omei, Wu-t'ai, and Chiu-hua, more pilgrims have come to P'u-t'o. (*PTSC* 1698, 2:4; Saeki 1961, 372, 373)

The emergence of P'u-t'o as a national and international pilgrimage center for the worship of Kuan-yin was a late and slow one, beginning in the tenth century, picking up momentum in the sixteenth, and reaching a peak only after the eighteenth. By contrast, the other "famous mountains," particularly Wu-t'ai and Omei, were already well known during the T'ang (618–907), the same time when the cult of Kuan-yin also became popular. Because of this popularity, a number of cultic centers for Kuan-yin worship were established on the mainland. While there did not seem to be strong local cultic centers for Mañjuśrī and Samantabhadra against which Wu-t'ai and Omei had to compete, the case was far different for P'u-t'o. Because P'u-t'o eventually emerged as the most important pilgrimage site for the cult of Kuan-yin, it became linked with the other great pilgrimage centers in later periods.

P'u-t'o was able to supersede mainland cultic centers because it claimed to be the Potalaka, the island home of Kuan-yin mentioned in the *Hua-yen ching* 華嚴經, the same scripture that provided legitimacy for Mount Wu-t'ai and Mount Omei. The forty-*chüan* version of the sutra translated by Prajna during the period 795–810 is particularly important. It describes the pilgrimage of the youth Sudhana (Shan-ts'ai 善財) in search of truth. Kuan-yin is presented there as the twenty-eighth "good friend" the young pilgrim Sudhana visits. Kuan-yin's home is Mount Potalaka, situated in the ocean. Sitting on a diamond boulder in a clearing amid a luxuriant wooded area, Kuan-yin preaches dharma to Sudhana. Mount Potalaka was also the setting for one of the most important esoteric scriptures, the *Ch'ien-shou-ch'ien-yen Kuan-shih-yin p'u-sa ta-pei-hsin t'o-lo-ni ching* 千手千眼觀世音菩薩大悲心陀羅尼經 (Sutra of the thousand-hand-and-thousand-eye Kuan-yin great compassionate-heart dhāraṇī), translated by Bhagavaddharma about 700. In this sutra, Kuan-yin reveals the all-powerful saving dhāraṇī to the great assembly of bodhisattvas and other beings gathered around Sakyamuni Buddha in Kuan-yin's palace on this sacred island.

While connecting the island to these influential scriptures, the builders of the Chinese Potalaka also incorporated mythical and iconographical elements of Kuan-yin developed by local pilgrimage centers on the mainland. Miracles attributed to Kuan-yin gave rise to such centers and to the local traditions connected with them. I would argue that only when Kuan-yin

became associated with certain sites and when people began to make pilgrimages to these places did the cult of Kuan-yin really take root in China.
The extensive acculturation that the bodhisattva experienced in China provides another reason for the proliferation of pilgrimage sites for Kuan-yin. Of
all the great Buddhist deities, Kuan-yin alone underwent a sexual transformation and in doing so succeeded in becoming completely Chinese (Stein
1986). Because of her great popularity in China, many cultic centers devoted
to her worship appeared in different localities. Miracles firmly anchored
Kuan-yin to these sites and in the process provided Kuan-yin with indigenous life stories and iconographies.[1]

Miracles and pilgrimage sites, therefore, played important roles in the
Chinese cult of Kuan-yin. They contributed to the domestication and sinicization of Kuan-yin. Miracle tales, local lore, literature, and art were the
media through which information about pilgrimage sites was made known
to pilgrims. They created the potential pilgrims' expectations and probably
shaped their experiences during the pilgrimage. Pilgrims, both monastic and
lay, were the agents who transmitted local traditions to other parts of the
country. These traditions were also carefully collected and preserved by the
compilers of mountain gazetteers, which, as I shall argue below, constitute a
powerful source for the legitimation of each site.

The relationships among the various pilgrimage centers devoted to the
same deity deserve careful study. Can we talk about local, regional, national,
and even international pilgrimage sites in China? Do they always compete
with each other for prestige and patronage? Or do some draw on the greater
fame of older and better established sites to confirm their newly acknowledged *ling* 靈 (efficacy)? The cult of Kuan-yin with its multiple pilgrimage
sites provides an ideal case for our study. Although this chapter concentrates
on the mechanisms and processes through which P'u-t'o became the Chinese
Potalaka, I will examine these developments in the light of other pilgrimage
sites on the mainland. As the chapter by Faure in this volume shows, the
study of the birth and decline of pilgrimage centers can provide us with
much-needed information about the social history of Chinese religion.

ESTABLISHMENT OF PILGRIMAGE SITES
FOR THE CULT OF KUAN-YIN

The founding myths recounting the establishment of most Kuan-yin pilgrimage sites contain two basic motifs: either Kuan-yin appeared in person and
performed miracles for the benefit of the people, or the site became known
through its possession of a miracle-working image of Kuan-yin, which either
came into being spontaneously (*tzu-tso* 自做) or was made by Kuan-yin
himself/herself.[2] Founding myths of pilgrimage sites therefore reflect the prevailing view of the miraculous. Sometimes both motifs are used in the found-

ing myths of the same site. I will first briefly discuss the establishment of three sites on the mainland. Each represents one motif. I will then examine the case of P'u-t'o, where it was primarily the possibility of having a vision of Kuan-yin that first attracted pilgrims and, to some extent, continued to do so throughout the succeeding centuries.

The creation of the first of such medieval Kuan-yin cultic centers is comparatively well known, for the legend of Miao-shan 妙善 and its relationship to the pilgrimage center Hsiang-shan 香山 has received considerable scholarly attention (Stein 1986; Dudbridge 1978, 1982; Tsukamoto 1955).

Hsiang-shan Monastery was situated on a mountain 200 *li* south of Mount Sung and a few miles southeast of Pao-feng county, in Ju-chou, Honan. Attached to the monastery was the Ta-pei Pagoda (Pagoda of the Great Compassionate One), which housed an image of the thousand-armed and thousand-eyed Kuan-yin. The term *Ta-pei* 大悲 refers to this iconography specifically. Following the introduction of Esoteric Buddhism during the T'ang, images of this type became very popular (Kobayashi 1953; Soper 1960). Li Chien (1059–1109), the author of *Hua p'in* (On paintings), described this image as being "made in person by a human manifestation of Ta-pei." He compared it to two other Ta-pei Kuan-yin images he had seen, one done by the famous painter Fan Ch'iung during the Ta-chung era (847–59), an image less than a foot in length and with thirty-six arms, and another housed in the T'ien-hsien Ssu 天僊寺 in Tung-ching, Hsiang-yang, which was also made "by a human manifestation of Ta-pei." T'ien-hsien Ssu was a nunnery. In the Wu-te era (618–28), when the nuns wanted to have an image of Ta-pei Kuan-yin painted on the wall of the main hall, they sought a good artist. A couple with a young girl came to answer the call, and the girl who did the painting was apparently a manifestation of Kuan-yin (Dudbridge 1978, 16; Stein 1986, 46; Tsukamoto 1955, 269).

The case of Hsiang-shan was unique, however, for Kuan-yin not only created an image but lived an embodied life there. As Dudbridge convincingly argues, the cult began with the joint promotion by a local official and the abbot of the temple in 1100, a pattern, as we shall see, often found in the creation of other pilgrimage centers as well. Chiang Chih-ch'i (1031–1104) served as the prefect at Ju-chou briefly and met Huai-chou, the abbot of Hsiang-shan Monastery, early in 1100. The abbot gave Chiang a book called *Life of the Ta-pei Bodhisattva of Hsiang-shan*, containing answers supposedly given by a divine spirit to the questions put forward by the famous Lü master Tao-hsuan (596–667) of Mount Chung-nan. The book, in turn, was brought to the abbot from a mysterious monk who came to Hsiang-shan as a pilgrim. The book tells the story of how Kuan-yin appeared as Miao-shan, the third daughter of King Miao-chuang. She practiced Buddhism and refused to marry. When her father became sick, she gave her arms and eyes to cure him. She manifested herself to her parents in the form of a thousand-armed and thousand-eyed figure, then reverted to her original form and died. The site where her stupa stood (together with the image made by her?) drew pilgrims who came every year in the second month. Chiang wrote the story of Miao-shan/Kuan-yin based on what he was told and had the famous calligrapher Tsai Ching pen it for a stele. By the early twelfth century, Hsiang-shan had apparently become a flourishing pilgrimage center.

Chiang did not stay in Ju-chou long. Less than three years after his transfer, Chiang served as the prefect of Hangchow between November 1102 and October 1103. It is highly likely, as Dudbridge argues, that Chiang brought this story from Honan to Hangchow. In the Upper T'ien-chu Monastery (Shang T'ien-chu Ssu 上天竺寺) there once stood a two-stone stele which might have read "Life of the All-Compassionate One, re-erected" (the first half of the stele was destroyed; it does not survive among extant rubbings). The stele, erected in 1104, repeated the story of Kuan-yin who was Princess Miao-shan (Dudbridge 1982, 591–93). Although the Upper T'ien-chu Monastery had already been an important Kuan-yin pilgrimage center for more than a century before Chiang's arrival, this story was probably not known in Hangchow. Once it reached Hangchow, however, it became closely connected with the Upper T'ien-chu, for the popular version as elaborated in the *Hsiang-shan pao-chüan* 香山寶卷 (The precious volume of Hsiang-shan) was supposedly revealed to P'u-ming, a monk of the temple. This story took deep root at the Upper T'ien-chu perhaps because the Kuan-yin worshiped there was already understood to be feminine. Hsiang-shan declined after Kai-feng fell to the Chin and Hangchow became the capital of the Southern Sung in 1138. The Upper T'ien-chu Monastery in Hangchow then became the undisputed national pilgrimage center for Kuan-yin worship until P'u-t'o emerged as a serious competitor in later centuries.

NAN WU-T'AI SHAN 南五台山 (SOUTHERN MOUNT WU-T'AI)

Yin-kuang (1861–1940), a Pure Land master and a great devotee of Kuan-yin, sponsored a new edition of the gazetteer of P'u-t'o during the 1930s. In the preface, he wrote,

> The bodhisattva is all-merciful and compassionate and thus beloved by people of the entire country. Therefore, there is a common saying that Kuan-yin is found in every household. The places where Kuan-yin carries out the work of enlightening beings are not limited to one. For instance, Southern Mount Wu-t'ai, Great Hsiang-shan, and Upper T'ien-chu are all well known. However, Mount P'u-t'o in the South Sea is the foremost in terms of its efficaciousness and the number of pilgrims going there. (*PTSC* 1924:16)

Nan Wu-t'ai Shan, a five-peaked mountain, was situated at the southern side of Mount Chung-nan 終南山, some 50 *li* to the south of Sian. In the same preface Yin-kuang appended an account about the creation of Mount Southern Wu-t'ai using material recorded on a stele written by a Yuan monk and erected in 1271. The following is a partial translation:

During the Jen-shou era (601–4) of the Sui, a poisonous dragon lived in the mountain. Relying upon his paranormal powers, he assumed the form of an immortal and came to Ch'ang-an to sell drugs made of cinnabar. He fooled the ignorant by saying that whoever took his drug would be able to ascend to heaven in broad daylight right away. Many people took his bait. They all ended up in the dragon's lair and became his food. But the people were deluded and did not wake up to the truth. The Great Being used the power of the compassionate vow and appeared in the form of a monk. Gathering grasses and building a hut on the top of the mountain, he tamed the evil power with his wondrous wisdom. The wind of purity swept away heated vexation. Wherever the thought of compassion spread, poisonous ether disappeared. The dragon obtained release in clarity and coolness (ch'ing-liang 清凉) and stayed in his cave peacefully. The residents were no longer endangered.

The news of the monk's efficacy reached the court, which decreed that a monastery should be built for him in gratitude for his benefit to the country and the people. Local gentry admired him, and some managed to extricate themselves from the net of attachment and, shaving off their hair, entered the Way. The Great Being liked to stay among the rocks. Monkeys and wild animals would sit around him. Birds in the forests would not cry as though they were listening to his dharma talk. They would disperse only after a very long time. Unfortunately, the very next year after the monastery was erected, on the nineteenth day of the sixth month, he suddenly entered nirvana. Strange fragrance filled the room. The sky became overcast. Birds and animals cried piteously, and the mountain forests changed color. Members of the sangha reported the sad news to the court, and eunuchs were dispatched to offer incense.

At the time of cremation heaven and earth darkened. But suddenly, in one instant, the whole area turned into a silver realm. Music resounded in the sky; the mountain shook; auspicious clouds flew; and the air was filled with strange fragrance. A golden bridge suddenly appeared above the Eastern Peak. A host of heavenly beings stood on the bridge, carrying banners and scattering golden flowers that, however, did not touch the ground. Finally, on top of the Southern Terrace, brilliant jewels of a hundred varieties filled a space whose breadth and height could not be measured. A glimmer of a dignified form in royal ease could be discerned. His compassionate face was grave and beautiful. Wearing a suit studded with coins and covered with necklaces, he moved in the wind and looked at everyone with bright illumination. At that time, there were more than a thousand people, both monks and laypeople, who witnessed the true form of the bodhisattva. They were overwhelmed with emotion and realized that the monk was a manifestation of Kuan-yin. Fragrance lingered for several months.

Mr. Kao, the left executive assistant of the Department of Ministries, wrote a memorial about this to the emperor, who read it and offered praise. The bones of the monk were gathered together and housed in a stupa. The emperor bestowed a plaque naming it Kuan-yin-t'ai Ssu (Monastery of Kuan-yin Terrace) and gave the monks a hundred square *li* of land for their sustenance. Every year the emperor sent messengers who came as pilgrims to make offerings and celebrate the ordination of new monks. The dharma was greatly promoted.

The monastery was renamed Nan Wu-t'ai Shan Sheng-shou Ssu (Monastery of Holy Longevity on Mount Southern Wu-t'ai) in Ta-li sixth year (771) of the T'ang. During the Five Dynasties, it was burned down in the war. In the summer of the third year of T'ai-p'ing hsing-kuo era of the Sung (978), auspicious signs of five-colored circles and clouds appeared six times consecutively. Monk Huai-wei reported these marvels to the governor, who memorialized the court. A gold plaque was bestowed on the monastery renaming it Wu-t'ai Shan Yuan-kuang Ssu (Monastery of Circled Light of the Five-Terraced Mountain). The halls were rebuilt, and a painting of the true appearance of the bodhisattva was installed. Incense has been offered there without interruption. Whenever there was drought, supplicants would come here to pray for rain. The prayers were always answered without fail. Such happenings have been recorded in the documents kept by the county and provincial offices. Pilgrims come in the month of the festival of Clear and Bright (*ch'ing-ming*) as well as on the death anniversary of the monk in the summer. Holding the young and helping the old, pilgrims come from hundreds of miles away. Defying danger and carrying offerings, they crowd the roads leading to the monastery for more than a month without a break. (*PTSC* 1924, 18–20)

I quote this account at length because the case of Southern Mount Wu-t'ai can serve as a prototypical example of the establishment of a Kuan-yin pilgrimage center. It began with the manifestation of Kuan-yin and the miracle he performed for the benefit of the community. Kuan-yin appeared as a wonder-working monk, a common guise for the bodhisattva recorded in miracle tales collected in the Six Dynasties (222–589) (Makita 1970).[3] The site was most likely Taoist originally, and the Buddhists' takeover was implied by the myth about the deceitful immortal who was in fact a man-eating dragon. The rivalry reminds us of the similar instances that occurred on Mount Lu (see Faure, chapter 4 of this volume). Southern Mount Wu-t'ai developed, furthermore, with imperial recognition and patronage, while being perpetuated by the promotion of its monks. It was revived by reports of new miracles, and finally, it was maintained by the enthusiasm of pilgrims, large numbers of whom came regularly.

THE UPPER T'IEN-CHU MONASTERY IN HANGCHOW

The fame of the Upper T'ien-chu Monastery was connected with a miraculous "spontaneously formed" image of Kuan-yin. The monastery underwent a major revival in 939 under the monk Tao-i, who was responsible for the discovery of this image (*HCLAC* 80/6b–13b; *HHYLC* 11). In that year Tao-i came from Mount Chung-nan, a famous mountain north of the Southern

Mount Wu-t'ai mentioned above and a numinous place frequented by Tao-hsuan and the mysterious monk who provided information about Princess Miao-shan. One night while Tao-i was meditating, he saw a bright light coming from the stream. When he looked into the water, he found a piece of marvelous wood several feet long with a strange fragrance and radically different color and grain. He asked a local artisan, K'ung, to fashion it into an image of Kuan-yin. When K'ung cut the wood open, he found a ready-made "naturally formed image" of Kuan-yin. The crown and drapery were gorgeous, and the bodhisattva's face was compassionate and beautiful. K'ung decided to keep the image for himself and replace it with another one made of ordinary wood. But Kuan-yin warned Tao-i of the deception in a dream. When the substitution was revealed, K'ung had to turn over the self-formed image. Some years later, during the Ch'ien-yu era (948–50), Tao-i had another dream in which a "white-robed person" (*pai-i jen* 白衣人) told him that a monk named Tsung-hsun would arrive from Lo-yang the next day and that he should ask for an ancient relic of the Buddha that was among the latter's possessions. When Tsung-hsun arrived and saw the image of Kuan-yin, he was greatly moved and offered the relic to be installed on its crown (*STCC* 1980, 26: 29, 86, 227).

Although the chronicle of the Upper T'ien-chu does not describe the appearance of the original Kuan-yin image, it was most likely that of the feminine White-robed Kuan-yin. This supposition becomes clear when we examine another group of founding myths concerning the establishment of the monastery that centered on Ch'ien Liu (851–932), the founder of the Wu Yueh kingdom. Before he came to the throne, he dreamed of a woman in white who promised to protect him and his descendants if he was compassionate. She told him that he could find her on Mount T'ien-chu in Hang-chow twenty years later. After he became the king, he dreamed of the same woman; this time she asked for a place to stay and in return agreed to be the patron deity of his kingdom. When Ch'ien made inquiries, he discovered that the only White-robed Kuan-yin image was found in T'ien-chu. So he established the T'ien-chu k'an-ching yuan (Cloister for Reading Scriptures at T'ien-chu), which was the earlier name for the Upper T'ien-chu Monastery (*STCC* 1980, 26: 31). From this account, the image housed in T'ien-chu appears to have been the feminine White-robed Kuan-yin. A pilgrim who saw it during the Wan-li era (1573–1615) described it as seated; two feet, four inches tall; and accompanied by Shan-ts'ai and Lung-nü 龍女 (Dragon Princess) (*STCC* 1980: 26, 228).

The White-robed Kuan-yin, one of several feminine forms of Kuan-yin that emerged in late T'ang, enjoyed widespread popularity from the tenth century on (Yü 1990a, 256–71). Paintings, statues, miracle tales, and founding myths of Kuan-yin temples dated from the Northern Sung (960–1127), the same time when P'u-t'o became slowly established, all attest to this fact.[4]

Beloved by pious believers and celebrated by Ch'an monks and literati painters, many paintings of the White-robed Kuan-yin have survived (fig. 5.1).
At first, during the Sung, they were more stylistically similar to the earlier Water-moon Kuan-yin (Shui-yueh Kuan-yin 水月觀音). Both depicted
Kuan-yin sitting alone, surrounded by waterfall, ocean, bamboo, and other
reminders of nature. There were, however, some major differences between
the two: the Water-moon Kuan-yin, who might wear either white or multicolored robes, was always sitting under a full moon or gazing at a reflection
of the moon; the White-robed Kuan-yin, who was invariably draped in a
white cape, was very often depicted without the moon. During the Ming,
after P'u-t'o gained national fame as Kuan-yin's home, the iconography of
White-robed Kuan-yin began to be increasingly merged with that of Potalaka Kuan-yin.

The Kuan-yin of the Upper T'ien-chu became known for her efficacy in
averting natural disasters and for her oracles transmitted to pilgrims in
dreams. Based on the reports of miracles reported by the prefect, Emperor
Jen-tsung bestowed the plaque Ling-kan Kuan-yin yuan (Cloister of Kuan-
yin of Efficacious Responses) in 1062 and reclassified it as a Ch'an temple.
The friendship between Su Shih (Su Tung-p'o, 1036–1101) and the abbot of
the temple, the Ch'an master Pien-ts'ai (d. 1091), promoted the fame of the
Upper T'ien-chu among the literati and officials. Just as the devotion to
Kuan-yin prevalent among Ch'an monks and literati officials helped her cult
generally, the same classes of people were responsible for the Upper T'ien-
chu's becoming a center for Kuan-yin worship. After Hangchow became the
capital of the Southern Sung (1127–1279), the temple received frequent visits
and favors from the emperors. Hsiao-tsung (r. 1163–88) praised Kuan-yin as
"T'ien-chu Kuang-ta Ling-kan Ta-shih" 天竺廣大靈感大士 (T'ien-chu's
Great Being of Broad and Extensive Efficacious Responses). Emperors in the
succeeding dynasties continued the patronage. The gazetteer of the monastery records Kuan-yin's success in granting rain in 998, 1000, 1135, 1374,
1455, 1477, 1503, 1539, 1542, 1545, and 1626; in saving the people of Hangchow from flood in 1065, 1580, and 1608; from locusts in 1016; and from
plague in 1588. When there was no rain for five months in 998, the reviewing
policy adviser moved the image to Fan-t'ien Monastery (Monastery of
Brahma Heaven) in the city and prayed for rain with all officials. This set the
pattern for subsequent requests for Kuan-yin's miracles. Her image was welcomed into the city and invoked by officials (*STCC* 1980, 26: 33–40).

During the Ming, the nineteenth day of the second month was known as
Kuan-yin's birthday. It was the most important day for all sorts of pilgrims,
who arrived from far away as well as nearby. They fasted and came to the
monastery the day before. Because there were hundreds of thousands of pilgrims, they could not be accommodated in the monastery but had to stay

Fig. 5.1. White-robed Kuan-yin,
by K'o Chiu-ssu (1290–1343),
with colophon by Ch'an master
T'ien-ju Wei-tse. Collection of the
National Palace Museum, Taipei,
Taiwan, Republic of China.

outdoors and wait for daybreak. This was called "spending the night in the mountains" (su-shan 宿山) (STCC 1980, 26: 41).[5]

The annual arrival of huge crowds created the Hsi-hu hsiang-shih 西湖香市 (pilgrims' fair of the West Lake, also known as the pilgrims' fair of T'ien-chu). The economic aspect of pilgrimage is a subject worthy of study by itself. Just as political patronage could influence the changing fortunes of pilgrimage sites, the economic activities that went on as a byproduct of pilgrimage might very well be one of the determining factors in the longevity of a site. We are fortunate in having some eyewitness accounts of the Upper T'ien-chu pilgrims' fair. The Ming writer Chang Tai, an avid traveler whose pilgrimage to Mount T'ai is described by Wu in this volume, described the fair as he saw it in the seventeenth century this way:

> It began on the twelfth day of the second month and ended on the fifth day of the fifth month. During these three months, Shantung pilgrims on their return trip from P'u-t'o and Chia-hsing and Hu-chou pilgrims on their way to offer incense at T'ien-chu arrived daily. Men and women, old and young, their number could reach several million. Once they came to Hangchow, they traded with the locals. That was why it was called a pilgrims' fair. Trading went on at the three T'ien-chu monasteries, the Temple of Yueh Fei, and the pavilion in the middle of the West Lake, but particularly at the Chao-ch'ing Monastery. From local products such as scissors, to religious implements such as scriptures and wooden fish, all the way to antiques and imported rare goods, everything could be found among the stalls inside the temples or the open-air markets set up temporarily for the occasion. It was truly a sight! (HCFC 1924, 2/14a–15a)

Fan Ts'u-shu, writing in the first half of the nineteenth century, told a similar story. He said that pilgrims came primarily from the Soochow area in Kiangsu and the three prefectures of Hangchow, Chia-hsing, and Hu-chou in Chekiang. But pilgrims also came from Shantung, Anhui, Fu-kien, Kwangtung, and Kwangsi. Pilgrims took two routes in coming to Hangchow—the northern route by the Grand Canal, disembarking at Sung-mu-ch'ang, and the southern route by the Yangtze River, disembarking at the banks of the Ch'ien-t'ang River. Fan put the figure of daily arrival at several tens of thousands. Among all the commodities on sale, candles, incense, rosaries, and spirit money decorated with tinfoil headed the list. They were produced primarily in Hangchow and Shao-hsing.

According to the same witness, pilgrims from Shao-hsing had a custom of offering huge candles weighing several tens of catties to the Upper T'ien-chu. Fastened to a scaffold, each candle was carried by two men and, accompanied by other pilgrims who beat on drums and gongs, it was delivered to the monastery. As soon as the candles were lighted, they were extinguished. Pilgrims then carried the candles back home and used them to light the rooms where silkworms were kept. There were other offerings. For example, pilgrims entwined several rolls and even several tens of rolls of white

and yellow cloths together and made them into a long rope. They walked
to T'ien-chu holding the rope, which they offered to the monks. This was
called "offering banners" (she-fan 捨幡). Pilgrims also offered two kinds of
incense: powdered sandalwood incense (t'an-hsiang 檀香) and incense sticks
(hsien-hsiang 線香). The former could weigh several hundred catties, and the
latter could consist of several thousand sticks. Immediately after the incense
was lighted, it would be put out and turned over to the monks. Thus, during
the pilgrimage season tens of thousands of catties of candles and incense
ended up in the temple's storehouse. This accumulation of wealth explains
why monks of the Upper T'ien-chu did not give tonsure to strangers but
kept the lineages within their own temple. Merchants who came to the fair
from outside Hangchow accounted for only 10 percent. The local merchants of Hangchow made more in the spring pilgrimage season than the
other three seasons combined (*HCFC* 1924, 2/15 a–b).

There is no need to go any further. From all evidences, the Upper T'ien-
chu was the national pilgrimage center for Kuan-yin worship during the
Southern Sung. Although it continued to be visited by pilgrims in the Ming
and Ch'ing (1644–1911), P'u-t'o eventually overtook it and succeeded in
being the only true home of Kuan-yin in this period. How this came to pass
will be the substance of the rest of this chapter.

We will examine the processes and mechanisms of the creation of P'u-t'o
as Mount Potalaka. On one level, there is the mythical and ideological construction of the island to fit the model provided by scriptures, thus the trans-
figuration of the landscape. Specific spots became singled out and identified
as places of numinosity and efficacy. Foremost of these places was the Ch'ao-
yin tung 潮音洞 (Cave of Tidal Sound) where Kuan-yin appeared to vision-
seeking pilgrims. Over time, other places were added: the Diamond Boulder
and the Purple Bamboo Grove both signified Kuan-yin's place of preaching;
Dragon Princess's Cave, Sudhana's Rock, and Parrot Stone, all near the
Cave of Tidal Sound, provided additional places for pilgrims to make divine
contact after the Dragon Princess, Sudhana, and the parrot began to appear
as Kuan-yin's attendants in pilgrims' visions.

On another level, we want to examine how P'u-t'o became physically
established, was built up, destroyed, and then rebuilt in several cycles. Each
time P'u-t'o rose from ruins, new monasteries became established under
new leadership. New spots of efficacy were discovered and promoted. For
instance, the Fan-yin-tung 梵音洞 (Cave of Brahma's Voice), situated
near the Northern Monastery, became known as a place where Kuan-yin
appeared to pilgrims in the late sixteenth century, during a major cycle of
rebuilding. It lent prestige to the Northern Monastery, and with the rising
fame of that monastery, more pilgrims came to this cave instead of the earlier
and more famous Cave of Tidal Sound for visions of Kuan-yin. The physical
building and rebuilding of the site tell us much about the dynamics between

pilgrims, among whom we count all the founders of the monasteries, and the island.

P'U-T'O SHAN

While P'u-t'o Shan literally means Mount P'u-t'o, it is actually the name given to one of the many small islands forming the Chusan archipelago. The island is long and narrow, 13.8 km from north to south and 5.6 km from east to west; the land area totals 77.3 square km (map 5.1). Ningpo is seventy miles due west. The development of P'u-t'o was very much connected with the emergence of Ningpo as a national and international trading center. During the Sui and T'ang, two changes contributed to the event. The construction of the Grand Canal extended the main overland trading route to the east coast. By linking the producing south with the consuming north, it also stimulated economic development of the Lower Yangtze delta. In the meantime, as a result of improvements in navigation following the invention of the steering compass, the maritime trade that connected the Yangtze delta with ports along the Chinese coast, in East Asia, and on the Indian Ocean became active. Ningpo reaped the benefits of both changes. Through waterways linking it with Hangchow, Ningpo became in effect the southern terminus of the Grand Canal. Because of shallows and tidal currents in Hangchow Bay, ocean-going junks from southeastern China had to transfer their cargoes at Ningpo for smaller boats sailing for Hangchow and other inland ports. For the same reason, products from the Lower Yangtze region had to be shipped to Ningpo for overseas trade. Because of its important location, the Office of Overseas Trade (Shih-po ssu), which supervised the coastal trade and controlled the maritime tribute of Korea and Japan, was in Ningpo almost continuously from 992 to 1523. By the Southern Sung, shipping flourished, and both international and domestic markets had expanded. Ningpo and the region near it including P'u-t'o were greatly stimulated by these developments. Among the commodities traded, incense was frequently mentioned, and Ningpo artisans were famous for making Buddhist altar fittings (Shiba 1977, 392–410).

The island, though small, was thus strategically placed in the crossroads of sea traffic between north and south China as well as between China and Japan. In early T'ang, Japanese ships came to China by the northern route, arriving in Shantung via the Korean peninsula. But after the mid-T'ang, when Silla united the three Korean kingdoms, Japanese ships began to use the southern route, arriving at Ningpo and Yueh-chou (present Yang-chou) via Okinawa. If they sailed this southern route under a northeast wind, it would take five days and five nights before they arrived at Shen-chia-men (the harbor next to P'u-t'o), where they had to wait to be inspected by Chinese customs before proceeding. On their return trip to Japan, they also

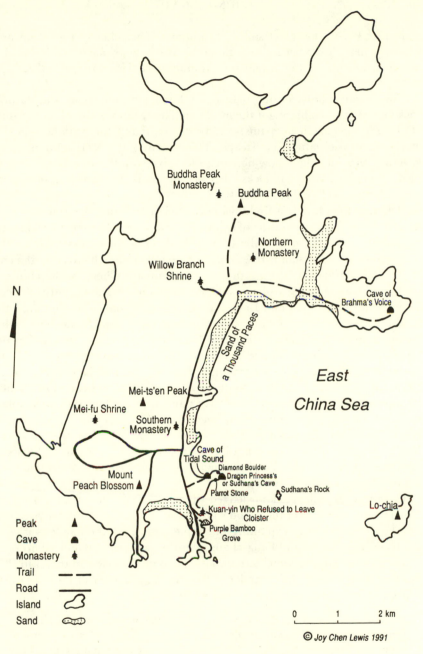

N

Buddha Peak
Monastery

Buddha Peak

Northern
Monastery

Willow Branch
Shrine

Cave of
Brahma's Voice

Sand of a Thousand Paces

East

China Sea

Mei-ts'en Peak

Mei-fu Shrine

Southern
Monastery

Cave of
Tidal Sound

Mount
Peach Blossom

Diamond Boulder
Dragon Princess's
or Sudhana's Cave
Parrot Stone

Sudhana's Rock

Lo-chia

Kuan-yin Who Refused to Leave
Cloister

Purple Bamboo
Grove

Peak
Cave
Monastery
Trail
Road
Island
Sand

0   1   2 km

© Joy Chen Lewis 1991

Map 5.1. P'u-t'o Shan

waited at P'u-t'o for good sailing conditions. Thus during the Ming and Ch'ing, when P'u-t'o became a national Kuan-yin pilgrimage site, it was also an important international maritime trading port (Hsu Ming-te 1987, 135–37).

The island is hilly, dotted with many low-lying mountains and natural rock formations. To highlight the mountainlike features of the island, writers of the P'u-t'o gazetteers painstakingly differentiated the various types of elevations of the natural landscape. The most recent (1924) edition of the gazetteer provides the following categories: sixteen hills (*shan* 山), eighteen peaks (*feng* 峯), twelve hillocks (*ling* 嶺), fifteen rocks (*yen* 岩), and thirty stones (*shih* 石) (*PTSC* 1924, 81–103).

Before its founding as a Buddhist holy site in the T'ang, the island seemed to have enjoyed the reputation of being a Taoist haven. The most well known mountain on the island was Mei-ts'en Feng 梅岑峯, the highest peak on the southern part of the island. It was named after Mei Fu, who lived at the end of the first century B.C. during the reign of Emperor Cheng of the Han dynasty and was reported to have sought refuge on the island and practiced alchemy near the mountain. In the late Ming, the monk Ju-chung built the Meifu Shrine to commemorate him. In fact, the whole island was called Mei-ts'en in pre-Sung sources before it became known exclusively as P'u-t'o. Other Taoist luminaries in addition to Mei Fu were also connected with the island. An Ch'i-sheng escaped from the chaos on the mainland at the end of Ch'in (249–209 B.C.) and went to the island to practice alchemy. Once when he was drunk, he was supposed to have painted peach blossoms with splattered ink on the rocks. This legend accounted for the name Mount Peach Blossoms (T'ao-hua Shan 桃花山), situated southwest of the Southern Monastery. Tradition claims that if one looks carefully, one can still discern the faint outlines of the peach blossoms. Ko Hung Well was named after the famous Taoist (A.D. 253–333?).[6]

Gazetteer compilers acknowledged the island's connection with Taoism. Not only did they accept the island's pre-Buddhist past, they actually seemed to take some delight in exploiting this reputation. Like the fabulous isles of the blessed, P'eng-lai and Fang-chang, P'u-t'o was seen as hallowed ground. But unlike the former, which are impossible to locate, one can travel to P'u-t'o. Sheng Hsi-ming, the compiler of the earliest gazetteer of P'u-t'o (1361) expressed this sentiment when he declared:

> P'eng-lai and Fang-chang are reported to lie in the mythical waters, but they can be reached only by flying immortals. In the past, both the First Emperor of Ch'in and Emperor Wu of the Han tried to find them for many years. They sent expedition parties far and wide. But with much toiling of the spirit and belaboring of the body, the project was like chasing after a shadow and trying to capture the wind. The legendary islands could never be located. Now Mount Small White Flowers [P'u-t'o] is not far from Ssu-ming. It is a place where

sages and worthies hid their traces. Although it is situated amidst terrifying waves and frightening tides, if one sails with the wind, one can reach it within a few days. (*T* 2101:1136a–b)

The Buddhist "takeover" of the island, if indeed one may use such a term, was, however, apparently a peaceful one. There is no evidence of a struggle with any previously existing Taoist religious authority. The difficulty was, therefore, not how to subdue or supplant an earlier cult, but how to legitimize new claims once made. During the eleventh and twelfth centuries, the identity between P'u-t'o and Potalaka was already taken for granted by a number of educated people, both monks and literati, and this convergence led to P'u-t'o's legitimacy. Nan-hu Tao-yin, who wrote *Ts'ao-an lu* 草菴錄 (Record of a grass hut) during the period 1165–73, for instance, made such an identification. The *Fo-tsu t'ung-chi* quoted the following passage from it:

Mount P'u-t'o is in the great ocean. It is situated southeast of Chin [Ning-p'o], about a thousand kilometers by the water route. It is no other than the mountain called Potalaka that is declared by the *Hua-yen ching* to be the "isolated place at the end of the ocean" where "Kuan-yin Bodhisattva lives." It is also no other than the Mount Potalaka that is declared by the *Ta-pei ching* to be the place where the palace of Kuan-yin in which Sakyamuni Buddha reveals the heart-seal of the Mantra of Great Compassion is located. The Cave of Tidal Sound is on the island. Ocean tides pound in and rush out day and night making deafening noises. In front of the cave is a stone bridge on which pilgrims stand facing the cave to pray. If they are sincere, they sometimes can see the Great Being sitting leisurely. Or they will see Sudhana come forward as if to welcome them. Other times one will only see the pure vase of green jade or the kalavinka bird flying as if performing a dance. Some six or seven *li* from the cave there is a large monastery. Merchants, diplomats, and tribute bearers sailing to and from the various countries in the Eastern Sea would come here to pray for safety. Those who are reverential and sincere all receive protection without fail. (*FTTC* 42 in *T* 2035:388b–c)

As in most early accounts of the island, the Cave of Tidal Sound was here too singled out for emphasis, for this was the place where Kuan-yin appeared to pilgrims. Merchants and diplomats receive special mention, for indeed they were responsible for building the island into a pilgrimage site and continued to serve as its chief patrons down the ages.

From the Sung on, important officials, famous literati, and well-known personages who visited P'u-t'o also began to write about the island. A large body of poems and commemorative essays left by these pilgrim-visitors to the island are collected in the island gazetteers. Wang An-shih (1021–86), the Sung political reformer; Chao Meng-fu (1254–1322), the celebrated Yuan painter; and Ch'en Hsien-chang (1428–1500), the Ming Neo-Confucian thinker, are just three notable examples culled from a long roster of writers who recorded their impressions of the island. While their writings undoubtedly contributed to the fame of the island (and for this reason were carefully preserved by the gazetteer compilers), most of the poems are about the natural setting and give impressionistic and formulaic descriptions of the scenery. Very frequently a set of poems would be composed to celebrate the ten or twelve "views" (*ching* 景) of the island. Such literary exercises follow an established convention and rarely reveal the writer's inner feelings. Wang An-shih's poem "On Visiting Mount Lo-chia" is a typical example of this genre.

> The layout of the mountain overpowers the ocean,
> The Ch'an palace is established at this place.
> Odors of fish and dragons do not reach here.
> But the sun and the moon shine on the island before anywhere else.
> Colors of trees reveal the coming of autumn,
> Sounds of bells are answered by those of waves.
> I never expected that I could use the convenience of my tour of duty,
> To momentarily brush away the stains of red dust.
>
> (*PTSC* 1607, 5:389)

Although monks, merchants, diplomats, and officials began to come to P'u-t'o in the Sung and some of them even celebrated it in their writings, the first history of P'u-t'o was not written until 1361. Its author, Sheng Hsi-ming, was the grandson of an immigrant from Kashmir. Sheng traveled widely and was particularly interested in the cult of Kuan-yin. He knew some of the noted Kuan-yin cultic centers on the mainland, including Southern Mount Wu-t'ai and Upper T'ien-chu, but even he was initially skeptical about P'u-t'o's claim to be Mount Potalaka until he was converted by a miraculous dream. Sheng then wrote a short history of the island, providing scriptural bases and founding myths for the identification. Sheng's is the first of eight gazetteers of the island. Together they form one of the most persuasive means of transforming the island into Mount Potalaka, a powerful medium proclaiming and broadcasting this identity. Even though the gazetteers range across some six hundred years, they form a self-contained cumulative tradition. Later ones referred to and quoted earlier ones; each, of course, omitted some old materials and added new as the island underwent changes and evolved into a national and international pilgrimage center. Since these gazetteers constitute one of the most useful primary sources for this chapter, I will discuss their general characteristics and contents.[7]

MOUNTAIN GAZETTEERS AND THE CREATION OF THE CHINESE POTALAKA

As Timothy Brook has pointed out in a recent study, mountain gazetteers, like the institutional and topographical gazetteers of which they form a part, were written in large numbers during the Ming and Ch'ing.

They have antecedents from the Song [Sung], which is when the term *zhi* [*chih*] 志 comes into use for identifying gazetteers generally, though it is not until the sixteenth century that topographical and institutional gazetteers become common. . . . In the sixteenth century, the production of topographical and institutional gazetteers becomes regular, increasing steadily through the Jiajing [Chia-ching] and Wanli [Wan-li] eras, and rising markedly during the opening decades of the seventeenth century. A second peak of greater magnitude is reached at the end of that century. Smaller rises occur during the middle of the eighteenth century and again at the beginning of the nineteenth, though the most striking peak comes in the closing decades of that century. (Brook 1988, 52)

Although the compilation of P'u-t'o gazetteers follows the general pattern, the specific dates coincide with the cycles of building and rebuilding of the island center.

Gazetteers of P'u-t'o were written by pilgrims and were about pilgrims. Among the compilers we find local magistrates, naval commanders, and men of letters who wrote either on their own account or at the request of resident abbots. With the exception of Sheng, the first gazetteer writer, all of them had gone to P'u-t'o as pilgrims. This point needs stressing, for it demonstrates most dramatically the dynamics between pilgrims and sites. Sites attracted pilgrims who in turn promoted the sites and thereby attracted more pilgrims. Gazetteer writers, through the printed word, might reach a broad audience of readers (mostly monks and members of the elite). "Ordinary" pilgrims, even illiterate ones, might also help promote the fame of a site through word of mouth by repeating stories they heard about it or marvels they themselves witnessed while there. Like most works of this genre, monastic gazetteers of P'u-t'o provide a description of the topographical layout, a history of the monasteries, a record of royal patronage and important donations, biographies of abbots and other famous residents, lists of flora and fauna, and poems and essays about the island written by pilgrim-visitors. These are not, however, entirely impersonal, objective, and factual descriptions. On the contrary, there is, one might say, an almost confessional air about them. Like collections of miracle tales about Kuan-yin, a genre begun in the Six Dynasties that reached great popularity in the Ming, gazetteers of P'u-t'o can be regarded as a type of testimonial literature. Because their aim was not only to inform but also to convince, they contain extensive collections of miracles wrought by Kuan-yin both in founding the island and in reviving it after successive cycles of decline and recovery. Even nature was miraculously transformed. For instance, the gazetteers inform us that there were no tigers on the island. Although one or two might occasionally land after swimming across the ocean from the mainland, they never stayed long. Snakes, on the other hand, were plentiful, but they didn't harm people (*PTSC* 1832, 12: 4b–5a).

P'u-t'o gazetteers contain another type of invaluable material that provides further evidence of pilgrims' effort to transfigure the landscape and create a sacred place out of natural space—epigraphical records left by pilgrims describing their visions of Kuan-yin or miraculous deeds performed by Kuan-yin for their benefit or for others they knew. Since the buildings on the island have been damaged by wars and piracy many times in the past thousand years, all the stone stelae on which such testimonies were originally carved have been destroyed or at least severely damaged. The transcriptions kept in the gazetteers furnish the only clue to a possibly extensive body of devotional literature. In this regard, P'u-t'o gazetteers definitely do not fit Brook's observation that "monastic gazetteers, though intended in part to be reading matter for the faithful, were not devotional publications" (1988, 55).

The gazetteers did not only record the long history of the creation, establishment, and development of P'u-t'o as the Chinese Mount Potalaka; they first proclaimed and then promoted the identification. Indeed, when Sheng came to write the first account of the island in 1361, he had to overcome his own doubt about the identity of P'u-t'o as Mount Potalaka. The difficulty for him, as no doubt for others, was the discrepancy between the mythical grandeur of the sacred island home and the prosaic reality represented by the remote and desolate P'u-t'o.

Sheng said that when he made a pilgrimage to Mount Wu-t'ai, he heard from a Tibetan master the description of Mount Potalaka found in a "barbarian" (*fan* 番) book, *Pu-t'o-lo-chia shan hsing-ch'eng chi* 補陀落伽山行程記 (A travel account to Mount Potalaka). Sheng then briefly summarized what he remembered from the book. The fantastic journey had to begin in India. One first had to go to the country called Ke-ts'u-to-chia-lo and circumambulate the stupa there day and night. Eventually one would be told the direction and duration of the journey. The pilgrim would travel through a country inhabited by yakṣa, who would entice him with food, drink, music, and sights, temptations he had to refuse. After this the pilgrim would encounter other types of demonic obstructions, but he was enjoined to be of good courage and not give up. He would then come to a jeweled pond from which he could drink sweet dew and become strengthened. During the rest of the journey he would encounter marvelous experiences. He was not to linger and become attached to these, but to push on. When he approached the holy land, he would be met by a horse-headed vajrapāṇi, who would lead him to the entrance to a grotto. There he would be comforted and encouraged by holy Tārās. Finally he was to enter the grotto, where purple bamboo and sandalwood trees grew in abundance, clear streams flowed, and tender grasses covered the ground like soft cushions. There he would receive the teaching of the wonderful dharma from Kuan-yin, who, surrounded by heavenly dragons, lived all the time with a coterie of bodhisattvas, and become enlightened. Whatever he desired would come true.[8]

Sheng was much impressed by this account and felt that Mount Potalaka was definitely not an ordinary realm that could be reached by anyone easily. Later he went to Ningpo, and several times friends invited him to go to P'u-t'o on pilgrimage. But because he doubted that the island could be Potalaka, he never made the trip. One evening he dreamed of a person who said to him,

> "Have you forgotten what the scriptures say? Bodhisattvas are skillful in manifesting in many places, for wherever people seek them propelled by their faith, that will be the place where bodhisattvas manifest themselves. This is like when one digs a well for water and finds water, but water is actually present everywhere. Furthermore, this cave [Cave of Tidal Sound] has been noted for miraculous happenings for a very long time. Spirit-like, transformative, free and comforting, it is indeed impossible to be fathomed by ordinary intelligence."

After Sheng woke up, he realized that bodhisattvas indeed could be present anywhere. He then gathered information about P'u-t'o and wrote a history of the place, attaching to it stories about cultic centers of Kuan-yin worship on the mainland (*PTSC* 1361; *T* 2101:1138c–39a).

Sheng mentioned Upper T'ien-chu and related a miracle that had happened there. In 1360 Hangchow suffered from the ravages of war, and all the monasteries on the Western Hill were destroyed. No one knew what had happened to the image of Kuan-yin housed in Upper T'ien-chu, but after K'ang Li, the grand councilor, offered gold as reward, someone found the image among wild grasses. After a propitious date was determined through divination, K'ang fasted; then, followed by officials, soldiers and townspeople, he went outside the north gate of the city on foot to welcome the image and installed it in Western Heaven Monastery (Hsi-t'ien Ssu) on Mount Ch'ing-ping, a temple he established himself. On that day, the holy image issued forth a bright light that, piercing through clouds, separated into three beams. One pointed far to the east, indicating the direction of P'u-t'o; the second beam pointed toward Upper T'ien-chu; the third rested on Hsi-t'ien Ssu. The main point of this tale was of course to establish a connection between P'u-t'o and these two important centers of Kuan-yin worship.[9] It is significant that Sheng chose to write an account of P'u-t'o one year after this miracle took place and that he used this story to link P'u-t'o with Upper T'ien-chu, perhaps the most famous Kuan-yin cultic center on the mainland.[10]

Two gazetteers were compiled during the Wan-li period of the late Ming, a time of major revival for P'u-t'o. The first was compiled by Hou Chi-kao, regional commander of Ting-hai, in 1589, some two hundred thirty years later than the one by Sheng. Even though it bore Hou's name, it was actually written by T'u Lung (1542–1605; *DMB*, 1324–27), poet, dramatist and lay Buddhist. It consists of six *chüan*; the first two contain imperial edicts, maps, scriptural references, miracles, and histories of the monasteries; the last four are devoted exclusively to literary works about the island. The second, similar in format but named "newly amended" (*ch'ung-hsiu* 重修), was compiled by Chou Ying-pin, who was a vice-minister of personnel in 1607. The justification for compiling this gazetteer so soon was that "whereas the earlier gazetteer emphasizes the mountain in order to make known the efficacy of the Buddha, this gazetteer emphasizes the monastery in order to glorify the imperial gift" (*PTSC* 1607, 5–6). Chang Sui, a eunuch serving as the director of one of the twelve directorates for imperial accouterments, wanted to celebrate the completion of the imperially sponsored rebuilding of the Southern Monastery.

A quick summary of the fortunes of P'u-t'o in the previous centuries and a closer examination into the causes for Emperor Wan-li's interest in the island are in order. The strategic location of P'u-t'o in the open seas, which had stood it in good stead in earlier times, created problems for its security in the Ming. In 1387, at the suggestion of T'ang Ho (1326–95; *DMB* 1248–51), Duke of Hsin, Emperor T'ai-tsu ordered that the entire population of the island be moved inland to strengthen the coastal defenses against the Japanese pirates. The image of Kuan-yin was also transported to a temple in Ningpo. During the reign of Shih-tsung (1522–66) the coastal regions again suffered from the disturbances of Japanese pirates and their Chinese collaborators who, under the leadership of Wang Chih, totally destroyed P'u-t'o. More than three hundred temples on the island fell into ruins. During this long period of darkness in the first half of the sixteenth century, only one temple remained standing; there, one monk and one servant stayed to keep the incense burning. The situation did not change for the better until the pirate chief was captured in 1557.

In his preface to the 1589 gazetteer, Hou Chi-kao credited the success in capturing Wang to Kuan-yin's help. As if to signify the return to peace and prosperity, on the seventh day of the seventh month in 1586 auspicious lotuses had appeared in bloom in Empress Dowager Li's palace in Peking. Two days later, on the ninth day, other unusual lotuses bloomed in the palace. Emperor Wan-li was greatly pleased and instructed eunuchs to invite officials to view the flowers and write poems about them. His mother, Empress Dowager Li, dispatched eunuchs to sail twice for P'u-t'o, carrying with them images of Kuan-yin, who was the chief deity of the lotus clan in the Womb-treasure Mandala of Esoteric Buddhism; forty-two cases of the newly printed additions to the Tripitaka; and 637 cases of scriptures from the Buddhist Canon, printed under imperial sponsorship earlier in the same year. The pilgrimage was made to thank Kuan-yin for the favor received and to pray for her continued protection.

The connection between the miraculous appearances of rare lotuses in the

palace and imperial patronage of P'u-t'o was clear and direct. The lotuses
were taken as an auspicious sign from Kuan-yin. They might also have
served as the religious basis for the cult of "Nine-lotus Bodhisattva" (Chiu-
lien p'u-sa 九蓮菩薩), which was vigorously promoted by Emperor Wan-li
and his mother. Stelae with inscribed images of this bodhisattva, modeled
closely after Kuan-yin, have survived.[11]

Emperor Wan-li and his mother, while being benefactors to Buddhism
and popular religion in general (Li and Naquin 1988, 142), continued to
shower favors on P'u-t'o for the next three decades. Twice in 1599 P'u-t'o
was chosen to receive two more sets of the Tripitaka. Among the collection of
scriptures contained in the forty-two cases forming the "continuation of the
Tripitaka" (*hsu-tsang* 續藏), which were printed under their sponsorship, the
pride of place was occupied by a Ming apocryphal scripture glorifying Kuan-
yin. Entitled *Ta-ming Jen-hsiao Huang-hou meng-kan Fo-shuo ti-i hsi-yu ta-kung-
te ching* 大明仁孝皇后夢感佛說第一希有大功德經 (The sutra of the great
merit of foremost rarity spoken by the Buddha, which the Jen-hsiao empress
of the great Ming received in a dream), this text had a very unusual origin,
for it claimed to be transcribed by Empress Hsu (1362–1407), wife of Emperor Yung-lo, as a result of a revelation she received from Kuan-yin in a
dream.[12]

Indigenous sutras glorying Kuan-yin had a long history in China. This
tradition seemed to have enjoyed a major renaissance in the Ming. Perhaps
inspired by the example of Empress Hsu, Emperor Wan-li and his mother
also created and promoted a scripture devoted to the Nine-lotus Bodhisattva,
an emanation of Kuan-yin. Because it was not introduced into the Tripitaka,
it was not as widely known. One extant copy of this sutra, entitled *Fo-shuo
Ta-tz'u Chih-sheng Chiu-lien P'u-sa hua-shen tu-shih chen-ching* 佛說大慈至聖
九蓮菩薩化身度世真經 (The true scripture of the great compassionate and
utmost holy Nine-lotus Bodhisattva's transforming the body in order to save
the world as spoken by the Buddha), was printed in 1616 by the order of
Emperor Wan-li.[13] Advertisements of the miraculous lotus flowers, the carving of stelae and printing of new sutras promoting the cult of the Nine-lotus
Bodhisattva, and the energetic patronage of P'u-t'o under the Wan-li emperor and his mother can be seen as connected parts of a grand plan. Religious faith and the desire for self-aggrandizement probably were inextricably
intermingled in their motives.

Before I turn to the four gazetteers compiled during the Ch'ing, I would
like to comment on an account of a trip to P'u-t'o that Hou Chi-kao made in
the spring of 1587; he wrote it down the following year, one year before he
compiled the gazetteer. The confessional tone of this account resembles that
of Chang Shang-ying, discussed by Gimello in chapter three of this volume.
It differs radically from other travel accounts written by the literati, who

usually took a detached and even ironical stance toward pilgrimage sites (discussed below and in the chapter by Wu). It is probably for this reason that the gazetteer compilers did not collect these other travel accounts.

Hou started out by identifying the island as the place where Kuan-yin preached the dharma. Since the T'ang, people had vied with each other in visiting P'u-t'o to pay homage to the bodhisattva. Hou's own family had lived by the ocean for many generations, and since he was little he had heard about the sacred island from his elders and admired it from the bottom of his heart. But not until the spring of 1587, when he was appointed governor of Chekiang, did he finally have a chance to make a pilgrimage to P'u-t'o and thereby fulfill his life-long dream. He catalogued the famous spots of the island, singling out the Cave of Tidal Sound and Sudhana's Cave, both identified in the gazetteer, as the places where Kuan-yin would appear to pilgrims who prayed with sincerity. Displaying his familiarity with the *Lotus Sutra*, he wrote, "Feeling ashamed on account of my military status, I did not dare to look inside the caves because I have not left the 'burning house'." Hou mentioned the names of two important abbots, Chen-sung and Ta-chih, who were responsible for reviving Pao-t'o (the former name for the Southern Monastery) and establishing Hai-ch'ao (the former name for the Northern Monastery). He then related his interest in collecting portraits of Kuan-yin. He had earlier obtained a portrait done by the famous T'ang painter Wu Tao-tzu and later another one by Yen Li-pen. He characterized the former as simple and elegant, the latter as splendid and beautiful. He had both portraits inscribed on stone stelae for future generations (*PTSC* 1589, 3:5a–11a). Even though these did not survive, the stele with Yen Li-pen's drawing of Kuan-yin apparently served as the basis for another stele carved in 1608 by Liu Pen-wen, an assistant regional commander, which he gave as a thank offering to Willow Branch Shrine (Yang-chih An 楊枝庵), a temple he established after his prayer for an heir was answered (*PTSC* 1924, 572). Popularly known as Willow Branch Kuan-yin (Yang-liu Kuan-yin 楊柳觀音), it is one of the few treasures remaining on P'u-t'o today, and reproductions of it are offered to present-day pilgrims as souvenirs.

Interest in the images and portraits of Kuan-yin and efforts to preserve and disseminate them were important mechanisms in linking Kuan-yin to P'u-t'o. As we shall see in later sections of this chapter, wonder-working images of Kuan-yin first brought the island to notice, miraculous visions of her attracted pilgrims, and the eventual emergence of P'u-t'o as Mount Potalaka was concretely symbolized by a new iconography.

All four gazetteers compiled during the Ch'ing were entitled *Nan-hai P'u-t'o Shan chih* (Gazetteer of Potalaka of the South Sea), for by this time the identity between P'u-t'o and Potalaka had become accepted. At the end of Ming, P'u-t'o had again suffered from the havoc wrought by pirates, resistant forces of the Southern Ming regime, and "red barbarians" (Dutch traders), all of whom regarded the island as a desirable headquarters. The government carried out the "sea prohibition" as a defense measure and in 1671 again moved the population inland. But in 1684 Taiwan and P'eng-hu were recaptured, and five years later, Emperor K'ang-hsi granted the request to restore P'u-t'o submitted by Huang Ta-lai, the regional commander of Ting-hai.[14] The next year, Lan Li, Huang's successor, installed Ch'ao-yin, a very able monk, as the abbot of the Southern Monastery. K'ang-hsi renewed his support by giving more gold and bestowing a new name—P'u-chi (Universal Salvation)—on the monastery in 1699. One hundred years later, Hsing-t'ung, a monk originally from Mount Omei, became the abbot. He discovered a broken stele of Ta-chih's tomb inscription on the abandoned site of Fa-yü Ssu or the Northern Monastery. He was also told about Ta-chih's prediction that the temple would be revived one hundred years after his death. Hsing-t'ung took all of these as omens for better days. He sent his disciple Ming-i to Fukien for donations of timber. General Shih Shih-piao dispatched battleships to transport the more than a thousand pieces of timber to P'u-t'o to rebuild Fa-yü (*PTSC* 1924, 375–77). P'u-t'o continued to receive imperial patronage under emperors Yung-cheng and Ch'ien-lung and eventually became more famous than before. Hui-chi Ssu 慧濟寺, commonly known as Buddha Peak Monastery, the third largest monastery on the island, was erected in 1793, the fifty-eighth year of Ch'ien-lung. P'u-t'o had reached the zenith of its fame.

When P'u-t'o had to compete with mainland pilgrimage centers and strive to establish its identity as Potalaka, there was only one major monastery—P'u-chi—on the island. During the late Ming and particularly in the Ch'ing, a second major monastery became increasingly important. P'u-chi became known as the Southern Monastery; the newer Fa-yü was called the Northern Monastery. When P'u-t'o reached the height of its development and achieved public recognition as Potalaka, competition between these two major monasteries began to emerge. The compilation of the four gazetteers in the Ch'ing reflected this rivalry. The first two, both in 15 *chüan*, were compiled in 1698 and 1705, during the reign of K'ang-hsi; the next two, both in 20 *chüan*, were compiled in 1739, during the reign of Ch'ien-lung, and 1832, during the reign of Tao-kuang, just some twenty years before the upheavals brought about by the T'ai-p'ing rebellion in the 1850s to 1860s. The 1698 gazetteer was compiled at the request of two successive regional commanders of Ting-hai who campaigned for the rebuilding of P'u-t'o, and of Kao Shih-ch'i, the vice-minister of the Ministry of Rites, a devout Buddhist believer. This gazetteer was jointly sponsored by the two monasteries, and Fa-yü Monastery published it immediately; but the abbot of P'u-chi sponsored a second, revised edition in 1705. The 1739 gazetteer was compiled by a Han-lin academician at the request of the abbot of Fa-yü Monastery. The last Ch'ing gazetteer, compiled in 1832, was written at the request of P'u-chi.

Each gazetteer had a partisan editorial stance and gave more emphasis to the sponsoring monastery.[15] At the same time, because the two monasteries competed, they served as each other's watchdog. In the process, materials blatantly damaging to either one would be screened out. For instance, an article originally contained in the 1589 gazetteer that gave a biased and un-critical depiction of the abbot of the Southern Monastery was deleted from all Ch'ing editions.[16]

Gazetteers preserved valuable information about the process through which P'u-t'o island became transformed into Mount Potalaka. They con-stituted an important mechanism to legitimize the claim, for they also served as an influential medium to broadcast the island's fame and attract more pil-grims. Many actors appear in their pages: emperors and empresses, officials and writers, monks and ascetics, ordinary men and women. But looming above all of them is Kuan-yin him/herself, for it was with the miraculous manifestation of Kuan-yin's efficacy that the island first entered the stage of history. In the rest of this chapter, let us look at a few key elements in the successful transformation of P'u-t'o into Potalaka—the founding myths of P'u-t'o, pilgrims' visions of Kuan-yin, pilgrims' testimonies of Kuan-yin's miracles, and promotion by resident monks and ascetics.

FOUNDING MYTHS AND THE CREATION OF THE CHINESE POTALAKA

All gazetteers of P'u-t'o have a section called "efficacious wonders" (ling-i 靈異) in which are reported miracles performed by Kuan-yin to indicate the special status of the island. These myths were kept in oral traditions by pil-grims or had earlier been gathered in collections of miracle tales. For these reasons, even ordinary pilgrims who usually had no access to mountain gazetteers might be familiar with these stories. The founding myths of P'u-t'o invariably head this section of P'u-t'o gazetteers. They, like many of the miracles found here, are about Kuan-yin's theophanies. In this sense, the promoters of P'u-t'o would agree with Mircea Eliade when he said, "Every sacred space implies a hierophany, an irruption of the sacred that results in detaching a territory from the surrounding cosmic milieu and making it qual-itatively different" (Eliade 1959, 26). Moreover, they would also, again like Eliade, stress that it was Kuan-yin who revealed him/herself and the island to pilgrims, not the pilgrims who discovered the deity on the island and thereafter built it into a sacred site. But perhaps to fashion such a dichotomy is to miss the complexity of the situation. One cannot declare dogmatically either that the site was intrinsically efficacious or that efficacy was imposed from outside; a more fruitful course might be to examine the mutuality of both claims.

The founding myths of P'u-t'o, like those we have seen in relationship with Upper T'ien-chu, contain Kuan-yin's epiphanies or miraculous images. One traced the founding of P'u-t'o to Emperor Wen-tsung of the T'ang (r. 827–39). Although this story had more to do with the spread of the cult of Kuan-yin in T'ang China, it was nevertheless linked with the special destiny of the island. The emperor loved to eat clams, and fishermen on the southeast sea coast had to offer them as tribute, an offering that became a heavy burden. One day a huge clam was served at dinner. It could not be opened with a knife. When the emperor knocked on the shell, the clam opened by itself; inside the shell was a portrait of Kuan-yin. The emperor was greatly astonished and had the shell stored inside a sandalwood box decorated with gold. He then invited the Ch'an master Wei-cheng to court and asked for an explanation. The Ch'an master said, "Events never happen without responding to something. This is to awaken your faith so that you will be frugal and love the people. The [Lotus] sutra says, 'For those who can be saved by the form of a bodhisattva, Kuan-yin will appear to them as a bodhisattva and preach the dharma to them.'" The emperor said, "I have seen the form of the bodhisattva, but I have not heard the preaching." When the emperor was asked if he had faith in what he saw, he answered yes. Then the master said, "If this is the case, then you have already heard the preaching." The emperor was much pleased and understood. It was said that he gave up eating clams from then on and decreed that all the monasteries in the country should install images of Kuan-yin for worship. The 1739 gazetteer concluded, "The founding of Lo-chia [P'u-t'o] began with this" (5:1).[17]

Two other founding myths pointed to the second half of the ninth century as the time when P'u-t'o began to be associated with Kuan-yin. Both were connected with foreign monks, the first possibly Indian and the second Japanese. Considering the need to affirm P'u-t'o's identity as the mythical Mount Potalaka, the gazetteers' special interest in highlighting the island's "foreign connection" might not have been fortuitous: if P'u-t'o was indeed the Potalaka of scriptural renown, this fact had to be recognized not only by the Chinese, but also by foreign devotees. The 1361 gazetteer stated, "In the first year of Ta-chung [848] of Emperor Hsuan-tsung, a foreign monk (*fan-seng* 番僧) came to the Cave of Tidal Sound. He burned his ten fingers in front of the cave. When the fingers were burned off, he saw the Great Being who preached dharma to him and gave him a seven-hued precious stone. This was the first of many miracles of P'u-t'o. The monk built a hut and stayed." This monk, whose name was not given, clearly came to P'u-t'o (and specifically to the Cave of Tidal Sound) as a pilgrim. How and when the reputation of the cave as a place for pilgrims wishing to obtain a vision of Kuan-yin became known was unclear. However, the monk-pilgrim must have been aware that the island was a holy site, for his behavior—burning off fingers—clearly indicated that he came with determination and expectation.

The second miracle happened to another foreigner, the Japanese monk-pilgrim Egaku. While Egaku was on a pilgrimage to Mount Wu-t'ai, he obtained an image of Kuan-yin, which he intended to take back to Japan. But when the boat came near P'u-t'o, it became stuck. Water lilies covered the ocean. Egaku prayed, saying, "If my countrymen have no affinity with the Buddha and are destined not to see you, I will follow your direction and build a temple for you." After a while, the boat started to move and finally came to a spot under the Cave of Tidal Sound. A man surnamed Chang saw this and marveled. He converted his house into a shrine to house the image which became known as the Kuan-yin Who Refused to Leave Cloister (Pu-k'en-ch'ü Kuan-yin Yuan 不肯去觀音院). All later editions of P'u-t'o gazetteers give the year 916 as the date for this miracle.[18] The area in the ocean where Egaku's boat became stuck came to be known as Water-lily Ocean (Lien-hua yang 蓮花洋), situated to the west of the island.

This image from Wu-t'ai supposedly did not stay on P'u-t'o but was taken to the mainland and installed at K'ai-yuan Monastery in Ningpo by its abbot. The compilers of P'u-t'o gazetteers, while acknowledging this fact, countered with evidence that the image that later became enshrined on the island was equally miraculous. Soon after the old image left the island, a monk-pilgrim (yu-seng 遊僧) arrived on P'u-t'o. He obtained a piece of rare wood and shut himself indoors to carve an image of Kuan-yin. Within a month the image was finished, and the monk disappeared. In the early thirteenth century, one finger of the image became lost. The monks felt very unhappy. But later, something resembling a flower was seen floating among the waves in front of the Cave of Tidal Sound. When it was inspected closely, it turned out to be the lost finger. It was put back on the image that, according to tradition, was the one being worshiped on P'u-t'o down through the ages (PTSC 1924, 177).

Over the centuries, then, it was not only P'u-t'o's reputation as Potalaka but also its reputation as a place where Kuan-yin appeared to pilgrims that contributed to its growing popularity. There were a great number of sightings of Kuan-yin at the Cave of Tidal Sound. Reports about these visions led to the royal patronage of the island. They also motivated pilgrims down the ages to go to P'u-t'o, hoping to obtain a vision of Kuan-yin.

VISIONS OF KUAN-YIN

The earliest recorded sightings of Kuan-yin were not the deliberate results of pilgrims' "vision quests." Rather, Kuan-yin appeared to royal emissaries caught in life-endangering situations and saved them from sure death on the open sea. All editions of P'u-t'o gazetteers, aimed at elite audiences, related the following in the opening paragraphs of their chapters on miracles.

In 1080, Wang Shun-feng was sent from Hangchow as an emissary to the three states of Korea. When the party reached P'u-t'o they suddenly ran into

a fierce storm. A big turtle came underneath the boat and made it impossible
to move. The situation was extremely dangerous. Wang became greatly
frightened and, kneeling down and facing the Cave of Tidal Sound, prayed to
Kuan-yin. Suddenly he saw a brilliant golden light. Kuan-yin emerged from
the cave and, wearing glittering pearl necklaces, manifested the form of the
full moon. The turtle disappeared, and the boat could sail again. After Wang
returned from the mission and reported this miracle to the court, the emperor
bestowed the plaque Pao-t'o Kuan-yin Ssu 寶陀觀音寺 (Monastery of Kuan-
yin of Precious P'u-t'o) on the temple, later known as the Southern Monastery. This was the first time that it received imperial recognition, and royal
patronage continued. The monastery was given land and grain. Each year
one monk was allowed to be ordained. According to the gazetteers, whenever
sailors ran into storms or pirates, as soon as they took refuge facing the
island, dangers would disappear.

   Another miracle attested to the same fact. During the Ch'ung-ning era
(1102–6), Liu Ta and Wu Shih were emissaries to Koryo (in Korea). When
they came to the islands near P'u-t'o on their return, the moon became dark,
and the sky was overcast for four days and nights. No one knew where the
boat was headed. The sailors were much frightened; facing P'u-t'o in the
distance, they kneeled down and prayed. After a while, wondrous light filled
the ocean. Everywhere one looked, it was as bright as in the daylight. Mount
Chao-pao could be seen clearly. They thus succeeded in landing at Ningpo
safely (*PTSC* 1361, *T* 2101:1137a).

   The growing interest of the gentry in P'u-t'o was very likely linked to the
fact that famous monks started to establish it as a Ch'an center about this
time. In 1131 the famous Ch'an master Chen-hsieh Ch'ing-liao, a native of
Szechuan, arrived at the island from the mainland after his pilgrimage to
Mount Wu-t'ai. Quoting a phrase from the *Hua-yen sutra*, he called the hut
where he stayed "an isolated place by the seashore" (*hai-an ku-chueh-ch'u*
海岸孤絕處). He attracted many brilliant students of the Ch'an tradition.
The prefect petitioned to the court and had P'u-t'o changed from the original
Vinaya classification to Ch'an, a more prestigious school in the Sung. At that
time there were some seven hundred fishing families living on the island. But
tradition says that as soon as they heard the dharma from the master, they all
changed their profession (or left the island and moved elsewhere). Chen-
hsieh was regarded as the first patriarch of the Ch'an lineage of the Ts'ao-
tung branch on the island. He later went back to the mainland and became
abbot of famous monasteries in Chekiang, such as Aśoka Monastery and
Kuo-ch'ing Monastery on Mount T'ien-t'ai. In 1137 another Ch'an master,
Tzu-te Hui-hui (d. 1183), came to P'u-t'o. Prior to this, he had been the
abbot of Ching-tz'u Ssu, a well-known Ch'an monastery in Hangchow.
Largely because of his teaching activities, P'u-t'o was said to have reached
the same reputation as T'ien-tung Monastery, the training center of the

Ts'ao-tung lineage in Ningpo (*PTSC* 1924, 341–42). As P'u-t'o became linked with important mainland Buddhist communities, it began to attract more pilgrims, both monastic and lay. One powerful factor in its favor was undoubtedly its reputation as the place where Kuan-yin appeared to sincere pilgrims.

While early reports emphasized Kuan-yin's saving grace symbolized by brilliant light, accounts from the twelfth century on provided more detailed descriptions about pilgrims' encounters with the bodhisattva. These people can be properly called pilgrims, for, although educated, they deliberately came to P'u-t'o to obtain a vision of Kuan-yin. By this time, reports about Kuan-yin's epiphanies must have spread to the mainland, for these pilgrims knew where to go once they reached the island. Without exception, they all went to the Cave of Tidal Sound, the focal point of their vision quest. These were not ordinary pilgrims; they were men of fame and status. Moreover, they wrote about their experiences and advertised P'u-t'o among people of their own class. The gentry-officials' contribution to the creation of the site cannot be underestimated. The first official who visited the island in the early years of Shao-hsing (1131–62) as an unabashed pilgrim was Huang Kuei-nien, a supervising secretary.

Huang Kuei-nien's pilgrimage to P'u-t'o, his vision of Kuan-yin, and the tribute he wrote to commemorate the miraculous event, *Pao-t'o Shan Kuan-yin tsan* 寶陀山觀音贊 (Tribute to Kuan-yin of precious P'u-t'o), are found in the local gazetteers of Ssu-ming (Ningpo) compiled in 1169 and quoted in some later P'u-t'o gazetteer (*CTSMTC* 7:2a–b; 9:26a–b). *Tsan* (贊 tribute), *sung* (頌 hymn), and *chieh* (偈 metrical chant, *gāthā*) are favorite literary genres used by Buddhists to sing the praise of the object of their adoration. They are shorter and more succinct than works of prose. They also tend to be more personal and emotional. In the tribute, Huang described how he prayed in front of the cave together with his companions with respect and trepidation. They chanted the name of Kuan-yin and spells (*mi-yü* 密語). They first saw a brilliant light, and suddenly Kuan-yin appeared in the form of royal ease, sitting leisurely on the rock overcropping above the cave, her body a purplish gold (*tzu-chin*).[19] Overwhelmed with gratitude, Huang kneeled down and vowed that he would from then on devote himself to studying Buddhist scriptures and would refrain from killing and take up a vegetarian diet. He also emphasized that this was not a private vision, but that everyone present, both old and young, had witnessed the same miracle.

In 1148, not long after Huang's pilgrimage to P'u-t'o, another member of the gentry-official class went to P'u-t'o as a pilgrim and also left a record of his vision. Shih Hao (1106–94), a native of Ningpo and a scion of the illustrious and powerful Shih clan, was a *chin-shih* degree holder.[20] Following a common pattern of using an official tour of duty as an opportunity for a private side trip, Shih, serving as the supervisor of salt, visited P'u-t'o with a friend in the third month of 1148. When they first went to the Cave of Tidal Sound, they could not see anything. So they burned incense and prepared tea. Tea leaves floated to the top of the cup, which they took as a sign intimating something wondrous was about to happen. After they returned to the temple, they talked with the abbot Lan who told them stories from the *Hua-yen ching*. After the noon meal they went back to the cave. They looked around and only saw wild rocks heaped upon each other. Disappointed, they decided to leave. But a monk told them about an opening on the top of the cliff and said they should look down from there. Dutifully they climbed to the top on all fours and suddenly saw an auspicious golden form. The whole cave was illuminated by the brilliance. They could see Kuan-yin's eyes and eyebrows clearly. Shih Hao clearly thought what he saw was the form of a woman, for he described her teeth being "as white as jade." They were filled with happiness and gratitude. After paying homage to Kuan-yin, they sailed back to Ningpo. Fearing that this event might be forgotten through time, Shih wrote it down and had it inscribed on the wall of the cave.[21]

Like Chang Shang-ying's pilgrimage to Mount Wu-t'ai discussed by Gimello (chapter 3 of this volume), Shih's experiences were facilitated and shaped by the guidance of resident monk guides. Like Chang, Shih also wrote the account for posterity. There was, however, no trace of ambivalence in Shih's attitude, a characteristic noticeable among the literati of late Ming as described in the chapters in this volume by Dudbridge and Wu. What might account for the difference in attitudes? One may be tempted to say that people of the Sung perhaps lived more comfortably with a sense of mystery and awe. But I am not convinced that people living in the late Ming had lost it. I think the answer may lie in the medium of their expression. Both Chang and Shih wrote for fellow believers or potential believers. Their writings were collected by gazetteers, which constitute, after all, a very different genre from novels and travel accounts. Mountain gazetteers have a more limited, but at the same time, more definite, audience. I suspect that if we comb through more of them, we may find other writings that express religious feelings with equal openness and honesty.

Probably as a result of Shih's promotion, the Cave of Tidal Sound became even better known. In 1209 monk Te-chao, a dharma heir of Ch'an master Fo-chao, became the abbot. Because it was very difficult for pilgrims to worship Kuan-yin at the cave he had a bridge built among the rocks so that pilgrims could stand on the bridge facing the cave. The project took six years. When it was finished, Emperor Ning-tsung personally wrote a plaque naming it Ta-shih Ch'iao 大士橋 (Bridge of the Great Being). One hundred thousand pine trees were planted. In the meantime, Te-chao had earlier, in 1210, started to build the great hall. Shih Mi-yuan, son of Shih Hao, had become the prime minister. He followed his father's example and was a devotee of Kuan-yin. He made donations to the project, providing money to build halls, rooms, and corridors and provided for lamps and ritual implements. When the emperor learned about the project, he also gave his support, and bestowed golden robes, silver bowls, rosaries made of agate, and brocaded banners. At that time, 567 *mu* of arable land and 1,670 *mu* of forest land were granted to the monastery (*PTSC* 1361, *T* 2101:1137c–38a).

ICONOGRAPHY, LITERATURE, AND THE CREATION OF THE CHINESE POTALAKA

Mountain gazetteers, miracle tales, and testimonials written by elite pilgrims all helped legitimize P'u-t'o's claim. Other media also played important roles in promoting the attractiveness of the site among people in society at large. Art and literature were two powerful means of communicating this new message. Imagination was superimposed on memory. Fantasy was built upon reality. The Potalaka in art and fiction might have little to do with the actual island in the ocean. No matter. Just as myths about Shangri-la stimulated and molded the Western fantasy about Tibet, similarly, depictions of P'u-t'o as Potalaka in art and literature fueled the Chinese pilgrims' longing for the sacred realm (Bishop 1989). These media drew the pilgrims to the island. They also taught them where to look and what to see.

   Changing iconography of Kuan-yin was closely reflected by how pilgrims saw the deity. From the twelfth century on, Kuan-yin appeared to pilgrims on P'u-t'o increasingly as Our Lady in White, just as she did at Upper T'ien-chu.[22] But there was a difference: Kuan-yin on P'u-t'o began to be accompanied first by Shan-ts'ai, the boy pilgrim Sudhana, and later by both the boy and Lung-nü, the Dragon Princess. With the appearance of Kuan-yin's attendants, another cave near the Cave of Tidal Sound that began to attract pilgrims became known as Sudhana's Cave. (Some gazetteers identified it as Dragon Princess's Cave and named a rock nearby Sudhana's Rock.) For instance, in 1266 Grand Marshall Fan, who suffered from eye disease, sent his son to pray in front of the Cave of Tidal Sound. When Fan washed his eyes with the spring water the son had brought home from the cave, he recovered. The father sent the son once more to the cave to offer thanks to Kuan-yin. Kuan-yin appeared to the son on the left side of the cave. She wore a cape formed by light haze and seemed to be standing behind a curtain of azure gauze. After that he went to worship at Sudhana's Cave, where first Sudhana and then Kuan-yin appeared. Kuan-yin wore a white robe with long tassels and many strands of pearl necklaces.

   In 1276, during the Yuan, Prime Minister Po-yen captured southern China, and General Ha-la-tai came to worship at the cave. When he did not see anything, he took out his bow and shot an arrow into the cave. When he boarded the boat to go back, suddenly the ocean became filled with water lilies. He was much frightened and regretted his behavior. He went back to the cave in repentance. After a while he saw White-robed Kuan-yin who, accompanied by Sudhana, walked gracefully by. As a result of this vision, Ha-la-tai had an image made (doubtless according to what he saw) and erected a hall for Kuan-yin above the cave. In the fourth month of 1328, executive censor Ts'ao Li came with an imperial order to offer incense and donations. He prayed for a vision at the cave. Kuan-yin appeared wearing a white robe and covered with necklaces. He next went to Sudhana's Cave and saw the boy, who looked like a living person (*PTSC* 1361; *T* 2101:1137a–b).

Sometimes a direct reference to contemporary art was made. For instance, we are told that on the sixth day of the tenth month in 1355, Liu Jen-pen of T'ien-t'ai returned from his duty as the supervisor of the circuit granary transport. He came to P'u-t'o and saw Kuan-yin at the Cave of Tidal Sound. The appearance of Kuan-yin was "the same as that painted in pictures" (*PTSC* 1739, 5:4b). But what kind of pictures? Was it White-robed Kuan-yin painted by artists since the Sung? What the pilgrim saw in his vision of Kuan-yin and how Kuan-yin was depicted in religious and secular art became closely connected. For as Kuan-yin was increasingly sighted together with Shan-ts'ai and Lung-nü, a new iconography of the Nan-hai Kuan-yin (Kuan-yin of the South Sea, Potalaka Kuan-yin) (figs. 5.2, 5.3) began to be identified with P'u-t'o from the Ming on.

Kuan-yin is called Nan-hai Kuan-yin in the Chinese novel *Hsi-yu chi* (*Journey to the West*). It has been suggested that Wu Ch'eng-en, the author, probably visited P'u-t'o, for he provided detailed descriptions of the island in no fewer than nine places in the novel.[23] Kuan-yin appears here as a compassionate and omnipotent savior. There is no doubt about Kuan-yin's gender, for as Potalaka Kuan-yin, she is the beautiful goddess from P'u-t'o.

> A mind perfected in the four virtues,
> A gold body filled with wisdom,
> Fringes of dangling pearls and jade,
> Scented bracelets set with lustrous treasures,
> Dark hair piled smoothly in a coiled-dragon bun,
> And elegant sashes lightly fluttering as phoenix quills,
> Her green jade buttons
> And white silk robe
> Bathed in holy light;
> . . . .
> With brows of new moon shape
> And eyes like two bright stars,
> Her jadelike face beams natural joy,
> And her ruddy lips seem a flash of red.

Fig. 5.2. Nan-hai Kuan-yin, by Chao I, dated 1313. Collection of
the National Palace Museum, Taipei, Taiwan, Republic of China.

Fig. 5.3. Nan-hai Kuan-yin. Woodblock frontispiece of *Kuan-yin sutra*, dated 1445.
Fa-yuan Monastery Rare Book Library, Peking.

Her immaculate vase overflows with nectar from year to year,
Holding sprigs of weeping willow green from age to age.
....
Thus she rules on the Mount T'ai,
And lives at the South Seas.
....
She is the merciful ruler of Potalaka Mountain,
The Living Kuan-yin from the Cave of Tidal Sound.

(Yu 1977, 185)

In this hymn of Kuan-yin, the author connected her with golden light, white robe, willow branch, pure vase, South Seas, Potalaka Mountain, and finally, the Cave of Tidal Sound. Wu Ch'eng-en was not being original here, for by the late Ming, Kuan-yin had come to be seen in this way by society at large. Painters were using these epithets in creating a new iconography of Potalaka Kuan-yin. The same cluster of almost stock phrases was also used in pilgrims' accounts of their vision of Kuan-yin. The similar depiction of Kuan-yin in different media was most likely due to mutual influence; and once this iconography became established, mutual reinforcement by different media undoubtedly helped its universal acceptance.

Nan-hai Kuan-yin was clearly a composite image, combining both scriptural elements that had been subjected to indigenous modifications and iconographical elements drawn from diverse sources. The emergence of this iconography coincided with the resurgence of P'u-t'o in the sixteenth century under the patronage of the Wan-li emperor and his mother after the island had suffered long periods of neglect. Its triumph over other forms of Kuan-yin probably happened during the seventeenth and eighteenth centuries when P'u-t'o enjoyed the patronage of the successive Ch'ing emperors K'ang-hsi, Yung-cheng, and Ch'ien-lung. In this reestablishment of the sacred site, local officials and able abbots collaborated closely. An extensive corpus of new literature in the form of *pao-chüan* 寶卷 (precious volumes) also appeared to explain and advertise this new iconography. These texts identify P'u-t'o as Hsiang-shan, thus linking Kuan-yin with Princess Miao-shan. Her attendants Shan-ts'ai and Lung-nü also underwent full sinicization. Rather than referring to these attendants' origins in Buddhist scriptures, the texts provided them with Chinese life stories. Stylistically, Nan-hai Kuan-yin had come to resemble White-robed Kuan-yin, the deity worshiped primarily at Upper T'ien-chu. As P'u-t'o became Potalaka, it superseded Hsiang-shan and Hangchow by absorbing the myths and images of Kuan-yin connected with these two mainland pilgrimage sites (Yü 1990a, 233–39).

Popular texts such as *pao-chüan*[24] did not only inform ordinary pilgrims about the Kuan-yin lore connected with P'u-t'o; more important, they also served as effective means to generate financial donations to build temples on the island. *P'u-t'o pao-chüan* 普陀寶卷, a well-known work published probably in late nineteenth century, presented Nan-hai Kuan-yin as responsible for the rebuilding of P'u-t'o. By providing expected rewards and retributions appropriate to the protagonists, this *pao-chüan* clearly teaches the virtue of making donations to monks from P'u-t'o, who may indeed be the manifestation of Kuan-yin herself. Although the extant editions of this text are late, they were perhaps based on oral traditions or even on an earlier written version (now lost) dating back to the two periods of intensive temple rebuilding on P'u-t'o.

The story told in *P'u-t'o pao-chüan* was supposed to have taken place during

the reign of Chen-tsung (r. 997–1021) of the Sung, the time of P'u-t'o's
founding. Assuming the form of a poor monk accompanied by two other
monks (who were Shan-ts'ai and Lung-nü in disguise), Kuan-yin went to the
Wang family to seek donations to build the Kuan-yin Hall. The old couple
were pious Buddhists who had divided their property between their two sons,
Yu-chin and Yu-yin, and devoted their lives to worship of the Buddha. The
parents soon passed away. Yu-chin remembered his father's instruction; he
loved to do good deeds and believed in Buddhism. Yu-yin was the opposite.
Influenced by his wife, who was greedy, hated monks, and delighted in killing animals, Yu-yin was interested only in enriching himself by exploiting
others. When Kuan-yin came seeking a donation, Yu-chin agreed to assume
the entire cost of the building project, to the derision of his younger brother.
The total cost of building the temple was 100,000 ounces of silver. To fulfill
this pledge, Yu-chin had to sell not only his jewelry, grain, land, and house,
which came to 99,600 ounces, but also his thirteen-year-old son and ten-year-
old daughter for 200 ounces each to make up the shortage. Yu-chin and his
wife were reduced to utter poverty and supported themselves by selling bamboo. But eventually the daughter was chosen to be the new empress, and the
son became a *chin-shih*. The parents were reunited with the children, and the
new emperor invited them to live in the palace. They converted everyone to
Buddhism. When they died they went to the Western Paradise. The emperor
had a Ch'an monastery specially built in which an image of Yu-chin made of
sandalwood was enshrined to receive people's worship (46b).

The fate of the younger brother and his wife was, alas, very different.
Although Yu-yin indulged in evil ways in this life, he had done good deeds in
his past life, so Kuan-yin decided to save him. She assumed the appearance
of Yu-yin and took up residence in his house while the real Yu-yin was out.
She instructed servants not to allow anyone in. When the real Yu-yin came
back, he was driven out and had to spend the night at Earth God's temple.
He went to court and lodged a complaint. But the judge decided that the one
staying at home was the real Wang Yu-yin and sentenced the complainant to
forty beatings by a heavy board (36). Yu-yin remembered his older brother's
devotion and turned his heart to Buddhism. He decided to go to P'u-t'o on
pilgrimage. Kuan-yin had Shan-ts'ai turn into a woodcutter and direct Yu-
yin to P'u-t'o. He suffered many trials and tribulations on the way. After
instructing Yu-yin's wife to keep a vegetarian diet and to chant Buddha's
name, Kuan-yin appeared as an old lady and aided Yu-yin on his pilgrimage
(48b). In the meantime, the wife also underwent a change of heart and decided to go on a pilgrimage to P'u-t'o. She sold everything and set out. She
endured a perilous passage on the boat, during which she prayed all the time.
Once on the island, she met her husband, who repudiated her. Heartbroken,
she jumped into the ocean intending to kill herself. She was saved by Lung-
nü, disguised as a fisherman, and woke up in her own bed. Realizing that

Kuan-yin had arranged everything, she became the goddess's devotee. Yu-yin remained on P'u-t'o and became a monk (53a).

Thus we see that the island and its advertisers were mutually dependent. The fame of P'u-t'o inspired people to write about it. At the same time, novels, plays, travel accounts, gazetteers, and popular texts served to bolster the newfound fame of the island. A similar relationship existed between the island and its pilgrims, many of whom were illiterate common people. The reported efficacy of Potalaka Kuan-yin drew many people to the island. But the island achieved new fame through the continuous discovery of new places of efficacy by these pilgrims.

ORDINARY PILGRIMS AND THE CREATION OF POTALAKA

Many ordinary pilgrims (among whom we should count the rank and file monks and nuns) went to P'u-t'o down the centuries. Being uneducated, they could not write about their experiences or paint a picture of Kuan-yin as they saw her in their visions. But they assuredly made as much contribution to the creation of the Chinese Potalaka as their more articulate fellow pilgrims. They did so by going to P'u-t'o en masse and thereby existentially confirming the ideological transformation of the island into Potalaka effected by abbots and elites. They also participated in the physical construction of the island by making financial contributions. We can catch a glimpse of these devout, but mute, humble pilgrims in the pages of travel accounts about P'u-t'o left behind by their more educated contemporaries.

Like other pilgrims, they also congregated around the Cave of Tidal Sound because Kuan-yin was believed to appear there. This remained the most popular place on the island until the Cave of Brahma's Voice became a serious contender in the seventeenth century. Hou's gazetteer described the height of the former's fame in the late Ming. Every spring monks from all over the country would come to the island carrying images of Kuan-yin cast in silver and gold. They would welcome Kuan-yin by throwing these images into the water as offerings to her in front of the Cave of Tidal Sound. They would also offer brocade banners and bells and tripods cast in gold or bronze in the monastic halls. Some monk-pilgrims who came from thousands of miles away would kneel and kowtow all the way until they were covered with blood. Some pilgrims, overcome with religious enthusiasm, would jump into the water to seek deliverance from this world. More pilgrims would burn their arms and fingers to show their sincerity and induce Kuan-yin to appear to them (*PTSC* 1598, 3:27a).

Two late Ming writers left accounts of their travel/pilgrimage to P'u-t'o that confirm the descriptions about the religious zeal of pilgrims provided by the gazetteers. The first was *P'u-t'o yu-chi* (A P'u-t'o travel account), written by Hsieh Kuo-chen (d. 1632). He said that aside from the two large monasteries, there were more than five hundred small shrines (*an*) scattered all over the island. Although the island was very beautiful, people looked upon sailing on the ocean with dread; thus even natives of Ningpo did not come to the island often. "Western monks," however, regarded coming to the South Sea on pilgrimage as highly desirable. For pilgrims, walking across the narrow stone bridge in front of the Cave of Tidal Sound was deemed especially meritorious. Hsieh described it this way:

> The bridge is about ten *chang* [one hundred Chinese feet] in length and two to three feet in width. It faces a sheer cliff on the north side on which a small temple dedicated to Kuan-yin sits. I sat by the window of Shang-fang-kuang Monastery and saw with my own eyes that some twenty monks walked on the bridge as if it were level ground. But one monk walked only a few steps before he started to quake and stood stock still. After a few minutes, he moved again and finally managed to walk to the other side. Everyone's eyes were focused on him, and some people were muttering words that I could not hear. When I asked the local monk in the temple, he said, "He almost did not succeed in achieving a rebirth as a human being in his next incarnation." (Hsieh Kuo-chen 2:242–43)

It seemed that in addition to hoping to obtain a vision of Kuan-yin, pilgrims also tried to predict their chances of being reborn as human beings in the next life by performing this daredevil act of walking on the stone bridge in front of the cave.

Hsieh also provided some information about pilgrims' economic contribution to P'u-t'o. Seven thousand to eight thousand *shih* of rice were needed each year, but since the island did not produce any grain, this had to be supplied by donors. Most of the rice was donated by women. Pilgrims from Fukien and Kwangtung provided other daily necessities (ibid.).

Chang Tai, in his inimitable style, gave an account of his trip to P'u-t'o. He went there for the holy day celebration of 2/19, the festival on Kuan-yin's birthday in 1638.[25] Like pilgrims to the Upper T'ien-chu Monastery in Hangchow, P'u-t'o pilgrims also observed the all-night vigil known as *su-shan* (spending the night on the mountain). It was quite a sight!

> The Great Hall is filled with incense smoke that is as thick as a heavy fog spreading over five *li*. Thousands of men and women sit in rows like packed fish. From under the Buddha's images all the way to the outside corridors, not one inch of space is unoccupied. During the night many nuns burn incense on their heads or burn their arms and fingers. Women from good families imitate them. They recite scriptures and try not to show signs of pain. If they can refrain from even knitting their eyebrows, this is considered as having faith and very meritorious. I wondered if the compassionate bodhisattva would be pleased by the offering of burnt human flesh. The sound of heads knocking against the ground reverberates throughout the valley. Monks of the temple do not sleep that night either. With hundreds of candles burning, they sit facing

the Buddha. In a state of sleepiness, some see Buddha [Kuan-yin] moving, while others see her send out brilliant light. Each regards what he or she sees as miraculous. They disperse only at daybreak. (*Lan-hsuan wen-chi*, 208)

Chang went to the Cave of Tidal Sound, noting that Sudhana's Rock and Dragon Princess's Cave were nearby.[26] When Chang asked the attending monk if he had ever had a vision of Kuan-yin as described in the gazetteers, the monk answered, "The bodhisattva used to live here, but during the Wan-li period [1573–1615], because the dragon wind was very strong, it blew away the stone bridge. Since then Kuan-yin has moved to the Cave of Brahma's Voice." Chang refrained with difficulty from bursting out laughing at what the monk said, so he bade the monk a hasty farewell (ibid., 209). This story accorded well with the time when the Cave of Brahma's Voice emerged as the new place to seek a vision of Kuan-yin following the establishment of the Northern Monastery.

Although Chang Tai was skeptical of reported miracles and openly critical of the credulous and fanatical pilgrims he saw on the island, he nevertheless regarded himself as a pilgrim. He seemed to disapprove of vulgar pilgrims, but not of pilgrimage itself. This same ambivalent attitude was present during his trip to Mount T'ai (see Wu, chapter 2 of this volume). Here also Chang was unabashedly condescending to the uneducated pilgrims. Although he came emptyhanded to P'u-t'o, he saw his act of writing about the island as no different from making religious offerings. In fact, it might be even more valuable:

> Master Chang [referring to himself] says: P'u-t'o is renowned because of the bodhisattva, yet it is neither truly nor exhaustively known because of her. . . . If there is no bodhisattva, then who would bother to come sailing through the ocean? For if there is no bodhisattva, there would be no pilgrim. Although this is the case, those who come here to worship her leave as soon as their purpose is fulfilled. While here, they either bow once every three steps or fold their palms once every five steps. Some also make full prostrations while shouting the name of the bodhisattva at the top of their voices. However, not one out of one hundred pilgrims who come to P'u-t'o can tell you much about the place. . . . Arriving on the island, I have nothing to offer the bodhisattva, but I know how to describe the natural scenery (*shan-shui*, 山水 literally, "mountains and streams"). So I will perform a Buddhist service (*tso fo-shih* 做佛事) by writing about the scenery of P'u-t'o. Perhaps I am the first person among the literati from ancient times until today who, while unable to worship the Buddha by offering money or rice, yet manages to do so through pen and ink. (ibid., 205)

Literati writers such as Chang, while disdaining the vulgar beliefs and practices of ordinary pilgrims, nevertheless were fascinated by them. Like modern-day ethnographers, they were very much interested in noting down what they observed and discovered. For instance, Chang tells us that village men and women believed that as soon as they went on pilgrimage to P'u-t'o, Kuan-yin accompanied them all the way. Therefore, if they stumbled, they believed it was because Kuan-yin had pushed them, but if they fell flat on the ground, then it was because she lent them a hand [so that they would not be hurt]. On board the ship, if the punting pole or the rudder got lost, and in fact, when any little thing happened, it would be interpreted as either a good or bad omen from the bodhisattva. (ibid., 213)

A later writer, making the trip to P'u-t'o in 1822, reported taboos observed by similar types of pilgrims who sailed for P'u-t'o.

Banisters in the rear part of the boat are reserved for gods and buddhas. One can lean on them or step over them, but must never sit on them. There is a special place in the back of the boat where one may dump the night soil or perform one's personal hygiene. One may not do so in any other place carelessly. When one sits on the gangplank, never wrap arms around one's knees, for this will bring stormy weather. When one sits, never dangle one's legs in midair, for this will cause delay in the trip. When one finishes eating, never put chopsticks across the rice bowl, for this will also cause further delay. When anyone commits these mistakes, he/she will make the boatmen really angry. (Cheng Kuang-tsu, 38a–b)

It is also possible to get a sense of the involvement and dedication of this vast number of ordinary pilgrims by combing through the miracle tales contained in the gazetteers. All the stories are ostensibly about the efficacious response of Kuan-yin to the pilgrims' devotion. At the same time, they provide some interesting data, albeit of an anecdotal nature, about the kind of simple pilgrims who, through their faith and devotion, sustained the pilgrimage tradition.

I select a few examples from a large body of material. All happened during the sixteenth and seventeenth centuries, one of the major cycles of P'u-t'o's revival. The first is about the mother of a P'u-t'o monk named T'ien-jan, who came originally from Hangchow. The mother kept a vegetarian diet at home and worshiped the Buddha. She often sought donations from people and would turn whatever she received over to her son and ask him to donate it to temples on the island. One day she was given an image of Kuan-yin whose neck was cast in gold. When she gave it to her son, he became greedy for the gold and asked a worker to scrape off the gold. The worker died as soon as he did so. A while later, the mother came over from the mainland. Even before she arrived on P'u-t'o, T'ien-jan already knew of her coming. He called out in a loud voice and cursed her, "The enemy who will harm me is now coming." When he saw his mother, he struck her on the cheeks and then, grabbing a knife, he cut his own neck. He ran around the island and called out, "Do not imitate my example. If you act like me, hell is right in front of your eyes." After saying this, he died. The gazetteer reported matter-of-factly that this happened in 1586, the fourteenth year of Wan-li (*PTSC* 1607, 155–56). This story is about a pious mother's unstinting effort to find donations; it is also a cautionary tale about greedy monks who pocketed pilgrims' offerings; above all, it is a story of Kuan-yin's unfailing efficacy.

Other stories provide some information about the geographical spread and occupational diversity of the pilgrims. For instance, a shopkeeper from Anhuei desired to go on a pilgrimage to P'u-t'o. He kept a vegetarian diet for three years to prepare himself for the momentous endeavor. He also moved to K'ung-shan (in Chekiang) to be closer to the island. On the new year's day of a certain year at the end of the Ming, he was finally all set to depart. Just then someone rushed to the docks and told him he should turn back because a fire had broken out next door to his shop. He refused to give up his trip, saying that even if the shop should burn to the ground, he would not turn back because he had been waiting for this pilgrimage too long. When he returned from P'u-t'o, he discovered that while all the neighboring houses had been burned to the ground, his shop remained intact (*PTSC* 1924, 188).

There were two stories about merchants; one was a cloth dealer from Kiangsi and the other a Cantonese overseas trader. We do not know the date, but the setting is probably late Ming. The first man came to P'u-t'o to offer incense as a side trip of his business ventures. He saw a decrepit statue of a heavenly king. Remembering a folk saying that dust from images of famous monasteries when mixed with medicine could cure illnesses, he took a handful of dust. But as soon as he got back to his boat, he became dizzy and suffered tremendous headaches. A very angry heavenly king of enormous height scolded him for cutting flesh from the god's shin. The cloth merchant was very frightened and repented his behavior. He asked a monk traveling with him to take the dust back to P'u-t'o, promising to make a new statue of the god. The story of the Cantonese trader is a little different. On his way home from Japan, he dreamed of a giant who asked to borrow his ship to carry a huge bone. He woke up in a fright. It was midnight. Suddenly the ship was about to sink because of a weird storm. Everyone on board started to cry. Then, just as suddenly, the wind changed, and they landed safely at P'u-t'o at daybreak. Overcome with relief, the trader went to a temple to worship Kuan-yin. There he saw the statue of a heavenly king whose leg had become detached and was lying in front of it. It looked exactly like the giant who had appeared to him in the dream. He marveled at the miracle and immediately donated money for a new statue (*PTSC* 1698, 10:12a–b).

The final story I cite happened in the spring of 1898. A group of pilgrims from San-chia, Huang-yen county, T'ai prefecture, went to P'u-t'o to offer incense. On their way back, when they had sailed no more than several hundred *li*, the boat was enveloped in thick fog and could not go any farther. When the boatman asked if anyone among the pilgrim group had done anything impure while on the island, an old woman hastily opened her bag and threw a yellow tile into the ocean. As soon as she did so, the fog cleared, and they sailed safely home. When asked, she explained that she did not intend to steal anything. It was just that she loved the smoothness and coolness of the yellow tile and wanted to use it as a pillow to keep cool in summer. However, even such a trivial deed was not overlooked. Everyone in the group was struck anew by Kuan-yin's efficacy (*PTSC* 1924, 200).

ASCETICS, ABBOTS, AND THE CREATION OF THE CHINESE POTALAKA

The fame of the Cave of Tidal Sound also attracted ascetics and serious religious practitioners who came as pilgrims and then chose to stay. The 1607 gazetteer contains an account of two such persons entitled "Biography of Two Great Beings," written by the monk Chen-i. In this account he described his encounter with two ascetics, one female and one male, whom he regarded as manifestations of Kuan-yin. The woman came to P'u-t'o in the sixth month of 1605 and the man four months later, after he had made a pilgrimage to Mount Chiu-hua. Both man and woman had dark faces and matted hair. They lived in two separate thatched huts perched on top of the hill south of the cave. The huts were no higher than three feet, leaking on top and damp underneath. The ascetics sat inside meditating all day. When people gave them food and money, they would accept the offerings but then give them away to mendicant monks. Sometimes the two would go without eating for several days, yet they suffered no ill effect. Ordinary people took them for beggars. Chen-i paid them a visit one night with a lay devotee. They sat in silence for a long time. The hosts did not show any surprise, but neither did they address the guests. When Chen-i made conversation with them, the man only smiled without speaking, but the woman was sharp-witted and quick on the uptake. In true Ch'an fashion, when asked about her name, she answered, "What name?" When asked about her age, she answered, "What age?" She answered the question about her native place the same way. She did say, however, that she had lived on Mount Chung-nan, a holy mountain not far from Mount Wu-t'ai, for a number of years. When asked about her realization, she said, "My eyes see the great ocean, and my ears hear the sound of wind, rain, tide, and birds." When asked about her method of religious practice, she answered, "Sometimes when I think of Kuan-yin, I will chant the name a few times. But the rest of the time, I merely sit. There is no particular method in my sitting." Chen-i was greatly impressed by her straightforwardness. She seemed to harbor not a thought in her mind. In the following spring, when many pilgrims visited the cave during the second month, the height of the pilgrimage season, the two ascetics left (*PTSC* 1607, 3:268–70).

Ascetics such as these two might have added an aura of mystery and sanctity to the island, but it was mainly through the energetic promotion of able monks that old places of renown became revived and new places of efficacy became discovered on P'u-t'o. The activities of Ta-chih Chen-jung (1523–92), founding abbot of Fa-yü, can serve as one example of the large part monks played in the creation of Potalaka.[27] Ta-chih was an intrepid pilgrim, having spent many years going on pilgrimages to Wu-t'ai, Omei, and Chiu-hua. In 1580 he came to P'u-t'o. After praying at the Cave of Tidal Sound and the Cave of Brahma's Voice and asking Kuan-yin for a sign, he saw one evening a large bamboo flow in with the tide and rest on a beach known as Sand of a Thousand Paces (Ch'ien-pu sha 千步沙), to the left of Southern Monastery. Taking this as the sign from Kuan-yin, he built a hut and named it the Cloister of Ocean Tide (Hai-ch'ao An 海潮庵), the forerunner of Northern Monastery. Soon many faithful began to donate money, which enabled him to expand the original modest temple. At that time, Ch'an practice was in a decline, but Ta-chih insisted on strict discipline and became as well known as Yun-ch'i Chu-hung (1535–1615), Tzu-po Chen-k'o (1543–1603), and Han-shan Te-ch'ing (1546–1623), the other three great masters of the late Ming (*PTSC* 1598, 3:27a–32a).

The above biographical account of Ta-chih was written by a writer who called himself Layman Ku-lo Fa-seng Yang-ti. He visited P'u-t'o as a pilgrim and sought out Ta-chih for an interview. After their conversation, Ta-chih gave the writer a document that chronicled his austerities and religious activities during the previous sixty years. Ta-chih chose the pilgrim as his biographer because of a dream Ta-chih had had the night before. In the dream, Kuan-yin told him that a layman by the name of Fa-seng (Monk with Hair), with whom he had a predestined relationship, would visit him. When Ta-chih saw the writer, he immediately realized that this was the predicted person. Ta-chih was an unflagging pilgrim and an energetic temple builder, but he was also an unabashed promoter of P'u-t'o and himself. Ta-chih, like many of his contemporaries, carried out this promotion by recourse to the miraculous. Citing the dream of Kuan-yin to legitimize his request for a favorable biography is one example. Another example, to which I alluded earlier, was Ta-chih's prediction that P'u-t'o would be revived one hundred years after his death. He had this prediction inscribed on his funerary stele. The rediscovery of this stele by Hsing-t'ung in 1691 provided the needed impetus to bring about the restoration of Fa-yü in 1692, exactly one hundred years later (*PTSC* 1698, 12:55a–57b).

Ta-chih was one of several able monks who helped to build P'u-t'o into a great pilgrimage site. Like others, he was himself a pilgrim. His relationships with pilgrims and officials were probably also typical of other abbots. The revival of the island always happened as a result of concerted effort by pilgrims, officials, and abbots. As Northern Monastery was established, the Cave of Brahma's Voice also became more famous. In 1626 an Indian pilgrim from Benares came to the cave and, impressed by the topography, offered relics of the Buddha and enshrined them in a stupa built on top of the cave.[28]

The 1705 gazetteer refers to the two caves as two eyes of the sacred island (2:13b). Like the Cave of Tidal Sound, the Cave of Brahma's Voice also attracted fanatic pilgrims who sometimes chose to commit religious suicide to show their devotion to Kuan-yin. Mui Sui, the prefect, was so disturbed by such actions that he wrote an impassioned plea, "She-shen chieh" 拾身戒 (Prohibition against sacrificing one's body) and inscribed it on a stele erected near the Cave of Brahma's Voice (12:35a–38a). This prohibition was apparently not effective. Robert F. Fitch, who made six trips to P'u-t'o between 1922 and 1928, described the cave this way:

> Into the depths below, in even recent times, pilgrims would throw themselves and commit suicide with the hope that they could not only quickly end their earthly miseries but also become immediately transformed into Buddhas and awaken in the Western Paradise. Hence, such acts are now most strictly forbidden. In former years, it was the custom for a priest to be let down in a basket to gather up the remains for cremation. (Fitch 1929, 70–71)

Fitch was much impressed by the Cave of Tidal Sound. "At high tide, when the wind is blowing inward towards the shore, the waves will enter the cave with great violence. At the inner end of the cave is a small exit upward and the writer has seen, in a typhoon, the water emerging like a geyser to a height of over twenty feet" (ibid., 50–51).[29]

Competition between the two caves did not diminish the attraction of either one for pilgrims. On the contrary, reports of Kuan-yin's appearances at both caves highlighted their efficacy and made a visit to both obligatory. The relationship between the Southern and Northern Monasteries was similar. Although there was a sense of rivalry between them, they actually reinforced each other's reputation. As the island became increasingly developed, all the holy places contributed to the aura of sanctity of the pilgrimage site. At the same time, each individual place derived its attraction from the site as a whole.

Since the Ch'ing dynasty, the two major monasteries have managed the smaller temples and hermitages on the island jointly. The 1924 gazetteer of P'u-t'o listed 88 small cloisters (*an* 庵) and 128 hermitages (literally, "thatched huts," *mao-p'eng* 茅蓬, simple dwellings for monks engaged in solitary meditation) under the jurisdiction of the Southern and Northern monasteries (77 hermitages belonging to the former and 51 to the latter). Similar figures were cited by missionaries, foreign tourists, and Chinese pilgrims around the turn of the century.[30] A system was worked out by which pilgrims, especially those who came from the northern provinces, were assigned to the two monasteries equitably. The 1739 gazetteer provided an interesting glimpse of how this system worked.

> Pilgrims who come from northern Chihli, Shansi, Shensi, Shantung, Honan, and other provinces north of the Yangtze River are called northern pilgrims (*pei-k'o* 北客). They should be hosted by the Southern and Northern monasteries equally. This system was already in use in former times. Moreover, rules stipulating how the two monasteries should receive the pilgrims were inscribed on stelae: the arrival of each pilgrim boat is registered in a book, and the monasteries take turns in receiving the pilgrims. In the case of northern pilgrims, if there are fewer than two in the group, it does not count. But if there are more than three, the group will be counted as one boat no matter whether there are many or few in the group. The two monasteries must receive pilgrim groups in turn. Regardless if the pilgrim group is large or small, or if it arrives early or late, the monasteries should not pick and choose. If among a pilgrim group there is someone known to one of the monasteries, or if the pilgrim is a donor to that monastery, this rule can be overlooked. But in that case, another similar group must be substituted to make up the difference. (*PTSC* 1739, 10:13)

CONCLUSION

The transformation of P'u-t'o into the Chinese Potalaka took many centuries. Many different kinds of people contributed to this effort, and many different types of media were used to bolster and broadcast the claim. All these were intimately connected with pilgrimage. Because of pilgrimage activities, an isolated island in the ocean came to be identified as the sacred home of Kuan-yin by Chinese as well as foreign pilgrims.

Leading Buddhist leaders in the late Ming were not always happy about the overemphasis on making pilgrimages. Faure has discussed the Ch'an tendency to dissolve place back to empty space (see chapter 4 of this volume). Indeed, from the enlightened perspective of *śūnyatā*, Potalaka is nowhere as well as everywhere. Chu-hung criticized the zeal of pilgrims in risking their lives by sailing the stormy ocean. He asked rhetorically:

> Did not the sutras say that bodhisattvas appear everywhere? Then there is no need to go very far. If you always maintain the heart of compassion and practice the deeds of compassion like the bodhisattva, even if you do not leave your own home, you are already looking at Potalaka; and even if you do not see Kuan-yin's golden visage, you are already with the bodhisattva moment to moment. (*Yun-chi Chu-hung*, 4:48a)

In true Ch'an fashion, in order to prevent people from forming attachment, Chu-hung deconstructed the myth of Potalaka and denied that Kuan-yin was found there only. But it was the great popularity of P'u-t'o pilgrimage in his time that incited his criticism. Even though Kuan-yin might not be found only on P'u-t'o, many people, especially pilgrims, found it comforting to believe that she was always there. To anchor Kuan-yin on P'u-t'o, a constant effort of constructing the island (both physically and metaphorically) was needed. The identity between the island P'u-t'o and the scriptural Potalaka had to be therefore repeatedly claimed. As the 1698 chronicle put it:

> P'u-t'o is the bodhimaṇḍa (*tao-ch'ang* 道場) of Kuan-yin. This is mentioned clearly in the Buddhist scriptures. An obscure place in China thus became known in the world because of secret texts hidden in the dragon's palace and Sanskrit scriptures from the Western regions. Thus we know that the perfect and bright in the ten directions all are manifestations of the Buddha. They are not restricted to the golden ground of Jetavana or the Indian palace of Sravasti. Take a look at P'u-t'o today: Is there any difference between it and the description found in the Buddhist scriptures? Does the bodhimaṇḍa today differ from that of yore when the great bodhisattva preached the dharma surrounded by the holy assembly? Someone may object, saying that auspicious gatherings do not occur often and the dharma feast can no longer be repeated. Therefore there is a difference between the present and the past. But can we really deny that the flowers, fruits, trees, streams, and ponds that we see now are not the realms of the bright and perfect? The Ch'an master Fo-yin Liao-yuan once said, "Green hills filling your eyes are there for you to see." Master Ch'eng Ming-tao was said to have immediately achieved enlightenment when he heard this. Travelers who come to P'u-t'o today must see everything with attention. Ordinary mortals are attached to phenomena. That is why some of them may have doubts. Recalling that the bodhisattva is said to have sat on a precious diamond throne, they think that the rocks on the island are crude and strange. But they fail to realize that mountains, rivers, grasses, and trees are originally formed by people's deluded thoughts. Because the Buddha's mind ground is wondrously bright, all that the Buddha sees are gold and jewels. One should study well the *Avataṃsaka*, *Sūraṅgama*, *Lotus*, and *Nirvāṇa* sutras. Only then will one know that all the famous mountain bodhimandas are indeed the places where Buddha lives. (*PTSC* 1698, 4:2b–3b)

Construction and deconstruction, founding and decline, building and rebuilding—these are some of the cycles P'u-t'o has experienced. Through all these changing fortunes, pilgrims were always in the midst of everything. What we see in the case of P'u-t'o is one example of how the Chinese created a Buddhist sacred landscape on their own land.

NOTES

1. This chapter is part of a book on the cult of Kuan-yin where I deal in greater depth with the issues raised here. In 1986–87 while I was doing research in China, I lived in Hangchow for six months and did fieldwork interviewing pilgrims coming to Upper T'ien-chu Monastery and P'u-t'o. (In the book I discuss myths about Kuan-yin told through women pilgrims' songs and miracles attributed to her. Readers may

also find relevant material in my videotape *Kuan-yin Pilgrimage* (1989) and other publications. I gratefully acknowledge the support I received from the American Council of Learned Societies, the Committee on Scholarly Communication with the People's Republic of China, and the Research Council of Rutgers University in carrying out my research on Kuan-yin.

2. References to such miraculously formed images can be found in standard collections such as *Fa-yuan chu-lin* 法苑珠林 and *T'ai-p'ing kuang-chi* 太平廣記. Similar phenomena are reported in Hinduism and Catholicism.

3. Pilgrimages to this sacred site have continued down the ages. In September 1986, I interviewed Hsu Li-kung 許立功 and Ming-ta 明達, the chairman and the secretary of the Shensi Buddhist Association. Both were natives of Shensi and were familiar with the local tradition, referring to Kuan-yin as "dragon-taming Kuan-yin" (Hsiang-lung Kuan-yin 降龍觀音). But in their version, Kuan-yin appeared as an old woman, not a monk. A temple (called Sheng-shou Ssu) previously stood at the base of the mountain. Inside the temple were the wall paintings depicting Kuan-yin's act of salvation that Hsu saw in the 1940s. Near the temple was a cave at whose entrance an image representing Kuan-yin's "flesh body" was enshrined. (Both the temple and the image were destroyed during the Cultural Revolution.)

From the base of the mountain to the top terrace where the Yuan-kuang Ssu was, seventy-two small temples called *t'ang-fang miao* 湯房廟 (soup-house temple) lined the way. Each temple maintained relationships with specific villages. During the Ta Kuan-yin miao-hui 大觀音廟會 (Great Temple Fair of Kuan-yin) pilgrimage season, which lasted from the twenty-fifth day of the fifth month until the nineteenth day of the sixth month, pilgrim associations (*hsiang-hui* 香會) from these specific villages would donate soup and water to these temples, which provided lodgings to pilgrims who brought their own food. This was a very similar arrangement to the *ch'a-p'eng* maintained by pilgrim associations that Naquin discusses in the chapter on Miao-feng Shan (chapter 8 of this volume). Ming-ta participated in the pilgrimage activities of 1948. He recalled that the area was crowded with people. Pilgrims came with bands of musicians. The tune they played was always the same, but the lyrics varied; the last sentence, however, always ended with "Everyone calls on Buddha's name (*jen-jen nien-fo* 人人念佛)." In the valley were *mao-p'eng* 茅蓬 (thatched huts) where ascetics meditated. Hsu told me that pilgrims had begun to return to Nan Wu-t'ai in the early 1980s, even though only a few of those small temples remained. Monks had also started their efforts to rebuild the two large monasteries.

4. For more examples of Hangchow temples that grew as a result of their White-robed Kuan-yin images, see *Yen-yu Ssu-ming-chih* 16:15a–b.

5. This tradition has apparently continued to the present. In the spring of 1987, from mid-February to early May, I observed and interviewed pilgrims who came to Hangchow for the spring pilgrimage (*ch'un-hsiang* 春香). I described the organization of pilgrims' groups and the activities of pilgrims who came to Upper T'ien-chu in the paper I prepared for the conference on Pilgrims and Sacred Sites in China (Bodega Bay, California, January 2–7, 1989). The most interesting discovery for me was that the women pilgrims were familiar with the story of Princess Miao-shan, whom they immortalized by the songs they sang, called *Kuan-yin ching* 觀音經. I recorded about twenty and transcribed a few in the conference paper "Miracles, Pilgrimage Sites, and the Cult of Kuan-yin" (see also Yü 1989).

6. The 1704 gazetteer mentions all three, but earlier gazetteers only Mei Fu. The 1924 gazetteer shows skepticism about the legend of Ko Hung (*PTSC* 1924, 525).

7. Mountain gazetteers are important sources for the study of Mount Wu-t'ai, Mount T'ai, Huang Shan, and Wu-tang Shan, which are discussed in the chapters by Gimello, Wu and Dudbridge, Cahill, and Lagerwey respectively.

8. Such travel accounts to Mount Potalaka were well known in India and Tibet. Tucci mentions two Tibetan accounts: one *Po ta la'i lam yig*, contained in the *bsTan-'gyur*, was written by Spyan ras gzigs dban p'yug, supposed to be Avalokiteśvara himself; the other, an account written by Tāranātha (b. 1575) in which the travel of Śāntivarman to Potala is narrated, is later than the first. The book Sheng mentioned could be the *Po ta la'i lam yig*. On the other hand, it could be some earlier book, for "a travel to Potala is already known to Hsuan-tsang, viz., to an author who wrote some centuries before the *Po ta la'i lam yig* of which we are speaking; this, in fact, is certainly late as its contamination with Śaiva ideas (the linga) clearly shows." In this account known to Hsuan-tsang, Mount Potalaka is east of Malaya Mountain. One reaches its summit via a winding and narrow path over cliffs and gorges. At the summit is a lake from which flows a river that runs twenty times around the mountain. In a stone temple Kuan-tzu-tsai Bodhisattva dwells. Many devotees attempt to reach that place, but very few succeed. The people living at the foot of the mountain who worship him are sometimes blessed by a vision of the Bodhisattva in the aspect of Paśupata Tīrthika or Maheśvara (Tucci 1958, 409–500).

9. By the late Ming, however, the fame of Upper T'ien-chu was overshadowed by that of P'u-t'o. Promoters of Upper T'ien-chu argued that it could substitute for P'u-t'o. Although Kuan-yin of Upper T'ien-chu and Kuan-yin of P'u-t'o were the same, "when one comes to Upper T'ien-chu, one does not have to go to P'u-t'o. This is because the small can contain the great, for this accords with the rounded view (*yuan* 圓). However, if one goes to P'u-t'o, one must then come to Upper T'ien-chu. This is because one should not neglect what is nearby in favor of what is far away, for that would make one fall into the one-sided view of partiality (*p'ien* 偏)" (*STCC* 1980, 66).

10. The existence of regional Kuan-yin cultic sites that did not achieve national stature was proven by the story about a third pilgrimage site that Sheng mentioned in passing; Mount Wu-ling 霧靈 (Misty Efficacy), near Peking, was devoted to the cult of White-robed Kuan-yin. Sheng related the custom of yearly pilgrimages made by devotees who came to the mountain to seek visions of Kuan-yin. She sometimes appeared to them clad in white, but she seldom showed her face. At night "heavenly lamps" (*t'ien-teng* 天燈) flickered mysteriously like stars or torches. Water in the streams flowing in the valley rose and ebbed with the tides; it was rumored that the streams were connected with the ocean, implying perhaps another connection with P'u-t'o (*PTSC* 1361, *T* 2101:1138c). Except for Sheng, Mount Wu-ling would have remained unknown to us. There must be other sites like it waiting to be discovered. The proliferation of similar regional pilgrimage centers and their possible competition would be a fascinating topic for research. Which site survives and which site disappears into the crevices of history would make an interesting story. Mountain gazetteers surely constitute one powerful mechanism to safeguard a site from possible oblivion.

11. Shiyu Li and Susan Naquin discussed the relationship between the Empress

Dowager Li and this mysterious Nine-lotus Bodhisattva in their article on the Bao-ming Temple (Li and Naquin 1988, 160–61).

Chou Shao-liang, curator of the Buddhist artifacts and library of Fa-yuan Ssu, Peking, provided further information about Empress Dowager Li's effort to promote this cult. Among his collections was the text of the scripture allegedly dictated by the bodhisattva to the empress dowager in her dream. I am grateful that he allowed me to make a copy. Chou also told me that there were at least three stelae still in existence. The first stele, titled "Nine-lotus Bodhisattva," was carved in 1587 and was originally found inside a stupa in Yen-shou Ssu in Pa-li-chuang, in the Peking suburbs. The second stele, named "Boy Worshiping Kuan-yin," was carved in 1589 and was originally housed in Sheng-an Ssu but is now in the courtyard of Fa-yuan Ssu. The third stele, called "Image of Nine-lotus Kuan-yin," was carved in 1592 and originally housed in Kuang-hua Ssu (also in Peking). The carvings are similar in composition and execution. They make it very clear that the Nine-lotus Bodhisattva is no other than Kuan-yin. They show the White-robed Kuan-yin sitting leisurely on a balcony. She looks at the pond below from which nine enormous lotuses rise in bloom. Behind her, luxurious bamboos fill the background; a white parrot sits prominently on the branches. On her right, a vase containing willow branches sits on a lotus pedestal. In the lower left corner, the boy pilgrim Sudhana (the 1592 stele alone also shows both Sudhana and Dragon Princess, who stands in the lower right corner) worships her with folded hands. As we shall see later, with the exception of the lotuses in the pond, all the iconographic characteristics of Potalaka Kuan-yin are present. The 1587 stele also contains a tribute to his mother penned by the Wan-li Emperor himself. It says that because of the queen mother's benevolence and compassion, Heaven has been moved to send down auspicious lotuses. To commemorate this lucky event and pre-serve its memory for future generations, an image of Kuan-yin is thereby inscribed on stone.

12. In the preface dated 1403, the empress explained the origin of this sutra. She received a visit from Kuan-yin, who conducted her to the Western Paradise and dictated the text of the sutra. Kuan-yin encouraged the empress to chant the sutras and mantras. Such chanting, she noted, will protect the faithful from all worries and sufferings. Like the "Universal Door" chapter of the *Lotus sutra*, this scripture will save the person from all kinds of danger. It will help dead ancestors of nine genera-tions back achieve deliverance. It will bring intelligent sons to the couple who have no heir. It will prevent a person from going to the Avici Hell. I discuss this sutra in the chapter "Buddhism in the Ming," *Cambridge History of China*, vol. 8 (forthcoming).

13. This copy is in the private collection of Chou Shao-liang in Peking. Another scripture glorifying the same deity but from the Taoist point of view was written at the same time. It was entitled *T'ai-shang Lao-chün shuo Tzu-tsai T'ien-hsien Chiu-lien Chih-sheng ying-hua tu-shih chen-ching* 太上老君說自在天仙九蓮至聖應化度世真經 (The true scripture of the Heavenly Immortal of Perfect Freedom, Nine-lotus Su-preme Sage's responding to transformations and saving the world as spoken by the Very High Old Lord). The copy kept at the Rare Book Section of the Chinese Bud-dhist Artifacts and Library in Fa-yuan Ssu, Peking, is also dated 1616. It contains the same imperial dedication at the back as that found in the Buddhist scripture.

The Buddhist apocryphal sutra begins with a dialogue between the Buddha and Kuan-yin who, grieved by the sufferings of mankind brought about by their own ignorance and evil deeds, asks the Buddha for succor. Buddha, in reply, makes a prediction about the appearance of the Nine-lotus Bodhisattva, who will bring peace and happiness to the world. Using identical language traditionally applied to the Western Paradise, Buddha describes the kingdom ruled by this bodhisattva. The sutra ends by urging people to chant diligently the sutra and especially the mantras revealed here. Without spelling it out in detail, the scripture nevertheless implies a close relationship between Kuan-yin and Nine-lotus Bodhisattva who, in turn, is made to point to Empress Dowager Li and her son, Emperor Wan-li. The sutra provides a possible explanation about the strange name "nine-lotus" and the presence of large lotus flowers on the stelae depicting Kuan-yin. The bodhisattva is described as intimately connected with lotus flowers, for they issue forth from her heart, are realized by her nature, seen by her eyes, heard by her ears, smelled by her nose, spat out by her mouth, grown from the top of her head, sat on by her body, and stepped upon by her feet (*Fo-shuo Ta-tz'u Chih-sheng Chiu-lien P'u-sa hua-shen tu-shih chen-ching*, 13).

14. The gazetteer of P'u-t'o attributed this to Kuan-yin's intervention. Kuan-yin was supposed to have appeared in the form of an old woman to Emperor K'ang-hsi while he toured Chekiang. The two had a conversation, and she suddenly disappeared. When Huang Ta-lai came forward to protect the emperor, the emperor asked about his position and then inquired about the conditions on the Chusan archipelago. Huang used this opportunity to make a detailed report about P'u-t'o. This report led to the emperor's gift of a thousand ounces of gold to build the monastery. The gazetteers described a similar encounter between Lan Li, the new regional commander, and an old lady carrying a fish basket in front of the Cave of Tidal Sound in 1690. Both Huang and Lan helped in rebuilding P'u-t'o, and they received sacrifices from the grateful monks at their "living shrines" (*sheng-tz'u* 生祠) (*PTSC* 1924, 190–91; 462–66). Porcelain figures depicting Kuan-yin holding a fish basket and attended by Sudhana and the Dragon Princess were made during the K'ang-hsi period. This was the "Fish-basket Kuan-yin." In *pao-chüan* and popular literature composed during the Ch'ing, Kuan-yin was often described as being an old woman (*lao-mu* 老母) or referred to as "Old Mother," echoing the Venerable and Eternal Mother worshiped by the sectarians. In fact, Kuan-yin was proclaimed by the same people as an incarnation of their goddess. The female founder of some sectarian sects, in turn, was believed to be the incarnation of Kuan-yin (Li and Naquin 1988, 180). The relationships between Kuan-yin and other female deities, as well as between her and female devotees, are complicated and deserve further study.

15. The most recent gazetteer was compiled in 1924 by Wang Heng-yen, an instructor at the local academy. The project was under the joint sponsorship of the magistrate of Ting-hai and Master Yin-kuang, one of the most eminent monks in modern China, who lived on P'u-t'o for more than thirty years. Wang used the materials found in previous gazetteers but also carried out on-site investigations (*ts'ai-fang*). He showed judicious judgment in his selections and took an impartial attitude toward both monasteries. To differentiate his gazetteer from those before, he called it *P'u-t'o Lo-chia hsin-chih* 普陀洛迦新志 (A new gazetteer of Potalaka).

16. This was in relation to an event in 1590: Ta-chih, the abbot of Fa-yü, was supposed to have played a major role in helping a local official who punished P'u-t'o monks and then suffered from divine retribution as a result. The 1698 gazetteer noted

the incident but refrained from either praising Ta-chih or blaming Chen-piao (*PTSC* 1698, 10:10a–b). T'u Lung, the original writer of the article, was far from being so judicious. He devoted six pages to this story, which he called "An Account of Efficacious Response on Mount P'u-t'o." There were two abbots on P'u-t'o—Ta-chih and Chen-piao. T'u described Ta-chih as a model of strict discipline and religious austerity. Being humble and patient, he was beloved by everyone. Conversely, Chen-piao was described as being arrogant, violent, and obstinate. He did not observe monastic rules, but ate meat and drank wine. Moreover, he would beat novices at the slightest excuse and often injure them. A very different picture of this abbot was found in later gazetteers. He was said to be honest and straightforward. He was known for his strict observance of discipline. He was friendly to serious practitioners, therefore was respected and beloved by famous monks. He built fifty-three hermitages on the island. When Ta-chih arrived at the island to build the Northern Monastery, he was said to have received much help from Chen-piao (*PTSC* 1832, 15:6a–7a; 1924, 353).

17. This story was recorded in *Fo-tsu t'ung-chi*, *chüan* 42, under Kai-cheng first year (836). It made no direct reference to P'u-t'o (*T* 2035, 385). The Ch'an master was described as from Mount Chung-nan, a site holy to both Buddhists and Taoists and near Southern Mount Wu-t'ai. At the end of the story, the master returned to Mount Chung-nan. Earlier gazetteers of P'u-t'o mentioned this story, but they did not date the founding of the island from this event (*PTSC* 1589, 3:20).

18. However, *Fo-tsu t'ung-chi* gives 858 and *Pao-ch'ing Ssu-ming chih* 寶慶四明志 (Gazetteer of Ningpo; compiled in 1225–27) gives 859. The latter provides more details about the history of the image. Under the entry on K'ai-yuan Monastery, one of the monasteries in Ningpo, we read that it was originally built in 740, during the K'ai-yuan era, and was destroyed in the Hui-ch'ang persecution. But in the early years of Ta-ch'ung (847–59), at the request of the governor, it was allowed to be rebuilt on the old site of another temple. Among the treasures of K'ai-yuan Monastery was the image of the "Kuan-yin Who Refused to Leave." The gazetteer then explained the origin of the image. In 859 the Japanese monk Egaku made a pilgrimage to Mount Wu-t'ai. When he came to a temple on the Central Terrace, he saw an image of Kuan-yin looking elegant, beautiful, and joyous. He begged to take this image back to his country. The monks agreed. So Egaku put the image on a sedan chair and carried it all the way to Ningpo to board the boat. But the image became so heavy it could not be lifted up. He had to ask all the merchants traveling with him for help before the image could be put on board. When they passed P'u-t'o, waves rose in anger, and there was a great storm. Boatmen became greatly frightened. Egaku had a dream in which a foreign monk said to him, "If you put me safely on this mountain, I will send you off with favorable wind." Egaku wept in gratitude and after waking told the people about his dream. Everyone was much astonished. After building a room on the island and respectfully settling the image there, they left. That is why the image was called the "Kuan-yin Who Refused to Leave." A while later, monk Tao-tsai of the K'ai-yuan Ssu dreamed that Kuan-yin wanted to come to stay in his temple, so he went to P'u-t'o to welcome the image and took it home to be installed. Townspeople in Ningpo prayed to the image and always received responses. So the temple came to be known as "Kuan-yin of Auspicious Responses" (Kuan-yin Jui-ying yuan). During the T'ai-p'ing hsing-kuo era (976–83) of the Sung, the monastery was refurbished and had the name changed to Wu-t'ai Kuan-yin-yuan, indicating that the image

originally came from Mount Wu-t'ai (*Pao-ch'ing Ssu-ming chih* 11:10a–b). Saeki Tomi regarded the date 916 as unreliable, for Egaku, who was a historical person, was reported to have gone to China in 839. It is unlikely that he stayed for 77 years (Saeki 1961, 383–84).

19. The purple gold–hued form is the iconography for Kuan-yin in the *Kuan-shih-yin san-mei ching* 觀世音三昧經 (Sutra of the samādhi of Kuan-yin), a scripture composed in China during the Six Dynasties; it provided one of the textual bases for Kuan-yin worship at that time. As Makita points out, many miracle accounts about Kuan-yin's epiphanies during that period described Kuan-yin's appearance in this way (Makita 1970, 111–55).

20. Shih Hao held a series of government posts; he started as an instructor in the Imperial University in 1157 and ended up serving jointly as the chief councilor of the right and commissioner at the Bureau of Military Affairs in 1165. He was a friend of Chang Chiu-cheng (1092–1159), a prominent Confucian literatus and lay Buddhist who followed the Ch'an master Ta-hui Tsung-kao (1089–1163). Shih also sponsored the careers of Lu Chiu-yuan (1139–93), Yeh Shih (1150–1223), and Chu Hsi (1130–1200). Thus by all accounts, he was well connected with the establishment (Davis 1986, 53–75).

21. *Pao-ch'ing Ssu-ming chih*, the local gazetteer compiled during Pao-ch'ing era (1225–27), recorded Shih's pilgrimage (20:9b–10a). Another local gazetteer compiled in the Yuan, the *Ch'ang-kuo chou t'u chih*, retold the story and provided a verbatim transcription of Shih's essay (6:7a–8a). It is of course also recorded in the gazetteers of P'u-t'o.

22. Among the accounts given in the chapter on "Miracles" in the chronicles, only one refers to Kuan-yin as sitting in the pose of royal ease (*PTSC* 1924, 177). Kuan-yin images created with this iconography are perhaps most familiar to modern visitors to major museums, for many fine specimens have survived from the Sung. In view of the great popularity of this type of Kuan-yin image at that time, it is strange that not more pilgrims saw Kuan-yin appear in this form.

23. See chapters 17, 22, 26, 42, 49, 57, and 58. See also Kung Lieh-fei and Wang Tao-hsing (50).

24. There have been many studies on *pao-chüan* in the last two decades. These popular texts provide insight on the religious and social realities of late imperial Chinese society. See works by Overmyer, Shek, and Sawada.

25. The account of this trip was called *Hai chih* (Record of a sea journey). Chang's description of the pilgrims' boat (*hsiang-ch'uan* 香船) could frighten away any would-be pilgrim. "A pilgrims' boat is a living hell. 'Good men' sit on the top deck and 'good women' the deck below. The boat is enveloped with sails and covers, and no air is allowed to circulate. Within the close quarters, several hundred unwashed people urinated and defecated. The persons who take care of pilgrims' food, drink, and all other kinds of need are called *hsiang-t'ou* 香頭 (pilgrims' leaders). They are monks from this or that temple" (213). Despite his critical attitude, Chang apparently observed the formalities of a pilgrim. He kept a vegetarian diet for more than a month, the entire length of his P'u-t'o trip. When he finally ate herring, his favorite fish, in Ting-hai, he had become so unaccustomed to its taste that he threw up (212). The sea voyage must have been very uncomfortable and frightening. Another literatus, who made the trip in 1737 in a presumably much better-equipped boat, re-

marked wryly that he was tossed up and down like "a grain of rice in a winnowing basket" and vomited throughout the crossing (Ch'i Chou-hua, 1987, 152). I am indebted to Pei-yi Wu, who told me of Chang Tai's account of his trip to P'u-t'o.

26. By the seventeenth century, with the appearance of the new iconography of Potalaka Kuan-yin, in order to provide symmetry for the two attendants, the original Sudhana's Cave came to be known as Dragon Princess's Cave and a rock nearby became known as Sudhana's Rock; there the boy was supposed to have worshiped Kuan-yin when he first came to the sacred island.

27. Ta-chih was a native of Ma-ch'eng, Hupeh, and received tonsure at age fifteen. He went to Mount Ox-head in Nanking in 1547; the next year, after he received full ordination in Peking, he went to Mount Wu-t'ai, where he stayed for five years. In 1558 he made a pilgrimage to Mount Omei and stayed on top of the mountain for twelve years without leaving the area. In 1574 he made a pilgrimage to Mount Chin-hua in the north of Szechuan (about eighty *li* from Mount Omei). Many pilgrims traveled between these two pilgrimage sites, but because there were no resting places along the way, it was a very arduous journey. Ta-chih established the Golden Lotus Monastery to benefit pilgrims.

28. The 1705 gazetteer contains two stele inscriptions of the stupa (11:44a–47a, 47a–48a). The relics "did not always present the same appearance to different people. Persons of inferior character saw nothing but a black object; those of higher moral standing saw a white object; to those of moderately good character the relics assumed a red appearance; and saintly people saw the figure of Buddha" (Johnston 1976, 315).

29. Johnston was far less impressed by the Cave of Tidal Sound and offered a rational explanation for the visions of Kuan-yin: "As a cave the Ch'ao-yin-tung is disappointing, for it is merely a perpendicular rent in the rocks by the sea-shore, and would attract no particular attention but for its sacred associations. At times the tidal waters rush into it with resounding roar and dashing spray, and the waves, says a monkish chronicler, lash the cliff walls like the tossed mane of a wild animal. If the critical Western enquirer insists upon extorting a prosaic explanation of the ghostly appearances of Kuan-yin, he may perhaps find one in the fact that at certain times, when atmospheric and tidal conditions are favorable, a shaft of sunlight streams into the cave through a gap in the roof called the *t'ien-ch'uang* 天窗, or 'heaven's window,' and strikes athwart the flying foam. The cave then seems to be filled with a tremulous haze, in which the unbeliever sees nothing but sunlit spray, but which to the devout worshipper is a luminous veil through which the 'Pusa of Love and Pity' becomes visible to the eyes of her faithful suppliants" (299).

30. Karl Gutzlaff visited P'u-t'o to convert the monks to Christianity in the 1830s. He noted that there were two large monasteries and some sixty small ones. About two thousand monks lived on the island (Gutzlaff 1968, 443). Boerschmann visited P'u-t'o in 1908 and reported that there were more than seventy small temples and more than a hundred hermitages. About fifteen hundred monks lived on the island, with two hundred to three hundred each in the two large monasteries (Boerschmann 1911, 11). A Chinese monk went to P'u-t'o on pilgrimage in 1915 and observed that aside from the three large monasteries, there were more than eighty small temples and a hundred hermitages. The small temples could house as many as thirty to forty monks at capacity (ten to twenty usually), and one hermitage could house several people without any problem. Theoretically, ten thousand to twenty thousand monks could be accommo-

dated by the various temples. But except during the height of the pilgrimage seasons of the second and sixth months, when six thousand to seven thousand monks would come to stay on P'u-t'o, only about two thousand monks usually lived on the island. He commented that there were more images of Kuan-yin and other deities than monks on P'u-t'o (Hsin-fan 1915, 17).

BIBLIOGRAPHY

Sources Cited by Abbreviation

CTSMTC   *Ch'ien-tao Ssu-ming t'u-ching* 乾道四明圖經. By Chang Chin 張津 et al. Compiled in 1169. 12 *chüan*.

DMB   *Dictionary of Ming Biography, 1368–1644*. Edited by L. Carrington Goodrich and Chaoying Fang. 2 vols. New York: Columbia University Press, 1976.

FTTC   *Fo-tsu t'ung chi* 佛祖統記. Compiled by Chih-p'an 志磐 ca. 1260. *T*. 2035.

HCFC   *Hang-chou fu-chih* 杭州府志. Separate issue on customs and products. 8 *chüan*. 1924.

HCLAC   *Hsiang-ch'un Lin-an chih* 咸淳臨安志. Compiled by Ch'ien Shuo-yu 潛說友 in 1268.

HHYLC   *Hsi-hu yu-lan chih* 西湖遊覽志. Compiled by T'ien Ju-ch'eng 田汝成 in 1526. 24 *chüan*.

PTSC   *P'u-t'o shan-chih* 普陀山志. There are 8 editions:

1. *Pu-t'o Lo-chia Shan ch'uan* 補陀洛迦山傳. Compiled by Sheng Hsi-ming 盛熙明 in 1361. 1 *chüan*. *T*. 2101.

2. *Pu-t'o Lo-chia shan chih* 補陀洛迦山志. Compiled by Hou Chi-kao 侯繼高 in 1589. 6 *chüan*. Tokyo: Naikaku Bunko.

3. *Ch'ung-hsiu P'u-t'o shan chih* 重修普陀山志. Compiled by Chou Ying-pin 周應賓 in 1607. 6 *chüan*. Reprinted in *Chung-kuo fo-ssu shih-chih hui-k'an* 中國佛寺史志彙刊, 1st collection, vol. 9. Taiwan: Ming-wen, 1980.

4. *Tseng-hsiu Nan-hai P'u-t'o Shan chih* 增修南海普陀山志. Compiled by Ch'iu Lien 裘璉 in 1698. 15 *chüan*.

5. *Tseng-hsiu Nan-hai P'u-t'o Shan chih* 增修南海普陀山志. Compiled by Chu Chin 朱瑾 and Ch'en Chün 陳璿 in 1705. 15 *chüan*.

6. *Ch'ung-hsiu Nan-hai P'u-t'o Shan chih* 重修南海普陀山志. Compiled by Hsu Yen 許琰 in 1739. 20 *chüan*.

7. *Chung-hsiu Nan-hai P'u-t'o Shan chih*. Compiled by Ch'in Yao-tseng 秦耀曾 in 1832. 20 *chüan*. Reprinted in *Chung-kuo ming-shan sheng-chi chih tsung-kan* 中國名山勝蹟志叢刊, 6th collection, vols. 50–53, edited by Shen Yun-lung 沈雲龍. Taiwan: Wen-hai, 1982.

8. *P'u-t'o Lo-chia hsin-chih*. 普陀洛迦新志. Compiled by Wang Heng-yen 王亨彥 in 1924. 12 *chüan*. Reprinted in *Chung-kuo fo-ssu shih-chih hui-k'an*, 1st collection, vol. 10. Taiwan: Ming-wen, 1980.

STCC   *Hang-chou Shang-t'ien-chu Chiang-ssu chih* 杭州上天竺講寺志. Compiled by Shih Kuang-pin 釋廣賓. 15 *chüan*. Reprint of 1897 edition. Contained in *Chung-kuo fo-ssu shih-chih hui-k'an*, 1st collection, vol. 26. Taiwan: Ming-wen, 1980.

Other Sources

Bishop, Peter. 1989. *The Myth of Shangri-La: Tibet, Travel Writing, and the Western Creation of Sacred Landscape.* Berkeley: University of California Press.

Boerschmann, Ernst. 1911. *Die Baukunst und religiöses Kultur der Chinesen.* Vol. 1, *P'u T'o Shan.* Berlin.

Brook, Timothy. 1988. *Geographical Sources of Ming-Qing History.* Ann Arbor: Center for Chinese Studies, University of Michigan.

Ch'ang-kuo chou t'u chih 昌國州圖志. 1297–1307. Compiled by Feng Fu-ching 馮福京 et al. 7 *chüan.*

Chang Tai 張岱. 1957. "Hai chih" 海志. In *Lang-hsuan wen-chi* 瑯嬛文集. Included in *Chin-tai san-wen ch'ao* 近代散文抄, edited by Shen Ch'i-yuan 沈啟元. Hong Kong: T'ien-hung Press.

Cheng Kuang-tsu 鄭光祖. 1845. *I-pan-lu tsa-shu* 一斑錄雜述.. In *Chou-ch'e suo chih* 舟車所至.

Ch'i Chou-hua 齊周華. 1987. "Yu Nan-hai P'u-t'o shan chi" 遊南海普陀山志. In *Ming-shan tsang fu-pen* 名山藏副本. Shanghai: Ku-chi.

Davis, Richard L. 1986. *Court and Family in Sung China, 960–1279: Bureaucratic Success and Kinship Fortunes for the Shih of Ming-chou.* Durham, N.C.: Duke University Press.

Dudbridge, Glen. 1982. "Miao-shan on Stone." *Harvard Journal of Asiatic Studies* 42, 2 (December): 589–614.

———. 1978. *The Legend of Miao-shan.* Oxford Oriental Monographs, no. 1. London: Ithaca Press.

Eliade, Mircea. 1959. *The Sacred and the Profane.* New York: Harper & Row.

Fitch, Robert F. 1929. *Pootoo Itineraries, Describing the Chief Places of Interest with a Special Trip to Lo-chia Shan.* Shanghai: Kelly & Walsh.

Gutzlaff, Karl. 1834. *Journal of Three Voyages along the Coast of China in 1831, 1832, 1833.* London. Taipei reprint, 1968.

Hsieh Kuo-chen 謝國幀. 1985. "P'u-t'o yu-chi" 普陀遊記. In *Chung-kuo ku-tai yu-chi hsuan* 中國古代遊記選 2:239–45. Peking: Chung-kuo lü-yu she.

Hsin-fan 心梵. 1915. "P'u-t'o li-fo kuei-lai te kan-hsiang" 普陀禮佛歸來的感想. *Hai-ch'ao-yin* 海潮音 11, 9:17–24.

Hsu Ming-te 徐明德. 1987. "Lun shih-ssu chih shih-ch'i shi-chi Ning-po-kang tsai Chung-Jih ching-chi wen-hua chiao-liu shih shang te chung-yao ti-wei" 論十四至十七世紀寧波港在中日經濟文化交流史上的重要地位. *Tang-tai Shih-chieh T'ung-hsun* 當代世界通訊 (Chekiang: Chekiang tang-tai kuo-chi wen-t'i yen-chiu-hui), no. 3:120–41.

Johnston, Reginald Fleming. 1976. *Buddhist China.* London: John Murray, 1913. Reprint. San Francisco: Chinese Materials Center.

Kobayashi Taichiro 小林太一郎. 1953. "Tōdai Daihi Kannon" 唐代大悲觀音. *Bukkyō Bijutsu* 20:3–27.

Kung Lieh-fei 龔烈沸 and Wang Tao-hsing 王道興. N.d. *Hai-t'ien fo-kuo P'u-t'o Shan* 海天佛國普陀山. Chekiang: Writers' Union of the Chou-shan Region.

Li, Thomas Shiyu, and Susan Naquin. 1988. "The Baoming Temple: Religion and the Throne in Ming and Qing China." *Harvard Journal of Asiatic Studies* 48, 1 (June): 131–88.

Makita Tairyō 牧田諦亮. 1970. *Rokuchō koyui Kanzeon okenki no kenkyū* 六朝古逸觀世音感應記の研究. Kyoto: Heirakuji Shoten.

Overmyer, Daniel L. 1976. *Folk Buddhist Religion: Dissenting Sects in Late Traditional China.* Cambridge: Harvard University Press.

———. 1978. "Boatmen and Buddhas." *History of Religions* 17, 3–4: 284–302.

Pao-ch'ing Ssu-ming chih 寶慶四明志. 1225–27. Compiled by Lo Chün 羅濬 et al. 21 chüan.

P'u-t'o pao-chüan 普陀寶卷. 1894 ed. Private collection of Wu Xiaoling of Peking. Blocks kept at Soochow, Ma-nao ching-fang.

Saeki Tomi 佐伯富. 1961. "Kinsei Chūgoku ni okeru Kannon shinkō" 近代中國に於ける觀音信仰. In *Tsukamoto Hakase Shōju Kinen Bukkyōshigaku Ronshū* 塚本博士頌壽紀念佛教史學論集, 372–89. Kyoto: Hozoken.

Sawada Mizuho 澤田瑞穂. 1975. *Zohō hōkan no kenkyū* 增補寶卷の研究. Tokyo: Kokusho kankokai.

Shek, Richard. 1980. "Religion and Society in Late Ming." Ph.D. dissertation, University of California at Berkeley.

Shiba, Yoshinobu. 1977. "Ningpo and Its Hinterland." In *The City in Late Imperial China*, edited by G. William Skinner, 391–439. Stanford: Stanford University Press.

Soper, Alexander C. 1960. "A Vacation Glimpse of the T'ang Temples of Ch'ang-an," *Artibus Asiae* 23:15–40.

Stein, Rolf A. 1986. "Avalokiteśvara/Kuan-yin: exemple de transformation d'un deus en déesse." *Cahiers d'Extrême-Asie*, no. 2:17–77.

Tsukamoto Zenryū 塚本善隆. 1955. "Kinsei Shina taishu no nyoshin Kannon shinkō" 近代支那大衆の女身觀音信仰. In *Yamaguchi Hakase Kanreki Kinen Indogaku Bukkyōgaku Ronsō* 山崎博士還曆紀念印度學佛教學論叢, 262–80. Kyoto: Hozoken.

Tucci, G. *Minor Buddhist Texts.* 1958. Part 2. Rome: Instituto Italiano per il Medio ed Estremo Oriente.

Yen-yu Ssu-ming chih 延祐四明志. 1320. Compiled by Yuan Chueh 袁桷.

Yu, Anthony C., trans. and ed. 1977–83. *Journey to the West.* 4 vols. Chicago: University of Chicago Press.

Yü, Chün-fang. 1989. "Miracles, Pilgrimage and the Cult of Kuan-yin." Paper delivered at the Conference on Pilgrims and Sacred Sites in China, Bodega Bay, Calif., January 1989.

———. 1990a. "Images of Kuan-yin in Folk Literature." *Chinese Studies* 8, 1 (June): 221–85.

———. 1990b. "Feminine Images of Kuan-yin in Post-T'ang China." *Journal of Chinese Religions*, no. 18 (Fall 1990): 61–89.

———. Forthcoming. "Buddhism in the Ming." In *Cambridge History of China.* Vol. 8, *Ming*, edited by F. W. Mote. Cambridge: Cambridge University Press.

Yun-ch'i Chu-hung 雲棲袾宏. 1973. *Chu-ch'uang san-pi* 竹窗三筆. In *Yun-ch'i fa-hui* 雲棲法彙. Published as *Lien-ch'ih Ta-shih Ch'üan-chi* 蓮池大師全集. 4 vols. Taiwan.

SIX

Huang Shan Paintings as Pilgrimage Pictures

James Cahill

Paintings of Huang Shan 黃山, the range of bare, precipitous, pine-clad and mist-hung peaks in southern Anhui province, are seen everywhere in China today; climbing the mountain is nearly obligatory for Chinese landscapists, most of whom have done pictures of it, some of them virtually devoting careers to it. Huang Shan is a familiar subject also in earlier painting, but there it is more localized and also limited in period: most Huang Shan paintings that survive before recent times are from the late Ming and early Ch'ing dynasties, the seventeenth and early eighteenth centuries, and most of them are by artists of the Anhui region or artists who spent periods of their lives there.

Paintings of Huang Shan have been studied in a number of their aspects: stylistic studies (Cahill 1982a and 1982b; Cahill 1981; Hsu 1975; Wright 1984; etc.); topographical studies that identify the places represented with actual places (Kohara 1971; Cahill 1981, chapter 4; Miyazaki 1985; Kōno 1986); biographical and chronological studies that try to determine when particular artists were there and when they painted their pictures (Kohara 1971; Chang 1987); studies of the religious and political meanings that came to be attached to the place (McDermott 1989). Here we will focus first on the character of the paintings as records of travel or guides to travel to Huang Shan and then on their aspect as recording or inspiring pilgrimages to Huang Shan. And, in keeping with the theme of this volume, we will attempt answers to the questions, What kinds of pilgrimages do these paintings represent, and what function did they perform in relation to the pilgrimages?

We will begin by setting a background against which these questions can be considered. The paintings of Huang Shan belong late in China's history and in Chinese painting history, but they are preceded by long, related developments: the founding of Buddhist temples on Huang Shan in the early centuries and the role they played in later times; literary accounts of travels to Huang Shan dating from the late Sung and after; the practice of making paintings depicting particular places or recording travel to particular places other than Huang Shan. The last include representations of sacred mountains, but we will not limit our discussion to those.

HUANG SHAN AS A SACRED MOUNTAIN

From the early part of Huang Shan's history we have no travel records, but we know that Buddhist temples were founded there as early as the eighth century. The Taoist presence on Huang Shan claims much greater antiquity but is difficult to separate from later accretions of legend. According to texts dating from the fourth century A.D. onward, the legendary Yellow Emperor came to Huang Shan late in his reign in search of the pill of immortality; he succeeded in his quest and established the seventy-two peaks as dwelling places for immortals or transcendants (McDermott 1989, 153). Among the accounts we will consider below, the writers of the earlier ones seem constantly aware that they are climbing a sacred mountain and express their sense of the numinous in the Huang Shan peaks. But as early as the late Sung, the date of the earliest of the extant travel records, a tendency toward secularization can be marked in perceptions of Huang Shan. McDermott (146) observes that the hold of Buddhism and Taoism on the mountain "began to slip by no later than the thirteenth century, when Huang-shan began to become the concern of literati from the surrounding prefectures, especially Hui-chou." This observation is borne out by changes in the content of the travel records, as we will see, and, although less clearly, probably also by changes in pictorial representations of the mountain.

A vision of Huang Shan constructed from the later literary accounts, then, would present it as more a secular than a sacred mountain or as sacred only in a special sense somewhat apart from organized religions, as we will argue below. In this respect, Huang Shan differs from the sacred mountains treated in other papers in this volume, which were centers of religious cults focused on some particular deity. To be sure, this secularized version of Huang Shan is doubtless colored by the special concerns of the literati, who, here as elsewhere, have the advantage of controlling our sources of information. A similar situation obtains in the history of Chinese painting: students of the subject are well aware that the accounts on which we base our understanding are affected, one might even say censored, by literati biases. We can assume that devout Buddhists continued to visit the Huang Shan temples, perhaps on purposeful trips that we could properly term pilgrimages, in the centuries after the Hui-chou literati had come to dominate travel to the mountain. But since, on the basis of known materials, it would appear that these Buddhist visitors did not write the travel accounts or paint or commission the paintings, they can occupy only a shadowy, hypothetical region as background to the concerns of this chapter.

In the 1679 gazetteer of the mountain, *Huang-shan chih ting-pen*, information on the Buddhist temples of Huang Shan is included in a short chapter titled "Buildings," along with information on a few Taoist temples and many pavilions, private villas, rest shelters, and bridges. This chapter is preceded by a long one on the Huang Shan scenery, chiefly the greater and lesser peaks, and followed by others on notable people associated with the mountain, travel accounts, and (longest of all) poems and other literary productions that Huang Shan had inspired. This weighting supports McDermott's observation; the temples of Huang Shan appear to have been, at least in later centuries, not so much objectives of pilgrimages in themselves as stopping places on pilgrimages pursued out of other, not primarily religious motives. From the travel accounts we know that they served as hostels, restaurants, and tourist information bureaus.[1] Nevertheless, since the temples appear in both the literary accounts and the paintings we will consider, a brief listing of the most important of them is in place here (map 6.1).

Hsiang-fu Ssu 祥符寺 (Auspicious Emblem Temple). Built during the K'ai-yuan era of the T'ang dynasty (713–42), it was the oldest of the Huang Shan temples. Originally named the Ling-ch'üan yuan 靈泉院 or Holy Spring Monastery, it was renamed in the Hsiang-fu era (1008–17) of the Sung dynasty. The temple is mentioned in the 1340 account of Wang Tse-min (see below) and others; situated at the base of the great peaks, near the hot spring, it was the standard setting-out place and hostel for climbers of Huang Shan.

Tz'u-kuang Ssu 慈光寺 (Compassionate Radiance Temple). Originally named the Chu-sha an 硃砂庵, Red Gravel Retreat, it was situated at the foot of the Red Gravel Peak part way up on the path to the summit. It was rebuilt by the monk P'u-men 普門 and renamed by the Wan-li Emperor (r. 1573–1620). It appears centrally in seventeenth- and eighteenth-century prints of Huang Shan and was a base from which serious climbers set out in their assaults on the great peaks.

Wen-shu Yuan 文殊院 (Mañjuśrī Monastery). Built on the Wen-shu t'ai 臺 or Mañjuśrī Terrace, the Mañjuśrī Monastery provides the best vantage point for viewing the great Huang Shan peaks. The T'ien-tu feng 天都峰 or Heavenly Capital Peak is directly across from it, and the Lien-hua feng 蓮華峰 or Lotus Peak is to the right. The temple was a latecomer to the mountain, built by the monk P'u-men at the beginning of the seventeenth century. The late Ming traveler Hsu Hung-tsu (Hsu Hsia-k'o) wrote, "Until one reaches the Mañjuśrī Monastery, one has not seen the real face of Huang Shan," and the couplet is still repeated. The Yü-p'ing lou 玉屏樓 or Jade Screen Hall is still there today; it is one of the two places on the mountain where climbers, at least foreigners, can stay overnight.

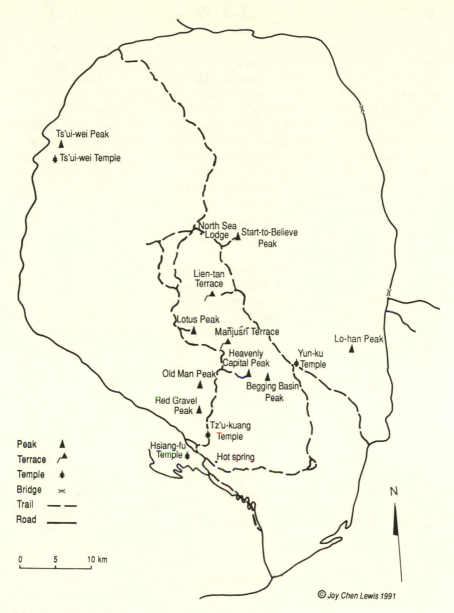

Ts'ui-wei Peak
▲

Ts'ui-wei Temple
♣

North Sea
Lodge   Start-to-Believe
              Peak
         ▲

Lien-tan
Terrace
▲

Lotus Peak
    ▲   Mañjuśrī Terrace
         ▲
         Heavenly   Yun-ku
         Capital Peak   Temple
Old Man Peak   ▲   ♣   ▲
    ▲   Lo-han Peak
Red Gravel   Begging Basin   ▲
    Peak ▲   Peak

         Tz'u-kuang
         Temple
Hsiang-fu   ♣
Temple ♣   Hot spring

Peak   ▲
Terrace   ⌃
Temple   ♣
Bridge   )(
Trail   – –
Road   —

0   5   10 km

N
▲

© Joy Chen Lewis 1991

Map 6.1. Huang Shan

Ts'ui-wei Ssu 翠薇寺 (Blue-green Temple). Built at the foot of the Ts'ui-wei Peak, the Blue-green Temple is said to have been founded by the Hemp-robed Monk 麻衣僧 when he came to Huang Shan from India in 882. A famous well was there, the water of which never flooded or dried up. This temple is also mentioned in Wang Tse-min's account.

Yun-ku Ssu 雲谷寺 (Cloud Valley Temple). Originally named the Chih-po Ch'an-yuan 擲鉢禪院 or Throw the Almsbowl Ch'an Monastery, it was given its present name in the Ming period. Situated between the Lohan Peak and the Po-yü 鉢盂 (Begging Basin) Peak, it was a mid-point resting place for those taking the east or "back" route up the mountain, as opposed to the frontal assault. (Today it is the base of a cable lift.) It was also called the Ch'eng-hsiang yuan 丞相院 (Prime Minister's Spring) because the Sung-period prime minister Ch'eng Yuan-feng 程元鳳, who was from Hui-chou, once studied there.

The Taoist lore of the mountain is preserved in an anonymous text ascribed to the Sung period titled *Huang-shan t'u-ching* (Picture classic of Huang Shan), which originally accompanied a set of (printed?) pictures, now lost and replaced, for the presently existing edition, with a series based on works by late Ming and early Ch'ing artists. The text provides a Taoist-geomantic reading of the mountain, peak by peak through all the thirty-six great ones, enumerating caves and springs, places where alchemy was practiced or medicinal herbs gathered, dragons sighted, miraculous cures performed. Sites of several Taoist temples are mentioned, in two cases later replaced by Buddhist temples. The text ends with a list of the rivers flowing outward from Huang Shan in all directions, a grand image that would reappear in Ch'ien Ch'ien-i's travel account, to be cited below. This Taoist vision of Huang Shan is the earliest, at least as it is recorded in texts; elements of it, as we will see, are found in the travel accounts of the following centuries, especially in the Ming, and in a few pictorial representations. Stories of the Yellow Emperor and immortals continued to make up an important part of the culture of Huang Shan in the Ch'ing. But there is little evidence for religious Taoist activity there in the later centuries.

LITERARY ACCOUNTS OF TRAVEL TO HUANG SHAN

A great many travel accounts by visitors to Huang Shan survive, the majority of them from the late Ming and after.[2] A selection of the most interesting has recently been published (Li I-min 1983), and what follows is based chiefly on the accounts included in this recent compilation. Li I-min points out in his preface that among sacred mountains Huang Shan was late in attaining prominence, being opened to relatively convenient travel only from the late sixteenth and early seventeenth century. Before that, climbers had no place to stay on the mountain and had to carry all their food, water, and bedding. Although several of the temples had been founded much earlier, the buildings as they existed in the late Ming mostly did not antedate that dynasty.

The succession of travel essays, from the thirteenth to the eighteenth century, documents the profound changes in how travelers described the mountain and to some degree, surely, how they experienced it, although we must make allowance for the constraints and conventions of the travel account genre itself.[3] Most of the early climbers were from nearby places in Anhui and Kiangsi. Wu Lung-han 吳龍翰, a historian from She-hsien in nearby Hui-chou prefecture, made the climb in 1268 with two friends and wrote a brief account. They spent three days on the mountain without meeting anyone else; they played the flute and drank wine and felt far from the human world, like immortals. Before descending they drank a toast to the grandest of the peaks, the Heavenly Capital Peak, vowing never to forget it. A Yuan-period scholar-official named Wang Tse-min 汪澤民, in a longer account written in 1340, gives detailed information on how to get there and writes of the awesome vista of the thirty-six peaks; the Heavenly Capital, he was told by a monk in a temple, was climbed only by herb gatherers who spent three days on the ascent. For him, too, Huang Shan was an abode of immortals and gods and a place the legendary Yellow Emperor, Huang-ti, had once visited.

Two early sixteenth-century accounts are found in the *Huang-shan chih ting-pen* (ch. 4). One by P'an Tan 潘旦 dated 1519 tells of how he traveled to Huang Shan through the snow in winter with his younger brother, his son, and three friends. After bathing in the hot spring they climbed to a height from which they could view the thirty-six peaks; they were awestruck at the sight and lost all awareness of the existence of the human world. Uncertain how to proceed, they returned to the Hsiang-fu Temple and drank hot wine. By the next morning the snow had cleared, and they gazed over scenery of indescribable vastness. Another traveler, Wang Hsuan-hsi 汪玄錫, made the trip in 1532 with friends; they, too, bathed in the hot springs, stopped at the Hsiang-fu Temple, and climbed high enough to view the great peaks. They visited someone living there who had collected poems about Huang Shan. Neither this account nor any of the earlier ones suggests the existence of any set route or sequence in which the scenic places were visited; probably they were not yet accessible enough for that.

A doctor from She-hsien named Chiang Kuan 江瓘 records in an essay a trip made in 1548 with two companions. By this time, although the climb was still difficult, it was eased somewhat by steps cut in the stone and stairways of wood and by buildings where one could rest. Chiang, not surprisingly, writes of medicinal herbs that could be picked there, but also of inscriptions carved on a cliff, a place that the poet Li Po had visited, legends of immortals, rocks named for their resemblance to a tiger or a drunken man—

all this making up a cultural overlay on the natural scenery. The naming of the thirty-six great peaks and other natural features centuries earlier had already begun to impose symbolic meaning on the natural forms; a gradual accretion of literary lore around them can now be seen to have furthered this process. Received information and recognition of named places seem to have somewhat supplanted firsthand observation of untouched nature. Chiang's account begins to have the character of an itinerary, moving from one named place to another.

The same is true of the short essay by the noted late Ming poet and critic Yuan Chung-tao 袁中道 (1570–1623): it is like a brief travelogue with poetic commentary. Other late Ming accounts have the same character; the route varies, but the travelers tend to see and record the same sights, while continuing to be overwhelmed by their awesomeness. An especially full record is by Wu T'ing-chien 吳廷簡, a climber from Hui-chou, who followed what had become a somewhat set route, stopping at the Hsiang-fu Temple, bathing in the hot spring, climbing to the Mañjuśrī Terrace, and so forth. He records inscriptions on the cliffs, which seem to have proliferated.[4] He is advised by the monks against attempting to climb the Heavenly Capital Peak and is content to gaze at it and the other great peaks from a lower eminence, the Lien-tan t'ai 煉丹臺 or Refining Cinnabar Terrace, where, legend had it, the Yellow Emperor had practiced alchemy. From there all the peaks could be viewed clearly, wonderfully arranged; "even Wu Tao-tzu or Ku K'ai-chih [great painters of the eighth and fifth centuries respectively] couldn't describe one ten-thousandth of this." He sits under a pine tree drinking wine, forgetting that there is a human world.

The famous late Ming traveler Hsu Hsia-k'o (1586–1641) made the climb twice, in 1616 (after a visit to Mount Po-yueh 白岳) and in 1618; the second time he ascended the Lotus Peak and, still a very difficult climb, the Heavenly Capital Peak. He records at length the wonderment and excitement he felt as one scenic marvel after another appeared before him. On the whole, however, his account is rather matter-of-fact, noting such mundane matters as where he ate and slept and the cold and fatigue he experienced. His responses to the scenery, as he states them, seem conventional: "Peaks competing in beauty and wonder surround the Heavenly Capital, for which they are the sentinels." Only in his account of the second trip, when he attains the summit of the Lotus Peak and looks out over the others, does he break into a kind of rapture: "It was a most overpowering sight; I cried out in ecstasy and could have danced out of sheer joy and admiration" (Li Chi 1974, 82). It is for moments like this, one feels in reading Hsu's travel narratives, that he persevered over so many years and endured the rigors and dangers of seeking out remote places. The sacredness of some of the places is of lesser interest to him; his responses tend to be visual and aesthetic: "There I looked down the vale where peaks and rocks enfolded each other in all kinds of postures and feasted my eyes on their many tints" (82–83).

The Huang Shan travel account by Ch'ien Ch'ien-i 錢謙益 (1582–1664) will be introduced later in another context. Essays by later writers, such as a long one by Liu Ta-k'uei 劉大櫆 (1698–1779) or the account by Yuan Mei 袁枚 of a climb made in 1783, take on an even more schematic character, recording—and prescribing?—a set passage from one designated place to the next; the places need only be named, description seeming no longer necessary. Temples provide lodging, and the monks are there to advise climbers on their routes.

The sense of firsthand wonder at the sublimity of the scenery or of religious awe is felt less in these late accounts than in the early ones. To note this is not to degrade the actual experiences of the individual climbers, which may well have been as deeply inspired by feelings of transcendance as those of a Sung-period pilgrim or of any sensitive climber of Huang Shan today. But the structure of the typical experience, as it is reported, with its sequence of sensations and associations, seems to have become somewhat conventionalized. Moreover, the changes in the travel accounts appear to bear out McDermott's observation that Huang Shan became increasingly secularized in the post-Sung period. In the Ming, he points out, there were literary societies at Huang Shan and even a lecture series (McDermott 1989, 147; see also Cahill 1981, 4–46). McDermott cites a mid-seventeenth-century monk who "could lament the passing of the Buddhist monk from the mountain and the appearance in his stead of the secular literatus." We will consider later how these changes appear to be reflected in paintings of Huang Shan.

TYPES OF TOPOGRAPHICAL PAINTINGS

The study of topographical painting as a subject category within the large subject of Chinese landscape is only beginning. I have attempted a very preliminary mapping-out of the material (Cahill 1982a, chap. 1; Cahill 1982c), and a fuller treatment of it by Kenneth Ganza is under way.[5] We use the term *topographical* for convenience to designate both representations of particular places and paintings presenting stages in a journey to some particular place. The two types could be considered separately—Ganza prefers to do so—but the distinction is not crucial to our present purpose. The relationship of topographical paintings to other landscape paintings is thus similar to that of portraiture to figure painting: they present themselves as depicting the real, the individual, the specific, as opposed to the imaginary, the unspecific. A difference, of course, is that we can still check the topographical pictures against the real places, as we cannot check portraits against people, except in other representations of them. But the difference is not in fact so

great as it seems, since in Chinese practice topographical pictures and portraits both normally follow schemata more than appearances, allowing us to
distinguish between degrees of schematization more easily than we can determine whether or not a work is a *true* image of a particular person or place.
Series of topographical pictures and portraits are among the standard
schematic images included in the late Ming pictorial encyclopedia *San-ts'ai
t'u-hui* 三才圖會 (1607); the word *t'u* 圖 in fact denotes such a schematic
image. Topographical paintings in China, then, are often more maplike than
properly pictorial, and a major theme in any study of them must be an investigation of the schemata for the representation of noted places as we can see
these in woodblock-printed pictures in local histories and guidebooks and
how individual paintings conform to these or depart from them.

Instead of attempting a chronological, developmental survey of topographical painting—a project severely hampered by the spottiness of the surviving material—we will instead consider a few types, as defined by purpose
or assumed purpose, offering examples. A simplistic assumption about the
creation of a topographical painting might be that the artist goes to the place,
observes it, makes sketches, then produces his painting based on observation
and sketches as a visual report of what he has seen. But paintings that present themselves as having come into existence that way represent only one
type, and they are in fact exceptional.

One useful way of organizing the types of topographical paintings is to
arrange them on a scale from the more schematic and functional to the more
pictorial and descriptive. In doing this we assume large conceptual differences between the types, differences that strongly affect, in part determine,
the character of the paintings.

Closest to the schematic end of the scale are picture-maps done as guides
for travel or simply as aids to understanding the layout of the terrain, its
prominent features, and landmarks. Two long handscrolls in the Freer Gallery of Art (reg. nos. 11.168 and 16.539), both ascribed to great early masters
(Chü-jan 巨然 of the tenth century and Li Kung-lin 李公麟 of the eleventh,
respectively) but really anonymous works probably of thirteenth-century
date, both representing the upper course of the Yangtze River, can serve as
early examples (Cahill 1982c, figs. 4 and 5). In both, written labels identify
mountains, towns, and so forth. They must represent a much larger class of
functional map-pictures that have mostly not been preserved; the survival of
these two is presumably due to their illustrious attributions, which gave them
a borrowed status as treasurable objects that others of the type did not enjoy.
Both have accordingly received little attention in recent scholarship, since
their attributions are no longer accepted and their formal repetitiveness
makes them relatively uninteresting as paintings, stylistic variation and differentiation of pictorial materials being irrelevant to their purpose. A later
example, a picture-map of the Yellow River dating probably from the seven-

teenth century, is more maplike but otherwise similar (Cahill 1982b, pl. 112). Another, probably early Ming in date and again in the Freer Gallery of Art (reg. no. 11.209), takes the viewer on a complete tour of the shores of the West Lake at Hangchow, enumerating in simple images the temples, villas, walls, boats, and the like that crowded the shores. The striking difference between this kind of painting and the kind that presents the scenery as if in a visual record of what the artist saw can be illustrated by comparing this West Lake scroll with another by the Southern Sung Academy master Li Sung 李嵩 (Cahill 1982a, fig. 1.34) in which distant scenery is dimmed and detail blurred as they would be in actual optical experience. Topographical paintings of this first type are not properly descriptive, nor do they record particular journeys. Many picture-maps of this kind must still exist in archives and historical museums in China and elsewhere, unnoticed (at least by art historians) and unpublished.

A second type is the painting or series of paintings, typically in handscroll or album form, that designates and depicts notable sights of a city or region. These are usually accompanied by texts, either inscriptions on the paintings or sections of text alternating with the pictures in a handscroll or album. In 1344 Wu Chen 吳鎮 (1280–1354) painted his "Eight Views of Chia-ho" in handscroll form (Cahill 1976, pl. 28), remarking in the opening inscription that if the Hsiao-Hsiang Rivers region could have its Eight Views (the famous Sung-period set of poetic scenes), why not his home town Chia-ho (i.e. Chia-hsing)? Numerous other Eight Views series followed, as other cities and regions, inspired by local pride, drew up their sets as tourist attractions and the local artists represented them.[6] When in the early fifteenth century the Yung-lo emperor was making his plans for moving the capital to Peking (as he would do in 1421), he took with him on trips to that city, in 1409 and again in 1413, a group of Han-lin academicians and the painter Wang Fu 王紱 ; in 1414 the academicians composed a series of ponderous poems about the Eight Views of the region, and Wang Fu made pictures of them.[7] Whether or not the project was carried out at the emperor's request is unclear, but in either case, the production of poems and pictures served a specific political purpose—to surround the city with a cultural aura, an enclosing structure of poetic allusions and conventionalized images, a set itinerary for visits and outings, as befitted an imperial capital. Yung-lo may have hoped also to soften with culture the raw political-military aims of the relocation. The choice of Wang Fu, a scholar-artist and stylistic heir to the prestigious Yuan masters, furthered that aim; if it had been properly descriptive, informative pictures that were required, pictures useful perhaps for strategic planning, an artist of another kind would have been invited along.

Wu- or Soochow-school masters of the middle and late Ming, with Shen Chou 沈周 and the followers of Wen Cheng-ming 文徵明 prominent among them, swelled the volume of paintings of this type with a large output from which many survive. They are mostly rather schematic in character, some nearly as much so as the picture-maps of our first type. They record tirelessly the identifying features of the Tiger Hill, or the Stone Lake, or the Stone Cliff at the Pond of Heaven; sometimes, as in Shen Chou's "Scenery of Wu" hand-scroll (Cahill 1978, pl. 41) or albums by later masters, the viewer is taken on a tour of sights of the region with distances between them (in the case of the handscroll) telescoped, but with the sequence laid out as one might in reality move from each place to the next. Paintings of this kind could have been acquired by visitors to Soochow, commercial travelers and others, to take home as remembrances or to give to friends who planned to make the trip. Since we have (to my knowledge) no inscriptional evidence for determining the purposes or identifying the patrons of such paintings, we can only hypothesize about these matters, but we will return to them in discussing examples from the seventeenth century, for which more evidence exists.

Far less common are topographical paintings of a type that are truly de-scriptive, supplying viewers with detailed visual information about the place and giving them a sense of "what it really looks like." These are exceptions, occurring only sporadically in the history of Chinese painting. I have sug-gested reasons why they were not more common or more appreciated in discussing the late Ming Soochow-school master Chang Hung 張宏, who painted them in some number (Cahill 1982a, chap. 1). They are done in a diversity of styles, since the Chinese tradition of painting contains no single "realistic" or "true-to-life" mode of representation. The mid-Sung master-work of *chieh-hua* 界畫 painting, the "Ch'ing-ming shang-ho t'u" 清明上河圖 (see Weng and Yang, 1982, pls. 87 and 88), supposing that it represents (as most scholars believe) the city of K'ai-feng in the late Northern Sung period, belongs to this type, but so does the aforementioned "West Lake" handscroll by Li Sung. The one supplies an abundance of sharply delineated detail, the other only a blurred view with implications of partly obscured richness of observation. But both permit the viewer a sense of visual participation in the scene: this, they suggest, is what you would see if you were there.

T'ang Yin 唐寅 (1470–1523), painting a farewell picture for an official who had served in Soochow, depicts the Chin-ch'ang Gate 金閶門 of the city and the clutter of habitations outside it with enough specificity to inspire, we may suppose, nostalgia in the recipient (Cahill 1978, pl. 91). Chang Hung, in a 1650 portrayal of Mount Kou-ch'ü 勾曲山, another name for the great Taoist mountain Mao Shan 茅山 (Cahill 1982a, pl. 2 and figs. 1.1, 1.10, and 1.12), records with an air of immediacy what he saw from a window in the house of the patron with whom he was staying instead of basing his picture on some schematic image of the mountain and its temples as another Soo-chow artist would have done.[8] Both T'ang's and Chang's works, like other paintings of this type, are sports, neither following a tradition nor creating one.

Paintings presented by the artists as travel reports, recording genuine voyages of discovery, are a subgroup of the preceding type, especially pertinent to our present inquiry. Lu Chih's 1554 album of his trip to Mount Po-yueh, to be discussed below, belongs to this type. In these the painter assures us, whether in an inscription or solely through the persuasiveness of his forms, that he could not have done the picture without going to the place and seeing it with his own eyes. Chang Hung makes this point in his inscription on the final leaf of the album "Ten Scenes of Yueh" 越. He painted the album, he writes, on his return from a trip there because what he saw did not agree with what he had heard, and he wanted to record his visual observations. He concludes that "relying on your ears is not as good as relying on your eyes"—a strangely un-Chinese sentiment perhaps best understood in the context of clear evidence of European influence in the paintings (Cahill 1982a, figs. 1.14–1.19). The same artist's depiction of Mount Ch'i-hsia 棲霞 near Nanking, painted in 1634, is another that owes its origin to a trip to the place; he visited it in the rain with a friend and looked down at the mountainside with its rock-cut Buddhist sculptures; upon his return he set down in a painting what he had seen (Cahill 1982a, pl. 1 and fig. 1.7). A few decades later, in 1651–53, the famous filial son Huang Hsiang-chien 黃向堅 traveled by foot for a year and a half to remote parts of Yunnan province to bring back his aged father, who had been left there in the wake of the Manchu conquest; in the years following, Huang painted handscrolls and albums depicting his journey (Cahill 1982a, fig. 1.30; Ganza 1988). A painter lacking in distinct style, he devotes an earnest literalness to his portrayals of the rugged, mountainous terrain in keeping with his aim of impressing on his viewers the rigors he had endured in rescuing his parent.

Of all surviving Chinese travel pictures, however, the series that might seem to best deserve the designation *pilgrimage paintings* is the album of forty scenes of Hua Shan by the late Yuan–early Ming master Wang Li (or Lü 王履). Wang, born in 1322 in Kun-shan, was a medical doctor. In the autumn of 1383 he traveled to Shensi province to climb Hua Shan 華山, one of the Five Sacred Mountains of Taoism. On his return, Wang Li painted an album of forty scenes representing places on the mountain, writing in addition a series of essays and poems making up twenty-six additional leaves. The album, Wang's only recorded and surviving work as a painter, is now divided between the Palace Museum, Peking, and the Shanghai Museum.[9] Wang Li's original motivation for traveling to Shensi and climbing Hua Shan appears to have been to consult doctors of that region and to gather medicinal herbs on the mountain, but the experience changed his life and his artistic style. The compulsion he felt to convey something of the grandeur of what he saw led him to adopt a more representational mode of painting, based on the styles of the Southern Sung Academy masters Hsia Kuei 夏圭 and Ma Yuan 馬遠. The scholar-amateur styles current in his time, with their emphasis on cultivated brushwork and stylistic allusions to old masters, must have seemed to him grossly inadequate for realizing that aim, although they would ordinarily have been considered "proper" for a man of his standing. In his essay accompanying the album he explicitly repudiates the literati approach, which he himself had evidently followed in his earlier painting. He writes that painters who "become famous in the world by 'following the ancients' are really groping in the dark." When asked who his teacher had been, he replied: "My teacher is my mind; its teacher is my eyes; their teacher is Hua Shan. That's all."

Wang Li's "pilgrimage" to Hua Shan, then, appears to have been inspired more by professional (medical) than religious motives and his experience there to have affected his artistic more than his religious life. He was quite aware of Hua Shan's sanctity as a Taoist mountain, but in his writings he expresses some skepticism of the Taoist religion and the idea of immortals. If his ascent can be regarded as a spiritual pilgrimage at all, it must have been in quest of the kind of spiritual attainment reached through contact with the sublime in nature, independently of organized religions. The experience of the sublime as an element in the Chinese poets' and artists' responses to mountain (including sacred mountain) scenery will be considered later.

Other types of topographical paintings than these four could probably be added, but these suffice to indicate the options open to artists in the period of our Huang Shan pictures and to supply a framework within which those pictures can be understood.

PAINTINGS OF MOUNT PO-YUEH AND HUANG SHAN IN YUAN AND MING

As we have seen, Huang Shan among the sacred mountains of China was late in achieving renown as a pilgrimage place and in developing amenities for travelers. Early climbers (through most of the Ming dynasty) had to bring their own food and water, sleep outside, and make their ascents mostly without the benefits of paths and cut steps (Li I-min 1983, preface). The sixteenth-century accounts tell of staying at the Hsiang-fu Temple at the base of the mountain and being supplied with wine by the monks. Toward the end of the sixteenth century the monk P'u-men obtained both local and imperial support to build temples on the mountain and construct walkways for the convenience of climbers (McDermott 1989, 147). According to Ch'ien Ch'ien-i (*Huang-shan chih ting-pen*, ch. 7:41b) the rock-cut steps that allowed an easier ascent of the Heavenly Capital Peak were not completed by P'u-men until 1614.

Early climbers of Huang Shan were mostly literati from Hui-chou and other nearby regions; from the late Ming on, they come from more distant places. If we ask what, apart from the spread of knowledge about the mountain and its increased accessibility, can have drawn these visitors from far away in this period, the answer must be the marked increase in travel, especially commercial travel, along the routes between southern Anhui and other regions, most of all the Yangtze delta cities, that made up the trade network of the Hui-chou merchants. The region of Hui-chou in southeastern Anhui province, also known as Hsin-an with She-hsien and Hsiu-ning as its principal cities, was from the middle Ming onward a center of mercantile activity that eventually dominated the whole Kiangnan region, the richest part of China. The Hui-chou merchants had networks of markets throughout this region, which they supplied and from which they reaped the profits, amassing fortunes beyond any thitherto known. Along with this commercial intercourse through the region went a lively movement of scholars and artists. We read of numerous visits back and forth from the late sixteenth century through the seventeenth—Chan Ching-feng 詹景鳳 and Ting Yun-p'eng 丁雲鵬, both from Hsiu-ning, spend time in Sung-chiang and come to know Tung Ch'i-ch'ang 董其昌 and his circle; Tung and his friend Ch'en Chi-ju 陳繼儒 from Sung-chiang visit the great families of Hui-chou to see their collections of art and enjoy their hospitality; Ch'eng Chia-sui 程嘉燧 travels often between Chia-ting and his family home in Hsiu-ning; and so forth.[10]

Mount Po-yueh 白岳, a range of peaks northwest of Hsiu-ning in southern Anhui, seems to have preceded Huang Shan in popularity both as a place for mountain climbing and as a subject for paintings; we can regard it for our present purpose as a kind of nearby, lesser forerunner of Huang Shan. Some of the writers of the Huang Shan travel accounts compare the two ranges, always to disparage Po-yueh. Hsu Hsia-k'o devotes a brief account to Po-yueh, which he climbed in March of 1616, before going on to his much longer report of his ascent of Huang Shan. Huang Ju-heng 黃汝亨, writing also in the late Ming, says that people who have never been to Huang Shan pair it with Po-yueh, but that Huang Shan has in fact no rivals in the world. Po-yueh's peaks, he observes, are steep and strong but like piles of stones, while Huang Shan's seem as if carved and are endlessly varied in shape. It is, he concludes, like comparing a courtesan with the Nymph of the Lo River, a mortal with a divinity. Ch'ien Ch'ien-i's essay quotes a friend's letter on the subject: "Po-yueh is strange and precipitous, but it's like the small [foreground] scenes of painters, with steep and rugged boulders like the daubings of low-class Taoists. Huang Shan's peaks thrust upward from the earth, the loftiest of them for several thousand feet, even the lesser ones for hundreds of feet. One can't get to the top of them, there is no place for the foot to rest. The color of the stones is richly dark" (Li I-min 1983, 40).

What is probably the earliest extant painting of Mount Po-yueh may also be the earliest true travel painting to survive—one that records, that is, in both painting and inscription, a trip that the artist made to the place. Furthermore, it may be the single identifiable "pilgrimage painting" we will encounter, in that its artist, in his inscription, explicitly states that it was made to record a pilgrimage to Po-yueh. And, to make the case still stronger, the artist (or purported artist) was himself a famous Taoist. The painting is signed by the semilegendary Yuan-period Taoist Leng Ch'ien 冷謙 and dated 1343 (see fig. 6.1). A problem of authenticity hangs over the work, as indeed over the whole persona of Leng Ch'ien (who is supposed to have been more than a century old in the Chih-cheng era [1341–68], but to have lived to serve as a court musician under the Hung-wu Emperor [r. 1368–98]). But the painting cannot easily be fitted by style into a later period either, and it seems acceptable to treat it as an early work without either trusting altogether or rejecting the date and authorship.[11]

According to the inscription, Leng Ch'ien made the trip with the famous statesman Liu Chi 劉基 (1311–75), who has also inscribed a poem on the painting. The two "arranged to make a pilgrimage" (*ting-ch'ao* 訂朝) to Po-yueh and made their way by boat, spending, he writes, seventeen days and nights on the journey. Arriving there, they "paid homage to the sacred images"—presumably in the Taoist temples at Po-yueh—and gazed awestruck at the mountains. Towering peaks in the distance were identified by the locals as the peaks of Huang Shan, so they were inspired to continue on, a day's trip, encountering on the way

> strange pines and wondrous rocks; lofty, majestic peaks and cliffs; flying waterfalls and bubbling streams; . . . the chattering of monkeys and birds. All of these arrested my thoughts and compelled me to remain there, body and soul. We pulled ourselves up on creeping vines to get to the summit of the mountain. . . . Liu said, "Up ahead we would stray into the mountains of the immortals," and he went on humming and chanting as before. Then he compelled me to sketch a likeness of the scene, so I made the effort at dabbing some paint. (Ganza 1986, 9–10)

In this inscription we find at last the designators of a true pilgrimage painting: The artist announces that he and his friend are making a pilgrimage to the mountain; they pay reverence to the sacred images at temples there; they encounter unearthly sights and feel that they have found their way into a realm of immortals; the artist's friend asks that he "sketch a likeness" of the scenery as a record (the painting was presumably done as a gift for Liu Chi, since Leng Ch'ien's reference to him at the end of the inscription follows a pattern common in dedications). Correspondences between the inscription and the early-period literary accounts of travel to Huang Shan are obvious; Leng Ch'ien's is in fact another of them, since he and Liu Chi did attain those grander peaks. The picture, then, should reveal to us the proper characteristics of the successful pilgrimage painting, one that transmits the spiritual exaltation of the experience and perhaps inspires others to follow the example it presents. And the painting doubtless did that for some viewers and would continue to do so today, if Leng Ch'ien (or whoever painted it) had been a better artist.

As it is, it is convincing enough as the work of an amateur who wants to convey to us in images the strangeness and diversity of what he saw. But where an episodic presentation of heterogeneous materials may be effective in a travel essay, it works against formal unity in a painting, and Leng Ch'ien's picture is more odd than compelling. He seems to be attempting to represent in a single composition the journey to Po-yueh by river, the arrival at the foot of the mountain with temples (?) among trees, the ascent of Po-yueh, and the Huang Shan peaks in the distance (presumably, they are the peaks seen in the upper right of the painting, partly hidden in clouds). The attendant problems of scale would have challenged a master painter; they defeat this one. That the dominant mountain mass in upper left represents Po-yueh itself is suggested by a comparison with a depiction of the peak in an early eighteenth-century print:[12] the buildings at the base; the path leading upward through pines; the angular, topheavy crags; the encircling clouds, all correspond. The art historian will add that Leng Ch'ien, for all his air of free, firsthand "copying of the scenery," uses an established compositional type, one we can see also in a better-known (and far better) work painted in 1365 by his Taoist contemporary Fang Ts'ung-i 方從義 (Cahill 1976, pl. 59) or, earlier in the Yuan dynasty, in one painted about 1309 by their illustrious predecessor the statesman-artist Kao K'o-kung 高克恭 (pl. 19). In all these compositions the foreground is divided by a river flowing between banks topped with trees, and buildings are seen in mist among groves and trees and bamboo in the middle ground, above which the peaks rise steeply. It is not a composition well suited to representing stages in a journey, as the muddled character of Leng Ch'ien's picture betrays; the hanging scroll form more generally is ill-adapted to that purpose, and travel paintings in later times were to favor the handscroll and album forms.

An album of pictures portraying scenes viewed on a trip to Po-yueh was painted in 1554 by Lu Chih 陸治 (1496–1576); his sixteen-leaf album is now in the Fujii Yūrinkan, Kyoto (Yuhas 1979, 100–105, 341–48, and pl. 21a–n). Both the paintings and Lu's inscriptions on them seem properly descriptive in intent, within the limits of his pictorial and literary styles; he gives no clue to why he made the trip. In his notes written on the last leaf Lu Chih tells of seeing many inscriptions by Sung writers carved on the cliffs of Po-yueh, so travelers to the mountain must have been numerous already by that time. A few decades later, in 1573, Sung Hsu 宋旭, an artist from Chia-hsing who spent his later years in Sung-chiang living as a professional painter, was engaged by a man from Anhui named Wu Yung-ho 吳用和 (or Chi-ho 季和), who himself traveled in Wu-Yueh (Kiangsu and Chekiang) and was probably a merchant, to paint a handscroll portraying the landscape on the road to Po-yueh. Sung Hsu in his inscription remarks that he was asked to do the picture because he had once made the trip himself and had a rough memory of its appearance. Writers of colophons on the scroll (which is known only from a literary record)[13] are reminded by it of their own travels in Hsin-an or southern Anhui. One of them, the artist Ch'eng Cheng-k'uei 程正揆, inscribed it twice—once in 1666, expressing his delight with the painting, which was owned by a relative of his, and again in 1669, after he had made the trip to Po-yueh and Huang Shan himself and was able to recognize the truthfulness with which Sung Hsu had portrayed the scenery. This set of inscriptions provides us with clues to how such a painting came into being and how it was appreciated by its viewers.

Another clue to the genesis of such paintings is found in the writings of the late Ming landscapist Li Liu-fang 李流芳 (1575–1629), whose family was from She-hsien in Anhui but who lived in Chia-ting in Kiangsu. He writes that in 1614 his brother gave him a blank album saying, "When you encounter places of particular scenic beauty in Hsin-an, sketch them for me. Then return the album so that I can look at the pictures and feel as if I were traveling there myself."[14] Whether Li painted the album and whether representations of Mount Po-yueh and Huang Shan were included in it are not recorded.

Among other late Ming artists who traveled to Po-yueh was Hsiang Sheng-mo 項聖謨 (1597–1658), who went there in 1623 and recorded his visit in a painting now in the British Museum (Li Chu-tsing 1976, 534–35 and fig. 1). Both the painting and its long inscription, however, are so heavy with literati-painting conventions and so thin in evidences of firsthand observation that Hsiang could almost have done them without making the trip at all. The painting, titled "Reading in the Autumn Woods," follows the compositional type associated with that hoary theme, reducing references to Po-yueh to some imposing mountain masses in the upper part. The long inscription reiterates the traditional values of living in seclusion, using time-worn images such as the herd-boy and buffalo.

None of these paintings of Mount Po-yueh, after the 1343 one by Leng Ch'ien, gives prominence to the temples there or offers any suggestion that visiting them was a prime goal of the trip; the later travelers were drawn mainly, it would appear, by the scenery. But all the paintings have the character of travel pictures, Leng Ch'ien's and Hsiang Sheng-mo's by portraying the approach to Po-yueh with the mountains in the distance, Lu Chih's album and Sung Hsu's handscroll (judging from its recorded inscriptions) by depicting stages of the journey. Huang Shan paintings, by contrast, whatever their form, concentrate on the peaks themselves, with less attention to the approach. An exception is Shih-t'ao's album, "Eight Views of Huang Shan," in the first two leaves of which the artist is seen on his way to the mountain and in the third, bathing in the hot spring before beginning the ascent (Edwards 1967, fig. 1 A–C, and p. 73). The album then continues, like typical Huang Shan painting albums, by offering the famous sights in sequence; making the rounds of these, rather than traveling to the mountain, is the experience normally presented. The form belongs, then, to the second of the three types of topographical paintings considered earlier, the one that depicts a set or series of notable places in a region. This was a form well established for literati appreciations of topography, and the use of it in Huang Shan paintings links them further to the "literati conquest" of the mountain.

What, then, would popular-culture representations of Huang Shan have looked like? If there were ever iconic cult images of the mountain or of other sacred mountains in China, like the Shinto shrine-mandalas of Japan, they do not appear to have survived, or at least to have been published. We can assume some production of simple, functional picture-maps like the ones that exist for other places and quite possibly exist for Huang Shan, kept in provincial libraries, perhaps, unremarked and unpublished because they are of small interest to high-culture devotees. We can speculate also that painted picture-maps of this kind, and perhaps crudely printed ones like those offered for sale at such places today, were available to people making their way to the properly religious pilgrimage sites studied in other papers in this volume; but again, no existing examples are known to me. The significance that such schematic pictures would have had for a sacred mountain is explored in William Powell's paper for our conference (Powell 1989). Chiu-hua Shan or Nine Floriate Mountain, the subject of that paper, was a Buddhist holy mountain believed to be the sacred realm of the savior-bodhisattva Kṣitigarbha or Ti-tsang and is near Huang Shan; it was a flourishing pilgrimage site and continues so to the present. But Chiu-hua, to my knowledge, was never represented in paintings of the kind Huang Shan inspired nor were any of the other mountains that were popular as pilgrimage places—P'u-t'o Shan (except as a simple setting for images of Kuan-yin) or Wu-tang Shan or Miaofeng Shan, the mountains treated in the chapters by Chün-fang Yü, John Lagerwey, and Susan Naquin. By contrast, substantial bodies of high-level painting were devoted to Huang Shan and Lu Shan, both Buddhist-Taoist sacred mountains in their early history and beloved of the literati later.[15] No cult of any deity is associated with either; instead, both came to be surrounded by rich accretions of poetry and prose, the vestiges and memories of famous visitors and sojourners, historical and literary lore.

To this hypothetical and doubtless over-simplified scheme—picture-maps for pilgrimage mountains, literati paintings for "high-culture" mountains— we can add an intermediate area occupied by the woodblock-printed pictures found in gazetteers, local histories, and other compilations devoted to these sites. Woodblock-printed pictures of Huang Shan exist in three forms: single-print distant views of the group of central peaks; prints in series making up a continuous panorama; and series prints providing separate, more close-up views of notable places.

Fig. 6.1 (*left*). Leng Ch'ien (active 1340s–50s?). "A Trip to Mount Po-yueh." Hanging scroll, ink on paper, dated 1343. Collection of the National Palace Museum, Taipei, Taiwan, Republic of China.

Fig. 6.2 (*right*). Ting Yun-p'eng (1547–ca. 1621). "Morning Sun over the Heavenly Capital." Hanging scroll, ink and colors on paper, dated 1614. The Cleveland Museum of Art, Andrew R. and Martha Holden Jennings Fund (65.28).

Fig. 6.3. Anonymous, sixteenth century. "Peaks of Huang Shan." Handscroll, ink and light colors on silk. Museum of Fine Arts, Boston (08.87).

Fig. 6.4. Another section of the same handscroll as fig. 6.3.

Fig. 6.5. "Tz'u-kuang Ssu and Wen-shu Yuan." Woodblock print from *Huang-shan t'u-ching*, early Ch'ing period. Heavenly Capital Peak is at top right, Lotus Peak top left, with the Mañjuśrī Terrace in between. Red Gravel Peak is in the center.

Fig. 6.6. Mei Ch'ing (1623–97). "Lotus and Heavenly Capital Peaks, with the Mañ-juśrī Terrace." Leaf from an album of scenes of Huang Shan, dated 1693. Shanghai Museum.

Fig. 6.7. Hung-jen (1610–64). "Kuang-ming Ting." Leaf from album of scenes of Huang Shan. Ink on silk. Ching Yuan Chai Collection, Berkeley.

Fig. 6.8. Hung-jen. "Lien-tan Terrace." Another leaf from the same album as fig. 6.7.

Fig. 6.9. Cheng Min (1633–83). "Lotus Peak." Leaf from the album "Eight views of Huang Shan." Ink on paper, dated 1681. Private collection, Alberta, Canada.

Fig. 6.10. Shih-t'ao (1641–1707). "Lotus Peak." Leaf from the album "Eight Views of Huang Shan." Ink and light colors on paper. Sen'oku Museum, Kyoto.

Fig. 6.11. Shih-t'ao. "Peaks of Huang Shan." Section of a handscroll, ink and light colors on paper, dated 1699. Sen'oku Museum, Kyoto.

The single-print type appears to be the earliest; examples are known from 1462, 1607, 1633, and 1648, and the differences between these reflect changing perceptions of the mountain.[16] The 1462 print portrays Huang Shan in a manner essentially in agreement with the early travel accounts: a foreground with buildings and bridges; the Hsiang-fu Temple further up; and beyond, only the sheer, seemingly inaccessible peaks, several with caves identified on them. This is Huang Shan contemplated as a Taoist numinous vision. The 1607 print, found in the "Geography" section of *San-ts'ai t'u-hui* (ch. 7), presents Huang Shan as even less accessible, with no buildings at all, only an array of needle peaks and pine trees and a few paths in the foreground, an austere image that may be based on some model even earlier than the 1462 print. In the picture of Po-yueh that directly precedes that of Huang Shan in *San-ts'ai t'u-hui*, temple buildings are by contrast spread over the slopes of more modest, climbable eminences, as they are in the picture of Chiu-hua Shan; this, we might conclude, is the image better suited to proper pilgrimage sites. The later single Huang Shan prints presumably reflect the progressive opening-up of the mountain; buildings and paths are enlarged and the scale of the peaks reduced. What becomes a standard configuration can be seen in these later prints: the Tz'u-kuang Temple in the center (replacing the Hsiang-fu Temple, which occupied this position in the 1492 print but now is seen at the bottom if it is present at all), the Heavenly Capital Peak at the right, the Lotus Peak at left. One print in the early Ch'ing series in the *Huang-shan t'u-ching* repeats this plan (see fig. 6.5), and one in the 1679 *Huang-shan chih ting-pen*, in turn, repeats that. The same symmetrical setting of the two greatest peaks occurs in many Huang Shan paintings, usually, however, with the Mañjuśrī Terrace centered between them (see fig. 6.6); this is the configuration that most immediately identifies Huang Shan in the later pictures.

Examples of series of prints forming a continuous panorama are to be seen in the first half of the *Huang-shan t'u-ching* series—the later pages represent individual scenes—and in the whole of the *Huang-shan chih ting-pen* series. Among Huang Shan paintings it is less common, with the anonymous sixteenth-century handscroll (see figs. 6.3 and 6.4) and Shih-t'ao's 1699 handscroll (see fig. 6.11) being, perhaps, the only major examples. The group of prints of particular places that concludes the *Huang-shan t'u-ching* series in the *An-hui ts'ung-shu* printing and the series after designs by the eighteenth-century monk-painter Hsueh-chuang 雪莊 in the *Huang-shan ts'ung-k'an* printing both correspond in plan to the painting album in which the individual leaves do the same, such as Hung-jen's album (figs. 6.7 and 6.8). The former group of prints is in fact based on paintings, probably originally album leaves, by well-known and lesser-known artists who are identified in the inscriptions—Hung-jen 弘仁, Mei Ch'ing 梅清, Cheng Chung 鄭重, and Chiang Chu 江注 among them.

A general trend in the history of woodblock printing in China can be noted in this quick survey of the Huang Shan prints: the earlier ones are anonymous or by minor masters; increasingly from late Ming into early Ch'ing, artists of repute engage in designing the prints, and the level of quality rises markedly. But as the artistic interest of the prints increases, their functional value diminishes, until they lose their usefulness as picture-maps to become objects for aesthetic contemplation, like literati paintings. In the end the prints, too, become part of the literati culture of Huang Shan.

Painted representations of Huang Shan do not survive from periods before the sixteenth century (unless we include the Leng Ch'ien painting of Mount Po-yueh in fig. 6.1, which shows Huang Shan's peaks in the background), and most from the Ming are known only from literary records such as those cited above. The earliest recorded representation of Huang Shan is a wall painting commissioned by the prefect of Hui-chou in 1154 (McDermott 1989, 153). A set of paintings of Huang Shan scenery is recorded as having been painted in 1497 for the sixtieth birthday of a wealthy Hui-chou couple; the pictures were by a certain Wang Ch'ung and were accompanied by poems by the noted Hui-chou literatus Ch'eng Min-cheng 程敏政 (1445– after 1499).[17] Ch'eng specifies that the aim of the paintings and poems was to felicitate the couple and wish them longevity; presumably it was the Taoist associations of Huang Shan that made its scenery appropriate for this purpose. The paintings apparently have not survived.

The earliest extant painting of Huang Shan known to me is a long, anonymous handscroll on silk in the Museum of Fine Arts, Boston, with a spurious signature of Hsu Pen 徐賁 (d. ca. 1378) and a false date corresponding to 1376. A dating by style would place the work in the first half of the sixteenth century; it would appear to be by some late Che-school master, perhaps a follower of Chiang Sung 蔣嵩. It presents essentially the same vision of Huang Shan as the 1462 print and the *San-ts'ai t'u-hui* print mentioned above: temples and other buildings in the foreground, with a few figures of travelers; sheer peaks projecting upward, some past the upper limit of the painting, seeming unscalable, although a few figures and buildings appear part way up or at their summits. A strong sense of the supernatural is evoked by crags that eerily take the forms of human figures or animals, and some of the peaks are hollowed with caves, one with what appears to be a temple inside or beyond it. The names of peaks and other places are written in red beside or above them, a feature common in topographical paintings; but the intent does not seem truly topographical. The composition of the scroll, with a succession of peaks appearing one after another as one rolls it, is in agreement with the peak-by-peak account in the Sung-period *Huang-shan t'u-ching*; the original picture or pictures that accompanied that text must have had the same character. It is a form that, in keeping with the Taoist character of the work, emphasizes the individual images more than their spatial relationships or modes of passage between them; the painting, that is, seems more iconic, like a succession of images of deities, than topographical. The similarity of the three early representations and the earliest text, all predating the "opening of the mountain" by P'u-men, confirms our belief that they all preserve the original Taoist vision of Huang Shan before it was secularized by the literati.

In 1614 Ting Yun-p'eng (1547–ca. 1621) painted a huge hanging scroll representing "Morning Sun over the Heavenly Capital" (see fig. 6.2; see also *Eight Dynasties of Chinese Painting*, no. 203) for the birthday of an official. The distant peaks of Huang Shan, dominated by the Lotus and Heavenly Capital peaks, appear at the top of the painting, with waterfalls and rivulets streaming down the slopes below. Ting's conception of Huang Shan's auspicious character is like Ch'ien Ch'ien-i's in a passage that will be cited later: the rivers flowing from this "capital of Heaven" are cleansing the earth of all evil. Thick clouds cover the middle ground, and the water issues forth below as a flooding river that flows beneath flourishing pines and other trees. Two gentlemen on the bank gaze into the clouds. The political implications of the scene, praising the official in a familiar metaphor as benefiting the people like clouds that bring them rain, are underscored in the poem. As in the recorded 1497 album, the image of Huang Shan, with its Taoist-geomantic symbolism, is here employed for a quite secular purpose.

According to the *Huang-shan chih ting-pen* of 1679 Ting Yun-p'eng also painted a series of scenes of Huang Shan, probably as an album, but they do not seem to have survived. The late Ming painter Cheng Chung (fl. 1565–1630), who came from She-hsien, painted scenes of Huang Shan that are, so far as I know, preserved only in the single woodblock-print rendering in *Huang-shan t'u-ching*. But these are scattered examples, and the great age of Huang Shan paintings was unquestionably the early Ch'ing.

EARLY CH'ING REPRESENTATIONS OF HUANG SHAN

The masters who painted Huang Shan in the early Ch'ing period include Hung-jen, Mei Ch'ing, Tai Pen-hsiao 戴本孝, Hsiao Yun-ts'ung 蕭雲從, Hung-jen's nephew Chiang Chu, Cheng Min 鄭旼, and other Anhui artists, as well as painters from elsewhere who traveled to Huang Shan, notably K'un-ts'an 髡殘, who was there for more than a year in 1659–60 (Chang 1987) and Shih-t'ao 石濤, who lived in Hsuan-ch'eng in Anhui from 1666 to 1680, climbed Huang Shan in 1667 and again in 1668–69, and painted its scenery many times. The appendix to this chapter provides a partial list of extant works by these artists depicting Huang Shan.

It is important to note the preponderance of albums among these and that paintings in hanging scroll form are often parts of sets or series. The implications of this serial character of the typical Huang Shan pictures will be explored later.

First, however, we will lay out still another set of coordinates within which representations of Huang Shan and (underlying these) travel to Huang Shan must be understood. Without attempting at this point to define the actual meanings and motivations for either making the pictures or taking the trips, we can consider three kinds of meaning that *might* attach to them in this period: the political, the religious, and the pursuit of the sublime.

The political associations of Huang Shan have been outlined in a paper by Joseph McDermott (McDermott 1989). Huang Shan was a refuge and gathering place for Ming loyalists in the early decades of the Ch'ing; the resistance hero Huang Tao-chou 黃道周, captured in Hui-chou county by the Ch'ing troops in 1646, composed poems using Huang Shan as a metaphor for his loyalist feelings on his way to his execution. Anti-Ch'ing troops hid out there in the 1650s and 1660s, and treasonous funeral rites for the last Ming emperor were performed at one of the Huang Shan temples (McDermott 1989, 159–60). The Heavenly Capital Peak served as an emblem of political power in Ting Yun-p'eng's painting of 1614 (fig. 6.2), done for the birthday of an official, and images of Huang Shan peaks symbolize Chinese national strength in countless paintings today. For Chinese to make pilgrimages to a site with such political significance should scarcely be surprising, if we think of how many have made their way to Yenan or Mao's birthplace during the past four decades. (Rudolf Wagner, in chapter 9 of this volume, writes about "secular pilgrimages" to places defined by the government as "of crucial importance for the revolution.") Recollections of Huang Shan's significance as a focus of anti-Manchu sentiment must indeed have resonated in the minds of many early Ch'ing visitors to the mountain, along with echoes of Taoist and other religious associations from earlier times. But I know of no inscriptional or other evidence that would encourage us to read political meanings into the paintings.[18]

The question of religious content in Huang Shan paintings of the early Ch'ing is best approached in a similarly circumspect and circuitous way; we would not be justified either in denying its presence or in claiming for it a dominant role in the import of the paintings. We have seen that in its early history Huang Shan had been a sacred mountain, a place set apart from the profane world where one might get closer to the divine realm. The authors of the earlier travel accounts write of feeling like immortals and of seeming to lose all contact with the mundane world. And, as we noted, some Taoist meanings may underlie the use of Huang Shan paintings as wedding gifts in the 1497 case cited above. But these religious associations, as we noted earlier, had been eroded by late Ming and early Ch'ing times and replaced largely by literary and secular concerns.

The relative lateness of Huang Shan as a sacred and scenic attraction for travelers is a factor here; the great age of landscape Buddhism and Taoism lay far in the past. How the transcendent experience of a mountain can once have been understood as furthering Buddhist enlightenment is well illustrated by a brief text from about A.D. 400 titled "Record of an Ascent to the Stone Gate," translated by Susan Bush in her article on the early landscapist Tsung Ping 宗炳, who is the author of an important essay on landscape painting and was a member of the community of lay Buddhists led by the monk Hui-yuan on Mount Lu 廬山 (Bush 1983, 149–52). The "Stone Gate" text tells how a group of believers climbed to the Stone Gate 石門 at the summit of Lu Shan and experienced a kind of collective exaltation they then interpreted in a Buddhist light. In Bush's summary of the last part of the text, "these unsought-for perceptions arouse a selfless delight, which is then analyzed by the group as a correct response to phenomena. At sunset the view from on high suggests the vast scale of the universe; in turn this stimulates thoughts of eternal time and the remoteness of the Buddha." The group composes a poem to record their perceptions.

No paintings survive from this period that might testify to how such an experience could have been embodied in pictorial form; we have only Tsung Ping's essay, in which Buddhist references are oblique if present at all. Among surviving paintings, the ones that best express the ideal of transcending the mundane realm by climbing remote and difficult mountain peaks are, needless to say, the great monumental landscapes of the Northern Sung period, the later tenth and eleventh centuries, the works of such masters as Yen Wen-kuei 燕文貴, Fan K'uan 范寬, and Kuo Hsi 郭熙. The nature of the paintings, the contexts of their creation, and the appreciations of them by later writers all suggest that the spiritual ascents for which they are visual metaphors are universal, not specific to Buddhism or Taoism. The realm of mundane experience is represented, usually, in the lower section of the painting by a village, the thatched houses of fishermen, travelers with laden donkeys. Paths lead upward to temple buildings in mountain valleys or hollows near the summit; climbers, sometimes wearing the broad hats of Buddhist pilgrims, are often seen making their patient way toward them. The untrodden peaks loom above, readable as representing a level of spiritual attainment beyond organized religion. The pattern recurs often enough—virtually every major landscape of the period is invested with some variant of it—that we can draw from it our basic understanding of the meaning of Northern Sung landscape. But the pattern does not survive, except in distant echoes and quasi parodies, into landscape painting of the Southern Sung, Yuan, and Ming periods. Landscape painting of these later ages, by pursuing effects and meanings profoundly different from those of the monumental landscape tradition, sacrificed most of its capacity to convey to its viewers the grandeur of awesome mountain scenery and the transcendental feelings it inspires.

Certain of the Individualist masters of the early Ch'ing, especially those working in Anhui and nearby Nanking, where a revival of Northern Sung landscape style had been under way since the late Ming—artists such as Hung-jen, K'un-ts'an, Kung Hsien 龔賢, and Shih-t'ao—were able, in their different ways, to recapture some of the qualities long absent from landscape painting: convincing effects of space and height and volume, the sense of real presence, of "being there," that Sung art critics had recognized as the sensation aroused in the viewer by the works of their best landscapists. But paintings endowed with these qualities are exceptional in this late period. We cannot say, then, that conveying in landscape imagery a religious experience of Huang Shan scenery was beyond the capacity of early Ch'ing painting but that we should not come to the paintings expecting that all or most of them will convey such experience. A recognition of this profound change in the nature of landscape painting surely underlies the statements of travel account authors who exclaim that the scenery surpasses the skill of any painter to capture it; significantly, they choose masters from the distant past rather than recent ones as those who had some chance of achieving it: "Even Ku K'ai-chih and Wu Tao-tzu couldn't have caught one ten-thousandth of this!" (much less, they might have added, our contemporary artists).

The problem of identifying and defining religious content—in the sense of pictorial expression of religious experience—in early Ch'ing paintings of Huang Shan and thus opening the way for a consideration of them as pilgrimage paintings might be eased if we expanded our concept of the religious beyond Buddhism and Taoism, immortals and alchemy, to encompass the quasi-religious experience of the sublime. This concept, well established in Western aesthetic discussions, has no exact equivalent in Chinese writings on art or literature, but expressions of closely comparable responses to nature are common in the poetry and painting of China.[19] The sublime in nature, as distinct from the beautiful or the pretty, comprises the vast, the awesome, that which transcends comprehension, inspiring in extreme cases the negative feelings of fear and disorientation. Apprehension of the sublime could be absorbed into religious perceptions, as with the climbers to the Stone Gate on Mount Lu cited earlier, but we need not follow those writers who want to read all Chinese responses to nature as somehow religious, ruling out the varieties of elevated but secular sensations of a poetic order, including those that we in the West term Romantic. The latter would be appropriate to Huang Shan as a center of literati culture, of poetry clubs and individualist escape from mundane affairs. However we understand them, the authors of Huang Shan travel accounts often report their responses to the mountain in terms of transcendence that agree with European expressions of the sublime in nature: they feel that they have left the real world behind them; the sights are beyond description; even the greatest artists could not describe one ten-thousandth of their grandeur, and so forth.

Ch'ien Ch'ien-i's essay is especially rich in expressions of this kind. He made the climb in 1642, after an abortive start in the previous year with the poet-painter Ch'eng Chia-sui. It was probably Ch'eng, a native of Hsiu-ning living in Chia-ting, who first aroused in Ch'ien the urge to climb the mountain. Another friend wrote Ch'ien a letter asserting that Huang Shan had no rivals for impressive scenery, that no description could be adequate to it, and that it would surpass anything he could imagine. Ch'ien was not disappointed. He begins his encomium on the mountain with a grand geomantic vision. Rivers issue from Huang Shan, he points out, in all directions. Builders of capital cities would situate them so that all evil would be drained away by rivers flowing out from the center (the palace); Huang Shan is like that, with the Heavenly Capital Peak in the center, cleansed of all noxious elements by the flow of its waters. This is indeed the capital of Heaven, Ch'ien tells his companion, the dwelling-place of gods. At the Mañjuśrī Terrace, the darkness and quiet make him feel that he is not in the human world; at the Lao-jen feng 老人峰 or Old Man Peak, he has a sense of viewing all of creation in one vast vision. He feels as if in another world, as if reborn. He seems to have left behind his physical self, to be moving about as pure spirit. In echoes of Chuang Tzu's "butterfly dream," he wonders whether he is experiencing reality or illusion, whether the peaks are rooted in earth or in his imagining. He has come to a heavenlike place; how can he escape worry over whether he will be able to return to the real world? Ch'ien's account transmits more than others in the late period of the sense of numinosity that Huang Shan climbers feel, and although some of the power of his essay can be credited to his superior skills as a writer, we can accept it as reporting a genuine experience of transcendence and the sublime.

Reading Ch'ien's essay and knowing that he wrote it during a great age of landscape painting in China, one looks for pictorial representations of Huang Shan that match his literary one in the elevated sensations and intensity of experience it conveys. And, with a few exceptions (certain works by Shih-t'ao and K'un-ts'an, notably) one looks in vain. Expressions of the sublime in nature are, as we noted, for the most part to be found earlier in Chinese painting—in Sung landscapes, in some leaves of Wang Li's Hua Shan album and some others of the Ming, in still fewer of the Ch'ing. Even those early Ch'ing artists who declined to follow their Orthodox-school contemporaries in loading their paintings with stylistic allusions to old masters tended to adopt other conventionalized modes; thus their paintings are difficult to read as products of any deep and direct responsiveness to nature. Or, if they respond, it is obliquely, manipulating style and form in intricate ways to create expressive structures that somehow convey their responses. Hung-jen, for instance, reports in a quatrain the stupefying effect that the scenery of the Nine Bends River 九曲江 at Wu-i Shan 武夷山 in Fukien (where he had fled from the Manchu invasion and where he was ordained a monk) had on him: "How could Creation have composed the Nine Bends River?/ The spindly peaks and bulging cliffs are glassy in appearance./ The Taoist's brush lies unused on the boat windowsill;/ He can only stare with wide eyes, too bemused to poeticize." But there is not much of the sublime in the painting that this quatrain accompanies (Cahill, 1982a, fig. 5.24); an austere, intellectual, visually fascinating work in the Ni Tsan manner, it bemuses the eye through abstract devices of spatial ambiguity, not through any visual description of those aspects of Wu-i Shan that awed the artist or through any truly pictorial evocation of its grandeur. Hung-jen's paintings of Huang Shan scenes (see figs. 6.7 and 6.8) have the same character. Mei Ch'ing sometimes attempts, with far less success than Hung-jen, to find metaphors in artistic form to convey some hint of the sublimity of Huang Shan scenery; for the most part, his stylistic resources are too narrow for his aim, and his pictures become in the end more fanciful and quirky than awe inspiring (see fig. 6.6).

In pursuing the possible pilgrimage aspects of early Ch'ing Huang Shan paintings we are brought back continually to an irreducible problem: the factors that properly motivate pilgrimages—political or religious motivations or the search for transcendence through experience of the sublime—do not appear to underlie the production of the paintings. These were still good motivations for traveling to Huang Shan and climbing the mountain, but they cannot be substantiated as reasons for *depicting* the mountain or as making up the principal content of the paintings. Besides the evidence of inscriptions, the somewhat schematic character of most of the paintings argues against any such reading of them. That the artists were little concerned with visually persuasive and evocative portrayals of Huang Shan scenery is obvious if we compare the paintings with the places or even with each other. What is repeated from one picture to another (see figs. 6.5 and 6.6) is not the "real appearance" of the place (which is, in any case, an ideal construct that can never be fixed) but a schema, a configuration that supplies the relative location of scenic materials, the characterizing shapes of the peaks (often exaggerated), and so forth. The naming of the peaks and places and the adherence of bits of history and legend and poetry to them matter more than visual truth to the artists, who will alter the forms to emphasize these imposed attributes, making the Lotus Peak look more like a cluster of lotus petals than a mountain peak or the Sounding Strings Spring 鳴弦泉, with its strands of falling water, more lutelike than waterfall-like. Or an artist (Shih-t'ao) will add whiskers and a nose to the Tiger Head Rock 虎頭石 to underscore the presumed resemblance.

In treating the scenes this way, the portrayers of Huang Shan follow established Chinese practice for this late period (cf. Cahill 1982a, chaps. 1 and 2), from which exceptions diverge only in more or less isolated cases of artists and paintings. How and when the schemata are formed are questions beyond determination. Like signs in a semiotic system (which in truth they are) they come into being and are accepted within a society without anyone being aware of the moment or manner of their appearance; like religious images in an iconographic system they take on a status of correctness without anyone asking why they should be the correct way to represent that deity or that place. Nevertheless, and even acknowledging that the paintings and prints we can see are a small fraction of those that were produced, we could trace in a broad way the formation of the standard configurations for representing particular places.

More to our present purpose, however, is to note that the formulation of such standard configurations is a process akin to naming: to name is to know, and to possess an established image of a thing or place is to gain a kind of social knowledge of it, to partake of a collective understanding. The word *t'u* in Chinese denotes such established images, as we noted earlier, and woodblock-printed collections of them, whether small-scale like the *T'u-hui tsung-i* 圖繪宗彝 (1607) or large-scale like the pictorial encyclopedia *San-ts'ai t'u-hui* (also 1607), were like vocabularies for a shared visual language. The primacy of the word in China dictates that the image will not be self-sufficient; it must be joined to the name of the thing depicted (understood, if not actually present as a written title) and some information about it, usually in an accompanying inscription. In the case of topographical painting, a conjunction of these three makes up an adequate cluster of information about the place: its physical configuration presented in a schematic image; its name; and some cultural resonances that it should arouse, in the form of poetic or literary or legendary or historical references. The creation of such clusters of visual and written information around a sequence of designated places in a site such as Huang Shan reinforced the cultural structure that had come to be superimposed on the physical terrain (a process we can trace, as noted earlier, in the succession of travel accounts); disseminated and accepted within a social group, these clusters structured in turn the movements and experience of travelers to the place. Seeing the real place only confirmed, in fact, the essential truth of the schemata—unless, that is, one was a maverick (for China) like Chang Hung and came back from the trip complaining about the mismatch between the received information and the place. For most travelers the experience of confirmation, of experiencing with one's own eyes and mind what one had already been shown and told was a major goal of traveling to some well-traveled place. The schematic pictures, then, served to set up expectations that could then be satisfied in the actual trip; they became picture-maps for cultural pilgrimages.

Again, as in our consideration of the travel accounts, we should note that writing this way about the function of the paintings is not to argue that the real perceptions and sensations of travelers were necessarily limited to those conveyed in the paintings. *We* are not treating the experience of climbing Huang Shan reductively; we are arguing, on the contrary, that the *artists* mostly did so, by reducing what could be a profound spiritual quest, a purgation, a communion with the otherworldly, a sublime transcendence of mortal bounds, to the controlled and comfortable patterns of literati culture. But we should expect nothing else from Chinese artists working late in their painting tradition. Since the literati or scholar-amateur movement had begun to dominate Chinese painting in the fourteenth century, the naturalistic and evocative effects achieved by Sung masters had come to be disparaged as signifying a lower level of taste in both artist and audience; brushwork and antique style, refinements and restraint were the proper concerns of the cultivated painter and of the true connoisseur. The passions, the intensity, the diversity of human experience that earlier paintings could convey were tamed and accommodated to literati taste. Painters such as Kung Hsien and Shih-t'ao who refused to be bounded by these dictates won their independence at a cost, giving up some of the rewards of widespread acceptance and success in their time. For the most part, the constraints of the literati style were regarded as positive in value, endowing the subjects portrayed with high-culture associations. Wang Fu's paintings did that, in the Eight Views series cited earlier, for the scenery around Peking, making it better suited as a location for the imperial capital; paintings by literati masters of the Wu School did it for the scenery and social observances of Soochow. Now the depiction of Huang Shan in variants of the literati styles by Anhui-school masters and others helped similarly to validate the mountain as a proper objective for the cultural pilgrimages of the literati and those who would emulate them.

If we accept this characterization of the paintings—that they are usually not to be understood as firsthand reports of the artists' visual experiences of the places—it follows that the artist could depict places where he had never been, relying on the established schemata. And indeed, we know of numerous cases of that kind. Hsiao Yun-ts'ung writes in an inscription that he has never been to Huang Shan, yet he painted a sixty-leaf album of its scenery (the album, in the Peking Palace Museum, is misleadingly ascribed to Hung-jen on the basis of spurious seals; see Cahill 1985). Some of the leaves in that album are replicated in an album in the same collection by Hung-jen's nephew Chiang Chu; and an early eighteenth-century Anhui master produced an album by adopting compositions from Hsiao Yun-ts'ung, Hung-jen, Shih-t'ao, and others.[20] Mei Ch'ing inscribes some of his Huang Shan scenes as based on leaves by Shih-t'ao and as representing places where he himself has never gone. The author of a preface to the *Huang-shan t'u* series by the eighteenth-century monk-painter Hsueh-chuang (printed by woodblock and reproduced in *Huang-shan ts'ung-k'an*, ch. 1) praises his pictures as based on actual experience of the places, "unlike [the earlier Huang Shan pictures by] Hsiao [Ch'en 蕭晨] and Cheng [Chung], which were achieved through imagination." The last work of the late Chang Ta-ch'ien 張大千 was a huge representation of the scenery of Lu Shan, a place Chang never visited. Shih-t'ao, in a famous album dated 1701–2, painted a series of scenes based on travel poems composed by his patron Huang Yen-lü 黃硯旅, poems describing places where the artist himself probably had never been. And in another painting representing the Min River in Fukien, done in 1697, he introduced to another patron who was about to travel there the scenery of a place he probably never visited himself.[21] Many other examples of this phenomenon could be cited.

On the other hand, an artist who had climbed a mountain had an obvious advantage in portraying it over one who had not. Sung Hsu was commissioned to paint the handscroll representing a trip to Mount Po-yueh, in the case cited earlier, because he had once made the trip. An artist might travel to the place and make sketches in order to add the scenery of that mountain to his repertory of subjects and perhaps to establish himself as qualified to produce pictures of it for anyone who wanted them. The Anhui master Tai Pen-hsiao made a tour of famous mountains in the early 1660s, at the outset of his career as a painter, presumably for that purpose. Another Anhui painter, Cheng Min, painted an album of eight scenes of Huang Shan in 1681 for a patron named Ch'u-chen 楚珍 who had asked him for one of his works (see fig. 6.9); in an accompanying inscription Cheng writes that although he has never traveled far, he did climb Huang Shan twice, in 1670 and again in 1673, a kind of pilgrimage that was necessary, he suggests facetiously, to validate his status as a She-hsien (Hui-chou) native—and, we may assume, as a Hui-chou painter. He remarks that the pictures will convey to Ch'u-chen, who had not yet visited the place, some of the excitement of going there; at some future time, Cheng writes, when Ch'u-chen has cast off his worldly attachments as he, Cheng Min, has already done, he too can climb Huang Shan, using this album as a guide.

Shih-t'ao, as we noted before, first climbed Huang Shan in 1667 and continued to portray its scenery, from recollection but also, we can assume, from sketches, for the rest of his career. His "Eight Views of Huang Shan," an album now in the Sumitomo collection (see fig. 6.10; also Cahill 1982a, figs. 6.14 and 6.15), presents itself so convincingly as an immediate, firsthand account, in both paintings and inscriptions, that it was once dated by Japanese scholars to the time of his ascent of the mountain in the late 1660s (Kohara 1971); now, on the basis of style, we date it to the 1680s, after he had left Anhui and settled in Nanking, and we see it as an extraordinary re-creation of the experience. The same is true of another of Shih-t'ao's masterworks, the "Scenery of Huang Shan" handscroll dated 1699, also in the Sumitomo collection (see fig. 6.11), painted for a monk-friend who had just returned from a trip there. In 1700 Shih-t'ao wrote on a handscroll depicting the Huang Shan peaks: "When I traveled to Huang Shan in the past, I climbed the Start-to-Believe Peak (Shih-hsin Feng 始信峯) and looked out over the area of the Eastern Sea. Yesterday I was telling Mr. Su I-men 蘇易門 about the wonders of the different peaks of the Yellow Sea [i.e., Huang Shan]. I drew on my imagination to paint this vision which I saw thirty years ago, and as the brush wandered my spirit followed. Old I [-men] was enthusiastic, and requested the painting to use as a guide for his future travels in the mountain."[22]

It was Shih-t'ao's practice to employ the scenery of places he had been and the styles associated with local schools in nostalgic evocations done for patrons who were from those places, or whom he had known there, or who were going there.[23] In the early 1690s he painted a handscroll depicting "Gazing at the Hills in Yü-hang" 余杭 (Shanghai Museum) for someone who was traveling to that region in Chekiang; in a later inscription dated 1693 he writes that the man had brought the scroll back to him saying that the scenery had turned out to be exactly like the painting. Leaving aside this unmanageable issue of "fidelity to nature," we can observe that it was part of Shih-t'ao's genius to paint always, even when he was using elements of established styles, as though he were simply setting down the data of immediate experience, so that his recollected or even imagined visions persuade us of their truthfulness to some reality.

A pattern emerges from these and other cases that brings us a step nearer to understanding the pilgrimage aspect of these paintings. The artist makes the pictures for someone who plans a trip to a famous place to familiarize him in advance with the notable sights there, to identify those sights and inform him about them. Or else the paintings are done for someone who returns from a trip, to remind him of his experiences, perhaps to show to friends while he recounts his travels. These are not so much images of present, direct experience as anticipations or reminiscences. The artist, for his part, may or may not know the places firsthand; in either case he tends to rely on established schematic imagery, presenting variants of it drawn in his individual style. The paintings and their inscriptions reinforce the cultural configurations and associations that had come to cohere around the notable sights of Huang Shan, serving, in effect, as guides to cultural pilgrimages.

Important to this function is the sequential character of the pictures, which typically are made in series: leaves of an album, sections of a handscroll, a set of hanging scrolls. As we noted in discussing types of topographical paintings, a sequence of pictures might present stages in the journey to a place and what the traveler would see along the way. Lu Chih's "Trip to Mount Po-yueh" album and presumably Sung Hsu's handscroll of the same subject (known only from a literary record) belong to that type. Most Huang Shan painting series, by contrast, are not devoted to getting to the place but to going around it, making a circuit of its designated stopping places. There is no single destination; the experience is cumulative, like a Buddhist making the rounds of a sequence of shrines or Sudhana's pilgrimage in search of enlightenment. In actuality, one comes to know Huang Shan gradually, part by part, one's exhilaration sustained in the connecting passages by the breathtaking vistas but raised to further heights at the stopping points, where the visual experience is enhanced by recalling the name and associations of the place. Yuji Takashina finds this the basic difference between pilgrimage paintings in Asia, which typically portray a series or circuit of sacred places, and those in the West, which represent the destination or some sight along the way. The picture scroll (*emaki*) is ideally suited to the former, he notes, just as the easel painting is suited to the latter.[24] The handscroll and album in China are both appropriate for analogizing in pictorial forms the cumulative experience of reaching full knowledge of a place through a tour of its parts; the handscroll emphasizes spatial and temporal continuity, the album

a series of moments, of discrete observations. Gardens in China, as structured spaces, are also depicted most often in these formats, which have the
effect of keeping the viewer moving, allowing a person no single "right" vantage point, obliging one to undergo, as elements in the apprehension of the
whole, the passage of time and even physical movement (rolling the handscroll, turning the leaves of the album).

If the paintings were, in this special sense, pilgrimage pictures, who were
the pilgrims? For whom, that is, were the paintings done? The answer can
only come from a detailed study of the dedicatory inscriptions on some of
them, to identify the recipients; such a study has not been made. McDermott
establishes that Hung-jen's major patrons in his later years were the Wu
family of She-hsien, who owned a good part of Huang Shan and whose
wealth and power came both from producing degree-holders and from commerce, the latter chiefly through dealings in the salt monopoly office at Yang-
chou but also through pawnshops and other commercial ventures (McDermott 1989, 161 ff.). Two recent studies of the patronage of Anhui artists have
led to similar, not unexpected conclusions: the artists' clientele was made up
of a mix of gentry, scholar-officials, and merchants.[25] The flourishing of a
school of painters in this region and the attracting of others from elsewhere
must have been closely related to the region's economic prosperity; just as
Soochow became the major center of painting in the sixteenth century, Yang-
chou in the eighteenth, and Shanghai in the nineteenth, so did the Hui-chou
region, in the decades around the Ming-Ch'ing transition, nurture local
painters and lure others from outside. Similarly, the popularity of Huang
Shan both for climbers and for consumers of paintings must have been stimulated in large part by the great increase in travel, especially merchant travel,
to and from the nearby Hui-chou region, from where an excursion to Huang
Shan would be an easy and attractive side-trip. The essay "Shang-ku chi"
(On merchants) by Chang Han (1511–93) describes the situation in the late
sixteenth century: "From all directions people came [to the Lower Yangtze
region] like spokes to a hub, from all places in the world they pour into this
region. . . . Hsiu-ning and She-hsien are where those who grasp stunning
profits are most numerous; merchants from here almost entirely cover the
empire" (Brook 1981a, 197). That Huang Shan had become an objective for
cultural pilgrimages among the literati doubtless enhanced its drawing
power for merchants, who were anxious to emulate high-culture practice.
Like the tireless seekers after spiritual enlightenment in the West today, men
of the early Ch'ing lived in an age when material values seemed dangerously
in the ascendancy and when desires for escape, transcendence, purification—
for all of which Huang Shan stood—were especially gnawing.

An accompanying phenomenon, from the sixteenth century on, was the
publication of route books and travel guides, some of them with picture-
maps; these have been studied by Timothy Brook (1981b, c, and 1988). They

were written mostly by those merchants who had acquired the necessary literary polish and were intended chiefly for the traveling merchants; they listed places through which the traveler would pass on a given route and mentioned famous sights and temples along the way, even though, for the most part, their concern was (as Brook puts it) with "how to get across the landscape rather than how to admire it" (Brook 1981b, 42). Apart from their function as practical guides, they must have given the traveler some comforting sense of foreknowledge, of at least knowing the names and sequences of the places he would encounter.

The same was surely an important part of the motivation for many of our paintings, profoundly different from the route books as these are in character. When Li Liu-fang's brother asks for pictures that will make him "feel as if he is traveling there himself," when Sung Hsu paints a handscroll of scenes from a trip for a patron about to make the trip, when Cheng Min expresses the wish that his album of Huang Shan scenes will inspire his patron to climb the mountain with Cheng's album as a guide, when Shih-t'ao's friend asks for a picture of Huang Shan to use as a guide for future travels there, or when another asks for a painting of the hills of Yü-hang and then after seeing them reports that they were exactly like the painting, they are all testifying to an understanding of the paintings that ascribed a quasi-guidebook function to them. Alternatively, the paintings can help the traveler-patron to recall a trip already made, as Shih-t'ao's 1699 handscroll of Huang Shan did. The travel represented can be either anticipatory or retrospective; in either case, the pictures serve less to record any actual event than to evoke or reinforce cultural imaginings or reminiscences of the mountain, to invest it in the viewer's mind with a set of associations and a sense of familiarity. They help to structure an experience that the intended viewer will have, or has had, or imagines having.

CONCLUSION

This paper has in the end taken the form of one of the excursions it describes, likewise arriving at no looming or sharply visible destination, deriving whatever value it has from the circuit itself, through which a kind of cumulative, second-class enlightenment may have been attained. We began by asking, In what sense can the experience of climbing Huang Shan, as we can reconstruct it from writings and pictures, properly be termed a pilgrimage? And if the Huang Shan paintings are pilgrimage pictures, in what sense are they? To the first question we can answer only: in the sense that we ourselves may be driven by the pressures of practical affairs of everyday life to make "pilgrimages" to certain historical, scenic, or otherwise inspirational places in pursuit of a loosely conceived spiritual transcendence, escape from materialism, communion with the sublime in nature, the recapture of cultural values feared lost. Religious impulses, or political, or poetic and literary may be elements in the motivation of such a pilgrimage, but none of these is essential to it. And to the second question the answer is again a qualified one; if we understand the Huang Shan paintings as participating in a complex of ideas and motivations of this kind as they had come to be attached to the practice of climbing Huang Shan and as serving (although not in any practical sense) as "travel guides" for the ascent, we can term them, in this limited sense, pilgrimage pictures. Perhaps the late period in Chinese history, or art history, allows no answers less muddied than these, and clearly motivated actions and expressions in both belong to a safely mythologized distant past.

APPENDIX:
PARTIAL LIST OF EARLY CH'ING PAINTINGS OF HUANG SHAN

Hung-jen

Album of scenes of Huang Shan. Ink on silk. Two leaves in Ching Yuan Chai collection, Berkeley (see figs. 6.7 and 6.8); other leaves unknown.
"Pines and Cliffs of Huang Shan." Hanging scroll, dated 1660. Shanghai Museum (Cahill 1981, fig. 5).
"The P'i-yun Peak." Dated 1663 (ibid., no. 25).
"The Shih-hsin (Start-to-Believe) Peak." Dated 1663. Canton Art Museum (see *I-yuan to-ying*, no. 25, p. 19).

Hsiao Yun-ts'ung

Album of fifty scenes of Huang Shan. Palace Museum, Peking. Spurious seals of Hung-jen, usually ascribed to him (see Cahill 1985).

Chiang Chu

Album of scenes of Huang Shan, Palace Museum, Peking. Some leaves reproduce the compositions in the Hsiao Yun-ts'ung album above; the relationship between these two and others requires further study. The album is discussed briefly, and two leaves reproduced, in Hsu Pang-ta, "Huang-shan t'u-ts'e tso-che k'ao-pien," *Tuo-yun*, no. 9 (December 1985): 125–28. This is a rejoinder to my article on the "Hung-jen" album (Cahill 1985).

Mei Ch'ing

A number of albums of scenes of Huang Shan dated between 1672 and 1695 (cf. fig. 6.6 in this chapter).
Two series of Huang Shan scenes in hanging scroll form, one on silk, one on paper. Five from the former series, four from the latter were shown

in an exhibition of Anhui School painting in winter 1984–85, Palace Museum, Peking.

Ten-panel screen of Huang Shan scenery. Canton Art Museum (see *I-yuan to-ying*, no. 16, pp. 12–13). Some of the many tall, narrow hanging-scroll paintings of Huang Shan scenery by Mei Ch'ing that survive were probably originally panels in screens of this type.

Cheng Min

Album of eight scenes of Huang Shan. Dated 1674 (see fig. 6.9). Private collection, Alberta, Canada (see Sotheby's auction catalog, New York, June 3,1985, no. 44).

A number of hanging scrolls of Huang Shan peaks and scenes. Several in Palace Museum, Peking.

Tai Pen-hsiao

"The Orchid Peak." Vannotti collection, Lugano (see Cahill 1967, no. 15).

"The Wen-shu yuan" (see Cahill 1981, no. 54).

Sun I 孫逸

"The Cinnabar Peak." Dated 1657 (see Cahill 1981, no. 18).

Shih-t'ao

Album of twenty-one scenes of Huang Shan. Palace Museum, Peking. Unpublished; it will be included in a planned (1992) exhibition of works by Tung Ch'i-ch'ang, his contemporaries, and artists he influenced scheduled to open at the Nelson-Atkins Art Museum in April 1992. I have not seen the Shih-t'ao album in the original; no signature or seals appear on the leaves, but there is presumably some accompanying documentation. It would appear from photographs to be an early work, done during the artist's stay in Anhui and perhaps dating from only a few years after he climbed Huang Shan in the late 1660s. In any case, it is an important predecessor of the better-known work listed next.

Album of eight scenes of Huang Shan. Sumitomo collection (see fig. 6.10; see also Cahill 1982a, figs. 6.14 and 6.15, and Kohara 1971).

"Scenery of Huang Shan." Handscroll, dated 1699. Sumitomo collection (see fig. 6.11; see also Cahill 1982a, fig. 6.30, and Miyazaki 1985).

"Scenery of Huang Shan." Handscroll, dated 1700. Ho Kuan-wu collection, Hong Kong (see *Chih-lo lou*, no. 20).

K'un-ts'an

A number of hanging scrolls with inscriptions mentioning Huang Shan, probably representing Huang Shan scenery (discussed and reproduced in Chang 1987).

NOTES

I want to thank the Center for Chinese Studies and the Committee on Research, University of California, Berkeley, for research support received during the presentation of this paper. I would also like to thank Joseph McDermott for useful comments on an earlier draft.

1. Note, however, that according to Timothy Brook, this was a more general phenomenon, not particular to Huang Shan. "Despite the religious association of their name, however, monastic gazetteers were basically secular in nature. Aside from biographies of monks and devoted laymen, texts dealing with specifically religious matters are rarely included" (Brook 1988, 54–55). This in spite of the fact that about one-third of them were compiled by monks (62–63). Chün-fang Yü (chapter 3 of this volume) disagrees.

2. The most important are collected in the 1679 *Huang-shan chih ting-pen*, edited by Min Lin-ssu. The four volumes of travel accounts in the 1935 *Huang-shan ts'ung-k'an*, edited by Su Tsung-jen, supplement these, mostly with later essays; this is by far the most complete collection.

3. P'ei-yi Wu comments on the conventionalization and secularization of *yu-chi* or travel accounts in a larger context, noting that the writer recording a trip to a famous mountain "is often obliged to touch all bases and compare his impressions with the comments of previous writers. Responses to sites and scenes are more often didactic than introspective." He defines "the usual content of a *yu-chi*" as "making the rounds of the historical sites and scenic spots, all catalogued and celebrated in earlier writings" (see chapter 2 of this volume, pp. 68 and 82). He postulates a "cultural gap" that separated the people who wrote the accounts from those who made the pilgrimages and notes that the former seem all but unaware of the latter.

4. The defacement of nearby Mount Po-yueh by "scholarly graffiti" was the subject of a bitter complaint from Yuan Hung-tao (1568–1610) (see Li Chi 1974, 62). Chang Tai, writing a bit later, makes the same complaint about graffiti on T'ai Shan (see Pei-yi Wu, chapter 2 of this volume).

5. Ganza's doctoral dissertation, "The Artist as Traveler: The Origin and Development of Travel as a Theme in Chinese Landscape Painting of the Fourteenth to Seventeenth Centuries," was written for the School of Fine Arts at Indiana University. He has published one paper (Ganza 1986) and delivered another (Ganza 1988) in the session on Genres in Chinese Painting at the College Art Association's annual meeting, Houston, February 1988.

6. Cf. the interesting discussion of series of *ching* 景, "views" or (as Brook renders it) "prospects": "A prospect is an established and well-defined view onto a known landscape, not a view that the artist selects and defines himself. Being conventional, it

provides precise terms, both visual and emotive, within which a landscape might be translated into painting or poetry while leaving the artist a narrow range of freedom in which to express himself through limited variations" (1988, 59). Brook's definition of *ching* is in agreement with my treatment of "views of Huang Shan" paintings later in this chapter.

7. For studies of this handscroll see Shih Shu-ch'ing, "Wang Fu Pei-ching pa-ching t'u yen-chiu," *Wen-wu*, no. 5 (1981): 78–85; Julia Marie White, "Topographical Painting in Early Ming China: Eight Scenes of Peking by Wang Fu," Master's thesis (University of California, Berkeley, 1983); and Kathlyn Liscomb, "The Eight Views of Beijing: Politics in Literati Art," *Artibus Asiae* 44, 1/2 (1988–89): 127–52. Liscomb argues convincingly that the scroll now in the Historical Museum, Peking, is not the original; but its authenticity is not our concern here.

8. For a study of the early history of Mao Shan and the Taoist religion practiced there, see Edward H. Schafer, *Mao-shan in T'ang Times*. 2nd ed., rev. Society for the Study of Chinese Religions Monograph No. 1 (Boulder, Colo., 1989).

9. For a brief account of the album and reproductions of two leaves, see Cahill 1978, pls. 1 and 2 and pp. 5–7. A good treatment of the album and its history is Shan Guo-lin, "Wang Li ho 'Hua-shan t'u-ts'e'," *Mei-shu ts'ung-k'an* 1 (1978): 17–21. A volume on Wang Li and his album for the Chung-kuo hua-chia ts'ung-shu series by Hsueh Yung-nien is in press; I am grateful to Elizabeth Weiland, who is herself writing a doctoral dissertation on the album for Columbia University, for making Hsueh's text available to me.

10. For the close relationship between the Sung-chiang and southern Anhui schools of painting in the late Ming, see Cahill 1981, Introduction. See also McDermott 1989, 152, for the relationship of Tung Ch'i-ch'ang to Hui-chou collectors.

11. For Leng Ch'ien, see the entry by T. W. Weng in L. Carrington Goodrich and Chaoying Fang, eds., *Dictionary of Ming Biography* (New York: Columbia University Press, 1976), pp. 802–4. The painting, which is in the National Palace Museum, Taipei, has been studied by Kenneth Ganza (Ganza 1986, 1988).

12. See *Po-yueh ning-yen* 白岳凝烟, postface 1714, facsimile reproduction in Chung-kuo pan-hua ts'ung-k'an series (Shanghai, 1960), p. 36. Other leaves in this book depict famous places on the mountain, most of them with names that suggest Taoist associations.

13. *Shih-pai-chai shu-hua lu* 十百齋書畫錄 by Chin Yuan 金瑗, late eighteenth century, ch. 8, p. 3b.

14. Li Liu-fang, *T'an-yuan chi* 檀園集, ch. 10, p. 16, quoted in the essay by Jane DeBevoise and Scarlett Jang in Cahill 1981, p. 43.

15. Li-tsui Flora Fu has studied paintings of this mountain in "Landscapes of Mount Lu," Master's thesis (University of California, Berkeley, 1989). She traces the "privatization" of the image of Mount Lu in later Chinese representations and the ways in which later artists drew on a rich store of "culturally encoded motifs."

16. The 1462 print is in a rare book in the Naikaku Bunko, Tokyo; see McDermott 1989, fig. 63. For the 1607 and 1633 prints see Cahill 1981, figs. 3 and 4. The 1648 print is in the T'ai-p'ing shan-shui series by Hsiao Yun-ts'ung; see Cahill 1982c, fig. 19. Joseph McDermott's discussion of woodblock prints of Huang Shan (McDermott 1989, 150–51) makes use of materials inaccessible to me.

17. McDermott 1989, 154; the information is from Ch'eng Min-cheng's *Huang-tun hsien-sheng wen-chi*.

18. Other paintings by Anhui artists may contain loyalist or other political messages—for instance, album leaves by Hsiao Yun-ts'ung discussed in the second chapter of my book on early Ch'ing painting (in progress). But the political meanings are not attached to images of Huang Shan.

19. See Kin-yuen Wong, "Negative-positive Dialectic in the Chinese Sublime," in *The Chinese Text: Studies in Chinese Literature*, ed. Ying-hsiung Chou (Hong Kong: Chinese University Press, 1986), pp. 119–58.

20. This album, by Huang Ch'i 黃錤, I know only through a copy by the twentieth-century master Huang Pin-hung 黃賓虹 that was exhibited at the She-hsien City Art Museum in 1984. Later I saw at the Palace Museum in Peking the album attributed to Chiang Chu, in which more than one hand seems to be represented. The complex problem of the relationship of these albums must be cleared up through careful comparison and research by someone who has access to them. What is clear is that compositions are repeated from one album to another and that the authorship of the albums is clouded. A similar replication seems to have taken place in Soochow-school albums and handscrolls representing scenery of that region, works by or ascribed to Shen Chou, Lu Chih, Ch'ien Ku, and others; but this material also requires detailed study to straighten it out. In both cases we should probably assume a large-scale local production of series of paintings after the designs of noted masters of the region to fulfill a demand from travelers and others.

21. For the 1702 album painted for Huang Yen-lü, see *Chih-lo-lou*, no. 21. For the 1697 painting of the Min River in Fukien, now in the Cleveland Museum of Art, see *Eight Dynasties of Chinese Painting* 1980, no. 239.

22. Slightly altered from the translation by Jonathan Hay in Hay 1988, p. 286. The painting is in the Ho Yao-kuang collection, Hong Kong; see *Chih-lo-lou*, no. 20.

23. Richard Vinograd discusses this practice of Shih-t'ao in "Reminiscences of Ch'in-Huai: Tao-chi and the Nanking School," *Archives of Asian Art* 31 (1977–78): 6–31.

24. "E no tabi, tabi no e," *Nihon no bigaku* 1, 1 (1984): 102–9. He is concerned with the Saigyo Monogatari and other Kamakura-period picture-scrolls.

25. Chi-sheng Kuo, "Hui-chou Merchants as Art Patrons in the late 16th and Early 17th Centuries," and Sewall Oertling II, "Patronage of Anhui Artists in the Wan-li Era," papers presented at the ACLS workshop "Artists and Patrons: Social and Economic Aspects of Chinese Painting," November 1980, forthcoming.

BIBLIOGRAPHY

Brook, Timothy. 1981a. "The Merchant Network in 16th-Century China: A Discussion and Translation of Zhang Han's 'On Merchants.'" *Journal of the Economic and Social History of the Orient* 24, 2 (May 1981): 165–214.

———. 1981b. "Guides for Vexed Travelers: Route Books in the Ming and Qing." *Ch'ing-shih wen-t'i* 4, 5 (June 1981): 32–76.

———. 1981c. "Guide for Vexed Travelers: A Supplement." *Ch'ing-shih wen-t'i* 4, 6 (December 1981): 130–40.

————. 1988. *Geographical Sources of Ming-Qing History*. Ann Arbor: Center for Chinese Studies, University of Michigan.

Bush, Susan. 1983. "Tsung Ping's Essay on Painting Landscape and the 'Landscape Buddhism' of Mount Lu." In *Theories of the Arts in China*, edited by Susan Bush and Christian Murck, 132–64. Princeton: Princeton University Press.

Cahill, James. 1967. *Fantastics and Eccentrics in Chinese Painting*. New York: Asia Society.

————. 1976. *Hills Beyond a River: Chinese Painting of the Yüan Dynasty, 1279–1368*. New York: Weatherhill.

————. 1978. *Parting at the Shore: Chinese Painting of the Early and Middle Ming Dynasty, 1368–1580*. New York: Weatherhill.

————. 1982a. *The Compelling Image: Nature and Style in Seventeenth-Century Chinese Painting*. Cambridge: Harvard University Press.

————. 1982b. *The Distant Mountains: Chinese Painting of the Late Ming Dynasty, 1570–1644*. New York: Weatherhill.

————. 1982c. "Late Ming Albums and European Printed Books." In *The Illustrated Book: Essays in Honor of Lessing J. Rosenwald*, edited by Sandra Hindman, 150–71. Washington, D.C.: Library of Congress.

————. 1985. "Lun Hung-jen *Huang-shan t'u-ts'e* ti kuei-shu" 論弘仁"黃山圖册"的歸屬 [On the album of scenes of Huang Shan attributed to Hung-jen]. *Tuo-yun*, no. 9: 108–24.

————, ed. 1981. *Shadows of Mt. Huang: Chinese Painting and Printing of the Anhui School*. Berkeley: University Art Museum.

Chang, Joseph (Chang Tzu-ning 張子寧). 1987. "K'un-ts'an ti Huang-shan chih lü" 髡殘的黃山之旅 [K'un-ts'an's trip to Huang Shan]. Paper for symposium on Anhui school painting, Hofei, 1984. In *Lun Huang-shan chu hua-p'ai wen-chi* 論黃山諸畫派文集, 359–71. Shanghai.

Chaves, Jonathan. 1988. "The Yellow Mountain Poems of Ch'ien Ch'ien-i (1582–1664): Poetry as *yu-chi*." *Harvard Journal of Asiatic Studies* 48, 2 (December 1988): 465–92.

Chih-lo-lou ts'ang Ming i-min shu-hua 至樂樓藏明遺民書畫 [Paintings and calligraphy by Ming I-min from the Chih-lo Lou Collection]. 1975. Hong Kong.

Edwards, Richard. 1967. *The Painting of Tao-chi*. Catalog of an exhibition. Ann Arbor: Museum of Art, University of Michigan.

Eight Dynasties of Chinese Painting: The Collections of the Nelson Gallery-Atkins Museum, Kansas City, and The Cleveland Museum of Art. 1980. Catalog of an exhibition. Cleveland, Ohio: Cleveland Museum of Art.

Ganza, Kenneth. 1986. "A Landscape by Leng Ch'ien and the Emergence of Travel as a Theme in Fourteenth-Century Chinese Painting." *National Palace Museum Bulletin* 21, 3 (July/August 1986): 1–17.

————. 1987. *Journeys of the Spirit: Landscape Portraits of Places in China*. Catalog of an exhibition. Memphis.

————. 1988. "Travel as a Genre: Defining Theme in Chinese 'Topographical' Landscape Painting." Unpublished paper, revised from paper presented at session on Genres in Chinese Painting, College Art Association annual meeting, Houston.

Hay, Jonathan Scott. 1988. "Shih-t'ao's Late Work (1697–1707): A Thematic Map." Ph.D. dissertation, Yale University.

Hsu, Wen-chin. 1975. *Tao-chi and Huang-shan*. Master's thesis. University of California, Berkeley.

Huang-shan chih ting-pen. See Min Lin-ssu.

Huang-shan t'u-ching 黃山圖經. Anonymous text ascribed to Sung period. In *An-hui ts'ung-shu*, series 5, Shanghai, 1935. Also in *Huang-shan ts'ung-k'an*.

I-yuan to-ying 藝苑掇英 [Gems of Chinese fine arts]. Shanghai, 1978.

Kohara Hironobu 古原宏伸. 1971. "Sekitō to Kōzan hasshō gasatsu" 石濤と黃山八勝畫冊. Explanatory booklet accompanying facsimile reproduction of eight views of Huang Shan album in Sumitomo collection, under editorship of Tanaka Isshō, Tokyo.

Kōno Keiko. 1986. *Kōzan zukan* [The Huang Shan picture scroll (by Shih-t'ao)]. Kyoto, Sen-oku Hakko Kan (Sumitomo Collection).

Li, Chi. 1974. *The Travel Diaries of Hsü Hsia-k'o*. Hong Kong.

Li Chu-tsing. 1976. "Hsiang Sheng-mo chih chao-yin shih-hua" 項聖謨之招隱詩畫 [Hsiang Sheng-mo's Poetry and Painting on Eremitism]. *Proceedings of the Symposium on Paintings and Calligraphy by Ming I-min*, 531–60. Hong Kong: Chinese University, Institute of Chinese Studies.

Li I-min 李一氓. 1983. *Ming Ch'ing jen yu Huang-shan chi-ch'ao* 明清人游黃山記鈔. Ho-fei.

McDermott, Joseph. 1989. "The Making of a Chinese Mountain, Huangshan: Politics and Wealth in Chinese Art." *Asian Cultural Studies* (Tokyo) 17 (March).

Min Lin-ssu 閔麟嗣 (1628–1704), ed. *Huang-shan chih ting-pen* 黃山志定本 preface 1679. In *An-hui ts'ung-shu*. Shanghai, 1935, series 5.

Miyazaki Noriko 宮崎法子. 1985. "Sekitō to Kōzan zukan" 石濤と黃山圖卷 [Shih-t'ao and his Huang Shan handscroll]. *Sen'oku hakubutsukan kiyō*, no. 2: 37–71.

Powell, William. 1989. "A Pilgrim's Landscape Text of Chiu Hua Shan." Paper prepared for the Conference on Pilgrims and Sacred Sites in China. Bodega Bay, Calif. January.

Su Tsung-jen 蘇宗仁, ed. 1935. *Huang-shan ts'ung-k'an* 黃山叢刊. 8 vols. Peking.

Wang Shih-hung 汪士鈜 (ca. 1662–1721), ed. *Huang-shan chih hsu-chi* 黃山志續集. In *An-hui ts'ung-shu*, series 5. Shanghai, 1935.

Weng, Wan-go, and Yang Boda. 1980. *The Palace Museum: Treasures of the Forbidden City*. New York: Abrams.

Wright, Suzanne. 1984. "Scenes of Huangshan." Master's thesis. University of California, Berkeley.

Yuhas, Louise. 1979. "The Landscape Art of Lu Chih (1496–1576)." Ph.D. dissertation, University of Michigan.

SEVEN

The Pilgrimage to Wu-tang Shan

John Lagerwey

In 1412 the Ming emperor Ch'eng-tsu (r. 1403–24) ordered a massive construction campaign on Wu-tang Shan, a mountain range south of the Han River in northwest Hupei. Within six short years, three hundred thousand corvée laborers had built seven large monastic complexes, a goodly number of small temples, and more than sixty kilometers of hewn granite walkways and steps on these mountains dedicated to the cult of Chen-wu 真武, the Perfect Warrior (map 7.1). In the year 1424, finally, not long before Ch'eng-tsu's death, the Forty-fourth Heavenly Master himself, Chang Yü-ch'ing 張宇清, having first selected at the emperor's behest some four hundred Taoists from all over the empire to staff the various abbeys and temples, celebrated a seven-day Offering of the Supreme Lo-t'ien Heaven to give thanks for the successful completion of the entire project.[1]

The reasons for this orgy of construction in the best imperial style are fairly clear—Ch'eng-tsu attributed to Chen-wu his successful usurpation of the throne—and so are the results: pilgrims began to stream to the mountain from far and wide, and Chen-wu became the object of one of the few truly "national" cults, involving all levels of society from the humblest butcher right up to the emperor.[2] All of this, of course, did not come to pass overnight, and we do well therefore to begin our investigation of the pilgrimage to Wu-tang Shan with a rapid survey of the history of the mountain and its god prior to Ming Ch'eng-tsu.

THE PRE-HISTORY OF THE CHEN-WU CULT

Chen-wu was originally called Hsuan-wu 玄武, the Dark Warrior (or Warrior of the Dark Heaven of the North). As such, he is well known already in

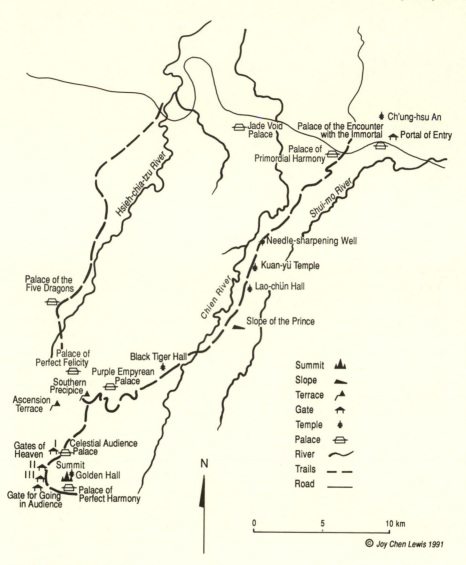

Palace of
Purity and Joy

Ch'ung-hsu An

Jade Void
Palace

Palace of the Encounter
with the Immortal

Portal of Entry

Palace of
Primordial Harmony

Hsieh-chia-tzu River

Shui-mo River

Needle-sharpening Well

Kuan-yü Temple

Lao-chün Hall

Palace of the
Five Dragons

Chien River

Slope of the Prince

Palace of
Perfect Felicity

Black Tiger Hall

Purple Empyrean
Palace

Southern
Precipice

Ascension
Terrace

Celestial Audience
Palace

Gates of
Heaven

Summit

Golden Hall

Gate for Going
in Audience

Palace of
Perfect Harmony

N

Summit

Slope

Terrace

Gate

Temple

Palace

River

Trails

Road

0   5   10 km

© Joy Chen Lewis 1991

Map 7.1. Wu-tang Shan

preimperial times, and he is portrayed in Eastern Han tomb engravings as the northern one of the "four divine animals" (*ssu-ling* 四靈; Rudolph and Yu 1951, illus. 74). By the early eighth century (and probably before), these four animals play a significant role in Taoist ritual as the guardians of the person of the high priest and of the purity of the sacred area (Lagerwey 1987, 94). This function of the Dark Warrior probably also explains why the northern gate of the T'ang capital of Ch'ang-an was called Hsuan-wu men (Huang Chao-han 1988b, 134).

According to the *Hsuan-t'ien shang-ti ch'i-sheng lu*, apparently the oldest extant collection of stories regarding the Dark Warrior,[3] a cult devoted to Hsuan-wu alone, to the exclusion of the other three divine animals, goes back at least to the seventh century.[4] The same collection, however, makes it very clear that it was the emperor T'ai-tsu of the Sung (r. 960–76) who first gave the cult national status (2.11b–12a, 14b, 3.10a, 19a). More official sources inform us that the emperor Chen-tsung (r. 998–1022), in response to the miraculous appearance of a snake and a tortoise in the year 1017, established a temple in honor of the Dark Warrior inside the capital city of K'ai-feng. In 1018 a spring suddenly bubbled to the surface next to the temple, and its water proved to have healing powers. The hall was renamed the Abbey of the Auspicious Spring (Liang T'ien-hsi, 1978, 55), and Hsuan-wu became Chen-wu, the Perfect Warrior, to avoid using the personal name of the Sung imperial ancestor, Chao Hsuan-lang 趙玄朗. He also received his first imperial title.[5]

The emperor Jen-tsung (r. 1023–64) himself is said in the *Ch'i-sheng lu* to have been cured by Chen-wu in the year 1056. This divine cure led to the first compilation of Chen-wu mirabilia, on which the 1184 collection of Tung Su-huang is largely based.[6] If the Warrior's prowess in battle with the demons that cause sickness was thus one of the main attractions of his cult, the *Ch'i-sheng lu* leaves no room for doubt that imperial gratitude was primarily the result of his assistance against the equally demonic "barbarians" (see Grootaers 1952). Indeed, so efficacious was the Perfect Warrior that even the Western barbarians decided during the T'ien-hsi period (1017–21) that they too would do well to worship him. They sent a mission promising peace in exchange for a portrait of Chen-wu and instructions on how to conduct his worship. The Sung chancellery accepted this proposal and ordered the Hanlin Academy to copy the official portrait of Chen-wu but to leave out of the painting his "vanguard," the tortoise and the snake (*Ch'i-sheng lu* 2.13b–14b).

In conclusion we may note that the greater share of the tales in the *Ch'i-sheng lu* take place along the northern and western frontiers, but the cult seems nonetheless to have spread already throughout the empire; stories of Chen-wu's miraculous interventions occur everywhere, from Shantung (2.17b)[7] to Kwangsi (3.19b) and from Szechuan (2.2b) to Fukien (4.20a).

THE PREHISTORY OF WU-TANG SHAN

Let us turn our attention now from the god worshiped on Wu-tang Shan to the mountain itself. In Ming times this mountain came to be known as the Great Peak, T'ai-yueh 太嶽, meaning that it was viewed as superior to the traditional Five Peaks. But what was its status in pre-Ming China?

Most of the ritual activity described in the *Ch'i-sheng lu* occurs in the Northern Sung capital of K'ai-feng. Mention is made of the dispatch of imperial inscriptions concerning Chen-wu to various sites throughout the empire, including Wu-tang Shan (2.22b), but nowhere is there any reference to imperial investment in the mountain. It is likely, nonetheless, that the Taoist ritual known as "the throwing of the strips"[8] was performed there throughout the Sung, for Wu-tang Shan is mentioned by Tu Kuang-t'ing (850–933) as one of the seventy-two "blessed plots";[9] and Liu Tao-ming, writing at the end of the thirteenth century, states that "successive dynasties have thrown the strips in the dragon well within the walls of the Wu-lung kung (Five Dragon Palace)" (Liu Tao-ming 1301, 2.9b).[10]

The history of Taoist occupation of Wu-tang Shan leads to similar conclusions as far as the dates of cultic development are concerned. The various monographs of the mountain all mention Yin Hsi as the first Taoist hermit to have lived in the Wu-tang range. He is followed by such other well-known figures from the Han to the T'ang as Ma Ming-sheng, Lü Tung-pin, and Sun Ssu-mo. Such references are, of course, notoriously unreliable, but we can nonetheless state with certainty that Taoist hermits have been associated with Wu-tang Shan at least since the Six Dynasties, for that is the date of the *Tung-hsien chuan*–derived biography of a hermit said to have lived on Wu-tang Shan in the second century B.C.E. (*Yun-chi ch'i-ch'ien* 110.19b).

The famous Ch'en T'uan (872–989) is reported by his biography in the *Sung-shih* to have lived on Wu-tang Shan for twenty years before moving to Hua Shan to escape from "an excessive number of visitors."[11] A text that occupies all of *chüan* 87 in the *Yun-chi ch'i-ch'ien* is attributed to one Chai Wei of Nan-yang, "hermit from Wu-tang Shan."

During the Yung-hsi period (984–87), one Chang Shih-sun (964–1049), a poor boy from nearby Kuang-hua who had learned to read on Wu-tang Shan, came in first in the imperial exams (Wang Kai 1744, 4.6a). In his youth, according to a story told by Chiang Hsiu-fu (1005–60) in his *Li-ch'üan pi-lu*, Chang narrowly escaped being "killed and sacrificed to demons by lying down in his bedchamber and reciting the Incantation of the Emperor of the Six Heavens of the North. The shaman (who wished to kill him), when he saw the stellar mansions [of the northern sector] hovering over Chang, took fright and fled."[12]

In the year 1141 Sun Chi-jan, a hereditary Taoist of Mao Shan, arrived on Wu-tang Shan with the Five Thunder Method of Shang-ch'ing.[13] He found the halls and temples on the mountain empty because of the war with the Chin but soon managed to restore the buildings of the Five Dragon Abbey—it was only later made a "palace"—thanks to his success in healing locals with Taoist "symbol-water" (*fu-shui*, water in which have been placed the ashes of a written symbol representing a divine name). Kao-tsung (r. 1127–62) summoned him to court and gave him permission to initiate ten Taoists. Sun's disciple, Teng Chen-kuan, carried on the tradition until Teng's death in about 1201; Teng in turn was followed by Ts'ao Kuan-miao of nearby Hsuan-shan, who died in 1236.

In 1275, apparently after another period of abandonment, the Five Dragon Abbey was restored by Wang Chen-ch'ang and six disciples. Shortly thereafter, several Wu-tang Shan Taoists learned the new Ch'ing-wei style of ritual from Huang Lei-ch'uang: Liu Tao-ming of Ching-men went on to write the *Tsung-chen chi* already mentioned; Yeh Yun-lai was summoned to court in 1285, where he won approval as an exorcist and rainmaker; Chang Tao-kuei of Ch'ang-sha had first studied with Wang Chen-ch'ang. Chang himself had more than two hundred disciples, of whom the most famous was Chang Shou-ch'ing, founder, as we shall see, of the Palace of the Perfect Felicity of the Celestial One (T'ien-i chen-ch'ing kung 天乙真慶宮) on Southern Precipice (Nan-yen 南巖).

Cumulatively, these stories show that Wu-tang Shan was a Taoist mountain of considerable importance from early Sung times on. As such, it was part of a network of Taoist mountains; new ritual styles from as far away as Mao Shan in Kiangsu made their way very quickly to Wu-tang Shan, and Wu-tang Shan Taoists of superior achievement attracted imperial attention.

But what drew Taoists to Wu-tang Shan? For the Sung we have only the tale of Chang Shih-sun, which suggests Wu-tang Shan's distinctive trait to have been the cult of the Emperor of the North. This "drawing card" will be massively confirmed under the Yuan.

IMPERIAL CONSTRUCTION ON WU-TANG SHAN

It is a curious, not to say startling fact that the cosmological dimensions of the mountain that was to become under the Ming *the* mountain, on which and on whose god dynastic legitimacy itself depended, were first clearly defined under the non-Chinese Yuan dynasty. According to the official texts treated below, indeed, the reasons for Mongol interest in Wu-tang Shan and its divine ruler were essentially the same as those of the Ming: association of the dynasty with the north. The north is the origin of the demonic in traditional Chinese cosmology, as it is the origin of "barbarian" invasion in Chinese political history. But this same unruly northland, once it is properly governed by the divine Emperor of the North and his terrestrial counterpart, becomes synonymous with safe borders and abundant rain. And whoever could ensure a safe northern frontier and rain in due time had, clearly, Heaven's approval—the Heavenly Mandate.

Proof of all this for the Yuan dynasty may be found in the *Hsuan-t'ien shang-ti ch'i-sheng ling-i lu (TT* 961). The first three texts in this book, all written in 1270, treat of the founding of a Chen-wu temple near the newly completed Yuan capital to commemorate the appearances of a "divine snake" and a "numinous tortoise" in Metal River in the dead of winter in the year 1269. These appearances were taken as signs of Chen-wu's approval of the new capital. The first of the three texts, by Han-lin academician Hsu Shih-lung (*chin-shih* 1227), cites the opinion of one Wen Yao-kou to the effect that this sign of divine approval was only natural, given the fact that "our dynasty was founded in the north, whose plenitude of power lies in water" (1b).[14]

A fuller and more explicit statement of the cosmological and political significance of the cult of the Perfect Warrior may be found in a text written in 1312 by the famous painter and calligrapher Chao Meng-fu:

> According to the *I-ching*, the celestial one gives birth to water, and the terres-
> trial six brings it to completion. All numbers begin with the celestial one; water
> is at the origin of the "taking shape" of all things. . . . The rise of the Yuan
> began in the north. The energy of the north being in the ascendance, the god of
> the north sent down prophetic signs: thus did Heaven announce [the dynastic
> change]. (*Ch'i-sheng ling-i lu* 14b–15b)

The fourth text in the *Ling-i lu*, written by the Han-lin academician Ch'eng Chü-fu in the year 1315, commemorates the founding of the Palace of the Perfect Felicity of the Celestial One on the Southern Precipice. During the reign of Sung Li-tsung (r. 1225–64), writes Ch'eng, the court ordered a Taoist called Liu the Perfect to set up a temple on the Southern Precipice. Liu failed, but a hermit from Han-tung, Lu Ta-yu, managed to live alone on this cliff for more than forty years. Lu had prophetic and other marvellous powers, and "his contemporaries considered him a god."[15]

When the Mongols entered the area, Lu Ta-yu left to study Ch'üan-chen (Integral Perfection) Taoism. He returned in 1275 and, after helping restore the Five Dragon Palace and the Purple Empyrean Altar (Tzu-hsiao t'an-yü 紫霄壇宇), took up his life as a hermit on Southern Precipice once again. In 1284 Chang Shou-ch'ing, then thirty-one *sui*, arrived from Hsia-chou (I-ch'ang county, Hupei) and asked to become Lu's disciple. "I've been waiting for you for a long time," said Lu, and transmitted to him the essentials of the Way. After Lu died, in the first month of the following year, Chang led his own disciples in opening paths to the Southern Precipice and fields around it for farming. They used the enormous sums of money contributed by the "tens of thousands of pilgrims who gathered on what is traditionally con-sidered the birthday of the god, to wit, the third day of the third month," to build an enormous complex on the Southern Precipice. It took more than twenty years to complete work on the "palace," and in 1308 the empress, having learned of Chang's reputation, ordered a Golden Register Offering be held. Chang was also summoned to the capital in 1312 to pray for rain—it had not rained from the ninth month of 1311 until the third month of 1312 according to Chao Meng-fu (Wang Kai 1744, 6.39b)—which he did success-fully in both that year and the next. An official title was granted to Chang's new "palace," and in 1314 Chang was ordered to return to the mountain bearing incense and gifts to "make sacrifice" (*Ch'i-sheng ling-i lu* 6a–9a).

Another Yuan text, by the Chi-hsien academician Chieh Hsi-ssu (1274–1344), recounts the reconstruction of the Five Dragon Palace, completed in 1336 (Wang Kai 1744, 6.21a–23b).[16] Chieh shows us the involvement of Chang Liu-sun and Wu Ch'üan-chieh—both men had close links to both Lung-hu Shan and the court—in this reconstruction and supplies a fairly complete list of the palace's abbots from 1286 on. He also mentions that the emperor Jen-tsung's (r. 1312–21) birthday fell on the same day as the Per-fect Warrior's, with the result that the characters *wan-shou* (long life) were added to the abbey's name, and from that time on it became the practice to perform Golden Register Offerings annually on that date.

Finally, the first bronze hall, now on a hill across from the Palace of Perfect Harmony, was built in the Ta-te reign era (1297–1307) according to T'an Yuan-ch'un (see his *Yu Hsuan-yueh chi*, 7a, in *Ming-shan Sheng-kai chi*).

Regular Ming worship of Chen-wu goes back to the founder of the dynas-ty, T'ai-tsu. He not only initiated the custom of biennial sacrifices on the days of Chen-wu's birth (3/3) and ascension (9/9),[17] he set up a temple in his honor in Nanking (*Ming-shih* 50.1304; cf. Wang Kai 1744, 5.21b). The third Ming emperor, Ch'eng-tsu, in addition to his vast building program on Wu-tang Shan, also built Chen-wu a "voyager's palace" (*hsing-kung* 行宫) in Pe-king. This temple was apparently built to protect the vulnerable northeast corner (= *ken* 艮, the Gate of Demons) of the capital. Ch'eng-tsu also ordered the regular expedition of sacrificial gifts from the two capitals on the new and full moons of the first month every year (Wang Kai 1744, 3.38b; cf. *Yü-chih Chen-wu miao-pei* [*TT* 960], written in 1415).

Wang Kai's *Chi-lueh* contains a whole series of decrees of the Yung-lo period (5.3a–8b; some are also found in *Ta-Ming Hsuan-t'ien shang-ti jui-ying t'u-lu* [*TT* 959]). One dated 1413 and addressed to the "officials, army people, and workers" refers to the destruction of the buildings on Wu-tang Shan at the end of the Yuan, the "invisible help" given by the god in the founding of the dynasty, and above all "the manifest aid given me by the god from the very beginning of the period of troubles" (Ch'eng-tsu is referring to the period between 1399 and 1402 when he, as "king of Yen"—Yen is the north-ernmost region of China—first fought and then overthrew the second Ming emperor, his nephew Hui-ti):

At that time I had already expressed my sincerity by vowing to set up a temple and an abbey in Peking, but because of the civil war, I was not able to satisfy my heartfelt desire. As soon as I came to the throne, I thought of Wu-tang, that it was the place where Chen-wu had manifested himself, and I conceived the desire to undertake a vast construction program. But the army needed rest, and I thought it better to wait. Now then, I should like to ask a part of the army to go there to build palaces and abbeys to repay the god's kindness, to serve the memory of my parents on high and ask for blessings on all who live here below.

The decree goes on to urge the officials in charge of the enterprise to take good care of the diet and health of their workers and exhorts the workers to "put your hearts into the work, for the gods will then protect and help you, and the undertaking will be easily completed. I did not embark on this enterprise because people persuaded me to do so, and it is not because of what people might say that I will halt it" (cf. the 1418 inscription, 5.19a–21a, which gives a full description of the construction program).

The final Yung-lo decree in Wang Kai's *Chi-lueh*, dated 1424, repeats the reasons for the building splurge—for the souls of his parents in heaven, for the happiness of the people on earth—and then orders local officials, now the work is done, to inspect the buildings regularly and keep them in good repair. The *Chi-lueh* has preserved only one subsequent renewal of this decree (that by Ying-tsung in 1445; 5.9a–b). But Fang Sheng, in his *Ta-yueh chih-lueh*, lists no fewer than nine additional renewals from 1425 to 1495 (1.14b–23a).

Maintenance of buildings and roads was financed primarily by an incense tax levied on pilgrims. A decree written in 1532 and based on a memorial of 1531 (Fang Sheng, 1556, 1.37a–39a) drawn up by Wang Min, vice-director of the Directorate of Palace Eunuchs, gives a glimpse of the history of the incense tax on Wu-tang Shan: originally, says the decree, the cult was designed "to pay respect to the god in order to pray for the people's welfare, not to feed incense burners and snare people's livelihood." All expenditures were overseen by the proper authorities, and there was no waste. But as the cult grew in importance, there was a great accumulation of wealth, which was then used for private ends. In 1493, therefore, it was decreed that the incense money from months one to four, when pilgrims were most numerous, be collected and sent to the Palace of Purity and Joy (Ching-lo kung 淨樂宮) in the city of Chün-chou for storage until needed for repairs. The money from month five on was to remain on the mountain for current expenses.

But there was still a surplus, and in 1522 a censor decided that troops stationed locally should be paid with the money. From then on, barely enough was taken in to meet current expenses; and when several years of famine led to a drastic reduction in the numbers of pilgrims, there was even a shortage of money. The decree of 1532 therefore ordered a return to the system instituted by the decree of 1493. This incense tax was finally abolished in 1736 (see below).

Fang Sheng has also preserved decrees relating to cultic matters, that is, to the kinds of services required of Wu-tang's Taoists in return for imperial patronage. A 1422 decree orders the Taoists of Wu-tang Shan to recite scriptures on the emperor's birthday (1.31b). A 1428 decree states more explicitly that they should recite scriptures and perform a seven-day offering on the emperor's birthday and do the same over a five-day period for Chen-wu's birthday (1.32a). Fang Sheng also supplies us with no fewer than seven decrees ordering special offerings (the dates range from 1473 to 1526), four of them on the occasion of the installation of newly cast statues in one or another of the mountain's "palaces." The inscription for one of these occasions—in 1479, when the emperor Hsien-tsung sent a new set of cast bronze, gold-covered statues to the Purple Empyrean Palace—has been preserved in Wang Kai's *Chi-lueh* (5.21b); in it the emperor renews his family's profession of allegiance to Chen-wu thus: "The country is at peace, our neighbors on all sides are submissive, order without intervention (*wu-wei chih chih*) has never been more perfect. How could this be possible were it not for the help of the god? It therefore behooves us to show our gratitude." The offering was celebrated on the occasion of the "welcome reception" given the statues in the eleventh month of the year 1479. The offering began on the seventh day of the month, and on the eighth and ninth days auspicious lights appeared at various places on the mountain—signs of Chen-wu's approval. After prayers for the longevity of the emperor had been offered on the tenth day of the month, the statues were formally installed on the fifteenth. The subsequent reflections of the censor Li Yen (1421–94) are not without interest for an understanding of the emotional investment in the Perfect Warrior's cult:

> Heaven and earth have at heart to give life to all creatures, and the Emperor [Chen-wu] is the heart of heaven and earth, for he is the lord chancellor of birth and growth. Positioned in the north, he is in charge of the decrees of winter, which is to say his function is to freeze. But such is the charity of Perfect Harmony [T'ai-ho 太和, another name for Wu-tang Shan] in the production of birth and growth that all things have no sooner come to an end [in mid-winter] than they begin again. If the Emperor's charity embraces all things, can it be exhausted? When our sovereign reverently worships in the Emperor's temple, he prays for long life for his beloved mother and for an abundance of imperial progeniture, he prays that the nation may know peace both within its borders and with its neighbors so that the birth and growth of all things may be assured.
>
> Our sovereign's heart is the Emperor's heart [or: What our sovereign desires is also what the Emperor desires]. And yet, although the sovereign can thus embody the Emperor's heart, if those who actually perform the worship and the placement of the statues are incapable of respectfully embodying the sovereign's heart, those below will not benefit. How then can we hope for peace for the people, or that the god will not be resentful?

All officials, whether of middle or noble rank, know that he who fears the gods of heaven and obeys the laws of the land, who does not rely on the gods and deal disrespectfully [with those below him], nor take advantage of public office for private ends, nor make use of force in order to obtain results may be described as "embodying the sovereign's heart." We have channeled the benefits of virtue so that they reach the people in abundance, and the god, rejoicing on high at what he has observed daily here, has manifested his marvellous power and vouchsafed auspicious signs. This bears recording. ("Sheng-te chao-ying pei-chi," Wang Kai 1744, 6.31a–b)

In conclusion, we may quote from an inscription written in the year 1600 by the Han-lin academician Liu Cheng-lien. Composed for a shrine to the Dark Emperor in the Ch'ung-hsu Cloister 冲虛庵 on Wu-tang Shan, it shows that the ideologically significant cosmology retained its importance right to the end of the Ming:

The Dark Emperor's cult is spread throughout the empire, but Wu-tang is its center. There can be no question but that the Emperor invisibly aided the Ming in securing the empire in the Yung-lo period, and it is therefore appropriate that his ritual rank be superior to that of all other gods. . . .

Each of the five elements has its virtue, but the greatest of the imperial virtues is that of water. In our times cult officials are most careful in their worship of the Dark Emperor. That is why Wu-tang is called the Great Peak: it soars high above the Five Peaks. Surely this is no accident! Surely this is no accident! (Wang Kai 1744, 6.34a–34b)

TAOISM ON WU-TANG SHAN

We have already noted that the Taoist tradition on Wu-tang Shan may be traced with relative clarity from the mid-twelfth century on. Wang Kai's *Chi-lueh* carries the story forward to Tuan Yun-yang of Sian, who for half a century, up to his death in 1741, "worshiped the Dipper and recited scriptures" in the Palace of Purity and Joy for whoever requested his services. In the intervening centuries, contacts are mentioned with Lung-hu Shan (Kiangsi), Mao Shan (Kiangsu), Hua Shan, and Chung-nan Shan (both in Shensi).[18]

According to a recently published work on the Taoist music of Wu-tang Shan, the Taoists who lived on the mountain regularly performed three kinds of rituals: daily offices in the evening and the morning; annual celebrations for the Jade Emperor (1/9), the Perfect Warrior (3/3 and 9/9), and the Three Officers (1/15, 7/15, 10/15; on these three days, cf. Lagerwey, 20–22); and Fasts and Offerings (*chai-chiao* 齋醮), especially for the dead (Shih 1987, 8).

Apparently basing himself on local, unpublished sources, Shih states that the Cheng-i Taoism normally associated with Lung-hu Shan had arrived on Wu-tang Shan already in the time of Sung Chen-tsung. By the mid-Ch'ing

Cheng-i Taoism had virtually disappeared from Wu-tang Shan, though not from the surrounding countryside. It had been supplanted by Ch'üan-chen Taoism, in particular the Lung-men school variety thereof, originally brought to Wu-tang Shan in the Hung-wu period (1368–99) by Ch'iu Yuan-ch'ing, a fourth-generation successor to the famous Ch'iu Ch'u-chi.

Shih also tells the tales of six living Wu-tang Shan Taoists. La Wan-hui, for example, born in 1902, is from Chün-hsien, at the foot of the mountain. Having been healed by a Taoist master on the mountain, he became an acolyte in the Golden Hall at age seven to "redeem the vow" his mother had made on his behalf. He was taught to read using the Confucian classics; he also learned to sing, to play half a dozen instruments, and to perform all forms of ritual. A member of the Hua Shan school of Taoism, La served as chief priest in many an offering before leaving Wu-tang Shan in 1933 because of the insecure conditions then prevailing in the area. He returned to live on the mountain only in 1980 (Shih 1987, 227–30).

Fang Chi-ch'üan, born to a very poor family in 1918 in Chün-hsien, was brought to live on the mountain at age five. The only surviving representative of San-Mao 三茅 Taoism on Wu-tang Shan, Fang followed much the same curriculum as La, but he also learned the art of siting (*feng-shui*). Shih mentions two other Taoist monks, both of them Ch'üan-chen and both of them of local origin (one entered the mountain at four years of age, the other at age twelve; Shih 1987, 230–33).

The last two figures Shih introduces (233–37) are both hereditary Taoists from Ku-ch'eng county. The first of them, Chou Ping-hsiang, who appears to be an even more versatile musician than La Wan-hui, is also a practitioner of all the various cosmological and healing arts.

Shih mentions, altogether, three schools of Cheng-i and six of Ch'üan-chen Taoism that have coexisted on Wu-tang Shan. In the absence of any precise information regarding these schools and the locus of their implantation, we can say little about their impact on the mountain. Was there rivalry between them, or between the monks who grew up on the mountain and those who came from other mountains to learn from a specific teacher, or between the monks and the married priests in the surrounding countryside, or between monks and hermits? We don't know. Nor is it clear when Wu-tang Shan became almost exclusively identified with T'ai-chi ch'üan 太極拳 and, as such, came to be known as the Taoist counterpart and rival of the Buddhist Shao-lin.[19]

To Shih Hsin-min's spare glimpses into the Taoist tradition of Wu-tang Shan we may add the tale of Hsu Pen-shan taken from the first issue of the magazine of the Wu-tang Shan Association for the Study of Wu-tang Boxing:

Hsu Pen-shan, *hao* Wei-chiao, alias Perfect Man of the Celestial One of Wu-tang Shan, was born in the year 1860 in Ch'i county, Honan. As a young child, he once accompanied his father on a pilgrimage to Wu-tang Shan to worship the Perfect Warrior. When they visited the Palace of the Encounter with the Immortal (Yü-chen kung 遇真宫), finding himself face to face with the statue of Chang San-feng, he felt reverence for this person with the aura of an immortal and the bones of a Taoist, whose stature surpassed that of ordinary people, whose Way and virtue were lofty and divine transformations mysterious, and the seeds of the desire to abandon the world and leave the family were planted deep within. In the first month of the year of his capping, he went on a journey by himself; he passed through Nan-yang and entered Wu-tang, where he took the decision to enter the Way. He subsequently became the student of the Lung-men masters Wang Fu-mao and Lin Fu-pao. (Huang Hsüeh-min 1983, 14)

In 1889 Hsu took charge of the repair of the path up the mountain. So well did he discharge his responsibilities that Hsiung Pin, head of the Taoists in Hsiang-yang department, appointed Hsu chief of all Taoists on the mountain. He completely reformed Taoist life on Wu-tang Shan, requiring of all the same strict observance of the rules that he followed.

One day near the beginning of 1909, at a time when "incense guests going in audience on the mountain" (*ch'ao-shan hsiang-k'e* 朝山香客) numbered a thousand a day, a group of more than two hundred pilgrims from Hsiao-ch'uan in Chün county began fighting in the garden behind Hsu's quarters. Eventually Hsu himself intervened, but the head of the association had under his orders more than sixty specialists of the martial arts, and they preferred fighting to listening. But Hsu leaped out of the menacing circle, seized a five-meter-long plank lying nearby, and invited the pilgrims to come at him. When they saw him twirling his plank like a toothpick, however, they immediately stopped, got down on their knees, and begged Hsu for mercy. "Only then did the Taoists of Wu-tang and the people in the surrounding countryside realize what great skills Hsu Pen-shan had in the martial arts, and he was known thereafter as 'Hsu the martial hero' or 'Hsu the teacher'."

The story moves rapidly to the year 1931, when in the month of May "Comrade" Ho Lung arrived with the Third Red Army at Wu-tang Shan. Hsu and the fifty Taoists then living in the Purple Empyrean Palace went out to welcome them. Headquarters and a hospital were set up in the Purple Empyrean complex. At one point Hsu helped Ho procure ammunition by organizing a raid on an arms convoy of the 51st Army of the Kuomintang. He also trained Ho and a select few of his men in the techniques of Wu-tang boxing. In the fall of 1932, concludes the article, not long after Ho's departure, Hsu was waylaid and assassinated by local bandits.

This *Shui-hu chuan*–like hagiography provides glimpses into Wu-tang Shan Taoism that none of the more sober accounts of Shih Hsin-min or the successive mountain monographs supply: a vocation born of a pilgrimage; the importance of martial arts on the mountain and in the surrounding countryside; the intermingling, right into the twentieth century, of religion and politics.

Most important for our understanding of Wu-tang Shan as a Taoist mountain, however, is the role played in Hsu's vocation by his "encounter with the Immortal" Chang San-feng.

Much has been written about Chang San-feng, most recently a book by Huang Chao-han. Like his predecessors, Huang questions whether this legendary character ever existed, let alone founded a school of martial arts (the famous T'ai-chi ch'üan mentioned above). Although Huang is apparently unaware that the fifteen-*chüan* edition of Jen Tzu-yuan's *Ta-yueh T'ai-ho shan-chih* is from the late fifteenth century, he is probably right in attributing the biography of Chang San-feng to Jen and using it to conclude that Chang was a real person, who did actually spend time on Wu-tang Shan at the beginning of the Ming (Huang 1988a, 18, 36). Jen, who may himself have known Chang, makes him out to be a partisan of the Three Teachings and a Taoist capable of predicting the future and of such remarkable feats as going for months without eating (Jen 1983, 428–32). Unfortunately for the T'ai-chi ch'üan legend, Jen breathes not a word of Chang's Taoist practice. He says only that "Chang Shou-ch'ing alone received his secret instructions, and from that time the 'celestial wind' [Taoism] expanded greatly, and the ancestral teaching (*tsung-chiao* 宗教) showed new vigor" (Jen 1983, 432).

Our look at Wu-tang Shan as a Taoist mountain would hardly be complete if we did not say a word about Chen-wu as a Taoist deity. The Taoist canon includes a number of texts—seventeen according to Huang Chao-han (1988a, 53, n. 43)—related to his cult, including the one that tells his story (*T'ai-shang shuo Hsuan-t'ien ta-sheng chen-wu pen-chuan shen-chou miao-ching* [*TT* 775]). The text was no doubt produced in a session of visionary writing. It relates, very rapidly, the history of the Dark Warrior's "enfeoffment" by the Jade Emperor. The eighty-second transformation of the "saintly ancestor of the Celestial Origin" (Hsuan-yuan sheng-tsu 玄元聖祖, Lao-tzu's title during the T'ang), Chen-wu was born a prince in a *chia-ch'en* year: "When he grew up, he left his parents and entered Wu-tang Shan. When he had practiced the Way for forty-two years, his Work was accomplished, its fruit ripe, and he ascended to heaven in broad daylight. The Jade Emperor enfeoffed him by decree as the Great Dark One, anchor of the north. His marvellous deeds began at that time" (3b).

Such, in succinct form, is the Taoist version of the myth of the Dark Warrior: a career modeled on that of a Taoist hermit. We shall see later how it compares with the popular version of the myth found in the late Ming novel the *Pei-yu chi.*

THE LITERATI AT WU-TANG SHAN

In the two previous sections we have been looking at an unambiguously Taoist mountain: its god was Taoist; Taoists lived there;[20] and emperors sent envoys there to ask Taoists to pray to the Perfect Warrior for the dynasty.

But as we now turn our attention to the literati, we find a quite different situation. Literati, of course, were by definition Confucians. That meant that they served the emperor; but it also meant that they had a clear sense of their own distinctiveness within Chinese society, a sense that included, especially in Ming and Ch'ing times, a negative attitude toward Taoism and popular religion. Insofar as service to the emperor implied praying to local gods for rain and prosperity, the literati who came to Wu-tang Shan willy-nilly confirmed its status as a Taoist mountain. But when they came as private citizens, they not infrequently challenged this status by ridiculing Taoist myths and popular ritual practices and by proposing, in their stead, an aesthetic and even ethical contemplation of the mountain.

Official Visitors

Wang Kai's *Chi-lueh* contains a number of texts originally written in connection with official visits to Wu-tang Shan. There is, for example, the following prayer for a plentiful harvest written by the censor Wu T'ing-chü (*chin-shih* 1487), probably in 1517:[21]

> In case of rain or drought we always pray; when ill, we call on you. We rush to you like rivers: answer us as an echo. For several years in a row we have had disastrous flooding, and our grain harvest has been lost. The people have become refugees, and I, T'ing-chü, have received the order of the emperor to succor them. But the storehouses have limited supplies, there is barely enough grain to enable people to survive. . . . What we fear the most is too much rain in the summer and drought in the fall. Humbly I, T'ing-chü, present incense and pray on behalf of the people. (Wang Kai 1744, 6.54b)

Half a century later another censor, Wang Shih-chen (1526–90),[22] wrote the following prayer for rain (the fifth and sixth months had been dry):

> There is no greater mountain on earth than the Great Mountain, and none of the famous rivers can outclass the Han. Their god must therefore be the most powerful. . . . The censor has come today without cart or vestments and with a reduced retinue. In utter simplicity I go about my task, in the hope of ensuring the condescendence of the god. I should like a three-day downpour to break the drought, and then I will come, followed by all the men and boys of the area to bow and salute you a hundred times to thank the god for his great gift. . . . To be a censor is nothing much, but I can still intervene before the Son of Heaven on behalf of the people of the five counties. It is therefore unthinkable that a god not be able to intervene before the Emperor on High on behalf of these same people. (Wang Kai 1744, 6.55a–b)

The prayer, apparently, was successful, for it is followed in the monograph by a prayer of thanksgiving for rain.

A similar prayer, dated 1681, by Wang Min-hao, magistrate of Chün-chou (see bibliographical note) also expresses gratitude for an end to a mid-summer drought: "Earnest prayers," he writes, "incantations, and scripture recitations had scarcely been going on for a week when the first dews came... and by the tenth day, a downpour" (Wang Kai 1744, 6.56b).

Perhaps the most important official visitor ever to come to Wu-tang Shan was Ts'ai Yü-jung (1633–99), who was named governor-general of Sze-chuan, Hunan, and Hupei in 1670. "I should have gone to worship on the famous mountains and by the great rivers within my jurisdiction," he writes, but not until the summer of 1673 did the occasion finally present itself.[23] He notes, first, that he made it as far as the Slope of the Prince (T'ai-tzu p'o 太子坡) on horseback; he proceeded by sedan chair to the Celestial Audience Palace (Ch'ao-t'ien kung 朝天宮), whence he was obliged to walk (other literati apparently had more obliging porters, for they were carried in special litters all the way to the summit). He ended his visit in Chün-chou on the plain, at the Palace of Purity and Joy, where he "prayed for ten thousand years for the emperor on high and asked for longevity for my parents below. Thus will the task of a son and a minister reach completion" (Wang Kai 1744, 7.32a). The introduction to his piece suggests that the early Ch'ing continued to identify dynastic fortune with the mountain: "Although this began in an earlier dynasty, during the Yung-chia reign era (307–312), the divine power of the Polestar, in perfect conformity with the god's reputation, has in very truth protected the nation and aided in the founding of this dynasty."

Private Visitors

Literati also went to Wu-tang Shan to pray for personal matters. Ma I-lung (1490–1562), for example, a member of the Directorate of Education, intro-duces his *Tai-ho shan fu* as follows (Wang Kai 1744, 6.14a):

> In the year 1507, having fallen sick, I prayed to the Dark Emperor and was blessed with healing. In the year 1510, therefore, I paid a visit to Mount T'ai-ho [Wu-tang] to offer thanks for the divine gift. How marvellous it is that such a mountain should exist between heaven and earth, yes, that in the creation such a god may be found.

Wang Tsai-chin (*chin-shih* 1592), an assistant education-intendant censor, was told by local officials that "when one goes to visit T'ai-ho, one must first burn incense in the Palace of Purity and Joy." Having risen early and bathed, he therefore proceeded to the "gate of the palace" (Wang Kai 1744, 7.16a). At each successive stop on his way to the Golden Hall (Chin Tien 金殿) on the summit, Wang was preceded by Taoists playing instruments and burning incense. When he reached the top, he noted that he had pre-viously ordered an offering be performed in the Palace of Perfect Harmony (T'ai-ho Kung 太和宮). Having rested and restored himself there, he then "straightened his clothes" in preparation for "going in audience in the hall of the Emperor." He admired the beauty of the early Ming architecture and then added: "The statue of the Emperor is solemn and dignified. With

utmost reverence I bowed before him, and all my worries fell away" (Wang
Kai 1744, 7.20a).

The same author described his descent as follows:

> Once we passed the third Gate of Heaven, we saw pilgrims (*ch'ao-li che* 朝禮者)
> from all over the country like ants in a row or fish on a string dragging them-
> selves upward. On all sides one heard scattered calls and the murmur of voices.
> Even the young and vigorous were panting. The noble, the capped and
> gowned, village women and commoners here rubbed shoulders. And so it was
> for several *li* until at last we arrived at the first Gate of Heaven. (Wang Kai
> 1744, 7.21b)

Wang Kai himself, his clearly negative attitude toward Wu-tang Shan's
Taoists notwithstanding (see bibliographical note), would seem, if we are to
judge by an inscription he left in the precincts of the Palace of Perfect Harmony, to have undertaken the project of reediting the mountain monograph
in order to press his prayer to Chen-wu for a son:

> Such is the Great Mountain's numinous brilliance: it produces clouds and
> sends down rain, it wards off calamities and fends off disaster, thus enriching
> the nation and aiding the people. From the T'ang through the Sung, the Yuan,
> and the Ming, right down to the present, every generation has transmitted tales
> of divine miracles. I, Kai, was first put in charge of this region in the year 1741.
> In that capacity it behooved me to worship the god, and on several occasions I
> was the beneficiary of his blessings. Meditating that I was already past forty
> and had as yet no son, I ventured to pray silently with utter sincerity. But
> thinking that if rich rites and humble words did not suffice to press my prayer,
> the reediting of the mountain monograph might, I made use of imperial favor
> to reach the highest possible standard. The *T'ai-ho shan chi-lueh* was completed
> in 1746. The blocks were cut, the fascicles bound, and I reported this by burn-
> ing a message before the divine throne in the Golden Hall of the Palace of
> Perfect Harmony. In the middle month of spring, 1748, I was blessed by the
> birth of a boy.
>
> The response of the mountain divinity made me wish to give thanks, for here
> was a case of luminous proof. Truly, a thousand prayers are not worth a single
> proof [that prayers are answered], and one such event engenders infinite feel-
> ings of gratitude. I herewith give expression to those feelings. And must I not
> henceforth be even more fervent in encouraging good works so as to open the
> way to good fortune?
>
> Reverently recorded in the ninth month of the year 1748.

But the literati, if they also came to Wu-tang Shan to pray, came primarily to see and describe, as we can see from the following observations made by
Wang Kai at the end of his selection of literati verse in the *Chi-lueh* (8.35a):

> Confucian ministers and literati have come here to visit and to write poems in
> every generation. They climb to the top and gaze out afar, and their thoughts,
> in like manner, float off into the distance: in the mountains they see how all the

peaks and summits gather round; in the water they see the crystal clarity of rivers and streams. And then, as the sun sets, they get a feeling of waxing and waning, of coming and going. Their eyes busy, their hearts pensive, thoughts of wind and cloud waft lightly and flow from the brush, with the result that those who come afterwards to behold in their turn are one and all taken by these writings. If we look at yesterday by means of today, we can also understand how the ancients felt and thought. What has this to do with the wild talk of spirits and miracles in the books of the Taoists?

A similar note is sounded by Yang Ho (*chin-shih* 1604), who writes of his visit to Wu-tang Shan in 1623 as follows:

Between the first and second Gates of Heaven strange peaks become visible, and distant ranges stand out in contrasts of height and shape. But the travelers' concern is for the path alone; they see only what is in front of them. "How wrong they are not to realize they are in a painting of Lu T'an-wei!" said I to my companions; "the Gates of Heaven are really steep, but if you stop every third step to look back and every fifth to sit down, you don't even feel tired from climbing." And I laughed at all the good pilgrims of both sexes who spend all their energy on the ascent and whose only fear is not to advance because they think the god is scrutinizing them. Dirty sweat pours down their faces, and they pant like they were about to die. How ridiculous! (*Ming-shan, Ts'an-hua*, 3b)[24]

A few lines and turns later, however, our superb Yang Ho, having stopped off in the "divine kitchen" (a part of the Palace of Perfect Harmony complex) to wash before making the final ascent, "climbs to the top and pays his respects to the Emperor with incense." That done, of course, he "loosens his robe and gazes out on all sides: I was atop a lotus flower of a thousand petals."

He marvels at what he sees, describes it, then checks with a Taoist to see whether his hunch regarding the northern sights was accurate: "Hua Shan it was!"

From high noon to dusk I looked at the mountains. The sky was clear, the breeze chilly, and there was nary so much as a wisp of cloud to block my wandering eyes. As dusk gathered, the mountains grew purple; when the sun went down, the blues deepened, the reds retreated, and suddenly, in the east, appeared the white of the moon, a glow of light fresh and pure, a bright mirror in the cloudless sky; to see it made one wish one's bones would change and one might [fly away], immortal.

ORDINARY PILGRIMS

It is difficult to know what the nonliterate masses in premodern societies thought and did. This difficulty is compounded in China by the fact that the literate ruling class and the largely illiterate population they governed did not share the same religion. As a result, the gap between popular piety and the spirituality of the literate was far greater than in medieval Europe, a fact that shows up in the literary record either as disdain or silence. Fortunately, pilgrim groups coming to Wu-tang Shan (and elsewhere; see Naquin, chapter 8 of this volume) did commission inscriptions commemorating their visits. A small number of these inscriptions have survived the ravages of time and the Red Guards and will enable us to lift a small corner of the literati veil and catch a glimpse of the face of ordinary pilgrims to Wu-tang Shan. But let us look first at what the literati have to tell us about them.

Literary Sources

References to ordinary pilgrims are scarce in the works of the literati. They are also not infrequently mean-minded, as we have seen. But all observers agree that pilgrims came to Wu-tang Shan in droves. The vice-censor Wang Chi-luo, for example, in his preface to the *Ta-yueh T'ai-ho shan chih*, describes conditions at Wu-tang Shan when he went there to oversee repairs in 1552: "Who under heaven and within the seas is not aware of the existence of this mountain? There is not a day in the month that there are no pilgrims coming to pay respects" (Wang Kai 1744, 6.42b).[25] Writing about a century later, T'an Yuan-ch'un says: "The people of the entire empire visit this mountain as though it were utterly familiar: toes tread on heels, and eyes follow eyes."[26]

Fighting in the Wu-tang Shan area at the end of the Ming led to the dispersal of most of the mountain's Taoists, according to Liu Chih-chung, judge in Hsiang-yang, but when a vigorous campaign in 1655 reopened the area, "pilgrims from all sides streamed [to Wu-tang Shan] as before" (Wang Kai 1744, 6.36b). Information on numbers of pilgrims in the Ch'ing is more difficult to come by, but to judge from the following imperial edict of 1736, they were still coming in numbers sufficient to justify central government attention:

We have already given orders that the incense tax collected [at Mount T'ai] in T'ai-an, Shantung, be abolished. Recently, we have learned that a similar tax is levied at T'ai-ho Shan in Hupei on all those, from near or far, who go to present incense. When the people go out of the sincerity of their hearts to pay their respects to the gods, they should give what they can and not be subjected to an incense levy which increases their difficulties. Following the example of T'ai-an, therefore, all incense levies are abolished at T'ai-ho Shan. (Wang Kai 1744, 5.1b)

Kao Ho-nien, a lay Buddhist who spent a week at Wu-tang Shan in the fourth month of 1904, gives witness to the continuing popularity of the mountain at the end of the Ch'ing: "An unending tide of pilgrims young and old, male and female" was to be seen on the mountain, according to Kao. There were still one hundred Taoists in the Palace of Perfect Felicity alone. Kao cites the following poem by another lay Buddhist: "The four great Buddhist mountains all gravitate around this pole; / The five Taoist sacred peaks all go in audience before their ancestor" (Kao Ho-nien 1983, 119–21).

It is difficult to ascertain, in the present state of our knowledge, to what extent Wu-tang Shan was the site of a truly national pilgrimage. According to Wang Ning-ch'u, writing in 1937, pilgrims came primarily from Hupei, Honan, Shensi, and Szechuan (86). But a recent article in the *Chiang-nan k'ao-ku* cites sources concerning a late Ming annual pilgrimage organized in Soochow. Every year in the second lunar month, on a previously selected auspicious day, upwards of a hundred "pilgrim ships" (*ch'ao-shan ch'uan* 朝山船) from all over Soochow prefecture would gather in the Pei-t'ang section of the port of Wu-hsi. Strung out in prearranged order, gongs on board sounding steadily, the pilgrim ships would parade from the southern end of Wu-hsi, past the eastern gate, and on to Pei-t'ang. In the evening, each boat attached "lantern trees" to bow and stern and hung out one lantern for each pilgrim on board. Firecrackers were set off. At the sound of the gongs, the people of Wu-hsi came out to meet the pilgrim ships in boats carrying orchestras and also bedecked with lanterns. Percussion and orchestras played together well into the night before the pilgrim boats finally set out on the nearly 3,500-kilometer round trip voyage to Wu-tang Shan up the Grand Canal, the Yangtze, and the Han to Chün-chou. Ku Wen-pi estimates it took them a month and a half to get to Chün-chou and three weeks to return, which means that the entire expedition probably took three full months (Ku Wen-pi 1989, 74–75).

Pilgrim Inscriptions

The inscriptions erected inside the temples or embedded in the mountain and temple walls of Wu-tang Shan provide a second source of information concerning ordinary pilgrims. During a three-day visit to the mountain in 1987, I counted about eighty such inscriptions, most of which were still sufficiently legible to be copied.[27] The vast majority of the surviving, legible inscriptions carry the names and sometimes the stories of ordinary pilgrims. It is clear from these accounts that most pilgrims came in groups, from a neighborhood or a village, for the typical plaque gives the place of origin of the group, the names of the participants, and the date of their visit (see also Naquin, chapter 8 of this volume).

Approximately three-quarters of the inscriptions indicate the place of origin of the pilgrims:

Place of Origin	Ming	Ch'ing	Republican	Uncertain	Total
Hu-kuang	5	27	6	6	44
Other	2	4	3	.	9
Unclear	3	4			7
Total	10	35	9	6	60

That the overwhelming majority of pilgrims came from the Hu-kuang (Hupei and Hunan) area is hardly surprising, but what does surprise is the apparent paucity of pilgrims from other provinces. In the Ming dynasty the only other place of origin is Honan (also nearby), and even in the Ch'ing there are few pilgrims from elsewhere. If the contributors to temple reconstruction listed in Inscription 34 were also pilgrims, 1761 would be the first year in which inscriptions mention pilgrims to Wu-tang Shan from places such as Kiangnan, Shantung, and Shansi. This means that imperial patronage notwithstanding, the pilgrimage (but not the cult) remained an essentially regional phenomenon well into the Ch'ing.

Another point worthy of notice is the large numbers of plaques commemorating Taoist rituals of offering (19), particularly in the Wan-li period (13). Thereafter, they would appear to have been less frequent, and the last one for which I found an inscription (no. 44) dates to 1823.

The following reasons are given for undertaking a pilgrimage: to pray for a son (nos. 11, 26, 32, 36); to give thanks (nos. 1, 32, 35, 38, 40); to fulfill a vow (nos. 19, 28, 43, 44, 69).

The seventeen pilgrimage-related inscriptions that give the names of all participants reveal group sizes varying from three to fifty; normal group size would appear to have been upwards of fifteen.[28] Group leaders are variously designated as "association heads" (*hui-shou* 會首: nos. 5, 21, 22, 29, 62), "incense chiefs" (*hsiang-chang* 香長, *hsiang-chu* 香主, or *hsiang-shou* 香首: nos. 10, 14, 16, 50), and "headman" (*shou-jen* 首人: no. 38). Pilgrims are referred to as "believers" (*hsin-shan* 信善, *hsin-shih* 信士, *shan-hsin* 善信), "laymen" (*chü-shih* 居士), "good people" (*chung-shan* 衆善, *shan-shih* 善士), "disciples" (*ti-tzu* 弟子), and, of course, "those who go in audience on the mountain to present incense" (phrase written in a variety of ways, the standard form of which is *ch'ao-shan chin-hsiang* 朝山進香).

Group organization is occasionally by family (nos. 36, 69) or by association (*hui*, whence *hui-shou*, "association head"; note in particular the Association of Universal Peace 太平會 from nearby Lao-ho-k'ou in 1922), but the most frequent mode would seem to be by temple (nos. 11, 14, 40, 60, 69) and by village, hamlet, or "god of the soil ward" (cf. esp. nos. 16, 各街社主; 19, 各坊土地祠下; 21, 土地下住; 25, 土地分下; 27, 各坊土地居住; 35, 土地居住). Although most of the designations in this last set might be understood as purely administrative divisions, taken as a whole they seem quite clearly to refer to religiously defined spatial units. As such, they remind us that, as at the level of the whole nation, so also on the level of the smallest local unit, "church" and "state" were inseparable in traditional China.

Let us look now a bit more closely at a few of the more significant inscriptions to see what they can tell us about why pilgrims came to Wu-tang Shan and what they did there. Inscription 21, directed to the Emperor of the Dark Heavens on High, reads:

The various territorial associations to the west of the capital of Chiang-ling county, Ching-chou department, Hu-kuang, under the dynasty of the Great Ch'ing: we worshiped the Way at the twelve palaces by celebrating a ritual of offering; we released lamps to float on the river and 'distributed food' [for hungry ghosts] every evening. We went in audience on the mountain and presented incense to repay our debt of gratitude and to ask for blessings and prosperity. Head of the Association for Welcoming Good Fortune, Wang Yueh, ritual name Chueh-i 覺儀.

The ritual name of each of Wang's thirteen companions is also given. Last on the list is the only woman, Lady Fu, ritual name Chueh-ao 覺粵 (disciple of Dark Heaven). The text is "inscribed and set up by the disciple Chou Chin-yung, on an auspicious day in the first decade of the ninth month, in autumn of the *chia-tzu* year, K'ang-hsi 23 [1684]."

Inscription 28 was written on request by one Su Hsun-mu for a group of pilgrims from I-ling county that included a Ch'üan-chen disciple, a "female believer," several holders of the lowest degree, and one student of the National University. Su begins with the affirmation that it is because no prayer goes unanswered on Wu-tang Shan that "streams of worshipers from all sides go there, thick as the clouds, in numbers incalculable." The leader of the group and his forty-odd companions therefore also

> made a vow in the year 1712 to pay a worshipful visit every third year from then on, and we have now done so several times. When we go, we prepare what is needed, we concentrate our wills, we wear our best clothes, and we fast, for sincerity and reverence are indispensable.

Right next to Inscription 28, which is dated 1725 and set in the wall of the Well Pavilion (Ching-lou 井樓) at the Needle-sharpening Well (Mo-chen ching 磨針井), is Inscription 30, dated 1736; it was also written by Su Hsun-mu. It reads:

> In spring and autumn an unbroken line of worshipers comes from all sides. . . . Six years ago I recorded the pilgrimage of the good people of our ward, but now that the accession to the throne of the saintly Son of Heaven has brought a simplification of government and a lightening of corvée labor, the benefits touch all the earth. Moreover, it is autumn, and the people are happy [?]. Thus once again do all the good people turn their faces toward Wu-tang to pay their respects.

As these two inscriptions clearly refer to groups of different origin, we may conclude both that Su Hsun-mu lived on Wu-tang Shan and that repeated pilgrimages at regular intervals were as regular a phenomenon on Wu-tang Shan as they were elsewhere. Su was perhaps one of the many Taoists on the mountain whose job it was to receive and look after pilgrims.

Inscription 35 is particularly interesting in that it shows a family with a multigenerational tradition of visits to Wu-tang Shan:

Virtue that overarches! Divine power that manifests itself throughout the universe! His divine thoughts resonate; he guards the northern sector. I, his disciple Wan, live in Ching-nan on the Chien [River]. For generations our family has been blessed and has gone to give thanks on Wu-tang. My great-grandfather, Chang Ying-hsiang, together with my grandfather, carved an inscription at the Needle-sharpening Well. Then my father, Tso-ch'ing, and his younger brother made another inscription at the Lao-chün Hall. . . . Then Hsun went with my younger brother and many fellow clan members to show their allegiance and inscribed a stone on the Mountain of the Immortal. It is not that we wish our names to stand out, nor that we fear to be ashamed with respect to our forebears, but merely to say that those who have turned toward goodness have someone to continue their work.

Another very interesting inscription is 36, also at the Needle-sharpening Well. The writer's father had first come to Wu-tang Shan in 1724 to pray for a son. Having been blessed with a son in the tenth month of 1725, the father undertook pilgrimages of thanksgiving in 1732 and 1737. "In obedience to my father's instructions," continues the inscription, in 1757, 1763, and 1774,

I led my fellow villagers on three pilgrimages, and the god blessed me with five sons and ten grandsons. In the decade since 1774 I have again been blessed with two grandsons. Our family having received such good fortune from the god, in the winter of 1783, so as to give thanks on my sixtieth birthday, I ordered my two eldest sons to go pay homage and give thanks to the Emperor.

The inscription is signed Ch'en Jung-tsung, Ch'ien-lung 49, *chia-ch'en* (1784), in the first month of spring.

Inscription 43 concerns an offering made in the tenth month of 1811 by all the "believers" of Kuang-i (nearby Lao-ho-k'ou). It opens with a reference to the antiquity of the Chen-wu cult and to its wide geographic spread. The inscription continues as follows:

We made a vow to visit the Emperor, to go in audience on the mountain and by the river to gain his divine assistance. . . . We of Kuang-i village have already presented incense three years in a row now, but we do not pretend to have fulfilled our vow or completed our task. In gratitude for the god's infinite kindness to us, we believers have collected money to inscribe this stone.[29]

Inscription 51 is to be found just to the left of the entrance to the cliff temple at Southern Precipice. Written by Chang Tsung-ts'ai, the man in charge of repairs to the temple, at the request of one Hsieh Ming-feng, it is dated 1880 and lists the names and contributions of some thirty-five individuals (and one company, the Jui-fa kung-ssu), most of whom are also surnamed Hsieh. Hsieh Ming-feng would seem to be the only person to have actually made the pilgrimage to Wu-tang Shan, and it was on one of his three visits that he saw the buildings at Southern Precipice in such a state of disrepair that he decided to collect money to restore them: "All the gentlemen in his village," writes Chang, "in the desire to plant vast fields of good fortune, contributed silver to help defray the costs of reconstruction."

It may be noted in passing that the majority of inscriptions in the last century have to do with financial contributions for repairs to buildings and paths. Inscription 65, for example, tells of one Hsiung Hsieh-pao who, having seen the sorry state of the mountain path leading to the summit while making a pilgrimage with his wife and daughters, went home to Honan to collect funds from "all the good people of Hsiang-yang." Inscription 69 shows that such fund collecting might also have had private motivations: partially defaced, it tells the story of someone who, after having been healed in 1909 by swallowing a Taoist symbol (*fu* 符),[30] "went on a pilgrimage to the Mountain of the Immortal in fulfillment of my vow. The second and third times I went, I lingered to contribute and collect funds for the reconstruction of the temples."

The Pilgrim Experience

Useful as these inscriptions may be for getting a glimpse of ordinary pilgrims, their laconic, not to say formulaic style tells us virtually nothing about what made the pilgrimage to Wu-tang Shan unique. For that, our only recourse would seem therefore to be an examination of the mountain itself. What did pilgrims see and visit on the mountain?

That the entire mountain was built up on the orders of an emperor preoccupied to the point of obsession with the cult of the Perfect Warrior greatly simplifies the task of "reading" Wu-tang Shan for, as we shall see, the mountain was organized from plain to peak as the unfolding story of the god's own ascension from human crown prince to divine emperor. The ascension of Wu-tang Shan meant, therefore, a progressive encounter with the Perfect Warrior. In our own ascent of the mountain we shall rely heavily on the late Ming novel *Pei-yu chi* (*Travels to the North*), a virtual guidebook to Wu-tang Shan; we may be quite sure that its reading influenced greatly the experience of late Ming and Ch'ing pilgrims on the mountain.[31]

For many a pilgrim the encounter with Chen-wu began in the town of Hsiang-yang, some seventy kilometers downstream from Chün-chou: people who go to Wu-tang Shan, Wang Kai informs us (3.10b–11a), go first to the Chen-wu Abbey near Hsiang-yang to "present memorials." The *Hsiang-yang fu-chih* of 1759 (9.9b) mentions a Chen-wu temple on Chiu-kung Shan, just west of the city. Founded in the Hsuan-te period (1426–35) by one Hsiao Hsu-shih, it was burned down at the end of the Ming and rebuilt at the beginning of the Ch'ing. "Its incense burner grew brighter with each passing day," adds the monograph, "and people called it 'little Wu-tang'."[32]

The encounter with "big Wu-tang" usually began in the river valley, at the Palace of Purity and Joy in the departmental seat of Chün-chou. This enormous abbey—its 520 rooms occupied no less than half of Chün-chou!—

was named after the country of which Chen-wu's legend made him out to be the crown prince, and pilgrims could even visit the tombs of the Prince's parents not far from town (see bibliographical note). In the *Pei-yu chi*, the future Chen-wu goes through several previous reincarnations before being born, in chapter 7, in the land of Ching-lo. He is in fact sent into the world at once to bring back thirty-six celestial generals who have gone to earth and to "complete his share of suffering" with forty-two years of misfortune (Seaman, 87). Born, like Lao Tzu, from the left side of his mother, the Prince is told by the goddess of the Dipper disguised as a Taoist that to "get rid of the four evil things: wine, lust, money, and anger," he must break all family ties. He therefore leaves the palace and is led by the goddess to Wu-tang Shan to "cultivate the Way" (Seaman 1987, 91–92).[33]

From Chün-chou the paved granite road ran due south some twenty-five kilometers before arriving at the foot of the mountain, marked, since 1552, by an entry arch on which were inscribed four characters based on the Ming emperor Shih-tsung's calligraphy: *chih-shih Hsuan-yueh* 治世玄岳, "the Dark Peak that governs the world." Once inside the portal, pilgrims were truly on sacred territory, and T'ao Chen-tien (1984, 12) cites a telling proverb: "He who passed through the gate of the Dark Mountain put his life in the hands of the gods; it was only when he exited the gate that he was once again a person of this world." To ensure that pilgrims understood, adds T'ao, a temple to Powerful Officer Wang (Wang ling-kuan 王靈官) was built just beyond the gateway. Officer Wang was in charge of keeping order on the mountain, and his statue showed him to be ferocious indeed: he had glaring eyes and protruding fangs, and he held an iron whip in his right hand.[34]

Past this gateway, the road turns east. The Palace for the Encounter with the Immortal, built to express Ch'eng-tsu's longing to encounter Chang San-feng, is just a kilometer in from the portal. Not far from this abbey is the Grotto of the Black Tiger, a demon under the orders of Chao Kung-ming 趙公明 according to the *Pei-yu chi*. Chao was a divine killer who preyed on travelers crossing the Yangtze at Hsu-chou until the future Perfect Warrior, acting on advice from the Three Pure Ones, defeated him. He then demasked the Black Tiger demon as well, and both were obliged to enter the crown prince's service (Seaman 1987, 125–30).

A second kilometer beyond the gate of entry brings one to the Palace of Primordial Harmony (Yuan-ho kung 元和宮) and a fork in the road: the "road of the gods" (*shen-tao*) turns southward up the mountain; the valley road goes on to the town of Lao-ying (Old Camp) and its 2,200-room Jade Void Palace (Yü-hsu kung 玉虛宮). Both the Yuan-ho and the Yü-hsu palaces are named after posts held by the Perfect Warrior in the celestial bureaucracy; the Yuan-ho kung, according to T'ao Chen-tien (16), served as a prison for monks who had broken monastic rules.

Some five kilometers separate this erstwhile prison from the first major complex actually in the mountains. It is called the Needle-sharpening Well, a name that refers to the following tale: When the Prince first left the palace in the Land of Purity and Joy, he went deep into the mountains to "refine his breath" (*lien-ch'i* 鍊氣) in solitude. (The place he went to, now called the Slope of the Prince, is five kilometers beyond the Needle-sharpening Well.) At one point the Prince grew discouraged with his progress and decided to go home. When he had descended as far as the well, he saw an old lady seated by the well sharpening a large iron bar. His curiosity awakened, the Prince asked the old lady, who was in reality his divine mistress, what she was doing: "I am sharpening a needle," she replied. "But isn't that too hard?" asked the Prince. "When I shall have sharpened the iron bar into a needle," responded the old lady, smiling knowingly at him, "the work will come spontaneously to fruition." Awakened by these words, the Prince headed back into the mountain to carry his work of sublimation to its conclusion (T'ao 1984, 21; a considerably more complicated version of this story is told in the *Pei-yu chi*; Seaman 1987, 98–104).

Not far from the Needle-sharpening Well the pilgrim passed a temple dedicated to Kuan Yü. Kuan Yü, the Confucian hero of the Three Kingdoms period, was the officially recognized god of war who, as such, had an officially funded temple in every seat of government throughout Ch'ing China. What is his temple doing less than halfway up the mountain of the Perfect Warrior? The *Pei-yu chi* tells a tale that makes this presence intriguing indeed: According to the late Ming novel, Kuan Yü was the disciple of the Buddhist P'u-an 普庵祖師. In a battle with Kuan Yü the Crown Prince is first mortally wounded by Kuan Yü's magic sword and then restored to life by his own divine master, who is acting on orders of the Three Pure Ones, Lao Tzu in particular. His master then tells him to go for help to Western Heaven, where Kuan Yü is practicing Ch'an meditation. When he arrives, the buddha of the future presents him to Kuan Yü as the "supreme emperor":

> "The Supreme Emperor is a reincarnation of the Jade Emperor. . . . You are a minister, and he is the lord. . . . Now that he has come for you, how can you not go with him?" "If I must go, then I must go," said Kuan Yü, "but I have not yet finished hearing the Expounding of the Law, so how can I be reunited with you here in the future?" "Although you are not yet versed in the Law," said the Buddha, "if you will bow down before the Supreme Emperor as your master, then from generation to generation you will not need to enter the mortal world. Even if you do not study the Law and listen to the sutras, you still will be able to avoid the suffering of reincarnation." (Seaman 1987, 135)

Kuan Yü goes back with the Prince, subdues his own assistant, and, having received new title from the Jade Emperor, is charged with "aiding the Supreme Emperor in exorcising demons" (Seaman 1987, 136). The Confucian god of war, in short, had converted to Buddhism, but he is told that to

enlist in the army of the Perfect Warrior is every bit as efficacious a way to
achieve salvation as Buddhist wisdom (no doubt because exorcising demons
is a highly meritorious exercise).

The Prince is said to have completed his work of sublimation—his
struggle with the dark forces of the north—on the precipice that bears his
name (T'ai-tzu yen 太子巖), just behind what is now the Purple Empyrean
Palace. We have already mentioned (n. 10) that the mountain's "blessed
plot" was moved in the Ming to Yü's Pool, just outside the outer gate of what
is now the largest remaining complex on the mountain. Not far from Yü's
Pool there used to be a temple dedicated to the god of wealth (Ts'ai-shen
Miao), here identified with Chao Kung-ming. The temple is also called
Black Tiger Hall, after Chao's assistant. This temple, in other words, recalls
the Black Tiger Grotto at the foot of the mountain and demonstrates graphically that the Perfect Warrior's gradual ascension implies that of the demonic
forces he vanquishes and takes into his service as well.

The inscription over the entrance to the Purple Empyrean Palace reads:
"Here began the judgment of the Six Heavens" (*shih-p'an liu-t'ien* 始判六天).
Pilgrims in the late Ming and Ch'ing probably understood this inscription in
the light of chapter 14 of the *Pei-yü chi*, where the Prince defeats "six demons,
who called themselves Heaven, Earth, Day, Month, Year, and Hour" (Seaman 1987, 145).[35] These "Six Poisons" live on K'un-lun Mountain, the axis
mundi of Taoist mythology, and their poisonous vapor knocks the Prince
unconscious. Kuan Yü goes to heaven to report the disaster to the Three
Pure Ones, who descend "in person" to breathe their breath of life back into
the Prince. They then give the Prince a magic fan, which one of the Prince's
assistants uses to defeat the Six Poisons and their master, Chu Yen-fu. Chu is
then given a title in the Taoist bureaucracy and vows his readiness "to exterminate false sorcerers" who "collect demonic forces and call them the Forces
of the Six Poisons, using my name and reputation to falsely control and subdue poisonous forces" (Seaman 1987, 149).

Several temple complexes on Wu-tang Shan have a Hall of the Parents
behind the main temple, but the most popular one was that at the Purple
Empyrean Palace, for to the left of Chen-wu's parents, in the Chapel of the
Hundred Sons, sat Sung-tzu niang-niang, the Lady Who Sends Sons (T'ao
1984, 30).

If the Prince completed his Work on the precipice that bears his name, it
was from the Southern Precipice, some two kilometers farther in, that he
actually ascended to heaven. The path that leads there passes by a small
temple built into a cliff. The temple is dedicated to the Duke of Thunder
(Lei-kung 雷公), yet another of the forces of the universe the prince defeated
and then took into his service (Seaman 1987, 137–38).

The place of the prince's ascension is marked by an Ascension Terrace

(Fei-sheng t'ai 飛昇臺), built on a spur that reaches precipitously out into the void. In the early Ch'ing no less a personage than the governor-general Ts'ai Yü-jung felt it necessary to write the following order concerning this terrace:

Inscription Forbidding Suicide at the Terrace of Ascension

The Terrace of Ascension at Southern Precipice is the place from which the Perfect Warrior, the Emperor on High, ascended to heaven. People mistakenly call it Suicide Cliff, and the Taoists on the mountain perpetuate this error. They even make it something divine, and foolish men and women are led astray by the name and, whether because of muddled views or in a fit of spleen, do their lives injury in such a way that they are beyond saving. The number of precipitous summits on the famous mountains of the empire is incalculable, and disciples of the Buddhists and Taoists often go up to the steepest drop-off to commit suicide. This practice is a grievous error and delusion, and it is a custom not confined to the Southern Precipice.

But at the Southern Precipice the site of the ascension has also been given a heterodox name, and the beautiful gates and terraces are strewn with flesh and blood. This is an insult to the Perfected on High and a pitfall for the ignorant. Whoever first gave rise to this name was utterly inhumane, but people blindly follow in his tracks. Alive, they are ignorant fools; dead, they become dangerous ghosts. It is without doubt their deeds in previous lives that brought on their heads this plunge into hell here and now. The Emperor on High is compassionate, but it would be better not to show sympathy. If we do not forbid this practice, many lives will be lost. I have therefore examined and rectified the monograph and changed the name to "Ascension Terrace."

Gentlemen who study the Way have their hearts fixed on what is beyond this world; when they have extinguished their light in this world, their names are registered in the Purple Court. Let them, when they are ready to mount on high, ascend this terrace: it is the profound desire of the Emperor on High to see them soar into the clouds driving a team of cranes and phoenixes. But if their Work is not accomplished, if they have yet to gaze out toward the mountains and rein in their hearts, then how much more so the ignoramuses mired in the world of the senses: how can they do away with their corporal foulness and soar above the mountain cliff?

From henceforth this is no longer to be called Suicide Cliff. The abbot of this palace and all its Taoists must regularly warn pilgrims that these [suicides] are forbidden forever. If anyone disobeys, whoever is responsible will be charged with a capital crime that cannot be commuted. Let there be no carelessness in the application of this decree! (Wang Kai 1744, 6.37a–38a)

Nor was Suicide Cliff the only danger on Southern Precipice; there was also a "dragon-head stone" that jutted out from the Palace of Perfect Felicity built into the cliff: "Those who come to pay their respects walk into space on the stone dragon and present incense in order to show their utter sincerity. A

Taoist points out Suicide Terrace down below."[36] This practice, too, was forbidden by Ts'ai Yü-jung in an "Inscription Forbidding the Dragon-head Incense Burner on Southern Precipice" (Wang Kai 1744, 6.38a–38b).

If madmen and saints sought thus to "soar up to heaven in broad daylight" in the same manner as the Crown Prince, ordinary mortals had to retrace their steps through the Southern Gate—the gate that gave access to heaven—marking the entry to the Southern Precipice and from there continue their plodding way up to the top of the Peak of the Celestial Column and its Golden Hall. For them, the worst was yet to come: first a long drop and then a steep five-kilometer climb that led through four mountain passes—the Gates of Heaven one, two, and three, and, finally, the Gate for Going in Audience before the Emperor (Ch'ao-sheng men 朝聖門). Once pilgrims had passed through this last gate, they could see the top of the mountain and the wall surrounding this Purple Forbidden City (Tzu-chin ch'eng 紫禁城).[37] Yet another turn, and they were in the Palace of Perfect Harmony, built with its back against the southern wall of the "city."

Here, if we are to judge by the two literati reports cited above, pilgrims prepared themselves physically and spiritually for the encounter with the god. They then went through the southern gate of the wall and underwent final scrutiny in a second hall dedicated to the Powerful Officer Wang[38] before ascending by the nearly vertical Nine-bend Staircase—nine is the number of Taoist heavens—to the Golden Hall. Inside it sat the bronze statue of the Perfect Warrior, on a throne, with a bronze tortoise and snake—his vanguard—at his feet (the story of their defeat by Chen-wu is told in chapter 10 of the *Pei-yu chi*). Once pilgrims had paid their respects to Chen-wu, they went to divine their fortunes in a small building to the left and have their pilgrim's sacks stamped in a similar structure to the right of the Golden Hall. Finally, before beginning their descent, the pilgrims went to burn incense before Chen-wu's parents in the hall to the back. (The walls of this latter shrine were covered with recent *ex-voto* when I first entered it in the fall of 1985.)

Ordinary pilgrims did not linger at the top of the mountain to gaze out over the surrounding peaks and contemplate their beauty or meditate on the relationship between high and low, rise and fall of fortune. Ordinary pilgrims knew their place, and they knew better than to tarry in the court of the Emperor. Indeed, many made the entire trip in a single day, starting out before dawn and returning to the foot of the mountain well after dark. Such precipitation, we have seen, was an expression of reverence, and perfect sincerity alone could protect the pilgrim from harm on this holy ground. Nonetheless, if they did not linger to gossip in the Forbidden City itself, we may be sure that, all along the way, they had been hearing and exchanging the legends that made the landscape come alive. And before they had left the top, the following tale may well have flitted across their minds and informed their sense of wonder and of participation in the vast company of their fellow pilgrims (it provides, in any case, a fitting manner for us to take our leave of the Emperor):

> Every year around the first day of fall flying ants swarm around the Golden Hall on the summit. At the end of the morning they fall to the ground. If they are many, there is more than a bushelful; if they are few, there will still be enough to fill several pecks. They are swept up to be thrown off a steep cliff, and their numbers are used to divine how many "incense guests" will come during the next year. If the divination is correct, the golden phoenixes on the four corners of the temple sometimes let out a cry. (Wang Kai 1744, 4.35b)

On their way down the mountain, when they reached the Southern Precipice, many pilgrims left the road they had taken up and picked their way down into the ravine below to make a final stop at the Five Dragon Palace. This temple, we may recall, was the original center of Wu-tang Shan, and we have no real proof that it was from the very beginning a part of the Perfect Warrior's myth. But by the time the *Pei-yu chi* was written, the Five Dragons had been incorporated into the single, overarching cult of Chen-wu, and they appear in the novel as the messengers who bring to the prince the decree of the Jade Emperor by which he learns of his investiture as Emperor of the North and Prime Minister of Jade Void (Yü-hsu shih-hsiang 玉虛師相, whence "Jade Void Palace"). We see the Prince, just before receiving this decree, "sitting on a rock combing his hair. Suddenly it occurred to him that his body of flesh and blood was useless, and he felt disinclined to comb his hair. He threw the comb behind him. Sunk in deep thought, only half-aware, he saw his body falling over the cliff" (Seaman 1987, 109).

The cliff, of course, is the Southern Precipice, and we are left to imagine the same Five Dragons bearing the Emperor heavenward, to his throne on the Peak of the Celestial Column (it should be noted here that in Taoist ritual, five is the number of *ch'i* 氣, "energies," in the north). The decree lauds the Perfect Warrior for having "practiced austerities for over forty years, so that not a particle of worldly desire remains." It also informs him that he will be charged with regular inspection tours of the world on the ninth day of the ninth month and the twenty-fifth day of the twelfth, in order to "investigate cases of good and evil in the world" (Seaman 1987, 109–10).

CONCLUSION

Most of China's many sacred mountains, even those specifically associated with Buddhism or Taoism, do not admit of a single, unified interpretation. The cult of the immortal Mei Fu, for example, is still very much alive on P'u-t'o Shan, as is that of the Yellow Emperor on Omei Shan, even though these are two of "the four great Buddhist mountains." On Heng Shan, the southern of the Five Peaks generally identified as "Taoist," there are more Buddhist shrines and temples than there are Taoist. And it is fair to ask whether the cult of Pi-hsia Yuan-chün, which came, as Naquin shows (chapter 8 of this volume), to dominate the eastern of the Five Peaks, can meaningfully be described as Taoist. Other famous mountains—T'ien-t'ai in Chekiang, Lu Shan in Kiangsi—were traditionally shared by Buddhists and Taoists; still others, too numerous to mention—indeed, many mentioned nowhere in any written source—were centers of local cults that did not spread and were never covered over by national cults or integrated into larger pantheons.

Wu-tang Shan is thus a very special, not to say unique case: a mountain whose every shrine and every scene has been integrated into the dramatic tale of a single god, a god whose Taoist identity is incontrovertible and whose imperial connections are impeccable. Is there no weak link in the chain for our hermeneutic ingenuity to break? None. For if Wu-tang Shan was not yet clearly identified with the Perfect Warrior in T'ang times, when it already belonged to a national network, it has never been explicitly identified with any other cult. Even the original focus of the mountain on the Five Dragon Abbey cannot be convincingly adduced as evidence for a significantly different cultic "prehistory," not only because the Five Dragons have, by late Ming, been successfully integrated into the Chen-wu myth, but also because, as already noted, "five dragons" is "Taoist" for "five energies of the north," and Chen-wu is, above all, the Emperor of the North.

But he is not the Emperor of the North worshiped on the northern of the Five Peaks. He is the Emperor of the North who, as the Yuan tales show best, has grown out of the ancient tortoise-and-serpent combination known in Han times as Hsuan-wu. Hsuan-wu, we noted, is one of the "four numinous beasts" who have played a crucial role in Taoist ritual from ancient times down to the present (see Lagerwey 1987, index: "Four Potentates"), and it is therefore no accident that the Perfect Warrior makes his first "modern" appearance during the reign of Sung Chen-tsung as one of the "four saints" (*ssu-sheng* 四聖).

Ever since that first appearance, the Four Saints have occupied an important place in the Taoist pantheon and in Taoist ritual (see below), and what we should like to do, in conclusion, is to show the relevance of these liturgical facts to our understanding of the pilgrimage to Wu-tang Shan. To do so, we shall once again have recourse to the *Pei-yu chi*. In the final chapter of the novel Chen-wu is described as the conqueror of "the many demons that prowled the Yangtze River":

> If officials met with difficulties while crossing the river, the Venerable Teacher would let down his hair and take up his sword and manifest himself in mid-air to save them . . . ; he frequently saved officials and their entourages, as well as

travelers and merchants. These people molded a statue of the god at the foot of Wu-tang Shan and built a temple there to worship him. (Seaman 1987, 203–4)

Rewriting history, the chapter then tells how Ch'eng-tsu was helped in battle by a god whose identity he learned by summoning the Heavenly Master to court. "This god has achieved perfection through his own efforts," the Heavenly Master told the emperor, "and is devoted to saving the people" (Seaman 1987, 205). Ch'eng-tsu thereupon undertook a pilgrimage to Wu-tang Shan, where he discovered "that the visage of the statue of the Venerable Teacher was the same as his own, which pleased him very much" (Seaman 1987, 206; see below, n. 2). After his return to court, the emperor ordered the huge construction campaign and the seven-day offering to which we have already alluded, and the novel concludes:

> Indeed, the spirit of the Venerable Teacher on Wu-tang Shan has manifested his spiritual powers. He saves those who meet with difficulties from their difficulties. He saves those who meet with disasters from those disasters. He makes the wind gentle upon the four seas and causes the waves to ebb. In those homes where the god is worshiped, the sons are filial and the grandsons obedient. Parents who have no offspring and who pray to him will all be provided for. . . . Thus it has continued up to the present day, some two hundred years from that time. Incense has been kept burning there, now as then, and the perpetual offerings of the imperial court have kept all under heaven at peace. (Seaman 1987, 207–8)

In his introduction, Seaman shows the importance of both exorcism and spirit-medium writing in the Chen-wu cult. Using the preface to an edition of the novel published by a Chen-wu temple in Taiwan, he also recounts the tale of a man who, after making a pilgrimage to Wu-tang Shan in 1871, founded the temple in question and reprinted the novel "so that there will be no mistakes in his chronicle and so that great benefits will come to the world through the example of his self-cultivation" (Seaman 1987, 23).

The *Pei-yu chi* thus provided both an incentive to pilgrimage and a key to the pilgrim's experience of the mountain (for those traveling by boat along the Yangtze, it also provided assurance of safe travel). In this role, of course, it was seconded by the many temple murals that also told the Perfect Warrior's story (see Grootaers 1952). Most important for our purposes, however, it reveals precisely what must be understood by the term "Taoist mountain" with reference to Wu-tang Shan: it is a mountain whose god ruled over the unruly world of the spirits much as the emperor ruled over China and who lived, like him, in a Forbidden City.

But Chen-wu, we must remember, is but an incarnation of the Jade Emperor in the novel (and the eighty-second transformation of Lao Tzu in the Taoist scripture that lies behind the novel). He is regularly knocked out by his demonic opponents and just as regularly saved by the Three Pure Ones.

In the end (as we have seen in the opening paragraphs of this chapter), just as the historical Ch'eng-tsu calls on the Forty-fourth Heavenly Master to select Taoists for the abbeys on Wu-tang Shan, so does the romanesque Ch'eng-tsu call on the Heavenly Master Chang (Tao-ling, no doubt) to identify his divine benefactor; both Ch'eng-tsus ask the Heavenly Master to perform the offering of thanksgiving in 1424.

The Perfect Warrior, in other words, is dependent—on the Three Pure Ones for his life and on the Heavenly Master for his identification and worship. The manner in which the Taoist sacred area is constructed in one modern Cheng-i tradition[39] will help us to understand why and to understand what this dependence implies for our understanding of Wu-tang Shan. The "inner altar" is presided over by portraits of the Three Pure Ones, with the Jade Emperor in fourth position; the "outer altar" is created by hanging portraits of marshals (most of whom figure in the *Pei-yu chi*) as well as of Chen-wu and Chang Tao-ling (Lagerwey 1987, 36–45). Chen-wu represents the exorcistic function of the Taoist, Chang his role as a civil official, and their paintings are hung above tables representing their respective mountains, Wu-tang Shan and Lung-hu Shan. Analysis of Taoist ritual shows that the role of the civil official is to communicate with heaven, that of the exorcist to "war against the dark forces" of the north (Lagerwey 1987, 64).[40]

In general, it may be said of the Taoist offering that it is, already in the eighth-century liturgy of Chang Wan-fu, a ritual designed for the worship of an integrated pantheon. It gives ritual expression to the search for unity, whether on an individual, communal, or imperial level. From the Sung dynasty on the lists of gods invited to Taoist offerings include the gods of the people in ever greater numbers, a change closely linked to the gradual displacement of imperial interest from the aristocratic, eremetic Taoism of Mao Shan to the popular and communal Taoism of Lung-hu Shan (Lagerwey 1987, 259–64).

The cult of Chen-wu as described in the *Pei-yu chi* and as experienced on Wu-tang Shan gives considerable insight into the nature of Taoist spiritual unification, for each victory of the Perfect Warrior leads to the "annexation" of yet another god—Chao Kung-ming, Kuan Yü, the various marshals, and the plague god Chang Chien (Seaman 1987, 142). Significantly, many of the demonic creatures the Perfect Warrior defeats and integrates into his "unified command" live in caves, just as the Taoist hermits who first domesticated Wu-tang Shan by "breathwork" that was the model for Chen-wu's did.

Indeed, the Chen-wu myth is best read as a poetic description of Taoist "internal alchemy" (*nei-tan*). The Taoist hermit, like Chen-wu, lived in solitude in order to come to terms with the forces of death and desire within himself, and he lived in caves because caves gave him access to the raw forces of nature that circulated deep within the mountain. These forces, when they emerged, could cause death and destruction to ordinary people; but the

Taoist hermit, like Chen-wu, mastered and made use of them. He was able to do so because he came, by practice, to realize in his person the order of the universe—cosmology.

To put it another way, the work of the Taoist hermit was the origin of all three visions of Wu-tang Shan: his heroic battle with the forces of death and desire within himself was projected onto the landscape and lived by the ordinary pilgrim as the myth of the Perfect Warrior, and his integration of his own forces with those of nature at once paved the way for the literati's aesthetic contemplation of nature and provided living proof of the efficacy of the cosmic system of which imperial ideology was an elaboration.

NOTES

Bibliographical Note: I would like to express here my gratitude to Professor Piet van der Loon for his many helpful suggestions and, in particular, for bringing to my attention articles by Ku Wen-pi and Huang Chao-han. This chapter also owes much to Gary Seaman, both for his comments at the conference and for his translation and study of the *Pei-yu chi.* Thomas Hahn was my guide on my first trip to Wu-tang Shan in 1985 and also sent me copies of Wang Kai's monograph and the article by Wang Ning-ch'u.

Of the four other monographs on Wu-tang Shan (Brook 1988, 157–58), I have had access to the first *chüan* of Fang Sheng's work and was able to read through and make notes on Jen Tzu-yuan's. It should be pointed out that the latter work is not the original of Jen Tzu-yuan, who was put in charge of all Wu-tang Shan in 1428 and died in 1430 (Wang Kai 1744, 4.17a), but a considerably augmented version from the Hung-chih period (1488–1505), whose latest internal date is 1495.

My principal source, the *Ta-yueh T'ai-ho shan chi-lueh,* was compiled in 1744 at the behest of Wang Kai, commissioner in the Lower Ching-nan circuit specifically charged with the oversight of the irrigation system (see the preface, 2a). Wang says in his preface (4b) that the woodblocks of the Ming monograph had been burned during the fighting and consequent destruction in the Wu-tang area at the end of the Ming. Wang Min-hao, magistrate of Chün-chou in 1680–81 (see *Chün-chou chih* 8.16a), had had a new version compiled, but its blocks had in their turn disappeared in a fire that destroyed the Ching-lo Kung (Palace of Purity and Joy) in Chün-chou:

> I was able to find manuscript copies kept on the mountain and thought at first to have new blocks cut. But I was dissatisfied with its lack of veracity and also with the fact that it contained many references to rituals rather like the "pure words" [Taoist prayers] of Sung authors. I suspected that Taoists had invented them and inserted them surreptitiously, and that they were therefore untrustworthy.
>
> Great rituals are simple; true reverence does without literature. T'ai-ho [Perfect Harmony, another name for Wu-tang Shan] is a famous mountain; Chen-wu is a venerated god. It is to be feared that the truth be lost when there are too many literary flourishes; and tall tales do not do justice to the substance of the matter. But a mountain classic has been lacking for some time now, and it is our duty to meet the need. In making this record of the mountain, it is our aim not to be as superficial and vulgar as the old monograph. We have selected that in it which was elegant and instructive, and we have

added to it from the various histories and also from the traditions of the people in order to make this "Concise Record" in several rolls. If in preferring the concise we have avoided the heterogeneous and in preferring the substantive avoided the flowery, then we have accomplished our task. (Preface, 5a–6a)

According to Wang Kai's "ground rules" (*fan-li*), the Ming monograph, called *T'ai-ho chih* 太和志, in 5 *chüan*, had been written in the Hsuan-te period (1426–35) by the Taoist Jen Tzu-yuan (the date given in Jen's text itself, p. 364, is 1428, and the text is called *T'ai-ho shan-chih*); Wang Min-hao's version had 20 *chüan*. As examples of legendary material unworthy of inclusion the ground rules mention the "Taoist tale of the Emperor crossing the sea and wandering in the east" and the story that locates the graves of the Perfect Warrior's parents near Chün-chou. Also eliminated are "all texts used in Chen-wu temples and having nothing to do with T'ai-ho." We shall see below that Wang Kai had private reasons for reediting the mountain monograph as well. See also Chün-fang Yü's general discussion of mountain gazetteers, chapter 5 of this volume.

1. See Jen Tzu-yuan 1983, 51 ff., 511 ff.; *Huang-Ming en-ming shih-lu* 4.2a–4b, 8b–9b; and *Ming-shih* 187; 25.7603. The number of Taoists is based on Wang Kai (1744, 3.9a–22b; Mano 1979, 403, n. 9, gives somewhat lower figures based on Ling Yun-i's *Ta-yueh T'ai-ho shan chih* 大嶽太和山志. By 1490 the number of Taoists living on the mountain had apparently doubled to around 800 (*Ming-shih* 185; 16.4903); the number of Taoists and acolytes reached 10,000 by 1580 (Ku 1989, 72); it had fallen to 230 in 1950 (Shih 1987, 2).

2. Huang Chao-han (1988b, 149) cites evidence that butchers and pork-sellers were corporate worshipers of Chen-wu.

For a full discussion of the reasons for the building project, especially the role played by the emperor's futile search for Chang San-feng, see Seidel (1970, 492–96), Seaman (1987, 23–27), and Mano (1979, 341–45). Particularly worthy of note is the legend—or is it a fact?—that statues of the Perfect Warrior were modeled on Ch'eng-tsu, who may well have thought of himself as the incarnation of the god. A fact unnoticed until now is that all Ming emperors after Ch'eng-tsu announced their accession to the throne by sending a sacrifice to Chen-wu (Wang Kai 1744, 3.36a–37a). During a September 1989 visit to Wu-tang Shan, I discovered that inscriptions of the texts of six Ming emperors' accession announcements are preserved inside the Hall of the Powerful Officer Wang near the top of the mountain (see below). Two of the six stelae are illegible; the remaining four give a stereotyped description of the dispatch of an official "to make sacrifice" (*chi* 祭) to Chen-wu.

This means, simply put, that the Ming Sons of Heaven believed they owed their possession of the heavenly mandate to the Perfect Warrior, who came, as we shall see, to be called the Supreme Emperor, Shang-ti, as his mountain came to be known as T'ai-yueh, the Great (or First) Peak.

3. In its present form the *Ch'i-sheng lu* (*Tao-tsang* 958, hereafter *TT*) is probably late Yuan or early Ming, for it contains notes that refer to the *Wu-tang fu-ti tsung-chen chi* (*TT* 962) compiled by Liu Tao-ming in 1291 and prefaced by Lü Shih-shun in 1301. In the text itself, however, we read of a first compilation ordered by the emperor Jen-tsung in 1055 (6.2a) and of a recasting, no doubt of this original collection, in 1184 by one Tung Su-huang (1.21b). See note 6.

4. The text contains three references to a Sui dynasty devotee of Chen-wu (1.23a, 3.8a, 6.9a). It also mentions a Taoist ritual of offering performed—anachronistically—at the Purple Empyrean Palace on Wu-tang Shan in the Chen-kuan period (627–49; see 1.20a). *Chüan* 2, however, opens with a story of the reincarnation of Chen-wu during the reign of Empress Wu Tse-t'ien and states clearly that the cult dates to that time (2.1a–2a; cf. 3.22a, 5.12b–14a, 6.4b–6a).

5. Wang Kai (1744, 3.31a–33b) records successive imperial titles given in 1018, 1202, 1257, and 1304; for the latter, see also the *Hsuan-t'ien shang-ti ch'i-sheng ling-i lu* (*TT* 961).

6. Apart from the references cited in note 4, the *Ch'i-sheng lu* contains but one pre-Sung date (904) (3.20b) and one other T'ang-era anecdote (7.7a). All other dated stories take place during the reigns of the first four Sung emperors, and the latest in date of these stories occurs during the Chia-yu period (1056–63) (5.11a). The events of 1055–57 that led to the first compilation are mentioned with noteworthy frequency (2.9a, 12b, 3.14b, 5.5a), and the text concludes with a hymn elsewhere ascribed to Jen-tsung (*Hsuan-t'ien shang-ti pai-tzu sheng-hao* 1a [*TT* 1482]), but here simply to the "emperor" (8.24b). It therefore seems safe to conclude that the *Ch'i-sheng lu* reflects, basically, the state of the cult as of the mid-eleventh century.

7. The story tells of the spread of the cult to northeastern China.

8. Concerning this ritual, see Chavannes. The ritual, which dates back at least as far as the fifth century, consists in reporting, in situ, to the gods of China's various holy sites (see n. 9) on the dynastic merit acquired by the performance of Taoist fasts and/or offerings in the capital. The report was written on strips of jade, which were then "thrown" into caves or rivers together with a bronze dragon, the messenger who carried the jade strip message to the divine lord of the site.

9. *Tung-t'ien fu-ti yueh-tu ming-shan chi* 9a (*TT* 599); Tu situates Wu-tang Shan in Chün-chou but, contrary to his usual practice, associates no immortal, god, or hermit with the mountain. Ssu-ma Ch'eng-chen's list of *fu-ti* (*Yun-chi ch'i-ch'ien*, ch. 27 [*TT* 1032]) does not include Wu-tang Shan.

Lists of holy sites have a long history in China. The first such list to have survived is the famous *Shan-hai ching* (Classic of mountains and waterways) of the second century C.E. By the mid-T'ang dynasty (Ssu-ma Ch'eng-chen) the number of such sites had come to be limited conventionally to thirty-six "cave-heavens" (*tung-t'ien*) and seventy-two "blessed plots" (*fu-ti*).

10. In Ming and Ch'ing times the blessed plot was shifted to a place in front of the Purple Empyrean Palace called the Pool of Yü's Footprints (Yü-chi ch'ih; see, for example, *Ming-shan sheng-kai chi*: T'an Yuan-ch'un, 5a, and Wang Shih-chen, 3b).

11. One of the principal sights on Wu-tang Shan would seem to have been Ch'en T'uan's "Terrace for Reciting the Scriptures" (Wang Kai 1744, 3.16b); according to his biography (ibid., 4.5b), Ch'en spent more than twenty years on Wu-tang Shan before moving to Hua Shan to avoid the crowds.

12. I owe this reference to Piet van der Loon.

13. This and the following paragraphs are based on Wang Kai 1744, 4.7b–10a. On the so-called Thunder Rites, cf. Boltz 1987, 413.

14. The second text, written five months after the first, is also by Hsu, but he has been promoted in the meanwhile to the post of minister of personnel.

15. Ch'eng probably writes from personal experience, for he had been surveillance commissioner in Hupei from 1300 to 1304 (*Yuan-shih* 172, 13.4015). He had also memorialized concerning the drought of 1313 (on which, see below).

16. Chieh was made Chi-hsien academician sometime between 1335 and 1342.

17. According to the *Chün-chou chih* 7.21a, in the late nineteenth century the various articles required for each of these sacrifices cost 18,060 cash.

18. A note on what is meant by "Taoist mountain" is perhaps in order here. It is traditional to regard the Five Peaks (*wu-yueh*) as Taoist, in contrast with the "four most famous (Buddhist) mountains" (*ssu-ta ming-shan*). While both history and cosmology can be called on to justify this identification of the Five Peaks with Taoism, these mountains already constituted a distinct group in the Former Han dynasty (see the *Shih-chi*), before Taoism had taken on an organized ecclesiastical form, and it is only from the late sixth century on that Taoists made a concerted effort to claim these mountains as theirs.

The Taoists were never entirely successful in pressing this claim, and of the five only Hua Shan and T'ai Shan, albeit in very different manner, play a significant and ongoing role in Taoist religious history. Perhaps even more to the point, even these two mountains are nowhere near as important to Taoist history as are such mountains as Mao Shan and Lung-hu Shan, centers, respectively, of Shang-ch'ing and Cheng-i Taoism. Together with Ko-tsao Shan (in Kiangsi), the ordination center of Ling-pao Taoism, these mountains constituted the "tripod" on which officially recognized forms of Taoism rested from the early twelfth century on. As for Chung-nan Shan, associated as it was with Lao Tzu's revelation of the *Tao-te ching* to Yin Hsi, it remains to this day an important Taoist mountain, but its real time of glory was the T'ang, when Lao Tzu was regarded as the divine ancestor of the reigning family.

There are, of course, many more famous Taoist mountains, from Ch'ing-ch'eng in Szechuan to Wu-i in Fukien, and from Lo-fu in Kwangtung to Lao Shan in Shantung.

19. On Shao-lin, see Faure, chapter 4 of this volume. The two types of "shadow-boxing" associated, respectively, with Shao-lin and Wu-tang are generally contrasted as "internal" (Taoist) and "external" (Buddhist), that is, aimed at internal or external defense and mastery.

20. Wu-tang Shan was thoroughly but not exclusively Taoist, for we know of at least one Ch'an hermit who resided there for most of the latter half of the sixteenth century (see the inscription by Yuan Hung-tao in Wang Kai 1744, 7.24b–26a; cf. Wang Shih-chen's description of his visit with this hermit in his *Yu T'ai-ho shan chi* 6b–8a).

21. Biography in *Ming-shih* 201; 17.5309. Wu is there credited with destroying no fewer than 250 "heterodox cults" (*yin-ssu*) at his first post in Shun-te county, Kwangtung.

22. According to his biography in *Ming-shih* 287, 24.7380, Wang was named vice–censor-in-chief of the right in Yun-yang prefecture in 1574.

23. To rule, in traditional China, meant at once to recognize and enfeoff local gods and to delegate one's authority to appointed officials. These officials, as representatives of the emperor, had in turn to ensure that all sacrificial obligations to local deities were met, in particular those of making regular sacrifice and reporting on important events to the gods of the mountains and rivers of a given territory.

Ts'ai Yü-jung's biography in *Ch'ing-tai ch'i-pai ming-jen chuan* (1.72) says he was appointed governor-general in 1670 and governor of Hu-kuang in 1674. Ts'ai spent altogether seventeen years in the area, most of them devoted to combatting rebellions there and southwest as far as Yunnan. The biography makes it very clear Ts'ai's appointment as governor in the second month of 1674 was linked to the uprising of Wu San-kwei, which began in the twelfth month of 1673. For the date of Ts'ai's visit to Wu-tang Shan, see Wang Kai, 7.30b.

24. The snide remarks concerning pilgrims are excised in the version of this text in Wang Kai (1744, 7.28b).

25. Wang was prefect of the Lower Ching-nan circuit from 1554 to 1556, that is, shortly after the events mentioned in the *Chi-lueh* (*Hsiang-yang fu-chih* [1886] 19.44b).

26. *Ming-shan*, T'an Yuan-ch'un, 1a–b. T'an, who addresses these words to his companion, a Buddhist monk, goes on: "Master, may I ask you to change my feet and eyes so as to enchant my heart!" The monk replies: "After we leave the Palace of Primordial Harmony, we come to the Golden Sand Flats. Tomorrow we will go out back of the Watching-for-Immortals Pavilion and follow the woodcutters' path: slowly on we will stop seeing other people." The phrase translated in the text refers thus not only to the fact that Wu-tang Shan was overrun with people, but also to the fact that they all saw the same thing, that is, what those who went before them had seen (and described); that is, they saw nothing at all.

27. The numbers in the discussion that follows are my own. The list includes virtually all inscriptions to be found at Southern Precipice, on the path from there to the summit, in the Palace of Perfect Harmony, at the Slope of the Prince, and at the Needle-sharpening Well, with the exception of a number of literati poems and several government-related inscriptions. It should be noted as well that time and weather have rendered illegible as many visible inscriptions as I was able to copy and that the mountain walls are pockmarked with rectangular holes from which inscriptions have disappeared.

28. A curious tale in the *Hsiang-yang fu-chih* (1759, 40.25a–b) tells of a woman from Chi-ning, Shantung, who, having heard her husband's tales of two group pilgrimages to Wu-tang Shan—the first is said to have taken place in 1686—insists on going along on the third. When her husband does not consent, she commits suicide. But when the pilgrim group reaches Honan, the man suddenly sees his wife by the side of the road. Certain he's seeing a ghost, the man begins to tremble, but his fellow travelers say: "We're more than a hundred. Even if it is a ghost, what have we to fear?"

On the question of pilgrim groups, their nature, and their size, see further the chapters by Dudbridge, Wu, Yü, and Naquin in this volume (chaps. 1, 2, 5, and 8).

29. The practice of making three successive pilgrimages in fulfillment of a vow is a common one, even today. In 1987 I met an individual who had made just such a vow. He had gone in 1986 to pray for the restoration of his wife's health. In 1987 he was going again, both to give thanks for the improvement in his wife's health and to have his "mouth opened" (*k'ai-k'ou*) by a local Taoist. The following day, as I was coming down from the summit, I met the man again in the Palace of Perfect Harmony: "It's finished!" he announced triumphantly and pointed to his cheeks as though passing a skewer through them. In reality, it had just begun, for to have one's "mouth opened" means "to undergo initiation as a medium": he was going home as the Perfect Warrior's "mouthpiece."

30. Taoist symbols are generally written in red on thin slips of yellow paper; if they are to be swallowed, they are first reduced to ashes and mixed with water (see above).

31. See Yü, chapter 5 of this volume, on the influence of the companion work, *Hsi-yu chi*, on the P'u-t'o pilgrimage. We may recall here as well that the many Perfect Warrior temples throughout the empire served as relays for the transmission of Chen-wu's legend, not least through the murals that decorated temple walls (see above).

32. According to the same monograph, 9.25a, the Yun-wu kuan on Hsiang-lu Shan, twenty *li* northwest of Nan-chang, was also known as "little Wu-tang."

33. See above concerning the Taoist scripture that made the Perfect Warrior out to be the eighty-second transformation of Lao Tzu, the divine founder of Taoism. The goddess of the Dipper, Tou-mu, is one of modern Taoism's most important and most popular deities. The story of Chen-wu's birth and induction into religion serves, thus, to establish his Taoist credentials.

34. According to Wang Kai (1744, 4.31b), "Those who go in audience on the mountain often hear at night the sound of whips and say, 'It's the Powerful Officer making the rounds of the mountain.'" There was yet another shrine to this divine guard on Mao-fu Peak, near the Five Dragon Palace. Again according to Wang Kai, if those who "ascend the mountain are not pure, they are driven out by snakes or tigers, or trapped at the foot of a tree and released only if they pray" (4.35b).

What the literati thought of such morality enforcers may be gathered from the following editorial note: "To do good without expecting a reward, to be afraid of no one and yet not to do what is not good—this, for gentlemen, goes without saying. But if ignorant men and women, upon hearing these tales of the Black Tiger and the Powerful Officer, look toward the mountain with fear and trembling, and if they are led thereby to regret their wrongdoings and turn to the good, even if this happens to only one or two persons in a million, or on only one or two days in a million, or in one or two thoughts in a million, that still is enough to bring invisible help there where the penal code does not reach, and it need not necessarily be of no assistance to the secular instruction of the human heart" (4.36b–37a).

35. These "Six Poisons" clearly refer to the demonic energies of the northern Six Heavens, the very energies said to have been defeated by the pure energies of the Three Heavens in early Heavenly Master Taoism (see above; see also Lagerwey 1987, 360).

36. The statement is Wang Tsai-chin's (Wang Kai 1744, 7.22a). See also Fang Sheng (in *Ming-shan* 5a), writing in 1535: "Those who are most scrupulous in their worship of the god go out to the dragon-head to place a stick of incense as a sign of their reverence."

37. Wu-tang Shan has many features—the Suicide Cliff, the three Gates of Heaven, the Southern Gate—common to a large number of mountains in China. But it is the only mountain, to my knowledge, that has a Forbidden City. This feature, therefore, more than any other, underscores what is meant by Chen-wu's title as Supreme Emperor: he is the spiritual counterpart of the Son of Heaven.

38. Concerning the stelae preserved in this shrine, see above, n. 2.

39. The description is based on the Cheng-i altar as constructed in southern Taiwan; the principles of construction, however, are essentially the same wherever Taoist sacred areas are laid out.

40. The opening chapter of the novel *Shui-hu chuan* contains a poem describing the Shang-ch'ing Kung (Supreme Purity Palace) on Lung-hu Shan. It mentions both a Hall of the Three Pure Ones and a Shrine of the Four Saints. This temple complex was completely destroyed during the Cultural Revolution, but in the nearby T'ien-shih fu, where the Heavenly Master used to live, separate temples to the same two sets of deities were among the first to be restored.

BIBLIOGRAPHY

Boltz, Judith. 1987. *A Survey of Taoist Literature, Tenth to Seventeenth Centuries*. Berkeley: Institute of East Asian Studies, University of California.

Brook, Timothy. 1988. *Geographical Sources of Ming-Qing History*. Ann Arbor: Center for Chinese Studies, University of Michigan.

Chavannes, Edouard. 1919. *Le jet des dragons*. Paris: Leroux.

Ch'ing-tai ch'i-pai ming-jen chuan 清代七百名人傳. 1936. Edited by Ts'ai Kuan-lo 蔡冠洛. Ch'ing-tai chuan-chi 清代傳記 edition, Ming-wen shu-chü, vol. 194.

Chün-chou chih 均州志. 1884. 16 *chüan*. Compiled by Chia Hung-chao 賈洪詔.

Fang Sheng 方升, comp. 1556. *Ta-yueh chih-lueh* 大嶽誌略. 5 *chüan*.

Grootaers, Willem A. 1952. "The Hagiography of the Chinese God Chen-wu." *Folklore Studies* 12, 2:139–82.

Hsiang-yang fu-chih 襄陽府志. 1759. 40 *chüan*.

Hsiang-yang fu-chih 襄陽府志. 1886. 26 *chüan*.

Hsu Tao-ling 許道齡. 1947. "Hsuan-wu chih ch'i-yuan chi ch'i t'ui-pien k'ao" 玄武之起源及其蛻變考. *Shih-hsueh chi-k'an* 史學集刊 5 (December): 223–40.

Hsuan-t'ien shang-ti ch'i-sheng ling-i lu 玄天上帝啟聖靈異錄. *TT* 961.

Hsuan-t'ien shang-ti ch'i-sheng lu 玄天上帝啟聖錄. 8 *chüan*. *TT* 958.

Hsuan-t'ien shang-ti pai-tzu sheng-hao 玄天上帝百字聖號. *TT* 1482.

Huang Chao-han 黃兆漢. 1988a. *Ming-tai tao-shih Chang San-feng k'ao* 明代道士張三丰考. Taipei: Hsueh-sheng shu-chü.

———. 1988b. "Hsuan-ti k'ao" 玄帝考. In *Tao-chiao yen-chiu lun-wen chi* 道教研究論文集, 121–56. Hong Kong: Chung-wen ta-hsueh ch'u-pan she.

Huang Hsueh-min 黃學民. 1983. "Wu-tang shan wu-tao jen, Hsu Pen-shan lue-chuan" 武當山武道人,徐本善略傳. *Wu-tang* 1 (Wu-tang shan Wu-tang ch'üan-fa yen-chiu hui hui-k'an 武當山武當拳法研究會會刊): 12–14.

Huang-Ming en-ming shih-lu 皇明恩命實錄. *TT* 1462.

Jen Tzu-yuan 任子垣, comp. 1983. *Ta-yueh T'ai-ho shan chih* 大嶽太和山志. 15 *chüan*. Augmented edition reprinted in *Tao-chiao wen-hsien* 道教文獻. Taipei: Tan-ch'ing t'u-shu.

Kao Ho-nien 高鶴年. 1983. *Ming-shan yu-fang chi* 名山遊訪記. Taipei: Fo-chiao ch'u-pan she.

Ku Wen-pi 顧文璧. 1989. "Ming-tai Wu-tang shan ti hsing-sheng ho Su-chou jen ti ta kui-mo Wu-tang chin-hsiang lü-hsing" 明代武當山的興盛和蘇州人的大規模武當進香旅行. *Chiang-Han k'ao-ku* 江漢考古 no. 1:71–75.

Lagerwey, John. 1987. *Taoist Ritual in Chinese Society and History*. New York: Macmillan.

Liang T'ien-hsi 梁天錫. 1978. *Sung-tai tz'u-lu chih-tu k'ao-shih* 宋代祠祿制度考實. Hong Kong.

Liu Tao-ming 劉道明, comp. 1301. *Wu-tang fu-ti tsung-chen chi* 武當福地總真集. 3 *chüan. TT* 962.

Mano Senryū 間野潛龍. 1979. *Mindai bunkashi no kenkyū* 明代文化史の研究. Tokyo: Tōmeisha.

Ming-shan sheng-kai chi 名山勝槩記, *chüan* 28:

    Fang Sheng 方升, *Ta-yueh chih* 大嶽志.

    Wang Shih-chen 王世貞, *Yu T'ai-ho shan chi* 遊太和山記.

    Wang Tao-k'un 王道坤, *T'ai-ho shan hou-chi* 太和山後記.

    Yang Ho 楊鶴, *Ts'an-hua* 叅話.

    T'an Yuan-ch'un 譚元春, *Yu Hsuan-yueh chi* 游玄嶽記.

Ming-shih 明史. 1985. Shanghai: Shang-hai jen-min.

Rudolph, Richard C., and Wen Yu. 1951. *Han Tomb Art of West China: A Collection of First- and Second-century Reliefs*. Berkeley: University of California Press.

Seaman, Gary. 1987. *Journey to the North: An Ethnohistorical Analysis and Annotated Translation of the Chinese Folk Novel "Pei-yu chi"*. Berkeley: University of California Press.

Seidel, Anna. 1970. "A Taoist Immortal of the Ming Dynasty." In *Self and Society in Ming Thought*, edited by W. T. De Bary, 483–531. New York: Columbia University Press.

Shih Hsin-min 史新民, ed. 1987. *Chung-kuo Wu-tang shan tao-chiao yin-yueh* 中國武當山道教音樂. Peking: Chung-kuo wen-lien chu-pan kung-ssu.

Ta-Ming Hsuan-t'ien shang-ti jui-ying t'u-lu 大明玄天上帝瑞應圖錄. *TT* 959.

T'ai-shang shuo Hsuan-t'ien ta-sheng Chen-wu pen-chuan shen-chou miao-ching 太上說玄天大聖真武本傳神呪妙經. *TT* 775.

T'ao Chen-tien 陶真典, ed. 1984. *Wu-tang shan* 武當山. Hupei jen-min ch'u-pan she.

Tu Kuang-t'ing 杜光庭. *Tung-t'ien fu-ti yueh-hsu ming-shan chi* 洞天福地嶽瀆名山記. *TT* 599.

Wang Kai 王槩, comp. 1744. *Ta-yueh T'ai-ho shan chi-lueh* 大嶽太和山紀略. 8 *chüan.*

Wang Ning-ch'u 王寧初. 1937. "Kuan-yü Wu-tang shan" 關於武當山. *Ching-i* 經逸 29:84–88.

Yuan-shih 元史. 1985. Peking punctuated edition. Peking: Jen-min wen-hsueh.

Yun-chi ch'i-ch'ien 雲笈七籤. 120 *chüan*. Compiled by Chang Chün-fang 張君房 (ca. 1025). *TT* 1032.

Yü-chih Chen-wu miao-pei 御製真武廟碑. *TT* 960.

EIGHT

The Peking Pilgrimage to Miao-feng Shan: Religious Organizations and Sacred Site

Susan Naquin

The modern city of Peking sits on the northwest edge of the North China plain. This area, though long inhabited, was at the far frontiers of the Chinese empire for many centuries; indeed, it was as the southern foothold for non-Chinese kingdoms based in northern Asia that the city first came into prominence. Only when the third emperor of the Chinese Ming dynasty decided to make this spot his Northern Capital in 1403 did the city's orientation finally shift southward. Over the next six centuries Peking became the headquarters of successive regimes: the Ming (1368–1644), the Ch'ing (1644–1911), various regional governments (1911–49), and the People's Republic (1949 to the present). During this period, not only did the city become larger and more populous, but the natural terrain of the area was continuously enriched by both the physical remains and the memories of an increasingly long and complex history.

On the featureless plain, a series of walls defined the city; they enclosed a regular grid of streets around the imperial residence at the core and sharply demarcated the urban area from the countryside. Over time, this space became charged with ritual, symbolic, and historical meanings. In the mountains that rimmed the walled city to the northwest, geography was similarly reshaped by culture. This chapter, part of a larger work on Peking, will look at one aspect of this process, namely, the transformation of a mountain west of Peking into a terrain sacred to devotees of a popular local deity. The physical site was built in the course of several centuries by a variety of pilgrims who visited it, while, as we shall see, the views of others besides pilgrims combined to shape the more complicated meaning that the mountain pilgrimage came to have in local culture.[1]

Miao-feng Shan 妙峯山, Mountain of the Marvelous Peak, lies about forty kilometers northwest of Peking. At 1,330 meters, it is the highest of the range of peaks behind the better-known Western Hills (Hsi Shan 西山) that rise up in sight of the capital (Bouillard 1925).[2] By comparison with many mountains in China, the history of this peak appears shallow, layers of cultural significance few, and competition over sacred power weak. This simplicity is deceptive. Nevertheless, because it was as the location of a temple to the goddess Pi-hsia Yuan-chün 碧霞元君 that Miao-feng Shan became significant, we must certainly begin our story with this cult.

THE CULT OF PI-HSIA YUAN-CHÜN

The female deity who came to be preeminent in North China[3] by the late nineteenth century was a relative latecomer to the celestial pantheon of Chinese popular religion; only in Ming and Ch'ing times did her worship became common and, even then, her following was distinctly regional.

This cult began, it seems, with the early eleventh-century discovery of a female statue lying at the bottom of a mountain pool. Recovered and installed as an object of worship, this "jade woman" (*yü-nü* 玉女) was able to demonstrate the potency that revealed her as a god. Although other stories were told about her, most devotees identified this deity as the daughter of the god of the mountain on which the statue was found. But this was no ordinary mountain; it was Mount T'ai 泰山, the venerable Eastern Peak (Tung-yueh 東嶽), looming above the plain in central Shantung province (some five hundred kilometers from Peking), a centuries-old site sacred to emperors and citizens alike. The identity of this Jade Woman, obviously no ordinary being, was thus from the outset closely linked in myth and symbol to Mount T'ai.

The locus of special imperial worship since the first millennium B.C., Mount T'ai was firmly established as the preeminent mountain of the North China plain, "the Prime of the Five Peaks." The spirit of the mountain was understood to be a male god who, by at least T'ang times (seventh–eighth centuries), was the judge of the dead and the lord of the tribunals of hell (ST 1684, no. 323; Chavannes 1910, 3–16; *CWK* 88.1484–91). Emperors bestowed successive titles on him, and Ming and Ch'ing rulers worshiped him regularly. His formal appellation was "Emperor of Humane Holiness, Equal to Heaven" (T'ien-ch'i jen-sheng-ti 天齊仁聖帝).

To this powerful and stern figure the much more recently discovered Jade Woman was attached as a daughter. She was called, respectfully, "Heavenly Immortal Jade Woman of T'ai Shan" (T'ai-shan t'ien-hsien yü-nü 天仙玉女). Because Mount T'ai was the Eastern Peak, in Ming times the Jade Woman acquired the further title of "Sovereign of the Clouds of Dawn" (Pi-hsia Yuan-chün).[4] Not unnaturally, her temples were particularly associated with mountaintops.

By contrast with her fearful father, Pi-hsia came to be viewed as a compassionate female figure. By 1600, she was being addressed as "Heavenly Im-

mortal and Holy Mother" (T'ien-hsien Sheng-mu 天仙聖母) and called by
many simply Niang-niang 娘娘 (Our Lady)[5] (*T'ai-an fu-chih* 1760, 7.7–8;
Chavannes 1910, 30–38). "The Five Peaks are all revered, but the Eastern
Peak is revered the most in our age. Of the various Eastern Peak gods, the
Heavenly Immortal Holy Mother is most revered by our age. How could this
not be, when the east gives birth to all and the ten thousand things are born
from a mother?" (PL 1599, no. 5827). She had also become closely associated
with a set of other female deities, two of whom were her constant companions: Tzu-sun Niang-niang 子孫娘娘 (Goddess of Children) and Yen-kuang
Niang-niang 眼光娘娘 (Goddess of Eyesight). Eventually, as many as nine
Niang-niang (not always the same ones) came to be found regularly in temples dedicated to Pi-hsia; most were specialists in matters related to childbirth (Goodrich 1964, 53–59).

These two cults, one old and one new, were often described in polarities:
male and female, yang and yin, death and life, father and daughter, father
and mother.

> Some say that the Clouds of Dawn Jade Woman is the god of Mount T'ai, but
> since there is also His Humane Holiness Equal to Heaven, how can this be? We
> respond by saying that it is the rule of heaven and earth that there be yin and
> yang; thus to worship the Clouds of Dawn Jade Woman is to treat the yin,
> while to worship the Great Emperor of Humane Sageliness is for the yang. (PL
> 1690, no. 936)

Pi-hsia was never part of the regularly funded imperial worship of Tung-
yueh (although images to her were often placed in his temples), and her cult
spread unsystematically. Her shrine on the summit of Mount T'ai grew with
popular and imperial support in the Ming—the large temple to her father
was situated at the foot of the mountain (Chavannes 1910, 102 ff., 126 ff.).
(See map 1.1.) We find that although Pi-hsia temples begin to appear in the
Peking area in the late 1400s, it was not until a century later, during the
Wan-li reign (1573–1619), that the tempo of such foundings became significantly livelier (*WS* 19; *Ch'en-yuan shih-lueh* 12–15; *HTL* passim; *CWK* 89–
107; *STFC* 1885, 17; *KCK* 6).

The active temple to the God of the Eastern Peak, built in Peking in the
early fourteenth century, made it easier for the Pi-hsia cult to take root. That
impressive complex was a few minutes' walk beyond the eastern walls of the
city (map 8.1). The celebration of the god's birthday in the late spring (on
the twenty-eighth day of the third lunar month) had also become, by late
Ming times, a festive event when the temple courtyards were packed with
visitors, probably the biggest such celebration in the capital (*TC* 2.67–68; ST
1607, no. 294; Chiang I-k'uei 1980, 4:79).[6]

Although the temple depended on the throne for major renovations, residents of the city contributed in an organized fashion to the upkeep of the

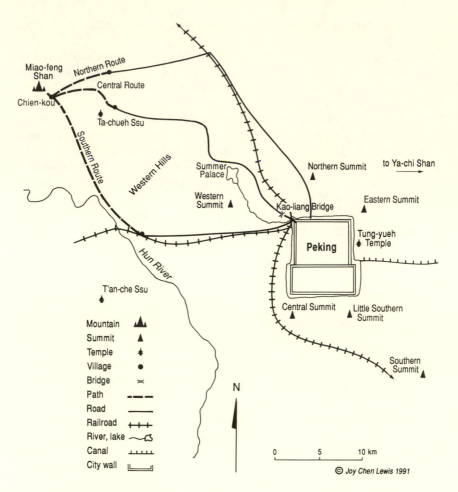

Map 8.1. Miao-feng Shan

shrines and expenses of the god's birthday. All Chinese temples needed regular endowments and donations to maintain a supply of daily offerings, but the provisions made for the Tung-yueh Temple were very well organized. Religious associations (*sheng-hui* 聖會)[7] that drew on both neighborhood and citywide membership annually donated a variety of ritual paraphernalia: pens, ink, paper, and record books that were placed in front of the seventy-two judicial officers, as well as flags, banners, incense, and offerings. "When the god needs something, it's there" (ST 1634, no. 305; 1587 Tung-yueh Miao cauldron in the Bai-yun Kuan; ST 1591, no. 288, 1592, no. 289). The concentration of rich, powerful, and pious patrons in the capital encouraged the formation and maintenance of such groups. Those who began to record their activities on large stone stelae placed in the temple courtyard were wealthy individuals; many were eunuchs of the inner court. In the seventeenth century we can begin to see similar groups of nobles and court personnel patronizing Pi-hsia Yuan-chün.[8]

More and more temples were built to this female deity; most remained small affairs, but a handful became famous, attracted patrons and pilgrims, and grew in size and endowed wealth. Of the two dozen temples to Pi-hsia Yuan-chün in and around Peking in the late Ming,[9] those most prominent in the life of the city were in the countryside beyond its high fortifications. Her official birthday was 4/18, but from as early as the Wan-li reign, 4/8 (already celebrated as a Buddhist holiday) began to be favored in Peking as the date when the deity's blessings were most accessible (Chavannes 1910, 70–72; *WS* 17:168; *TC* 3:133).

A relationship with Mount T'ai continued to be important in defining the identity of these temples to Pi-hsia, each of which had an attached shrine to the god of that mountain. When her Temple of Vast Compassion was built in 1608, it soon became nicknamed the Western Summit (Hsi-ting 西頂), as if to form a pair with the Eastern Peak temple across town.[10] The idea that there were five peaks in China, at each of the four directions and in the center, was an old and powerful one, an idea that suggested a stable underlying structure of the physical world to which government and human society could orient itself.[11] By at least the 1630s Peking residents had recreated in their region a smaller version of this cosmological structure through the cult of Pi-hsia Yuan-chün. They had selectively designated other Pi-hsia temples as the Southern, Eastern, Northern, and Central summits (*TC* 3.132–34).

As map 8.1 shows, these designations were at best approximate in terms of actual geography, but their power to realign the untidiness of nature into a system that, as it existed in people's minds, was not only symmetrical and regular, but deeply reassuring is quite clear. By using temples that were fictive mountains, these designations with a single stroke both invoked the larger cosmology of the five peaks of which Mount T'ai was a part and created a new and independent set of anchors for this small portion of the North

China plain around the capital. A sacred terrain had been invented and imposed. The divine protection implied by these five points where the deity was immanent was thus directed toward the capital, the center of the micro-cosm. The Pi-hsia cult would in turn derive strength from this resonant system, even if the perceived efficacy of individual temples rose and fell.[12]

As the new temple on Miao-feng Shan—to which we will turn our attention in a moment—was launched in the mid-seventeenth century, the deity was thus already beginning to rival the cult of the Eastern Peak with her own "mountain" temples, history, iconography, reputation for compassion, crowded birthday celebrations, and independent religious associations. During the Ch'ing, Our Lady of Miao-feng Shan gradually eclipsed these older temples and became preeminent. Let us examine how this came about.

THE PILGRIMAGE TO MIAO-FENG SHAN

Although arguments from silence are dangerous, the evidence is convincing to me that substantial religious activity on the Mountain of the Marvelous Peak began only in the seventeenth century,[13] especially the latter half of that century, after the Ming had been conquered by a powerful Manchu-led confederation from the northeast. We know that in 1689 the mountain was attracting Peking devotees of Pi-hsia. In the spring of that year, more than seven hundred men from a temple just outside the city walls who were part of a group that regularly burned incense at the Northern Summit commissioned a stone stele to record their visit to the Pi-hsia Yuan-chün temple at Miao-feng Shan (ST 1689, no. 653). The donors were identified as villagers (*li-jen* 里人), the text was composed and written by a lowly sixth-rank secretary in the Board of Works, and their stone was small and unprepossessing, a far cry from the huge tablets with elaborately decorated borders seen in the temple of the God of the Eastern Peak.

This new Pi-hsia temple was in quite a remote spot. These bare mountains behind the Western Hills had been explored and spottily named over the centuries; rough paths had been tramped out, and small settlements established, but to residents of Peking the area remained bleak and distant (*MITC* 1461, 1.24–27; *TC* 7.321–25). The new temple was not in fact on the summit of Miao-feng Shan, but rather on the end of a southern spur, a spot that gave a dramatic view of the winding valley beyond which lay the gleaming ribbon of the Hun River. (I have found no stories explaining the choice of location.) The journey to the mountain wilderness was more than an easy stroll: it took the better part of a day just to reach the foothills from Peking and another full day to climb up the poorly marked trails from there.

Nevertheless, stelae erected by pilgrim groups at the Miao-feng Shan temple give ample evidence of the traffic generated by the growing popularity of the Niang-niang housed here. Unlike the association of 1689, later groups were created specifically for the pilgrimage to this mountain on Pi-hsia's birthday. In the course of the next century, eighteen surviving stelae and donated objects were the unprepossessing gifts from groups that originated inside and outside the Peking city walls (in about equal measure). They appear to have been started by people from the same neighborhood or village who would make the journey together every year. The great majority were men, and most were Bannermen—that is, members of the new ruling group, some Manchu, some Chinese, that had moved en masse into Peking from the northeast in the 1640s.

By the 1730s, such groups were large and increasingly formalized: they ranged from a few dozen to more than seven hundred people,[14] adopted association names, and had designated leaders. The Yin-shan lao-hui 引善老會 (Venerable Association for Leading [People] To Do Good Deeds), for example, set up their first stele in 1737, with 144 members listed, including a few women. They erected another twelve years later, naming 163 men, 18 of whom served as association officers. By 1755 the group had grown to 268, 88 of whom were women. They identified themselves as people of the Banners from the Pao-fu temple community outside the northwest gate of Peking.[15]

In the nineteenth century, the continuing development of Miao-feng Shan was both mirrored in and made possible by the elaboration of a set of routes to it, for the physical infrastructure and symbolic structure of the pilgrimage grew in tandem. As early as 1822, stele texts spoke of five routes (*tao* 道) up the mountain, a characterization later repeated even though this number was more symbolic than real. In fact, a shifting constellation of paths led to the temple, of which three were more or less permanent. They were named variously the Southern, Northern, and Central Routes.[16]

The Central Route, which seems to have been the oldest, could be reached directly and easily from Peking. One left the city by way of the Summer Palace, a road that had become increasingly well traveled in the Ch'ing period as emperors K'ang-hsi (1662–1722) and Ch'ien-lung (1736–95) built and expanded their summer villas nearby. In the early nineteenth century, resting places for pilgrims began to be built along the steep path that rose west from the foothills, up and then down, and then up again to Miao-feng Shan. The Southern Route was longer but not so arduous. It involved travel on more commercial roads leading due west from Peking, crossing the Hun River by ferry, and walking up the long valley toward which the Miao-feng Shan Pi-hsia temple faced. In the early nineteenth century, most of the way stations built for pilgrims were along these two routes. It was only at the end of the century that improvements in transportation spurred the use of a Northern Route as well.[17] All three routes converged at Chien-kou, a poor and sleepy village that lay in the shadow of the peak temple.

Once off the plain, the paths to the summit passed near few ancient sites,

and only an occasional ruined building or crumbling stupa might be seen in
the distance. Miao-feng Shan was a far cry from Mount T'ai, Mount Wu-
tang, or P'u-t'o Shan (described in other chapters of this volume). Place
names here were of no particular antiquity and merely called attention to
natural features and the trials of the ascent: the "eighteen turns" and "360
elbow-bumpers," "melon-squashing rocks," "fortress ravine," and "double-
dragon ridge." The rest houses and shrines built by pilgrimage associations
became the highlights of the trip, and these relatively recent "sights" directed
attention entirely toward the pilgrim's goal. During the climb one looked up
to see if the peak really resembled a lotus flower. At the summit, one went to
peer over the steep temple precipice from which the truly pious could leap
without harm, and one sought out the protruding rock behind the main hall
that because of its appearance when struck by sunlight had given the spot the
name "golden summit" (Lowe 1941, 1:87; KU 172; Mei Ts'un 1983, 136–
39).

A stele erected in 1822 commemorating the construction of a new hall on
the peak illustrates the broad scale of activity by that time. Many contributors were named, including incense associations from Peking and its suburbs,
men and women, old and young, Manchu and Chinese, residences and
shops, even lime and coal mines from the nearby hills. With increasing frequency religious associations were concentrating their activities on specific
tasks necessary to the comfort of their fellow pilgrims. The 1822 stone listed
thirty-eight rest houses (literally, "tea stalls," *ch'a-p'eng* 茶棚) and other
altars set up at regular intervals by groups. The stele also indicated that the
goods and services provided already included not only incense, fruit, flowers,
altar decorations, and prayer mats for the temple interiors (at the top and en
route), but also tea, medicine, millet porridge, lanterns, road repair, railings
along the river, and ropes for the ferry (ST 1822, no. 667 and no. 694).

These groups continued to use the term *sheng-hui* (sacred [or religious]
association), although others sometimes called them *hsiang-hui* 香會 (incense
associations). Their full names usually mentioned both pious goals and services contributed: the Religious Association for Wholeheartedly Donating
Medicinal Plasters, the Single Heart United-in-Charity Religious Association for [Providing] Feather Dusters and Green Tea, the Venerable Association for Donating Fresh Flowers, and so forth (KU 41–52).

As the organizations became more specialized, they also became more
internally differentiated. Beyond the position of association head (*hui-shou*
會首) and deputy head, which had long been in use (for other kinds of organizations as well), more titles appeared, some reflecting particular tasks:
money manager, tea supervisor, treasurer, cook, head carter, and the like
(KU 23–25 and countless inscriptions).

Each group had a specific responsibility—tending a single rest house, for
instance, or repairing one segment of the stony path. Although coverage was

Fig. 8.1. Entertainers performing en route to Miao-feng Shan. Reproduced from *Yen-tu*, no. 2 (1990), back cover.

initially very spotty, the growing popularity of the pilgrimage (in turn encouraged by these very activities) extended such services to more and more of the pilgrims' paths until a great variety of what might be called tourist facilities were provided. Without any obvious coordination, several hundred schedules were staggered to reduce the crush at the peak and provide a continuity of services over the two weeks when the mountain was open (KU 74–108). Residents of Peking learned about the pilgrimage from large paper announcements (shaped like stone stelae) that were posted by members all around the city in the early spring, inviting people to sign up and make the journey.

In 1852 we begin to have records of the many entertainer groups who were by then (and probably had been for some time) a regular part of the pilgrimage (*CCT* 1852, no. 83202). Such groups included—for example—the "road openers" (*k'ai-lu* 開路), who frightened off malevolent spirits along the way. To this end, they painted their faces with fearsome stripes, unloosed their hair, and tossed and twisted heavy pitchforks with awesome dexterity. There were also brightly costumed folk-opera troupes, drum-singers, tightrope walkers, jugglers, and a host of other amazing, noisy, and colorful performers (fig. 8.1; see Imbault-Huart 1885, 62–71, and many later accounts).[18]

The life expectancy of these associations varied considerably, probably in relation to the degree that membership was reinforced by preexisting social ties (especially residence and occupation). Without any significant corporate property, continuity probably depended on the strength of such links and the availability of energetic leadership. Most associations appear only once or twice in the historical record, and newer groups sometimes reused the names of long disbanded organizations. The Erh-jen 二人 sheng-hui, established in 1730, for example, set up stelae in 1737 and 1782; the name reappears as a contributor to an 1899 stele and is used again in 1936. These Bannermen (both Chinese and Manchus) who provided free tea and porridge may have truly earned the title "venerable association" (*lao-hui* 老會) (ST 1737, no. 658, 1782, no. 665, 1899, no. 700; 1936 stele at site). Although there were more and more groups, the associations of the later Ch'ing period were not very different in size from their predecessors.[19]

From at least the eighteenth century, the pilgrimage season—defined in Chinese terms as the period when the temple was "open"—took place during the first part of the fourth lunar month (first to fifteenth). The 8th was already the main day of celebration.[20] In the mid-Ch'ing, an "autumn" pilgrimage (actually in the seventh month, usually August) had also developed in a kind of forced symmetry with the spring season, which it never came close to matching in popularity.[21]

Miao-feng Shan had been benefiting from the growing involvement in the public life of the capital and the region of what we may probably call an urban bourgeoisie (see Rankin 1986; Rowe 1989). In the course of the late

Ch'ing, we see more and more evidence of business firms and occupational groups making donations and coming on pilgrimages. Some shops acted on their own; some cooperated with members of the same guild (e.g., iron-workers: ST 1862, no. 695; pawnshops: ST 1885, no. 683; actors: ST 1892, no. 718; mat-shed shops: ST 1862, no. 731, ST 1867, no. 732, Imbault-Huart 1885, 64). The restoration of one part of the peak temple complex in the 1880s was made possible by more than a thousand donors, including several dozen Peking firms (most probably money shops) (ST 1882, no. 717).

Not only did wealthy merchants and even government offices (ST 1892, no. 723) join in supporting the festivities, so did more ordinary occupations. The Public Welfare Religious Association for Continuing Good Works by [Donating] Leaf Tea (Kung-i ch'ang-shan ch'a-yeh sheng-hui 公議常善茶葉聖會) appears to have begun as an organization of the porters who worked for the Ch'ing court carrying the baggage of tribute missions. They formed an association in 1857 and around the turn of the century cornered the specialized work of carrying goods for the furniture stores of Peking. They treated Pi-hsia as a patron saint, and their pilgrimage association was at the same time a guild for the protection of the porters' small monopoly. Their headquarters were in a Niang-niang temple (which they appear to have owned) in the Chinese section of Peking; there, newcomers were initiated and annual meetings held (there were 180 members in 1926). They made the pilgrimage to Miao-feng Shan every year and as their form of meritorious activity donated leaf tea to some forty rest houses along the way, using funds tithed from members in the course of the year (Burgess 1928, 80–91). The tinkers and the boot-and-shoe guilds had a similar relationship to the deity (Imbault-Huart 1885, 64; ST 1921, no. 757 and no. 758; Burgess 1928, 171).

Toward the end of the nineteenth century, the increasing popularity of the Miao-feng Shan pilgrimage was further enhanced by improved transportation and more lavish patronage. The high tide of religious activity may have been in the last decade of that century. An 1899 stele illustrates the scope and scale of pilgrimage associations in that year: it was subscribed to by 24 entertainment organizations, 61 tea stalls, and 56 associations, groups that came from inside and outside Peking, throughout the western suburbs, and along the pilgrimage routes, as well as 180 other individuals, shops, and temples (ST no. 700). At this time a contemporary source guessed that there were more than 90 rest houses along the main routes (Jang-lien 1899, 5); others estimated that one to two hundred thousand people came annually (TLC 1900, 38–40; Douin 1910–12, 136).

The building complex at the summit had grown with the pilgrimage. Nine other smaller shrines had been constructed around and behind the main hall to Pi-hsia and her attendants, and three more rooms were used for feeding and housing pilgrims. By 1900 the main courtyard contained a forest of several dozen commemorative stelae and a stone pit that served as an immense incense burner. Off to the side were three other separate shrines, and behind, slightly up the slope, was the Hui-hsiang T'ing 迴香亭 (Returning Incense Pavilion), where Tung-yueh was worshiped (KU 131–32; *MFSCN* diagram; TLC 1900, 38–39; ST 1882, no. 717, 1925, no. 687; FK 96).[22]

A burst of largess from the court had also given encouragement to the pilgrimage. In the 1890s, Empress Dowager Tz'u-hsi formed the habit each spring of watching the passing pilgrims from a special viewing stand at the Summer Palace. Entertainers stopped to perform before her—and found a most receptive audience. Soon groups of singers, stilt-walkers, weight lifters, actors, lion dancers, drummers, and martial artists were bestowed the privilege of carrying large banners of imperial yellow inscribed with the words—emblematic of imperial favor—"Long Life Without Limit" (*wan-shou wu-chiang* 萬壽無疆). Those selected also received cash awards (KU 204; CH 2, 40–41; *NWF* 1937).[23]

This high tide was soon cut short. In late May of 1900 a great many pilgrims froze to death in a freak snowstorm. Soon afterward the Boxer rebels besieged the diplomatic legations in Peking, the emperor and empress dowager fled, and the capital was occupied by foreign troops; the dynasty came to an end in 1911. Recovery from the decline at Miao-feng Shan caused by these events came only after 1917 (FK 102–4; CH 3).

As the vigor of the pilgrimage revived in the 1920s and 1930s, wealthy Tientsin groups played a role in the pilgrimage disproportionate to their numbers and contributed significantly to the maintenance of the infrastructure on the mountain even as they helped promote the fame of the deity in a larger region. Such participation was encouraged by developments in transportation in the capital area. Whereas previously pilgrims from Tientsin had traveled to Peking by boat along the Grand Canal (riding for free) and then circled around to the north of the city, after 1896 a railroad speeded this process and furthered the development of the Northern Route, which was near the new train line. In the first decades of the twentieth century, other railroads out of the city improved the journey of travelers to the Miao-feng Shan foothills (*Tu-shih ts'ung-t'an* 1940, 65–66; *Pei-ching li-shih chi-nien* 1984, passim). Although mention is occasionally made of pilgrims from Pao-ting and Kalgan (each about 150 kilometers away), the pull of Our Lady of Miao-feng Shan did not significantly extend much beyond Peking and Tientsin.

In the 1920s, the crowds that flocked to the mountain each spring did not go unnoticed. Police from the city came to maintain order, while European, American, and Japanese residents of Peking joined in, fascinated by the noise, color, and strange sights. They marveled at pilgrims who were laden with chains and ascended with painful slowness, walking one step, prostrating themselves on the path, then walking another. They noticed pilgrimage association members in their uniforms, carrying chests of supplies, their bells ringing and flags waving in the breeze. They watched jugglers toss heavy iron locks, young acrobats balance precariously on poles, and dramatic troupes, some leaping about on stilts, perform skits and plays (Bouillard 1921; Gamble photographs;[24] Bogan 1928, 28; Eigner 1939; Murakami 1940, 158–67). Chinese guidebooks (some put out by the new railway companies) similarly advertised these festivities (*Ching-Sui t'ieh-lu lü-hsing chih-nan* 1922; *LHCN* 57–58).

Despite repairs and modern improvements, visitors in the 1920s saw much that was dilapidated and were usually told that the size of the pilgrimage had been larger in the past (KU and FK passim; CH 24–25). Although the number of groups may have declined, the scale of services was extraordinarily complete. Several dozen different kinds of entertainers participated, often many groups of each kind. Loose contemporary estimates of the total number of rest houses and pilgrimage associations (categories that overlapped) range from two hundred to four hundred.

The role of these organizations in the development of the Miao-feng Shan Pi-hsia Yuan-chün cult seems hard to overestimate. As we have seen, they had, from the beginning, not only given money to build the temple complex and the paths to it, but by their public involvement widely advertised the power of this deity. The increasing fame of the mountain temple in the course of the seventeenth, eighteenth, nineteenth, and twentieth centuries was surely both a cause of these societies' efforts and a result. The cult grew together with these groups, which can be described without embarrassment as its promoters. Of course, without the large-scale involvement of individual, unorganized pilgrims, Miao-feng Shan would never have become so well known, but it was the pilgrimage associations whose services as travel agents and tour directors advertised and facilitated this broader popularity.

Over these centuries, the Pi-hsia Yuan-chün cult at Miao-feng Shan had made a vital place for itself in the popular culture of Peking, but its growth had only been from a local to a regional cult before its trajectory was interrupted by civil war and revolution. It became almost impossible to continue the pilgrimage in the 1940s: the Communists held the hills while the Japanese or the Nationalists held Peking, and severe damage was inflicted on the temple site during the resultant guerrilla warfare. Whatever remained after the Communist victory did not survive the virulent attacks on religion of the Cultural Revolution period (1966–76). In the more tolerant climate of the 1980s, however, publicly sponsored efforts to rebuild the temple complex were initiated, electricity was brought in, and a rough road to the top was built along the Southern Route. In the spring of 1988 images of Pi-hsia Yuan-chün and her companions were installed and, even as the old stelae lay broken in the courtyard, a freshly carved stone tablet recorded the visit of the 150-person United Heart Religious Association from a nearby village in May (the fourth lunar month) of that year.[25]

Thus, an uninhabited mountain became the site of a temple that grew steadily in size and renown, so that in the course of three hundred years the Mountain of the Marvelous Peak became synonymous with the cult of Pi-hsia Yuan-chün. Surely a great many pilgrimage sites in China began thus, but the relatively intense growth of this temple seems to have been made possible by the fame of Mount T'ai and the rich history of Tung-yueh and Pi-hsia. Iconography, beliefs, rituals, organizations, and expectations could all be drawn from older, well developed traditions and simply transplanted to this mountain. Since the site was culturally bare, there was virtually no competition. Miao-feng Shan's growth was further expedited by the proximity of a very large city (probably one million residents in Ch'ing times) that could provide a constituency for the deity. Pilgrimage associations channeled funds and energy single-mindedly into the promotion of this site.

This story of Miao-feng Shan seems quite straightforward, for the mountain appears an uncomplicated sacred site, free of the competition over meaning that this volume shows to have been normal at Chinese (and other) pilgrimage centers. But this impression is misleading. The history of the mountain temple that we have presented thus far is, in fact, the story *as told by* the pilgrimage associations themselves. They were our major actors, their stelae have been our principal sources, their successes have provided our plot.

The associations did not, in fact, "build" this sacred mountain single-handedly, but we will need to listen closely to hear the more muffled voices of other pilgrims. Even more important, the central place that Miao-feng Shan came to occupy in Peking culture was "constructed" by more than just pilgrims. Many who never visited the mountain knew about it and interpreted it within their own, often very different frameworks. We will turn first to these interested parties, the vocal audience for the unfolding drama of the mountain's history—outsiders, observers, and competitors—whose own evolving ideas about our mountain were an integral part of its story. Then we will return to the diversity of the pilgrims themselves. By thus both broadening and narrowing our focus, we should be able to uncover the contentious reality of this site—and others as well.

CONTENDING FRAMEWORKS

Outsiders who witnessed and gradually incorporated Miao-feng Shan into their worlds included monastic communities in these same mountains, devotees of other temples to the Sovereign of the Clouds of Dawn, reigning emperors who were local patrons of religion as well as guardians of orthodoxy, and the educated elite of the capital. These groups had different perspectives, competing interests, and their own ideas about what constituted a sacred site, yet they too were part of the collective construction of this pilgrimage.

There had never been a monastic community on Miao-feng Shan itself. In the barren mountains around it a few Liao and Chin temples had been built in the ninth through eleventh centuries (*STFC* 1407, 11.270–71), and by the mid-Ming, some were still maintained as refuges whose sanctity came in part from their distance from mundane affairs. A stele commemorating one restoration in 1513 declared:

> We do not know when [this temple] was founded, it was too long ago. The location is remote and visitors are few. It is a place for sincere Buddhists to come to and be far from the world; only those who can renounce [the world] with firmness and determination are able to live here. (ST 1513, no. 874)

Those with a taste for such solitude were indeed few, but there were other Buddhist establishments elsewhere in these mountains in late Ming and Ch'ing times. Old, accessible, and successful, they embodied their own ideas about pilgrims and sacred space, and a brief look at two of them can reveal an influential perspective on our popular cult.

T'an-che Ssu 潭柘寺 was a large temple complex nestled on a mountain-side across the Hun River well south of Miao-feng Shan. Its many ancient inscriptions and enormous trees testified to the antiquity of this monastery, of which it was said, "First there was T'an-che, and then there was Yu-chou [Peking]." Oral tradition claimed that the site commemorated the conversion to Buddhism of a local dragon god (a common myth), but the monks pointed instead to their stable community of clerics, gathered for meditation, and the consequent concentration of piety and ritual expertise as their source of sanctity. Stelae recorded the substantial land holdings, respected abbots, regular imperial patronage, and large Buddhist assemblies. It was monks and the Buddhist teachings that made this site special (HTL 2:91–92; FM catalogue and stelae; *Wan-p'ing hsien-chih* 1684, 3.18; Arlington and Lewisohn 1935, 197–98). Similarly, the Ta-chueh Ssu 大覺寺, much nearer Miao-feng Shan, also presented itself as a large, old, rich, and respected monastery. Visitors were expected to be impressed by its many stelae and plaques in imperial calligraphy, fine Buddha images, biographic accounts of famous abbots, and precious set of the huge Buddhist Canon (FM catalogue; *CWK* 106.1764–67).

Considered in this framework, the complex at Miao-feng Shan suffered by comparison. The temple was small, rather new, and had attracted no distinguished clergy or patrons. Although a few monks had been in residence from at least 1734, their role in the life of the temple or pilgrimage—as participants or organizers—was minimal (ST 1734, no. 656; Imbault-Huart 1885, 70–71; KU 148).[26] The resident god, Pi-hsia Yuan-chün, was not mentioned in the Buddhist Canon. Moreover, although she had one scripture in the Supplement to the Taoist Canon [*Pi-hsia*]), no Taoists were in residence. Instead of an old, orthodox pedigree, a shrine in the peak temple could claim to commemorate only the hybrid efforts of a Buddhist monk, Taoist priest, and ordinary layperson to found the temple in 1662 (KU 176; Bouillard 1921).

And yet the written record partially conceals monastic links to this supposedly more vulgar world of popular religion. Accounts of travelers note that T'an-che Monastery was itself increasingly attractive to pilgrims and other visitors who came in the fourth month to pray and to admire its huge ginko trees and picturesque setting. Moreover, some stelae do record that by the middle of the Ch'ing these monks were receiving financial support from the annual visits of Peking religious associations—although their numbers were few and here (unlike Miao-feng Shan) the monks themselves managed the donations.

Those clerics who lived at the Ta-chueh Ssu actually found themselves caught up in and affected by Miao-feng Shan's transformation. Their temple was quite close to the village where the Central Route began to ascend, and just behind their monastery loomed the mountain itself. Pilgrims going to pay respects to Pi-hsia often detoured and stopped at Ta-chueh Ssu.[27] The initial disdain with which the monks may have greeted the arrival of such visitors surely changed to interest in the contributions they brought, for rooms were eventually built to lodge and feed the pilgrims (Bredon 1922, 338–41). For these two temples—and others like them—such extra income may have become increasingly important as imperial and private patronage declined in the nineteenth century (stelae at site; P'an Jung-pi 1758, 19; TLC 1900, 30–32).

A belated formal acceptance of Miao-feng Shan into the framework of the capital's Buddhist establishment came in 1934 when a white stupa was built on the front terrace of the peak temple and a monk from the capital's most prestigious monastery came to inaugurate it by lecturing on the dharma (*Hua-pei tsung-chiao nien-chien* 1941, 12). Founded on different ideas of sanctity, these monastic communities thus both competed with and accommodated themselves to another kind of religious power.

Other temples to the Sovereign of the Clouds of Dawn in the Peking area, which were probably treated with the same cautious condescension by large Buddhist monasteries, had their own kind of rivalry—and dialogue—with Miao-feng Shan. Like the many temples to popular deities, they took it for granted that supernatural beings would respond to gifts and sincere prayers made before images of them placed on temple altars. It was the power to answer prayers that made a temple god *ling* 靈 (efficacious, successful), not fame or antiquity or wealth or an impressive setting (although these might follow, and would certainly help). Within this framework, Pi-hsia was but one of many gods to whom the people of Peking prayed—and most people prayed to more than one. Kuan-ti and Kuan-yin had many more altars, other gods had many fewer (Naquin 1986). To those who shared a devotion to Pi-hsia Yuan-chün, the emergence of Our Lady of Miao-feng Shan must have been of particular interest.

Devotees of her other temples agreed about Pi-hsia's power and how to gain access to it, but disagreed about where. Each temple was implicitly challenged by seemingly more efficacious manifestations in other places. The dynamics of Chinese religion meant that a god's efficacy and popularity were mutually reinforcing, producing over time the pattern of a few (a changing few) very successful temples among a host of others. In the late Ming, the field of potential competitors to Our Lady of Miao-feng Shan was already small and, over time, became smaller.

The temple near Kao-liang bridge outside the northwest corner of Peking, much patronized in the seventeenth century but never one of the summits, and later on the pilgrim route into the mountains, hosted only unremarkable festivities by the twentieth century. The Eastern Summit, probably an unremarkable temple given this designation to round out the symbolic system, had never been very popular and eventually disappeared. The celebrations at the modest Northern Summit were in time transformed into an agricultural implements fair. The Southern Summit, the oldest temple to Pi-hsia near Peking and the home of a lavish pilgrimage in Ming times, had later been replaced, symbolically and ritually, by a newer, closer Little Southern Summit. Here, as well as at the Western and Central summits, there were continuous spring festivals in Ch'ing times, but only the Western Summit temple still celebrated in the fourth month; the other two had been shifted to the fifth and sixth months. By the twentieth century, the only two temples near Peking that honored Pi-hsia's birthday were the Western Summit and an old temple on Ya-chi Shan 丫髻山, a mountain eighty kilometers east of Peking, and their pilgrims were still far fewer than those at Miao-feng Shan (TLC 1900, 28–56 passim).

Despite the prestige that presumably attached to being one of the Five Summits, by the 1880s the "Golden Summit" (chin-ting 金頂), as Miao-feng Shan had come to be called, was brightly outshining the others. Ya-chi Shan had accumulated ten stelae left by pilgrimage associations; the Western Summit nine (none after 1725); the Northern Summit three (ranging from 1773 to 1942); the Central Summit and Kao-liang Bridge temples each three (none since the early Ch'ing) (fieldwork at sites; PL card catalogue).[28] Miao-feng Shan had at least twenty-four.[29] Unlike the pilgrim associations at Miao-feng Shan, those at the other sites aided the temple itself (with incense, lanterns, etc.); they provided no services to pilgrims except on the temple grounds (tea, for example). Ya-chi Shan, although much farther from the city, appears to have had no pilgrimage route lined with tea stalls for weary visitors.[30]

The resident monks and active patrons of these Pi-hsia temples probably regarded the elaborately coordinated network of rest stops, entertainment, and other services found along the roads to Miao-feng Shan with amazement and envy. How, in the face of such competition, did devotees articulate the special qualities of their own temples? Each shrine stressed the deity's general powers, of course, especially her generosity and responsiveness; some noted her connections with the mighty God of the Eastern Peak; others emphasized the auspicious setting of the capital itself or the constellation of the Five Summits.

Most then called attention, if they could, to the popularity of *their* manifestation of Pi-hsia, as illustrated in volume of incense burned and crowds on the annual birthday. They surely told tales of miracles performed, but this subject is poorly preserved in the historical record for this cult. (Contrast the stories about Kuan-yin described by Yü in chapter 5 of this volume.) We know that the initial popularity of the Western Summit was connected with a mysterious (to me) wave of belief that presenting sacks of dirt at the temple would bring benefit (*YHP* 1619, 29:746). The Kao-liang Bridge temple had, in late Ming times, become famous specifically for the Niang-niang's ability to grant children: "According to popular tradition, on 4/8 Our Lady sends down births; women who are without sons must on this day beg for a response" (*WS* 17:168). Devotees at the Western Summit also noted the god's ability to deliver sons (PL 1688, no. 2791, 1689, no. 2787).

Because each temple was most clearly distinguished from the others by its physical layout and setting, history and location became important components of identity. The Central Summit was near Peking's flower-growing suburbs, and so its patrons usually noted its fragrant blooms, shady trees, and general greenery (PL 1664, no. 3681). Devotees of the Western Summit praised the setting, near springs and mountains, efficacious and famous, superior to that at the other summits: "It is not on a mountain, but peaks can be seen in the distance; it is not on the water, yet streams run all around it" (PL 1665, no. 2759 and 1673, no. 2767). The Ya-chi Shan shrine had the considerable advantage of actually being on a mountaintop (albeit a rather small one), and most accounts noted its curious and characteristic shape: "[The mountain] has two peaks that pierce the clouds and from a distance look like topknots, whence its name." It was "a mountain that to the north leans against the Great Wall and to the south faces the sacred capital, [a place] where twisting mountains embrace" (1715 stele at site).

Of all these temples, only Ya-chi and Miao-feng were, like distant Mount T'ai, real mountains, an important advantage in a culture that—as this volume demonstrates—associated divinity with remote heights, and one surely not lost on devotees of a cult that so stressed the links between their god and such summits. Ya-chi Shan was near enough to Peking to be visited by the faithful every year, and, although it was twice as far as Miao-feng Shan, the flat and then gently ascending road was much easier to travel. This unprepossessing double-humped hill sat within a valley dwarfed by higher mountains and took only a few hours to ascend. By contrast, Miao-feng Shan had an imposing presence and was reached by shorter, more arduous routes.

Location may underlie the only explicit comparison by devotees of Pi-hsia of the two mountain temples, a difference articulated in terms of pilgrim constituencies. Ya-chi Shan came to be known for its "rich pilgrims" (*fu-hsiang* 富香), Miao-feng Shan for its "poor pilgrims" (*k'u-hsiang* 苦香) (Bouillard 1923, 308).[31] (The simplistic categories of "rich" and "poor" were a common way of talking about stratification and inequality in this society.) Other information bears out this distinction. Situated near well-traveled imperial routes to Ch'ing tombs and summer hunting grounds, Ya-chi Shan was decorated with many stelae donated by those well connected to the throne. Such high-status pilgrims could ride in carriages, stay at inns along the way, and be carried the short distance to the summit; they did not need the services of pilgrimage associations.[32] Miao-feng Shan, by contrast, attracted large numbers of more ordinary patrons.

Miao-feng Shan's relationship to these other temples was thus an uneasy one. The language of "dividing incense" or branch-to-mother-temple relationships was not used (in sources known to me) to connect different temples to this deity. A pilgrimage association simply tied one small temple (sometimes for another god) to one major Pi-hsia temple through one annual celebration. No processions marking circuits or nested hierarchies linked them or structured competition.[33] Nevertheless, there was the system of the Five Summits, into which even the new Little Southern Summit and the Golden Summit had squeezed their way. Others were linked in popular religious literature, as, for example the four Peking Pi-hsia temples (including Ya-chi Shan) mentioned repeatedly in the late Ming "Precious Scroll of Our Efficacious and Responsive Lady of Mount T'ai" (*Ling-ying*). Another informal cluster (including both Ya-chi and Miao-feng) reflected a local shamanistic subcult (Li Wei-tsu 1948). All Pi-hsia temples benefited, of course, from the enhanced fame of this god, so although each temple tried to articulate a distinctive identity, the unseemly sentiments that expressed rivalry were generally muted and indirect (at least in written sources).

Government policy toward the Miao-feng Shan pilgrimage, expressed in imperial edicts and statutes, was, by contrast, clearly and publicly defined. For many centuries, Chinese states had attempted to arrogate to themselves the power to define (or at least ratify) what was to be considered sacred and holy. Any religious site was potentially unsettling to such authority, and the Ch'ing state was officially unsympathetic toward popular pilgrimage.[34] Furthermore, because religious celebrations were occasions for large gatherings of men and women from all social classes and for performances by entertainers and martial arts specialists, they represented just the sort of heterogeneous assembly that governments had long discouraged as deleterious to public morals. The Ch'ing Code prohibited the formation of associations (*hui*

會) generally, and specifically banned religious activities involving processions of god images accompanied by music and percussion (de Groot 1903–4, 138).

The first Ch'ing emperor had articulated such concerns when he declared that "the capital is an important area. We must immediately prohibit those who use the excuse of offering incense to unfurl banners and bang gongs, for this permits men and women to mix together and makes noise that fills up the alleys and lanes as [people] act brazenly in public" (*CSL* 1656, 104.12–13). Such prohibitions were repeated in 1709 and 1724 and frequently announced in edicts posted thereafter in public places (*HT* 501.7–8). Although unambiguous rhetoric did not translate into effective action (as this volume illustrates), the laws defined the government perspective and provided the grounds for intermittent crackdowns.

But even in this sort of imperial pronouncement, one can see grudging acknowledgment of a world in which popular organizations were common and useful. When the Ch'ien-lung emperor came to the throne in 1735, he made it known that he had no objections to the large numbers of people who climbed Mount T'ai every year to pray to Pi-hsia there, although he urged the residents of north China not to make pilgrimages over long distances ("the gods' efficacy comes down everywhere") (*KCTTC* 1735, 25:369–70; *CSL* 1736, 21.10; 1739, 92.19–20). While not altering the law, in later ministerial communications he overlooked reports of the activities of associations dedicated to the Sovereign of the Clouds of Dawn in and near Peking. As imperial power waned in the nineteenth century, fear of minor disturbances paled beside the threat from major rebellions that shook the empire, and later rulers could do little more than repeat the hollow prohibitions. Nevertheless, from the legal perspective, the central meaning of the pilgrimage at Miao-feng Shan was unambiguously its illegal and dangerous dimension: the opportunities supposedly presented for proper behavior to be ignored and social order threatened.

The attitudes of Ming and Ch'ing emperors toward popular religion generally was actually more ambivalent (Li and Naquin 1988). After all, they made their own pilgrimages and usually favored cooptation over confrontation. Government regulations and accounts of imperial ritual chart the history of the incorporation of local cults deemed worthy of imperial support. The god of Mount T'ai was part of this official pantheon: temples to him were built not only in the capital but at every unit of provincial government, and regular offerings were made by officials and paid for by the government. Empirewide patronage of this male god, a firm-minded judge represented as an awe-inspiring ruler, did not extend to the regional cult of Pi-hsia Yuan-chün. Imperial support for her was much more muted and recorded only semiofficially in the stelae and plaques that commemorated specific visits and donations.

In Ming times, patronage offered in the name of the ruler often came in fact from the women and eunuchs of the inner court. The temple to Pi-hsia at Kao-liang Bridge was extensively renovated in 1592 when an imperial son survived smallpox after prayers for him had been made there (*STFC* 1885, 17.549–50). In 1608 eunuchs connected with the imperial textile bureau founded the Western Summit (*YHP* 1619, 29.746). Ch'ing emperors were also solicitous of this deity. The Western Summit had been restored with imperial support in 1712 and given a number of other gifts by K'ang-hsi, while the Central and Southern summits were restored with funds from the imperial treasury during the Ch'ien-lung reign. These emperors also founded, or restored, or donated calligraphy to other Pi-hsia temples in the Peking suburbs and in the capital area more generally (*CWK* 90.1530–31, 99.1639–41; *T'ung-chou chih* 1879, A.23–24).

We should not automatically construe such attentions as signs of a special devotion to the Pi-hsia cult, for Ming and Ch'ing emperors were lavish toward temples of all kinds, and Manchu rulers particularly prized a pose of impartial generosity. When court officials commemorated K'ang-hsi's sixtieth birthday in 1713 by building a temple on Ya-chi Shan, they did so by constructing a shrine to the Jade Emperor on the second of the mountain's two peaks, opposite the one to Pi-hsia. In their stele, they praised the power of the place, not the god (*Huai-jou hsien-chih* 1604, 1.17; 1715 stele at site). Ch'ien-lung's restoration of the Southern Summit in 1773 accompanied a rebuilding of the important bridge by which the temple stood; he even noted in his edict that others had objected that there were already too many temples to this god (*T'ung-chou chih* 1879, A.23–24).

In contrast, more private records suggest some degree of private and personal imperial devotion to Pi-hsia Yuan-chün in Ch'ing times. In 1819 the Chia-ch'ing emperor (r. 1796–1820) came in person to the Western Summit on 4/3 to burn incense, and he had, at least once before, done the same at the Southern Summit—but only the diary of imperial movements recorded the visit (*CCC*). As a prince, the Tao-kuang emperor (r. 1821–50) had also visited the Southern Summit on trips to the adjacent hunting park, but we know about this only through a poem he later wrote (*Chi-fu t'ung-chih* 1884, 11:2:359–60). A prayer to Pi-hsia for rain also written by that prince could speak of her powers as more official statements could not: "Yuan-chün is a god who protects the north; the merit of her quiet assistance is known to all. For this reason, from as high as the son of heaven to as low as the ordinary people, there are none who do not nod in acknowledgment, performing rites at her summits without interruption" (11:2:340).

The history of imperial patronage of Ya-chi Shan suggests even closer links with this particular Niang-niang. In 1704 the K'ang-hsi emperor visited the mountain shrine, a decade later he gave more funds on the occasion of his fiftieth birthday, and ten years after that incense was burned on his behalf

(*STFC* 1885, 24.7–10; 1723 stele at site). Ch'ien-lung wrote two poems about the mountain. According to a private account, during the reign of her son, Tao-kuang, the empress dowager oversaw a restoration of the Ya-chi Shan temple after a fire and attended the opening ceremonies in 1837 (Lin-ch'ing 1849, 3B.31). Empress Dowager Tz'u-hsi (1835–1908) was also said (unofficially) to have visited in 1886; she had an imperial prince visit regularly thereafter (Wu Chen-yü 1896, 7.9). A temporary palace for use on imperial travels was nearby (*CWK* 129.2248–49).

In the imperial framework, the cult of Pi-hsia Yuan-chün was thus both kept at a distance, to be controlled through restrictions on public behavior and quasi-formal support, and embraced as an object of private worship. Yet imperial patronage of the Miao-feng Shan temple is conspicuously absent. Only in the late nineteenth century do we see private interest by the powerful empress dowager. In the 1880s large bells were donated to the temple on the peak, and at some time three wooden plaques said to be in her hand also came to adorn its interiors. Tz'u-hsi's greatest effect on Miao-feng Shan pilgrims, however, was her sponsorship (mentioned above) of entertainers who made the annual journey. These are, however, the first examples of direct imperial patronage in the temple's two-hundred-year history.[35] Several surviving paintings of the pilgrimage were probably done for the court at this time.[36]

It may also be true that as imperial gifts and visits drew Ya-chi Shan and the Five Summit temples into the state orbit, those temples' general popularity declined. The arrival of royalty drove out ordinary pilgrims, after all, while imperial donations preempted community support and court functionaries might supplant local managers. Miao-feng Shan, far enough away from the center and paths of power, grew unencumbered by such patronage, and its pilgrimage associations multiplied. It is thus tempting to see the triumph of the Golden Summit at the expense of the Five Summits as a reflection of a popular preference for temples that were free of official or clerical oversight.

This imperial system collapsed in 1911. Subsequent Republican and warlord governments, by contrast, rarely supported community temples and were even less willing or able to prohibit springtime pilgrimages. Few challenged the well-articulated skepticism toward popular religion of many twentieth-century intellectuals. Indeed, government attitudes had long been influenced by a tradition among educated Chinese—also discussed elsewhere in this volume—of ambivalence toward the kind of phenomenon that Miao-feng Shan represented. Peking elites, whether local families or officials, literati, or businessmen from elsewhere in the empire, had their own framework (also contradictory) for understanding mountains, cults, and popular religion more generally.

Initially, it had been the lower, nearer Western Hills to which capital elites were drawn, not the wild mountains beyond. Already in the thirteenth century, these hills were sought out by members of the court as retreats from the city, prized not for sacred territory but for their cooler climate and scenic prospects. The many configurations of earth and running water also made these hills ideal burial grounds. By late Ming times, they had become a favored spot for "strolling" (*yu* 遊) by literati and the subject of short essays and poems (for example, *STFC* 1638, 6.68–117; *CWK* 86 and 87). Emperors and their families amused themselves within sequestered parks, enjoying the careful re-creation of nature that Chinese gardens involved: lakes, walkways, pavilions, private temples, boats, flowers, and rocks. Literati took short trips through a wider area, delighted in the relative wildness, and enjoyed hills, valleys, and cliffs for their shade, their quiet, their vistas, their surprises. They stopped in temples—often the only habitations to be found in such parts—for a vegetarian meal or an evening's lodging, taking a special interest in old trees, art objects, and the conversation of an occasional monk. They tracked down historic sites, although there were few here besides the hunting grounds of Chin emperors or graves of famous men. Well-known monasteries like Ta-chueh Ssu were of course visited, as well as smaller, more ordinary establishments (see *CWK* 101 passim or *TC* 6–7.) Gods and miracles, on the other hand, were rarely discussed in their writings.

Popular as the Western Hills were, literati poems or accounts of Miao-feng Shan were virtually nonexistent. It was, after all, even more remote and not on the way to anywhere. The lack of year-round lodging and the crowds of the pilgrimage season may both have seemed incompatible with solitary, dignified literati travels (see Wu, chapter 2 of this volume). Instead, Miao-feng Shan was first labeled by the educated in the geography sections of local histories. A cluster of peaks seen from afar and collectively called the "Mountains One Looks Up To," Yang Shan 仰山, was once famous for its "five peaks and eight pavilions," vanished Chin dynasty sights, one of which was called Miao-kao Feng (Marvelous High Peak) (*STFC* 1407, 11:270–71). Later scholars took Miao-kao Feng to be an antecedent name of Miao-feng Shan.[37]

Local histories written by literati usually listed temples, categorized either as famous places or the sites of annual festivals. Temples to Tung-yueh and Pi-hsia were enumerated in both these contexts in late Ming books such as the *Miscellaneous Account of Wan-p'ing* (*WS* 1593), the *Account of the Sights of the Capital* (*TC* 1635), or their various Ch'ing successors. The 1758 *Famous Sites in the Annual Calendar of the Capital* was the first to list "Miao-feng," in passing, as one of several temples a person could visit, perhaps as part of an "incense association"; it was not named as one of the famous shrines to Pi-hsia (P'an Jung-pi 1758, 18–19). While countless temples to this god were mentioned in the massive and extremely detailed eighteenth-century imperial compilation *A Study of the Old Records of the Capital* (*CWK* 1785), Miao-feng Shan was not.

In the nineteenth century, a new kind of travel literature began to be written, one that defined scenic spots slightly differently: visitors' guides to Peking intended for a less refined and more practical reader. Some collected short verses commemorating local sights; others were largely lists. Miao-feng Shan was initially mentioned, briefly, in the 1870s (*Tu-men chu-chih-tz'u* 1877, 13), but the first clear description of the pilgrimage comes in a guide not to Peking but to Tientsin, published in 1885 (*CMTC* 2.35).

A still different attitude was exhibited at the end of the Ch'ing period by several careful scholarly studies of the pilgrimage done by Manchus, by now self-defined spokesmen for Peking culture and long patrons of this cult.[38] These authors, who visited Miao-feng Shan both as pilgrims and as scholars, wrote with energy about the journey's landmarks and with understanding of its religious purposes. Their books recast the Miao-feng Shan pilgrimage in a more favorable light. They marveled at the crowds and entertainments and pronounced on the popularity of the pilgrimage with enthusiasm: "All these associations consider the pilgrimage as a noble thing"; "the flourishing state of the incense fires of Peking's Miao-feng Shan have been heard of all over the empire" (Jang-lien 1899, 5–6; T'ang Yen 1907, 9.17; plus TLC 1900, 38–40 and the wonderful later study by Feng-k'uan, FK 1929).

Comprehensive tour books in the Western style appeared in the 1910s, some in Chinese, many in foreign languages. Here Miao-feng Shan was proudly hailed as "one of the chief attractions near Peking" and "certainly the most exciting of the temple fairs" (*Guide Book to the New Official Plan of Peking* 1917, 45; *Pei-p'ing chih-nan* 1929, 4.19; also *Ching-Sui t'ieh-lu lü-hsing chih-nan* 1922). These accounts, some long, some short, were intent on persuading readers that the pilgrimage center at Miao-feng Shan was a source of local pride and distinction. Foreign tourists took their cues from these attitudes, but it was still a hardy few who made the trip. The *Cook's Guide* of 1924 counseled that for the journey one needed "no little time, a full travelling equipment, and the patience to struggle with a hard road," but Juliet Bredon called it "perhaps the most beautiful of all the trips in the Western Hills" (Bredon 1922, 335–38; Cook 1924, 46).

It was in the context of this blossoming of accounts of Miao-feng Shan that the pilgrimage was discovered by China's new folklorists of the 1920s. In 1925, the American sociologist Sidney Gamble persuaded his Chinese colleague Li Ching-han (Franklin Lee) to ignore his friends, who "thought it bizarre to spend effort studying such superstition," and climb Miao-feng Shan during the pilgrimage season. Li wrote an article about this 1925 trip while Gamble preserved a record in movies and photographs. That same May, the historian Ku Chieh-kang (not a Peking native), with the sponsorship of the Peking University Society for the Survey of Popular Customs, assembled four colleagues to accompany him up the mountain. Their essays, published first in a local newspaper and later in a double issue of their new journal, "Folklore" (*Min-su*, no. 69–70, July 1929), redefined Miao-feng Shan yet again. Now it was to be understood as a splendid example of popular folklore, worthy of the intellectual's serious consideration, "a new kind of very lively source material" (KU 9). Ku Chieh-kang himself was particularly astonished by the pilgrimage associations (his text is full of exclamation marks),[39] and he collected all the data he could on these admirable manifestations of a folk culture too long neglected by scholars.[40]

The images of Miao-feng Shan refracted through the writings of China's educated elites over three centuries thus mirror both the development of the pilgrimage itself and changes in this increasingly heterogeneous elite. The Ming-Ch'ing literature by Chinese retained (and urged on the reader) a studied diffidence toward discussions of religious matters; Manchus conveyed (and tried to generate) more warmth and local pride; foreigners encouraged curiosity and promised amazement.

All these outsiders, their records, and their readers reflect very different frameworks for viewing Miao-feng Shan—different from each other and different from those of other pilgrims. Simplifying, we might say that to monks, the crucial frame of reference was the distinction between Buddhist monastic institutions and the temples to ordinary gods. To devotees of the deity, it was the relative efficacy of her different manifestations. To the state, the pilgrimage was a problem of social order. To the rulers themselves, this temple belonged to one cult in a field of many, worthy of support, whose importance was to be defined by them. To the literati, the mountain temple was belatedly evaluated as one of many scenic places in the capital area.

It should now be easier to see how the history of Miao-feng Shan presented in the first part of this paper reflected its sources: the data enthusiastically collected by twentieth-century fieldworkers, including this author; the affectionate late Ch'ing Manchu accounts of Peking culture; and the stone stelae erected by pilgrimage associations that ignored the competition and saw themselves as the crucial agents of the god's popularity. Of course, the story as originally told is not false, only one-sided. The wider context reveals that the successes of the Miao-feng Shan pilgrimage were not effortless and uncontested, but took place in a field where there was ambivalence, hostility, and envy as well as devotion and faith. But this one-sided view was also challenged from within, by pilgrims who themselves had no unitary view of the meaning of Miao-feng Shan. Here too, closer attention can reveal the sound of many voices.

INTERNAL DIVERSITY

How important were the incense associations in structuring and defining the pilgrimage for participants? For pilgrims who joined a group, the climb up Miao-feng Shan was certainly a collective affair, undertaken either with neighbors, or co-workers, or people one might see only once a year. Typically, these pilgrimage associations disbanded after their annual trip, then reassembled in the early spring of the following year. The time given over to the pilgrimage and related charitable activities was substantial and usually extended well beyond the three days needed to make the trip. Most devoted nearly two weeks' time, leaving home before the mountain was "open" on 4/1 and not returning until the fourteenth or fifteenth.

The shoemakers' association, for example, started preparations on 2/1; on 3/25 it was ready to post impressive yellow paper announcements that described the schedule and invited old and new members to sign up. Lists of participants were then prepared, and it seems likely that at this time the current year's officers were selected, duties assigned, and funds, goods, and equipment prepared. These groups first convened at the place (often but not always a temple) where their group's image (often of Pi-hsia Yuan-chün) was housed during the year. The shoemen met on 3/30 and spent the night together before setting out. On 4/1 they began the journey; the following day, on the mountain, they set up an altar with their own statue of Pi-hsia and then for the next fourteen days and nights repaired the shoes and sandals of other pilgrims on demand. On the eleventh, the group made its own trip to "pay respects to the summit" and then returned to their rest house. On the thirteenth, the names of participants were recorded on a petition sent by burning to the deity, and on the sixteenth they all "thanked the mountain" before returning home (KU 14–16, 75–103; FK 49, 84, 105–6; Tung Fu-ming 1939, 25; Lowe 1941, 1:81).

All groups organized such a timetable according to similar stages with common names: spend the night together, start out, begin to provide services, visit the summit, terminate services, and return home. Schedules like these were important sources of order and predictability, and the movements of pilgrimage association members were, in consequence, highly circumscribed.

Within a common framework, each group had not only its own schedule but its own terrain. The paths followed—always ascending by one route, descending by another—were similarly announced in advance. Moreover, most of these associations had a temple or rest house that served as their headquarters. Some were the temporary thatched buildings suggested by their name "tea stall"; others had developed into small (or even large) stone buildings. The group's possession of the spot was advertised in permanent stone commemorative stelae, wooden plaques, and incense burners, or in the flags, lanterns, and decorations hung each year at pilgrimage time (CH 27).

Group travel to and from the peak was, moreover, supposed to be highly ritualized. Every association had to stop at each rest house on its way—one every few kilometers—and take some refreshment. Upon arrival, they entered in a fixed order and were greeted with calls of "First pay a visit to the god, then come over here and rest and drink some tea." And indeed they would go straightaway to bow and make offerings at the altar, to the reverberation of gong or bell, and then sit down. To descending pilgrims, the host association attendants sang out instead, "Carry good fortune back home, and come drink some tea over here." Sometimes short songs were exchanged (KU 143; Ch'en Lei 1986, 255–59; Li Ching-han 1925, 8–9; Lowe 1941, 1:88). If two groups met on the road, etiquette prescribed a formal meeting and polite deference.

Republican period photographs indicate that some members (probably the officers) wore uniforms: dark pants and jackets with the association name written on round medallions sewn onto the clothing. Proper behavior was in order at all times and was sometimes spelled out on a group's announcement: "Our people must not push and shove or be noisy or frivolous; neither is it permitted to pick flowers or fruit along the way. As for eating meat and drinking wine, these are also forbidden." Violators would be struck from the group list (KU 22).

For these pilgrims, personal motives were to be subsumed in the gratification of collective good deeds. The names and language used by these associations vigorously emphasized group solidarity: everything was undertaken "with a united heart" or "with a common purpose." Members referred to themselves collectively as "doers of good deeds." Their stated goals were actions that would earn them merit, and Buddhist language of good works appears in oft repeated phrases like "broadcast the merit of our virtuous worthies' deeds during these fifteen days and nights." Such activities were intended to be public and so were proudly recorded on plaques, stelae, and posters.

A fundamental identity between the entertainer groups and these service-oriented pilgrims was asserted not only in the similar names and procedure for making the pilgrimage, but in their classification, following a common Chinese preference for dichotomization, into "martial" (entertainment) and "civil" (service) associations.[41] The performers' journeys were also staggered across the pilgrimage season; they carried their own flags, had their own special clothing, and behaved according to the same rituals of politeness. The rest houses were also the nodes of their routes, and upon arrival, they too first made their obeisances to the deity, then performed both for the god and the crowd (CH 21, 25–28; Tung Fu-ming 1939, 33–40). As associations created an invisible underlying structure for the pilgrimage, the music and costumes and energy of the entertainers publicly punctuated and enlivened the more subdued procession of pilgrims.

While we might marvel (as did Ku Chieh-kang and his colleagues) at the unorganized coordination among these associations, it is important to pause and distinguish how things were supposed to work from a reality that was undoubtedly much messier. Not all services were continuously available—

tea stalls collapsed and paths washed away—and new groups did not always form as old ones disappeared. Like all promoters, these associations presented a very upbeat, and surely deceptive, picture. Similarly, we should see in their emphasis on common purpose as much ideal as reality.

These annual displays of merit and talent and organization would naturally have produced competition that could not have been wholly submerged in rituals and rhetoric of unity. I think we must assume, for example, that the young toughs skilled with cudgels or spears or pitchforks who took the time to dress up and perform were proud to advertise their prowess and eager to be thought better than other teams (see Lao She 1985, 151, from a 1935 story). Costumes, repertory, skill, size, possession of an imperial banner—there were many ways to compete. The stone tablets that charitable associations endowed were themselves public declarations of wealth that varied considerably in size of stone, grace of decoration, quality of carving, and elegance of prose.

Generally speaking, the members of these associations represented a heterogeneous assembly of occupations, villages, and neighborhoods. Without a full study of the range of religious (and other) organizations in Peking, it is not possible to say if those who went to Miao-feng Shan represented some particular slice of capital society. But we can say that natives (as opposed to sojourners) predominated, if we allow that Bannermen were, as they indeed felt themselves to be, an important segment of the local community. With time, the appeal of the deity grew broader in the region, and gradually residents from the nearby city of Tientsin came to play a prominent role.

This commercial town, perhaps half the size of Peking and a hundred kilometers southeast of the capital, and had entered a new phase of economic growth after the 1860 settlement with the foreign powers that opened it up as a treaty port and made it the dominant city of the region (Hershatter 1986). In the 1880s, Tientsin pilgrims began to be noticeable at Miao-feng Shan (*CMTC* B.35). The growing wealth and influence of Tientsin merchants in Peking might suffice to explain this change, but devotees would have pointed to a new subcult of "Granny Wang" (Wang San-nai-nai 王三奶奶), a deified devotee of Pi-hsia from that city. After her death (said to have occurred while she was on this pilgrimage; her grave is on the Central Route), Granny Wang demonstrated a special responsiveness to prayers from her fellow natives, and they in turn rewarded her with incense, offerings, statues, and shrines (FK 27, 97; Chou Chen-ho 1929; Li Wei-tsu 1948; Sawada 1965, 59; Li Shih-yü 1987).

Regardless, Tientsin pilgrims helped develop the Central and then the Northern Route. They built new rest houses and supplied lanterns and then lamps the entire length of these two paths, making it possible for pilgrims to travel safely at night (CH 38; ST 1906, no. 745 and 1925, no. 687; KU 54).

Most of the eighteen pilgrimage associations from that city active in the 1920s had combined to form a single "united association" (KU 51–52). They built and maintained many of the new halls at the peak, a fact few visitors could fail to notice (ST 1920, no. 689 and 1925, no. 687; Li Ching-han 1925, 8). Given the spirit of common purpose that was supposed to prevail during the pilgrimage, we can only imagine the mixed emotions with which such ostentatious patronage was received by the older, probably less affluent groups from Peking.

Bearing in mind not only these kinds of internal divisive pressures but also the not-always-sympathetic views of outsiders who did not make the pilgrimage, we can begin to hear in these associations' statements about what they were, echoes of what they did not want to be mistaken for: we are public-minded and respectable citizens (not monks without families, not trouble-makers), sincere in our devotion (not tourists), dedicated to this Niang-niang (not her other manifestations, not other gods); we are truly motivated by the desire to aid our fellow pilgrims (not selfish), and of one heart and mind (not competitive).

It may have been possible for the pilgrimage associations to constrain somewhat the activities and attitudes of their members, but affecting all pilgrims was another matter altogether. Although the groups would have us believe that the experience of every pilgrim was set firmly in the context and atmosphere of this organized public-spiritedness, the overwhelming majority of pilgrims—at least 80 percent—were *not* members of such associations.[42]

Of course, pilgrims, organized or not, did have common experiences. The five routes and regular rest houses and the two weeks surrounding the eighth day of the fourth month together were to make up the temporal and spatial grid upon which those who climbed Miao-feng Shan on their own also planned their pilgrimages. Like groups on their way up or down, individuals stopped at these small temples to pay their respects, have a bowl of tea or porridge, and make a small donation. They joined the god as an audience for the acrobats, weight lifters, jugglers, and swordsmen. They listened to folk songs, watched lion dances and stilt walking. At the summit, they too crowded into the courtyard, and jostled for a place at the altar, and paid a call at each of the individual shrines. All were deafened by the sounds of gongs and drums, horns and bells, and engulfed in the waving banners and flags and the clouds of pungent incense smoke. Coming down, similarly fatigued, everyone wore auspiciously shaped red souvenir cut-outs and at night formed a stream of lights visible across the valleys that bobbed in the dark like a moving dragon.

There were, of course, differences. The journey of the individual pilgrim (or, more likely, a small family group) was much shorter than that of a large association, followed no prescribed route or schedule and could occur at any time during the year.[43] While some wore sandals and carried the flask, incense satchel, and walking stick that identified them as pilgrims, no special apparel was required, and pictures reveal considerable variety in attire.

Moreover, these pilgrims concentrated their attention not on their fellow travelers but on the deity whose temple was their objective. The story of Miao-feng Shan was to them surely not about fellowship but an account of divine efficacy, of well-known miracles, and of a personal relationship. One came because Our Lady would respond to individual prayers for help; was her temple not called "Palace of Efficacious Responsiveness" (Ling-kan Kung 靈感宮)? Her promise was inscribed on countless plaques and banners: "If you make a request, you will get a response" (*yu ch'iu pi ying* 有求必應).

Moreover, as elsewhere in China, the language of the individual pilgrim was one not of good deeds but of heartfelt promises made and kept, of earnest vows and generous rewards. The core of this transaction between human and deity was the pilgrim's vow. A request to the god could be made anywhere, anytime, but this prayer was supposed to be accompanied by a sincere promise of thanks, expressed as an act of penance or an act of charity. A request and promise (*hsu-yuan* 許願), if followed by a divine response, would be repaid by the fulfillment of the vow (*huan-yuan* 還願) (Lowe 1941, 1:79; Yang 1961, 87).

Some penances were performed during the pilgrimage up the mountain, and although there were relatively few penitents, they appear to have set an important tone of religiosity for all who saw them (KU 159–60). The man who put on the clothing of a criminal, placed a set of stocks around his neck, and sat by the roadside soliciting donations to fulfill his vow to repair a local temple; the person who carried a saddle on his back and crawled up on all fours like a horse, without speaking a word, in thanks for the cure of a relative's illness; the woman on tiny bound feet who followed each third step up the mountain with a full prostration (FK 61; Li Ching-han 1925, 10; Eigner 1939; *MFSCN*; Lowe 1941, 1:86–87)—such inspiring exemplars, who staggered exhausted to the summit, were to be treated with particular respect by other pilgrims; the obvious pain expended almost guaranteed such a response. They were living symbols of Pi-hsia's power and of the active bond between the god and each pilgrim. They acted out in extreme form what seem to have been the attitudes of the ideal pilgrim: sincerity, devotion, fortitude, wholeheartedness, gratitude.

If the ascent was sometimes marked by pain, the descent was joyous. Pilgrims were rewarded by the god with "blessings" and "good fortune" (*fu* 福). The souvenirs sold in great numbers at the peak were emblems of these blessings: bats (also pronounced *fu*), butterflies, tigers, flowers, goldfish, and the like. Red sashes were sold announcing that the bearer had "paid respects to the mountain, presented incense, and is bringing good fortune home" (KU

162). Pilgrims returned decorated with dozens of these festive objects on their clothing and in their hair, hats, and turbans.

The greetings prescribed for pilgrims who encountered one another on Miao-feng Shan encapsulated these values. On the way up to the peak, each murmured "O Pious One!" (*ch'ien-ch'eng* 虔誠); coming down, "May You Take Blessings Back Home!" (*tai-fu huan-chia* 帶福還家). The former greeting also substituted for "excuse me" and "please step aside" (*MFSCN*). In a society where strangers were routinely ignored and hierarchy was marked by forms of address, such phrases insisted on a uniform interchange between those involved in this common activity. Piety was more important than status, and all would be rewarded with blessings.

Other language used in connection with the pilgrimage (and not unique to this site) can suggest other underlying values transmitted to (and expressed by) pilgrims. The deities lived in "palaces" and "halls," pilgrims came "presenting incense" (*chin-hsiang* 進香) in order to "have an audience at the summit" (*ch'ao-ting* 朝頂); finishing, they "sealed up their petition," "thanked the mountain," and finally "returned incense" (*hui-hsiang* 迴香). Such terms, partially borrowed from court rites, lent solemnity and authority to the rituals. While this language of respectful subservience could assert the orthodoxy of pilgrimage activities, it, like the mountain itself, also emphasized the mightiness of the god and the humility of her petitioners.

The distance from familiar scenes and the presence on the mountain of bright temple halls, divine images, rising incense smoke, old stone stelae, and ancient pines had a reinforcing message. Here was a zone of transcendent time and space, replete with written and physical symbols that emphasized what was eternal and forever, universal and omnipresent, a realm of auspiciousness and blessings, sanctity and virtue, of concentrated divine power.

The universality of the god's appeal was another important part of the rhetoric of the pilgrimage. Pi-hsia Yuan-chün, the focus of individual devotions, was characterized as virtuous, nurturing, merciful, and benevolent. Her generosity was theoretically available to any petitioner, like "the golden light shining everywhere," "her efficacious responsiveness extended in all directions" to "men and women, young and old, near and far." All were equal in the face of the deity. The formal greetings that made no distinction by class or sex, the common humble fare of tea and porridge, and the primitive accommodations further contributed to this leveling. The act of burning incense was, moreover, a single simple ritual that united all comers and made every one a pilgrim.

Unfortunately, we have no accounts by ordinary pilgrims describing their feelings. The testimony of observers emphasizes that pilgrims conformed to expectations. Coming home decorated with souvenirs, singing and laughing, they seemed to exude gaiety and cheer, "minds full of beautiful thoughts."

The sense of unusual good feeling, of a kind with what Victor Turner has, on the basis of other pilgrimages, termed "communitas" (1974), made a sharp impression on even very skeptical visitors. A Buddhist monk in 1919 thought it "seemed like another world" (Hsiu-ming 1986), as did Ku Chieh-kang, who was struck with the harmony and friendly behavior (KU 73). His friend Li Ching-han was amazed at how orderly and peaceful things were (1925, 5–6). Another observed that everyone performed the same rituals and had a "single mind, a single purpose"; the experience "transforms people of all social levels into one family" (CH 4). A Western-educated intellectual noted, "A mysterious atmosphere will make every one who goes to visit the goddess kowtow, even one who may not be a follower of the faith" (Tung Fu-ming 1939, 28). "On the whole," wrote two Westerners, revealing their own standards for communitas, "a perfect democracy exists among the travelers. Along the road, people share alike, and snobbery is non-existent" (Bredon and Mitrophanow 1927, 285).

Such unanimous testimony cannot be ignored, but here too it is important to remember that individuals (and even more so members of associations) were subtly pressured into such behavior by their own and others' expectations. Private feelings of discomfort, annoyance, or disappointment were to be suppressed.

Advance publicity about the spring pilgrimage, created largely by the organizations against the backdrop of monastic, governmental, and scholarly views, was intended to instruct the would-be pilgrim as well as heighten expectations. Religious books and manuals described the routes and told stories of Miao-feng Shan.[44] One small undated (ca. 1940) booklet called "A Guide to Miao-feng Shan" (*MFSCN*), rather scholarly in its presentation, advised pilgrims on the do's and don'ts of proper behavior. But most pilgrims probably also learned what to expect from colorful woodblock prints and from songs and miracle tales heard back home or told during the pilgrimage.[45] Might some not have been disappointed when the reality proved less marvelous?

Furthermore, pilgrims—like associations—came in all varieties, and the habits of social and sexual hierarchy could not lie far beneath the egalitarian surface. Diversity, while evidence of the god's wide appeal, threatened the ideals of equality and fellowship. Indeed, association members proudly differentiated themselves from ordinary pilgrims and, as everywhere, the rich reduced their discomfort more easily than the poor.

And should we assume that women came to Our Lady with the same expectations as men? At the very least, the opportunity to leave the confines of the home for a holy-day should have been especially welcome to women (hence official concern about public morals). Those pilgrims who sought Pi-hsia and her attendant Niang-niang for problems relating to children and childbirth may have actually represented a special constituency. The Heavenly Immortal Holy Mother had, after all, become the predominant female deity in this part of China. Such topics are usually left out of our sources, but the *Cook's Guide* to Peking tells us that on the peak "plaster dolls and eyes [for Pi-hsia's companion deities] strung upon the goddess testify to the number of their miraculous cures and benefits" (1924, 46; also Eigner 1939, 171). But such petitioners may have been mostly men. The best evidence suggests that the number of women was actually small, not exceeding the fewer than 10 percent of association members who were female.[46]

It is also worth remembering that Pi-hsia was not the only deity worshiped on the pilgrimage. Some associations had their homes in temples to other gods, and various tea stalls accordingly had these deities on the main altar. At the peak (as in any Chinese temple) there were, with time, many adjunct shrines. Sakyamuni Buddha, Kuan-yin, and the gods of wealth and medicine were worshiped here; Tientsin pilgrims made donations to Granny Wang, the actors' guild to their patron, craftsmen to theirs. The Hui-hsiang T'ing dedicated to the Emperor of the Eastern Peak was a mandatory stop for all pilgrims (KU 130, 173). Thus, although everyone went immediately to the main hall and burned incense in front of each altar, different individuals and groups still had special relationships with gods other than Pi-hsia.

Nor should we forget that not all of those on the mountain were there to make a pilgrimage. It was expected that beggars would congregate on occasions when public charity was encouraged, and the crippled and destitute appeared annually along the roads leading up Miao-feng Shan. In the twentieth century (at least), they lined the paths and cried out for descending pilgrims to share their blessings ("Devout and pious sir, pity this miserable worm who is repaying a debt in this lifetime") (Lan 1921; Li Ching-han 1925, 5–13).

And what of the villagers and peasants who lived near the temple? The hard, rocky mountains around Miao-feng Shan had only gradually come to play a role in the economy of Peking, and then a marginal one as a source of walnuts, apricots, hawthorns, and peaches, boulders and limestone. Local residents thus welcomed the annual influx of pilgrims, and entrepreneurs sought customers among the travelers. Able-bodied men could hire themselves out as "mountain-climbing tigers" transporting the well-to-do. Some vendors sold local fruit by the roadside while others hawked the peach-wood walking sticks that returning pilgrims expected to buy. Still others made hats, baskets, and souvenirs out of paper, felt, or woven wheat straw (Tung Fu-ming 1939, 28; Hsiu-ming 1919; *LHCN* 57–58). In the main jumping-off points, inns and restaurants could do a substantial business during the season, and in smaller settlements, rooms were rented out and temporary eating places set up. The sleepy hamlet of Chien-kou, where all pilgrims rested before making the final ascent, came to life once a year. No wonder that locals referred to the pilgrimage season as the "harvest from the temple" (*LHCN* 57–58).[47]

In sum, individual pilgrims were themselves a heterogeneous lot and came to the mountain with a variety of very different expectations, interests, and preoccupations. The language of pilgrimage that they used emphasized not collective but individual relations with the deity. There was no necessity to share the goals and values of the associations that facilitated the journey. Pious penitents were expected to be single-mindedly oblivious of the entire infrastructure, while casual tourists could do as they pleased. Not only should we therefore not let the formal voice of the pilgrimage associations speak for pilgrims as a whole nor overestimate the unifying effects of a Turnerian process, we might also reflect upon the actual vitality that diversity brought to the experience as a whole.

This multifaceted look at the history of the pilgrimage to Miao-feng Shan should warn us of the dangers of accepting the normative view of any one partisan group. It may also suggest a better understanding of the popularity of this site. Miao-feng Shan actually drew strength from the multiplicity of meanings imputed to it and from the diversity of pilgrims who went there. Internal variety, the combination of organized associations and individual pilgrims, gave energy to the pilgrimage. Similarly, Pi-hsia's broader cult as well as competition with other temples and other gods and the mixture of hostility and patronage by rulers and elites gave dynamism to the mountain's growing popularity.

CONCLUSION

Contention and complications notwithstanding, Miao-feng Shan's pilgrimage associations remain its distinguishing feature and, thus, worthy of a few concluding thoughts.

A full evaluation of the significance of these *sheng-hui* is hampered by lack of data on such phenomena in other times and places in China. (Similar organizations are common in other cultures.) The historical record for the city of Peking gives no sign of such groups before the late Ming. From the 1580s, stelae left by these associations increase in number, while eyewitnesses also note their existence. A markedly disproportionate percentage of such groups were connected with the cults of the Eastern Peak (first) and (later) the Sovereign of the Clouds of Dawn; in time, they were organized for other temples in the capital. In the course of the Ch'ing period, the scope of voluntary organizations more generally grew steadily in Peking. This process, too, complex to be documented here, is in keeping with the trends shown for guilds in other cities (viz., Johnson 1986 and Rowe 1989 for Shanghai and Hankow) and for late Ch'ing elite organizations in other regions (Rankin

1986). Such developments are only in part a reflection of better documentation. Chinese society was changing.

There is, of course, no question that voluntary religious organizations existed in China well before the sixteenth century, although accounts of them in the primary and secondary literature are scattered and unsystematic.[48] Without further work, it is not possible to place the developments in this essay in a longer-term context or to test my assertion that something different was happening in the early modern period.

Comparisons with activities at other pilgrimage sites in the Ming and Ch'ing periods are also difficult without other research. Most references to what seem to be pilgrimage associations in the North China region were, in fact, to those organized for the Pi-hsia cult at Mount T'ai (Smith 1899, 142–44; Duara 1988, 122–28; Dudbridge, chap. 1 of this volume and conference paper; Wu, chapter 2 of this volume). The studies in this book (and those produced for the conference that preceded it) suggest that this scale of organizational activity may have been atypical for China as a whole.[49]

Twentieth-century fieldwork has provided some data. Ku Chieh-kang suggested (KU 12) a distinction between northern incense associations (*hsiang-hui*) and the processions (*sai-hui* 賽會) of southern China, in which god images were taken from a temple and paraded through the community along a circuit. Although the distinction has some potential—such processions were indeed rare in Peking—the familiar north-south categories seem very crude.

Because of many fieldwork studies there, we have a sounder basis for understanding the religious organizations of Taiwan in recent times. There, where processions were common, anthropologists have been most interested in activities organized around ascriptive rather than voluntary ties. They find that new shrines are formed by a process of dividing the incense of the parent temple and see such groups as the component units of pilgrimage (for example, Schipper 1977; Sangren 1987).

The pilgrimage associations described in this chapter do not conform to this pattern. They were created (it is unclear how) on the basis of various kinds of ties: villagers participated as part of a temple community, guild members traveled together, coworkers came from the same government office; but troupes of amateur musicians and sword fighters and large numbers of city shopkeepers and residents *who had no other activities in common* also joined. These groups did not always speak for clearly defined communities. What P. Steven Sangren has called the "ritual societies" (*she-t'uan* 社團) of early twentieth-century Taiwan may have been more similar, involving urban and rural groups "weakly" joined for an annual celebration (1987, 84–86), but a good deal more research is needed before meaningful comparisons can be made and broader patterns discerned.

Until then, this chapter can serve to introduce one deceptively simple regional pilgrimage center in early modern China and to call attention to the organizations that appear to be its most significant patrons. In the end, my story is still their story.

NOTES

1. Some of the material in this chapter was first reported in Naquin 1986. I have greatly benefited from the comments of Glen Dudbridge, Helen Dunstan, Benjamin Elman, Barend ter Haar, and Victor Mair and from interesting discussions at the Johns Hopkins University, Columbia Modern China Seminar, and our 1989 Pilgrimage conference. I would also like to thank the National Endowment for the Humanities, the Committee on Scholarly Communication with the P.R.C. of the National Academy of Sciences, and the University of Pennsylvania for financial support for this research and the librarians of the Peking Library and Shou-tu Library in Peking for their invaluable assistance.

2. Mount T'ai in Shantung is only two hundred meters higher.

3. Certainly within the North China macroregion, as defined by G. W. Skinner, and Manchuria. I am uncertain about the extension of the cult into adjacent Shansi.

4. Pi-hsia 碧霞 means "the colored clouds that precede the dawn." Yuan-chün 元君 is a common Taoist term for a female deity; I have translated it as "sovereign" because the characters themselves suggest a male personage. In Chinese cosmology, the east was the direction associated with birth and with life, "where the ten thousand things are born" (ST 1592, no. 289). For Pi-hsia generally: T'ai-shan chih 2.55–59; Chavannes 1910, 29; Lo Hsiang-lin 1968, 6–10. The early history of these two cults needs proper study; I am merely summarizing the secondary literature. Both are also discussed in the Wu and Dudbridge contributions to this volume.

5. I borrow this translation from Glen Dudbridge. See Dudbridge 1991.

6. The Tung-yueh Temple has been firmly closed to the public for more than twenty years and currently (1990) houses a school run by the Ministry of Public Security. Photographs and a fine Chinese drawing from before 1949 are to be found in Goodrich 1964.

7. Sheng was written interchangeably with the character for "holy" 聖 and the character for "triumphant" 勝. For early names, see the list in Liu Hou-tzu 1936.

8. There was a dramatic increase in stone stelae recording religious organizations, but further work on such organizations before 1600 (when they certainly existed) will be necessary before one can appreciate how new these developments were. Judged on the basis of such records, Tung-yueh and Pi-hsia associations vastly outnumbered comparable (and derivative) groups operating out of other temples in Peking in the Ch'ing period. Between 1636 and 1704, sixteen stelae were set up at one Pi-hsia temple alone (PL card catalogue for Hsi-ting).

9. Using rather detailed sources, I have counted nine inside the city walls and eighteen in the surrounding countryside (up to a distance of fifty li). These temples were named variously T'ien-hsien, Niang-niang, or T'ien-hsien Sheng-mu temples (miao 廟, an 菴, or hsing-kung 行宮). See WS 19:204–5; STFC 1638, 2.55; CWK 96.1602; HTL 2:89, 2:28; and the PL stelae rubbing collection card catalogue.

10. The earliest reference I have seen to any of these various "summits" is to the

Western summit in 1614, but the use of the other summit names was common by the 1630s (T'ao Yun-chia 1633).

11. See note 18 in Lagerwey, chapter 7 in this volume. While the designations of some of these five had varied, Mount T'ai had always been the eastern mountain.

12. As they did; by the mid-eighteenth century there were two Nan-ting temples.

13. The earliest reference I have found to Mount Miao-feng comes from 1512; tradition dates the temple to 1662, but the oldest dated object in the peak temple is from 1689. If there was an earlier cult that Pi-hsia Yuan-chün supplanted, I have found no hint of it. The literati T'ao Yun-chia and Yü I-cheng both traveled through these mountains (T'ao in the autumn of 1614, Yü in the next decade or so), visiting a number of Pi-hsia temples and climbing along routes that pilgrims would later travel, yet neither mentions any such temple here (T'ao Yun-chia 1633; *TC* 7.319–25). Nor is Miao-feng Shan mentioned in any of the rather detailed late Ming descriptions of Peking religious establishments. The late Ming "Precious Scroll of the Efficacious and Responsive Niang-niang of Mount T'ai" (*Ling-ying*), not an official or literati source, similarly talks of four important Pi-hsia temples in the Peking area but makes no reference to Miao-feng Shan.

14. For the first century, the average was 173. I have figures for thirteen groups who donated stelae over this period. These and similar generalizations are based on the total corpus of Miao-feng Shan stelae, preserved at the site or on rubbings in the Shou-tu Library, supplemented with information from FK and KU. I was able to go to Miao-feng Shan in May (the fourth lunar month) of 1987 and 1988. These trips were much enhanced by the assistance and the company of Yen Ch'ung-nien 閆崇年 and Li Shih-yü 李世瑜.

15. This was not a temple to Pi-hsia. They carved two other stelae, in 1806 and 1836, with fewer names (ST 1737, no. 657; 1749, no. 660; 1755, no. 661; 1806, no. 669; 1836, no. 671).

16. Different names were used for them at different times, including North Central, Old Northern, New Northern, New Central, South Central. These terms actually referred just to the last, mountainous, stages of the pilgrim's journey; access to these "routes" was provided by ordinary flatland roads.

17. The twelve stelae from the nineteenth century that mention route names refer only to the Southern and Central. For distances: FK 21.

18. For the road openers: CH 27–28; Jang-lien 1899, 5; Tung Fu-ming 1939, 34. They acted out a tale drawn from the Mu-lien story cycle (Grübe 1901, 112–17; Hsu Tao-ling 1947, 239). For a drawing of them, see below, n. 36, item no. 2.

19. I have figures on seventeen named associations between 1797 and 1882; the average size was 204.

20. *CCT* 1817, 51173; reference kindly provided by Liu Cheng-yun. See the schedules in KU 74–108, which culminate on the eighth and are over by the sixteenth. Stele records are vague about the date of the deity's birthday—probably to hide the fact that the local celebrations were earlier than the ones on Mount T'ai.

21. The earliest object with a commemorative date in the autumn was an incense burner donated to the hall of the god of wealth in the eighth month of 1767 (ST 1767, 693). See also *KCTTC* 25:369–70, dated 1735, and ST 1824, no. 740 for references to autumn and spring pilgrimages. Imbault-Huart 1885, 63 says the temple was open 7/1–7; Bouillard 1921 says 7/21 to 8/1; KU 103–5 says 7/25–8/1.

22. *Hui-hsiang* 迴香 (lit. return + incense) seems to have been the opposite of *chin-hsiang* 進香 (presenting incense, making a pilgrimage) and implied both bringing back incense and returning home from the pilgrimage. In the novel translated by Dudbridge in chapter 1 of this volume, the term is used to refer to the celebration held at a local temple upon the pilgrims' return. Current religious practice in Taiwan suggests that incense from the peak temple was then placed in the home temple's burner. But the temple to Tung-yueh on Miao-feng Shan was probably called the Hui-hsiang Pavilion because it was the first step on the route home, not because it was the source of incense.

23. See illustration no. 1 described in n. 36 below. Eunuchs had again become important patrons of pilgrimage. In 1864, 1870, and 1892, for example, three of them undertook major repairs to the stone paths along several of the routes up the mountain (ST 1870, no. 721; FK 133).

24. Sidney Gamble's impressive photographs of China (1917–27), including a great many of Miao-feng Shan, as well as twenty lively minutes of silent movie footage of the pilgrimage itself, are held by the Sidney D. Gamble Foundation for China Studies. I am most grateful to Catherine Gamble Currin of that foundation and to Nancy Jervis of the China Institute in America for access to these materials. For some of these photographs, see *China Between Revolutions* 1989.

25. Following the well-known Chinese principle by which later arrivals claim ever earlier antecedents, this group asserted that it was founded in 1573.

26. Edkins claims that the monks lived at the temple only during the fall and spring pilgrimage seasons and left it "shut up and unoccupied" the rest of the year (Edkins 1893, 271). The presence of numerous resident managerial clergy helps us distinguish monasteries from temples.

27. Pictured in illustration no. 3 described in n. 36.

28. A few, including three at Ya-chi Shan, are in too poor condition to date.

29. Twenty-four had set up stelae prior to 1890. Several hundred association names are attested, but in sources of a sort that do not exist for the other temples.

30. One record of such a rest stop does survive (PL 1696, no. 8186), and there are a number of reasons why others might have disappeared from view. There were also inns along the way that catered to this traffic.

31. Chin-hsun says that *k'u-hsiang* refers only to penitents (CH 21), and indeed there may have been more of such pilgrims at Miao-feng Shan as well.

32. There were a few. See PL 1696, no. 8186.

33. Such relationships were common in Ch'ing and twentieth-century Taiwan; see, for example, Sangren 1987, 88.

34. We will here consider only the Ch'ing period, when the pilgrimage took shape; Ming policy on popular religion was in any case even more multifaceted (Li and Naquin 1988).

35. Chia-ch'ing's empress had previously bestowed a similar honor on one such association but had not made it a common practice (CH 35–36).

36. These paintings (my nos. 2 and 3 below) are among five contemporary representations of the pilgrimage that I have seen. Unfortunately, it has been possible to reproduce only one of them here.

One (no. 1) is a color woodblock print showing imperially sponsored entertainer groups (including a *yang-ko* 秧歌 troupe) on the road by the Summer Palace; the title

"Long Life without Limit" suggests a late Ch'ing date. The original is in the Hermitage in Leningrad (*Chinese Popular Prints* 1988, no. 113).

Two come from different Ch'ing colored paintings of the Miao-feng Shan pilgrimage; the originals are probably in the Palace Museum, Peking. The one illustrated in this chapter as fig 8.1 (no. 2) shows several sets of pilgrims en route up the mountain: a group of performers sponsored by the Board of Works is prominently featured, but stilt walkers, road openers, and acrobats are also shown (*Yen-tu*, no. 2, 1990, back cover). The other (no. 3), as published, shows a detail of a theatrical troupe performing in front of the Ta-chueh Ssu (*Yen-tu*, no. 4 [1986], opposite p. 25). No information about these paintings is provided by the magazine.

Another set of paintings (no. 4), representing Ch'ing dynasty scenes (which I have seen through a xerox of a photograph sold in Peking ca. 1930), shows the pilgrimage in four hanging scrolls. Each has mountain peaks in the rear and a lively pilgrimage scene before a temple at the front. Similar to nos. 2 and 3 above, three represent a condensed vision of the Northern, Southern, and Central routes; the latter is set in front of the Ta-chueh Ssu. The fourth focuses on Chien-kou and shows at the top the peak temple set dramatically on an overhanging cliff. All give center stage to entertainer groups and pilgrim onlookers and show the path leading away through countless peaks in which rest houses look like impressive temple buildings. (I have had access to this photograph, in the possession of Victor Ch'üan, through Chün-fang Yü; my thanks to them both. No further information about the painting is currently available.)

By contrast, a foreigner's photograph from 1939 (no. 5) shows a rough woodblock print used by a pilgrimage association pasted above their posted announcement. In it, several crudely drawn uniformed men carrying the beflagged chests typical of these groups, drawn very large and out of scale, wind through mountains toward a summit marked with a pennant (Eigner 1939, opposite p. 170).

37. The first recorded use of the term "Miao-feng Shan" is in a stele of 1513 (FK 13).

38. Bannermen, both Chinese and Manchu, are prominent in lists of association members. The existence of temples to Pi-hsia in the cities of southern Manchuria in the late Ming suggests that the deity was not new to them when they occupied Peking in 1644 (*Feng-t'ien t'ung-chih* 1934, 93.18, 93.32).

39. He wrote in colloquial Chinese, so any punctuation was a novelty.

40. Since 1949, Chinese intellectuals have not publicly shared Ku's enthusiasm. Conversely, contemporary academic trends in the West have encouraged the rediscovery of this material, while the author of this essay herself shares a scholarly interest in popular culture.

41. It is possible that this *wen wu* 文武 differentiation was formalized during the period of imperial patronage in the 1890s and thus reflects symbolic tidying by the throne.

42. Li Ching-han estimates that 10–20 percent were pilgrimage association members (1925, 9); Tung Fu-ming says 5 percent (1939, 26).

43. The journey from Peking usually entailed two nights and three days on the road, but those who could afford transport needed less time, especially after the advent of the train and automobile.

44. A pilgrim manual is mentioned in Bredon and Mitrophanow 1927, 286. There

is said to be a scripture about this Pi-hsia (Douin 1910–12, 135–36) and another (dictated by a planchette cult) about Wang San-nai-nai (Chou Chen-ho 1929, 74–75, 94–96). I have been unable to locate any of these.

45. For recent transcriptions of a few of these tales, see Chang and P'eng 1985, 190–92. My research has not included fieldwork to collect more data of this sort. Illustrations nos. 1, 2, and 3 described in n. 36 emphasize the entertainment to be seen by placing groups of performers at the center. Like the paintings described in the Cahill essay (chapter 6 of this volume), these pictures could be enjoyed both before and after the trip.

46. Judging from the forty-seven stelae set up for this pilgrimage between 1689 and 1936, which listed about 7,000 names, 300 (4 percent) were women. But only twenty of these stelae listed any women at all, and of these names, about 7 percent were women. Li Ching-han estimated 7–8 percent (1925, 9), and Sidney Gamble's photographs of that same year show very few women (see above n. 24). Derk Bodde's photographs a decade later are similar (private communication, 1989).

47. Seemingly at the instigation of Tientsin merchants, a twentieth-century rose-growing industry developed in the Miao-feng Shan area. The roses were used to make expensive wine, tea, and perfume, for the air and water of the mountain gave them a special fragrance. The rose harvest followed the pilgrimage, and the temple courtyard was used for sorting and drying (Hubbard 1923, 59–65; FK 45). According to a local legend ("Why the Roses on Miao-feng Shan Bloom in the Sixth Month"), Pi-hsia (obviously a friend of these merchants) made the flowers bloom late so that they would not be picked clean by the pilgrims (Chang and P'eng 1985, 193–94). Otherwise, the area was still rather deserted ten months a year.

48. For such organizations in medieval times, see Gernet 1956, 251–69. Edward Shaughnessy kindly called these groups to my attention.

49. Some of the stelae at Wu-tang Shan studied by John Lagerwey (see chap. 7 of this volume) use terms like "association head" and seem to represent communities. Chün-fang Yü's chapter mentions "soup-house temples" supported by specific villages situated along the path up to Southern Wu-t'ai Shan in the 1940s that seem to resemble our mountain's tea stalls.

BIBLIOGRAPHY

Citations of reprints of Ming and Ch'ing works give the original *chüan* plus the page number in the reprint.

Sources Cited by Abbreviation

CCC   *Ch'ing-tai ch'i-chü-chu ts'e* 清代起居註册. Taipei: National Palace Museum, 1985.

CCT   *Chün-chi-tang* 軍機檔 [Archive of Grand Council copies of palace memorials]. Taipei: National Palace Museum. Numbered by reign.

CH   Chin-hsun 金勳. *Miao-feng-shan chih* 妙峯山志 [An account of Miao-feng Shan]; appended: "Huang-hui k'ao" [A study of the imperial associations]. N.d. but ca. 1929. Handwritten MS.

CMTC   *Chin-men tsa-chi* 津門雜記 [Miscellaneous account of Tientsin]. 1885.

CSL   *Ch'ing shih-lu* 清實錄 [Veritable Records of the Ch'ing dynasty]. Mukden, 1937; reprint ed., Taipei, 1964. Date followed by citation; separate pagination for each reign.

CWK   *Jih-hsia chiu-wen k'ao* 日下舊聞考 [A study of the Old Record of the Capital]. Ca. 1785; reprint ed., Peking: Ku-chi, 1983.

FK   Feng-k'uan 奉寬. *Miao-feng-shan so-chi* 妙峯山瑣記 [Random jottings about Miao-feng Shan]. Peking: Pei-ching, 1929.

FM   *Catalogue of Chinese Rubbings from the Field Museum*. Edited by Hartmut Walravens. Field Museum of Natural History, Fieldiana Anthropology, new series, no. 3. Chicago, 1981.

HT   *Ch'in-ting Ta-Ch'ing hui-tien t'u shih-li* 欽定大清會典圖事例 [Collected statutes of the Ch'ing]. 1899; reprint ed., Taipei, 1963.

HTL   Hsu Tao-ling 許道齡. *Pei-p'ing miao-yü t'ung-chien* 北平廟宇通檢 [A catalogue of Peking temples]. N.d. but ca. 1936. Peking: Kuo-li Pei-p'ing yen-chiu-yuan shih-hsueh yen-chiu-hui.

KCK   Li Tsung-wan 厲宗萬. *Ching-ch'eng ku-chi k'ao* 京城古蹟考 [A study of old records of the capital]. Before 1745; reprint ed., Peking: Ku-chi, 1981.

KCTTC   *Kung-chung-tang Yung-cheng tsou-che* 宮中檔雍正奏摺 [Palace memorials of the Yung-cheng reign]. Taipei: National Palace Museum, 1977–80.

KU   Ku Chieh-kang 顧頡剛, ed. *Miao-feng-shan* 妙峯山. Canton: Chung-shan ta-hsueh min-su ts'ung-shu, ca. 1929; reprint ed., Taipei: Fu-lu t'u-shu kung-ssu, 1970.

LHCN   *Pei-p'ing lü-hsing chih-nan* 北平旅行指南 [A tourist guide to Peiping]. N.d. but ca. 1935. Not consecutively paginated.

Ling-ying   *Ling-ying T'ai-shan niang-niang pao-chüan* 靈應泰山娘娘寶卷 [Precious scroll of our efficacious and responsive lady of Mount T'ai]. Ming. Copy held by the Chinese Academy of Social Sciences Institute of Religions, Peking.

MFSCN   Chin Ch'an-yü 金禪雨. *Miao-feng-shan chih-nan* 妙峯山指南 [A guide to Miao-feng Shan]. Ming-sheng tao-yu-she, n.d. (ca. 1936). 19-page booklet.

MITC   *Ta Ming i-t'ung-chih* 大明一通志 [National gazetteer of the Ming]. 1461; reprinted 1505.

NWF   *Nei-wu-fu chang-i-ssu ch'eng-ying ke-hsiang hsiang-hui hua-ming ts'e* 內務府掌儀司承應各項香會花名冊 [Lists of names of the pilgrimages associations that were submitted to the Imperial Household Department of Ceremonials]. Documents organized by Hou Chih-chung of the Peking Library. 1937.

Pi-hsia   *Pi-hsia yuan-chün hu-kuo pi-min p'u-chi pao-sheng miao-ching* 碧霞元君護國庇民普濟保生妙經 [Marvelous sutra of Pi-hsia Yuan-chün, who protects the nation and the people, preserves life, and saves all]. In *Hsu Tao-tsang* 續道藏 [Supplement to the Taoist Canon], 1607; reprint ed., Taipei: National Central Library, 1961. HY 1433.

PL   Peking Library (Pei-ching t'u-shu-kuan) stele rubbing; date followed by catalogue number.

ST   Shou-tu 首都 Library (Peking) rubbing; date followed by catalogue number.

STFC   *Shun-t'ien fu-chih* 順天府志 [Shun-t'ien prefectural gazetteer]. Editions:
    1407. *Shun-t'ien fu-chih*. Peking: Pei-ching ta-hsueh, 1983; reprint of the sections of
        the 1403–7 "Yung-lo ta-tien" as found in the 1885 edition
    1638. *Wan-li Shun-t'ien fu-chih*
    1885. *Kuang-hsu Shun-t'ien fu-chih*; reprint ed., Taipei, 1965
TC   Liu T'ung 劉侗 and Yü I-cheng 于奕正. *Ti-ching ching-wu-lueh* 帝京景物略
        [Account of the capital]. 1635; reprint ed., Peking: Ku-chi, 1980.
TLC   Tun Li-ch'en 敦禮臣. *Yen-ching sui-shih-chi* 燕京歲時記 [Record of the
        annual calendar of festivals in Peking]. 1900. Translated and annotated
        by Derk Bodde as *Annual Customs and Festivals in Peking*. 2d ed. Hong Kong:
        Hong Kong University Press, 1965.
WS   Shen Pang 沈榜. *Wan-shu tsa-chi* 宛署雜記 [Miscellaneous account of
        Wan-p'ing]. 1593; reprint ed., Peking: Pei-ching, 1961.
YHP   Shen Te-fu 沈德符. *Wan-li yeh-hu-pien* 萬歷野獲編 [Gleanings from the
        Wan-li period]. 1619; reprint ed., Peking: Chung-hua, 1979.

Other Sources

Arlington, L. C., and William Lewisohn. 1935. *In Search of Old Peking*. Peking; reprint
    ed., New York: Paragon Book Company, 1967.
Bogan, M. L. C. 1928. *Manchu Customs and Superstitions*. Peking.
Bouillard, Georges. 1921. *Péking et ses environs. Première Série: Le Yang Shan et ses temples*.
    No pagination.
———. 1923. "Usages et coutumes à Pékin durant la 4ᵉ lune." *La Chine* 38:299–311.
———. 1925. Sheet 141 of "Carte de la Chine" (1:100,000) prepared for the French
    Ministry of Communications.
Bredon, Juliet. 1922. *Peking: A Historical and Intimate Description of its Chief Places of
    Interest*. 2d ed. Shanghai: Kelly & Walsh.
Bredon, Juliet, and Igor Mitrophanow. 1927. *The Moon Year: A Record of Chinese Cus-
    toms and Festivals*. Shanghai: Kelly & Walsh.
Burgess, John Stewart. 1928. *The Guilds of Peking*. New York: Columbia University
    Press.
Chang Pao-chang 張寶章 and P'eng Che-yü 彭哲愚. 1985. *Hsiang-shan ti ch'uan-shuo*
    香山的傳說 [Tales of Hsiang-shan]. Shih-chia-chuang: Ho-pei Shao-nien erh-
    t'ung.
Chavannes, Edouard. 1910. *Le T'ai Chan: Essai de monographie d'un culte chinois*. Paris:
    Leroux; reprint ed., Peking, 1941.
Ch'en Lei 陳雷. 1986. "Miao-feng-shan ti ch'a-p'eng yü ch'a-p'eng hsiao-tiao"
    妙峯山的茶棚與茶棚小調 [Miao-feng Shan's tea stalls and their songs]. *Wen-shih
    tzu-liao hsuan-pien* 30:255–59. Peking: Pei-ching.
Ch'en-yuan shih-lueh 宸垣識略. 1788; reprint ed., Peking: Ku-chi, 1981.
Chiang I-k'uei 蔣一葵. 1980. *Ch'ang-an k'e-hua* 長安客話 [Talk about the capital].
    Ming, Wan-li reign; reprint ed., Peking: Ku-chi.
Chi-fu t'ung-chih 畿輔通志 [Gazetteer of the capital region]. 1884; reprint ed., Shih-
    chia-chuang: Ho-pei jen-min, 1985.
China Between Revolutions: Photographs by Sidney D. Gamble 1917–1927. 1989. New York:
    China Institute in America.
Chinese Popular Prints. 1988. Leningrad: Aurora Art Publishers.

Ching-Sui t'ieh-lu lü-hsing chih-nan 京綏鐵路旅行指南 [Peking to Sui-yuan railroad guide]. 1922. 3d ed.

Chou Chen-ho 周振鶴. 1929. "Wang San-nai-nai" 王三奶奶 [Granny Wang]. *Min-su* 69–70:68–107.

Cook, Thos., and Son. 1924. *Cook's Guide to Peking, North China, South Manchuria, Korea.* 5th ed. Peking: Thos. Cook and Son.

Douin, M. G. 1910–12. "Cérémonial de la cour et coutumes du peuple de Pékin." *Bulletin de l'association amicale franco-chinoise* (Paris) 2:105–38, 215–37, 327–68; 3:134–55, 209–33; 4:66–84.

Duara, Prasenjit. 1988. *Culture, Power, and the State: Rural North China, 1900–1942.* Stanford: Stanford University Press.

Dudbridge, Glen. 1991. "A Pilgrimage in Seventeenth-Century Fiction: T'ai-shan and the *Hsing-shih yin-yuan chuan.*" *T'oung Pao* 77.

Edkins, Joseph. 1893. *Chinese Buddhism: A Volume of Sketches, Historical, Descriptive, and Critical.* 2d ed. London.

Eigner, Julius. 1939. "Strange Ceremonies Connected with Buddhist Pilgrimage to Miao Feng Shan." *China Journal* 30, 3:168–72.

Feng-t'ien t'ung-chih 奉天通志 [Gazetteer of Feng-t'ien prefecture]. 1934.

Gernet, Jacques. 1956. *Les Aspects économiques du bouddhisme dans le société chinoise du Ve au Xe siècle.* Saigon: Ecole Française d'Extrême-Orient.

Goodrich, Anne Swann. 1964. *The Peking Temple of the Eastern Peak: The Tung-yueh Miao in Peking and Its Lore, with 20 Plates.* Nagoya: Monumenta Serica. Research done in the 1930s.

Groot, J. J. M. de. 1903–4. *Sectarianism and Religious Persecution in China.* Reprint ed., Taipei, 1963.

Grübe, Wilhelm. 1901. *Zur Pekinger Volkskunde.* Königliche Museum für Volkerkunde zu Berlin Veröffentlichen, vol. 7, nos. 1–4. Berlin.

Guide Book to the New Official Plan of Peking. 1917. Edited by the Geographical and Topographical Society of China. Shanghai.

Hershatter, Gail. 1986. *The Workers of Tianjin, 1900–1949.* Stanford: Stanford University Press.

Hsiu-ming 修明. 1986. "Ch'ao-pai Miao-feng-shan Niang-niang-ting tsa-chi" 朝拜妙峯山娘娘頂雜記 [Miscellaneous account of a visit to Miao-feng Shan's Niang-niang summit]. *Wen-shih tzu-liao hsuan-pien* 30:249–50. Describes a 1919 trip.

Hsu Tao-ling 許道齡. 1947. "Hsuan-wu chih ch'i-yuan chi ch'i t'ui-pien k'ao" 玄武之起源及其蛻變考 [A study of Chen-wu's origins and transformations]. *Shih-hsueh chi-k'an* 1, 5:223–40.

Hua-pei tsung-chiao nien-chien 華北宗教年鑑 [Yearbook of religious activities in North China]. 1941. Peking.

Huai-jou hsien-chih 懷柔縣志 [Huai-jou county gazetteer]. 1604.

Hubbard, Gilbert E. 1923. *The Temples of the Western Hills.* Peking: Librairie française.

Imbault-Huart, Camille. 1885. "Le pèlerinage de la montagne du Pic Mystérieux près de Pékin." *Journal Asiatique*, 8th series, 5:62–71.

Jang-lien 讓廉. 1899. *Ching-tu feng-su chih* 京都風俗志 [Customs of the capital].

Johnson, Linda Cooke. 1986. "The Decline of Soochow and the Rise of Shanghai: A Study in the Economic Morphology of Urban Change, 1756–1894." Ph.D. dissertation, University of California, Santa Cruz.

Lan, F. 1921. "Souvenir d'un pèlerinage à Miao fung shan." *La Chine* 4:272–74.

Lao She. 1985. *Crescent Moon and Other Stories*. Peking: Chinese Literature.

Li Ching-han 李景漢. 1925. "Miao-feng-shan 'ch'ao-ting chin-hsiang' ti tiao-ch'a" 妙峯山'朝頂進香'的調査 [A survey of the Miao-feng Shan pilgrimage]. *She-hui-hsueh tsa-chih* 2, 5–6:1–42.

Li Shih-yü 李世瑜. 1987. "Wang San-nai-nai ti ku-shih" 王三奶奶的故事 [The story of Granny Wang]. MS.

Li Shiyu and Susan Naquin. 1988. "The Baoming Temple: Religion and the Throne in Ming and Qing China." *Harvard Journal of Asiatic Studies* 48, 1:131–88.

Li Wei-tsu. 1948. "On the Cult of the Four Sacred Animals (Szu Ta Men 四大門) in the Neighborhood of Peking." *Folklore Studies* 7:1–94.

Lin-ch'ing 麟慶. 1849. *Hung-hsueh yin-yuan t'u-chi* 鴻雪因緣圖記 [Illustrated notes on my life].

Liu Hou-tzu 劉厚滋. 1936. "Pei-p'ing Tung-yueh-miao pei-k'e mu-lu" 北平東嶽廟碑刻目錄 [A catalogue of the stelae of the Peking Tung-yueh Miao]. *Kuo-li Pei-p'ing yen-chiu-yuan yuan-k'an hui-pao* 7, 6:116–38.

Lo Hsiang-lin 羅香林. 1968. "Miao-feng-shan yü Pi-hsia Yuan-chün" 妙峯山與碧霞元君 [Miao-feng Shan and Pi-hsia Yuan-chün]. In *Min-su-hsueh lun-ts'ung* 民俗學論叢, edited by Lo, 1–57. Taipei: Chuan-chi wen-hsueh. Originally written in 1929.

Lowe, H. Y. [Lo Hsin-yao]. 1941. *The Adventures of Wu: The Life Cycle of a Peking Man*. Peking; reprint ed., Princeton: Princeton University Press, 1983.

Mei Ts'un 梅邨. 1983. *Pei-ching Hsi-shan feng-ching ch'ü* 北京西山風景區 [Scenic spots in Peking's Western Hills]. Peking: Pei-ching lü-yu.

Murakami Tomoyuki 村上知行. 1940. *Pekin saijiki* 北京歳時記 [Annual calendar of festivities in Peking]. Tokyo.

Naquin, Susan. 1986. "The Pilgrimage to Miao-feng-shan." Paper presented at the Second International Conference on Sinology. Taipei.

P'an Jung-pi 潘榮陛. 1758. *Ti-ching sui-shih chi-sheng* 帝京歳時紀勝 [Famous sites in the annual calendar of the capital]. Reprint ed., Peking: Ku-chi, 1981.

Pei-ching li-shih chi-nien 北京歴史紀年 [Chronology of Peking history]. 1984. Peking: Pei-ching.

Pei-p'ing chih-nan 北平指南 [Peiping guide]. 1929. Pei-p'ing min-she.

Rankin, Mary Backus. 1986. *Elite Activism and Political Transformation in China: Zhejiang Province, 1865–1911*. Stanford: Stanford University Press.

Rowe, William T. 1989. *Hankow: Conflict and Community in a Chinese City, 1796–1895*. Stanford: Stanford University Press.

Sangren, P. Steven. 1987. *History and Magical Power in a Chinese Community*. Stanford: Stanford University Press.

Sawada Mizuho 澤田瑞穗. 1965. "Ban-to-ku no kamigami" 蟠桃宮の神神 [The gods of P'an-t'ao-kung]. *Tōhō shūkyo* 26:55–75.

Schipper, Kristofer M. 1977. "Neighborhood Cult Associations in Traditional Tainan." In *The City in Late Imperial China*, edited by G. W. Skinner, 651–76. Stanford: Stanford University Press.

Smith, Arthur H. 1899. *Village Life in China: A Study in Sociology*. New York: Revell.

T'ai-an fu-chih 泰安府志 [Gazetteer of T'ai-an prefecture]. 1760.

T'ai-shan chih 泰山志 [Gazetteer of Mount T'ai]. Ming, Chia-ching (1522–66) ed.

T'ang Yen 唐晏. 1907. *T'ien-ch'ih ou-wen* 天咫偶聞 [Hearsay from the capital]. Reprint ed., Taipei: Ku-t'ing, 1969.

T'ao Yun-chia 陶允嘉. 1633. "Hsi-shan chi-yu" 西山紀遊 [Record of a walk in the Western Hills]. In *Ming-shan sheng-kai t'u* 名山勝槩圖. T'ao's trip took place in 1614.

Tu-men chu-chih-tz'u 都門竹枝詞 [Verses from the capital]. 1877.

Tu-shih ts'ung-t'an 都市叢談 [Talks on the capital]. 1940. MS.

Tung Fu-ming. 1939. "Chinese Itinerant Players at Miao Feng Shan. Evidences of Greek Influence in the Pilgrimage Plays at the Temple of the Jade Lady." Reprinted from *Collectanea Commissionis Synodalis* (Peking) 12, 1:20–43.

T'ung-chou chih 通州志 [T'ung department gazetteer]. 1879. Reprint ed., Taipei, 1968.

Turner, Victor W. 1974. "Pilgrimages as Social Processes." In *Drama, Fields, and Metaphors*, edited by Turner, 166–230. Ithaca: Cornell University Press.

Wan-p'ing hsien-chih 宛平縣志 [Gazetteer of Wan-p'ing county]. 1684.

Wu Chen-yü 吳振棫. 1896. *Yang-chi-chai ts'ung-lu* 養吉齋叢錄 [Account from the Yang-chi studio]. Reprint ed., Taipei, 1968.

Yang, C. K. 1961. *Religion in Chinese Society*. Berkeley: University of California Press.

NINE

Reading the Chairman Mao Memorial Hall in Peking: The Tribulations of the Implied Pilgrim

Rudolf G. Wagner

Secular political movements since the French Revolution have often seen traditional religion as their ideological competitor and the administrators of this religion as their institutional opponent. There ensued strong antireligious and anticlerical propaganda, which in a successful revolution was often followed by an outright ban on religious ceremonies, a closure of sites that would provide a focus for religious sentiment and community, and attempts at demolishing religious institutions.

Efforts were made to match the religious structure with revolutionary institutions. The old gods were replaced by new notions (like Reason, Liberty, Class Struggle, or Revolution), the old buildings by new centers, and the new state authorities took it into their hands to establish new cults. While this substitution has been well documented for the French Revolution (Ouzouf 1976; Nora 1984), there is less research about the youth movements that have sprung up since the turn of the twentieth century and much less for the postrevolutionary efforts of the socialist camp. In Europe, the new socialist states had to cope with often well-legitimized, ubiquitous, and highly organized churches. The Communist parties tried to match the organizational and religious offerings of their opponents at each level, from ceremony and ritual to philosophical, patriotic, and moral guidance and social organization.

In terms of religious space, the new state ordained a new holy map with a number of holy sites and places associated with revolutionary activities (battles, important meetings, etc.) or with revolutionary leaders to replace or compete with the traditional pilgrimage and tourism centers. Like a map showing the levels of religious charge of different areas, this secular map has some international centers—Lenin's Mausoleum in Moscow, for example, or the wall where many of the Paris Commune activists were shot—and a network of national and regional centers, such as the Petersburg Winter Palace or Ching-kang Shan. On the microlevel, it has local replicas of larger revolutionary institutions, replacing the local shrine or church with a house of culture or a revolutionary museum.

The secular pilgrimage in China was[1] closely modeled upon its predecessor/competitor. The pilgrimage was to counteract the natural decay of revolutionary fervor by taking the pilgrim temporarily out of normal life circumstances to engage in a new type of purified social relations with other pilgrims. The entire revolutionary advance to the distant goal of communism is structurally so closely linked to pilgrimage in China that the most famous pilgrimage novel of China, *Journey to the West* (*Hsi-yu chi* 西遊記), has served since 1949 as the standard metaphor for the long pilgrimage to communism (Wagner 1990, 140 and 146 ff.). The purpose of an actual pilgrimage—to bridge the painful chasm between the distant goal and present-day triviality through short-term exultation—fully anticipated Communist individual behavior and social relations for a short time, and was to energize further advance.

The Communist movements inherited the commitment of the modern— and in China also the traditional—state to organize the religious sphere and pushed the principle further than any of their predecessors had ever done. This commitment implies a substantial distrust of the subversive potential of unsupervised religious activities like sect formation or pilgrimages and has always been combined with a heavy-handed persecution of such private activities (see Naquin, chapter 8 in this volume).

Some peculiarities prevail under the Chinese circumstances. First, the Chinese Communists did not have to cope with a church as organized and articulate as the European churches were. Second, the prevailing religions in China were not monotheistic. Nonetheless, the organizational and ideological counterstructure set up by the Chinese Communists is modeled upon the European, and in particular Soviet, precedent. It reacts not to particular Chinese realities, but rather to the set of precedents considered binding in the socialist camp. Whatever the reasons for its introduction, however, it operates under Chinese conditions. Accordingly, the origin of these structures might have little to do with their actual function in Chinese society.

The focus of this study is on secular pilgrimages and pilgrimage centers in the People's Republic of China (PRC), in particular the Chairman Mao Memorial Hall. The decision to build this monument in Peking on T'ien-an-men Square implied that the chairman should be lying in state in the heart of the heart of the nation and that the hall was designed as a secular pilgrimage center in a new religious geography mapped out during the Cultural Revolution. Without going into any great detail, I will try to sketch this background of the Memorial Hall, as many of its features become telling only in this context.

THE RELIGIOUS GEOGRAPHY OF NEW CHINA

On October 22, 1966, *Jen-min jih-pao* carried an editorial—"Hung-wei-ping pu-p'a yuan-cheng nan" (Red Guards do not fear the hardships of a Long March)—praising a group of students from Dairen who had walked all the way from the far north to Peking, doing propaganda for Mao Tse-tung Thought on the way, helping with the harvest, and learning about the revolutionary experiences of the villagers. The editorial quotes one of them as saying, "Although we left our bright classrooms, our comfortable beds, and superb living conditions and did not use comfortable transportation, we achieved a great spiritual liberation, tempering, and elevation [of our revolutionary attitude]." The editorial supports this contention.

> And that is indeed how it is. People who have not gone through hard and bitter struggles cannot become real revolutionaries. Whoever thinks one has to "make revolution all in great comfort" and that there can be "peaceful evolution all in great comfort" will slip into the morass of revisionism.

The reenactment of the Long March silently implied a similarity of structure that at the time was not expressed. To make a new Long March necessary, the levers of power again had to be in hands akin to those of the Kuomintang in the early 1930s. In 1966, the "revolutionaries" saw themselves again in a difficult and threatened position, and in a minority to boot. Only by mirroring the Long March would they be able to spread the word of Mao's thought so that it would become the "masses'," only by going through a process of prolonged self-purification would they acquire enough legitimacy and strength to become "successors of the Revolution" who could "lead the masses" and thus overcome the enemy entrenched in his administrative positions. Evil was reigning again, corrupting the souls with the "revisionism" of warm beds.

They had come to Peking, the central seat of world revolution, to see Mao Tse-tung, who embodied the highest virtues associated with world revolution. On the way, they had purified themselves physically by enduring the various hardships involved with walking for about a month and had purified themselves spiritually by studying Mao's works and spreading his gospel in the places through which they passed. The comfort of their schools and dorms is described as the natural condition for turning people "revisionist" and slackening their revolutionary fervor. Their way from Dairen to Peking was not organized by a travel agency or the Youth League. They were in the situation described for pilgrims who leave their everyday life and circumstances, enter into a new "freedom" and establish new social relations based on the common goal of the tour, willingly incur and endure hardships and fasting, and prepare themselves mentally with reading appropriate religious texts on the way to the holy center. Socially, the Red Guards had left their controlled and familiar habitat; they were out in the open, and they described this new environment both in this text and in interviews as a thrilling "liberation." This ecstatic departure from the morass of everyday life with its threat of "revisionism" or loss of religious fervor was also a departure from the narrow controls imposed by parents and schools, both of which would soon become associated with the same evils of revisionism. The Red Guards claimed the right to operate outside the boundaries of law and custom because of their revolutionary purity.

These and other students' mirroring of the Red Army's Long March was *ch'uan-lien* 串聯, to establish contacts and exchange revolutionary experiences with others. Because the students were not randomly traversing whatever difficult terrain was at hand but were going to specific geographical points, in particular to Peking, people from very diverse regions were able to come together and make contacts. By engaging in horizontal communication, they were blunting one of the key instruments of social control in the hands of Party administrators, who enforced the traditional ban on such communication very efficiently after 1949.

Lin Piao's and Mao Tse-tung's support of these horizontal links in late 1966 shows that they felt the vertical structure at the time to be so much dominated by their political opponents that their challenge would be unsuccessful unless they could establish a counterstructure of information and allegiance. The development of direct and horizontal communication among the migrating students made them into a highly mobile, cohesive social force with the energy, the self-righteousness, and the ascetic fervor and legitimacy of youth. At the same time, the imposition of a rigid code of behavior stressing ideological and military obedience to the chairman and his thought established a direct link between them and the top of the hierarchy (Mao and his "trusted successor," Lin Piao), bypassing the many layers of command in between. Upon their return home, the new acolytes would claim the nobility, high purpose, and purity of the new convert and turn into obedient political propagandists. There was, of course, a latent contradiction. Once the power struggle in the center changed back to more conventional forms of intrigue and plot, and once disillusionment spread among the acolytes, horizontal communication would become a threat, and efforts would have to be made to curtail this temporary freedom.

At this early stage of the Cultural Revolution, the various elements of the Long March pilgrimage were still discrete, and it took months until they merged to form a unified whole. On the day the editorial quoted above appeared, a second editorial entitled "Ling-hun shen-ch'u nao ko-ming" (Wage revolution in the depths of the soul) praised the woman worker Wei Feng-ying for remodeling her thinking and soul through the study of Mao's works. "The most outstanding characteristic of Wei Feng-ying's study of Chairman Mao's writings," it noted, "is that she *had the courage to wage revolu-*

tion in the depth of her own soul" (emphasis added). No one is "red" automatically, Wei maintained; only a truly revolutionary transformation of all of one's spontaneous urges and attitudes could make a real revolutionary. In the reports and the copious materials about her, there was not at first an established and standardized Maoist canon to account for Wei Feng-ying's magical transformation and provide guidelines for others. But such a set of texts was in the making. Lin Piao seems to have been behind all three segments: the New Long March of the Red Guards, the revolution in the depth of the soul (which engendered the famous hand gesture in the revolutionary Peking operas where the words come straight from the revolutionized innards), and the *lao san p'ien* 老三篇, the three articles by Mao one should study time and again[2] together with the newly compiled *Quotations from Chairman Mao* and Mao's poems.

Within a few weeks, these three elements were fused. The Red Guards would use the *lao san p'ien* as their core study material on their New Long March ("Pa 'lao san p'ien'" 1966). The mental and physical hardships of this combined exercise would transform their souls. An editorial note prefacing the leader in *Jen-min jih-pao* on December 2, 1966, summarized the experiences of the millions of Red Guards who had by then trekked to Peking to see the chairman in person at the big rallies organized for them:

> Their experiences were ultimately to raise high the grand banner of Mao Tsetung Thought, conscientiously learn from the Liberation Army, and put politics first in every respect. Beginning with the preparatory work before setting off, the study of the writings of Chairman Mao must be the most important thing in all activities so that *the process of the Long March becomes the process of the transformation of one's own soul through Mao Tse-tung Thought.* ("Pien-che an" 1966, emphasis added)

By December, when this article was written, the *lao san p'ien* had become the embodiment of Mao Tse-tung Thought. In an odd interplay of spontaneous pilgrimage activity with guidance and encouragement by a section of the Center (i.e., the Party/state leadership), millions of youths set out on pilgrimages to Peking and other revolutionary sites to imbue themselves with revolutionary spirit, see the chairman, and *ch'uan-lien.*

Peking, the capital and the residence of the chairman, was the focus of Red Guard pilgrimages. And just as national political structures were mirrored on local levels throughout the PRC, Peking, the pilgrimage center, was replicated in the provinces. Under strictly administrative rules, such replication would have led to the establishment of the provincial capitals, county capitals, and so forth as regional or local pilgrimage centers; and in fact there have been frequent efforts to effect such replication. This administrative mirroring, however, clashed with the "religious" criterion, namely, a direct association with the revolutionary enterprise. Typically, a map of religiously charged points, being extremely uneven and often marginal in the distribution of the charged points, differs fundamentally not only from the administrative division, but also from the idealized market pattern once described by Skinner (Skinner 1964 and 1965). In the first weeks of the Long March activity, the students added Shao-shan (Mao Tse-tung's birthplace), the Ching-kang Shan area, and Yenan as pilgrimage sites ("Che-li sheng-ch'i-lai" 1966; "Mao Chu-hsi tsai Ching-kang-shan" 1966). In November, the first maps "for the purpose of revolutionary *ch'uan-lien*" were printed. These were little books of thirty-four pages with a map of China, of the Long March, and of the different provinces. An insert showed the basic grid of the streets of provincial capitals, on which the train stations were marked. The editors apologized that their maps were simply reproductions of earlier materials and that the new names with which many towns and places had adorned themselves since the onset of the Cultural Revolution had not been entered (*Chung-kuo ti-t'u ts'e* [*kung ko-ming ch'uan-lien yung*] 1966).

The religious hierarchy of different places is indicated on these maps. There are three levels on the national grid. Peking, marked with a big red star, is a category all its own. Second-level places are marked with a red flag indicating "Memorial Places of Revolutionary History"; the third level contains places without nationally relevant revolutionary charge. The places of the second order continually shift with the shifting status of leaders in the Center associated with these places. The Red Guard maps added Mao's birthplace (Shao-shan) and the places of Lin Piao's triumphs (P'ing-hsing Kuan 平型關 and Lu Shan 盧山) to the original list as given in the 1965 edition of the *Tz'u-hai* (sub loco); the 1979 edition of the same encyclopedia eliminated Lin Piao's holy sites (sub loco). Outside either list other, dormant sites waited to be included as the contention in the Center went on.

Concerning the role of the PRC state machinery in redefining the religious geography of China, we may consider the following points established.

First, after the founding of the People's Republic, the Center defined a series of places as of crucial importance for the Revolution.[3] The selection of these places reflected the status of those leaders, such as Mao Tse-tung, who had emerged victorious in the various inner-Party quarrels, as well as their ideological priorities. These places were made targets of collective visits organized by the Communist Party and its mass organizations as well as by state institutions (schools, etc.). Such trips were intended to instill visitors with the faith that the leaders had sacrificed many decades of their lives in the service of the Revolution, had purified themselves in the process, had become powerful enough to overcome a seemingly invincible opponent, and could be trusted also to overcome the tribulations of the "new society." Their purpose was furthermore to set up a model of rarefied behavior for the visitors that, if successfully imitated, would lead them to similar glory. In pre–Cultural Revolution China there seems to be little evidence that the visit to these museums was in itself considered to contribute to the "steeling and temper-ing" so necessary for the "revolutionary successors." It should be borne in mind, however, that a museum in general is separated from the triviality of everyday life, the evidence for which is less its formal structure than the formalized behavior of visitors, which is derived from that in a temple or a church. In the case of the new Chinese revolutionary museums, the guards rigidly enforced this behavior.

Second, the list of places accepted as belonging to the orthodox faith is set up by the Center, which also defines the hierarchy among these places with administrative means (terminology used for the different sites, volume of financing, and fixing of distances from which visits to these places can be organized by the units, ranks entitled to paid visits, level of reporting on the site [national, regional, local]). The list of accepted national places is less a positive list of such places than a shadow list of places excluded. Thus the various sites of worker action in the 1920s, the places associated with Sun Yat-sen, and the sites of soviet areas other than those in which Mao Tse-tung played the leading role, were not included.

Third, any major change in the power constellation of the Center will lead to a rewriting of revolutionary history, a redefining of the features of the ideal model, and a rearrangement of the hierarchy of memorial sites. Sadly, as my study focuses on the Mao Memorial Hall, I have not gone through the te-dious work of assembling all these sites, their change in status, and the (prob-able) growth of irregular sites not included in any official hierarchy but sup-ported by locals and by local officials. The list of national sites on the 1966 map eliminates a substantial number of other sites that at the time still had official status in the hierarchy, elevates a number of low-level places (Mao's birthplace, P'ing-hsing kuan) to the top rank of the hierarchy, and even in-cludes some completely new sites (Lu Shan). The role of the PRC state in the administration of the religious geography and in establishing the hierarchy of the places mirrors the role of the traditional Chinese state. Given the discre-tionary monopoly of the PRC state, the internal ruminations among the top leaders play a primordial role in the definition and reevaluation of the sites.

Fourth, the pilgrimage activities of the students, spontaneous as some of them might have been, were met by efforts from parts of the top leadership to direct their fervor and energy to purposes to the liking of these leaders. The various sites had all been present as dormant, potential pilgrimage sites. It can be presumed that they had not all been built directly after the founding of the PRC. Their establishment, definition, and exact status must have been decided at the highest levels as they involved important issues of Party his-tory. As can be seen from Mao's birthplace, new sites could spring up and perhaps become part of the hierarchy if they caught the proper wind. Shao-shan certainly received an economic boost from the millions of visitors and the railroad built during the Cultural Revolution to connect it to the main line. Through the rearrangement of the accepted sites and the public communication of the approved list through the maps in question, which were printed in large numbers, the Red Guard pilgrimage enterprise was instrumentalized for the very particular political interests of a few leaders. The most evident feature was Lin Piao's insertion of his own person into the hagiographic hierarchy, matched by the daily photographs in the papers showing him with the chairman and eventually the statement in the Party platform making him Mao's chosen successor.

From the crass and fairly well documented evidence of the interference of the Chinese top leadership into the pilgrimage process, we may infer that similar, albeit less pronounced, controversies have happened and still happen within church bodies that have to negotiate the status and orthodox acceptability of their pilgrimage sites and mediate these considerations with their own theological, political, or regional interests, an aspect hitherto hardly touched in pilgrimage studies.

It would certainly be exaggerating to maintain that traditional pilgrimage activities were spontaneous, while those of the socialist states were planned and ordained. The churches took and take an active role in steering and guiding the pilgrimage activity of their members and in trying to prevent them from leaving the narrowly circumscribed field of orthodoxy. Conversely, there were periods in some socialist states, China included, during which a substantial spontaneous outburst of revolutionary/religious fervor interacted very uneasily with state planning and orthodoxy. The breakdown of a unified system of control at the outset of the Cultural Revolution, when all sides in the Center began to go public and recruit irregular support from outside the Party hierarchy, greatly enlarged the leeway of the Red Guards. This lack of control is evident in their refusal, in early 1967, to abide by Chou En-lai's order to go home and resume normal activities, in their unabashed use of free travel privileges to pursue very personal (love, touristic) interests, in their refusal to abide by the official canon of thinking (i.e., Mao's *Selected Works*), in their printing hitherto unpublished texts and speeches by the chairman as additional sources for orthodox thinking, and in the flood of material published during this period outside the narrowly controlled traditional official channels. Such publication and dissemination of holy works hitherto withheld in the face of the powers that be is characteristic of many millennial movements both in China and abroad.

The early phase of the Cultural Revolution (even down into the early 1970s) is thus characterized by fever, contention, and turbulence in religious geography and its ideological underpinnings. Viktor Sklovskij quoted Boris Eikhenbaum as saying that "every text is written against the background of another" (Sklovskij 1966, 12). We will apply what follows from this observation for our reading of the Chairman Mao Memorial Hall (Mao Chu-hsi chi-nien t'ang 毛主席紀念堂). This building operates within the traditions and constraints outlined above and reacts to the specific turbulence prevailing in religious orthodoxy.

Frederic Wakeman has studied the hall in the context of other similar structures of both the imperial and revolutionary traditions, focusing on the question of the ownership and treatment of the body of the deceased (Wakeman 1988). Lothar Ledderose has studied the Washington, D.C., precedent for the spatial setting of the hall in Peking and the architectural antecedents for the integration of a tomb and a memorial hall in the history of Chinese architecture (Ledderose 1988). With the rear brought up in such fine manner, I can concentrate on more contemporary aspects of the hall while enjoying the privilege of vandalizing their information and argument wherever I see fit and adding to it wherever I can.

The sources used for this endeavor are nothing to boast of: the hitherto unused official record on the underlying symbolism of the Sun Yat-sen Memorial Hall from the Nanking archives ("Tsung-li feng-an shih-lu" 1930), a collection of documents relating to the Sun Yat-sen Mausoleum ("Nanching shih Chung-shan ling kuan-li ch'u" 1986), and a very detailed but undocumented description of the history of this mausoleum by Chou Tao-ch'un (1989); the detailed pictorial albums of the different memorial halls (Yao and Ku 1981; "Mao Chu-hsi chi-nien t'ang" 1978) including the rejected options in the case of the Mao Memorial Hall; the master plan for the intended symbolism of the Mao Memorial Hall in a Chinese architectural journal ("Mao Chu-hsi chi-nien t'ang tsung-t'i kuei-hua" 1977); and sundry articles in various newspapers. I have visited both memorial halls to determine how far the master plans present a post facto harmonization of diverse elements, but in most cases this determination could be made as well (or better) from the written and photographic record. In other words, the sources were strictly "historical." No living participant in the construction or pilgrimage use of the buildings was interviewed for this study; the implied pilgrim has thus not been confounded with the messiness of a real human being.

BURIAL OPTIONS

A monument does not grow, it is built. It is an intentional structure. In modern times, constraints imposed by building materials have been greatly reduced. Although the Mao Memorial Hall was built in an area that experiences frequent and often very strong earthquakes, and although the safety of Mao's remains were an important consideration, we may assume that the ensuing technical requirements had only a negligible impact on those features of the building visible to and perceived by a visitor. We are thus in the agreeable situation of being able to define the hall as a substantially pure intentional product operating within technical confines not exceeding the demands of grammar in a literary text. Thus we can trace every feature to an underlying purpose.

Methodologically, we can treat the building of the hall as the writing of a literary text. Frequently scholars will have at their disposal the various plans and drafts for a novel. While the final text might proceed in a different way, these documents conserve the text's rejected options, which in turn highlight the particular features of the options actually realized. We are in the happy situation of having similar drafts and plans for the Mao Memorial Hall ("Mao Chu-hsi chi-nien t'ang chien-chu she-chi" 1977) to which Ledderose first drew attention in a talk in Berlin in 1980. As a building typically is a silent text, knowledge of the rejected options will help us to articulate and document the intentional features of the final product.

The Mao Memorial Hall was planned and construction begun after Mao Tse-tung's death in September 1976; it was finished in August 1977. Mao's successor was Hua Kuo-feng, a man whose legitimacy in handling the precious remains was hotly contested on the one side by Mao's widow, Chiang Ch'ing, and on the other by Teng Hsiao-p'ing. Although Teng had been dismissed from all offices in April 1976 after the big demonstrations on T'ien-an-men Square in the wake of Premier Chou En-lai's death (when hundreds of thousands of people, disenchanted with Mao's close ideological and marital relationship with the Gang of Four, had gathered in the square to deposit their wreaths for Chou at the Heroes' Monument), his star was again rapidly rising subsequent to Mao's demise.

The Chairman Mao Memorial Hall was thus built, and built in Peking. Standing in T'ien-an-men Square as it does, the hall rejects a number of other options for handling the remains of Mao Tse-tung. Only against the adumbration of these unbuilt buildings can many of the specific features of the hall become visible.

In terms of location and treatment, the first rejected option was not to build a hall and to cremate the body. It had been a rule since the 1950s, when, after Stalin's death, the "cult of personality" was criticized, that bodies of Communist leaders were to be cremated, a rule applied to Premier Chou En-lai and Marshal Chu Te, both of whom belonged to the same generation of revolutionary leaders as Mao and who had died a few months before Mao in 1976 (Fallaci 1980). The leaders, Mao included, had signed such an agreement. The very concept of building the hall thus rested on the unspoken argument that a qualitative difference remained between Mao and the other leaders.

Early socialist theoreticians like Marx had rejected the then prevalent view of Thomas Carlyle in *On Heroes and Hero Worship*, according to which history was made by giants. In this view, the very individuality and particularity of such heroes would be decisive, and thus the preservation and public exhibition of their physical remains had some logic. Plekhanov eventually made the theory acceptable in socialist circles by arguing in his "On the Role of the Individual in History" that the individual would indeed play a decisive role in history if he or she embodied the best aspirations of all progressive classes (Plekhanov 1940). Given the obvious importance of personal traits and preferences of leaders like Lenin and Stalin in the Communist movement, this argument found some echo in the real world, thus making Plekhanov's theory acceptable independent of his objections to Lenin's policies in 1917. Lenin's remains were preserved and exhibited in the Lenin Mausoleum on Red Square in Moscow after his death in 1921. Sun Yat-sen (d. 1924), who considered himself the "Lenin of the East," specifically requested in his written and verbal testaments that he, like Lenin, be exhibited in a crystal coffin at the site he had selected near Nanking. The plan came to naught because the corpse was exposed to air and deteriorated when it was temporarily removed from the Pai-yun Temple 白雲寺 in Peking by the guards who tried to protect it from threatened destruction by an underling of warlord Chang Tso-ling (Chou 1989, 43, 93). The physical remains were finally enshrined in the Sun Chung-shan Mausoleum outside Nanking. Ho Chi Minh, who had died in 1969, had explicitly requested to be cremated, but the Politburo overruled his testament and had him embalmed and exhibited in a crystal coffin. In this context a cremation of Mao could be read as a statement that he was inferior to Lenin as a theoretician, to Sun Yat-sen as a politician, and to Ho Chi Minh as a revolutionary. Preserving the remains and building the hall would make Mao take up the challenge on all three levels. It would imply that he added to Lenin by providing a theory for class struggle under socialism; achieved for China what Sun had aspired to, a successful revolution; and showed the way to world revolution in third-world countries.

The second rejected option was to return the body to Mao's native place in Shao-shan to be taken care of by the family. As Wakeman has pointed out, however, Mao's "family" was politically in no position to claim the body (Wakeman 1988, 263). His last wife, Chiang Ch'ing, had been dismissed from the Politburo and incarcerated as a political criminal only a few weeks after Mao's death. Mao's nephew Mao Yuan-hsin, who had been with his uncle most of the time during the latter's last months, was relieved of his post as first secretary of Liao-ning province and arrested shortly thereafter. This dilemma was not new. Lenin's wife, Krupskaya, was a constant threat to Stalin's claim to the succession, as manifested in the supervision of the burial ceremonies and the later handling of Lenin's remains. Sun Yat-sen's wife, Soong Ch'ing-ling, had publicly denounced the Kuomintang leadership after the 1927 falling-out with the Communists. She threatened not to take part in the grand ceremonies in June 1929, when Sun's remains were enshrined in Nanking. She eventually took part after having publicly repeated her denunciation of the Kuomintang leadership and having been reelected to the

Kuomintang Central Committee in spite of it. By then Chiang Kai-shek had taken control of the committee handling the ceremonies, and he not she (or Sun's son Sun K'o) went for the last farewell into the burial chamber "representing the family, the party, and the state," the two others being the Dutch dean of the diplomatic corps and Inukai Tsuyoshi 犬養毅, a Japanese friend of Sun's (Chou 1989, 123).

The third rejected option, an option that was in fact among the proposals submitted after Mao's death, was to build a *ling-mu* 陵墓, an architectural ensemble with the tomb, in the hills outside Peking. Since the T'ang dynasty (seventh to ninth century) this form of "mountain mausoleum" *shan-ling* 山陵) had gradually become the custom for the imperial family (as opposed to the mounds erected during the Ch'in and Han). These mountain mausoleums were in the vicinity of the capital and were thus, in the geography of the imaginary, "central" (Lo 1984, 8; Yang 1985, 163). They were situated on a north-south slope with the imperial face looking south. A "way of the spirit" (*shen-tao* 神道) flanked by stone sculptures of officials and animals in mourning position led up to such mausoleums (Yang 1985, 144f). The remains were enshrined at the highest point of the *shen-tao*. As Ledderose points out, the reconstruction of Empress Wu Tse-t'ien's mausoleum near modern Sian shows that there was a ceremonial hall in front of the burial chamber (Ledderose 1988, 330).

To take this option would at best have put Mao into the tradition of the Ming emperors buried near Peking. Their most important paragon, however, the founder of the Ming Chu Yuan-chang 朱元璋, was buried in the Ming Hsiao-ling 明孝陵 on Tzu-chin Mountain 紫金山 outside Nanking, preceded there by the third-century founder of the state of Wu, Sun Ch'üan 孫權. Since one famous corpse attracts another, men who deemed themselves or were deemed by others to be important enough to be so elevated and whose ideals echoed with Ming (as opposed to "foreign") rule were entombed on Tzu-chin Mountain. Sun Yat-sen had chosen his own enshrinement site to be near Chu Yuan-chang's. When the Ch'ing dynasty abdicated, Sun had gone to this site to inform the spirit of the deceased Ming emperor of this momentous event (Chou 1989, 44). As Sun's merits were considered superior even to Chu Yuan-chang's, his mausoleum was situated higher up the slope. His mausoleum consists of a *shen-tao* leading from south to north where the stone carvings of officials have been replaced by trees, a ritual hall with his south-facing statue in the middle and his political program written on the wall, and a burial chamber.

Wang Ching-wei, who had broken with Chiang Kai-shek and set up in Nanking a government that cooperated with the Japanese, had himself embalmed and enshrined in 1944 in a mausoleum modeled on Sun's next to that of his mentor to assert his ongoing loyalty to Sun and to claim the legitimacy of the succession. He had the place renamed Plum Blossom Mountain

(Mei-hua Shan 梅花山) for a flattering echo of Plum Blossom Hill (Mei-hua Ling 梅花嶺), the place where Shih K'o-fa 史可法, the Ming dynasty general who fought the Manchu armies, was buried. But not even the allusive environment and the steel-reinforced concrete of his edifice could prevent victorious Chiang Kai-shek from having blown up and flattened to the ground in January 1946 the structure embodying Wang Ching-wei's claim to superiority and immortality and from having Wang's "flesh body" (mummified corpse) reduced to cinders (Chou 1989, 315 f.).

Chiang Kai-shek in turn selected a site for his own burial on the same slope, higher than that of Chu Yuan-chang, to whom he felt superior, but below the level of Sun's Memorial Hall. Chiang even included Tai Li 戴笠, the head of his secret police, in the category of supermen and heroes, allotting him a tomb on the same mountain (Chou 1989, 324).

Peking did not provide as rich and enticing a metaphoric environment as Nanking. The emperors buried there were Manchu or those Ming emperors like the Chia-ching emperor to whom historical dramas of the Great Leap period had satirically compared Mao (Wagner 1990, 264). The notion of a new central leadership under the unified Maoist guidance of Chairman Hua Kuo-feng furthermore had to be expressed with all the unity the country could muster. Finally, Peking with the new chairman had to establish its claim to primary position on the nation's religious map. The rejection of the mountain mausoleum option with its link to Sun Yat-sen and the imperial past and the acceptance against evident objections at all levels of society of a "grand and lasting contribution" made by Mao shows that the planners and political leaders operated under considerable environmental stress.

To reject cremation had evidently been hardest, not only because it meant rejecting revolutionary precedent—Chou En-lai had been cremated—but also because cremation gave Party leaders who objected to Mao's actions during the last decade or more of his life legitimate arguments for not building a memorial hall. A decision not to build also would have put Mao on a clearly lower level than Lenin.

The pilgrimages of the Cultural Revolution led to Peking not because the city boasted holy sites from the history of the Revolution—there were none—but because the chairman himself resided there and received them in the public mass rallies. With Mao's death in 1976 the administrative center was in danger of losing its standing at the top of the religious hierarchy. The building of the hall with the body of the chairman enshrined there kept intact the hierarchy that had made Peking the center during the Cultural Revolution. The chairman would continue to receive the pilgrims visiting the capital.

The building of the hall was intended to reestablish the hierarchy of religious sites. By the time of Lin Piao's death in 1971, some sites printed in the

1966 map had fallen into disrepute. With the reestablishment of the Center came the authorized redefinition of the other sites.

The hall was built under the new chairman's personal guidance. The decision to build the hall, the basic guidelines according to which plans were to be developed, the selection of the eventual design down to decisions about particular ornaments or symbols to be used were all in the hands of a committee chaired by Hua Kuo-feng, the highest state and Party authority in 1976 and 1977. True, once decisions had been made, people from all walks of life and from all regions of China were given roles in the execution of the plans, but the enterprise left them no room for expressing their own feelings and attitudes toward the deceased; they simply fulfilled their assigned tasks. This massive reassertion of the "unified leadership of the Party" under the new chairman came in reaction to and rejection of the highly irregular mourning activities that had followed the death of Chou En-lai. After that incident, Teng Hsiao-p'ing was dismissed as the instigator of the troubles; instead, Mao elevated Hua Kuo-feng to be his successor and to be prime minister. At the time of the building of the hall those activities, which had taken place on the very site where the Memorial Hall was being built on T'ien-an-men Square, still ranked as "counterrevolutionary." The rigorously centralized and supervised planning of the Memorial Hall for Mao under Hua Kuo-feng's guidance thus was intended to undo the pollution of the square caused by the turbulence and spontaneity of the 1976 T'ien-an-men Incident in form and the Chou En-lai option in content. Events in June 1989 certainly highlight the dimensions any action on T'ien-an-men takes on in the *imaginaire* of society (Wagner 1991).

The Memorial Hall reasserts central control over the religious geography and ritual in the same manner as the fifth volume of Mao's *Selected Works*, which was edited by Hua Kuo-feng in 1977 during the building of the hall, undid the irregular publication activities of the Cultural Revolution (Mao 1977). In fact, house-to-house collections of such irregular material were made throughout the country to reestablish the unity between centrally accepted and privately held material.

The placement of the hall stressed the centrality that Mao Tse-tung Thought was to have for China, while the direct guidance by the new chairman stressed the direct transfer of legitimate power to Hua Kuo-feng. Hua made the intentions clear when he said on October 9, 1977, at the inauguration ceremony for the building:

> We definitely have to hold on to the grand banner of Chairman Mao and have to make this a cherished tradition handed down from one generation to the next. To situate the Chairman Mao Memorial Hall on T'ien-an-men Square is the grand and lofty symbol of this firm resolution and holy oath of ours. (Hua 1978, 13)

The square on which the Memorial Hall was built was cleared only during the 1950s, after the founding of the PRC. In a symbolical imitation of Red Square outside the Kremlin in Moscow, T'ien-an-men was set up as the sacred center, the heart of the nation. The language of Chinese tourist guides gives an idea of its meaning. A 1957 guide to Peking writes about the ensemble of T'ien-an Gate and the square:

> T'ien-an-men is known to us all. Its beautiful features form an important part of our state emblem. People turn to T'ien-an-men and see it as the people's Great Dipper [guiding star]. The people of the entire world are very familiar with T'ien-an-men; T'ien-an-men symbolizes magnificent new China. (*Peiching yu-lan shou-ts'e* 1957, 13)

Independent of the directional aspects of the imperial axis discussed below, this square figures in the *imaginaire* of modern Chinese geography as the center of Peking, which is in the same universe the center of the nation. Stamps, embroidered emblems of the nation, posters, and money carry the symbol of T'ien-an gate and the square. The Memorial Hall was designed to form the "center of the square" (again in a symbolic way), and this orgy of centrality was continued throughout the building's structure (map 9.1). The room where Mao's remains were to be enshrined is the symbolic center of the Memorial Hall; in the symbolic center of the room would be Mao's remains; and on the center of Mao's remains would lie the Communist flag, in the center of which is the Communist symbol, the hammer and sickle. Centrality is the structural principle of the entire edifice.

Other Chinese leaders had chosen other symbolic devices for their remains. Chou En-lai had his ashes dispersed on Huang Shan, a mountain that, as McDermott has shown, became an icon for the "fatherland" in Yuan times (McDermott 1989, 174). The action tried to express that he had spent his life in the service of the country and the people and would eternally be part of the nation's metabolism.

The Chairman Mao Memorial Hall was to be a memorial hall. This statement might seem tautological. Lenin, however, is in the Lenin Mausoleum, and the *ling-mu* (mausoleum) had been the standard form for dealing with the remains of Chinese emperors. Even within this old form, however, a new practice had emerged: the emperors had been embalmed and entombed; the revolutionaries were embalmed and exhibited. The combined form of a mountain mausoleum with a (planned) crystal coffin became the model for Sun Yat-sen's *ling-mu*.[4]

But as the report on the planning of the hall published in late 1977 said:

> The leading comrade called everyone's attention to the necessity of drawing a clear demarcation line between [the Mao Memorial Hall] and the mausoleums of the ruling class. The ruling class and the people have an antagonistic relationship. In their mausoleums [the ruling class] still want to manifest that they

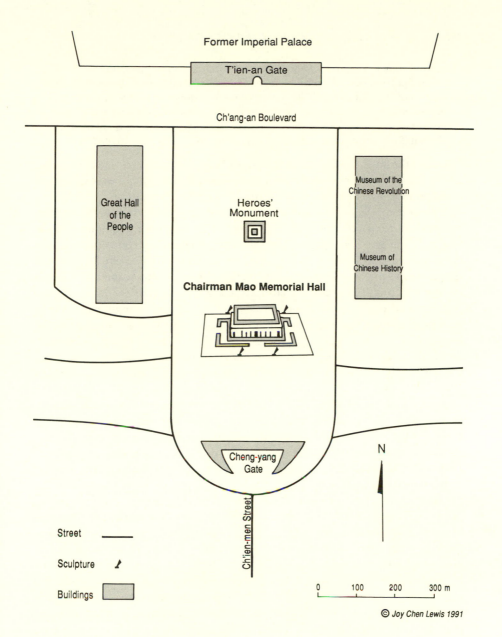

Map 9.1. T'ien-an-men Square, Peking

are the rulers. Therefore the foreign pyramids as well as the Chinese under-
ground palaces leave people with a gloomy and stifling feeling. Through incessant study it gradually dawned on us: we were to design a memorial hall, not a
mausoleum; we were [furthermore] to design a memorial hall for the commemoration of a leader and guide of the revolutionary people, and not a memorial hall for some common celebrity. (*Mao Chu-hsi chi-nien t'ang* 1978, 31 ff.)

Given the solid precedents of Lenin and Sun Yat-sen, this statement cannot well contain the real motive. It marks, however, the qualitative difference
between Mao and "common celebrities" in Carlyle's tradition.

The decision to build a memorial hall was not reached until early October, that is, after the four members of the Politburo then denounced as the
Gang of Four had been jailed. Given their previous strong control over publicized opinion and Chiang Ch'ing's evident claim to Mao's body and written
remains, one might surmise that the original plan as envisioned by Chiang
Ch'ing and her group had indeed been a *ling-mu* and that the many *ling-mu*
plans reproduced later were not freak products of some architect's fantasy.
An authoritative report indicates that Hua Kuo-feng, Wang Tung-hsing (the
head of the security guard for the Central Committee), Wang Hung-wen,
and Chang Ch'un-ch'iao (Politburo members closely associated with Chiang
Ch'ing) were involved in the planning of what to do with Mao's remains
(Fan 1990, 230).

A *ling-mu* in the mountains would enshrine Mao in an elevated but terminal and tangential position. The architect of Sun Yat-sen's mausoleum had
tried to overcome the terminality of Sun's death by giving the ground plan
for the mausoleum the shape of a liberty bell ("Tsung-li feng-an shih-lu"
1930, 40; Ch'i 1930; Chou 1989, 54; fig. 9.1), and the Kuomintang leaders
decided that the message it would send into the world—Sun's appeal on the
occasion of the founding of the state—would be written onto the walls inside
(as in the Lincoln Memorial). But in the view of the Communist leaders, this
attempt to overcome the limits of death by symbolic means had already
failed by the mausoleum's inauguration under Chiang Kai-shek's supervision and chairmanship. A mausoleum in the center of Peking (like Lenin's
in Moscow), however, would be too closely linked to Chiang Ch'ing, too
gloomy, and not specific enough in its political message (see *Chien-chu hsueh-
pao* 1977, no. 4 p. 26, for illustrations of options). It dealt neither with the
past nor with its slightly more fickle brother, the future.

Mao was to stay alive in the very center, embedded into the one and only
authoritative and truthful interpretation, to prop up the status of his handpicked successor and his political line. The result was to be a new type of
building combining the features of a *ling-mu* with those of a memorial hall
and making the Chairman Mao Memorial Hall the "eternal" public manifestation of the new orthodoxy as envisaged by Hua Kuo-feng. Rejecting the

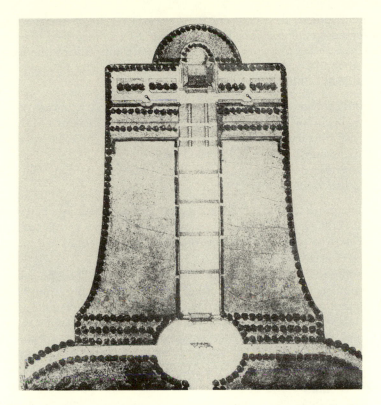

Fig. 9.1. Aerial view of plan for the Sun Yat-sen Mausoleum in the shape of a liberty bell. From Ch'i Kung-heng, *Chung-shan ling-yuan ta-kuan* (Shanghai, 1930).

pure *ling-mu* option also dealt a nice blow to the "feudal" thinking of Chiang Ch'ing.

As Hua was the successor handpicked by Mao himself, it was important that Mao's physical remains stay present as a reminder of his choice. The new orthodoxy would be enshrined in the building. The politics encoded in the overall setting of the Memorial Hall down to its smallest ornaments would then eternally link a particular interpretation of Mao's heritage with the flesh of his authentic body. The hall would become the center to which people from all over the land would make their organized pilgrimages to receive in a solemn and dignified atmosphere in symbolic form the orthodox teaching about Mao's glorious and successful past, the legitimacy of his successor, and a vision for the future, all authenticated by the presence of his physical remains. At the same time, that presence in this solemn environ-

ment would spur on their determination to carry out his bequests with revolutionary determination. The joint editorial of the newspapers *Jen-min jih-
pao* and *Kuang-ming jih-pao* in early October 1976 introducing the Center's
decision to build a memorial hall spelled this out. The Chairman Mao
Memorial Hall would be built

> to permit one generation after the other of the people's masses to rever-
> ently behold with their own eyes the remains of Chairman Mao,
> to cherish the memory of Chairman Mao's magnificent achievements,
> to study again Chairman Mao's teachings,
> and to inspire their [i.e., the masses'] revolutionary fighting will. ("Mao
> Chu-hsi chi-nien-t'ang" 1978, 2)

This statement made the "guiding thought for the planning of the [Mao]
Memorial Hall" clear to the architects, who were to come up with designs to
evoke the desired responses from visitors, and they proceeded to develop the
hall as it was eventually built.

Cherishing the memory of Mao's achievements referred to the past wars:
the Communists had emerged victorious after the civil war of the 1930s, the
anti-Japanese war, and the subsequent second civil war of the 1940s. To
study Mao's teachings again referred to the theoretical principles on which
these victories as well as the founding and construction of the socialist state
after 1949 were supposed to have relied and which should guide the future.

The inspiration mentioned in the last section refers to the application of
the lessons of the two first parts in the post-Mao future. Mao's teachings had
led to great achievements, and future successes would depend on strictly
following the directives he had given. The confidence inspired by these experiences would help the pilgrims upon their return to fight the various gob-
lins and monsters of heterodoxy and give them, at least in their own mind,
the standing and legitimacy to do so. They had seen the chairman and received authentic orders.

Of course, I am not talking here about the actual social process of the
pilgrimage to the Memorial Hall and the actual effects it had or might have
had on the pilgrims. I am dealing here with the implied pilgrim, a product of
fantasy as different from the actual pilgrim as the implied reader is from
someone actually leafing through a book.

The Chairman Mao Memorial Hall is built on the imperial axis, thus
establishing a continuity with the imperial tradition. In an important break
with tradition, however, the hall faces north. The original axis is directional,
going from north to south. The emperor looked south as did the main statues
in Chinese temples, which are also aligned on a north-south axis. The Communist government inherited the institutional position of the emperor. When
Mao proclaimed the founding of the PRC, for instance, he stood on T'ien-an
Gate facing south, where "the people" had assembled on the square. During

the big ceremonies of the PRC to this day, the leadership assembles on T'ien-an Gate facing south. The people gathering on T'ien-an-men Square in 1976 and 1989 challenged the government whose place in the imaginary constitution of the state was on T'ien-an Gate and beyond, in the imperial palace.

This Memorial Hall is not the first Communist building to face the "wrong" way. In connection with the ceremonies of the founding of the PRC in 1949, it was decided to erect a Stele in Commemoration of the People's Heroes (*Jen-min ying-hsiung chi-nien pei* 人民英雄紀念碑) on the imperial axis (the stele was finished only in 1958). The inscription, written by Mao himself, reads, "The people's heroes will be eternally handed to posterity without decaying," meaning that these heroes will live on forever in memory. The "heroes" are not just the Communist revolutionaries, but the "people's heroes," all those who had sacrificed their lives for the revolution between 1840 and 1949. Mao's inscription gives the stele a direction. It faces north and breaks the southward direction of the imperial axis. It is thus stripped of its imperial connotations, while still symbolizing grand national importance.

At the time of the founding of the PRC, one consideration in planting the stele on the axis might have been the symbolism that it breaks and stops the imperial ruling perspective in the same manner as the "people's heroes" had broken the imperial powers. However, already in 1949 the emperors had faded into memory, and they certainly were not sitting in audience thereafter. The people actually standing on T'ien-an Gate were the new lords of the country. They, not the old emperors in their coffins, faced the inscription. The monument and its inscription mark a commitment by the leadership to the "people's heroes." At the same time, the inscription is a challenge spelled out by Mao Tse-tung, who had ordered the northward orientation. The memory of these heroes of the people will stay alive, and the leaders assembled on T'ien-an Gate, who might be less immortal than these heroes, have to live up to the high standards and expectations expressed through and on the stele. By means of the monument and its inscription the chairman, who laid claim to having fulfilled the aspirations of these heroes, challenges his colleagues to follow his guidance. On those occasions when the stele could utter its admonitions, that is, when the leaders were assembled on T'ian-an Gate, the masses of the people were also congregating around the stele. This adds a fine twist, identifying the heroes commemorated on the stele as the best among the "people" (*jen-min* 人民) assembled on the square and insinuating that Mao's own words and orders represented the interests and aspirations not only of the dead but also of the living. It is a remonstrative stele, coming to life on the grand occasions when the leaders face the people. A rendering of all its implications would read: "The people's heroes will forever live on in memory long after you are dead! What have you done to live up to their aspirations?" The inscription is written by a leader who felt that he had been opposed in every one of his strategic suggestions by a major-

ity or near majority of his colleagues and felt vindicated by his eventual
victory to ask for more allegiance.

Standing behind the monument to the south, the Chairman Mao Memorial Hall was also to face the leaders on T'ien-an Gate. When translated into
an evaluation of the relative importance of the "people's heroes" and Mao for
the success of the revolution, the proportions between the stele and the hall
attest to Carlylean views. The building receives its own directionality from
something hidden from view but present in the mind, the large statue of Mao
Tse-tung sitting in the entrance hall of the building. The statue faces north,
again breaking the north-south flow along the axis and invisibly confronting
and challenging the assembled south-facing leadership.

The final report on the building in 1977 says about the role of the hall
during the mass rallies:

> There is a free space thirty to seventy meters wide around the gardens of the
> Memorial Hall that could be used to enlarge the capacity of the square, which
> otherwise would hold between 400,000 and 600,000 people, so that on the occa-
> sion of grand political rallies the Chairman Mao Memorial Hall would be sur-
> rounded by the broad masses. This would give expression to the theme that
> Chairman Mao is among the masses and that Chairman Mao forever lives in
> our hearts. ("Mao Chu-hsi chi-nien-t'ang tsung-t'i kuei-hua" 1977, 4)

Inside the Memorial Hall, the remains of Mao Tse-tung were to lie under
the inscription "Our Great Leader and Guide Chairman Mao Tse-tung will
live forever in our memory," the formula *yung-ch'ui pu-hsiu* 永垂不朽 (be
handed down forever without decaying) being the same as on Mao's inscription for the people's heroes' monument outside. This inscription also faces
north. Thus the hall duplicates the stele in axis, direction, content, and challenge; the live leaders now face the dead heroes and their dead leader, both of
which are on the axis of national importance in the midst of the masses of the
people, challenging the leadership's Maoist credentials and its adherence to
the "fast determination and holy oath" to follow Mao's directives that Hua
Kuo-feng had spelled out with none other than Teng Hsiao-p'ing sitting by
his side.

The inscription "Chairman Mao Memorial Hall" over the north-facing
entrance was written by Hua Kuo-feng in a replica of Mao's writing on the
heroes' stele. By the time the Memorial Hall was finished, however, Hua
Kuo-feng's star was waning. He had lost his usefulness to the military leaders
who in 1976 had staged the coup that removed Mao's widow and who
wanted one of their own, Teng Hsiao-p'ing, to run affairs. As Hua Kuo-feng,
however, was in control of the planning and construction of the hall (as well
as of the publication of the fifth volume of Mao's *Selected Works*), he had an
opportunity to install a lasting and defiant Maoist challenge in the heart of
the heart of the nation, much as Mao himself had done with the stele in 1949.

Ledderose has convincingly argued that the alignment of the stele and the Memorial Hall is modeled on the arrangement in Washington, D.C., of the Washington Monument and the Lincoln Memorial. The front of the latter furthermore provided an architectural model for the facade of the Chairman Mao Memorial Hall, and the inside with the statue of Lincoln sitting in his chair was the precedent for the entrance hall of the Mao Memorial with its statue of Mao.

One might go a step further. The Washington axis includes a third component, the Capitol, where the Senate and House of Representatives meet. In this context, the Washington Monument and the Lincoln Memorial assume a similar function to the stele and the Mao Memorial in Peking. They stand there as a double reminder to Congress: to keep in mind the freedom of the new nation, liberated from colonial domination (Washington Monument), and to maintain the commitment to equality of all citizens symbolized by Lincoln and the text written on the wall inside the Lincoln Memorial. The two monuments in Washington, D.C., thus share the remonstrative purpose of their Chinese equivalents, the only difference being in the addressee. In the United States, it is Congress; in China, the top leadership of the Center. This rearrangement certainly implies a realistic if modest assessment of the role of the National People's Congress in Peking.

The actual construction of the Memorial Hall was organized to enhance its symbolic importance. The materials were brought from all over the country, and in particular from areas loaded with sacred memories; the workers engaged in the building also came from all over the country to symbolize the great unity of the people in their exuberant love for the deceased chairman and devotion to his chosen successor. Organizationally, the entire process was a picture-perfect illustration of democratic centralism, which does operate quite well as long as no financial considerations enter the fray.

The year-long bustle of tens of thousands of people building the hall in the nation's center tried to undo the 1976 T'ien-an-men Incident, which had polluted not only the holy space and the structures of the state, but also the pedigree upon which rested the new chairman, who owed his promotion to this very incident. It engaged in a silent contest with the Kuomintang, who had tried to build the Sun Yat-sen Mausoleum in one year, but in fact needed four. And it was a race against time, as Hua Kuo-feng's days were numbered.

THE IMPLIED PILGRIM

It is time now to enter the building. We have used methods of analyzing the genesis of a literary text in order to explore the development of the Memorial Hall. We now proceed to study the building as it stands. It is designed as a building through which the pilgrims pass on a prescribed itinerary. Consequently, it is a building with a time structure, where one element after another confronts the pilgrim in a predetermined order. This is quite unusual, as most religious buildings do not have such a strong time structure. A pilgrim going to a Buddhist temple, for example, would enter through the south gate and be expected to make his devotions first in front of the main statue. He would then be free to wander around the halls on the sides. (Convention, however, did control the sequence at least somewhat.) The planners of the Mao Memorial Hall took complete control of the pilgrims' way. They could and did try to calculate and anticipate the effects of the various stations on their pilgrims. Although from a divine, or an architect's, perspective, all elements of the building are present simultaneously, they are dissolved for the implied pilgrim into a sequential order.

A novel shares this structure. As a finished product, it is present in its entirety, beginning and end simultaneously. But the reader is forced to wander through its narrow lines over time to get to the end. This is no awkward clumsiness on the part of the reader, but the way of handling a novel. Its time structure is essential, not accidental. The reader, with experience from other novels, from history, from life, at any given moment may try to anticipate what will happen next or in the end. The writer has some competition in the reader, an interlocutor. But because he is in control of the text, he can play with the reader's anticipation, fool him, mislead him, or otherwise vent his rage upon the reader's unruly fantasies. Some writers, like Fielding, go about this play quite openly. Literary scholarship refers to the phantom whom the writer installs as his reader and manipulates in this manner as the implied reader (Iser 1978).

The implied reader is no relation to any real reader, the latter having considerably more freedom. He may skip pages, fall asleep, drift off on a tangent, or throw the book away. As far as the discipline of reading line for line goes, the implied reader is the writer's victim, plaything, and slave. As the design of the Memorial Hall was not experimentally tested for effects on any real pilgrims, we will analyze the implied pilgrim of the Chairman Mao Memorial Hall. The main source for this is the report of the planning of the hall ("Mao Chu-hsi chi-nien-t'ang tsung-t'i kuei-hua" 1977). While this report is invaluable for its keys to the symbolical meaning of many features, it ignores the political controversies raging around the heritage of Mao in 1977. The report thus has to be checked against the available photographic evidence and supplemented by detailed studies of the ideological implications of the structural and ornamental features of the building. As the planners had to communicate with their pilgrims on the basis of known symbols, the building is and has to be readable without the report mentioned above. But it certainly helps if we are spared some of the labors of identifying the symbolic meaning, the place of origin, and the historical associations attached to this place by each of its elements. With regard to historical studies of pilgrimage sites for which this type of documentation is not readily available, this means that with a much higher investment of labor similarly detailed results could be obtained as for the Mao Memorial Hall.

Evidently, the implied pilgrim of the Memorial Hall is altogether different from the frivolous eighteenth-century reader in Fielding's mind. The implied pilgrim's attitude is one of belief, obedience, and affirmation. He will not come with a hostile glance, but will come to be overwhelmed, to be strengthened in his beliefs, and to be confronted with a power far beyond his own measure, a power that might well be beyond the traditional notions of good and evil. His knowledge about holy matters might be narrow, but it is calculable. It consists of the standard lore of notions and texts handed out during the Cultural Revolution. He is supposed to know the decisive moments in Party history, Mao's poems and the occasion for which they were written, the *Quotations from Chairman Mao* and the *lao san p'ien*, and perhaps some more. Armed with this knowledge, he will be able to decode the various symbols and come up with the proper response.

He will be attuned to the experience long before he enters the hall. No bicycles are allowed on T'ien-an-men Square. A green belt separates the hall from the surrounding area. Clothing is to be formal, marking the exceptional situation; visitors are to form long lines in twos; their handbags have to be checked in. They are expected to stay in line and to keep the exact speed of the others. The guardians keep rigid order, constantly exhorting the visitors with hard voices to stay in line, to move on. There is no milling around as there was during the 1976 T'ien-an-men Incident. In this collective shuffle, no personal emotions are encouraged, or possible. No one is to attach a handwritten poem to the chairman's statue, no one to deposit a wreath, light an incense stick, or throw a tantrum. "Superstitious practices" are as strictly outlawed as they had been at the Sun Yat-sen Mausoleum ("Tsung-li feng-an shih-lu" 1930, 14a; "K'o-ling kuei-tse" 415). The entire scene is the antithesis of the frenzy of Mao worship during the Cultural Revolution. It is an exercise in the imposed and accepted discipline of awe.

The itinerary of the pilgrim is a march through space/time, designed to achieve the same purification as the entire Long March of the Chinese revolution and its imitations during the Cultural Revolution were said to achieve. The vast physical spaces of the revolution shrink to some 250 meters, and its decades to some fifteen minutes.

The pilgrim enters the compound passing between two sculptures that mark his way as the *shen-tao* of the mausoleums. The first sculpture, outside the building to the east, sings the praise of "Chairman Mao's militant practice during the period of the democratic revolution, representing figures from the peasant movement, the Long March, the Anti-Japanese War, and the liberation struggle [or civil war]" ("Mao Chu-hsi chi-nien-t'ang tsung-t'i kuei-hua" 1977, 12)—in short, showing what the resolution on building the Memorial Hall called "the grand achievements of Chairman Mao."

The second sculpture, to the west, is on the next theme of this resolution, "study again the teachings of Chairman Mao." It deals with the "revolutionary practice of Chairman Mao during the period of the socialist revolution, and has sculptures about [the oil field] Ta-ch'ing, [the model brigade] Ta-chai, and the Great Proletarian Cultural Revolution [in the form of a Red Guard girl and the worker/peasant/soldier alliance in the front]" ("Mao Chu-hsi chi-nien-t'ang tsung-t'i kuei-hua" 1977, 12). The two sculptures technically stand at the same point in time in the itinerary of the pilgrim, but they are to be looked at in sequence so that they follow each other in terms of perception/time. There is an important difference between them. The "grand achievements" of the pre-1949 phase are to be remembered, but the teachings of this period do not seem to be of great relevance for the present. None of the figures in this sculpture carries Mao's works, although his image hovers above them. During this period, Mao still led them in person. The second sculpture, however, deals only with the post-1949 period. The symbolic progress is led by three persons representing the worker/peasant/soldier alliance. The worker, who as the "proletarian" stands in the middle and leading position, holds up one volume of Mao's works. The content of this volume must be Mao's teaching for the socialist period. And when the building was completed, there was indeed one such volume, the fifth volume of Mao's *Selected Works*, edited in 1977 by Hua Kuo-feng and containing only texts written after 1949. The other four volumes are historical matter. This fifth volume, the pilgrim is to understand, is the only book to be "studied again," for only it is relevant to the present.

The fifth volume of Mao's works comprises the symbolic lore of this second and most relevant stage of the revolution: the two big units of industrial advance and rural collectivization praised during the Cultural Revolution and set up as models, Ta-ch'ing and Ta-chai (Hua Kuo-feng had chaired the first Learning from Ta-chai Conference in September 1975 and given his first big speech there); the worker/peasant/soldier alliance which supposedly ruled the country through the revolutionary committees set up at all levels from the provincial leadership down; and the Red Guards. These all are enshrined here as Mao Tse-tung's essential teachings on socialism.

The pilgrims go through the hall and leave it at the other side, passing out into T'ien-an-men Square through two more sculptures. By way of simple symmetry, they must deal with the remaining part of the directive, namely, to "inspire revolutionary fighting spirit." Having learned the lessons from the sculptures at the entrance, the leading characters on both sides of the way at the exit of the compound each carries one volume of Mao's works—namely, the fifth—to lead the crowd into the future. Mao can no longer lead in person; his image is absent from both sculptures.

These are united-front sculptures with "workers, peasants and soldiers, minorities, revolutionary cadres as well as intellectuals and young people," as the official report says ("Mao Chu-hsi chi-nien-t'ang tsung-t'i kuei-hua" 1977, 12). The grammatical break after "cadres" indicates a status break: the intellectuals and young people do not qualify for leadership positions, but they are included in the united front. The two sculptures march off into the future with much forward urge and gesture, the latter leading the pilgrim's eye up to an inscription fastened onto the building standing to the south of the Memorial Hall, namely Cheng-yang Gate. The inscription reads: "Carry Out Chairman Mao's Behests, and Carry the Cause of the Proletarian Revolution Through to the End." The only thing to hold on to is Chairman Mao's "behests" as laid down in the fifth volume.

The time structure of a mausoleum is terminal. The pilgrim advances to the last and highest point, where the body is enshrined, and then returns the way he came from this excursion into the realm of the dead and immortal back to the realm of the living and mortal. The Chairman Mao Memorial Hall, in contrast, has a transitional time structure from the past to the future. In the interstice between the two, the eternal present, Mao is forever enshrined. This time structure and its implications mark the difference between the *ling-mu* concept and that of the Mao Memorial Hall.

The sculptures and the inscription in the south talk back to a silent but public interlocutor who argues that things change and Mao's behests are a matter of another time. The 1977/78 public controversy between the "Whatever Faction," the *fan-shih p'ai* 凡是派, chaired by Wang Tung-hsing and supported by Hua Kuo-feng, a faction that was supposed to argue that one should follow Chairman Mao's behests in "whatever" came along, and the faction around Teng Hsiao-p'ing, which maintained that a new period had come when not all of Mao's teachings were binding any more, is already present in the silent texts of the Memorial Hall.

The addressees of the final call on Cheng-yang Gate are represented on its right and left. Thirty red flags on high poles stand for the thirty provinces, government-administered cities, and autonomous regions that have to, as the explanation of the picture in the Chairman Mao Memorial Hall memorial volume says, "victoriously march ahead under the guidance of the Party Center headed by Chairman Hua."

The two sets of sculptures are on level ground. Their time is on the level where the mortals walk from the past into the future. Between the two sets of sculptures stands the hall, which is elevated above the plain of mortal time. The pilgrim has to rise to another and higher level to enter the hall, a common feature of buildings with the authority of the eternal like Buddhist temples, imperial palaces, and the Sun Yat-sen Mausoleum. This is the level of eternity, or, more threateningly, of continuous presence and validity.

The symbolic lore surrounding the building does all it can to help the implied pilgrim understand that he is entering a higher and eternal realm. The greenery surrounding the building separates it from the profane world and foreshadows the theme of eternity. As in the case of Sun Yat-sen's mausoleum, the landscaping has been designed as a part of the architectural ensemble; it consists of plants of traditional and well-known symbolic values. The outer ring has three rows of *Pinis tabulaeformis* (*yu-sung* 油松), an "evergreen of long life, high stature, sturdy and straight, verdant green in both winter and summer," in the words of the architects. Thirteen of these trees had been brought from Yenan, where Mao had spent thirteen years of his life and labors. Crab apple trees and hawthorne trees, brought from all corners of the empire, were planted near both entrances. They flourish in March, and the appropriately red fruit they bear in September every year symbolizes the ever-new red fruit sprouting from Mao's heritage ("Mao Chu-hsi chi-nien-t'ang tsung-t'i kuei-hua" 1977, 10).

The symbolism doesn't end there.

> The base of the memorial hall consists of a two-tiered platform, with a total height of 4 metres, the walls of which are faced with reddish granite. The platform is surrounded by white marble balustrades with designs of the *wan nien ching* evergreen plant in bas-relief. This is meant to symbolize the Chinese people's determination to keep the red state founded by Chairman Mao firm as the rock and longliving as the evergreen plant. (English Abstracts 1977, 2)

This phrase from the English summary to the architects' report about the planning of the Memorial Hall marks an important shift. The entire edifice is not just a memorial hall for Mao Tse-tung, but a symbol for the structure of the new state, with Mao Tse-tung enshrined in the center.

The base with its reddish granite is a quote from an old plan. Chou En-lai had intended to implant this symbolism into the base of the Great Hall of the People in the early 1950s, but no appropriate reddish granite was found. By the time the Memorial Hall was being constructed, such granite was available ("Mao Chu-hsi chi-nien-t'ang chien-chu she-chi fang-an ti fa-chan kuo-ch'eng" 1977, 36). As reddish granite does not change color, this fundament would effectively guarantee the state's long-term political complexion. Between the achieved past and the promise of future glory symbolized by the two groups of sculptures, the entire building hovers on the time axis as the pilgrim walks through.

The pilgrim enters the big anteroom through the door beneath Hua's big inscription in golden characters reading "Chairman Mao Memorial Hall." Mao had been state president for a while, but "chairman" only of the Party. The man enshrined here in the imaginary replica of the state edifice is simply

图 56　北大厅方案

Fig. 9.2. Proposed sculpture of Mao Tse-tung in stern posture, with painting of sun behind and radiating sunbeams on the ceiling. From *Chien-chu hsueh-pao* 1977, no. 4.

the head of the Communist Party. The Kuomintang had done the same with Sun Yat-sen. He was enshrined as the Party chairman, *tsung-li* 總理, not as the head of the Canton government. The implied claim is for the continuous control of the state structure by the Party led by the enshrined leader and his successors ("Tsung-li feng-an shih-lu" 1930, 1).

A statue of Mao Tse-tung in white marble sits in the middle of the wall, facing the door. When the doors are open, his challenging figure can be seen from T'ien-an Gate. Mao, a benign smile on his face, sits in an arm chair, his legs crossed. The sculpture intends to impress on the implied pilgrim the feeling that he is standing next to Chairman Mao and personally listening to his teachings. Behind the chairman is a large embroidered replica of a land-scape painting by Huang Yung-yü.

Both show the stress of rejected options. The calmly sitting chairman talks back to the many statues of Mao adorning public places in China, precast, standing, pointing ahead. It also talks back to the classical frontal sitting statue, with legs rigidly apart and both hands stiff on the upholstery, a stern figure of authority as expressed in the statues of the Jade Emperor, Lincoln, and Sun Yat-sen. Down to the last round of discussions about the hall, there had been several proposals to sculpt Mao sitting in this stern position ("Mao Chu-hsi chi-nien-t'ang tsung-chieh fang-an [ti-erh lun]" 1977, 45; see fig. 9.2). The relaxed Mao decided on instead symbolizes the words of the 1978 Constitution that people should "feel both unity and ease of mind and liveliness," implying a promise by (or a compromise of) the Hua Kuo-feng leadership that the tension and hectic activity of the Cultural Revolution with its fever-ish adoration of Mao and its persecutions were over (Constitution 1978, 6).

Mao wears a Chung-shan (i.e., Sun Yat-sen) suit. Originally designed by Sun Yat-sen himself as a "modern" outfit, it had by 1978 become a marker of Maoist orthodoxy.[5] The more radical reformers such as Hu Yao-pang were already sporting Western suits. Since then, the suit worn by a PRC leader on a given occasion has foreshadowed the political line he will be taking.

The painting in the background had to handle the traditional metaphoric image of the chairman as the sun. He had been widely described as this celestial body since the Great Leap years, and billions of Mao buttons during the Cultural Revolution portrayed his head as the sun rising in the east, radiating. As Ledderose pointed out in his lecture in Berlin in 1980, the proposals to have a stern, sitting sculpture were combined with proposals to paint a huge red sun rising behind the chairman's head with a grid on the ceiling imitating the beams radiating from the sun. This idea of the sun had even become the focus of one of the plans for the entire building, which was to be like the sun rising, recalling a plan for a Newton Memorial in Paris suggested during the French Revolution (Starobinski 1982, 59).

While construction went on, fundamental changes occurred in the political Center. After Mao's death and the jailing of his wife and her associates in the autumn of 1976, Hua Kuo-feng had promoted a continuation of the criticism of Teng Hsiao-p'ing. But by the time the hall was nearing completion in fall 1977, Teng Hsiao-p'ing was back in the top leadership. The reduction of Mao from the blazing red sun in the east to a friendly, smiling teacher, comfortably sitting cross-legged in his chair with a vast Chinese landscape behind him reflects in my understanding the strategies of Teng Hsiao-p'ing and his supporters. Unable to build no hall, they opted for toning things down.

As Ledderose (1988) has shown, the landscape behind the sculpture operates on a traditional trope of memorial sculptures. The picture on the theme "grand fatherland" does not deal with Mao's revolutionary activity, but with his patriotic commitment to the nation. Compared to the sculptures outside, which stress the Communist leader, the sculpture of Mao and the painting behind him make a different kind of united-front offer. Every patriot, Communist or not, can pay his tribute to Mao Tse-tung and be accepted by the co-pilgrims.

Some details of the entrance hall, however, still show holdovers from the original red sun concept. The entrance hall will hold about seven hundred pilgrims. They receive instruction and a pattern for proper behavior from the lamps on the ceiling, which are modeled on sunflowers. Sunflowers are known for their peculiar habit of staying always turned toward the sun. This characteristic made them an appropriate and frequently used image of the "people's" relation to Mao Tse-tung. Electrically, of course, the lamps have their own sources of energy, but in the imaginary structure, they receive their light from the sun. The people's lights and insights are just reflections of the grand shine emanating from the chairman; like sunflowers, they receive their nourishment from him; in turn, being lamps, they use their light to brighten his countenance. In socialist language this is called a dialectical relationship between leader and led.

But the sun is not there. The conflicts in the Center surface in the signs of stress in the entrance hall, where the actual sculpture of Mao Tse-tung contradicts the implications of the lamps. The lamps turn toward Mao Tse-tung, the red sun who never made it there. The implied pilgrim is at a loss, because his text is not manipulated by one supreme author and chairman, but by a goodly dozen authors battling for control of the symbolic load of the Memorial Hall with a success here, a compromise there, and an occasional toad to swallow. It would be pleasant and in tune with leadership presentations at any given moment to make the argument of harmony. This would mean that there is no controversy, but that various aspects of Mao's rich personality are shown. Given the unmediated coexistence of these mutually exclusive elements and the ruthless struggle for succession going on at the time in the Center, I don't find much merit in this interpretation.

While our deconstructive efforts have shown the "reform faction's" prevailing in the entrance hall, the room in the center shows the inverse.

The model of the implied pilgrim we have used presupposes a unified authorial will and the author's complete control over the material and the pilgrim. But even in a traditional text, the writer is a multifarious being. The conscious crafting, subconscious urges, and resistance and resilience of plot and character (which often insist on acting independent of the author's intentions) all operate as authorial wills and often are in conflict, leaving the implied reader in happy confusion. Furthermore, the implied reader is no dummy, no robot acting on a master's orders, but an individual invested with literary and, in our case, political experience; it is assumed that the reader will talk back to the text, and the texts often show signs of stress (like silent emphases or noisy lacunae) from this conflict. Our text was written by the entire Politburo, and the various factions battled for the implied pilgrim. No one was entirely in control, and in the process of building, the balance of power shifted. What looks like a silent building standing somewhere on T'ien-an-men Square is in fact a riot of conflicting messages, lukewarm compromises, and coded signs.

On his strictly controlled way, the pilgrim now enters a corridor leading to the room where Mao is enshrined. The corridor is fairly dark to let the eyes of the implied pilgrim adjust to the solemn dimness prevailing in the central room of the building/square/city/country.

The center room puts the revolutionary education of the implied pilgrim to the test. In tune with traditional *ling-mu*, this room is modeled on a private bedroom (Ledderose 1988, 331). The pilgrim is to understand that the person lying there is alive in a symbolic sense, but resting in a light slumber. The sculpture replacing Sun Yat-sen in the sepulchral room carried the same symbolism. The presence of Mao's flesh body operates as a reinforcement of the "behest" symbolized outside by the book. Mao is asleep now in eternity; the only person who could change the behest is gone, and his physical presence is to instill in the pilgrims the awe that, it is hoped, will prevent them from going astray (as their own wits might lead them).

With regard to time, the pilgrim in the central room has arrived at the present. Past the past of the entrance sculptures, on his way to the future of the exit sculptures, he stands in the middle, in the present, and in the presence of Mao Tse-tung. This is not the trivial, fleeting present prevailing outside, but the present of an eternal presence. What the pilgrim sees here at this most important moment of the voyage he will take with him into the future.

The remains of the chairman are enshrined on a massive slab of black granite from, as the papers amply reported, Mount T'ai ("Mao Chu-hsi chi-nien-t'ang chien-chu she-chi fang-an ti fa-chan kuo-ch'eng" 1977, 14). All its weight notwithstanding, the slab is but a quote.[6] In his talk "Serve the People," which Mao gave on the occasion of the death of a soldier in 1944 and which is one of the three articles to be studied time and again, he said:

> Death awaits all men but its significance varies with various persons. The ancient Chinese writer Ssu-ma Ch'ien said: "Although death befalls all men alike, in significance it may be weightier than Mount T'ai or lighter than a swan's down." In significance, to die for the interests of the people is weightier than Mount T'ai, but to work hard and die for the fascists, for those who exploit and oppress the people, is lighter than a swan's down. (Mao Tse-tung 1969a, 1)

With his quote in mind, the implied pilgrim knows that the chairman's service to the people must have been weighty indeed. With Mao Tse-tung enshrined on the granite, the texture of meaning becomes symbolically rich. The granite slab talks back to the no-hall. Mao's death is so important that the rules for the average Communist leader do not apply. He is unique, and his uniqueness is bound up in his physical existence.

The man enshrined there, however, is no united-front character. The dominant emblem to characterize him is the international Communist flag with its hammer and sickle referring to the workers and peasants. The core of Mao is thus not a patriotic commitment to China; first and before all, Mao is a Communist. All other things devolve from this core element. This emphasis is repeated in the emblems attached to the black stone. They represent the three bodies Mao is supposed to have founded: the Party, the army, and the state. The emblem in front is that of the Party. As the most important body, its centrality is stressed. The emblems of the army and the state are attached on each side. A unique figure in the international Communist movement committed to world revolution, Mao is credited with founding the Chinese Communist Party, which in turn under his guidance founded and led the People's Liberation Army, which won victory so that Mao could proclaim the People's Republic of China, the silent text reads. This structure is replicated in the relationship between the Memorial Hall as a whole, which is the symbol of the state edifice, and the position of Mao's remains in its core, where he is enshrined as a Communist. All factions then battling in the Center agreed on the eternal "leading role of the Communist Party" and knew that it hinged on public acceptance of Mao's political and theoretical contributions.

The emphasis on his unique position in international communism enters him into the lists for the title of "the greatest Marxist-Leninist of our time." This title had been contested since Stalin's death, and Mao Tse-tung certainly had done all he could to get the honor. Mao's theories had indeed played an international role for many years. With an interruption between 1956 and 1969, the Chinese Party had for decades proclaimed in its constitutions both that Marxism-Leninism and Mao Tse-tung Thought were its guiding theories, and Teng Hsiao-p'ing later even wrote this into the state constitution. Mao was thus said to have developed Marxism-Leninism to the point of joining the quartet of Marx, Engels, Lenin, and Stalin as a new classic. The arrangement in the center room supports this claim and rejects the view held by what was soon to become a majority in the Politburo that Mao's record from the mid 1950s on was far from grand.

Around the black slab on which Mao's remains lie under a crystal cover, beds of flowers in bloom have been arranged. According to the report about the building of the Memorial Hall, the implied pilgrim is to understand this as a reference to the last line of a poem by Mao: "But when the time comes when the mountains are filled with flowers, she will smile in their midst," the "she" referring to the winter plum. Mao Tse-tung with his surrounding of blossoming flowers assumes the role of the winter plum in the poem. The poem, "Ode on the [Winter] Plum," is part of the implied pilgrim's interior decoration. He will know the lines by heart and will remember the context in which the poem was written. During the Cultural Revolution, Mao's poems were often—and quite legitimately so—interpreted as direct references to contemporary events and developments. The innocent little flowers might indicate and hide the entrance to some basement or subtext. The poem deals with the *mei* 梅, the plum, blossoming in winter. It runs:

> Wind and rain send spring away,
> flying snow greets spring's return.
> Banks and ravines are already under a thousand feet of ice,
> still there it is, the beauty of a blossoming branch.

> This beauty does not want spring for herself,
> she only wants to announce spring's coming.
> She waits until the mountains are covered with flowers,
> then she will smile in their midst.
>
> (Mao Tse-tung 1969b, 51)

But recalling the poem is not the end of our labors in divining the text of the room. In a note under the title, Mao remarks that the poem, written in December 1961, is a reply and inversion of a poem of the same title by the Sung poet Lu Yu (1125–1210). Such annotation is a frequent practice in Mao's poems, and even the smallest Cultural Revolution edition of his poems will also print the poem to which he refers. The implied pilgrim can be relied upon to be familiar with the other poem, too. And we may hypothesize that the meaning of Mao's poem will become clear only in the confrontation with this other text. In a translation that does not even try to do justice to its poetic qualities, Lu Yu's poem runs:

> Outside the station next to the broken bridge,
> calmly she blossoms, there is no owner.
> Dusk has already come, she is sad in her loneliness,
> and more, she faces wind and rain.
>
> She is not eager to fret for spring herself,
> lets the other flowers have their jealousy.
> May her falling blossoms become mud and be ground to dust,
> as long as their fragrance lingers on.
>
> (Mao Tse-tung 1969b, 52)

Both poems praise the winter plum. But while Lu Yu stresses the jealousy and pettiness of the common flowers, they become the symbol of the people in Mao's poem. To fall down among them is for Lu Yu falling into the mud, while Mao's blossoms lie smiling in their midst.

Mao Tse-tung made use of the core symbol in the first part of Lu Yu's poem, the plum's blossoming before spring has set in. The tree blossoms in winter, but no travelers come by, the bridge is broken, and no one cares for the tree, which has no owner and stands alone in the dusk, wind, and rain. PRC commentators have defined Lu Yu as a "patriotic poet" and have rather successfully read the poem against the background of Lu Yu's time following the interpretive rule that the author is to be identified with the main protagonist, here the tree.

Lu Yu was born when northern China fell under the control of the Jurchen, who established the Chin dynasty. He lived through many years of flight and turmoil, represented by the weather in the first lines (Hsiang and Ch'in 1986, 116ff.). Amid these harsh and evil forces the aristocratic tree opens its blossoms calmly and sadly without much care whether there is someone to admire them. Its surroundings are neglected, but the tree goes about performing its purity. It is not even interested in living into spring, when better times come and everyone has a go at blossoming. It does not care for the jealousy of the plebeian flowers. It just hopes that even if its blossoms fall and die (that is, if Lu Yu should fall victim to some vicious political intrigue and be killed), they will retain its original fragrance of upright purity under adverse circumstances.

Mao Tse-tung wrote his poem in reply in December 1961. The Great Leap (1959–61) had led to a vast man-made famine; the other leaders held Mao responsible and pushed for drastic reforms, which he was to denounce later as a revisionist shift of focus from class struggle to production goals. It was the time when his star hung lowest. Still, in the midst of this revisionist "winter," Mao's pure thoughts flourished, a harbinger of better things to come. When they come, his blossoms will have fallen, dead, among the blossoming flowers of the "people," smiling in their midst. The poem portrays Mao in the middle of the "revisionist" winter, alone still, but sure to be eventually cherished by all.

The time frame of the symbolism implied by the poem remains ambiguous. It could be that the revisionist winter is still threatening, which in 1977–78 would be a not-too-oblique reference to Teng Hsiao-ping's rise. Or it could be that the glory had been achieved—the "First Cultural Revolution has been successfully achieved," as Hua Kuo-feng put it—and that the road to full communism was clear, so that Mao is now lying smiling among the flowers. The implied pilgrim reserves his judgment until further evidence is available. In any case, the poem could be read as a support for the preservation of Mao's remains.

Before the implied pilgrim can move on, he has to read another inscription. On the wall facing the entrance to the central room behind the chairman's remains is a large inscription: "The Great Leader and Guide Chairman Mao Tse-tung will be eternally handed down to posterity without decaying."

The terms "leader and guide" take up the theme of the entire hall: Mao was the leader in the past and will be the guide for the future. The *yung-ch'ui pu-hsiu* of the last line echoes the very same words written by Mao onto the Heroes' Monument on T'ien-an-men Square. Symbolically, the two thus form a pair: the masses of people commemorated in the stele gave their lives, and now their chairman has joined them. He, too, will not be forgotten. The stele, however, operates on a purely symbolic level. No hero is actually preserved and enshrined under that monument, and the "eternally handed down to posterity without decay" carries just the normal meaning of "will always be remembered." In the frenzy to get the symbolic message of the Memorial Hall straight, the designers confused the matter. Once they actually preserved the remains of the chairman and exhibited them, the phrase began to operate on both the literal and the metaphoric level.

Suddenly, the question of preserving Mao's ideological heritage is tied up for the pilgrim with the technical problems of keeping the chairman's flesh body intact. The constant rumors about a decay of the remains are but a reflection of the "decay" of the ideological heritage of Mao under the new leadership. Any change in basic ideology affects the remains, and vice versa.

Given the obvious quandary of the survivors in handling the remains of their giant, we might have to probe deeper for the causes that made them voluntarily land in it. In Chapter 4 of this book, Bernard Faure explores the role of the flesh bodies of famous Buddhist saints in the formation of pilgrimage centers. That their bodies had not decayed was seen as proof of the purity and rarefication they had achieved through their saintly lives. This belief in turn led to the conviction also encountered in medieval Europe that these bodies contained some magical power that could help in achieving worldly ends (Geary 1976).

But it was known that the bodies of Mao, Lenin, and Sun had been preserved by cooling and chemical treatment and not by a rarefied inner life. Therefore, we will have to determine the status of this type of burial in China within a different and political burial hierarchy.

The People's Republic has set up a formalized burial hierarchy. It starts with cremation and dispersal of the remains of "counterrevolutionaries," goes through various grades of cremation urns corresponding to the political status of the deceased, and ends with burial on the heroes' burial ground at Pa-pao Shan in Peking.

No one operating within this hierarchy will have the honor of having his body preserved in the flesh. On top of and beyond this hierarchy, however, are the few individuals who claim or for whom it is claimed that they made history "progress." It is not enough that they had a big impact on history; Hitler's remains would not have been embalmed and enshrined by the Allies. They have to be victorious, too, so that their adherents have the power to secure their preservation.

When Sun Yat-sen's remains were temporarily kept in the Pai-yun Temple in Peking, the northern warlords, badly battered by the northern expedition of the Kuomintang, had an emergency meeting in Peking in June 1927. One of them, Chang Tsung-chang, surmised the reason for their defeat to be the "excellent *feng-shui*" enjoyed by Sun's remains in their very midst in Peking. Chang Tso-lin agreed and suggested that the remains should be burned, but he was opposed by another general (Chou 1989, 92). Wang Ching-wei, who controlled Sun's remains after he set up his government in Nanking, used Sun's numerous contacts with Japan to bolster his own policies. The Sun Mausoleum, however, had been built before Wang established his government in Nanking. After the war, it could be claimed that he had just misused it for his own purposes, and it could be restored to Chiang

Kai-shek's control, rather than destroyed. After 1949, it could again be claimed that it had been planned and largely built before Chiang Kai-shek had come to power to impose his own interpretation of the heritage. The Communists restored it to what they saw as its original purpose. And although Sun's remains were again threatened during the Cultural Revolution, they have been the site of many united-front pilgrimages before and since.

Mao's remains were and are no less threatened. Had his wife and her associates managed the Memorial Hall and enshrined him, and had they been toppled shortly thereafter, his body would have been so "polluted" that only leveling of the hall and cremation of the body could have erased the blemish. As it is, Mao was embalmed at the nadir of his prestige. Numerous were those who wanted the "leading role" of his thoughts revoked. And numerous were his victims who even now would enjoy the desecration of whatever in the remains on exhibit is still original Mao. The importance placed on the security and safekeeping of the remains of both Sun and Mao attests to the awareness of the natural and political threats constantly endangering such a flesh body. The extreme care lavished on the flesh bodies of the luminaries in favor attests to their importance in authenticating and legitimizing their successors through their physical presence.

We have a fine test case to check the inherent value of such a flesh body or its parts, namely, Sun Yat-sen's entrails. They had been removed at the Peking Union Medical Hospital after his death when his body was prepared for preservation, and they had been kept there. After the Japanese occupied Peking, they took control of the hospital. When Wang Ching-wei heard that Sun's entrails were there, he secured agreement from the Japanese authorities to transfer them to Nanking to join the rest of the body in the mausoleum. With much fanfare against the American imperialists who had arrogated the possession of these holy entrails, *ling-tsang* 靈臟, he organized a big ceremony on April 5, 1942, in Nanking to welcome these parts of the deceased. Wang had kept the Kuomintang ritual of silently reciting Sun's behest and bowing to his picture at the beginning of grand meetings. Now he added another element, called "showing respect from afar to the holy entrails of the father of the nation."

The head of the committee set up by Wang Ching-wei to handle the Sun Mausoleum, Foreign Minister Ch'u Min-i, failed to notice that Sun's flesh body was inherently valuable only if attached to a political line in power. After Wang's death and the end of the war, Ch'u took the entrails and hid them with friends in Nanking. Landed in Chiang Kai-shek's "model prison" in Soochow and threatened with execution, he offered his "precious," *pao-wu* 寶物, to Chiang Kai-shek in exchange for his life. It is not clear how, but Chiang's emissaries learned where his "precious" was, found the entrails, identified them, and as they were a part of Sun Yat-sen identified with Wang Ching-wei, a national traitor, promptly burned them; even the ashes were not allowed to join the rest of the body (Chou 1989, 314 f.).

There is thus a dialectical relationship between the flesh body of the hero and the political line authenticated through his presence. His presence props up the authority of the powers that be, but these powers in turn authenticate its parts, physical and spiritual. Chiang Kai-shek's plans to take Sun's remains with him to Chungking and later to Taiwan attest to the importance of possessing the remains. The plans were thwarted by the very safety accorded the remains. Chiang and his men would have had to use explosives to get them out, and this force might have damaged the body (Chou 1989, 339).

At the same time there is a potential for conflict between the flesh body and his administrators. The embalmed body contains the public claim that the teaching of the hero is valid as long as the body is there and can be appealed to in times of need. In 1947, Chiang Kai-shek had demobbed many of his officers. They found themselves without the wherewithal to support their lives, and many turned to begging, selling their wives, and suicide. Eventually about four hundred officers went on a highly publicized weeping pilgrimage to the Sun Mausoleum to tell the father of the nation of their plight. The action implied that the administrators of his body had turned their backs on his behest (Chou 1989, 327 ff.).

Hua Kuo-feng, who was retained after 1981 on the Central Committee after having been dismissed as Party secretary and premier, was always the first to visit the Memorial Hall on the morning of Mao's birthday, the implication being that he alone, not the new leaders, embodied the true heritage of the man enshrined there. And in an ironic twist, the students occupying T'ien-an-men Square in mid-May 1989 turned to the Chairman Mao Memorial Hall and sang the famous paean on Mao, "The East is red, the great sun rises, China has brought forth Mao Tse-tung . . ." On the preceding day, Party Secretary Chao Tzu-yang had revealed to Soviet leader Mikhail Gorbachev that according to a secret decision made in 1987, the Party would turn to Teng Hsiao-p'ing for all major decisions. The students read this as an indication that the government's intransigence hinged on Teng Hsiao-p'ing's orders. Their song to the flesh body in the Memorial Hall implied that Mao Tse-tung, who had twice dropped Teng Hsiao-p'ing, had been right.

In fact, the enormous speed with which the Memorial Hall was built—the planning and execution taking altogether less than one year—shows that historical lessons had been learned. After Stalin's death, the entire leadership—and public—went through an extended public show of mourning, and there were plans to handle his remains in a manner akin to those of Mao Tse-tung. But within two years and after gruesome battles in the Center (including the arrest of Lavrenty Beria, which served as the precedent for the arrest of Chiang Ch'ing and her associates), Stalin's physical remains were in the same shape as his ideological teachings. In the views of the Hua Kuo-feng leadership, the instant preservation of the physical remains would help preserve the spiritual remains on which Hua's own polical future hinged.

Much thought went into solving the physical problems of preservation. The efforts to secure the hall against earthquakes are well documented ("Mao Chu-hsi chi-nien t'ang chien-chu she-chi" 1977, 18 ff.). The problem of preserving the Mao heritage through preserving the flesh body was translated into huge investments for the cooling machinery in the basement of the Memorial Hall. But even the foreign machinery had trouble solving the political problems.

The problems associated with the coexistence and codecay of Mao's remains and thoughts arise from a traditional notion in Chinese politics. If things went awry in the political/moral sphere of the old empire, Heaven signaled disapproval in the dark language of heavenly portents, locust swarms, or earthquakes. The political crisis of 1976—with the deaths of Chou En-lai, Chu Te, and Mao Tse-tung—was epitomized by nature's coming out of joint. The devastating earthquake in August 1976, which cost hundreds of thousands of lives and was centered close enough to the capital to collapse parts of the Peking Hotel near T'ien-an-men Square, was felt to be one such heavenly portent. Given the dark language of Heaven, it was never quite clear who exactly was responsible for the earthquake. A periodical directly controlled by Chiang Ch'ing and her associates quickly came out with a historical article about the T'ai-p'ing leader Hung Hsiu-ch'üan, who had interpreted the big earthquake of 1851 in a poem as a portent of Heaven's distress with the Ch'ing government and support for a dynastic change (Han and Ch'en 1976, 30 f.). This was read as a thinly veiled claim, on Chiang Ch'ing's side, for the throne. Hua Kuo-feng, on the other side, visited T'ang-shan, where the heaviest damage had occurred, to organize relief. In this context, the earthquake was a mandate to do away with the Gang of Four. The earthquake showed the instability of the Chinese political edifice, and the events in the weeks thereafter—with Mao's death and the military action against four Politburo members—epitomized this feeling.

Hua Kuo-feng's efforts after this cataclysm were directed to achieving some sort of stability under his leadership. The publication of the new volume of Mao's works was a step in this direction, as was the decision to establish the Memorial Hall. The hall, however, was to be built in an area where earthquakes (both political and seismic) were frequent. Because of the symbolic identification of the Memorial Hall, with Mao in the center, with the edifice of the state and its ideological core, the capacity of the Memorial Hall to withstand physical earthquakes became the measure for the state to survive the political turmoil of Mao's succession. Thus ability of the hall to "survive" an earthquake became loaded with political symbolism. The troubles in the relationship between Mao's remains and Maoist heritage are repeated in the relationship between the Memorial Hall and the state edifice. The overidentification of symbol and symbolized makes the (assumed) eternity of ideas and institutions dependent on the frailty of worldly constructs. All innocence is gone; the interpretive consequences of the most trivial acts (like repairs) send all heads spinning.

Intrigued about the durability of worldly things, the implied pilgrim moves on to the exit room to have his doubts about the plum poem and the exact status and constellation of the present resolved. He finds a huge replica of Mao's poetic "Answer to Kuo Mo-jo" (January 9, 1963), written to the melody of "Man-chiang-hung," carved into the wall (which makes removal difficult). Kuo Mo-jo's poem had referred to Mao as the red sun, compared him to the wise emperor Yao of old, and envisaged that the entire universe would become "red" as the red flag was unfolded by the east wind blowing out of China. The four volumes of Mao's works that had just been redone and published to mark the new orthodox dispensation (as opposed to the "revisionist" works emanating from the Soviet Union) are duly mentioned in the poem. They are "pure gold that does not melt in the flames" of class struggle and furthermore "point out the right way to the people" (Kuo Mo-jo 1969, 56).

Mao answered this exercise in flattery with one of his grandest poems. It again deals with revisionism. The Soviet Union has moved from just being a deviant group within the Communist movement to becoming an imperialist power, and Khrushchev is satirized as an "ant on an acacia tree bragging of her big empire." The second part of the poem calls on the hesitant and wavering to join in the revolutionary advance and "wipe out all insects harmful to people." The text also solves what remained as a question from the central hall. "Now," it repeats, "the west wind lets leaves fall on Ch'ang-an, flying, arrows come humming." Ch'ang-an is China's ancient capital, and it stands for the center of the nation. In the harsh and public polemics between China and the Soviet Union, the poem charges, the Soviet Union not only drowns China with hostile propaganda (leaves), but also takes hostile measures (arrows). And as the urgent appeal in the second part shows, there is great reluctance in China to follow Mao's adventures. In the "now" of the poem, the west wind still dominates, and the mood is hesitant. Only in some glorious future when all follow Mao's appeal will a great change come. The poem ends:

> How much is still to be done,
> always pressing;
> Heaven and earth roll on,
> light and darkness hurry on.
> Ten thousand years—too long,

we can but use each morning and each night.
The four seas are in turmoil as clouds and waters rage,
the five continents quake as wind and thunder let loose.
We have to wipe out all insects harmful to man,
utterly invincible we are.

(Mao Tse-tung 1969c, 54)

The implied pilgrim leaves the hall impressed by the dangers of revisionism lurking in the present and called upon to stay true to the behests of the late chairman to "continue the revolutionary cause to the end," a duty made explicit by the exit sculptures on both sides of the *shen-tao* and by the inscription on Cheng-yang Gate.

CONCLUSION

The Chairman Mao Memorial Hall is built in its main features from a defensive perspective in a manner similar to the one Mao himself used in the design of the heroes' monument on T'ien-an-men Square. The hall is the silent manifesto of a leadership group that knew it was on the way out and used what little time and opportunity it had to plant a strong, lasting, complex, and irritating symbol in the center of the center of the center, a symbol that would outlive their own tenure in power and provide a reminder, a focus, and some encouragement for those advocating a continuation of Maoist policies under a leadership personally approved by the late chairman.

The locale chosen by Hua Kuo-feng in the sacred space of T'ien-an-men Square that marks the heart of the nation showed his strategic wit. The legitimacy of the Party's "leading role," or rather discretional monopoly, hinged on the figure of Mao Tse-tung. The new leadership under Teng Hsiao-p'ing went as far as it could in dismantling the Hua Kuo-feng heritage of Maoism. The fifth volume of Mao's works could be withdrawn (which it was in 1982 after Hua Kuo-feng's replacement as chairman of the Party). Those parts acceptable to the new leadership would continue to be available (which they are). But the Memorial Hall could not easily be handled in this manner. Hua's inscription could be removed (which it was), the banner at the exit could be taken down (which it was). But the symbolism of the hall was hewn into stone, and the identification with the symbolized was so heavily reinforced that to this day the new leadership has to live with this remonstrative Maoist sore in the center of the nation, propagating the now-unavailable fifth volume, the Red Guards, Ta-chai, Ta-ch'ing, and all.

The only real option was to tear down the entire edifice. (Plans of this kind are occasionally still ventilated in the press by members of the leadership irritated by the continuous challenge of the hall.) But since the building is invested with such a heavy symbolic load, no one could predict what the costs and consequences of such an operation in the heart of the nation's sacred space would be. The post–Hua Kuo-feng leadership remains in a quandary. Since 1979, the Memorial Hall has more often been closed than not, but even if there were indeed "technical reasons" for the closures, they were not believed and were read as political subterfuges. And there has been pressure from the pilgrims. They might come for a variety of reasons: tourism, curiosity, hero worship, spite, or religious awe might enter into any combination. But even in 1987 and 1988, with reduced hours and no work-unit dragging its members to the hall, several hundred thousand people a year still visited it. The new leadership has the same problem with the hall that Chiang Kai-shek, Wang Ching-wei, again Chiang Kai-shek, and finally the Communists had with the Sun Yat-sen Mausoleum, the same problem the Catholic Church often has with pilgrimage sites. Doctrine has changed; the hall does not embody the orthodox faith but is rather a threat and a fundamentalist challenge to present teachings. But it has assumed a life of its own.

So the hall had to be kept, and it had to be open. The new leadership was left with the "choice" of diffusing the original message and refunctionalizing the building. The Sun Yat-sen Mausoleum illustrates that such can be done. It was built as a monumental counterpart to the Liberty Bell, inaugurated by Chiang Kai-shek as a monument to national unity achieved and his author-itarian rule established, taken over by Wang Ching-wei as a symbol of close Chinese-Japanese cooperation, retaken by Chiang as a monument to a China freed from foreign occupation, reassigned by the Communists the role of Sino-Soviet cooperation and the "new" three principles, nearly destroyed during the Cultural Revolution as a symbol of Chiang Kai-shek's fascist dictatorship, kept up by the revisionists in the Communist leadership, and retained after 1978 as a propaganda prop for a new united front between Communists and Kuomintang, a place where Taiwanese politicians and Communist leaders could meet.

In 1977 when the Mao Memorial Hall was built, the then minority argued that there had been an entire "generation of senior revolutionary leaders," not just Mao. Symbolically, they could find their image in the columns of the Memorial Hall. (Hua had to include the notion about this generation in his speech at the hall's opening.) But there was little in the main line of the pilgrims' way that the new leadership could do to expand this symbolism. Along both sides of the way through the building, however, are reception rooms where important guests might rest for a while. After what must have been a rather desperate search for means to patch over the central sore, the new leadership decided to add four memorial rooms (*chi-nien shih* 紀念室) to the Memorial Hall. They were opened in December 1983, nearly six years after the hall itself. Such developments are well known from pilgrimage cen-ters, where the authorities add new places of worship to replace the heterodox challenge or where new niches or side temples are added for new gods or saints by pilgrims who discover their potential, not rarely to the point of obfuscating the central figures.

The awkward rooms, which had not been designed for the purpose, are numbered one through four, and the numbers, as is the custom in China, represent a hierarchy. The first memorial room to the left of the entrance hall is dedicated to none other than the chairman himself. The second, on the same level to the right, is dedicated to Chou En-lai. The third, south of the first, is for Liu Shao-ch'i, and the fourth, south of the second, is for Chu Te. Simultaneously, the writings of these leaders were gathered into selected works (*hsuan-chi* 選集), elevating them to the same status as Mao's *Selected Works*. Photographs in these memorial rooms stress the "close comradeship" of these leaders with the chairman, a theme repeated on the second floor in a film about the glories of the Chinese Revolution. This rearrangement made Mao the embodiment of the collective wisdom of this generation of senior leaders, removed his authority personally to appoint a successor, retained the claim for the mandatory leadership of the Communist Party, and, most important, installed the surviving senior leaders of the old generation, and Teng Hsiao-p'ing in particular, as the true and legitimized successors of the chairman. The rearrangement also reduced the pressure of the hall on the present by adding features taken from the category of the revolutionary museum. Adding the four rooms through which people could wander at will also diffused the rigid time/space structure imposed before.

Meanwhile, the heart of the heart of the nation continued to palpitate on its own rhythm. The people occupying the square in 1989 had symbolically come from the entire country, specifically from the campuses of the nation. As in April 1976, they claimed with this act to represent the nation in a challenge to the leadership symbolically installed on T'ien-an Gate and in the palace behind. They erected their new remonstrative monument, the Goddess of Liberty, on the imperial axis facing north. It stood in front of the heroes' monument, implying the claim that the highest value for which these heroes had died was liberty. The government reacted less symbolically with tanks and guns. Afterward, it tried to clean and calm down the polluted and inflamed heart of the nation by cordoning it off for several months and to mark the reinstatement of government control on October 1, 1989, with merry dances by army children and the erection of a gigantic worker/peasant/soldier statue on the very spot where the Goddess of Liberty had been torn down (Wagner, in press).

NOTES

Most of the research for this paper was done while I was a research linguist at the Center for Chinese Studies, University of California, Berkeley, and a visiting professor at the John K. Fairbank Center for East Asian Research at Harvard University. To the scholars and librarians at both institutions I am greatly indebted for their continuing support of this line of inquiry. The German Research Foundation added its share by supporting a trip to Nanking (on other business) that made it possible for me to see the Sun Yat-sen Mausoleum and to study materials in the archives of the city.

1. The use of the past tense here does not exclude that attempts may be made by the PRC leadership to rekindle a similar kind of fervor. In fact, since the 1989 crackdown on the democratic movement, such attempts have been under way with the campaign to "learn from Lei Feng" and similar heroes. They are directed, however, at a populace that has grown cynical, and there seems to be nothing of the often feverish emotional involvement of earlier years.

2. These were "Chi-nien Pai-ch'iu-en" 紀念白求恩 (In commemoration of Bethune), *Mao Tse-tung hsuan-chi* 2:620–22; "Wei jen-min fu wu" 爲人民服務 (Serve the people), *Mao Tse-tung hsuan-chi* 3:954–55; and "Yü-gung i shan" 愚公移山 (The foolish old man who removed the mountain), *Mao Tse-tung hsuan-chi* 3:1049–52.

3. There seem to be two ranks for such sites: "units for the preservation of top-grade-emphasis cultural relics" (*Ti-i-p'i ch'üan-kuo chung-tien wen-wu pao-hu tan-wei* 第一批全國重點文物保護單位), which in 1986 included 33 revolutionary sites out of a total of 180 sites, and the same for "second-grade-emphasis cultural relics," which included 10 revolutionary sites in a total of 62 (*Chung-kuo ming-sheng tz'u-tien* 1986, 1148 f. and 1158).

4. There is to my knowledge one other *chi-nien t'ang* (memorial hall) in China, the Memorial Hall for the Revolutionary Heroes (Ko-ming lieh-shih chi-nien t'ang 革命烈士紀念堂) in Nan-ch'ang (Kiangsi). But no one is buried or enshrined there, and in fact it belongs to the well-attested category of *chi-nien kuan* 紀念館, a museum-like structure to commemorate a revolutionary hero like Lu Hsun.

5. In the committee handling Sun Yat-sen's Mausoleum two factions headed by Hu Han-min and Soong Ch'ing-ling had confronted each other on the question of dress. A compromise was reached: Sun was to wear a traditional official's dress with a silk jacket on Polish sculptor Paul Arlinsky's (Yao and Ku 1981, 3) (sometimes transcribed "Lang-t'e-ssu-chi" 朗特斯基 [Zhou 1989, 29]) big sculpture in the ceremonial hall and the Chung-shan suit on the sculpture over the coffin by the Czech sculptor B. J. Koči (transcribed Kao-ch'i 高崎), which was to replace his unpresentable remains. (Dr. Oldrich Kral of Prague was kind enough to help me identify the sculptor. Koči worked in China from 1920 on and, apart from the Sun Yat-sen statue, produced a number of bas-reliefs and sculptures of a feminist, a beggar, and a Shanghai riksha, among others. He was praised in the Chinese magazine *The Hexagon* [Toman 1936, 308]). Soong Ch'ing-ling, who had advocated the "revolutionary" costume, is said to have eternally regretted that things had not been decided the other way around (Chou 1989, 30).

6. Matignon reports that very expensive slabs from Mount T'ai were put in front of houses during the late Ch'ing as apotropaic devices against evil spirits (Matignon 1936, 63).

BIBLIOGRAPHY

"Che-li sheng-ch'i-lai yung-yuan-pu-lo ti hung t'ai-yang" 這裏升起來永遠不落的 紅太陽 [Here the red sun which will never go down has risen]. 1966. *Jen-min jih-pao*, Oct. 26.

Ch'i Kung-heng 齊公衡. 1930. *Chung-shan ling ta-kuan* 中山陵大觀 [The sights of the Sun Yat-sen Mausoleum]. Shanghai: Liang-yu.

Chou Tao-ch'un 周道純. 1989. *Chung-shan ling-yuan po-chi* 中山陵園博記 [A detailed account of the Sun Yat-sen Mausoleum]. Chiang-su: Chiang-su jen-min.

Chung-kuo ti-t'u ts'e (kung ko-ming ch'uan-lien yung). 1966. 中國地圖册(供革命串連用) [A map of China (for the purpose of [Red Guards] establishing links)]. Peking: Ti-t'u.

"The Constitution of the People's Republic of China." 1978. *Peking Review* 11.

"English Abstracts of Principal Articles." 1977. *Chien-chu hsueh-pao* 建筑学报, no. 4, supplement pp. 1–4.

Fallaci, Oriana. 1980. "Deng: Cleaning up Mao's 'Feudal Mistakes.'" *Washington Post Outlook*, Aug. 31.

Fan Shuo 范碩. 1990. *Yeh Chien-ying tsai 1976* 葉劍英在 1976 [Yeh Chien-ying in 1976]. Peking: Chung-kung chung-yang tang-hsiao.

Geary, Patrick. 1976. *Furta Sacra: Thefts of Relics in the Central Middle Ages*. Princeton: Princeton University Press.

Han T'ien-yü 韓天宇 and Ch'en Tsung-hai 陳宗海. 1976. "Ti-chen shih wei hsin-ti chao" 地震實爲新地兆 [The shaking of the earth is but the harbinger for a new earth to come]." *Hsueh-hsi yü p'i-p'an* 學習與批判, 9.

Hsiang T'ung 向彤 and Ch'in Ssu 秦似. 1986. *Lu Yu shih-tz'u shang-hsi* 陸游詩詞賞析 [Appreciating and understanding the poems of Lu Yu]. Nan-ning: Kuang-hsi jen-min.

Hua Kuo-feng 華國鋒. 1978. "Hua Chu-hsi tsai lung-chung chi-nien wei-ta ti ling-hsiu ho tao-shih Mao Chu-hsi shih-shih i-chou-nien chi Mao Chu-hsi chi-nien-t'ang lo-ch'eng tien-li ta-hui-shang ti chiang-hua" 華主席在隆重紀念偉大的領袖和導師毛主席逝世一周年及毛主席紀念堂落成典禮大會上的講話 [Speech by Chairman Hua on the occasion of the grand ceremony of solemn commemoration of the first anniversary of the death of the great leader and guide Chairman Mao and of the completion of the Chairman Mao Memorial Hall]. In *Mao Chu-hsi chi-nien-t'ang*.

"Hung-wei-ping pu-p'a yuan-cheng nan" 紅衛兵不怕遠征難 [Red Guards do not fear the hardships of a long march]. 1966. *Jen-min jih-pao*, Oct. 22.

Iser, Wolfgang. 1978. *The Implied Reader: Patterns of Communication in Fiction from Bunyan to Beckett*. Baltimore: Johns Hopkins University Press.

"K'o-ling kuei-tse" 客陵規則. Dated Sept. 30, 1929. [Rules for the visit to the mausoleum]. In *Chung-shan ling tang-an shih-liao hsuan-pien* 中山陵檔案史料選編, edited by Nan-ching shih tang-an kuan Chung-shan ling-yuan kuan-li ch'u.

Kuo Mo-jo 郭沫若. 1969. "Man-chiang-hung" 滿江紅. In *Mao Chu-hsi yü-lu*. Peking: Jen-min.

Ledderose, Lothar. 1988. "Die Gedenkhalle für Mao Zedong, ein Beispiel von Gedächtnisarchitektur." In *Kultur and Gedächtnis*, edited by Jan Assmann and Tonio Hölscher, 321–45. Frankfurt: Suhrkamp.

"Ling-hun shen-ch'u nao ko-ming" 靈魂深處鬧革命 [Wage revolution in the depths of the soul]. 1966. *Jen-min jih-pao*, Oct. 22.

Lo Che-wen 羅哲文 and Lo Yang 羅揚. 1984. *Chung-kuo li-tai ti-wang ling-ch'in* 中國歷代帝王陵寢 [The mausoleums of successive Chinese emperors]. Shanghai: Shanghai wen-hua.

Mao Chu-hsi chi-nien-t'ang 毛主席紀念堂 [The Chairman Mao Memorial Hall]. 1978. Peking: Chung-kuo chien-chu kung-yeh.

"Mao Chu-hsi chi-nien-t'ang chien-chu she-chi" 毛主席紀念堂建築設計 [The design of the Chairman Mao Memorial Hall]. 1977. *Chien-chu hsueh-pao* 建築學報, no. 4: 13–30.

"Mao Chu-hsi chi-nien t'ang chien-chu she-chi fang-an ti fa-chan kuo-ch'eng" 毛主席紀念堂建築設計方案的發展過程 [The process by which the Chairman Mao Memorial Hall was planned and designed]. 1977. Chien-chu hsueh-pao, no. 4:31–47.

"Mao Chu-hsi chi-nien-t'ang tsung-chieh fang-an (ti-erh lun)" 毛主席紀念堂總結方案(第二論) [The overall design of the Chairman Mao Memorial Hall (second essay)]. 1978. *Mao Chu-hsi chi-nien t'ang*.

"Mao Chu-hsi chi-nien-t'ang tsung-t'i kuei-hua" 毛主席紀念堂總體規劃 [The overall plan of the Chairman Mao Memorial Hall]. 1977. *Chien-chu hsueh-pao*, no. 4: 4–12.

"Mao Chu-hsi tsai Ching-kang Shan tien-jan ti ko-ming chih huo chao-liang ko-ming hsiao-chiang-men kuang-hui ti chan-tou ch'ien-ch'eng" 毛主席在井岡山點燃的革命之火照亮革命小將們光輝的戰鬪前程 [The beacon of revolution lit by Chairman Mao on Ching-kang Mountain illuminates the glorious fighting future of the revolutionary little generals]. 1966. *Jen-min jih-pao*, Nov. 25.

Mao Tse-tung 毛澤東. 1969a. "Ho Kuo Mo-jo t'ung-chih" 賀郭沫若同志. In *Mao Chu-hsi yü-lu, Mao Chu-hsi ti wu-p'ien chu-tso, Mao Chu-hsi shih-tz'u* 毛主席語錄, 毛主席的五篇著作, 毛主席詩詞 [Quotations from Chairman Mao, five works of Chairman Mao, poems by Chairman Mao]. Peking: Jen-min.

———. 1969b. "Wei jen-min fu-wu" 爲人民服務 [Serve the people]. In *Mao Chu-hsi yü-lu, Mao Chu-hsi ti wu-p'ien chu-tso, Mao Chu-hsi shih-tz'u*. Peking: Jen-min.

———. 1969c. "Yung mei." In *Mao Chu-hsi yü-lu, Mao Chu-hsi ti wu-p'ien chu-tso, Mao Chu-hsi shih-tz'u*. Peking: Jen-min.

———. 1977. *Mao Tse-tung hsuan-chi* 毛澤東選集. Vol. 5. Peking: Jen-min.

Matignon, J. J. 1936. *La Chine hermétique*. Paris: Librairie Orientaliste Paul Geuthner.

McDermott, Joseph P. 1989. "The Making of a Chinese Mountain, Huangshan: Politics and Wealth in Chinese Art." *Ajia Bunka Kenkyu* (Tokyo) 17:145–76.

"Nan-ching shih tang-an kuan Chung-shan ling-yuan kuan-li chü" 南京市檔案館中山陵園管理局. 1986. *Chung-shan ling tang-an shih-liao hsuan-pien* 中山陵檔案史料選編 [A selection of documents from the archives of the Sun Yat-sen Mausoleum]. Nanking: Chiang-su ku-chi Press.

Nora, P. 1984. *Les lieux de mémoire*. 4 vols. Paris: Gallimard.

Ouzouf, Mona. 1976. *La fête révolutionnaire, 1789–1799*. Paris: Gallimard.

"Pa 'lao san p'ien' tso-wei p'ei-yang kung-ch'an-chu-i hsin-jen ti pi-hsiu-k'o" 把"老三篇"作爲培養共產主義新人的必修課 [Make the three articles into mandatory study material for the education of New Communist Man]. 1966. *Jen-min jih-pao*, Nov. 20.

Pei-ching yu-lan shou-ts'e 北京游覽手册. 1957. Peking: Pei-ching.

"Pien-che an" 編者按 [Editor's preface]. 1966. *Jen-min jih-pao,* Dec. 2.

Plekhanov, Georgii Valentinovich. 1940. *The Role of the Individual in History.* New York: International Publishers.

Skinner, G. W. 1964, 1965. "Marketing and Social Structure in Rural China," Pt. 1. *Journal of Asian Studies* 24, 1 (Nov.); pt. 2, ibid., 24, 2 (Feb.).

Sklovskij, Viktor B. 1966 *Schriften zum Film.* Translated by A. Kaempfe. Frankfurt: Suhrkamp.

Stavobinski, Jean. 1982. *1789: The Emblems of Reason.* Charlottesville: University Press of Virginia.

Toman, P. 1936. *Nový slovník čsl. výtvarných umělců* [A new dictionary of Czechoslovak artists]. Prague.

"Tsung-li feng-an shih-lu" 總理奉安實錄 [A record of the ceremonies for the Chairman (Sun Yat-sen)]. 1930. Nanking. S.p. in Min-kuo Archive, Nanking.

Tz'u-hai 辭海. 1965. Reprint ed., 1979. Hong Kong: Chung-hua shu-chü.

Tz'u-hai. 1979. Shanghai: Shanghai tz'u-shu.

Wagner, Rudolf G. 1990. "Sun Wukong Three Times Beats the White-Bone Demon—A Study in PRC Mythology." In *The Contemporary Chinese Historical Drama: Four Studies,* edited by Rudolf G. Wagner, 139–235. Berkeley: University of California Press.

———. 1991. "Confrontation in the Imaginaire: Political Institutions and Social Change in the PRC." In *Rethinking Third-World Politics,* ed. James Manor. London: Longmans.

Wakeman, Frederic. 1988. "Mao's Remains." In *Death Ritual in Late Imperial and Modern China,* edited by J. Watson and E. Rawski, 254–88. Berkeley: University of California Press.

Wen-hua-pu wen-wu chü, ed. 1986. *Chung-kuo ming-sheng tz'u-tien ti-erh pan* 中國名勝詞典第二版 [China's famous sites, second edition]. Shanghai: Shang-hai tz'u-shu.

Yang K'uan 楊寬. 1985. *Chung-kuo ku-tai ling-ch'in chih-tu shih yen-chiu* 中國古代陵寢制度史研究. Shanghai: Shanghai ku-chi.

Yao Ch'ien 姚遷 and Ku Ping 古兵, eds. 1981. *Chung-shan ling* 中山陵 [Sun Yat-sen Mausoleum]. Peking: Wen-wu.

CONTRIBUTORS

James Cahill is professor of the history of art at the University of California, Berkeley, specializing in Chinese painting. His many books and articles include the most widely read popular introduction to the field, *Chinese Painting* (1960), *The Compelling Image: Nature and Style in Seventeenth-Century Chinese Painting* (1982), and *Three Alternative Histories of Chinese Painting* (1988). He is currently working on the fourth in a five-volume series on later Chinese painting, the first three of which have been published. In recent years he has spent a great deal of time in China seeing collections, studying, and lecturing.

Glen Dudbridge is professor of Chinese at the University of Oxford, fellow of University College, Oxford, and fellow of the British Academy. He was trained at the University of Cambridge and the New Asia Research Institute, Hong Kong. Among his main publications are *The Hsi-yu chi* (1970), *The Legend of Miao-shan* (1978; Chinese edition, 1990), and *The Tale of Li Wa* (1983). His current work is on the religious culture of T'ang China.

Bernard Faure is associate professor of religious studies at Stanford University. He was born and educated in France, where he received a Doctorat d'Etat ès Lettres et Sciences Humaines from the University of Paris in 1984. His publications include: *La volonté d'orthodoxie dans le bouddhisme chinois* (1988), *Le bouddhisme Ch'an en mal d'histoire* (1989), and *Rhetoric of Immediacy: A Cultural Critique of Chan/Zen Buddhism* (1991). He is currently working on the religious worldview of Keizan Jokin, an early fourteenth-century Japanese Zen monk, and on the use of diagrams in Buddhism as a medium between orality and writing.

Robert M. Gimello is professor of East Asian studies and religious studies at the University of Arizona. He received his Ph.D. from Columbia University and has taught at the University of California, Santa Barbara, and Dartmouth College. His publications include *Studies on Ch'an and Hua-yen* (with Peter Gregory), *Path to Liberation* (with Robert Buswell), and articles on Hua-yen Buddhism and comparative mysticism. He is currently working on the history of Buddhist thought in East Asia, seventh to twelfth century.

John Lagerwey is a member of the Ecole Française d'Extrême-Orient. He received his Ph.D. from Harvard University and did field work on Taoist ritual in Taiwan and in the People's Republic of China. His publications include *Wu-shang pi-yao, somme taoïste du VIe siècle* (1981); "The Oral and the Written in Chinese and Western Religion," in *Religion und Philosophie in Ostasien: Festschrift für Hans Steininger* (1985), and *Taoist Ritual in Chinese Society and History* (1987). He continues to do research in the field of Taoist history and bibliography.

Susan Naquin is professor of history at the University of Pennsylvania. She received her Ph.D. from Yale and is the author of *Millenarian Rebellion in China: The Eight Trigrams Uprising of 1813* (1976) and, jointly with Evelyn Rawski, *Chinese Society in the Eighteenth Century* (1986). She is currently writing a book about popular religion and public space in early modern Peking.

Rudolf G. Wagner is professor of Chinese studies at the University of Heidelberg and has published in the fields of early medieval intellectual and cultural history of China, late imperial social and intellectual history, and contemporary literature. His publications include "Lebensstil und Drogen im Chinesischen Mittelalter" (1972), *Reenacting the Heavenly Vision: The Role of Religion in the Taiping Rebellion* (1984), and *The Contemporary Chinese Historical Drama: Four Studies* (1990).

Pei-yi Wu is professor of classical and Oriental languages at Queens College and visiting professor of Chinese at Columbia University. His most recent publication is *The Confucian's Progress: Autobiographical Writings in Traditional China* (1990). He is currently writing a book on Chinese woman warriors.

Chün-fang Yü is associate professor of religion at Rutgers, the State University of New Jersey. She specializes in the history of Chinese Buddhism since the T'ang dynasty. She was educated at Tunghai University, Taiwan, and Columbia University, where she received her Ph.D. Her publications include *The Renewal of Buddhism in China: Chu-hung and the Late Ming Synthesis* (1981); "Ch'an Education in the Sung: Ideals and Procedures" (1989), and a chapter on Ming Buddhism for the forthcoming *Cambridge History of China*, vol. 8. She is currently writing a book on the cult of Kuan-yin in China.

Compositor:	Asco Trade Typesetting Ltd.
Text:	10/12 Baskerville
Display:	Baskerville
Printer:	Edwards Brothers, Inc.
Binder:	Edwards Brothers, Inc.

DATE DUE

GAYLORD			PRINTED IN U.S.A.